Harrogate Great Chronicle, 1332–1841

Harrogate Great Chronicle, 1332–1841

in two parts

part one: 'Early Harrogate, 1332–1841'
part two: 'Source materials and bibliography'

by
Malcolm G. Neesam

Carnegie Publishing Ltd

sponsored by Hornbeam Park Developments Limited

Harrogate Great Chronicle, 1332–1841
by Malcolm Neesam

First published in 2005
by Carnegie Publishing Ltd
Carnegie House, Chatsworth Road
Lancaster LA1 4SL
www.carnegiepublishing.com

The publishers gratefully acknowledge a subvention
towards production costs generously received from
Hornbeam Park Developments Limited, Harrogate

Part one, 'Early Harrogate, 1332–1841'
published in book form;
Part two, 'Source materials and bibliography'
published on CD-ROM (not available separately)

British Library Cataloguing-in-publication data
A catalogue record for this book is available
from the British Library

ISBN 10: 1-85936-145-5
ISBN 13: 978-1-85936-145-0

Designed, typeset and originated by
Carnegie Book Production
Printed and bound by CPI, Bath Press

Dedicated to
Her Majesty the Queen

Contents

List of illustrations   ix

Acknowledgements   xv

General introduction to the *Harrogate Great Chronicle*   xxi

Part one: Early Harrogate, 1332–1841

1   Genesis of a community   1

2   Harrogate and the Royal Forest   24

3   Early Harrogate, 1332–1571   52

4   Rise of the spa, 1571–1660   69

5   Restoration to enclosure   96

6   Harrogate and the enclosure of the Forest   124

7   Harrogate spa after 1778   147

8   Bathing at the spa   177

9   Entertainment at the spa   195

10 Township administration and the Poor Law   224

11 Religious life and church building in Harrogate, 1770–1841   239

12 Education in Harrogate   259

13 A hospital for the poor   270

14 The building of Harrogate, 1778–1841   285

15 Obtaining the 1841 Improvement Act   369

16 Conclusion   395

Notes and references   401

Index to part one   408

Part two (on CD): Source materials and bibliography

Class A: General material

Class B: Duchy of Lancaster documents

Class C: Literary documents

Class D: Township documents

Class E: Royal Forest documents

Class F: Spa books

Class G: Guide books

Class H: Protection of the Wells

Class I: Improvement Bill, 1841

Class J: The Stray

Class K: Faith and Religion

Class L: Wills

Class M: High Harrogate church

Class N: Low Harrogate church

Class O: Greeves family papers

Class P: Theatrical playbills

Class Q: Highways and transports

Class R: Newspapers

Class S: Property (enrolments, leases, mortgages, abstracts of title, 1623–1842)

Class T: Haverah Park title deeds, leases and enrolments

Class U: Bath Hospital documents

Class V: Starbeck Spa documents

Class W: Solicitors' documents

Class X: Education documents

List of illustrations

Plates

Frontispiece: The author, Malcolm G. Neesam, University of Leeds
      AD 2001   II

1   The Harrogate Hoard, *c.* 800 BC, courtesy Royal Ontario
     Museum   5

2   John of Gaunt's castle ruin, *c.* 1900   39

3   Arms of the Duchy of Lancaster   43

4   Original 1626 title page of *Spadacrene Anglica*   70

5   The earliest known depiction of the Tewit Well, *c.* 1640   72

6   Tewit Well, with Low Harrogate Sulphur Well Temple of 1807   73

7   The St John's Well, discovered in 1631   79

8   Harrogate Hall   85

9   Bilton Hall, courtesy C. B. Hopes   87

10 Red Cat Cottage was probably once a Beer House or Tavern   312

11 Prospect Farm   175

12 Starbeck Spaw   74

13 Early advertisement for the Starbeck Spaw   75

14 The earliest known plan of Low Harrogate's Sulphur Wells   77

15 Topographical sketch of Sulphur Wells   78

16 Thomas Rowlandson's drawing 'Dr Syntax at Harrowgate'
     Courtesy Harrogate Museums and Art Galleries   310

17 Early photograph of Harrogate water carrier   191

18 Dragon Hotel, *c.* 1870, original Dragon Farm visible third
     from left   102

19 Dragon Hotel at right, and 'Dragon' Theatre at left   210

20 Dragon Lodgings   290

21 The Devonshire Place, or 'Dragon' Theatre   209

22 Queen Hotel, *c.* 1833, ascribed to W. P. Frith   287

23 Queen Buildings, AD 2000   287

24 Church Square, or Spa Hill, *c.* 1833, ascribed to W. P. Frith,
     with the 'Toy Shop', and Bay Horse Inn   106

25	The Bay Horse, precursor of the 'Empress', Church Square	107
26	The Theatre Royal, Church Square, built 1788	211
27	Performances were usually on Tuesdays, Thursdays and Saturdays	213
28	Bilton Endowed School	262
29	Strawberry Dale Academy, c. 1900	166
30	1789 plan for an Assembly Room at Harrogate	203
31	The unknown artist's signature	204
32	High Harrogate 1829, Granby Hotel (left), Church Square (centre), St John's Chapel (right)	291
33	High Harrogate after the 1831 building of Christ Church	286
34	High Harrogate's Park Parade (left) and Devonshire Place (right)	286
35	Woodlands House	296
36	Wedderburn House	297
37	Lady Wedderburn and her circle at the St John's Well, c.1790	293
38	Langdale's Weekly list of Company, precursor of the Harrogate newspapers	340
39	Moses Griffiths' 1772 drawing of Well Hill	178
40	The Sulphur Well, c. 1770	189
41	John Field's drawing of Low Harrogate, c. 1820, the White Hart at left, Hopewell House at right	351
42	Low Harrogate c. 1815. From left to right, the White Hart, Old Bell, Well Hill and Sulphur Well	336
43	designs for an enclosed Sulphur Well pump room	167
44	designs for an open Sulphur Well pump room	168
45	The Sulphur Well Pump Room of 1808, from Well Hill, towards the back of the Old Bell Tavern	163
46	The 1808 Sulphur Well Pump Room, with Well Hill in the background	164
47	Woodcut of old Wellington Inn, Cold Bath Road, c. 1850	302
48	Promenade Inn, photographed c. 1890, long after its closure	306
49	The Crown Hotel, as sketched in c. 1820	179
50	Interior plan of the old Crown Hotel, c. 1820	180
51	The Swan Inn	343
52	The George Hotel's oldest section is on the right	309
53	The 1806 Promenade Room was re-fronted in 1874	275
54	The Crown, or Montpellier Pump Room	167
55	Dr Thomas Garnett, 1765–1802, has been credited with the first scientific analysis of Harrogate's waters	192
56	Pickersgill Palliser, founder of the *Harrogate Advertiser* and Secretary of the Royal Bath Hospital	279

57	The Harrogate Workhouse	273
58	The Starbeck Toll House	119
59	Notice of sale, the Old Bell Inn	337
60	Captain Thomas Thrush, R.N., courtesy of Mrs H. S. Livingstone	317
61	The old Bath Hospital, photographed from Bogs field, c.1860	270
62	The Brunswick Hotel, left, with York Place, right, ascribed to W. P. Frith, c. 1833.	324
63	The Sulphur Well and Well Hill, ascribed to W.P.Frith, c.1833	169
64	Low Harrogate's parish church, St Mary's, was built in 1825	251
65	John Williams used an elegant Ionic design for his 1834 Victoria Baths.	181
66	Joseph Thackwray's Crown, or Montpellier Baths favoured the Tuscan order.	183
67	The 1834 Crown Baths, with the 1822 'Chinese' Crown Pump Room	183
68	The 1835 Spa Rooms were the peak of Harrogate classicism	222
69	The interior of the Spa Rooms	349
70	The beginnings of James Street, the future Prospect Hotel at right, the reconstructed St John's Chapel at centre, Prospect Villas at left	323
71	Prospect Place, right, Parliament Street, centre, Montpellier Parade, left, ascribed to W. P. Frith, c. 1833	352
72	World's End (later Skipton) Road, with Smithy Hill at far left, Grove House at right, ascribed to W. P. Frith, c. 1833	103
73	The Dragon Hotel, childhood of W. P. Frith, R.A.	353
74	Regent Parade, with Westmoreland Street junction at right	357
75	Park Parade, c. 1833, Christ Church at right	361
76	Park House, Park Parade	257
77	Bilton House, Park Parade	362
78	Regent Parade	288
79	Park Parade	289
80	Salutation Buildings, known for many years as Gascoigne's, and then as the County Hotel.	104
81	The Granby, with Granby lodgings at left, and St Alban's Villa at right	105
82	Harlow Hill Observation Tower	367
83	The Crescent Inn, with T. H. Walker's Leamington Well Pump Room of 1838 at far right	115
84	Visitors faced many obstacles on the road to Harrogate	118
85	The arrival of the Harrogate Stage Coach was a keenly anticipated event	121

86 Doubtless the Harrogate doctors also dealt with patients
whose ailments were more of mind than flesh! 283

87 The presence of the militia and rich elderly female visitors
inevitably produced unlikely pairings 365

88 All the great Harrogate hotels provided a weekly ball night
for their guests and invited company 199

89 R. H. Swan's shop behind the Crown Hotel, the original
home of Harrogate Toffee 383

91 By 1831 much of lower Parliament Street had been developed 319

92 Park Parade's Methodist Chapel of 1796 320

93 The Brunswick Hotel at Harrogate corner 332

94 Betty Lupton 385

95 West Park, 1841, with Brunswick Terrace at left 325

96 The Harlow Hill tower, with the 'King's plantation' at left,
drawn by John Field, 1830 366

97 The Bath Hospital and Bogs field, with Harlow Hill at left,
drawn by John Field, 1830 271

98 The Swan Inn drawn by John Field, 1830 311

99 Low Harrogate Church, a drawing by John Field 250

100 The Queen Hotel at left, with Christ Church and Church
Square at right, drawn by John Field in 1830 246

101 St John's Well, with Christ Church at right, and Park Parade
in the background, drawn by John Field in 1830 172

102 The Granby at far left, and the Black Spring (High
Harrogate's well of fresh water) with Church Square and
Mansfield House at right, drawn in 1830 by John Field 190

103 An unidentified drawing from John Field's 1830 collection,
probably of Tewit Well 17

Plans

1 Townships of the Royal Forest xxii

2 Royal parks and woodland chases around Harrogate xxiii

3 Belmont Park 30

4 The Little Park 29

5 1587 Map from Plumpton dispute xxvi

6 Great Broad Way, 1587 xxvii

7 Warburton's map, *c.* 1720 xxxiv

8 Jeffreys' map, *c.* 1767 2

9 Forest of Knaresborough, 1767. Note reversion of north
and south. Courtesy of W.Y.A. Service, Leeds xxx–xxxi

10 Harrogate and the 1778 Award, copy of 1886 144

11	1778 Enclosure, Harlow Hill to West Park	131
12	1778 Enclosure, Harlow to Park Parade	132
13	1778 Enclosure, Bogs Field to Parliament Street	134
14	1778 Enclosure, Cold Bath Road	135
15	1778 Enclosure, King's lands, later Duchy estate	136
16	1778 Enclosure, Pannal Ash	138
17	1778 Enclosure, Pannal Ash to Leeds Road	138
18	1778 Enclosure, York Place to Tewit Well	139
19	1778 Enclosure, South Stray to Hookstone	140
20	1778 Enclosure, High Harrogate	141
21	1778 Enclosure, Granby Corner to Forest Lane Head	142
22	1778 Enclosure, World's End Road	143
23	Ingilby estates, central Harrogate, pre-1810	314
24	Haverah Park & Pannal, *c.* 1778. Russell, p. 126	8
25	King's Harrogate allotments, 1778. Russell's survey, p. 123	31
26	King's High Harrogate allotments, 1778. Russell's survey, p. 122 (see also B.31 and B.32)	299
27	The King's Low Harrogate allotments, *c.* 1782, Russell's survey, p. 122	300
28	The King's allotments, Hookstone to Crimple (see B.31 & B.32) Wedderburn's closes 243 and 245 granted 1781	294
29	King's allotments, Low Harrogate *c.* 1810. Russell's Survey, p. 132	295
30	Chapel lands, *c.* 1810. Russell's surveys, p. 132	298
31	Bilton Park, *c.* 1840. Courtesy West Yorkshire Archive Service, Leeds	54
32	Charles Greeves' 1821 plan of Low Harrogate	305
33	Charles Greeves' 1821 plan of Prospect Place	322
34	Charles Greeves' 1821 plan of the Leeds to Ripon turnpike road	315
35	Charles Greeves' 1821 plan of Park Parade	363
36	Charles Greeves' 1821 plan of the Granby locality	197
37	Twentieth-century reworking of Greeves' 1821 plan	198
38	Surrender of site for St Mary's Church, 1 August 1825	251
39	The Thackwray Well case plan, *c.* 1837	347
40	Survey of Low Harrogate area of Pannal, *c.* 1839	188
41	Survey of Harlow Hill area of Pannal, *c.* 1839, showing field boundaries between Otley Road and Irongate Bridge (now Cornwall) Road	35
42	Powell survey, *c.* 1839. Low Harrogate	326
43	Powell survey, *c.* 1839. Montpellier Quarter to Prospect Place	326
44	Powell survey, *c.* 1839. West Park and York Place	327

45   Powell survey, *c.* 1839. Central Harrogate and West Park   328
46   Powell survey, *c.* 1839. High Harrogate   329
47   Powell survey, *c.* 1839. Church Square and Granby   330
48   Duchy of Lancaster's proposed developments, Low
        Harrogate, John Howgate's 1839 plan   335

Acknowledgements

THE *Harrogate Great Chronicle's* scale and the several decades of its creation have understandably caused me to be indebted to many people and institutions, foremost of which is Her Majesty's Duchy of Lancaster. The Duchy's Clerks, Sir Michael Ridley, his successor, Paul R. Clarke, and my good friend Roy A. Smith, have indeed been gracious and patient during my seemingly interminable examination of the Duchy's archives and to Roy Smith in particular, I owe a great debt for his skill in guiding me to appropriate sources of information. Beyond purely personal expressions of gratitude, I am aware of the role of generations of Duchy officers since 1399, whose work has invariably been to the advantage of the Harrogate community, which is partly why the *Harrogate Great Chronicle* is dedicated, with gracious permission, to the Queen, in whom the Duchy title is invested. Duchy of Lancaster material is reproduced by permission of the Chancellor and Council of the Duchy of Lancaster who retain the copyright.

I would like to acknowledge specific help as follows, in alphabetical order:

Thank you to the *Harrogate Advertiser's* general editor Jean MacQuarrie for providing help with the typing of Class 'R' in 1990; to Peter Barnwell for his great service as textual reader and critic; to Bath Reference Librarian M. Joyce for valuable help in 1988 with the matter of statutes of Elizabeth I; to Bedfordshire Historical Record Society for permission to quote from their 47th volume; to Mr R. Beldon, for bringing my attention to the John Field drawings of *c.*1830; to Birmingham Public Library's Nesta Jenkins in 1989 for help with copies of *The Lounger* for 1785; to the Bodleian Library's department of Western Manuscripts for their guidance in 1994 through the Dodsworth manuscripts, and for the privilege of using Duke Humphrey's Library; to Matthew Bourne for his completion of the plans of the Royal Forest and the parks and woodland chases, as well as for his expertise in converting the author's floppy discs; to the Borthwick Institute, York, for their kind help and reproduction permission; to the Bradford District Archives branch of the West Yorkshire Archive Service, for their help on several occasions between 1987 and 2002, and for their kind permission to reproduce the plans of Harrogate Wells, and documents A.271, A.273, A.287 and C.37; to Brighton and Hove local studies reference librarian Stephanie Green for help with the 1796 *New Brighton Guide*; to the British and Foreign School Society for permissions regarding their material at Brunel University; to the British Library's department of Manuscripts between 1986 and 1998 for help with many inquiries, especially with the Rosslyn papers, and for permission to reproduce material owned by them; to Buxton Library for help with the Axon papers; to Cambridge University Press, for permission to quote from the R. J. Hollingdale 1983 edition of Friedrich Nietzsche's *Untimely Meditations*, published by Cambridge University Press; to George Capel – a good friend – Harrogate's long serving Reference Librarian, for unfailing help over forty years during my interminable examination of the library's collections; to Cardiff Council Libraries and Information Services, for help with the Colt Hoare journals; to DLA Piper Rudnick Gray Cary and the West Yorkshire Archive Service Leeds, for permission to reproduce document A.247; to the Diocese of Chester for their kind permission to reproduce material in Class M; to Mrs G. J. S. Close for kindly allowing me to reproduce extracts from the diary of Dr Simpson, her Great Grandfather; to Harrogate's Millennial Mayor, Councillor George Crowther, OBE, for his suggestion that part two of the *Great Chronicle* be issued on CD; to Cheshire County Record Office for their help with Bishop Bridgeman's Ledger Book and numerous inquiries relating to High Harrogate and the Diocese of Chester, and for permission to reproduce the extracts in Class M; to Mr and Mrs Chippindale for the loan of eighteenth- and nineteenth-century family papers; to the Church of England Record Centre, Bermondsey, for access to files on Harrogate schools; to the Reverend Canon Richard McDermid, Vicar of Christ Church, for permission to copy and reproduce extracts from the Vestry Meeting Minute Book, 1780–1852; to Mrs Ann Clark for information as to the descendants of Basil Cozens-Hardy, editor of the 1950 edition of Silas Neville's diary; to the Viscount Lord Cobham DL of Hagley Hall, and his PA, Joyce Purnell, for help with the manuscript letters of Sarah Lyttleton, and for permission to publish extracts C.98.C.; to Constable Robinson for permission to reproduce extracts from the correspondence of Sir Walter Scott; to Liza Copeland for kind permission to reproduce extracts from the notebook of the Reverend Samuel Ellis; to the Duchy of Cornwall for permission to reproduce documents E.36.c and E.66. and to Duchy Archivist and Records Manager Elisabeth Stuart for her kind help and guidance through the papers of Rollo Clowes; to Coutts & Co. for information about Baroness Burdett-Coutts; the author acknowledges the genius of George Cruickshank; to Mr R. Davidson, a good friend, for his unfailing and regular encouragement of my historical endeavours; to Devon County Council for their search,

Acknowledgements

fruitless alas, for information about James Franklin of Bere Ferrers; to the Duke of Devonshire, for permission to reproduce the Devonshire Mss, Chatsworth; to the Dickens House Museum for information about the pastiche 'The Pickwickians, or Sam Weller in Harrogate'; to Mr G. R. Fowler, a good friend, for information about the growth of retail developments on Royal Parade, and for regular encouragement; to Mr Robert Frost, Senior Librarian at the Yorkshire Archaeological Society, for decades of help and advice; to Gloucestershire Record Office for their help with identifying the notebooks of Rev. Samuel Ellis from 1781 to 1801, and other British diaries; to Mrs M. Graham for information about the Leeds Road Lodge; to Dr S. J. D. Green for guiding me towards a successful Master of Philosophy degree and for advice on relevant reading material; to Harrogate Council's Chief Executive Mick Walsh for granting access to deeds of council-owned property; to Harrogate Borough Council's Lynne Mee for her greatly appreciated and regular encouragement, and for help with typing class R; to Harrogate Librarians John Stuffins and Harry Whittleston for permission to reproduce local history material; to Jane Hatcher for bringing to my attention several useful items of local history; to the Controller of Her Majesty's Stationery Office and the Queen's printer for Scotland for permission to reproduce the Crown copyright extracts in part two, and for their splendid work in editing, printing and disseminating the Rolls series; the late Dr Phyllis Hembry, distinguished author of *Spas of England*, for her unfailing expertise in all matters related to British spa history, for her interest in and encouragement of the author's work, and for her generous permission to quote from her own work; to Mr M. Hine, a good friend, for his regular encouragement of my work, and for helping me obtain the special paper for the complete printed edition of the *Great Chronicle*; to C. B. Hopes for supplying the illustration of Bilton Hall, and for advice on a range of suitable illustrative material; to Bernard Horrocks, Copyright Officer of the National Portrait Gallery, for information on pictorial copyright; to Dr Richard Hoyle for permission to reproduce his valuable work on the riots of 1507; to R. J. Stanley, group librarian at Hull, for help with the Wray and Hollingsworth letters; to the librarian of the Brynmor Jones Library at the University of Hull, for information about Bentley's *Miscellany*; to Brian Dyson, and the staff of the University of Hull's Archive department, for making available the Courtney diaries; to Hutchinson for making available the diary of Joseph Farington; to Sir Thomas Ingilby Bt of Ripley Castle, for pointing me in the right direction regarding the Haverah Park Papers; to Adrian Blunt, Deputy Librarian at the Inner Temple Library, for his interpretation of several references in Conway Davies' *Catalogue*; to Thomas Quinlan of the National Archives, Dublin, for help with the Irish State Papers, and to the Director of the

National Archives of the Irish Republic for kindly granting permission to publish document C.87; to D. J. Johnson, Deputy Clerk of Records at the House of Lords for granting access in 1991 to several eighteenth-century Bills and Acts; and to the House of Lords Record Office for permission to reproduce extracts A.254; A.255; A.256; A.257; A.258; A.259; A.260; to Professor Bernard Jennings, for permission to reproduce extracts from the *History of Harrogate and Knaresborough* (Advertiser Press, 1970), and from the *History of Nidderdale* (Advertiser Press, 1967), both of which he edited; to Mrs Joan Kirby for help with the Plompton correspondence; to Leeds District Archives at Sheepscar on many occasions between 1978 to 2002 for help with many matters, particularly with the Bilton Park Papers, Pannal vestry minutes, and for permission to reproduce the 1767 pre-enclosure map; to Leeds City Library for access to their local history collections; to the University of Leeds and their School of History, for teaching me the art of historiography; to the Library of the University of Leeds for their help and patience in obtaining source material; to the Special Collections department of Leeds University Library for permission to reproduce extracts from material in their collections; to Lincolnshire Archives for their help with the Tennyson papers; to Lord Lytton, and the authors' agents Pollinger Limited, for permission to reproduce the Lovelace Letters reproduced in C.56; to Mrs A. London, fellow historian and friend, for her regular encouragement of my historical endeavours; to the Central Library at Manchester, for help with information about Tryphosa Jane Wallis; to John Murray, publishers, for permission to reproduce extracts from Lord Byron's letters and journals, edited by Leslie A. Marchand; to the National Archives, for invaluable and repeated help during frequent visits between 1987 and 2005, both at their former location in Chancery Lane, and their new one at Kew; and for their permission to reproduce the state's archives; to North Yorkshire County Council Record office for their courtesy and help with all communications, and for permission to reproduce extracts in several documentary classes; to the Public Record Office of Northern Ireland, and the Deputy Keeper of Records, for permission to reproduce extracts from the Castlereagh papers; to Dr Bruce Osborne of the Spas Research Fellowship for his enthusiastic encouragement of my research into the early history of Harrogate spa; to Oxford University Press for permission to reproduce extracts from their publications; to Pan MacMillan, for their kind cooperation with extracts from the letters of George Dempster; to Dr D. Crook for information about the Pipe Roll Society; to Pollinger Limited, authors' agents, for their kind cooperation with the Lovelace papers; to the successor to the firm of Powell & Son for their gracious patience during the author's many years of scrutiny of their records, and their kind permissions; to Princeton University Press for permission to reproduce lines from L. M.

Acknowledgements

Knapp's *Tobias Smollett*; to the Random House Archive and Library, for their help with reproducing extracts from the diary of Joseph Farington, and, from the chosen letters of Maria Edgeworth; to the Record Society of Lancashire and Cheshire for publishing the *Great Diurnal of Nicholas Blundell*; to Brigadier Ridley of Mansfield House for providing me with access to various deeds and papers connected with Harrogate's Georgian theatre; to St Robert's Church, Pannal, for permission to reproduce material in documents D.60–D.63 and K.18; to the Royal Historical Society for permission to reprint lines from J. Kirby's edition of the Camden Society's fifth series, eighth volume, *Plumpton Letters*, and also for permission to reproduce documents C.7, C.29.1, E.12, E.14, E.48–51; to the Royal Mail Archive for their kind permission to the author to reproduce material held in the British Postal Museum and Archive, identified by entry A.309; to the Royal Ontario Museum in Toronto for information about the Harrogate Hoard, and for permission to publish the photograph on plate one; to the Royal Commission on Historical Manuscripts on many occasions between 1987 and 1998, for help in locating material through the National Register of Archives; to Graham Saunders for giving me access to the archives of the former Royal Bath Hospital, and permission to reproduce extracts before 1841; to The Lord Saye and Sele for permission to reproduce extracts from the journal of Celia Fiennes; to Norman Scarfe for permission to reproduce an example of his work on the 1786 Harrogate visit of Alexandre de la Rochefoucauld; to the Scottish Record Office for help with the papers of Alexander Wedderburn and the diary of Cameron of Erracht; to Mrs A. Smith, a good friend, for her advice and help on matters concerning the history of Pannal Village; to Sheffield Archives for help with the Hofland papers, and Bilton Mill lease of 1597, and to the Head of Sheffield City Council's Department of Leisure Services for permission to reproduce documents A.109, C.83; to Mrs Elizabeth Sheilds for her splendid trans- lations of Latin and Anglo-French manuscripts, and for her general advice on interpretation; to the Society for Theatre Research for permission to reproduce C.59, and for information about the late Sybil Rosenfeld; to Mrs Suzy Stead, for her tireless work in converting the author's manuscripts into machine readable form; to Harrogate's late Librarian and Curator, John Stuffins, for stimulating my earliest efforts at historical research; to the Surtees Society, for their kind granting of permission to the author to quote extracts from society publications, and to the Honorary Secretary, Dr Anne Orde, for her advice on Symeon of Durham. to Maurice Taylor for help with the Yorkshire place-name 'Harlow'; to Mr W. F. Taylor for permission to reproduce lines from his 1996 edition of *Ducks and Pease*; to the family of the late Mr W. P. Thistlethwaite for permission to quote from his 1984 volume *Quaker Meetings of Knaresborough and Harrogate*; to Mrs Sylvia

Thomas, incomparable archivist, formerly of West Yorkshire, for her unfailing help and encouragement on every occasion; to the Thoresby Society for permission to quote extracts from their publications; to the memory of Harrogate Historian H. H. Walker, for his constant encouragement of my historical work, and for the privilege of serving as his reader; to the literary executor of the late Leslie P. Wenham, for permission to publish the Harrogate extracts from his work; to the Wellcome Institute Library, and Andrew Melvin, for access to books from their early printed book collection; to Wakefield Archives for help with Turnpike Trust papers, Quarter Sessions' records, and various property deeds; to West Yorkshire Archive Service for their valued help over several decades and for permission to reproduce material held by them, and also for material from the Diocese of Chester in their keeping; to Ruth Wilcock for providing several useful references to old Bilton; to the City of York Council: York Reference Library, for kind permission to reproduce the Hargrove papers, and for providing access to eighteenth-century Yorkshire newspapers; to York Minster Library and Archives, for information about post-Norman conquest diocesan organisation, and for help with the identification of several documents; to the University of York for help with the letters of Sir Walter Scott; to York City Archives for regular help during the 1970s and 1980s, and to City of York Archivist Mrs Rita Freedman in particular for her frequent advice, and sturdy defence of York's Archives; to the Council of the Yorkshire Archaeological Society for permission to reproduce references from the *Leeds Friends Minute Book, 1692–1712*, and from other documents in their collections.

To all these, and the many other individuals and organisations who have helped me with the Harrogate Great Chronicle, I offer my profound gratitude and thanks.

I have been particularly careful to respect the copyrights of all material used. Some copyright holders have proved impossible to identify or contact, and I apologise for any offence inadvertently caused by this failure.

Finally, I have a great debt of gratitude to Mr C. J. Bentley, of Hornbeam Park Developments Limited, without whose encouragement and help the *Harrogate Great Chronicle* would not have appeared.

Malcolm G. Neesam, Manor Place, 2005.

General introduction to the Harrogate Great Chronicle

T HE *Harrogate Great Chronicle* has two principal sections: a comprehensive collection of documentary source materials pertinent to the
history of Harrogate from earliest times to 1841, and a narrative history
based on them. This introduction should, however, be read before
consulting either the narrative history or the source materials, as it explains
the genesis, content and purpose of the entire work.

Part two, the *Source materials and bibliography*, was the first to be
completed. It consists of twenty-four classes of source materials relating to
Harrogate town, which are reproduced either as abstracts or in full. The
sequence includes all known references to Harrogate from 1332 until 1841.
The former date is the earliest surviving documentary reference to
Harrogate, and the latter is that of the 1841 Improvement Act, and the
beginning of H. H. Walker's monumental *History of Harrogate under the
Improvement Commissioners, 1841–1884*. Indeed, the *Harrogate Great Chronicle*
was written as a companion volume to the Walker study, and to form the
first of a series of authoritative books on the town's history.

Part one, *Early Harrogate, 1332–1841*, is a narrative history of Harrogate
based on the source materials reproduced in part two. It is the first serious
attempt to untangle the town's history from that of the neighbouring
communities of the surrounding Royal Forest.

The first history of Harrogate was written by Eli Hargrove for his guide
book, which appeared in 1775. Hargrove was a printer and bookseller,
whose principal interest lay in pleasing his customers, the majority of whom
were spa visitors. Accordingly, emphasis was placed on modern spa
amenities, on hotels and inns, on entertainments, on sightseeing. History

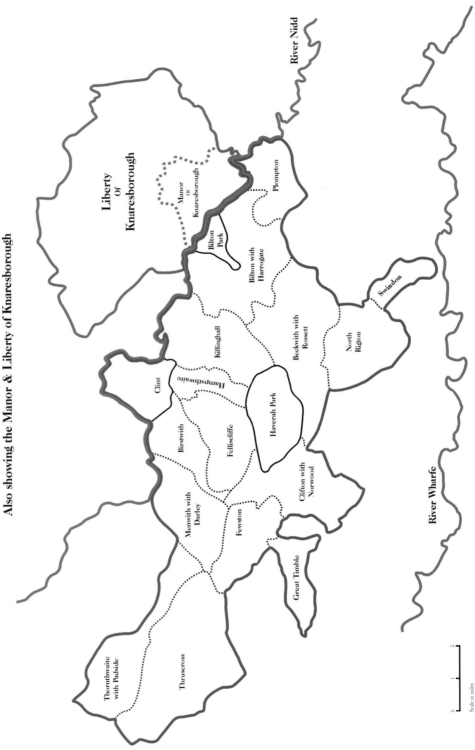

Townships of the Royal Forest
Also showing the Manor & Liberty of Knaresborough

River Nidd

Liberty
of
Knaresborough

Manor
of
Knaresborough

Plompton

Bilton
Park

Bilton with
Harrogate

Swindon

Killinghall

Beckwith with
Rossett

North
Rigton

Clint

Hampsthwaite

Haverah Park

Birstwith

Fewstone

Felliscliffe

Clifton with
Norwood

Menwith with
Darley

Great Timble

River Wharfe

Thornthwaite
with Padside

Thruscross

Scale in miles

2   1   0

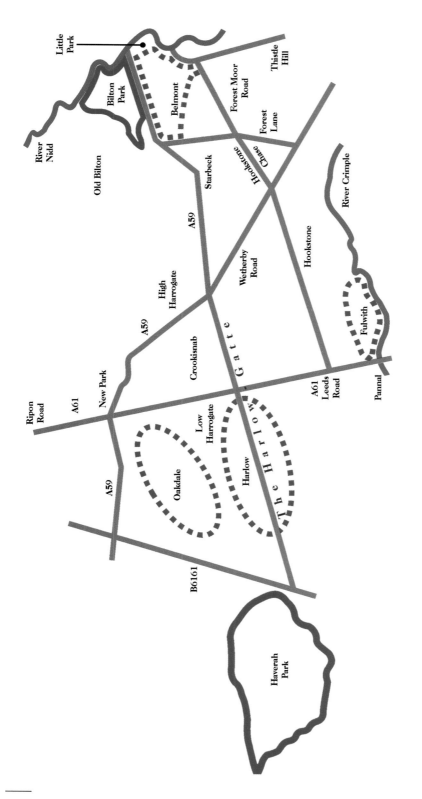

PLAN 2
Royal parks and
woodland chases
around Harrogate

Harrogate and its encircling Royal Parks and Woodland Chases,
showing the actual boundaries of the parks, and the conjectural bounds (broken lines) of the
woodland chases, with modern roads superimposed.

Little Park

River Nidd

Old Bilton

Bilton Park

Belmont

Forest Moor Road

Forest Lane

Thistle Hill

Starbeck

Hookstone Chase

River Crimple

A59

High Harrogate

Wetherby Road

Hookstone

Ripon Road

A61

A59

New Park

Crookisnab

G a t t e

Fulwith

A59

Oakdale

Low Harrogate

Harlow

T h e H a r l o w

A61 Leeds Road

Pannal

B6161

Haverah Park

was largely ignored, or reduced to a series of colourful anecdotes for the diversion of the reader, few of whom would have required anything more detailed. This fostered the belief that Harrogate had little history, and that its development was driven by Georgian spa mania. Nor was this error helped by the progressive tendencies of the townspeople, who, driven by the doctors and innkeepers, strove to extend patronage by improving and extending facilities. Old buildings were torn down ruthlessly to make way for improvements, and if visitors liked to see the ancient and the picturesque, they could always visit the surrounding communities recommended in Mr Hargrove's guidebook. What Harrogate's visitors wanted were ever better and modern spa facilities, and that was precisely what they got. There was little money in history.

The first antiquarian investigation into the town's past was undertaken by William Grainge is his 1871 volume *The History and Topography of Harrogate and the Forest of Knaresborough*. Grainge's text is a mixture of scholasticism, gossip, travel writing, and antiquarianism. He relates things that we would sooner not have, such as endless lists of monumental inscriptions within churches, and he omits things we wish he had not, such as histories of the old Harrogate inns. Nevertheless, Grainge's book was a good start to the process of providing Harrogate with a reliable historiography, and even if only 125 of its 511 pages related to Harrogate town, those 125 pages were valuable.

The second attempt at a history of Harrogate was Walter Kaye's superb *Records of Harrogate*, which appeared in 1922. This book is not a narrative history, but a scrupulously edited presentation of source materials pertaining to the town's pre-nineteenth-century history. It is perhaps the only work that the *Harrogate Great Chronicle* does not render obsolete, as it contains full transcriptions of Church Registers and Parish Accounts. Kaye's notes on Harrogate's pre-reformation chantry chapel were of outstanding importance.

In 1954, William Haythornthwaite's *Harrogate Story* appeared in the form of a slim, 121-page study of the township from 'Georgian village to Victorian town'. Haythornthwaite used the recently re-discovered township records to describe the working of the local authority system, paying special attention to the operation of the poor law and workhouse. The author of several brilliant newspaper articles on Harrogate's history, Haythornthwaite died before he could write the longer work to which his surviving notes indicate he was working.

The most significant attempt to replace William Grainge's *History and Topography* ... appeared in 1970, with the *History of Harrogate and Knaresborough*, written by the Harrogate W.E.A. Local History Group, edited by Bernard Jennings. Of the text's 452 pages, about 240 are concerned with Harrogate's history. The importance of the W.E.A. history lay in its extensive use of the hitherto neglected Rolls of the Court of the Royal Forest, which enabled the history of Harrogate to be pushed back several centuries.

The W.E.A. Jennings *History* ... appeared at the same time as H. H. Walker began to write his *History of Harrogate under the Improvement Commissioners, 1841 to 1884*. The book was the author's life's work, based on research notes collected over forty years. Unfortunately Walker died in 1980, before the book was finished, and his family entrusted its completion, editing and publication, to the present author, a task that took six years. When the Walker book finally appeared in 1986, the author had come to understand that the pre-1841 history of Harrogate also merited study, the *Harrogate Great Chronicle* being the result. At this point, it is necessary to step back two decades.

In 1964, the author worked as an assistant at Harrogate Library, which was then under the inspired control of John Stuffins, the Borough Curator and Librarian. About fifteen years earlier, Stuffins had acquired Harrogate's Township records, the majority of which were stored in the loft of the Old Town Hall, with others being discovered in a local antiquarian bookshop. This important collection was re-housed in the basement of Harrogate Library, where it was consulted by Haythornthwaite, and later, in 1959, catalogued by the National Register of Archives. By 1964, the bundles of documents had become untidy, with some of the wrappers showing signs of wear and tear. The author was then directed by Stuffins to put them into order, a process that lasted until the author left the library to attend the University of Leeds' Department of Librarianship. This early contact with the Township Records, which with the active encouragement of John Stuffins, he began to transcribe, provided the author with his first experience of local historical research.

In 1974, following the reorganisation of local government, the Township papers passed to the successor authorities, and for nearly ten years, no catalogue or finding list was available, which is why the author has not attempted to amend the abstracts done before 1972 by himself and William Haythornthwaite.

The concept of expanding class 'D' into the greater range of classes 'A' to 'X', developed after we came to appreciate both the extent of Harrogate's local history source material, and how very remote and obscure much of it was. At the same time we were aware of two other factors: first, the growing demand for source materials of local history, especially from those groups for whom visits to the British Library, Scottish Record Office, Chatsworth House, Duchy of Lancaster, or even West Yorkshire Archives, were impracticable; secondly, the extreme fragility of many source

PLAN 5. 1587 Map from Plumpton dispute.

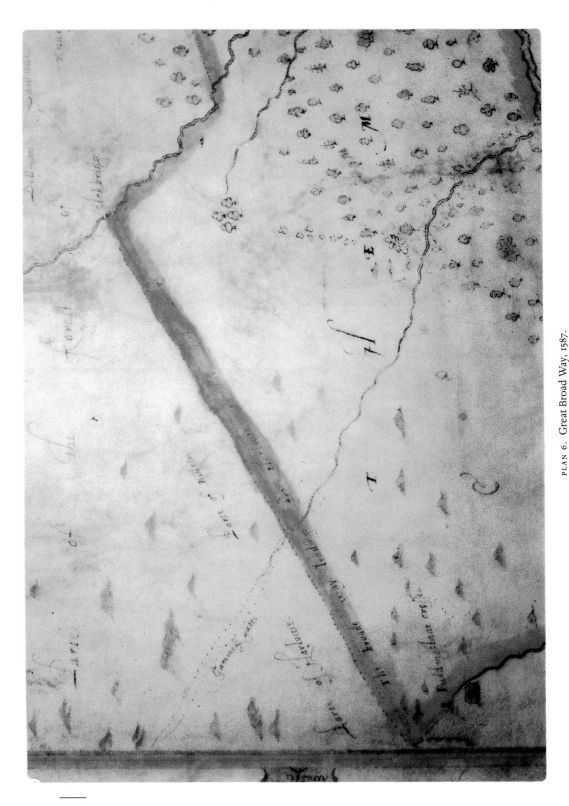

PLAN 6. Great Broad Way, 1587.

materials, allied to their careless handling by such users as school classes. These considerations led inevitably to one conclusion: the cause of local history would only be furthered by making available within the covers of a single published work, *the entirety* of relevant source materials. Such a collection would also empower local historians to an unprecedented degree, and provide means for the critical exploration of all published work, including that of the present author.

The narrative history that forms the first section of the *Harrogate Great Chronicle*, was written to demonstrate how source materials may be interpreted and exploited. In itself, the narrative history is complete, and can be detached from part two, the document classes 'A' to 'X'. However, for the reader who wishes to investigate in depth any subject referred to in the narrative history, access to part two is essential, via the link provided by means of the accompanying code references.

But why reproduce so much; surely the above criteria could be met by a more critically selective approach? Does not this gigantic comprehensiveness smack of negation of editorial responsibility? Our reply to such accusations is to explain that the *Harrogate Great Chronicle* serves the needs of conservers, as well as exploiters, of knowledge, and that no one can say with finality which fragment of information will be of use to future researchers. Our book is also intended as a counter to the fashion for the pamphlet school of local historiography, which is not without value, but needs balancing with more substantial work. We also hope to set an example for other communities and local historians, as a demonstration of how to locate, abstract, reproduce and interpret the source materials of local history. Indeed, it is possible that the *Harrogate Great Chronicle* is one of the largest historiographical studies ever completed on a single English community.

We began to develop the *Harrogate Great Chronicle* immediately after the 1986 publication of H. H. Walker's *History of Harrogate Under The Improvement Commissioners, 1841–1884*. In its complete form, the *Harrogate Great Chronicle* represents a considerable expenditure of our resources, which begs the question of its value. Let us therefore consider the value of history in general.

'In any case, I hate everything that merely instructs me without augmenting or directly invigorating my activity.' Goethe's words explain the stimulus for this book. The effective citizen should know his community and how it came to be. Such knowing encourages co-operation and participation, surely a necessity for civilised life. 'Instruction without invigoration, knowledge without attendant action, should be hated by us as a costly superfluity and luxury' – again, Goethe's words.

In the second of his *Untimely Meditations*, published in 1874, Nietzsche defined and considered three categories of historiography: the monumental, the antiquarian, and the critical.

Monumental history sees the great isolated achievements of higher humanity strung out across the millennia like mountain peaks linking a chain across a sea of mediocrity. This monumental conception of the past teaches the man of the present that greatness was once achieved, and that it therefore may be achieved again. It allows us to go on our way with a lighter step, and comforts in times of degeneracy. At the same time, monumental history can overwhelm and dismay, by holding before the reader such a dazzling image of former greatness that the viewer is tempted to give up the struggle of life in despair. And this proposition needs to be understood and pondered: history can be borne only by strong personalities; weak ones are utterly extinguished by it.

Antiquarian history reveres that which has survived – buildings, literatures, moralities, philosophies etc. The antiquarian tends with care that which has existed from of old, so that the conditions under which he himself came into existence may be preserved for those who will come after him. This desire to perpetuate the past for the service of the future, serves life, and is therefore good. Popular misinterpretation of the *Magna Carta*, or naïve belief in the value of written constitutions, are manifestations of faith in antiquarian history. Nowhere is this value higher than when it spreads a simple feeling of pleasure and contentment over the modest, rude, or even barren conditions in which men and nations live. Yet the moment antiquarian history is no longer animated by the fresh life of the present, and falls into mere scholarly-ness, it becomes degenerate. There then follows the repulsive spectacle of the mindless rage for collecting together everything that has ever existed. Man becomes encased in the stench of must and mould, in the indiscriminate raking together of fragments of bibliographical minutiae. Witness the activities of that embodiment of the modern bore, the obsessive genealogist; listen to his conversation – but no, we ask *too* much!

Critical history also serves life, for if he is to live and progress, man must have the strength to break up and break free of the past. But only a superior strength can judge; weaklings hide behind the mask of tolerance, which can often be, we suggest, nothing other than an inability to say no. And all this is quite apart from those who when they write history, do so in the naïve belief that all the popular views of precisely their own age are right and just views, and that to write in accordance with such views is the same thing as being just. *This* is their so-called objectivity.

We warn against over-saturating with history, be it in relation to an individual, a community, or a people. Over-saturation seems to be dangerous and hostile to life in five respects.

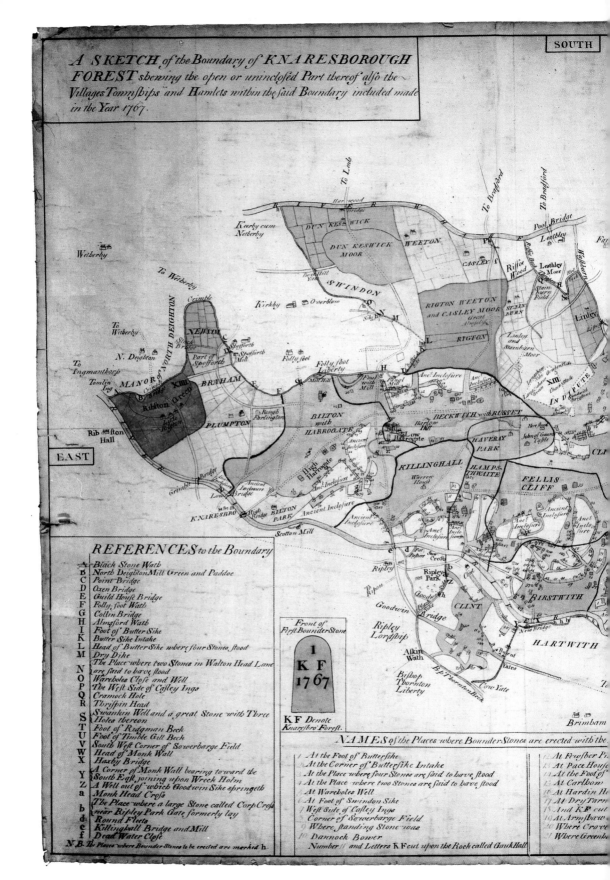

SOUTH

*A SKETCH of the Boundary of KNARESBOROUGH
FOREST shewing the open or uninclosed Part thereof also the
Villages Townships and Hamlets within the said Boundary included made
in the Year 1767.*

EAST

REFERENCES to the Boundary

- A Black Stone Wath
- B North Deighton Mill Green and Paddoe
- C Point Bridge
- D Oxen Bridge
- E Guild House Bridge
- F Folly foot Wath
- G Collin Bridge
- H Almsford Wath
- I Foot of Butter Sike
- K Butter Sike Intake
- L Head of Butter Sike where four Stones stood
- M Dry Dike
- N The Place where two Stones in Walton Head Lane are said to have stood
- O Wareholes Close and Well
- P The West Side of Casley Ings
- Q Cramock Hole
- R Thrissen Head
- S Swankin Well and a great Stone with Three Holes thereon
- T Foot of Ridgman Beck
- U Foot of Timble Gill Beck
- V South West Corner of Sowerbarge Field
- W Head of Monk Wall
- X Haxby Bridge
- Y A Corner of Monk Wall bearing toward the South East, joining upon Wreck Holm
- Z A Well out of which Goodwin Sike springeth
- a Monk Head Cross
- b The Place where a large Stone called Corp Cross near Ripley Park Gate formerly lay
- d Round Fleets
- e Killinghall Bridge and Mill
- f Dead Water Close

N.B. The Places where Bounder Stones to be erected are marked h.

Front of First Bounder Stone

1
K F
17 67

K F Denote
Knaresbro' Forest.

NAMES of the Places where Bounder Stones are erected with the

1 At the Foot of Buttersike
2 At the Corner of Buttersike Intake
3 At the Place where four Stones are said to have stood
4 At the Place where two Stones are said to have stood
5 At Wareholes Well
6 At Foot of Swindon Sike
7 West Side of Casley Ings
8 Corner of Sowerbarge Field
9 Where standing Stone was
10 Dannock Bower
11 Number 11 and Letters K F cut upon the Rock called Gawk Hall

12 At Fresher Pi
13 At Pace House
14 At the Foot of
15 At Carlbow
16 At Hardin He
17 At Dry Tarn
18 And K F cut
19 At Armsbur
20 Where Crave
21 Where Greenb

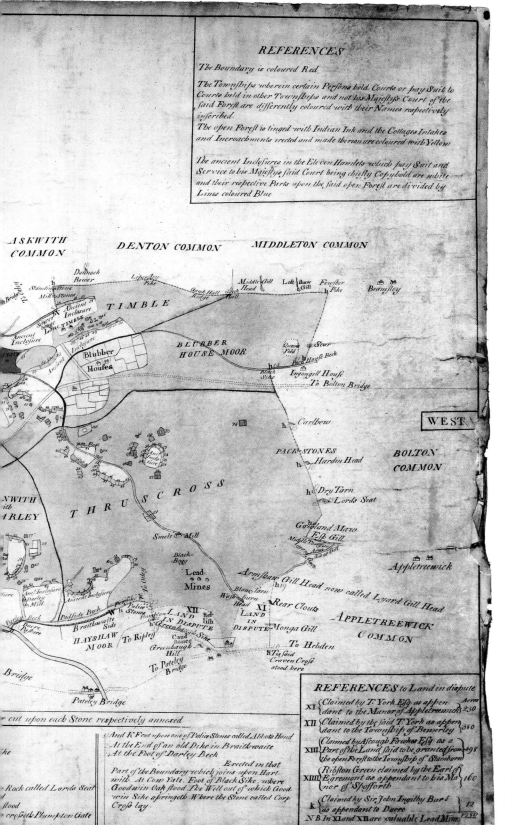

First, it can create a weakened personality whereby backward looking consideration on the past leads to a devaluation of the present, in the belief that nothing memorable can again be achieved.

Second, it can lead an age to believe that it possesses the rarest of virtues, justice, to a greater degree than any other age.

Third, it disrupts the instinct for spiritual progress and development, both in individuals and in communities, and thus hinders the attainment of maturity.

Fourth, it implants the deadly belief that mankind has reached old age, and that one lives in a late civilisation, causing boldness, adventuring, and the passing of new frontiers, to be banished.

Fifth, it leads to a dangerous cynicism in respect of the world and the place of the individual in it.

Thus Nietszche, on the uses and abuses of history!

These considerations deserve to be pondered by those readers into whose hands we now place this result of long labour. In writing the *Harrogate Great Chronicle*, we are giving the public two new tools for local historiography. The first is akin to the scalpel, as it enables the researcher to sift through the surviving records of the community's past, with the precision and deftness of a practised surgeon. The second tool is new to the historiography of locality – the hammer!

In our journey down the centuries of our community's past, we have witnessed many things and met many people. We have seen the lives of such grandees as the Lord Chancellor of England, as well as those of the least of the paupers in the Township's Workhouse. The high days and holidays of the townspeople have been before our eyes, as have the darker visitations of famine, murder and plague. Just as we have savoured the splendour of life at the great inns and hotels, so have we tasted the tragedy of bankruptcy, sickness and bereavement. We have attended the birth of children who became the saviours of their community, as well as those who became murderers. The obscure customs and deeds of the ancient Forest have been uncovered, and set down in print for all, as have the deliberations of the Township authorities, who dragged the often unwilling community into the modern age. We have unlocked secrets, opened private diaries and letters, setting forth the intimate thoughts of their long-dead authors. By way of balance, we have republished those newspapers and broadsheets whose print was once of import to the whole community. And yet – we are aware that our journey through more than five hundred years of the past has been superficial, and that much of significance has been lost beyond power of recall.

Beware of historians. Still more, beware of historians who are at pains to proclaim their impartiality, their objectivity. Such historians are deluding themselves, even if they do not delude the reader. A historian without an axe to grind has never, will never, exist. And what of our axe, or, if we may change the allusion, why forge this *hammer*. Ah, my friends, the truth is that we simply wish to give back to the community that which it has forgotten, and to do so with crushing thoroughness.

W A P O N

Dishforth

Carleton

Ripon
Bishopton

Cundall

Norton un Clay

Thornton Bridge

B U R

Henwick Bridge

Marton

Thorp

Brafferton
Helperby

TAKE

M E L

Studley Park

Kirby Hill

Hunburton

Newby Hall

Skelton

Ellenthorp

Myton

Ten Mile Hill

Fountain Hall
Fountains Abby

Brampton

Bur rowbridge

Micklehow Hill
Haddock Stone 8

Markenfield

Roecliff

Isurium

Fowler ton

Inglethorp

Bishop Mount

The Spaw

Devils Arrows or Brigantium

Aldborough

toft

Coplowe

Minskip

L. Dunsford

Alne Church
Langford

inton

Burton

Staveley

Arkendale

H. Dunsford

Oldwarke

Newton

Stanley

Leonal

Grafton

G. Ousburn

Ours R. Lin

Walkingham

Marton

A
P
O
N

Brearton

Lit. Ousburn

Kirby Hall

Mowton

The Park of The Hay

Marton Woods

Ripley

Furnham

Scotten

Allerton Mauleverer

Whixley Park

Whixley

Nun Monkton

Screven

The Priory

Flaxby

Colstrop

Greenhamerton

Bilton Park

Dropping Well

Knaresborough
S. Roberts Chap: an the Hermitage of one intire Stone

Gold-borough

Hopperton

Kirk Hamerton

Hunsin gere

Cattel

Wisthorp

Tarraygate Spaw

Plumpton Tonr

Washford

Ribston Hall

Couthorp

Midd R.

Over

1 | Genesis of a community

O N 30 September 1332 the Royal Forest Court enquired into a complaint by John of Harowgat concerning assault and trespass, the court's enquiry being recorded in the rolls (A.35). This is the earliest surviving documentary reference to Harrogate in any spelling, and although the matters detailed in the court roll were commonplace, the reference is of outstanding importance for the historian. The interesting aspect of the 1332 court roll is that it is the oldest *surviving* document of a series which once stretched back to the beginnings of the Royal Forest in *c.* 1100, and, had this series been preserved, it is likely that there would be even older references to Harrogate than that of the 1332 Roll. Before the author opens the narrative history of Harrogate from 1332 to 1841, it is necessary to consider how the Harrogate named in that 1332 court roll came into being, a task complicated somewhat by paucity of evidence.

The first task required of any reader seeking to interpret source materials of Harrogate's history is to define what is meant by Harrogate – or for that matter, what is meant by any term of locality, boundary or community. As these words were set down at the very end of the twentieth century, the place name Harrogate was applied to both the traditional town, with its population of over 70,000, and to the greater district, with its population in excess of 140,000. Yet the former had neither a separate Mayor or Council to represent its peculiar interest, and the latter included within its boundary the communities of Aldborough, Boroughbridge, Knaresborough, Masham, Pateley Bridge and Ripon. As for boundaries, they are of no more definitive use than place-names, given the number of boundaries that may exist, and the degree of disparity between one and another. Old Harrogate, for example, consisted of two villages: Bilton-with-Harrogate, also known as High Harrogate, and Low Harrogate, sometimes called Sulphur Wells. Bilton-with-Harrogate formed, for a time, part of the township of Killinghall, and Low Harrogate, or Sulphur Wells, formed part of Pannal, which itself was part of Beckwith-with-Rossett. For practical purposes, however, the boundaries of real significance were those of parish, diocese and township. Bilton-with-Harrogate was within the diocese of Chester,

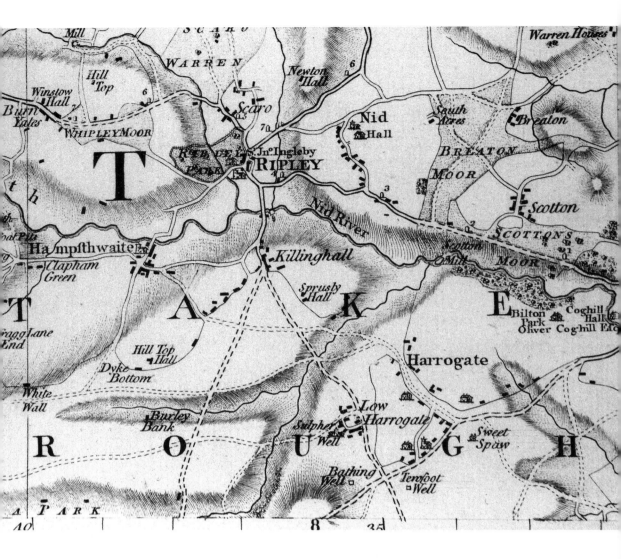

PLAN 8
A section of Jeffreys'
map, *c.* 1767.

Low Harrogate was within the diocese of York – at least until 1836, when both High and Low Harrogate came into the new diocese of Ripon.

And then there was the Royal Forest. Both High and Low Harrogate were within the Royal Forest, which because of the importance of neighbouring Knaresborough Castle was known as the Royal Forest of Knaresborough. Yet the town of Knaresborough was never part of the Royal Forest of Knaresborough, being divided from it to the south by the River Nidd. Knaresborough town had been a borough since 1169, later forming part of the greater Liberty of Knaresborough, which included the manors of Arkendale, Burton Leonard, Scriven, Ferrensby and Knaresborough. To add to the confusion, both the Royal Forest of Knaresborough and the Liberty of Knaresborough formed part of the larger Honour of Knaresborough, which was first mentioned in 1167, an Honour being a grouping of several manors under the administration of a single lord.

A further trap awaits the historian searching for documentary evidence, in that things are seldom as they are described. From the fact that Harrogate is not named within the Domesday Book of 1086, may be extrapolated the conclusion that Harrogate did not exist in 1086. Bilton is, however, referred to in Domesday, and when it is appreciated that the court rolls of the Royal Forest of Knaresborough, from the first surviving copy of 1332, until the eighteenth century, with their many hundreds of references to Bilton-with-Harrogate seldom refer to Bilton alone in their enrolments (S.1 etc.), the significance of clerical abbreviation may be grasped. And Domesday is full of such abbreviations. Added to this is the etymological fact that the place-names which comprise the town of Harrogate, including Bilton, Beckwith, Harlow, and Harrogate itself, are pre-Norman, having Anglo-Norse roots. Pannal is not mentioned in the Domesday Book, but Pannal was part of Beckwith-with-Rossett, and Beckwith and Rossett are both entered in the 1086 survey (A.9).

The Harrogate referred to in the court enquiry of 30 September 1332 (A.35) had not sprung into being in order to provide John and his companions with a convenient place of domicile, but had existed before their time. Before we relate Harrogate's history from 1332 until the time of the Improvement Act of 1841, it is necessary to peer further into the well of the past.

Hitherto, the principal reason for the lack of serious archaeological investigation into Harrogate's pre-Conquest history, has been the naïve acceptance of the belief that it had no such history, and that unlike all the other surrounding communities of Nidderdale, Harrogate sprang into existence at some point in the eighteenth century, as if from a black hole. The weight of this book in the reader's hands is proof to the contrary.

Over two hundred years before the appearance of the *Harrogate Great Chronicle*, the work of Eli Hargrove began a myth. The Harrogate sections of Hargrove's guidebooks always emphasised the town's up-to-date-ness, praising the modernity of its facilities and the current fashionableness of its life and society. History was left to the surrounding countryside. Hargrove's writings provided Harrogate with propaganda for its modern spa, and treated the surrounding communities as suitable subjects for the amusement of visitors to Harrogate in search of picturesque diversion from the rigours of spa life. This legacy was responsible in no small part for the neglect of Harrogate's earliest history (G.1 etc.).

Yorkshire contains many examples of pre-Roman antiquity, the Devil's Arrows near Boroughbridge being a celebrated example. Within the area of Harrogate town, few examples of such antiquities have been discovered, probably because the condition of the land, which was heavy clay, covered with damp scrub-growth, discouraged early settlement. Certainly mesolithic finds have been made on Greenhow Hill, sixteen miles north-west of Harrogate, which pollen analysis has dated to about 4500 BC and similar discoveries made at Blubberhouses Moor and Great Almscliffe. Neolithic – or New Stone Age – implements have also been found at Rigton Moor, and arrowheads, flint and stone axes, have been unearthed at Haverah Park, Killinghall, Kirkby Overblow, Knaresborough and Harrogate. Bronze Age material has also been discovered throughout the area, and some bronze axe heads found near to the St John's Well at High Harrogate.[1] The most interesting Bronze Age find at Harrogate consists of three artifacts from the late ninth or eighth century BC which were discovered in 1848 in a field ¾ of a mile north east of Bilton village, map reference SE 4798 5130 (A.6). The so-called Harrogate Hoard (see plate 1) comprised a bronze socketed spearhead with a basal loop; a bronze leaf-shaped sword; and a bronze socketed spearhead with gold foil ornament. The latter item has design elements in common with a spearhead discovered at Lough Gur, County Limerick, Ireland, and with a spear-head found at Pyotdykes, Angus, Scotland, all of which have a purely geometric style of decoration which can be seen in Beaker 'sun-disc' work of early Bronze Age context.[2] The Harrogate hoard was discovered on land owned by W. H. Fenton, but as its spectacularly interesting nature was not recognised by Harrogate's council: the whole collection was acquired in 1927 by the Royal Ontario Museum in Canada (A.6).

Apropos Celtish influences, *Nidd* and *Crimple* are rare examples of Celtic names in modern Harrogate, the former meaning 'brilliant' or 'shining' and the latter being a compound of 'Cwm', or 'crooked' and 'pwll' or 'pool'. Both the rivers Nidd and Crimple were boundaries of the ancient township of Bilton-with-Harrogate, which thus places Harrogate linguistically with the oldest named localities in Nidderdale.

Despite the claims of Victorian historian William Wheater, there is no evidence to show that Brigantia left any impression on the area of Harrogate town. Wheater, who appears to have had an imagination akin to a rampant hothouse, furnished Harrogate with a history whose gaudiness would have made Gibbon pale and Tolkien envious. His claim that Crescent Gardens 'in the very nature of its existence, will have served the kings of the Brigantes, later Queen Cartimandua and her nobles, who brought with them their allies, the soldiers and officials of Imperial Rome',[3] is an example of the approach to historiography which renders Wheater's work intolerable. So far as Brigantia is concerned, whose territory once embraced all Yorkshire, it is only necessary to note that the area of Harrogate town did once lie within its bounds.

It was probably the Roman era that brought about the conditions that enabled permanent settlements to be established within the vicinity of the modern town of Harrogate. These conditions were manifested most strongly in routes and trading, as well as a few permanent settlements such as that at Adel Beck, twelve miles south of Low Harrogate's Old Sulphur Well. The serious Romanization of Britain began in AD 43, when forces of the Emperor Claudius landed on the Kent coast, but it was not until AD 71 that the Romans were able to invade the territories of the Brigantes that became Yorkshire. By approximately AD 78 the Ninth Legion had transferred its headquarters to York, and it was between this time, and the beginning of the fifth century AD that were constructed the great series of roads and routes which were one of the Romans most influential legacies.

Harrogate lies eleven miles west of the Roman settlement of *Isurium Brigantum*, and sixteen miles east of the Roman fort of Ilkley. The fort at Ilkley, or *Olicana*, seems to have been established in the late first century AD after which it enjoyed sporadic occupation until the end of the Roman occupation in the fifth century AD. The location of the above-named Roman settlements, together with the position of such Roman roads as those from Manchester to Aldborough, or York to Catterick indicate that the town of Harrogate developed in an area which was an integral part of Roman life in Britain. But that is all they indicate.

The important Roman road from Manchester to Aldborough passed Ilkley, Blubberhouses Moor, and Hampthswaite (some three miles north-west of Harrogate) before crossing the River Nidd near Ripley, at which point all traces have disappeared until Aldborough is reached. Opinions vary as to the precise alignment of the Roman road at Ripley, although its existence has been verified in sections.[4] The memoirs of Blind Jack Metcalfe,

PLATE I
The Harrogate
Hoard, *c*.800 BC.
COURTESY ROYAL ONTARIO
MUSEUM

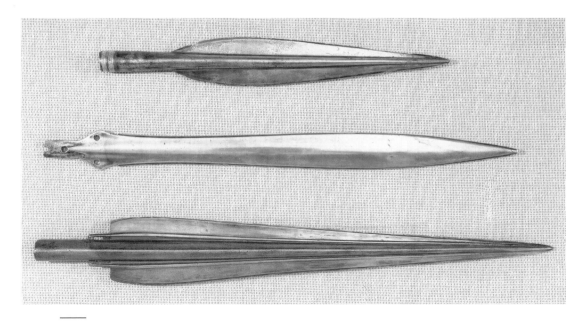

the Yorkshire roadmaker, published in 1795, contain a reference to the making of the Harrogate to Knaresborough turnpike road of *c.* 1751, which described the finding of a Roman 'causeway' on the route, whose materials were subsequently salvaged for re-use (C.30.p). Given the discoveries of sections of Roman road in the area of Hampsthwaite, to the west of Harrogate, it is possible that the later Harro-gate could be part of a track system which diverted from the Nidd at Ripley due south to Killinghall, Beckwithshaw, and then north-east to Aldborough via Harlow Hill, and Knaresborough. Roman artifacts uncovered at Harrogate include the head of a bolt, or 'catapulta', weighing eight ounces, which was found in 1788 in a field four hundred yards south of the St John's Well (then known incorrectly as the Old Spa) (A.4).

In 1952, a Roman coin of Augustus Hadrianus 'Cos III' was unearthed on Harlow Hill, which had been issued in the third year of the reign of the Emperor Hadrian. This places the date of issue at AD 119. In commenting on the coin, local archaeologist and historian Benny Kent was credited with saying, 'there was a Celtic settlement on the top of Harlow Hill during the second century A.D. ... other coins have been found in this area which suggested that Roman soldiers must have been there during that century ... these coins were not just odd ones belonging to collectors and dropped at a later date'.[5] Roman coins have also been found on Harlow Hill, Crag Lane and Claro Road, near to Stone Rings Beck.[6] Unfortunately, no accurate map or plan has been made of the location of Harrogate's Roman finds. Nor has there ever been any serious archaeological investigation of Harlow Hill, apart from the casual recording of many querns and hand-mills dug up in 1769 when the agent of the Duchy of Lancaster ordered the planting of fir trees on what later became the King's Plantation.[7] The Roman abandonment of Britain in the early fifth century AD – the year AD 409 being the most accepted date[8] – opens the era sometimes known as the 'Dark Ages', when the island of Britain was subjected to the incursions of the Saxons, Angles, Jutes, Danes and Norsemen. The earliest of these invaders were the Angles and Saxons from northern Germany, who had previously harried the Yorkshire coast during the Roman occupation, and whose people seem to have penetrated as far as Ripon by about AD 500. Indeed, some historians believe that the names of Ripley and Ripon derive from the Germanic Hrype tribe,[9] who may also have been the origin of Ribston, the early form of which was Ripestan, or Hyrpe-stone, indicating a tribal boundary at the confluence of the rivers Nidd and Crimple. Such ingenious explanations are insufficient material from which to build a convincing early history for the locality, any more than vague stories captured in the form of local hearsay. Antiquarian William Grainge, writing in the 1860s, recorded that 'tradition murmurs that the armies of Uter Pendragon encamped upon Harlow Hill, about the year 460; and the humble cottage of a husbandman bore the name of Pendragon's Castle until quite a recent period' (i.e. circa 1870). Uter Pendragon was, of course, the father of King Arthur, and it is unfortunate that Grainge recorded nothing more substantial than 'murmurs' (A.283), which in any case were lifted from the writings of Hargrove.

Anglo-Saxon place-names around Harrogate include Ripley, Bilton, Killinghall, Rossett, Rudfarlington, Knaresborough, and Scriven. Bilton probably comes from 'Billa's Ton', or the woodland clearing belonging to Billa, although we observe that according to the etymologists, virtually every place-name in Britain derives from a 'woodland clearing', if not a 'river crossing'! Neighbouring Killinghall, whose boundaries once embraced Bilton-with-Harrogate, is said to derive from 'the hall of Cylla's people'. Rossett, once Rossehirst, comes from 'horse wood'. Knaresborough, whose Domesday Book spelling is Chenaresburgh probably derives from the personal name of Cenheard, who held a castle, or burg.[10]

The monk Bede (*c.* 673–735), known as the greatest scholar of Anglo-Saxon England, recorded that in the year 705, a synod was held 'near river Nidd'. The precise location of this synod is not known, but it is likely to have been at some place adjacent to an accessible route, of which the Roman roads were still the best examples.

In 866 York was captured by the Danes, who went on to secure the rest of Yorkshire and the north midlands. By 876 there were many Danish settlements in Yorkshire, and it is from this period that so many of the area's Danish place-names originate, although it is not easy to distinguish between the earlier Norse and later Danish names. Certainly Scandinavian origins account for the widespread occurrence of *-kirk* (church), *-by* (village or farmstead), *-thorpe* (a secondary settlement) and *-with* (a wood) in the area. Examples of Danish names include Kirkby Overblow, Addlethorpe, and Barrowby. More obviously Norse names are Hampsthwaite, Felliscliffe, Kettlesing, and Haverah Park's *Siwardergs* or *Siwerdherges*.

Various theories have been considered to explain the name Harrogate, which is with good reason divided into two parts: *Harro* and *Gate*. The *-gate* is easy to explain, being derived from the Scandinavian word for 'way'. *Harro* presents the historian with difficulties, especially because of the variable spellings that have come down to us. The first surviving example of *Harrogate* occurs in the Court Roll of 30 September 1332, which refers to 'John de Harowgat', followed a few lines later by 'Johannis de Harugat'. The same record also employs the spellings of Harowgate, Harwegate, Harougat and Harrogate (A.36). Had the earlier rolls survived, it is not unreasonable to suppose that they too would have contained several different spellings. Which ever was the first preferred way of spelling the first part of 'Harrogate', it would still have had a specific meaning, but with a lack of positive evidence, it is only possible to provide a series of educated guesses. Certainly, Eli Hargrove believed that it meant either 'a place of invaders and spoilers' (G.1), from the Anglo-Saxon invasions, or, the way to the place of robbers, Haverah Park being anciently known as the place of robbers (G.3). Another possible explanation comes from 'Harrogate' being the road, or way, to Haverah (E.7). Although the Park of Haverah was established along with the Royal Forest only in *c.* 1100, its name may be much older, so Haverah is a possible candidate. On etymological grounds, the case for Haverah is less convincing, as it has never been usual for rural populations to convert an easily pronounced 'v' into a more demanding 'rr'. Haverah Park was also part of Professor Smith's explanation, who believed that *Harro* derived from the Norse *Horg*, a pile of stones, or cairn, and that such a cairn may either have been on Harlow Hill, or at the former 'Pippin Castle' in Havarah Park, which was removed when the Scargill Reservoir was constructed in *c.* 1898.[11]

The *Harrogate* of which we are writing was a word that appears to have

PLAN 24
Haverah Park and
Pannal, *c.* 1778.
Russell, p. 126.

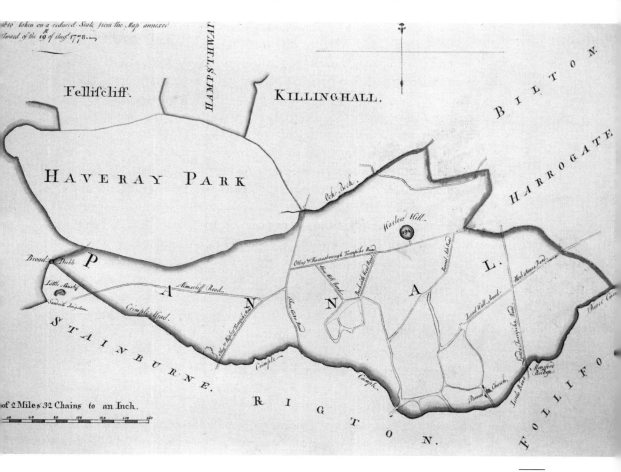

been first used as a geographical name. Given the degree of settlement in the area, we are assuming that the source of the *Harro* to which the *gate* led was of some size and significance. As Harlow Hill is unquestionably the most significant feature within the vicinity of Harrogate town, the *way to Harlow*, or Harlowgate, commends itself to our favour, especially because examples of this spelling occur in the court rolls – as for example during the reign of Edward II, when *Harlowgate* was used. As Harlow means in Anglo-Norse, the *Soldiers' Hill*,[12] and all the evidence points to the geographical name of Harrogate being adopted in Danish-Norse times, probably *c.* 900, the name Harrogate may reasonably be explained as meaning the road to the hill of the soldier. The name Harlow is found both in northern and southern England. At Leeds, some fifteen miles south of Harrogate, a Harlow Hill is located within the township of Headingly, referred to by Ralph Thoresby in his *Ducatus Leodiensis* of 1715 and by James Wardell in his *Antiquities of borough of Leeds* of 1853, who wrote that, 'Harlow-hill in the township of Headingly-cum-Burley appears to have been very strongly defended ... the ancient name is evidently Saxon'. Wherever the location, Harlow means one thing: 'soldiers' hill', although as Thoresby pointed out in 1715, the *hill* is really superfluous, as Harlow includes *hill* within its meaning. The Tudor map of 1587 (see plan 6) identifies the modern York Place in Harrogate as part of the great 'Broad Way', leading to the hill of the soldier. The length and direction of the great 'Broad Way' is uncertain, after the section from Harlow to Stokbrigge, although it is reasonable to assume that it continued from Stokbrigge to the Nidd, more or less concurrent with the later turnpike route.

On the southern approach to Harlow Hill, overlooking Crimple Valley, there is a further interesting site connected to Harrogate's Dark Age past. At Follifoot Ridge, on the north side of Follifoot Road, there is a field known as Alexander's Hill, which used to contain a fifty feet diameter barrow. The early name for this land was 'Bicker-flat', or 'Battle-flat', from which the still surviving 'Beaker Cottages' derive their name. Antiquarian James Wardell investigated the remains of this barrow in the 1860s, discovering that it had once contained fragments of 'urns, bones and pieces of brass'. He also discovered that the barrow had been pillaged by the highways surveyors of earlier times, the stones being used for the repair of local roads. Wardell concluded that the barrow 'was not of the most ancient kind, but perhaps covered the remains of British warriors slain in conflict with the Roman invaders.' As the artifacts have been lost, the 'brass' weapons having been melted down by the village blacksmith, the origins of the Battle-flat barrow remain a mystery (A.5).

The royal castle at Knaresborough was the most important man-made structure within the vicinity of Harrogate. It was first mentioned in 1129–30, when £11 were recorded as having been spent on 'the King's works at Chenardesburg',[13] although little is known about the castle's form or structure. Given that the origin of the name of Knaresborough is in the same Anglo-Norse tongue as that of Harrogate, and that the meaning of the name Knaresborough is most probably either 'Cenheard's Castle', or the 'Castle on the rocky promontory', the great stone castle of the twelfth and thirteenth centuries surely had a precursor. Such a structure would have been built of timber, probably for guarding the route of which the *Harro gate* was an important part, thanks to the eminence of Harlow Hill. The site of Cenheard's castle may have been adopted because of its advantageous situation on the rocky promontory overlooking the river Nidd, and also because the Nidd formed a boundary between two lordships, which may have been rivals. This rocky promontory may also have been the origin of the *Knar* in Knaresborough, as this is its meaning in the Anglo-Norse tongue. However, the more frequent use in the Harrogate district of another variant for the same subject, *crook* or *Kruk*, makes our first inter-pretation marginally more likely. A further explanation for the origin of Knaresborough's name may be obtained by comparing it with Selby's *Knarlending*, where the *cnearr* meant a landing place on the river Ouse.[14]

The soke of Bilton-with-Harrogate is of considerable antiquity, the earliest surviving documentary evidence dating from the tenth century AD. Because some historians have, for the past two hundred years, bound the communities of Harrogate and Knaresborough together, on the naïve assumption that geographical proximity is indicative of mutual inter-dependence, they have failed to appreciate the significance of the Nidd boundary, and of the important role of more distant communities. The first references to the fledgling communities that became Bilton-with-Harrogate and Beckwith-with-Rossett, occur in a statement concerning church lands in Northumbria, set down by Oswald, Archbishop of York, probably in the same year that he became Archbishop, AD 972. In what appears to have been a territorial readjustment, Oswald recorded that the large and important centre of Otley was to lose a number of sokes or parts of sokes, in the following named order: Haddincham, ... Hyllibleg ... Mensinctun ... Burhleg ... Gislicleh ... Scenfinc ... Middeltun ... Dentun ... Timmel ... Stanburn ... Becwudu ... Byllintun (A.7). In modern English, these sokes become Addingham, Ilkley, Menston, Burley, Guiseley, Chevin, Middleton, Denton, Timble, Lindley, Stainburn, Beckwith and Bilton. The significance of these manors to Otley may be seen on a modern map.[15] The first six sokes, Addingham, Ilkley, Menston, Burley, Guisley and Chevin, all ran south of the Wharfe in a west–east direction. The last seven sokes, Middleton, Denton, Timble, Lindley, Stainburn, Beckwith and Bilton, all ran north of the Wharfe in a west–east direction. It is likely that the majority, if not all, of these thirteen sokes had become associated with Otley during the post Danish settlement of the last third of the ninth century AD. Archbishop Oswald, in his territorial reorganisation, split three of the Otley sokes, detaching only half of Burley, Denton and Bilton. Which halves remained with Otley, and which halves passed into other lordships, in not known, but it is reasonable to surmise that the changes remained valid until the time of the Norman conquest.

The significance of the Otley connection with Harrogate lies in the system of roads which connect the two communities with Otley's former sokes, as well as with the important routes from Manchester and the north of England. Both the Otley Road from Killinghall (and let it be recalled that for centuries, Bilton-with-Harrogate formed part of the larger township of Killinghall) and the Otley Road from Harlow Hill (itself part of the ancient way to the soldiers' hill), lead into Otley township, and the line of the more recent A61 – Bradford road leads, via Pool Bridge, to the same place.

The Norman barbarians overcame England in the year 1066, and within twenty years, King William I saw the completion of the great survey of 1086, subsequently known as the Domesday Book. A mere four years after the calamity of 1066, the monk Simeon of Durham recorded an event in his *History of the Kings of England*, which although little more than a curiosity, is nevertheless worth relating, as it contains a reference which some have believed refers to Harrogate. Simeon relates that in the year 1070, an army of marauding Scots commanded by king Malcolm III marched southwards, through Cumberland, before turning east and devastating Teesdale and the parts bordering on it on each side. When the Scots horde reached

> the place called in English Hundredskelde, that is, the hundred springs, having there slaughtered some nobles of the English nation, the king (keeping part of the army) sent part home by the way they came with a vast booty.

Simeon went on to describe the progress of the horde in Cleveland and Holderness, all of which were pillaged, and the destruction by fire of the church of St Peter at Wearmouth (A.8). It is Simeon's reference to *Hundredskelde* that has caused some historians to think of Harrogate, since no other place is known to possess so many mineral springs, and no likely alternative has ever been proposed. It must, however, be emphasised that Malcolm's army was associated more with lands to the north and east of Harrogate.

Following the Norman conquest of England in 1066, it soon became clear that the greatest problem facing King William was that of security in the north. Briefly, the northern uprising of 1068, brought about through the royal taxation levies of 1067 and 1068, produced a violent reaction from the king, who feared that the north might break away from his grasp, and, with the support of the Danes or Scots, form an independent territory centred on York. After occupying York and sacking Durham, the barbarian king instituted the infamous 'harrying of the north', which the *Anglo-Saxon Chronicle* for 1069 noted 'laid waste to all the shire'. Writing later, the chronicler Orderic Vitalis noted:

> nowhere else had William shown so much cruelty. Shamefully he succumbed to this vice, for he made no effort to restrain his fury and punished the innocent with the guilty. In his anger, he commanded that all crops and herds, chattels and food of every kind should be brought together and burned to ashes with consuming fire, so that the whole region north of the Humber might be stripped of all means of sustenance. In consequence, so serious a scarcity was felt in England, and so terrible a famine fell upon the humble and defenceless populace, that more than 100,000 Christian folk of both sexes, young and old alike, perished of hunger.[16]

Simeon of Durham noted king William devastated the North:

> throughout the winter and slaughtered the people ... It was horrible to observe in houses, streets and roads, human corpses rotting ... no-one survived to cover them with earth, all having perished by the sword and starvation, or left the land of their fathers because of hunger ... between York and Durham, no village was inhabited.

The work of the Norman barbarian extended to the destruction of harvests, the smashing of ploughs and other tools, and the mass murder of the population.

We have described the foregoing events in order to place in context the appropriate entries contained in the great survey of 1086, known popularly as the Domesday Book. The Domesday Book contains the results of a unique survey undertaken to establish who held what land and livestock, its condition, and how much it was worth. Interpretation of the survey is complicated, not only because there are several versions, but also because of the language and terminology adopted by the clerks who assembled the incoming information. The term *waste* has proved particularly misleading, as it appears to have been applied not only to lands and vills that had been devastated, but also to lands and vills which had been subjected to amalgamation, division or centralisation. For example, the Lacy estates at Kippax and Tanshelf were administered centrally, so outlying estates had their details grossed up in the totals for the central manor, and were subsequently referred to 'waste', to prevent duplication. A further use for the term 'waste' was with the avoidance of geld, or taxation, in that land that was really waste could clearly yield no income on which geld could be paid. It was accordingly advantageous for the tenant, on the amalgamation of manors, to credit all the equipment and value to a single manor, and to write of all the others as 'waste'.[17]

'Waste' may also have been used to describe land that was afforested. In the case of the Royal Forest of Knaresborough, there is no evidence to show how long it had existed before the first reference of 1167 (A.10). Bilton-with-Harrogate lay within the Forest boundary, being located south of the river Nidd. According to the Domesday survey, Gilbert Tison's Bilton lands were valued at five shillings, whereas Archill's were waste, as was land at Beckwith and Rossett (A.9). This makes it unlikely that the Forest of Knaresborough existed in 1086, as the term 'waste' would have been applied uniformly throughout the forest, including Bilton-with-Harrogate. In fact, by 1086, of those lands which later became the Royal Forest, only those of Bilton, valued at 5s. and Whipley, valued at 2s., were not classed as 'waste', which gives some indication of the importance of Bilton-with-Harrogate in terms of the lands of the later Royal Forest of Knaresborough.

Bilton, in 1066, had been held by Gamelbar and Archill (or Arnketill) but by 1086, the former's lands were held by Gilbert Tison and the latter's lands were held by the same 'under the king' (A.3). Gamelbar held land not only in Bilton-with-Harrogate, but also in Hampsthwaite, Beckwith-with-Rossett, North Rigton, Plumpton, Walton, Todoure, Kirky-Overblow, Spofforth, Great Braham, Plumpton and Rudfarlington, all of which are south of the Nidd, and ring the modern town of Harrogate in all directions save the north. Gamelbar does not appear to have held any lands north of the Nidd. Archill, or Arnketill, in comparison, held lands south of the Nidd at North Rigton and Bilton-with-Harrogate, but also north of the Nidd at Whipley and Ripley. The Domesday entries for Bilton, Beckwith and Rossett provide information about their status in 1086 for geld assessment and ploughlands. 'Geld' was a Saxon term for money, and was a north country term for taxes. The geld assessment was calculated in 'carucates', a carucate being the amount of land that could be ploughed in a day by a single plough team, and support a family. Since the quality of soil was variable, the amount of land varied from area to area. On average, a carucate contained between 60 to 180 acres, or an average of 120 acres. At Bilton, Tison's lands were assessed at 3½ carucates, or 420 acres, Archill's lands held under the king being identical.

Domesday entries for the manors of Killinghall and Knaresborough – the former to the north of Harrogate and south of the Nidd, the latter being east of Harrogate and the Nidd – are of comparable interest. At the time of the 1086 survey, Bilton did not form part of Killinghall, but was listed as a separate manor, with Killinghall recorded as part of Aldborough, held by the King.[18] At Killinghall, the king held one carucate of land, and the Archbishop of York held 8 carucates.[19]

Knaresborough was held by the king, along with a number of 'outliers': Walkingham, Ferrensby, Scriven, Brearton, Susacres, Cayton, Farnham, and South Stainley, Fewston with Bestham. Of these 'outliers', the importance of the Nidd boundary is once again demonstrated by the fact that all are to the north of the Nidd, save for Fewston with Bestham. Apart from the king, Erneis de Burun held 10 bovates[20] of taxable land at Knaresborough, but none south of the Nidd in Bilton, Beckwith or Rossett. Bilton land-holder Gilbert Tison, however, held 4 carucates in Scotton, north of the Nidd. This same Gilbert Tison also held 3 carucates at Beckwith. Identification of the holders of the above-mentioned lands is not easy. The king was William I, the 'Conqueror'. Arnketill, or Archill may have been the Yorkshire thane who was involved in the uprisings of 1068 and 1069, but who submitted to king William at York, surrendering his son Gospatric as a hostage. By this means, Arnketill managed to retain his former lands at Bilton, but only as tenant-in-chief, under the king. Gilbert Tison, or Gilbert 'Firebrand', held extensive estates in Lincolnshire, Nottinghamshire and Yorkshire, and is believed to have died *c.* 1115–18.[21] Gilbert Tison's estates appear to have been confiscated by the Crown at some point between the compilation of the Domesday survey, and the year *c.* 1115.[22]

Little is known of Erneis de Burun (who held land at Knaresborough) other than that he became Sheriff of Yorkshire during the 1080s, and that in 1088 he acted with Ivo Taillebois to seize Durham Castle during an action against the Bishop of Durham.[23]

The most interesting of the Bilton Domesday references is that of Gamalbar, but here our enquiry can only be of speculative nature. The biographical entries in the Phillimore parallel text edition of Domesday, contain five Gamalls, of whom at least three may have been connected with the Gamalbar of Bilton. Other than the Domesday survey of 1086, the Gam prefix may be seen on the Plumpton map of 1587, where it is written as *Gammell gate* – or the way to Gamal's lands (see plan 5). This name is placed over what later became West Park, shortly before its junction with York Place, and a useful marker on the 1587 map is formed by Hookstone Beck, which as late as 1871 was recorded as running from the Prince of Wales' corner, across the Stray, and down into Crimple Beck.[24] A further '*Gam*' reference is found on the map which accompanied the 1778 enclosure of the Royal Forest, when allotment 544 containing 27 acres, 3 roods, 14 perches, was described as being near *Gams Gate*. This field ran from what is now Leeds Road, near Trinity Church, up Harlow Hill, and *Gams Gate* itself appears to be marked on the map, virtually conterminus with the site of Trinity Church (see plan 17). Other entries in the Great Award (B.31) refer to

Gams Gate, e.g. 541, 542, and 545. The oldest surviving documentary source for the *Gam-* prefix is in a grant of *c.* 1173, by William de Stutevill to Robert the forester of Blubberhouses, to lands with liberty to make improvements, plough and build houses without let, rendering a mark yearly. The bounds of these lands lay in part from, 'Gamels-wath by the road up to the highway between Knaresborough and Scotton and by the highway leading to the road to Barker's-wath [thence] to Nidd and descending Nidd to Gamels-wath ...'[25] *Wath*, in Anglo-Norse, means ford, and Gamels-wath must be what today is called Mill Wath below Scotton Mill. The 'road up to the highway between Knaresborough and Scotton' can only be the continuation of Milner's Lane north of the Nidd, and Milner's Lane led to the heart of old Bilton, where Gamelbar held lands in 1066.

It is not possible to identify which parts of Bilton-with-Harrogate and Beckwith-with-Rossett were held by the above named men, so we can provide the reader only with speculation. The 3½ carucates held in 1066 by Gamelbar and in 1086 by Gilbert Tison, equivalent to approximately 420 acres, could have been that part of old Bilton bounded by Bilton Beck, Bilton Lane, Spring Wood and the River Nidd. Gamelbar also held much of the land which later became the Royal Forest, including Beckwith, Killinghall, Birstwith, Fewston, and Rigton, as well as Plumpton, which was without the forest.

By the time of the survey of 1086, the division of Yorkshire into three parts, or ridings – originally the Viking 'thrithing' – was well established, with the Harrogate area being well within the West Riding. The ridings were sub-divided into wapentakes, with the Harrogate area located within the Wapentake of Claro. The wapentakes saw to the raising of armies, the levying of taxes, the maintenance of law and order and property transactions, although with these two last matters, Bilton-with-Harrogate and Beckwith-with-Rossett came within the jurisdiction of the Royal Forest Court after *c.* 1100. 'Wapentake' was a Scandinavian word which derived from the symbolic manner in which weapons were flourished to signify agreement to decisions taken by open-air public assemblies.[26] The surviving wapentake records relating to Bilton-with-Harrogate and Beckwith-with-Rossett are either sixteenth-century, being concerned with the mustering of men for military purposes, or seventeenth-century, concerning taxation, and both of the relevant classes of documentation are reproduced in the *Great Chronicle*'s Class A.

The establishment of the Royal Forest of Knaresborough, and its inclusion of Bilton-with-Harrogate, Beckwith-with-Rossett, Killinghall, and other neighbouring communities, was of such paramount significance for the development of Harrogate that it is necessary to give it consideration, before examining the area's post-Domesday life. As the matter of Harrogate and the Forest is the subject of chapter two, the following is restricted to generality.

We do not know when the Royal Forest was established, and it is likely that the records containing this information were lost when John de Lisleburn destroyed the records during his occupation of Knaresborough Castle in 1317–18.[27] The first surviving reference to the Royal Forest occurs in the pipe roll for Henry II of 1167 (A.10), but the Forest is more likely to have been established during the reign of Henry I, which lasted from 1100 to 1135. Given that William the Conqueror died one year after the completion of the Domesday survey of 1086, which contains no mention of the Royal Forest, and given that his son, William II reigned for the short period from 1087 to 1100, the opening year of the reign of Henry I is a reasonable point at which to place the Royal Forest's establishment. The reader may obtain a better impression of the Royal Forest by substituting *estate* for forest or waste, as both terms convey images which are likely to be far from reality (see plan 1).

Although there is no supporting documentary evidence for the Royal Forest of Knaresborough ever having been part of a pre-Norman hunting forest, this intriguing possibility was considered by landscape historian Dr Richard Muir, who speculated that as the co-axial field system between Ripley and Aldborough pointed to it belonging to a larger entity, the royal forest may have been part of the vast ancient estate of Burghshire.[28]

The importance of the Royal Forest to the communities of Bilton-with-Harrogate and Beckwith-with-Rossett, lay in two areas: employment and jurisdiction of Forest law. Employment was divided into three principal categories with one special sub-category. First came agriculture, which was influenced by the special status of the land as Royal Forest, followed by forestry, and finally mining. Because the Royal Forest also included a number of special enclosures called parks or chases, set aside for such activities as the Royal Stud, grazing animals, or for timber, work in the parks and chases formed a sub-category of general forestry work. To these three principal categories of employment must be added the whole range of work found in the medieval villages which found themselves within the bounds of the Royal Forest.

Jurisdiction meant more than the severe penalties exacted from those who infringed the law of the Forest. It also meant conditions for the conveyance of property, for inheritance, the regulation of wills, and rights to common pasture. Many of the customs observed by the Foresters were special to the Royal Forest of Knaresborough, and although the earliest known version of them dates from as late as 1559, they appear to be of a much older provenance. Just how old these 'customs' are cannot be known, principally because the chaotic conditions following the death of Henry I in

1135 threw the administration of the Royal Forests into the melting pot, especially during the difficult reign of King Stephen, from 1135 to 1154. When Henry II began his reign in 1154, he was faced with the difficult task of re-establishing the royal authority that had been dissipated during the struggle for power, and that meant the reorganisation of the royal forests. Consequently, it is reasonable to suppose that the jurisdiction to which the forest communities were subject dates from the reign of Henry II, from 1154 to 1189. Indeed, it was under Henry II that the royal forests extended to a size far greater than that enjoyed by his grandfather, so much so that the matter became contentious in the war waged by the barons against King John, requiring its settlement in Magna Carta, and later, in the separate Forest Charter of 1217.[29]

Over and above the matters of employment and jurisdiction, the influence of the royal forest on the communities of the future town of Harrogate had one pre-eminent role, which hitherto has escaped the attentions of historians. The location of the special parks and chases was critical in determining the rate and direction of the subsequent development of Bilton-with-Harrogate and Beckwith-with-Rossett. One example, at this stage, will suffice. Shortly after the discovery in 1571 of the first mineral well in Bilton-with-Harrogate, a valuable sulphur well was discovered at old

PLATE 103
An unidentified drawing from John Field's 1830 collection, probably of the Tewit Well.
COURTESY OF MR R. BELDON

Bilton, which is referred to in Stanhope's study of 1626 (F.4). As old Bilton was the centre with the highest population in the area which later became Harrogate town, and as the well was half as near again to the important centre of neighbouring Knaresborough, than was the two-mile distant Tewit Well, it would have been natural for spa development to have occurred at Bilton, extending down towards the river Nidd and Knaresborough. That this obvious development did not occur is explained by the fact that the Bilton sulphur well was in the middle of Bilton Park, an enclosure within the Royal Forest, where development was out of the question. Accordingly, when the first spa development occurred, it took place at Harrogate Head, where the Tewit and Sweet Wells were located, and also at the sulphur wells in Low Harrogate within Pannal village (F.3). Details of the parks and chases are provided in chapter two.

As the twelfth century progressed, and the reign of Henry II was succeeded by that of Richard I, the community of Bilton, living under two miles from the soldiers' hill and its road, found itself part of the new Forest of Knaresborough, as well as the larger Honour (see plan 1). The Honour was leased by the Crown to a number of men who not only farmed all the forest revenues, but also were keepers of Knaresborough Castle, and it was from these times that there developed a link between the borough of Knaresborough (first recorded in 1169)[30] and the villages of the royal forest. Serlo de Burgh is the first known holder of the Honour, and it was his nephew, Eustace Fitzjohn, who held the Honour from 1130, for which he paid the Crown £22 a year. The first reference of castle building comes from this time, with an account of £11 spent on 'the king's works'.[31] In 1173, the Honour was granted to William de Stuteville in exchange for an undertaking to provide the king (Henry II) with three armed knights.[32] In 1199, the first year of the reign of King John, Stuteville granted land that later became important parts of south Harrogate, to Nigel de Plumpton (A.11). In exchange for Plumpton's services, and one horse worth a hundred shillings, Stuteville granted land bounded by the river Crimple, Osbernescahebec (Stone Rings Beck), the great Puddingstone Cross on Harlow Hill, the peak of Harlow, the great road to Bilton (the Harro-gate, or present Otley Road and York Place), thence to Stokkebrigge (Starbeck) and thence to Holebec and so into Nidd and back to Crimple. All these features are clearly visible on the 1587 map (see plan 5), which was produced to settle a lawsuit brought by the Duchy of Lancaster about the enclosure of land near Rudfarlington. William Plumpton's witnesses described the Puddingstone Cross as formerly standing between Pannal tithebarn and the hedge corner of Harlow. This places the Puddingstone Cross, in modern terms, somewhere within the locality of the junction of Pannal Ash Road and Richmond Road.

One of the greatest difficulties in considering the boundaries of the period in question is that they were invariably determined by features of the natural landscape, such as rivers and hilltops, or well-known man-made features such as roads, churches, or crosses. Such features have, with the passage of time, been either lost, or developed beyond recognition, which makes it difficult to place ancient land grants. Put entirely in modern terms, Stuteville granted Plumpton Harrogate land bounded to the south of a line from the top of Harlow Hill, running down Otley Road, York Place and Knaresborough Road, as far as Starbeck, then along Holbeck into the Nidd, along the Nidd as far as the Crimple, and following the Crimple until its junction with Stone Rings Beck. The boundary then followed Stone Rings Beck to the Puddingstone Cross, before running across to Harlow Hill, and its beginning. The townships of Little Ribston, Plumpton and Rudfarlington were included within the bounds of Stuteville's grant. In the normal course of events, the possession of the Honour would have descended from Stuteville to Stuteville, but when William's son Nicholas died in 1205, his heir was subjected to an enormous 'relief', or 'succession fine' of 10,000 marks, by King John, which probably included arrears of Stuteville debts to the Crown. The king had probably set the relief at such a high rate in order to ensure that the Crown would regain control of both the royal castle, and the royal forest, wherein he hunted, which – in the event – he was able to do.[33]

William de Stuteville not only granted land to Nigel de Plumpton, but he also presented Robert the hermit with land around his cave at Knaresborough, north of the Nidd.[34] Less well known is the fact that Robert Flower is said to have had another hermitage and chapel south of the Nidd, near the Star beck and west of Rudfarlington, which was possibly given to him by the Plumptons:

> the chapel I grant thee of St Hylde,
> with all the land that lies partyll.

This chapel was believed to have been dedicated to St Hilda, and although it was probably destroyed on the orders of William de Stuteville, the ruins and their name survived for centuries as 'St Hile's nook'. Historian William Grainge recorded that this relic of St Robert remained undisturbed until 1826, when the trees were felled, and that in 1843, the stone was used to build the Roman Catholic chapel at Knaresborough (A.13).

In 1205–6, the Honour reverted to the Crown, bringing back into royal hands the Forest, and with it the ancient *Becwudu and Byllinctun*. King John installed Brian de l'Isle as custodian (rather than lord) of the Honour, who was followed by the Archbishop of York and Adam de Staveley, who paid £200 for the privilege.[35] Then, in 1229, the Honour was granted to the Earl of Kent, Hubert de Burgh, who forfeited it in 1232 at his disgrace.[36] The next grant proved longer lasting, when in 1234 the King, Henry III, gave the estates to his brother Richard, Earl of Cornwall, who was succeeded by his son Edmund, in 1272. Edmund died in 1300, and as his nearest heir was King Edward I, the Honour returned once again to the Crown.[37]

Following Archbishop Oswald's statement of 972 (A.7), Bilton-with-Harrogate appears to have become part of the parish of Knaresborough, along with Arkendale and Brearton,[38] and accordingly the inhabitants had to pay a tithe on the corn of Bilton, which in 1243 was set at six marks, to the Prebend of Knaresborough (A.19). Pannal church – which until the building of old St Mary's in 1825, was, technically, the church for all the inhabitants of Low Harrogate – also came under the patronage of the lord of Knaresborough, and in 1278 the lord, Edmund, Earl of Cornwall, gave the advowson (that is, the right to select the new incumbent when vacancy occurred) to St Robert's Friary, which was allowed to appropriate the church in 1319.[39]

Tenants of the Royal Forest were obliged to have their corn ground at one of the lord's mills, which they also had to keep in a state of good repair.[40] An early reference to the mill at Bilton was made in 1279, when an inquest was held on 'William, son of Adam Cam, [who] fell from a certain plank into the water near the Mill of Bilton …' and drowned. The verdict recorded an accident (A.19.b). There are some early references to forging in the accounts of the Earldom of Cornwall, from 1296/1297, where it is recorded that Pannal forge was held by William of Scaklethorpe and his fellows, who paid the Earl £13 4s. for thirty-three weeks at eight shillings a week, minus lost time for religious holidays. Benedict, son of Hugo, paid £6 8s. for sixteen weeks' lease of a forge at Haverah Park, and the entry closes with the cryptic statement that, 'from the rent of the potters nothing this year' (A.22). Possibly the local supply of clay had dried up, or the potters had turned their hands to other activities.

Something of the status of the former Otley sokes may be seen in an inquisition of 1301 into the lands and tenements held by Edmund, Duke of Cornwall. Beckwith, Rossett, and Pannal are all mentioned separately, as is Bilton. Since the first three localities are invariably referred to, in township terms, as Beckwith-with-Rossett, their separate listing in the inquisition is confusing (A.23).

Until 1307 the Honour was held by Edward I, but when Edward II began his reign in the same year, the new king granted it to his favourite, Peter de Gaveston, who was created earl of Cornwall. Gaveston held the Honour until his death in 1312, at which it returned to the Crown (A.20.b). More will be written of this period in chapter two, when the subject of Harrogate's royal parks and chases is considered. This was an exceptionally significant period for the development of Bilton-with-Harrogate, and before this

_____

opening chapter is finished, it is necessary to consider the difficult but elementary question of the origin of the Harrogate *community*, both the when and the why.

We have shown that the etymology of Harrogate is Anglo-Danish and/or Norse, from *c.* 835–950, and that its early population centre of Bilton is older, deriving from the same English of *c.* 490–700 as Killinghall, Knaresborough, Plumpton, Rossett and Scriven. The first surviving reference to both Beckwith – from which Pannal grew – and Bilton, occurs in the statement of 972 (A.7), some one hundred and fourteen years before the first reference to Knaresborough, in the Domesday survey of 1086, which contains no reference to Harrogate. The first surviving reference to Harrogate as a place of domicile, occurs in the Court Roll for 1332 (A.35). Only two explanations can account for these references. Either Harrogate existed as a community before 1086, but was included with Bilton in the survey, perhaps for clerical convenience; or it existed purely as a geographical name without any appreciable residential population. If the latter is true, then at some point between 1086 and 1332 the geographical field name of Harrogate became a residential community.

If the geographical feature called the Harro-gate had, from its earliest period as a named locality, some sparse population, which was too negligible by 1086 to be classed as a separate community (being included with Bilton) but which had by 1332 developed to the stage whereby it was named in a legal dispute, then it is necessary to provide a theory for its coming into existence. Equally, if the Harro-gate had no resident population beyond the ancient *Byllinctun* and the Pannal parts of *Becwudu*, until the existence of the community to which John of Harrogate belonged, it is also necessary to attempt to explain why this community suddenly appeared.

In attempting to answer the question of when and why the Harro-gate geographical feature became Harrogate the community, it is useful to examine a valuable set of calculations that were completed by the WEA local historical team in the 1960s (A.25). Using accounts and assessments other than the court rolls (A.1), the team found that the two villages of Beckwith-with-Rossett and Bilton-with-Harrogate underwent a phenomenal growth in their acreage figures between 1305 and 1349. For example, Bilton-with-Harrogate extended from 480 acres in 1305, to 575 acres in 1349. Over the same period, Beckwith-with-Rossett (which included Pannal, Harlow Hill and the future Low Harrogate) extended from 449 acres to 666. Between 1314 and 1349 Beckwith-with-Rossett underwent an extraordinary 45 per cent growth, if the figures are to be believed, and the figures tally with the sums paid to the receiver as rentals.[41] One explanation for this increase of township acreage may lie with an adjustment to the often unreliable and rough estimates used in the middle ages, which may have been subjected to accurate re-surveying. It also needs to be understood that the Royal Forest, in common with other localities, used its own customary acre measurement, which was said in the seventeenth century to be equivalent roughly to four statute acres. An incomplete survey of the Forest in 1611 (A.122) showed that one holding of just over 60 acres customary measure converted to 163 acres in statute measure. Another holding of 20 customary acres was in reality 72 statute acres.[42] This difference merely underlines the unreliability of the medieval records. Nevertheless, the 15 per cent increase in the rented acreage of Bilton-with-Harrogate between 1307 and 1312, must – if it was not the result of some unknown re-survey – have been the result of an increase in the assarting of the Forest (A.25). In short, there is evidence to indicate that at both the Pannal and Bilton-with-Harrogate areas, there was a sudden and unusual expansion of land under cultivation.

One explanation for the above-described measurements may be found in the accounts of catastrophic disruption suffered by the Royal Forest at this period in the early fourteenth century. According to the Chronicle of Lanercost, in

> A.D. 1318, ... in the month of May, the Scottish army invaded England further than usual, burning the town of Northallerton and Borough-bridge and sundry other towns on their march, pressing forward as far as the town of Ripon, which they despoiled ... they went off to Knares-borough, destroying the town with fire, and searching the woods in the district whither the people had fled for refuge with their cattle, they took away their cattle. And so forth to the town of Skipton ... which they plundered ... (A.30).

Further evidence of the devastation caused by the Scottish invaders lies in the order of 25 January 1319 to John de Wysham, keeper of the Honour, to acquit the men and tenants of affected communities from payment of their rents (A.31). Among the communities so named are Birstwith, Hampsthwaite, Killinghall, Rossett and Bilton, whose populace had been 'ruined to a great extent by the burning of their houses, the abduction of their beasts, and the carrying away of their goods by the attacks of the Scotch rebels ...'

It is possible that the sudden increase of rented acreage in Bilton-with-Harrogate between 1307 and 1312 was achieved by people who lived at either Pannal or Bilton, but who also rented land on or near the Harro-gate. This explains why the name of Harrogate does not appear in the statement of 1319, despite the expansion of the rented acreage. The Scottish invasion disrupted the area in 1318, bringing destruction to all the villages named in the order of 1319 (A.31). Thirteen years later Harrogate appears as the name of a community (A.35), one explanation for which may be that the victims of the Scottish invasion, having lost their homes and suffered the devastation of land close to those homes, turned to the recently assarted land at Harrogate, which being sparsely populated had suffered relatively little damage, and began its occupation. One set of calculations indicates that in the early 1300s the ratio of arable land to meadow land in Bilton-with-Harrogate was 1:2 (A.32), which points to a preponderance of simple pasture, far more difficult to destroy than cultivated crops.

To conclude our opening chapter, we cannot provide the reader with a certain explanation of how, when and why the ancient geographical Harrogate became the community of Harrogate. Our examination of the sparse, surviving relics has permitted no more than the formulation of a couple of alternative theories, which we will reject cheerfully on the production of new and compelling evidence to their contrary. Without such evidence, we are content to bring this chapter on the genesis of a community, to its close, and to progress to more certain matters with Harrogate and the Royal Forest.

Harrogate and the Royal Forest

2

THE Royal Forest of Knaresborough may have been established before the Domesday survey of 1086, which does not refer to it, or after, in which case the reign of Henry I from 1100, is a reasonable date to adopt for its beginning. Chapter one referred to the chaotic conditions in the Royal Forests of England during the troublesome reign of King Stephen, or, from the close of the reign of Henry I in 1135, to the opening of the reign of Henry II in 1154. The first surviving documentary reference to the Royal Forest of Knaresborough occurs in 1167, during the reign of Henry II (A.10), of whom it was written that 'during his long reign [he] extended the royal forests beyond the area they had attained under his grandfather'.[1] Plate one shows the extent of the Royal Forest, which was bounded to the north by the river Nidd, west by the Honour of Kirby Malzeard and Blubberhouses, south by the Liberty of Otley and the Forest of Wharfedale, and east by the Manor of Plumpton. Encompassed within these boundaries were the constabularies of Thruscross, with its seven hamlets of Bramley, Darley, Hill, Holme, Menwith, Padside and Thornthwaite; Clint, with its five hamlets of Birstwith, Fearnhill, Felliscliffe, Hampsthwaite and Rowden; and Killinghall, with its three hamlets of Beckwith, Rossett, and Bilton-with-Harrogate. Eventually, these hamlets grew into the eleven separate constabularies of Beckwith-with-Rossett, Bilton-with-Harrogate, Birstwith, Clifton, Clint, Felliscliffe, Hampsthwaite, Killinghall, Menwith-with-Darley, Thruscross and Timble.

North of the Forest's boundary at the river Nidd, was the Liberty of Knaresborough, which comprised the dependent Manors of South Stainley and Cayton, Burton Leonard, Brearton, Walkingham Hill, Scotton, Farnham, Staveley, Arkendale, Clareton-with-Coneythorpe, Great Ouseburn, and the special Manor of Knaresborough with Scriven and Ferrensby. Knaresborough was first recorded as being a Borough in 1169,[2] and Haya Park was a special Royal Park established *outside* the Royal Forest.

The name 'liberty' was applied to an area beyond a borough in which freemen had rights of pasture, so it may be understood that freemen of the Liberty of Knaresborough had no rights of pasture south of the river Nidd, since land there was part of the Royal Forest.

The above information is provided to emphasise the critical importance of precision when using such names as *Knaresborough*, as there were five possible administrative bodies to which it was applicable: borough, manor, liberty, forest and honour – to say nothing of the royal castle, which actually formed a sixth! In 1974, all these units became part of the new district of Harrogate.

The population of the Royal Forest was subjected to a body of law that was expressly written to protect the interests of nobody other than the monarch. Consequently, Forest Law was disliked by everyone other than the monarch. Indeed, the barons who, in 1215, forced the Magna Carta on a reluctant King John, insisted in clauses 47 and 48 that recent extensions of the forest should be abolished. Two years later, William the Marshall issued the Charter of the Forest, in the name of the infant Henry III, which called for much disafforestation, but when Henry III reached full age, he fought back and revoked earlier concessions. The story was repeated again with Edward I, who in 1297 confirmed Magna Carta, but excluded the clauses which dealt with disafforestation.

The most important source of information about early forest law is the 'Assize of the Forest' of 1184, which was not new law, but rather a contemporary statement of current practice. The 'Assize' forbade interference with the forests or forest game, hunting with bows, arrows, hounds or harriers, the selling or giving away of anything within the forest, the depasturing of cattle at specific periods, and the hunting of wild animals at night with a view to their capture. All males over twelve years of age were required to swear an oath that they would not harm game. Penalties for infraction were ferocious. Anyone caught poaching venison, either inside or outside the forest, could be mutilated, usually by castration and blinding, and collective fines or confiscations of property were frequently levied to avenge unexplained dead deer. There were, of course, exceptions, and privileged tenants could occasionally receive grants of free warren, for the hunting of foxes, hares, rabbits, pheasants and partridges – but never for the hunting of deer.

The populace of the Royal Forest of Knaresborough was not only subjected to the severe constraints of Forest Law, but also to the conditions of a peculiar set of regulations, or 'customs', which were first recorded in 1559, the first year of the reign of Elizabeth I (E.119). These 'customs' may have originated from a much earlier time, possibly even before the establishment of the Royal Forest in *c.* 1100, although a post-plague origin of *c.* 1370 cannot be rejected altogether. William Grainge's claim that the customs dated from the time of Edward III cannot be verified.[3] Because the residents of Bilton-with-Harrogate and Pannal lived with the ramifications of the 'customs of the forest', it is necessary to examine their provisions before considering the history of Harrogate and the forest up to the time of the Civil War.

All residents were tenants of the Crown. The Crown owned the freehold of the whole of the Royal Forest, and had – through the Forest Court and its officers – absolute dominion over the life of the tenantry. Yet the tenants also had rights, and provided they obeyed the law and conformed to the standards of the society in which they lived, life for the people of Bilton-with-Harrogate does not appear to have been any worse – and possibly a good deal better – than that of the majority of communities in fourteenth-century England. The 'customs of the forest' provided a degree of security of tenure which may have been the envy of less-favoured communities, especially those which were under the direct rule of a capricious lord. Although such lords may indeed have held sway over the people of the Royal Forest, they were essentially lease-holders, and therefore of temporary duration, since outright ownership was the king's prerogative, who preferred to lease the lordship to the highest bidder. The absent monarch, having derived a good income from the lease-holding lord, left the administration of the Royal Forest to the lord and his forest officials. Although the lord, regarding the forest as a speculative investment, might squeeze as much profit as possible from it, he would neither have desired, nor been allowed, to ruin it. For this reason, the forest 'rules' were probably known by the greater part of the population.

The preamble to the earliest version of the 'rules' recorded in 1559 by the Duchy of Lancaster's commissioners, explains that the foresters had petitioned the Duchy for 'a commission for the due examination of and trying out of certain ancient customs …'. This indicates a significant, and possibly long-standing issue of some contention, which may have involved disputes over the conveying of land and property following the death of a tenant. The fact that this issue surfaced shortly after the Reformation makes tempting the idea that it was possibly prompted by disputes about lands which had formerly belonged to the Church, including Harrogate's chantry chapel. However, there is no direct evidence for this assumption.

The first 'rule' required executors of deceased tenants who had been in possession of property and, or, land, to pay to the Crown 'the best beast [horse, ox, cow, etc.] … for and in the name of a Herriot' – a heriot being the name for the payment made to a landlord by all in-coming tenants. Rules two to six covered deceased tenants' heriots where the amounts of land and/or buildings varied in number, and where tenants died with land held in fee simple. Rules seven and eight governed the letting by customary tenants of lands and buildings to other persons. Rule nine provided for the fining of tenants who cut down trees and sold the wood, with a provision included for tenants to take firewood for their own use, as well as timber to repair their dwellings. Rule ten provided for the heirs of executed felons to take up inheritances on payment of six years' rent. Other rules provided for the surrender of lands and/or messuages (buildings) by tenants and their transference to wives, heirs, etc., the repair of fences and boundaries. Rule twenty-eight required tenants to have grain, grown within the forest, ground at one of the king's mills. Rule thirty-two required the 'metes and bounds' of the forest to be perambulated once in three years. The penultimate rule (no. 37) required tenants to repair the piles and windings of the King's mill dams, the materials to be provided by officers of the Crown.

The thirty-eight rules or 'customs' of the Royal Forest reveal the importance of tenurial rights to land and buildings, as well as for their transference from one tenant to another.

Disputes about land and rights of access for grazing appear as early as 1225, when the Archbishop of York, who then leased the royal forest from the Crown, received from King Henry III an order to 'allow the King's men of Killinghall, Felliscliffe, Birstwith and ... Greistenwra [?] to have common in the pasture of ... Siwerdherges and Haywra [Haverah Park] as they used to have it in the time of ... King John [1199–1216].' (E.3) The king's order may have resulted from a petition by the tenants of certain forest communities for the restitution of rights of pasture. If this was the case, then it implies that the creation of Haverah Park post-dated the reign of King John. Equally, it may have been that the foresters were awarded special rights in Haverah Park, when the Royal Forest was created, and that their petition was for restitution of these former rights as enjoyed during *and before* the reign of King John. The matter was not resolved to the foresters' satisfaction, as two years later King Henry III, during a visit to Knaresborough Castle, ordered the Archbishop of York to investigate whether a previous lord of the Royal Forest, William de Stuteville, had deprived the foresters of their rights, when he was granted the lease of the Royal Forest in 1173 (E.4). The outcome of the investigation is not known, but as the use of Haverah remained exclusively royal, the Archbishop of York probably failed to support the foresters.

Haverah Park, and the other parks, woodlands and chases of the Royal Forest, were specially designated areas, some of which may have been in existence before the Forest's creation in *c.* 1100 (see plan 2). West of Harlow Hill, beyond even the ancient *Becwudu* of Archbishop Oswald's statement of 972 (A.7), lay the 2,250 acres of Haverah Park, also known as Haywra (E.16), Heywra (E.13) or Haveray (E.17). East of Harlow Hill, and bounded by the

River Nidd, lay Bilton Park, with its 1,100 acres. The third local royal park, Haya, or La Hay, had 1,200 acres, but as it lay beyond the forest boundary, to the east of Knaresborough, it is beyond the scope of our study.

The Harrogate area of the Royal Forest contained three special woodland preserves: Harlow, Fulwith and Oakdale, whose exact dimensions are not known (see plan 2). Certainly Harlow was centred on Harlow Hill, and may have extended westwards, well towards Beckwithshaw. We have a hint as to the eastern boundary of Harlow, in the Tudor map of 1587, on which Gammell Gate separates Bilton from Harlow (see plan 5). As Gammell Gate appears to be the route of West Park, it may be that the eastern boundary of Harlow lay along the route of West Park Stray and the modern A61. Fulwith lay south-east of Harlow Hill, and was possibly bounded by the modern Hookstone road and Crimple Beck. Finally there was Oakdale, or Ockden, which may have extended around much of Oak Beck, and was therefore to the north-west of Harlow Hill. The significant point about the royal parks and woodlands of Harrogate was not their size, but their location, in that they acted as a major determining factor in communal development. Where *they* were, houses and homesteads could *not* be, save for those of a few privileged individuals.

The ancient boundary between Bilton-with-Harrogate and the manor of Knaresborough, certainly before the time of Archbishop Oswald's re-organisation of 972 (A.7), was the river Nidd, and this continued to divide the Royal Forest from the Liberty of Knaresborough after the probable establishment of the former during the reign of Henry I. Yet an anomaly developed which (as with the area's other special enclosures) so affected the future Harrogate township's direction of growth, that a considered assessment is required before moving on the examine the locality's royal parks.

The area of the Royal Forest south of the Nidd, bounded by the modern Knaresborough to Harrogate road from High Bridge, Forest Lane, Forest Moor Road, Bland's Hill to Low Bridge, included the two distinct units of Belmont and the 'Little Park under the Castle'. As it is likely that any documents relating the origins and history of these two areas were lost when Brian de Lisleburn destroyed the honour records at Knaresborough Castle in 1317–18,[4] an explanation for their existence must rely on deduction using much later material. It is likely that the so-called 'Little Park under the castle' came into existence shortly after the building of the second, or stone castle at Knaresborough, first mentioned in 1129–30,[5] and that the purpose of this thin strip of land, which falls away steeply from the edge of Belmont Field down to the Nidd, was connected either with the castle's supplies or defences; or, that it was created to assist some special activity within the new royal forest (see plan 4).

The latter is unlikely, due to the location of the 'Little Park' directly

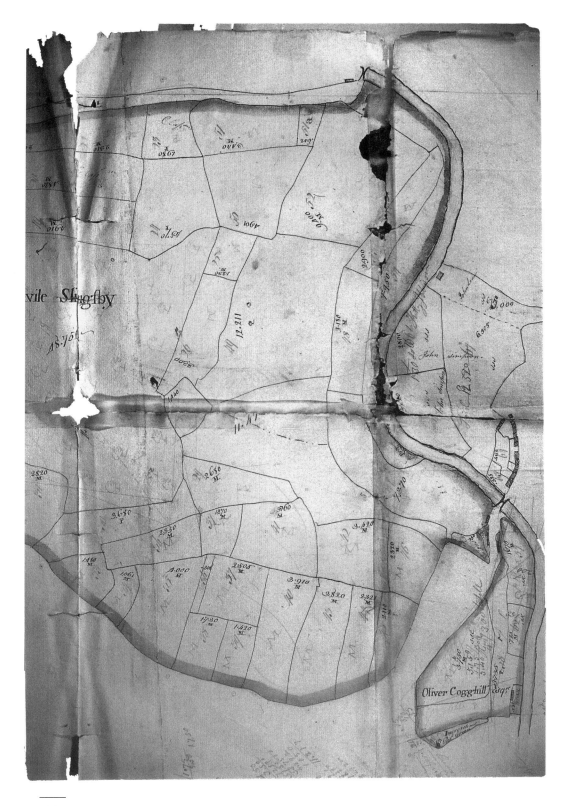

Oliver Cogghill Esqr.

29

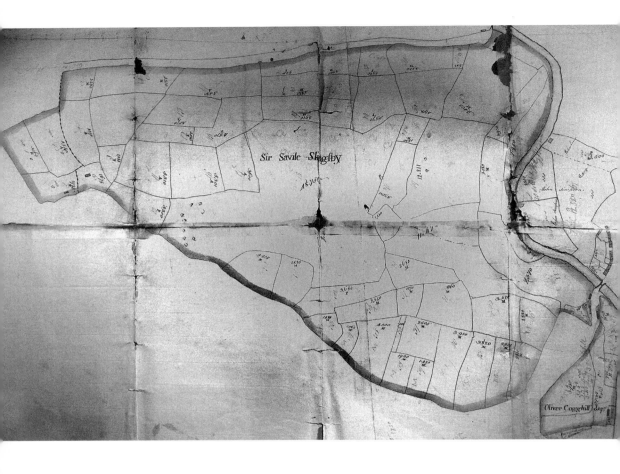

opposite the castle's footing, and the most reasonable explanation we can provide about the Little Park's origin is that it was created originally to ensure that *all* the surroundings of the castle were subject to the direct and immediate control of its occupants, and that having established such control by this annexation south of the Nidd of territory of Bilton-with-Harrogate, the Norman power was then content to lease the land to tenants from both Bilton-with-Harrogate and the Manor of Knaresborough. The distinction between the Little Park and Belmont seems to have lapsed after 1450, when Richard Faulkes, minister of the House of St Robert, leased the Little Park from the Duchy, for twenty years, on behalf of the Trinitarian Friars of Knaresborough. The conditions of this lease were that the order must enclose the Little Park with a pale or fence, which allowed the king's game to enter and exit. Within a year of the agreement of 5 February 1450, the minister was before the court for deliberately breaking his agreement, in that the required exit and entrance point had not been provided (A.37.150). The Belmont enclosure plan depicts the fields of the former Little Park (allotments 47, 48, 53 and 54, last with the dropping well) showing that they adhered to the fall of the gorge between High and Low bridges.

Belmont's boundary did not include the whole of the land framed by Forest Lane and Forest Moor Road, as a plan of the Belmont enclosures of *c.* 1775 shows (see plan 3) its south-western boundary sheering off from Forest Lane at a point near to Forest Lane Head, and running towards the Nidd at Low Bridge. The Duchy of Lancaster's meticulous survey of the so-called 'king's allotments' of *c.*1778 (see plan 25) also shows Belmont as a continuation of Bilton Park down to Low Nidd Bridge. It is therefore possible that Belmont field separated from the rest of Bilton Park by the Nidd end of the Harlaw Gate, had no special genesis until it was awarded to the Trinitarian Friars.

The Knaresborough Trinitarian Friars had a strong connection with Belmont. In 1257 Richard, Earl of Cornwall, gave to the Friars of the Chapel of St Robert all that land on the south side of the Nidd called 'Belmond ... between the Forest and the Little Park ... up to the road ... to Heywra ...' (E.8). Then, in 1314, an inquisition at the Honour Court examined the Friars' claim to build a barn in the area. The Trinitarian Friars were experiencing difficulty in transporting produce between the Friary, north of the Nidd at Knaresborough, and Belmont, south of the Nidd, which had been formerly part of Bilton-with-Harrogate. However, the Court had to consider the

PLAN 25
King's Harrogate allotments, 1778. Russell's survey, p. 123.

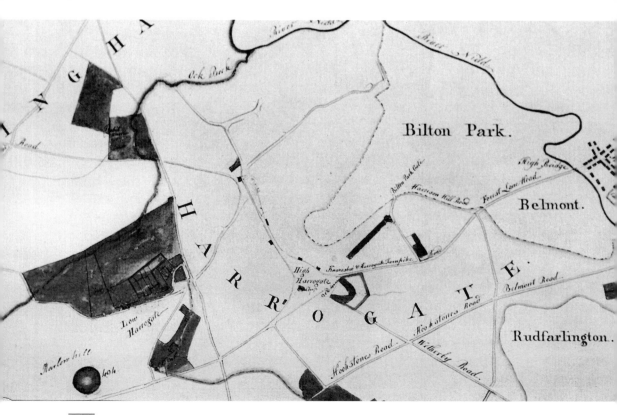

claims of other tenants, who comprised men of Knaresborough manor, as well as Bilton-with-Harrogate – and possibly Plumpton (A.27). Although the origin of Belmont is unknown, we offer the following theory as one possible explanation as to its existence. Belmont's French roots point to a Norman source, and at this location, directly opposite the Norman stronghold of Knaresborough Castle, and adjoining the 'Little Park', it is possible that Belmont developed as pasturage for cattle on the lush lands which rolled down to the Little Park's brow. Such lands may have been farmed by the same tenants as those who leased the Little Park, and who gradually pushed southwards towards the present Forest Lane. Historian William Wheater believed that the highest point of Belmont could have been a watch-point for Knaresborough Castle (A.37.186), which is an interesting possibility, especially if Belmont's boundaries were wider than those previously described. The long-term influence of the Trinitarian Friars, and Knaresborough Manor's control of much of this of part of Bilton-with-Harrogate, may be seen in the allotments following the Great Award of 1778 (B.31), which will be considered at the appropriate point in our narrative.

The most important single source of information about Harrogate's royal parks and woodlands lies in the Ministers' Accounts from the reigns of Richard II to Henry VI (A.1) and Henry VII to Henry VIII (A.2), from which it is possible to compile a general view of the Royal Forest of Knaresborough as a place of mixed agriculture and industry – mining and forging etc. – within which were a series of special parks and woodlands in which cattle were pastured, timber grown and deer protected, and the royal stud maintained. Outside the parks and woodlands, but still within the forest, were the fields and farms of Bilton-with-Harrogate, and Beckwith-with-Rossett, which appear to have been mostly arable, according to the court rolls. (Classes A, S). The open parts of the royal forest were home to wild animals which were enumerated by Thomas Parkinson:

> the wild animals then existing, and numerous in the district, were the wolf, wild boar, wild cattle – which Whitaker says were then called Oryx, and identical with the Aurochs or wild bulls of Lithuania – deer, stag, roebuck, hare, fox, badger, beaver, polecat or foumart, and the smaller animals then existing (E.12).

The Stuteville grant of 1199 to Nigel de Plumpton granted him permission to hunt

> the fox, and have throughout the whole of the Forest of Knaresborough, saving to the Lord the Royal Beasts of chase, the Stag, the Hart, and the Roebuck ... (A.11).

The earliest known reference to Haverah Park occurs in 1173, with the granting of the Honour of Knaresborough by Henry II to William de Stuteville (E.2). Haverah also featured in Henry III's order of 1225, when the tenant (the Archbishop of York) was ordered to allow 'the King's men of Killinghall, Felliscliffe, Birstath ... to have common in the pasture of the Lord King ... of ... Haverah as they used to have it in the time of ... King John.' (E.3) In 1234, Haverah Park passed to Richard, Earl of Cornwall and brother to Henry III, along with the parks of Bilton and Hay. Unlike Haverah, they were not named, but described as 'the Park' (E.6) and 'the New Park' (E.7), and it was to Bilton Park that Henry III sent forty deer. The timber which was grown in the parks and woodland enclosures seems to have been primarily oak, as is reflected in the name Oakdale. When Ripon Cathedral needed timber for work on the tower, it came from the Harrogate woodlands, an order of Henry III in 1227 called for thirty trees to be supplied from 'our forest of Okeden' (A.16).

The woodland preserves of Fulwith, Harlow and Oakdale (see plan 2) certainly contained much valuable timber, but they were also used to graze certain kinds of animals. When Edmund, Earl of Cornwall, confirmed a charter of his father, King Richard, in 1257, he allowed the Friars of Knaresborough's Holy Trinity to depasture forty pigs in Oakdale (E.8).

The earliest evidence for human activity at Haverah Park certainly pre-dated the establishment of the Royal Forest, and was a triple complex of earth mounds, known by the colourful name of Pippin Castle, whose origins may have been pre-Roman. They were swept away with the building of Scargill Reservoir in 1898. Adjacent to Pippin Castle was the Norse name-place of Siwardergs (Siward's '*erg*' or shieling) that was referred to as being within Haverah Park in a document of 1225 (E.3). Haverah's most significant structure was the lodge, more commonly known as 'John of Gaunt's Castle', which was probably built during the late twelfth century to accommodate official visitors to the park.

On Friday 19 September 1292 King Edward I, the 'Hammer of the Scots' journeyed from the Borough of Knaresborough to Haverah Park, travelling by way of the 'Harro-Gate'. The 'itinerary' of Edward I records that the King was at Haverah from Friday until Monday, when he moved to Skipton (A.21). His predecessor, King John, may have also travelled to Haverah Park via the 'Harro-Gate' during April 1210, June or September 1212 (A.15), but here there is no direct evidence.

A notice of 3 November 1298 sent from 'Heywra' (Haverah) by the Archbishop of York to the Abbot of Fountains Abbey (E.13), points to there being some kind of accommodation from where the Archbishop had his note penned. At this time, Haverah's most important industry must have been its forge, and as the Royal Forest had, since 1234, been controlled by the Earldom of Cornwall, the accounts of late thirteenth-century Haverah were included in the earldom's rental records, which contain a reference to Benedict, son of Hugo, paying a rental of eight shillings a week for sixteen weeks for one forge at Haverah (A.22). The same records mentions a forge at Pannal and Salterkeld (probably Saltergate Hill) at other locations within the Royal Forest, and these forges appear to have been powered by wood taken from the same forest, as well as coal from Bilton Park, which was mined as late as 1800 (E.99). Forging is known to have been practised within the Royal Forest of Knaresborough at least since 1206–7, during the reign of King John, with the largest being at Blubberhouses, first mentioned in 1227. By the end of the century the forest was home to a very active iron industry, with four large works in operation, and, in addition, some small forges of lorimers and nailsmiths.[6] To the south of Crimple Beck, a forge in Rigton Wood is known to have been working between 1284 and 1297, and in the latter year, the sum of 27s. was paid for nail-smithies.[7]

The Royal Forest of Knaresborough was not the only local place that had an active iron forging industry. At Spofforth, held by the Percys, a noble family of Norman descent, two forges were being worked in 1258.[8] However, after 1300, iron working in the area of the Royal Forest and on lands east and west of Leeds, appears to have been brought to a standstill, because the wood which supplied much of the fuel had been used up. By 1304–5 only two forges remained in the forest, one working, the other blown out.[9] As early as 1195, the Cistercians of Fountains Abbey had obtained a licence from William de Stuteville, to burn charcoal from 'dead wood' in the Forest of Knaresborough,[10] and the demise of the thirteenth-century iron forging industry in and around Harrogate was probably caused by over-exploitation of the forest's timber resources and exhaustion of supplies of iron-ore. By 1304–5, the forest's only working forge was at Haverah Park, which was leased for an annual rental of £20,[11] and by the middle of the century only a few iron-ore mines appear to have survived, including one at Haverah Park (where, in 1351, Thomas Arkyll paid 13s. 4d. rent for a year's working of a mine) and Oakdale (where Richard de Rothwell leased one at Le Northmoere in Okden at a rent of 3d. per week).[12]

A relic from the fourteenth-century forging industry may today be found in the route which connected Haverah Park and Kirkby Overblow, via Oak Beck, Cornwall Road (whose old name was Irongate Bridge Road, but whose route was almost certainly moved south after 1778), and probably either Cold Bath Road, Harlow Hill and Pannal, or, via what is now West Park and Leeds Road, to Walton Head. Material transported along this route included iron-ore, as well as fuel.

Haverah Park, together with the Royal Forest, reverted to the Crown at the death of Edmund Earl of Cornwall in 1300, as King Edward I was

PLAN 41
Survey of Harlow Hill area of Pannal, *c.* 1839, showing field boundaries between Otley Road and Irongate Bridge (now Cornwall) Road.

———

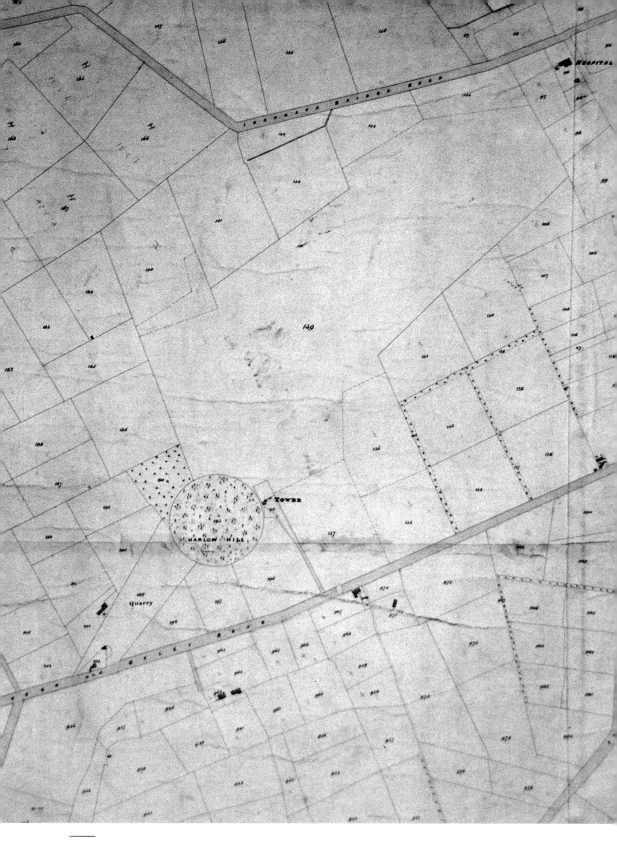

Edmund's nearest relative. Evidence for the reversion is found in the order of 4 June 1303, issued by Miles de Stapleton, Constable of Knaresborough Castle, requiring the pond of the King's Mill at Bilton 'and the head of the pond of his stew at Haverah' be repaired (E.16). An interesting petition relating to Bilton Park was issued in 1303. Henry de Scriven of Scriven petitioned the King, Edward I, stating that his ancestors had enjoyed the office of foresters of the Royal Forest of Knaresborough, which office paid them sixpence per day, together with common pasture in the forest, as well as in Bilton Park *before the said park was enclosed* (which points to Bilton Park have been established *after* the creation of the Royal Forest, *c.* 1100). The petition stated that after the enclosure of Bilton Park, the de Scriven rights continued, save for pasturing sheep and goats, but the Forest Steward Sir Miles Stapleton, interrupted these privileges. The Exchequer Chamber, in reply, decreed the petitioners should continue to enjoy their privileges without interruption, and that in addition, they be allowed to take from the King's woods all reasonable house-bote and hay-bote, without cutting down any oak, ash, hazel or fruit growing tree. It was also ordained that de Scriven should have pasture in the park of Bilton for his plough oxen and milk kyne (E.1.a). Henry de Scriven was again interrupted in the enjoyment of his Bilton Park privileges during the Lordship of Peter de Gaveston, causing him to issue a further petition. At an Inquisition of 1307, the de Scriven lineage traced the rights back to ancestor Gamel, causing Henry de Scriven to again be confirmed in his rights to pasture (E.1.b.). The summer letting of pasture land for grazing cattle at a fixed price per head, is known as agistment. By 1366, the agistment for Bilton Park was 8*d.* each for cattle, 4*d.* for a stirk (a young heifer or bullock), 1*s.* 6*d.* for a horse, and 9*d.* for a young horse (E.1.c.) The value of the agistment shows why rights of pasture were guarded so jealously.

The royal parks and woodlands had their keepers, and March 1307 saw a grant for life being given to John Brond, 'of the custody of the park of Haverah ... so that he keep it himself with another man, and receive as much as any two men formerly keeping it.' (E.18.a) Brond's duties were to keep the park's pale in good order, protect natural resources, and provide the King's officers with whatever information they might require about income and expenditure. An inquisition of 6 February 1307 stated that Haverah had two 'parkers' who received 11½*d.* a day (E.19), but this was probably on top of an established wage, which was referred to in 1296 as being £4 11*s.* per annum for two keepers at Haverah. Wages at the smaller Bilton Park paid a single Parker £1 10*s.* 4*d.*, plus one penny a day, and two carpenters who fixed and maintained the pale of Haverah Park were paid 38*s.* (probably each) for their work (E.12).

The same year of 1307 that saw John Brond taking custody of Haverah park also saw King Edward II granting the whole of the Honour, including Harrogate and its woodlands, to Peter de Gaveston, who was created Earl of Cornwall. Edward became King in July 1307, and in making the grant to his favourite Gaveston, he wisely retained control of the great castle at Knaresborough (A.20). The grant, which was confirmed on 16 August 1310, gave Gaveston, his wife Margaret and their lawful heirs, 'free chace in all the demesne woods of the Honour, with the parks of Le Haye, Bilton, and Haverah ...', as well as power to take and imprison all trespassers (E.20). The extraordinary career of the Gascon Gaveston has been the subject of much historical comment, including Christopher Marlowe's wonderful play, *Edward II*. His close relationship with Edward brought him great power, and indeed for the period of the King's absence in France, Peter de Gaveston was *de facto* ruler of England. Gaveston's enemies succeeded in having him banished in May 1308, but he was recalled the following July, only to be banished again in 1311. After final recall in January 1312, he was captured by the barons in May at Scarborough, and beheaded without trial in June. Such was the man who for a time had lordship over Harrogate.

The year 1308 witnessed the marriage of King Edward II to Isabella of France, who was granted enjoyment of the royal parks of Bilton, Haverah and Hay. It is very likely that King Edward II visited Haverah Park between 13 and 14 August 1310, as the privy seal, court and household were recorded at Haverah after moving from York (A.26). Eight years later, Edward granted custody of Bilton Park to new warden Constantine Le Harpur, at a fee of 2*d*. a day. Constantine received his grant on 18 March, a mere two months before catastrophe reached Harrogate in the form of the Scottish army, which in May had poured into Yorkshire (E.23.a).

According to the Chronicle of Lanercost, the Scottish invasion of May 1318 penetrated much further south than usual. Northallerton and Boroughbridge were burned, and the booty-laden horde pressed on to Ripon, which they despoiled, and it was only after paying a ransom of a thousand marks that the city was saved from destruction. After a three-day respite, the Scots turned towards Knaresborough, which they destroyed by fire. In addition, the Scots sent raiding parties into the forest to search out those who had fled with their possessions. One such party reached Pannal, burning down the church. The chronicler then relates that the Scots moved on to Skipton, which they burned, before returning north, with plundered cattle driven before them (A.30). The Lanercost Chronicle provides a possible explanation for the development of a populated settlement by the Harro-Gate, as we have already related in our first chapter.

Statistically the foresters were more at risk from the activities of local breakers of the King's peace than from armies of marauding Scots. However, it was probably true that many otherwise law-abiding people were driven by the Scottish raiders to take desperate measures, including trespass in the Royal Parks and Woodlands. Constantine le Harpur, warden of Bilton Park, had his wages disrupted by the troublesome times, requiring an order, dated 24 June 1322, to the keeper of Knaresborough Castle, to pay le Harpur 'his wages in arrear ... to wit, 2*d*. a day' (E.25). The warden probably had a hard time of things in the years following the Scottish invasion. From this period, there exists a singular pardon, which was given to William Snawe of Bilton for his sin of 'adhering to the Scots' (E.28.a). Nothing is known of the circumstances of Snawe's transgression, nor of the reason for his pardon, but doubtless his neighbours spoke of them for many years. Events of a more serious nature occurred in 1324, when a commission of Oyer and Terminer[13] was appointed to investigate the circumstances touching the persons who broke the parks of Queen Isabella at Bilton, Haverah and Hay, hunted therein, and carried away deer (E.27). A further commission for a similar offence was issued in July 1330, concerning further illicit hunting, and also the cutting down of trees and removal of timber (E.28.b).

In 1323 King Edward II again travelled to Yorkshire, arriving at York on 1 May, and staying at the Archbishop's Bishopthorpe Palace. The King spent three days in the royal parks, including Haverah, his itinerary being recorded in the first volume of *Collectanea Archaeologica*, which states that Edward stayed at Haverah on 25 and 26 September (A.26). Writing around 1870 in the full-blown style of High Victorian prose, historian William Grainge noted 'remote, lonely and insignificant as the place now appears, we can truly say, when standing on its ruins and looking on the landscape around, that King Edward more than five hundred years ago gazed upon the same hills and valleys as we do now – standing upon the same ground on which we now stand.' Grainge was writing not just of Haverah Park, but of the lodge, known locally as John of Gaunt's castle, although as John of Gaunt was Edward II's grandson and not born until 1340, it is probable that during the visit of Edward II it was known simply as the castle or fortress.[14] Certainly the details of a series of major repairs, itemised between 1333 and 1335, refer to 'the fortress of Haywra' (see plate 2).

Haverah Castle may have been damaged by the Scots during their incursions of 1318 (A.30), although the itemisation of expenditure on repairs over the period from 1333 to 1335 does not state the reason for such extensive repair work. The castle's chapel was re-roofed with a mixture of old and new lead, and eight masons were employed on the stonework, being paid 4*d*. a day for their labour, as distinct from the carpenters, who received 2*s*. 6*d*. each per week. It is known that 1,200 iron nails were used, and that the lead sheets for the roof were fixed with 500 'leadnails'. Two rooms were named: a hall called 'le Waerhall' and the Queen's Chamber, probably in

honour of Edward III's consort, Queen Phillipa. The fortified nature of Haverah Castle is indicated by references to the castle gate, brattice (a temporary wooden partition on a parapet) and palisade. Evidence for a strengthening of existing fortification is provided by the commissioning of a new piece of work, a surrounding ditch 26 feet broad by 12 feet deep (E.34).

On 22 September 1343 an order issued from the Tower of London appointed Roger de Normanvill custodian responsible for Haverah Castle, at a wage of 10 marks per annum. The previous custodian, Edmund de Tichemersh was mandated to hand over to de Normanvill the castle's armour, victuals, and 'other things in his custody' (E.36.a). Custodianship of Haverah Castle also included responsibility for the king's horses. In the fourteenth century, the Harrogate area's royal parks became increasingly important as a centre for the royal stud, although the surrounding royal forest was still dominated by agriculture and forestry.

A stud in the Royal Forest of Knaresborough was first referred to *after* the earliest references to deer, which occurred in 1244 when the Lord of the forest, Richard, Earl of Cornwall, received from his brother Henry III, forty deer from Pontefract Park to stock the new park at Bilton (E.6). Thirteenth-century accounts of court pleas contain many cases of deer and other wildlife being molested, but not a single case of depredations on the stud, or indeed on any other horses (E.10). It was not until 1318–19 that the Pipe Rolls of Edward II mention horses, recording that the herbage of Haverah Park was reserved for the sustenance of the King's horses and oxen (E.21). There-after, the stud received frequent mention, and on 5 September 1335, the 'keeping of certain great horses of the King, and of the King's stud on this side of the Trent ...' was committed to the care of William de Neusom (E.31.b) who succeeded his father John de Neusom in the same post (E.31.c). William de Neusom's father seems to have been in debt, for on the same day that his son was confirmed in his new office, an order was issued to the bailiffs to take into the King's hands the goods and chattels of the late John de Neusum, who 'was held to the King in divers debts on the day of his death and rendered not his accounts ...' (E.31.c). William had been left an awkward legacy. Five days after the order of 5 September, a further order was issued from Perth. The bailiffs were instructed to deliver those goods and chattels of the late John which had not yet been taken by William, and to deliver them to Alice, wife of the late John, and now a widow. The profits from the agistments of the parks were to be received by the bailiffs and delivered to Alice, so that she could answer for the arrears of her late husband (E.31.d). This reasonable action appears to have been typical of the royal administration.

William de Neusom does not seem to have retained his position for very long, as it passed within months (1335) to Edmund de Thedmarsh or Tichemersh (E.31.e), who indulged in sharp practice in his dealings with King Edward III, which came to light after his death in *c.* 1343. An inquiry revealed that although de Thedmarsh received one hundred marks per annum for the agistment of animals in the Harrogate area's royal parks, he had paid over to the King only forty marks, and that he had also taken for his own use hay, oats and other necessaries intended for the stud. In all Edmund de Thedmarsh had held back the sum of one thousand pounds, a huge sum in fourteenth-century terms (E.37.a), for which he would have incurred a severe penalty, had he not died before discovery of his misdeeds. De Thedmarsh's successor, Roger de Normanville held the office from 1343 (E.36.b) until *c.* 1348 (E.37.a), after which it passed to John de Barton (E.37.c), who controlled parks and stud during the terrible years of the great plague, described in chapter three.

Although the traditional 'customs of the Royal Forest' (E.119) make no reference to regulating the hunting of forest livestock with dogs, the matter was thoroughly covered by the law of the land, especially in the 1184 assize of the forest.[15] The fourteenth of the assizes' provisions required mastiffs to be 'lawed', a process which rendered them useless for hunting by the cutting of their claws and three toes of their forefeet. Insight into local custom is found within a court roll for 1345, headed *Expedition of Dogs*, which intimates that it was the custom for tenants to present their dogs for inspection. When Robert Fowlbaroun failed to produce his dogs for the expeditation of 1345, which was held at St Hilda's Chapel, near to the site of the twentieth-century Morrison's store, he was fined for his neglect of duty (E.36.c).

Maintenance of the royal park palings was an important aspect of the custodians' responsibilities, and the court rolls make frequent allusion to the work of repair. In May 1333 the king's council ordered that the park paling of Haverah should be repaired with posts and boards (E.26.d), but such defence was little protection against the violence of the times. On 15 October 1351 a commission of Oyer and Terminer was issued

> touching the evildoers who broke the parks of Queen Philippa at Knaresborough [the little park beneath the castle] and Bylton, and entered her free chases and warrens there ... hunted in these and carried away deer from the parks and chaces, and hares and rabbits, pheasants and partridges from the warrens (E.38).

A more serious event occurred in 1358, when the close rolls recorded that William de Aldeburgh, knight, ordered his men to break into the Queen's park of Haverah, on the night of the Wednesday before Easter, where with hunting dogs they took four bucks and twelve does. So great was their booty that five carcases had to be left behind. On the first Monday after Easter, again at William de Aldeburgh's order, a further foray was made into the royal parks, this time at Hay, where a buck, two sorels and four does were taken. The close roll for 16 May 1358 ordered the justices to 'supersede taking any process before Michaelmas' upon the indictments against the accused men. The entry ends '... for certain causes, the King of his favour has granted that no execution or process shall be made upon those indictments before that date.' (E.39.a) Some light is shed on this curious entry by one issued four days earlier, on 12 May 1358, when King Edward III issued a pardon to John de Stratherne, whose name was foremost on the order of Oyer and Terminer, describing him as 'yeoman of the King's kinsman, Edward de Balliolo, King of Scotland', who vouched for de Stratherne's entire innocence (E.40.b).

The court rolls and accounts contain fewer references to the woodland chases of Fulwith, Harlow and Oakdale, than to Bilton and Haverah parks. Nevertheless, those references are of interest. In 1333 widow Alice de Laresbyry was fined for cutting down a green alder in Harlow (A.37.2), and in 1342, Henry de Pensax was fined for cutting wood in 'Harla and Okdene' (A.37.23). The court roll for 1343 records that Agnes, daughter of Gilbert de Harugate 'for taking greenwood in Harlagh [Harlow] the same de Harugate broke the law regarding green underwood in Harlagh, fined xiid.' In 1350 William Carpenter of Pannal was fined for cutting down a tree in Harlow (A.50), and John of Gaunt's register contains many references to the oak trees of Oakdale (A.56). One hundred and fifty years before William Carpenter's time, King Henry III had issued an order, dated 1227, that the woodland preserves of Fulwith, Harlow and Oakdale provide trees for work on the tower of Ripon Minster, from which 'our forest of Okeden' supplied thirty (A.16). A brief entry in the 1361 rolls names Geoffrey de Dene as late keeper of the bailiwick of the Forest of Ockeden (Oakdale).

However, by 1443, the offices of forester for Fulwyth and Harlow appear to have been merged, as Thome Gelder was sworn into the post of 'forester of Harlowe and Fulwyth' (A.37.123). The post was confirmed in *c.* 1483 by Richard III (E.64). This may be an indication of the shrinking nature of both woodlands, possibly because of depredation. Clearly, timber was a very important contribution to the economy of Harrogate's royal woodlands, and some of the monies raised were used in the great building works at Windsor Castle, which king Edward III was completing. An order to joint keepers of the Royal Parks, John de Barton and Thomas del Bothe, dated 26 July 1361,

> to sell, in view and testimony of the king's clerks ... all the king's horses, mares and studs in the parks of ... Haverah [and other parks] (except ten of the best mares there) and to deliver the proceeds of the sale by indenture to the king's Clerk, William de Wykeham, surveyor of the king's works in the Castle of Wyndsore, towards the expenses of the said works. (E.41.a)

Three years after the sale of the king's horses, Edward III received news that the fortress (*'fortalice'*) of Haverah was in poor condition, especially with regard to the chapel, bridge and gate. On 13 June 1364 the Sheriff of York received an order requiring a survey to be made, and 'all defects therein to be repaired' (E.42).

The numbers of persons pasturing beasts in the royal parks can be assessed by means of the court rolls. For the summer of 1365 Haverah Park pastured 478 beasts and 274 stirks, which at 8*d.* a head for beasts and 4*d.* a head for stirks represented good income. Horses were charged at a higher rate, with eighty-seven persons paying pasturage fees, of whom Will Benttes paid the most, with his 172 beasts and 115 stirks. The agistment roll contains several old Harrogate family names, such as Benson (Will. Dicson-benson), Thackwray (Nichol de Thakwra), Pullan (Rico. Polayne) and Shutt (Adam Shotte) (E.43.a).

In 1372 an event occurred which had profound significance for Harrogate, as well as the nation in general. King Edward III granted the Royal Forest to his younger son, John, Duke of Lancaster, also known as John of Ghent, or Gaunt. The Earldom of Lancaster had been translated into a Duchy on 6 March 1351, when Henry Grosmont, the fourth Earl – a soldier, diplomat and administrator – was created first Duke of Lancaster (see plate 3). Henry died ten years later, in 1361, without a direct male heir, so the Duchy reverted to the King, Edward III, who in the following year of 1362 created his son, John of Ghent, or Gaunt, second Duke of Lancaster. The new Duke acquired valuable additions to his territory in 1372, when he surrendered the Earldom of Richmond to his father, King Edward III, gaining in exchange the Honours of High Peak, Pevensey, Tickhill and Knaresborough, which last Honour contained the Royal Forest and Harrogate. Duke John witnessed the end of the reign of King Edward III, and lived through the reign of the succeeding monarch, Richard II, but his son, Henry Boling-broke, was banished by the latter King. When the Duke died in 1399, King Richard tried to confiscate the Duchy inheritance, but the new Duke returned from exile and landed on the Yorkshire coast at Ravenspur in June or July. He was met by a band of loyal followers, among whom Duchy historian Sir Robert Somerville includes two hundred from the Forest of Knaresborough.[16] Henry Bolingbroke then marched on Pickering, Knaresborough and Pontefract castles, which he seized, his triumphal progress ending with the surrender of Richard II at Flint, and his subsequent coronation in Westminster Abbey on 13 October 1399. The first act of the new King, Henry IV, was to declare that the inheritance of the Duchy of Lancaster should be held by the monarch separately from other Crown possessions, descending directly to his male heirs. This decree was of incalculable good fortune for Harrogate, the importance of which cannot be over-emphasised.

One of the most important sources of information about Harrogate in the later fourteenth century is the register drawn up by Henry IV's father, John of Gaunt, between 1372 until 1383. Compiled at the London palace of Savoy, with entries in French, the register contains several interesting references to Bilton Park, Harlow, Haverah Park and Oakdale, whose management was clearly a matter of concern to the Duke (E.48, E.49). An entry for 1380 records that the keeper of the Royal Forest was ordered 'to give to the tenants of Bilton and Harrogate enough brushwood to enclose a place in Bilton Park, which it is their duty to do,

PLATE 3
Arms of the Duchy of Lancaster.

and ... see they do it quickly' (E.49.a). The repairs were needed to keep the livestock within the park, rather than exclude unauthorised persons, for whom a regular palisade would have been no deterrent.

During the twelfth and thirteenth years of the reign of Richard II (1388–89 and 1389–90) a series of outrages brought great unrest to Harrogate and the surrounding Royal Forest. A number of men attempted to murder the acting master forester, Robert Doufbiggyng, who had been appointed by Robert de Rokley, the King's master forester for Knaresborough Forest and all its parks and woodlands. Doufbiggyng's appointment appears to have been part of a strategy by de Rokley to end certain malpractices that had resulted from a foresters' gathering, or Parliament, known as 'Dodelowe'. In November 1388, an armed band visited Haverah Castle, probably via Harlow Hill, and besieged Doufbiggyng, who had taken refuge within. The plotters had already failed to silence their enemy the previous Palm Sunday, when they had ambushed Doufbiggyng at Fewston Church, which resulted in the victim and five other men being set upon and assaulted, the severity of which may be judged by the fact that, subsequently, some died of their wounds.

The patent rolls relate that the unofficial 'parliament' had appointed several foresters to unordained posts, and that they had been in

> subversion of the law and oppression of the people, disinherison of the ... duke and loss of life of his ministers; also for destroying ... the park of Haverah and doing mischief in other parks and chases ... entering the house and destroying the goods and utensils of Robert Doufbiggyng, value forty shillings, abducting the groom of Robert de Rokley, knight, and his greyhound, and detaining them for two days; and for coming with others on 1st June [1390] ... to the house of Robert Doufbiggyng ... and slaughtering sixteen oxen and cows and destroying household utensils, value £8 (E.52.a).

These details were recorded in a pardon of 1393 issued to one of the accused, Richard Walthewe, whose co-accused, John Stubbe, obtained a similar pardon two years later, which related further outrages committed against Doufbiggyng, including the murder of his son Edmund, on the first Sunday after Michaelmas 1390 (E.42.b). This series of outrages had probably been the result of the foresters' mounting resentment at the Master Forester's efforts to control their illicit activities, especially by his appointment of the unfortunate Doufbiggyng, on whom fell the full fury of their displeasure. Whatever the cause, a vendetta developed which was prosecuted with a ferocity which even for those violent times was remarkable for its disregard of life and property.

Before we continue our narrative into the fifteenth century, it is necessary to refer to the folk-hero figure of Robin Hood, if only because many readers concern themselves with the history of England's royal forests only because of the pervasive charm of his story. The separation of the literary, historical and mythical figures of Robin Hood is a task that has engaged several historians,[17, 18] for many years. The outcome is that so far as the historical figure is concerned, the most likely period in which Robin Hood existed was that covered by the reigns of King Edward II (1307 to 1327) and King Edward III (1327 to 1377).

Medieval historians now admit Yorkshire's forests are better candidates as settings for the exploits of the historical Robin Hood than anything in Nottinghamshire, most particularly the West Riding's Forest of Barnsdale, long notorious for its dangerous passage. The antiquary Leland stated that, 'Along the left hand, about three miles betwixt Milburn and Ferrybridge, I saw the wood and famous forest of Barnsdale, where they say that Robyn Hood lyvid like an outlaw'.[19] The former royal parks and woodlands which formerly ringed and penetrated medieval Harrogate are further possible settings for the Robin Hood story, precisely because they were royal, and consequently well endowed, and also because, as historians such as Dobson, Taylor and Walker have pointed out, Plumpton Park has several connections with Robin Hood. The British Library's Department of Manuscripts contains a reference to Robin Hood hunting in Barnsdale Forest and Plumpton Park[20] and indeed the earliest and most detailed account of Robin Hood, printed in 1495,[21] affirms that: 'When he came to Plompton Parke'. It is known that both Bilton and Haverah Parks lost deer to poachers, and that they were not unfamiliar to the brigand and robber. Edward II certainly visited Haverah Park in May 1322 and September 1323, at the very time when he was greatly concerned about the depredations to his northern forests (A.26). It may be that some local folk legend of Robin Hood led to the name being adopted for a Harrogate inn sign, as recorded by author David Lewis: 'I'll send all my friends to the famed Robin Hood' (C.92.b), which later became the Wellington Inn in Cold Bath Road. Indeed, the earliest known name for Cold Bath Road was Robin Hood lane, and as late as 1902 the name of Robin Hood Field was used in a lease (S.f.12). All this, however, proves nothing, but merely hints at possibilities.

The fifteenth century opened with Harrogate and the surrounding royal forest firmly subject to the ownership of the king and administration of the Duchy of Lancaster, who through the agency of the forest court, provided the community with the stability and judiciary which were to have such beneficial effect. Stewardship of the Royal Forest of Knaresborough was, since 1399, the responsibility of the Duchy, Their first appointee was Sir Peter de Bucton,[22] but in 1414 Sir Robert Plumpton succeeded,[23] whose extensive estates lay to the east of Harrogate. Sir Robert's son, William, seems to have made attempts to re-stock the parks during his term as Steward, for in 1439 he took charge of one hundred and sixty wild deer, which must have had a considerable effect on the pasturage of the royal parks (E.56).

There appears to have been a dispute in the 1470s between the foresters of Fulwith, Oakdale and Swindon (Harlow was not mentioned, but a document of grants by King Richard III, dated *c.* 1483, refers to the office of forester of 'Fulwithe & Harlowe' (E.64), so the two may have been combined), and the tenants, on the matter of the foresters' wages. It appears that whereas the chief forester was paid by the Duchy, the woodland foresters were paid by the tenants, presumably on the grounds that their work was of great benefit to those tenants. Ralph Birnand, forester of Fulwith and John Lounde, forester of Swindon, had been demanding the wage of four pence a day, and Hugh Owersby, forester of the smaller Oakdale, demanded threepence a day. The matter had come to light during a tour, or 'progress' made by the Duchy officials, in March 1476, when they traversed the parks and woodlands about Harrogate. Along with evidence of a general falling standard of maintenance (e.g. 'the park of Bylton ... is gretely hurted and the wodes thereof almost destroid be felling of the grete trees ... the pasture of the same park is gretely hurted by wrotyng of swyne ...'), the Duchy also recorded that the wage claims of the woodland foresters were the source of 'grete wrong and hurt of the said tenants' (E.61). The dispute was serious enough to require the Duchy to arrange an investigation into the claims of the foresters, and the objections of 'the Knights, Esquires & Gentlemen and others having and occupying lands and tenements within the said forest'. Both parties had agreed to accept the findings, which were that the three foresters were demanding too high a wage, and that it should be reduced by one penny a day. Moreover, payment of the foresters' wages was to be regularised, with payments being made at Michaelmas and Easter. The agreement closed with lists of tenants who were responsible for paying the foresters' wages, but unfortunately the lists for Fulwith and Oakdale have not survived (E.62). In comparison, the wages of the park keepers during the opening year of the reign of King Richard III show that John Brown, keeper at Bilton, received an annual wage of £2 5s. 6d., the Bilton Park palliser received annually £1 10s. 5d., and of the larger Haverah Park, the keeper, Ralph Pigot received £6 1s. 8d. and the un-named palliser £3 0s. 8d. (E.63).

Meanwhile, the Plumptons continued to show interest in Harrogate's parks and woodlands. By 1490, Haverah Park was leased by David Griffith, councillor to Thomas, Earl of Derby, and when this lease came up for renewal, Sir Robert Plumpton sought to obtain the post of Keeper, at a yearly rent of £8 per annum, for six years (E.66.b). Much of the negotiation appears to have been undertaken by Sir Robert's son, Edward, who urged his father to persist in his attempts. On 6 May 1490 Edward wrote to his father that,

> I laboured to David and spake with him according to your desire; and there is great labour made to him to put you from Haverah Park [i.e. there was opposition] and offered to him £10 and a reward of 100 shillings. Notwithstanding I have made such labour, and caused him to be so agreeable to let it to you for six years ... and you to send six marke to him at Whytsontide next to London, and then and there have your indentures sealed and delivered ... (C.1.b).

Sir Robert ignored his son's urgings, and on 11 June received a further letter from Edward: 'ye have a faythfull frynd and servant of David Griffith, but I marvell that ye sent not the money at Pentycost ...' (C.1.c). Again Sir Robert failed to send the money, and again his son urged him to do so, on 28 June: 'I marvell much that your mastership sendeth not ... what shall I say to him ... remember you may have his parke ... by my labour, and if he change and let it to another, blame me not ...' (C.1.d). The lease between Griffith and Sir Robert was agreed on 26 August, whereby Sir Robert acquired for eight years the office of keeper of the Park of Haverah, with herbage and pannage, all for the yearly rent of £8. (E.66.b)

The office of park keeper was sought because of the opportunity for gain brought with the keeper's power to sub-let. Responsibilities of the post still required the vigilance of the keeper, and in a single year such as 1482, there were several prosecutions for unlawful hunting. John Lindley and John Watson were accused of hunting in Harlow and Fulwith; John Baildon and Geoffrey Flaseby were accused of killing a buck at Harlow; the minister of St Robert's church, Panel, hunted a buck from Harlow to Haverah, which was killed by William Plumpton; Ralph Burnand left in Harlow four bucks he had dispatched (A.78). There were many more cases.

Depredation of the deer was not always the result of law breaking. Between 29 September 1507 and 11 May 1508, thirty-five deer died of 'murrain' at Bilton Park, two hundred and thirty-six at Haverah Park, with further losses at Hay Park (E.66.d) The 'murrain', or plague, may have been the cause of the trouble which occurred in May 1507, when six hundred people – many of them from the Harrogate area –

> riotously united themselves, assembled, congregated and associated at Killinghall, ... and with force of arms ... broke and entered three closes of ... the lord the King ... tore up a dyke ... destroyed hedges and defences ... trampled down ... the grass ... (A.85).

The indictment, and the following inquisition at York Castle on 31 May 1507, did not explain the cause of the foresters' riot, but given the several references to the breaking of boundary hedges, and the depasturing of rioters own cattle on the land they entered, it is possible that a mixture of fear over the murrain, and resentment at the isolation of the Royal Parks – a resentment made perhaps stronger by the keepers' efficiency in protecting the park palings – had sparked serious discontent.

The advent of the great Elizabeth, who reigned from 1558 to 1603, saw the Duchy undertaking a survey of the Queen's inheritance of the Royal Forest of Knaresborough. This was done in 1562 by Privy Councillor Ambrose Cave,[24] whose survey found that, 'our game and deere pale and lodge and about our parke of Haverah ... is in great ruyn and decay and that ther hath been made great wast and spoile of our woods there and diverse other spoiles and waste committed within our parke ... in diggings and invertings the soile ...' (E.69). A subsequent inquisition into the state of Haverah Park found that thanks to the disrepair of the pale, the deer had vanished (unlike the smaller Bilton Park which in 1561 still retained about a hundred (E.68)), and that it would take more than £400 to secure the park again for deer (E.70).

There are two principal reasons for the sixteenth-century decline of the royal parks and woodlands about Harrogate. First, the role of the Crown, as the days were long past when Norman and Plantagenet monarchs enjoyed the chase through the Royal Forest. The draconian laws of Henry I and Henry II had lapsed, and as the eventful reign of Elisabeth reached its twilight, the forest became just one more asset, administered on behalf of the monarch by the benign but distant Duchy, whose officials were involved increasingly with the Duchy courts and the judicial system. Second, there was the role of the declining ironworks industry, which as ore and fuel became ever more scarce, created an unscrupulous attitude towards the lands and materials of the royal forest. That much of the damage was caused by the iron-smelting industry, is not to be doubted. As late as 1693, Dr Neale was writing about the land around Harrogate's Sweet Spaw (the St John's Well), noting that 'many iron-stones were thrown up, all the ground thereabout being digged up, and all the wood destroyed in Queen Elizabeth's time, by iron-forges ...' (F.19). The Crimple Beck blast furnace (which will be considered in chapter three) built by the Earl of Cumberland, and referred to in a Duchy of Lancaster commission of 1598, may have been the cause of the destruction of Fulwith's woodlands.

Elizabeth's successor, James VI of Scotland and I of England (1603–25), when newly crowned, desired to learn the full extent of his inheritance. Accordingly, in 1604, the Duchy commissioned Richard Blower (who enjoyed the title 'Messenger of the Duchy and Usher of the Council House')[25] and his colleague Balam Colvile, to survey 'the King's wood in

Yorkshire'. Fortunately, their survey has survived intact, unlike the earlier one by Ambrose Cave, of which only the Haverah park section (E.69) has survived. Blower and Colvile examined the sale of timber by one Thomas Johnson, from the Parks of Bilton and Haverah, including the enclosures of Oakdale and Harlow, finding that Johnson had greatly exceeded his authority, and that the proceeds of his sales had not been returned for the king's use. The report of this highly unsatisfactory situation noted that the smaller Bilton Park retained 1,608 mature trees still standing, compared with the larger Haverah's 410 standing trees. Beyond Bilton Park, in the hamlet of old Bilton, the 'moor' contained only 207 'pieces of timber, being all the butt ends of trees'. This is further evidence of Johnson's unscrupulous forestership. Alarmed at Blower and Colvile's findings, the Duchy's feodary, Sir Henry Slingsby, wrote to Sir Robert Cecil (E.72) – the Earl of Salisbury – apparently unaware that Sir Robert had ceased to be the Duchy Chancellor in 1599.[26] The earl, however, did not allow such a paltry matter as his inability to sign Duchy warrants to interfere with looking after Duchy interests, and he wrote to Johnson, charging him with neglecting the king's property. The result of this correspondence was a special Duchy commission headed by Blower and Colvile, to enquire into the sale of timber by Thomas Johnson, the outcome of which confirmed his irresponsible behaviour. The Duchy forests and chases were to receive much attention in the reign of Charles I, and during the early years of his father's reign, James I, the Duchy had concerned itself with sales of timber and unauthorised felling.

In 1615 Sir Henry Slingsby himself, 'keeper, herbager and farmer of Bilton Park', was found guilty of 'divers offences, misdemeanors and wrongs done to our woods, game and other things committed to his charge', being fined £623 10s. 0d. by the Duchy Court. He was also removed from office, and the keeping of Bilton Park was granted to Esme Stuart, Lord Aubigny, at a rent of £11 12s. 2d. per annum (E.74). The Duchy moved immediately to set Bilton Park to rights, issuing a warrant to the Deputy Surveyor of Woods, Edmund Saltmarsh, for the repair of the lodges at Bilton Park, authorising the use of 'forty trees out of a moor adjoining to the said park called Alrome' (E.75). The location of Alrome, [or Olrom E.71] is not known precisely, but it seems to have been the name of the moorland which stretched from the Star Beck as far as the eastern boundary of Harlow, being perhaps of vulgar nomenclature. The repairs at Bilton Park were not restricted to the lodges, as it was necessary in 1622 to hold an inquisition at Knaresborough Castle for identifying those responsible for maintaining the pale. (E.76).

On 2 February 1626 Charles I was crowned king, thereby receiving the inheritance of the Duchy of Lancaster, which that amiable monarch then began to dismember. Desire for a greater income caused the old forest laws to be enforced with greater strictness, and whereas James I had, because of his interest in sport, discouraged disafforestation, his son Charles I had no such compunction. In the first year of his reign, Charles issued commissions that led to the disafforestation of Leicester in 1628, Duffield Frith, and – more significantly – Needwood. Under Charles I, the Duchy of Lancaster lost over one hundred manors, the 'consideration' money being paid directly to the Exchequer, and never appearing in the Duchy accounts. As if these extensive sales and grants were not enough, the Duchy was further dismembered – if only temporarily – by the settlement which Charles made in 1629 upon his queen, Henrietta Maria. Her jointure was fixed at £28,000, of which £6,000 represented Exchequer and Duchy lands. The 'antient Duchy' was so reduced by 1635, that in May, the lords of the Treasury observed that as Duchy receipts were £10,855, but outgoings amounted to £11,160, the Duchy's pensions should be stopped![27]

King Charles's treatment of his Duchy inheritance had a direct influence on the future growth of Harrogate. On 27 April 1627 the king demised, for a term of ninety-nine years, the Royal Parks of Haverah and Bilton, together with the entire Honour of Knaresborough (including both Forest and Liberty) to Sir Francis Bacon, Sir John Darombe, Thomas Murray, James Fullerton, and Thomas Taylor, a consortium of speculating businessmen (E.77). One year later, the king sold outright the three royal parks of Bilton, Haverah and Hay – subject to their existing leases – to the city of London. Bilton Park went for £1,350, with a fee farm rent of £40. By this action, king Charles severed totally the connection between Bilton Park and the Duchy of Lancaster, which had existed since 1372 and the time of John of Gaunt. The sale of Bilton Park occurred just at the time that the medical profession was beginning to promote Harrogate's mineral wells, as will be described more fully in chapter four. Although the Bilton Park well was described by early writers (F.4), it was after 1628 entirely in private hands, thus preventing its exploitation by such businessmen as those who converted High and Low Harrogate into urban clusters centred on the iron and sulphur wells respectively. Equally, when the time came after 1770 to lay out the Stray, the private ownership of the Bilton Park well removed old Bilton from any consideration of candidature for inclusion within the two hundred acres. Harrogate's former royal parks did not for long remain in the hands of the city of London, which soon sold them on at a profit. Thomas Stockdale purchased Bilton Park in 1631, securing the outstanding leases for £1,880 (E.78), largely with the help of Henry Benson – soon to become a bitter enemy (E.79). Haverah Park was purchased by the Ingilby family (T.761) with whom it remained for centuries.

The execution of Charles I on 30 January 1649 and the beginning of the

Commonwealth meant the end of the English monarchy, but not the extinction of the Duchy of Lancaster. But even if it had, the Duchy's role in the administration of the Royal Forest of Knaresborough, including the parks and chases in and about Harrogate, had already been of such significance as to ensure that the core urban growth of the twin communities of Bilton-with-Harrogate and Pannal had been in the right direction. Without the inviolable preserves of Haverah and Bilton Parks, and the equally untouchable acres of Harlow, Fulwith and Oakdale, the communities of the twin villages would have developed in less cohesive and more splintered manner. But by the reign of Charles I, both High and Low Harrogate were well-established communities, which was why the execution of their former owner was unable to hinder their continuing and successful growth. At this point we conclude our account of Harrogate and the royal forest, and turn to a more detailed consideration of the growth of High and Low Harrogate between the years 1332 and 1571.

Early Harrogate, 3
1332—1571

W HEN John of Harrogate made his appearance before the forest court in 1332, his community was unlikely to have been anything more than a number of dwellings, scattered across that part of the royal forest between the river Nidd, at Bilton Banks, and the brooding eminence of Harlow Hill. Although none of these buildings has survived, it is unlikely that they differed from those of other royal forest communities, being principally one- or two-storey constructions of either free stone and render, or timber and mud. The only Harrogate building of any consequence was probably the chantry chapel, the first surviving reference to which dates from 1439 (L.3). It is not, however, the appearance of early Harrogate's vernacular buildings which is of most significance to the historian, but rather their location. Apart from the cluster of building around Bilton village, Harrogate's growth appears to have been non-nuclear, in that the town had no single core which expanded over several centuries, but rather a series of dispersed satellite communities which were linked by routes connecting farms and homesteads. These 'cluster' communities[1] were at the junction of Milner's Lane and Bilton Lane (today's Old Bilton), which lay within a five hundred yard diameter circle;[2] the area of modern Harrogate bounded by Harrogate Hall Farm, Bilton Endowed School, Knox House Farm, and Hill Top Farm;[3] the green around the junction of today's Crab Lane, Bilton Lane, Skipton Road and King's Road, along Skipton Road into High Harrogate;[4] the sporadic 'ribbon' development along King's Road into Low Harrogate, and via Cold Bath Road to Pannal;[5] Pannal village, a community in its own right, references to which are herein restricted to the protruding tongue of land that later became known as Sulphur Wells and Low Harrogate;[6] the minor cluster at the Pannal Ash Lund House Green crossroads. Two further clusters may have had a significant role in the growth of early Harrogate, at Knox and Starbeck, although in the latter case especially documentary evidence is sparse.

Evidence of agricultural practice in old Harrogate has been largely obliterated through urbanisation. Traces of the ridge and furrow system in a field north of Bilton's 'Gardeners Arms', were observed by historian Jennings in his 1970 study,[7] as well as signs of reversed 'S' curves in the field hedges of Stubbing Field. And it was in the neighbourhood of Bilton field that 'John of Harrogate' suffered the assault which resulted in an appearance before the magistrates on Wednesday 30 September 1332, the record of which has survived as the earliest known example of the name of Harrogate. The Latin record refers to John le Long of Harrogate having to guard his field and animals from 'evildoers nightly lying in wait', one of whom – Richard del Wood – 'insulted him, beat, wounded and ill-treated him, contrary to the peace'. Because there was more to the case than simple assault, which was vigorously denied by Richard del Wood, the magistrates decreed that it would have to be put before the next judicial enquiry, the records of which have been lost. (A.35). The 1332 case spells the name of Harrogate *Harowgat, Harugat, Harogat* and *Harowgate*, all within the same document, a treatment which supports the geographical field-name origin theory, as distinct from one of populated locality. What is not beyond doubt, however, is that in the 1332 document, 'Harrogate' is used to denote a community, rather than any geographical field name, and that the same use applied to such other names as Bilton, Killinghall and Knaresborough. Further examples of the Harrogate spelling may be seen in document A.36.

The combined population of Harrogate in the early fourteenth century is unlikely to have been more than about thirty families, whose numbers, inclusive of dependants, possibly comprised 250 individuals. These residents occupied land which varied in size from a humble cottage plot, about one third of a rood in size (known locally as an 'oblate' of land), to plots as large as 30 acres (A.37). All tenants paid the lord of the Forest the annual rent of 6*d*. per acre and 4*d*. per messuage, as well as a share of the tallage (a community tax, replaced in the later fourteenth century), and transfers of land and messuages by copyholders also produced a 'fine', which was usually recorded on the margin of surrenders entered in the court rolls (Class S).

Between 1342 and 1344, and between 1345 and 1349, the assarting of Bilton-with-Harrogate continued, with a further six acres of forest land being converted into eight new assarts, the largest of which was 2½ acres in central Harrogate's 'Crokesnab'. This was slow progress, compared with more than seventy forest acres assarted in Clint, Felliscliffe, and Birstwith over the same period.[8] Harrogate's slow progress was probably the result of reluctance by the tenants to work the heavy cold soil and wet clay (still a feature of the area), rather than because of any shortage of labour.

One great advantage enjoyed by the Harrogate population of *c*.1350 was that their status as 'customary tenants' of the royal forest meant that they were not liable to labour services, other than those contained in the *customs* (E.119) relating to the maintenance of dams, and the boundaries of the parks and enclosures within the royal forest. Also, the amount of land suitable for assarting (clearing woodland for cultivation) within the forest encouraged population spread, as a man with several sons invariably attempted to use them to clear extra land that would support them when they became of age. As one historian has observed 'As a result of the labours of the Forest dwellers, there was on the eve of the Black death more cultivated or improved land in the Forest than there was at any subsequent period until the march of the plough was resumed after the enclosure of the Forest common more than four centuries later.'[9]

Members of Harrogate's community maintained themselves through the practice of agriculture, forestry, forging and mining, the last of which included the marl pits at Bilton. Marl is a mixture of mud and lime that was used to counter acid soils and to improve water retention in sandy soils, as well as in brick-making. Bilton's deposits appear to have been exploited at least from the fourteenth century, and a 1347 dispute between Robert Brown and Adam de Roudon concerned an accusation that the latter had stolen the former's marl, with the aid of a cart, Brown claiming damages of

Harrogate Great Chronicle
PART ONE

————

PLAN 31
Bilton Park, *c.* 1840.
COURTESY W.L.A. SERVICE,
LEEDS

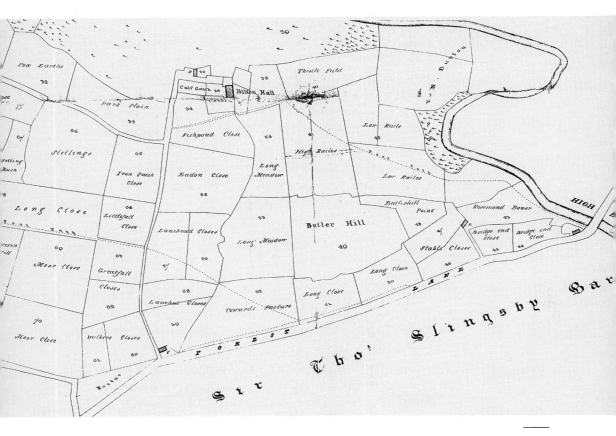

a shilling (A.40). The importance of the marl deposits is shown by the survival of the name into the nineteenth century, where the 1839 Bilton Park tithe apportionment identifies fields 18, 26 and 27, leased to Ann Marshall, all with the name 'Marlpit Close' (E.118). The fields are still identifiable at the time of writing, being between the Bilton Caravan Park and Bilton Banks (see plan 31).

The location of Harrogate astride the route between Kirkby Overblow and Haverah Park, used principally by workers employed in the forging industry, may have been the means by which Harrogate suffered its greatest calamity: the arrival of the Black Death. In 1318, some thirty years before the coming of the great plague, the population of what the 1332 document (A.35) identified as Harrogate, had suffered the Scottish incursion, when Knaresborough town was damaged, and Pannal Church burned (A.29, A.30). So great had been the devastation that the men of Bilton joined with those of other forest communities in petitioning the King, Edward II, for relief. The resulting inquisition taken in 1319 by Robert de Sapy and Gilbert de Wygeton reported that, 'the said men and tenants are ruined to a great extent by the burning of their houses, the abduction of their beasts, and the carrying away of their goods by the attacks of the Scotts rebels.' In response, an order was issued which acquitted the men of Bilton, Roshirst, Killinghall etc., from their last rents, which were worth a total of £72 3s. 7d. (A.31). That the area recovered from the Scottish incursion is shown by the entries in the Court Rolls, which record the continuance of the commonplace disputes and tenancies which had long been part of communal life. In 1347 the forest issued a set of rules for branding forest livestock (A.41), and in the spring of the following year the Court Steward seized a cottage and garden in Bilton, because Beatrice of Harrogate, who held the cottage and garden on a ten-year lease from her father, Robert, had failed to pay the Court the requisite 'fine' or rental at the end of the ten-year term, necessary for a term of renewal. The vacant property was then entered by Joan, daughter of Peter of Bilton, who paid an entry 'fine' of two shillings for the privilege (A.42).

The assarting process continued through the summer of 1348 without abate. For example, Percival de Pensax took a further assart of one acre in Bilton, paying an entry 'fine' of two shillings, and a yearly rent of sixpence. The forest officers appear to have encouraged the process, at least until the crisis of 1349, the first intimation of which may have reached Harrogate shortly after 28 July 1348, when from the fastness of Cawood Castle, Archbishop Zouche of York, proclaimed the imminence of a great pestilence (A.45).

The bacterium *pastuerella pestis* is primarily an internal parasite of rodents, especially rats. Transmission of the bacterium from rat to human is brought about usually by the intermediacy of the flea. *Pastuerella pestis* multiplies in the blood of an infected rat with great rapidity, so that when the flea feeds, it sucks up large numbers of the bacterium, which then become established in the flea's stomach. Multiplication of the bacterium causes the stomach to become solid, preventing the flea from retaining or digesting food. In this state the flea becomes ravenous, causing it to attack any animal within reach, including humans, on whom it will feed voraciously until its blocked stomach recoils, forcing the flea to regurgitate blood now infected with pestei. The flea also defecates, excreting more bacilli. Irritation of the victim's skin causes rubbing, which increases the likelihood of further infection. A single rat can harbour scores of fleas, but when the rat dies and its corpse cools, the fleas abandon it for a fresh victim. Spread of *pastuerella pestis* is halted by frost, and encouraged by warm weather of about 25°C. Even without the rat, fleas can be transported in clothing and other soft material, which on being handled by humans, provide starving fleas with means of sustenance. In 1348, of course, none of this was known, nor suspected.[10]

The plague, probably the 'Black Death', reached the south of England in the summer of 1348, reaching York by May 1349. After Archbishop Zouche's proclamation of 28 July 1348, Harrogate's population had probably lived in daily fear of the infection, producing a greater degree of hostility towards strangers than was the norm for fourteenth-century forest communities. By July 1349 the plague had reached Knaresborough – whether by road or river is not known – from whence it spread across the Nidd into the Royal Forest, reaching Harrogate probably by August or September (A.45). One possible route for the plague was that of the local iron ore industry workers between Haverah, Oakdale and Kirkby Overblow, the sacking used with the transportation of equipment and supplies being a likely home to infected fleas. The mining of ore from Oakdale and the removal of timber from Haverah Park were still taking place during the 1360s (A.52).

By whichever path the plague arrived in Harrogate, the effect was devastating. Infection is followed by a hard and painful haemorrhagic swelling of the lymphatic glands – the bubo, from which the name 'bubonic' derives. The pain increases as the bubo ruptures, the intensity of which could drive victims to throw themselves from windows, plunge into rivers, or run naked through lanes and streets. As the death toll mounted, observers would have witnessed the sight of shuttered houses, many with the mark of the plague upon their thresholds, from which the cries of victims could be heard, the horror of which might be heightened by the sudden frenzy of some soul in extremis.

We do not know the population of either the royal forest in general or Harrogate in particular, on the eve of the plague, so it is not possible to calculate the death rate. However, of Bilton-with-Harrogate's 575 acres, 274 acres were held by tenants whose deaths were recorded in the court rolls for 1349–1350. This figure of 274 acres represented 48 per cent of the community's total acreage. The court rolls for the period following the decline of the great pestilence in 1350, show that four-fifths of holdings vacated through plague death passed to members of the same family, usually sons, daughters, brothers or sisters. This was in contrast to other neighbouring townships, such as those to the west of Killinghall, where about two-fifths of land vacated by plague death was inherited by people other than wives, sons, or daughters, which indicates that whole families had been obliterated (A.47).

One sign of the labour shortage which followed in the wake of the plague was the increasing consolidation of isolated parcels of land, practised by tenants after 1350. An example of this was enacted by William de Pensax and Adam del Bene in April 1351, who exchanged one acre parcels in Bilton-with-Harrogate (A.51).

A further calamity occurred in 1361–62, when the plague returned, creating havoc among the young who had been unable to build up immunity during the outbreak of 1349, and it was for this reason that the plague of 1361–62 was known as the plague of children. The single most arresting fact from these misfortunes was that unlike virtually every other royal forest community, and many beyond its bounds, Harrogate had no land abandoned because of plague deaths (A.53). In townships to the west of Killinghall, two-fifths of land vacated by death was inherited by people other than sons, daughters or wives, which points to the extinction of whole families (A.47). Forest rules required a deceased tenant's land to be taken up within one year, and during the immediate post-plague years the rolls do not contain even a single example of unclaimed Bilton-with-Harrogate land (A.48).

Despite the staying power of the Bilton-with-Harrogate tenants, the plague exacted a very heavy toll of life, and it has been calculated that during the outbreak of 1369, the forest's death rate was three or four times the national average; the Vicar of Hampsthwaite was one of the victims.[11]

Shortly before the outbreak of the children's plague, Harrogate was the scene of a dispute which became one of the lengthiest to be considered by the forest court. A series of seven stained and dense membranes record that as a result of improperly maintained fences, corn fields in what is now central Harrogate, were invaded by cattle from neighbouring arable land. The tenant of the cornfields, Richard Milleson, made complaint against his neighbours, William del Wode and William Gaye, at which a counter charge was made by William Gaye that another neighbour, William Rbynson Johnson, was himself guilty of not maintaining proper fences in Crokesnab. After much further charging and counter-charging, Gaye won damages of four shillings and five pence, and William del Wode secured two shillings and three pence, from William Robynson Johnson, and three shillings and four pence from William de Pensax. During 1366, the 'Cows in the corn' case must have been one of Harrogate's main talking points (A.55).

Crokesnab – also spelled Crooksnab, or Crokisnab – was the name for the irregular promontory of land which separated High Harrogate from Low Harrogate, or more properly which comprised Bilton-with-Harrogate lands whose northern and western bounds fell sharply down towards the lands of Pannal within Beckwith-with-Rossett. Despite speculation as to the locality and extent of Crokesnab, there is little difficulty with identification. As late as 1810, the great surrender of lands by Sir John Ingilby to James Franklin included a close named 'Crooks Neb' (T.263), and in the previous year's survey by William Chippindale listed Harrogate field 23, tenanted by Robert Dearlove, under the name of 'Crookt Lands', with a further entry under tenant W. Roberts, as '69, Crooks Neb'.

Map twenty three shows the extent of the ancient Crokesnab, although only the northern and western boundaries reflect the geography of the area, the southern and eastern boundaries being probably the result of old assarting. Crokesnab, like Harro –gate, was a geographical term which became a place of settlement, but because it was absorbed within the expanding villages of High and Low Harrogate, it did not survive as a community name. Agriculture, mining and forging, and forestry, continued to be the economic mainstay of fourteenth-century Harrogate, and despite the depredations of the mining and forging industry, the area continued to possess a good amount of timber, the most significant of which was within the royal forest's parks and chases. John of Gaunt's register for 1372–76 refers to the woodlands of Oakdale still containing much oak (A.56). John of Gaunt, as has been noted in our second chapter, was the fourth son of King Edward III, who in 1362, made John the second Duke of Lancaster. Ten years later, in 1372, the Duke of Lancaster received the Honour of Knaresborough from his father, including the Royal Forest with Harrogate.[12] This gift had great consequence for the Harrogate community.

Edward III, who died in 1377, was succeeded by his son, Richard, during whose reign was introduced the controversial and highly unpopular levy known as the poll tax. Although a similar tax had been levied in 1222, for purposes of assisting the kingdom of Jerusalem, Parliament's tax of 1377 was in reality the first national poll tax. The details of this tax relating to Bilton-with-Harrogate are not known, but those of the subsequent poll tax of 1379 – which like the 1222 tax was graduated according to wealth – have survived, albeit in a form which incorporated the names of Bilton-with-Harrogate residents with those of Beckwith-with-Rossett and Pannal, as well as Swindon (A.58, A.59). The A. 59 list is especially interesting, as it contains several of the oldest known Harrogate names, including the de Neusums, whose predecessors had been keepers of the royal parks back in the 1330s (E.31), the del Wodes, who had been parties in the previous decade's 'cows in the corn' case (A.55), the Skelwras, Chilrays, Schutts and de Corbys. Of this latter name, John de Corby was named in a royal patent of King Richard II, which was a pardon to another local man, Robert de Pensax, 'for the death of John de Corby, killed at Harrogate, 10th August 1384.' (A.60). Death, like taxation, was an inescapable part of life in medieval Harrogate.

In 1380, a third poll tax, levied at a flat rate of twelve pence a head, virtually precipitated the so-called Peasants' Revolt of June 1381, which nearly cost Richard II his throne. However, the downfall of Richard II was brought about not through fiscal measures, but through a dispute which directly involved Harrogate as part of the possessions of the Duchy of Lancaster. After the death of the second Duke, John of Gaunt, his son and heir, Henry Bolingbroke, who had been banished by Richard II, learned of that monarch's attempt to reclaim the Duchy possessions, and returned from exile with his followers. He landed on the Yorkshire coast at Ravenspur in the summer of 1399, and, gathering more supporters, continued inland on a march which ended with the overthrow of Richard at Flint, and Bolingbroke's subsequent coronation on 13 October 1399 as Henry IV. At that coronation there occurred the event which proved to be of unparalleled significance for Harrogate. Henceforth, it was decreed, the possessions of the Duchy of Lancaster would be for ever merged with the English monarchy. And thus it was that from 13 October 1399, until the Great Award of 19 August 1778 (B.31), every square inch of Harrogate and the surrounding royal forest belonged to the monarchs of England.

Medieval Harrogate unquestionably shared the age's preoccupation with religion, and yet the local history of this subject is documented with a paucity that is almost suspicious. The first surviving reference to the existence of a chapel in Harrogate occurs not in the Court Rolls, but in a will dated July 1439, in which Thomas Lyndley left the sum of twelve pounds to chaplain John Brig who was daily to celebrate mass in the 'chapel of Harowgate' (L.3). From the evidence of later wills, such as those of John Benson in 1525 (L.8), Robert Kirkby in 1537 (L.9), and John Linley in 1541 (L.13), it can be deduced that Harrogate Chapel was a chantry chapel. As to who built this chapel, why they built it, and where they built it, these matters are mysteries.

The chantry chapel's purpose was to celebrate masses for the soul of the founder, his or her families, or members of the guilds or associations which had paid for the chapel's erection and maintenance, either during their lifetime or after their death. They were usually attached to a parish church, although they could also be located some distance from it. The first known chantry was that of Bishop Hugh of Wells at Lincoln Cathedral, *c.* 1235. Following the plague of 1349, the number of chantry foundations increased substantially, prompted by the potent combination of heightened awareness of life's temporality, and the ability of the priestly classes to prey upon the credulity of those over whom they held sway.[13] For example, whereas Lincoln Cathedral possessed a single chantry in 1290, the number increased to thirty-six by the time of Henry VIII's survey of church revenues, with a total for England and Wales of 1,733, of which the diocese of York boasted 425.[14]

It is reasonable to assume that Harrogate's chantry chapel was established at some point between the outbreak of the Black Death in 1349 and 1372, when Harrogate and the surrounding royal forest were granted by Edward III to his son John of Gaunt, the second duke of Lancaster. The significance of this latter date lies in the habit of the 'antient duchie' of maintaining meticulous records, none of which contains even the vaguest reference to the establishment of a chantry at Harrogate. Consequently, the first known surviving reference to Harrogate chantry chapel in 1439 comes as something of a surprise (L.3). The gap of sixty-seven years between 1372 and the first known reference to the chapel in 1439 may be because many of the court rolls for this period are missing, a condition which also applies to the pre-1372 rolls.

The date of Harrogate chantry chapel's foundation could be guessed more accurately if the name of the founder was known. The *Liber Regis* records a tradition that some chapels within the dioceses of York and Chester, having been erected originally for domestic use, later became parochial without being consecrated.[15] Between the time of the earliest known chantry chapels of *c.* 1235 and 1372, Harrogate was held by the Crown; from 1372 until 1399 it was held by the Duchy of Lancaster; and from 1399 onwards it was held by the Duchy of Lancaster as a royal inheritance. There is therefore the strongest likelihood that Harrogate chantry chapel was built between the plague year of 1349 and 1372 by one of the families who held the royal forest on a crown lease, or who had sufficient rank and means to build it within the forest on an illicit enclosure.

The period of the Stuteville lease of the forest, from 1173 to 1205 (A.14), was pre-chantry, as were the years from 1205 to 1235, at which latter time the first known chantry was installed at Lincoln.[16] The forest was held by the Earls of Cornwall from 1234 to 1300,[17] who are unlikely to have established a single chantry in Bilton-with-Harrogate. At the death of Earl Edmund in 1300, the forest reverted to the crown, as Edward I was the Earl's nearest heir, remaining in this state until 1307, when the new King Edward II granted it to his friend Gaveston, Earl of Cornwall, who held it until his death in 1312, at which it again reverted to the crown. Between 1331 and 1369 the forest was granted to Queen Philippa, and at her death in 1369 it reverted to her husband, King Edward III. From 1372 to 1399 the forest was held by John of Gaunt, whose son, Henry Bolingbroke, returned from banishment and seized the throne as Henry IV in October 1399. The Royal Forest of Knaresborough and all Duchy possessions merged with the possessions of the monarch (A.20). It may therefore be seen that during the time between 1349 and 1372 (the most probable period for the establishment of the Harrogate chantry chapel), the royal forest was held by Queen Philippa and King Edward III. Although it is tempting to suggest that the death of Queen Philippa in 1369 may have stimulated the erection of a chantry, dedicated to her memory in the lands she had once held, there is no supporting evidence for this possibility. Chantry chapels continued to be built within the Royal Forest until Tudor times, one of the last being that of St Margaret, which was erected in 1507 by Henry Banke at the hamlet of Hyll within Thruscross township.[18]

The location of the Harrogate chantry is a further mystery. Unlike the chapel of a hermit, such as St Robert of Knaresborough, chantry chapels were not found in remote or obscure locations, in that rate of use and degree of access were significant factors governing their construction. Accordingly, they were invariably convenient to a road or way. In fourteenth- and early fifteenth-century Bilton-with-Harrogate, the principal routes led from old Bilton, and what is now Bilton Lane and King's Road before reaching Cold Bath Road in Pannal. Equally, the ancient Harro-gate ran from the Nidd up to the crown of Harlow Hill. Of these two routes, the proximity of old Bilton to the church of St John in Knaresborough mitigates against the likelihood of Harrogate chantry being at Bilton, whereas the Harro-gate, being virtually equidistant between Pannal's St Robert's Church and Knaresborough's St John's Church, is a more realistic possibility. But where?

References to a great cross made from pudding stone have led some historians to assume that it was a relic of the Harrogate chantry chapel, and that the location of the cross – could it be identified – would furnish the location of the chapel. This is unlikely, as the earliest known reference to the cross occurs in 1199 (A.11), well before the fashion for founding chantries. The location of the great cross may be identified by examining the charters between 1199 (A.11) and 1587 (A.110), from which it is clear that it was on Harlow Hill. The map which accompanied the 1587 Plumpton dispute (A.110) also depicts the pudding stone cross, placing it south of the *broade way* (the Harro-gate) *leading from Harlowe to the Stokkbrige*, more or less at the point at which Stone Rings Beck rose from the hill side. Intriguingly, the map (see plans 5 and 6) also shows a building on an east–west axis, with what could be an apse, a little to the south of the great pudding stone cross, and as it is the only structure depicted in the whole area between Stone Rings Beck, the river Crimple, and the Star Beck, it was clearly a building of some importance. By 1587, the Harrogate chantry chapel had ceased to exist, having been dissolved in 1549, but it is reasonable to assume that its buildings may have survived. If this structure was indeed Harrogate's chantry chapel, then in terms of the late twentieth century, its location was somewhere in the vicinity of Rossett Acre County Primary school. Pudding stone cross seems to have vanished by 1610, as the surveyor John Moore noted that he was shown by Sir Edward Plumpton's men '... the place ... called Puddingstone Crosse by [i.e. near] Pannal, but the inhabitants of Pannall knoweth noe such place.' Further on, Moore again referred to 'the place they call Puddingstone Cross ...' (A.122, folio 199) which points to the name of the cross lingering as a place-name after the cross itself had vanished from the landscape.

The place shown on the 1587 map is certainly a possible situation for Harrogate's chantry chapel, which could have been built there in order to benefit from the presence of the great pudding stone cross. Other likely sites include the area around the junction of the modern Knaresborough and Skipton Roads. (But not, let it be noted, the site of Christ Church, nor indeed the site of the oblong tongue of land which obtruded into the Stray from what later became the site of the Harrogate District Hospital – this last was the site of the eighteenth-century 'New Cold Bath' (G.2).) A further possible site for the Harrogate chantry was Starbeck, within reach of the Stockbridge (meaning either an enclosure of wooden posts or a wooden bridge), near to what later became known as Spa Lane. This site was not only at some small distance from Knaresborough's St John's church, and Pannal's St Robert's, but it was also convenient for the great *broade way* and its traffic, as well as being situated in a pleasant sheltered valley. A third possibility is that the chantry was in the vicinity of the junction of the later Regent Parade, Devonshire Place, and Westmorland Street, at the northerly tip of what later became the High Harrogate triangle. Each of the foregoing sites is candidate for the site of Harrogate's chantry chapel, and each may equally be the incorrect one.

References to Harrogate Chapel, as distinct from the chapel of Bilton-with-Harrogate, or even Bilton Chapel, are significant, and may have indicated a chapel serving a wider geographical, rather than a tight communal locality. Such a reading would enable the central geographical feature of Harlow Hill to be a candidate.

It is worth noting that, apropos chantries and land in Harrogate, the parish church of Ripley possessed about four acres of land in Harrogate, which for a time was held by one Thomas Westow (K.2). St John's at Knaresborough also held 'a tenement, with appurtenances, in Bilton, in tenure of Robert Barrowse, at 11s. 4d.'[19] There are references to several chantry chapels at Knaresborough's St John's church, including those dedicated to St Edmund, St Mary Magdalene, and – possibly – St Nicholas, which latter was also confusingly named in connection with the castle in 1333.

Few of Harrogate's records of the tax known as the tenth, or 'moveables' tax[20] have survived, including those for 1475, or the fifteenth year of the reign of Edward IV. The record for Bilton-with-Harrogate includes *Richardus Mowbray, Capellanus*, who was probably a chaplain for Harrogate Chantry (A.75). Harrogate's first surviving fifteenth-century document of any significance is found within the patent rolls for 1422, during Henry V's final year, which confirmed the presentation of land in Shirwood Forest and Sutton-in-Colefield, from William Pensax of Harrogate to his brother Thomas. It seems that Thomas had entered these holdings without licence or payment of the customary 'fine'. After paying forty shillings, the trespass was pardoned, and Thomas Pensax could enjoy his gift (A.62). This trivial incident was typical of the importance attached to regulating and controlling the occupancy and transference of land. Such recording often allows the identification of particular parcels of land, because the common names survived through the centuries, until nineteenth-century urbanisation. For example, among Harrogate's many fifteenth-century transfers of land, the court rolls for 1442 record that John Milleson transferred to Richard Slyngesby 1 acre in Crokisnab, ½ an acre in le leyflate in Harugate, and ½ a rood in Sanbuttes in Bilton. In exchange, Richard Slyngesby transferred to John Milleson 1 acre, comprising 1 selion[21] called Jacoldall, 1 selion called Holland, and 1 selion called Holhedland (A.65). Some of these place names may be found in the catalogue of land sold by auction in March 1806: Crokisnab became Crook's Nebb, lot 2, plot 63; le leyflate became High Flatts, lot 5, plots 26–29 (T.2482). Sanbuttes became Sandy Buts lot A. plot 26 (T.2484).

Three Duchy charters of 1449, 1459 and 1460 (B.1), issued during the reign of Henry VI, confirmed that the feoffees of lands including the Royal Forest of Knaresborough, were entitled to enjoy the same rights and privileges as the owner (i.e. the king). The charters refer to feoffees enjoying 'the same liberties, privileges and jura regalia &c. as fully as when the said lands were in the King's hands ...' (charter of 1449, repeated with slight variation in the charters of 1459 and 1460), and continues to name not only the Royal Forest of Knaresborough, but Okeden, Fulwith, Haywra and Bilton (all of which were within the forest) as well as Hay Park, which lay beyond the forest's boundary. The issuing of these three charters during the reign of the ascetic King Henry VI (who of all English monarchs hitherto, was the least likely to have participated in the delights of the chase), may have been the result of a desire by those who leased the forest from the King to indulge an activity which hitherto had been the monarch's privilege alone. The superfluous naming of the parks and chases of the royal forest gives credence to this possibility. Hunting must have been possible during Henry VI's reign, as there are many recorded cases from the later reign of Edward IV, in 1482, when unlawful hunting came to the attention of the forest court. For example, the minister of Saint Robert's Church at Pannal was accused of hunting a buck on Harlow Hill which he chased into Haverah Park, where it was killed by one of the Plumpton family (A.78).

As may be expected of the century that experienced the Wars of the Roses, many of the time's surviving references to Harrogate are concerned with military affairs. Some of the excuses provided by local people for their failure to participate in Henry V's wars in France have survived. William of Beckwith, 'able of person and livelihood', said he would do the service 'with all his heart', had he not to appear before the council in London (A.63). It is likely that Harrogate men fought at the great battle of Towton on 29 March 1461, when their immediate leader, William Plumpton, was killed, and his father, Sir William Plumpton, was compelled to throw himself on the mercy of his captors (A.72). The Court rolls record that William Plumpton held land on Harrogate's Crokesnab, which was soon claimed by his brother Robert.[22] It is possible (the circumstances are unclear) that the 1479 general pardon granted to Thomas Beke, a Harrogate taylor, was for his failure to provide military service, but there is no doubt that the fine of one shilling levied upon Henry Redschawe, Henry Batte, William Lemyng, Robert Hoge, Richard Spynke and John Thompson was for their failure to obey the 'community of the village of Harowgat' in military service, and for their not contributing towards the wages of their neighbours when men were required to go 'towards Scotia' in the service of the king (A.77).

In 1507 men of Harrogate were involved in a gathering of about six hundred 'evil doers and disturbers of the king's peace' which assembled at Killinghall. The assembly included men from most of the forest communities, as well as Follifoot, Kirby Overblow, Knaresborough and Walton Head. Armed with axes, hatchets and mattocks, the foresters marched to three of the king's 'closes' and destroyed a newly made dyke and the hedges and defences surrounding it, allowing their beasts to pasture on the enclosed vegetation. According to the indictment, one of the three closes, 'Swynden' was completely destroyed. Swindon was a woodland south of Crimple Beck, as was Rigton Wood, and along with Yearwith (or Hampsthwaite) Hollings, Swinecliffe and Swarcliffe, formed a special royal forest 'preserve'. It is possible that the cause of the disturbance may have been some alteration to the water-courses, such as the newly made dyke at Swindon. The alterations must have been considerable to create so much opposition, which proved the sturdy independence of the foresters when their livelihoods were threatened (A.85). Swindon sike formed part of the boundary dividing the royal forest from Kirby Overblow and Walton Head, and the 1507 indictment named men from both of these two latter communities – five from Kirby Overblow and one from Walton Head – as having taken part; this shows that the disturbance involved men from beyond the royal forest's boundary. Boundaries were of great importance to royal forest tenants, as can be seen from the innumerable disputes brought before the court. In 1512 John and Margaret Waide sought an enquiry into the boundaries of their lands at 'the hamlet of Harrogate and Bilton', and those of sixteen neighbours, paying a fine to cover the enquiry's costs. The marking, confirming and re-confirming of boundaries was a normal aspect of medieval life. (A.87). Agricultural practice in sixteenth-century Harrogate included a considerable amount of consolidation of uneconomic strips of land, such as those exchanged between John Matthew and Thomas Knowles (A.101), which resulted in more compact holdings which were easier to maintain.

In 1534, the same year that the authority of the Pope was abolished in England, and Henry VIII was styled head of the Church, a military muster was held at Harrogate. The records divided the Harrogate area into three groups: *Bylton cum Harrogate, Pannall* and *Bekwyth cum Rossett*, each group also being sub-divided into three categories of man. It is instructive to compare the findings. Of archers with harness, Bilton and Harrogate had five, Pannal none, and Beckwith with Rossett six. Of archers without harness, Bilton and Harrogate had ten, Pannal five, and Beckwith with Rossett fourteen. Of men with bylls (a military weapon consisting of a long staff terminated by a hook-shaped blade which usually incorporated a spike) Bilton and Harrogate had fourteen (who were also with harness), Pannal had three (without harness) and Beckwith with Rossett had twelve (without harness). This shows that Bilton and Harrogate, with its high proportion of men possessing harness, was not an impoverished part of the forest, even before the discovery of the spa in 1571. By 1538, a further muster confirmed Bilton-with-Harrogate's status (A.93).

The reformation instituted by Henry VIII was continued under Edward VI, in the second year of whose reign (1549) the chantry chapels were dissolved. The court roll of 1550 records that Harrogate chantry chapel was included in the general dissolution, and that its last priest, Ralph Stewarde, still held the tenancy, which comprised the chapel and its surrounding garden of half an acre. It seems to have been the king's intention to have conferred the Harrogate chantry on one John Cotton, in recognition for his previous services, but only *after* the death of the former priest, who was to be allowed to have possession for life. Cotton, however, was dispatched to Scotland on the king's business, whereon he was slain, leaving his family in debt. Ralph Stewarde having also presumably died, two friends of Cotton, Thomas Derley and William Adame, undertook to pay his debts in exchange for the tenancy of Harrogate chantry chapel, which offer was accepted on 15 December 1549. Then, Derley and Adame were approached by William Tanckarde of Boroughbridge, who arranged for the tenancy to be transferred to himself, paying a fine of 8*d.* on 7 May 1550 (K.4). The fabric of Harrogate's chantry chapel might have been removed shortly after 1550, the materials being incorporated in other building, or it may have deteriorated slowly, being treated somewhat in the manner of a convenient quarry. In either case, not a trace remains of Harrogate's first building monument, other than a few references in the court rolls and royal forest wills.

Harrogate wills of the sixteenth century provide insight into the industry and living standards of the community, which – let it be remembered – was still one of copyhold tenancies in entirety. They reveal that agriculture, forestry, carpentry, weaving and – to a lesser extent – forging, were the main-stays of life. Goods bequeathed included livestock (principally cattle and horses), tools of trade, household utensils, clothes, monies, and the occasional book, such as in the will of Robert Kirkby (1537), who also required 'one priest to say a trentall of masses for my soul and to say them at Harrogate Chapel ...' The most important item to be bequeathed was the current tenancy, as allowed by the ancient *Customs of the Royal Forest* (E.119), which required payment of a heriot (customs 1–5), as well an entry fee, or 'fine' (customs 18 and 19), before any transfer became legal. Examples of livestock are found in Katherine Cook's will of 1566, in which a ewe and a lamb are bequeathed to Marie Dowson (L.30), or the 1591 Will of Richard Birnand, who decreed that 'I give unto Thomas Myers' little boy of Harrogate thirteen shillings and fourpence to buy him three ewes, and that Peter Hogg shall see them put to his best profit, not letting his father meddle with them in any case' (L.1.1). Examples of tools of trade may be found in the wills of farmer Robert Waide, in 1576, who bequeathed 'all my corn growing or sown upon the ground that is in my own occupation on the day of my death, be divided into three parts ...' (L.36) and weaver Richard Alleyn in 1612, who bequeathed a loom with gears, two pairs of cloth shears, a pair of tenters, etc. (L.61). Household utensils are represented by such entries as those in the wills of Dorothy Becke of 1600, who bequeathed 'a bed, a mattress, two coverlets, one blanket, two sheets, one brass pot etc. ...' (L.51) and John Mathew of 1580, who bequeathed 'thirtene pece of pewther [pewter]', among many other items (L.38). Clothes remained a regular item for bequest. John Pannell of 'Harlogaite' left his brother a green jerkin, a pair of hose, a doublet, as well as all the timber lying before his doors, and ten pounds of money 'that I did borrow of him' (L.42).

John Sporett 'of Harlowgaite' willed (in 1558) that on the day of his burial, his neighbours should have bread and ale (L.24) and many wills include charitable distribution of money, such as Thomas Benson's 'ten shillings for the poor of Bilton-with-Harrogate' (L.70). Some of these provisions give the reader the impression of having been left more for the well-being of the donor's soul than for true public-spiritedness, not that the poor would have minded either way!

The majority of farmers, judging from the evidence of their wills, practised more than one livelihood, as for example did John Lightfoot, who ran a farm with twenty cattle, nearly one hundred sheep, lambs, pigs, geese, bees, with rye, barley and beans, as well as a blacksmith's practice (L.34). The inventory of John Hill, one of Harrogate's most substantial yeoman farmers who died in 1589, included along with much agricultural material, two pairs of old cloth shears and a loom, a spinning wheel and comb stock, wool combs, wool cards, and heckles, as well as yarn and cloth (L.44). William Lightfoot of Harrogate died possessed of a 'woollen loom with four pairs of wollen gears', as well as two spinning wheels, cards, combs, woollen and hempen yarn' (L.54). This was not untypical, and shows the presence of the weaving industry which supplemented local agriculture, and which was an economic mainstay of life in sixteenth-century Harrogate.

Once of great importance to the economy of the royal forest, iron-smelting appears to have been abandoned by the late fourteenth century, and, to quote Jennings, 'by 1391 all activity in the forest itself had ceased'.[23] The industry revived, however, when mineral coal replaced wood as a fuel for powering the forges, and by the end of the sixteenth century, the most northerly furnace operating in the West Riding of Yorkshire could be found south-east of Harrogate.[24] The first attempt to use mineral coal in the smelting process was made in Yorkshire by Thomas Proctor who in 1589 obtained a patent to smelt iron and lead. Proctor failed, but a few years later, in 1595, the Earl of Cumberland, who owned a furnace in the royal forest, took a licence to smelt iron and lead with a mixture of mineral coal and peat.[25] These actions were noted by the Duchy of Lancaster, who in 1597 issued a special commission to their surveyor, Richard Stanhope, to enquire into the local situation. Stanhope advised the Duchy that the Earl of Cumberland's ironworks was near to the ancient corn mill at Fulwith, which had burned down about six years previously, and that there was a neighbouring three-acre site convenient for the erection of another ironworks. The Crimple Valley location was indeed ideal for heavy industry, as it had a good water supply from the river Crimple, was near to the route between Haverah Park and Kirby Overblow, had a local supply of ironstone 'within the waste' (i.e. the forest), and the area contained seams of mineral coal, such as that at Bilton (A.115). The Duchy Commission is interesting because it gives support to the later assertion of Dr George Neale who claimed that 'Many iron-stones were thrown up, all the ground thereabout being formerly digg'd up, and all the wood destroyed in Queen Elizabeth's time, by iron-forges ...' (F.19). This was written in *c.* 1693, in reference to the ground around the Sweet Spa (now known as the St John's Well), and it shows that during Queen Elizabeth's reign the forging industry was responsible for the loss of timber, and the disturbing of the ground. Such vigorous disturbance may have been responsible for the uncovering of a hitherto hidden well, which could have flowed unseen for centuries. We shall probably never know. But what is certain is that in 1571, a Mr William Slingsby recognised the mineral properties of Bilton-with-Harrogate's Tewit Well, and thereby changed, for ever, the course of Harrogate's history.

4 | Rise of the spa, 1571–1660

According to Edmund Deane, William Slingsby was the first person to recognise the 'medicinal quality' of the mineral well at High Harrogate, vulgarly known as the Tewit Well because of the propensity of pewits (known in the north as tewits) to consume the salt globules which formed at the well head. Deane wrote that Slingsby had 'travelled in his younger time, was thoroughly acquainted with the taste, use, and faculties of the two Spaw fountains' (F.3). The water was not a sulphur water, but an iron, or chalybeate water, which some writers termed vitriol, and which Slingsby compared with the Sauvenir and Pouhon Wells at Spa, a resort in the Spanish Netherlands (in what is now Belgium), which were patronised by visitors from all of Europe, including England, following visits by Dr Augustine Augustini, physician to Henry VIII[1] and distribution of a 1559 view of Spa by painter Aegidius Pierriers. Although later writers provided Mr William Slingsby with such spurious titles as 'Captain' (G.1) or even 'Sir' by the time of William Grange's influential 1862 'Memoir of the life of Sir [sic] William Slingsby Kt.', the man who identified the mineral qualities of the Tewit Well was plain Mr William Slingsby.[2]

Spa, in the Spanish Netherlands, was not only used by those in search of health, but also by those English malcontents whose strong Catholic sympathies led them to frequent a resort next to the great Catholic University of Louvain and within the domains of Philip of Spain. The use of Spa as a setting for possible 'plottes and stratagems' against protestant England caused Elizabeth and her ministers concern, who believed that the claims of some English visitors that they were at Spa to take the waters, were a cover for plotting. By 1565, Principal Secretary Cecil heard from Sir Edward Warner that there was a 'great repair' to Spa for benefit of the water[3] an exodus which further alarmed the government as English relations with Catholic Spain deteriorated after 1568, and the 1569 dispersal of English Catholic refugees after the failure of the northern rising. It was to Spa that many of these English refugees assembled, including the leader of the rising, the Earl of Westmorland and Lady Northumberland, whose presence was communicated to Cecil (now Lord Burghley) in August 1571. The presence at Spa of many more humble, and presumably illiterate rebels, some of whom sent 'Spa rings' to their English friends as a token of their survival, so alarmed the Queen and her government that in 1571 an Act was passed which controlled foreign travel by issuing passes only to those who has taken the oath of allegiance. And 1571 was the year Mr William Slingsby was credited with the discovery of the Tewit Well, insofar as Edmund Deane, the first writer on the subject, in his 1626 book (see plate 4) refers to 'about 55 yeeres agoe' (F.3), a date accepted by the majority of later authors.

Although a connection cannot be proved between Slingsby's 1571 discovery at Harrogate, and government concern at the number of English visitors to continental Spa, there is a possible link though Slingsby's friendship with Dr Timothy Bright, the rector of Methley, who had visited continental Spa (F.3) was also the inventor of short-hand and a physician close to Queen Elizabeth, Lord Burghley, and Sir Francis Walsingham[4] and was well placed to pass the news of William Slingsby's discovery to the appropriate circles. In the memoir of Bright, the author suggests that it may have been Bright's over-frequent attendance at Tewit Well which led to his 'grievous dereliction of parochial duties'.[5]

In order to appreciate the convenience of Slingsby's 1571 discovery, it is necessary to understand that it occurred at a period when the public sought replacements for the 'holy wells' which had been lost or defaced during the Reformation, especially those associated with saints and miracles, and of the corresponding vacuum this caused. Subsequent to the Harrogate discovery, wells with healing (and for healing, read miraculous) qualities were discovered in 1579 at King's Newnham, Warwickshire, and Newton, Huntingdonshire, in 1580 at Clifton, Bristol, and at Mile End in London, in 1611 at Wanstead, Essex, in 1624 at Wellingborough, Northamptonshire, in 1640 at Sydenham in Kent, in 1664 at Gilthwaite, Sheffield, in 1684 at Butterby, County Durham, and in 1698 at Aldfield, Yorkshire – to name only a geographically representative handful. The transformation of the patronage of English wells from objects of religious idolatry and superstition into resorts for the recovery of health, has been related skilfully by Dr Phyllis Hembry, to whose works the interested reader should refer.[6]

Slingsby's discovery of the mineral qualities of Harrogate's Tewit Well, coming as it did at a time when the English government was attempting to discourage its citizens from attending continental Spa, was clearly

Spadacrene Anglica.

OR,

THE ENGLISH
SPAW FOVNTAINE.

Being
A BRIEFE TREATISE
of the acide, or tart Fountaine in the
Foreſt of *Knaresborow*, in the Weſt-
Riding of *Yorkſhire.*

As alſo a Relation of other medicinall
Waters in the ſaid Foreſt.

BY
Edmund Deane, D^r. in Phyſicke, *Oxon.*
dwelling in the City of YORKE.

LONDON,
Printed for *Iohn Griſmand* : and are to be ſold by *Richard*
Foſter, neere the Minſter gate in *Yorke.*
1 6 2 6.

PLATE 4
Original 1626 title
page of *Spadacrene
Anglica.*

fortunate, and was given further publicity in 1598, when Dr Bright gave it the happy name of 'the English Spa'. This description was recorded by Dr Deane in his 1626 book *Spadacrene Anglica*, which was the first book about Harrogate and the first recorded application of the name of 'spa' as a common noun. It was thanks to Dr Deane that we know of William Slingsby's actions after his recognition of the water's nature, as he noted of him, 'it was his good fortune to live for a while at a grange house very neare to this fountain [i.e. well] and afterwards in Bilton Parke all his life long. Who drinking of this water found it in all things to agree with those at the [continental] Spaw. Whereupon ... he made some further triall and assay: That done, he caused the fountaine to be well and artificially walled about, and paved at the bottom ... with a fit hole in the side ... for the free passage of the water through a little guttered stone. It is open at the top, and walled somewhat higher than the earth, as well to keepe out filth, as cattle ...'

This shows that Slingsby consumed the Tewit Well water over a long period, the words 'in all things to agree ...' indicating not just taste, but pharmacology (F.3, chapter six). Deane referred not only to Dr Bright's patronage of the Tewit Well, but also to Dr Anthony Hunton of Newark upon Trent, and of how he would expostulate on the failure of Yorkshire doctors to further the fame of the well by 'publike writing'. Edmund Deane took up this challenge, as his epochal 1626 *Spadacrene Anglica* shows.

Deane's book was not the first book to be written about an English resort with a mineral water well. In 1562 William Turner published his *Book of the Natures and Properties as Well of the Baths in England as of other Baths in Germany and Italy*, printed at Cologne by Arnold Birckman (F.1). This was followed in 1572 by John Jones text *Benefit of the Auncient Bathes of Buckstones, which cureth most greevous sicknesses* ... (F.2). As neither Turner's or Jones' texts use the word spa as a noun, the national significance for England of Deane's text, which calls the Tewit Well the 'English Spa', may be appreciated.

Although later editions of *Spadacrene Anglica*, cobbled together crudely by pirates after Deane's death, confused some writers as to the exact location of the 'English Spa', the first and accurate edition of 1626 contains the author's true description.

> *Spadacrene Anglica.*
> Or. The English spaw-fountain.
> Being a briefe treatise of the acide, or tart fountain
> In the forest of Knaresborow, in the West-Riding of Yorkshire
> ...

Further, in chapter six, Deane places the precise location of the English Spaw at 'Haregate Head', which was at the foot of Harlow Hill, in the

Bilton-with-Harrogate community. Deane was not writing his book for local consumption, nor still for the residents of the Royal Forest, but for the wider readership of England, the vast majority of whom would have never heard of Harrogate, or Haregate Head, although they might reasonably be assumed to have heard of the Royal Forest of Knaresborough, or, if not, of the West Riding of Yorkshire. At no time did Deane, or any of his immediate medical successors, confuse the Royal Forest of Knaresborough with the town or manor of Knaresborough, and thus lead to the error of implying that the English Spa was within Knaresborough township. The well identified by William Slingsby, dubbed 'English Spa' by Dr Bright, and made the subject of a book by Edmund Deane, is High Harrogate's Tewit Well (see plate 6) which since the beginning of recorded history has only been within the boundary of the community of Bilton-with-Harrogate.

Spadacrene Anglica focused attention on the Tewit Well 'being the principall subject of this whole treatise', but also considered four other 'fountains', which had singular properties, or 'mineral vertues and faculties'. Deane first refers to the so-called 'Dropping-Well' opposite Knaresborough Castle, on the south, or Bilton-with-Harrogate side of the Nidd, which was within the 'little park beneath the castle' which divided Belmont Field from the river. Deane's reference to 'divers inhabitants … say, and affirme, that it has beene found to bee very effectual in staying any flux of the body …' indicates that the waters had been taken partly for medical purposes, but it is reasonable to assume that this use declined as the petrifying nature of the water became more widely known.

PLATE 5
The earliest known depiction of the Tewit Well, *c.* 1640, possibly St. John's Well.

PLATE 6
Tewit Well, with
Low Harrogate
Sulphur Well Temple
of 1807.

Deane then dealt with three sulphur wells, termed 'stinking wells', noting that 'one of them, and that which hath the greatest current, or streame of water, is in Bilton Park'– which by 1626 was within a year of being sold by its new owner, Charles I. The other two sulphur wells were the one which became famous as the Old Sulphur Well 'beyond Haregate Head, in a bottome on the right of it as you goe, and almost in the side of a little brook' (see plates 14 and 15), and the one at Starbeck (i.e. 'one that is neare unto the towne [of Knaresborough]'). The former sulphur well became famous as the Old Sulphur Well, now beneath the Royal Pump Room, and the latter was an important part of the Starbeck Spa (see plate 12).

Deane's interest was that of a medical man, so his references to the Harrogate wells are concerned with their pharmacological action, rather than their historical development, so, despite his care with the Tewit Well (which was the principal subject of his book), he fails to inform us when the other wells were first discovered or used. It is therefore reasonable to assume that although the nature of the sulphur wells must have been known to the local population for centuries before 1571, their medicinal qualities appear to have been recognised only between 1571 and Dr Deane's first printed reference of 1626 (F.3). There is a tantalisingly early reference to 'very sovereign waters; as ye Spa, Sulphur and St Mungo Wells' in the vale

PLATE 12
Starbeck Spa.

of York, the first two being at Bilton-with-Harrogate on the accompanying chart. Unfortunately, neither the list nor the chart have been dated, although a hand-written list of the archbishops of York, written on the verso side, ends with an entry for 1628 (A.132). Evidence to support attendance at the spa before Dr Deane's 1626 book comes from a letter from William Stanhope, dated 5 March 1622 at Harrogate, to Framlingham Gawdy, concerning a financial transaction, it being extremely unlikely that Stanhope (possibly a relative of Dr Michael Stanhope of York) was in Harrogate for anything other than the spa (A.131).

There is a single and tantalizingly brief reference to the spa in the 1605 deposition against John Ingleby, in which his servant, Jane Smythe, spoke of his having received a visit from the Roman Catholic Robert Winter in the summer of 1604, and their subsequent meeting at Ripley or Ripon, after which John's relative, James, stayed with Robert Winter to 'ride with him to the Bath' (A.118). Within Yorkshire and much of northern England, this term was applied only to Harrogate, so its use by Jane Smythe may indicate that the Bilton-with-Harrogate waters were being used for bathing long before the publication of *Spadacrene Anglica*, which itself hints at the possibility in chapter five of the first edition: 'The vulgar sort drinke these waters [i.e. the sulphur waters] ... and are soon holpen [helped] by washing the parts ill affected therewith, which thing they might much more

PLATE 13
An early
advertisement for the
Starbeck Spa.
Starbeck was termed
a detached portion of
Knaresborough town
by the Great Award
of 1778.

75

conveniently ... doe, if at Bilton Parke were framed two capacious Bathes, the one cold, the other to be made hot or warme, by art ...' (F.3).

The interest of Deane and his fellow doctors Bright and Hunter in the Harrogate waters was shared by Dr Michael Stanhope, also of York, which in the early seventeenth was a very important centre for medical practice. Shortly after the appearance of Deane's book, Stanhope, in company with Dr Deane, three other physicians, and 'a worthy knight', paid another visit to the wells. The party left York and travelled to Knaresborough, where they found a guide who took them across the Nidd and guided them to the Tewit Well, which was 'situate upon a rude barren moore, the way to it in a manner of a continuall ascent' (F.4, pp. 5–7). This is somewhat surprising, in that Dr Deane was one of the party, whose own book about the Tewit Well had appeared shortly before Dr Stanhope's visit. It is also surprising to read in Stanhope's account of this visit *Newes out of Yorkshire ...* that 'Upon our first approach to the Spring, we were satisfied that former times had taken notice of it, by reason it was enclosed with stone, and paved at the bottom, but withall we plainly perceived that it had beene long forgotten, which the filth wherewith it was choaked did witnesse' (see plate 5). After cleaning the well, the visitors sampled the water, and praised its quality and value. If Dr Deane was really present, having only just published an account of the well which included Dr Bright's earlier praises (F.3), why was Dr Stanhope's party so delighted by their 'discovery', and was it likely that Dr Deane would have simply attended as one of Stanhope's party? Probably not, and the more Stanhope's account is read, the more it seems to be panygeric to Stanhope's perception. Indeed, on page 4, Stanhope writes that although two neighbouring gentlemen, Slingsby and Ingleby 'did for many years ordinarily drinke', he could not 'perceive it gained any great credit, but hath since their decease been altogether involved in silence'. This is an incredible statement, in view of Deane's earlier book, *Spadacrene Anglica*, and adds weight to the possibility that Stanhope was an opportunistic self-publicist.

Stanhope's party continued their investigation, and proceeded to the sulphur well 'in the skirt of an hill, close by a Rivolet'. This alludes to the sulphur well's position below the modern Well Hill, and adjacent to the Valley Gardens stream, which runs through a culvert towards Coppice. On the following day, the party revisited the Tewit Well, each member drinking between eight and fifteen glasses of water, so that within the hour, the strongly diuretic nature of the Tewit Well water caused it to come 'so freely from us that we were like to many walking conduits' (F.4, pp. 17–19). The party also visited the spring in Bilton Park (which must have been the sulphur well already noticed by Dr Deane (F.3, chapter four), as well as one they termed the 'pigeon spring', which is something of a mystery in that its

a two Steps down
b two Steps down
Door of No 3 is 3 feet high, 1 f 10 wide
Door of No 4 is 2 f 6 wide, 3 f 6 high
N1 out Side 5 f each Angle also 5 f high to y Cover
  it rises 2 feet, door 4 f by 2 f also a Stone
  in the bottom rises 8 Inches the stones in the
  other Wells rises not so high.

Well No 1 Door Side 5 f, End 4.11. Door 4 f. by 2 f. High 5.6 to the pyramidal part.
No 2 Door Side 4.6. End 4.2. Door 3.8 by 2 f. High 5 f 6.
No 3 Door Side 3.5. End 3.8. Door 3 f 6. by 22 In. High 4 f 9.
No 4 Door Side 3.10. End 4.4. Door 3 f 6. by 2 f 6. High 5 f.

Thermometer stood in y strong
est Sulpher Well at 48
in the Brooke 53 D
in y neset Sulph: Well
at 50 ½

Causway   Bridge   Causway

77

PLATE 15
Topographical sketch
of Sulphur Wells.
COURTESY OF WEST YORKSHIRE
ARCHIVE SERVICE, BRADFORD
BRANCH

character and location are unknown. The reference to pigeons may be due to large numbers of these birds in the vicinity, or more particularly because the pigeons gathered round the well to peck the accretions of salts which formed at its rim, which implies a sulphur water. Although the location may have been in Bilton Park (and subsequently lost) it could also have been at Starbeck, which is more likely, where the sulphur springs became an important part of the Starbeck Spa. That it was not the Starbeck Chalybeate Well is made clear by a later passage in Stanhope's book, which notes that 'in the latter end of this summer [i.e. 1626] there was another spring discovered by Dr Leake, a physician of Yorke, a mile neerer the town of Knaresborough, than is the Tuit-Well'. Stanhope classed this spring with the Tewit Well, comparing both to the two chalybeate wells of continental Spa. This is irrefutable evidence that the new well discovered at Starbeck by the fortuitously named Dr Leake was a chalybeate, or iron water (F.4, pp. 29–30). From the above, it is reasonable to deduce that the Pigeon Spring to which Dr Stanhope referred, was the Starbeck Sulphur Well.

Stanhope and his party appear to have lodged themselves at Knaresborough, and indeed Stanhope, in *Newes out of Yorkshire* ... refers to the wells being 'conveniently seated neere a Town of amply receipt for

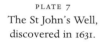

strangers'. Yet on closer examination, these words follow immediately an account of the dropping well, which although outside the boundary of the town and manor of Knaresborough, was directly adjacent on the south bank of the river Nidd (F.4, pp. 29–30). It is clear from a variety of seventeenth-century sources that some visitors to the Harrogate wells stayed in Knaresborough, but it is also clear that they stayed in Killinghall, Beckwithshaw, Otley and Wetherby, and continued to do so long after the great Harrogate inns were operating, especially during the busy summer months.

Six years after Stanhope's *Newes* ... appeared, he issued a further book, *Cures without Care*, which publicized his greatest triumph: the discovery of the St John's Well (see plate 7). The doctor describes how, in the summer of 1631, 'it was my hap to discover a new spring distancing itself about a quarter of a mile from the other [i.e. the Tewit Well].' Stanhope praised the value of his new well (which contained a chalybeate, or iron water) above that of the Tewit Well, and provided *Cures without Care* with some case histories. A 'gentlewoman from Suffolk' who was persuaded to try the new water, after a fortnight, voided many stones, to the number of a hundred'. Stanhope's case histories were not restricted to the new St John's Well, but included the waters of the Tewit Well and old Sulphur Well, mentioning the latter's use by a 57-year-old Edinburgh lawyer who bathed in it at his lodgings (F.5, pp. 9–19). The author regretted the open nature of the environs of the Old Sulphur Well, and also the lack of suitable sanitary accommodation: 'What unseemly shifts have I seen strangers of note put to for want of a convenient place of retirement ...'. Interestingly, and in

PLATE 7
The St John's Well,
discovered in 1631.

comparison to his comments about the neglected Tewit Well, Stanhope notes that the Old Sulphur Well was patronized by all classes of society, and that the appearance and behaviour of the lower orders needed regulation (F.5, p. 25). The account of the 1631 visit by the Countess of Buckingham implies that Harrogate's lack of suitable accommodation for visitors caused the Countess to pitch a tent or awning in the vicinity of the Tewit Well, so that she could enjoy the waters in comfort, but Stanhope did not relate whether or not she used it for daytime or nighttime accommodation (F.5). Harrogate's lack of proper accommodation for the Countess of Buckingham and other nobility and gentry does not mean that the facility was unavailable totally. The most likely cause of inn development was the desire of local farmers to take advantage of the arrival of visitors in their midst, and at first this may have shown itself by offering visitors basic accommodation within the family farmhouse. Over the years, further rooms, or even redundant agricultural buildings, may have been added to the original residence, and with the rise of the spa, so arose an under-standing that the harvest from the visitors was greater than that of the land. Further, the farmhouse, by its very nature, was well placed to provide visitors with good supplies of fresh food, an important consideration when diet was such a factor in the spa experience (F.27). That other medical recommendation, that of exercise, could also be encouraged, as the farmhouses, often set in attractive countryside, were ideal locations for walks or riding. The abstracts of title (Class S) of several hotels show that they had once possessed farms (Granby Farm, Queen Farm, Crown Farm, Dragon Farm, etc.) and that some remained contiguous to the hotels long after the two functions separated (S.1035, S.1071).

It is difficult to assess the immediate effect on Bilton-with-Harrogate made by William Slingsby's discovery, and by the further discoveries of Stanhope and Leake, and the publicity from Bright, Deane and Stanhope. At this time, Bilton-with-Harrogate and Pannal were simply two more communities within the Royal Forest, on whose territory all the wells were located, but as visitors increased, it is likely that their presence was more of a source of comment and speculation as to the wells' further healing qualities.

From what is known of the attitudes of later generations of Harrogate doctors and innkeepers, their self-interest encouraged visitors to stay in Harrogate, and discouraged attempts to send Harrogate to the visitors in the form of bottled mineral water. So long as Harrogate was owned by the Duchy, the wells were open for all to drink from, or for local landlords to source for their guests' bathing, the waters being transported to lodgings in barrels. The same openness enabled anyone to bottle the water, and dispatch it some distance, and although the standard twentieth-century publication on English spas states that evidence for the trading of bottled Harrogate water exists only from 1740,[7] there is earlier evidence. In a little known pamphlet published *c.* 1855, 'Records of Cures effected by the Harrogate waters in the reign of Charles the first', the case of one Smith, a York shoemaker, is described, who was

> exceedingly overgrown with scurvy ... usual medicines availing nothing. He was at length advised by a learned scholar ... to send for the Sulphur Water to his house, which he not very willingly did, thinking it a hard task to drink water in the cold of Winter. His ordinary draught was half a pint in the morning which had such good success with him that within lesse than a month he was ... cured ...[8]

The sulphur water consumed by the York shoemaker can only have been transported from Harrogate to York in bottled form, and as Charles I reigned from 1626 to 1649, with Dr Deane's epoch-making study published in 1626 (F.3), it is reasonable to date the above cure around 1630. This means that Harrogate mineral water was being bottled not only a full ninety years before the time quoted by Dr Hembry, but that it was also being bottled about twenty years before the very first example of such activity at Epsom, in 1651, or about forty years before that at Bath, in 1673. Thus, Harrogate water was not only the first spa water to be drunk in England, but it may well also have been the first to be bottled.

Harrogate's conversion from agriculture to spa occurred in the seventeenth century when the Harrogate community saw the possibility of improving its economic condition, and of reaping benefits from the visitors' presence over and above anything offered by forestry or farming. Before this is considered, it is necessary to consider the state of Harrogate between Slingsby's 1571 discovery, and the outbreak of Civil War in 1642.

Chapter two has dealt with the history of Harrogate and the royal forest up to 1628 when Charles I sold the royal parks of Bilton, Haverah and Hay – this last not being within the royal forest. Bilton-with-Harrogate, and the Low Harrogate section of Pannal continued to develop during the first half of the seventeenth century, and it is clear that when the Civil War erupted the Harrogate community was well established as a successful economic and social unit far in advance of its forest neighbours.

Eight years before William Slingsby's discovery, the rents of the royal forest totalled £232 0s. 9d., the principal payments coming from Killinghall, who paid £50 11s. 5¼d., Clint and its associated hamlets, who paid £42 12s. 9½d., and Timble, who paid £25 4s. 11½d., whereas Bilton-with-Harrogate paid only £12 9s. 2¼d, and Pannal, together with all of Beckwith-with-Rossett, paid £19 5s. 8d. Padside, by comparison, paid the small sum of £1 8s. 2d. (A.100). However, by 1577, Bilton-with-Harrogate's rents were £17 11s.

8¾d. and Pannal with all of Beckwith-with-Rossett paid £18 5s. 6d. By comparison, Killinghall's rents had dropped to £11 14s. 0¾d. and none of the other forest townships paid more than Bilton-with-Harrogate, and only Clint, with a payment of £17 8s. 1¼d., exceeded that of Killinghall (A.107). The fluctuations of these rentals, which tended to be stable for decades, may have been due to several reasons, and it is possible to construct a case in favour of increased land values resulting from the advent of the new phenomenon of spa visitors. Although this appears to be a reasonable inter-pretation for the increased rentals, we cannot be certain.

The court rolls continued to record the operation of the judicial system, and also provide insight to the social system both from the point of admin-istration of the townships and the control of law and order. For example, in 1563, five Harrogate men were each fined 3s. 4d. for being 'players of painted cards, called *le cards*, to the bad example of their neighbours and against the laws' (A.99). In 1583 the important water mill at Bilton was re-leased to Frances Pullen for £10, plus the annual rent of 46s. for twenty-one years. This was a good sum to pay, and widow Pullen must have been assured of a fair return for her outlay. (A.109). Three years later, in 1586, two Pannal women were convicted of being 'common milkers of other men's cows' and expelled from their home, an order being issued that no inhabitant of Pannal was to shelter them on pain of a fine of 20s. (A.109.b). In 1612, one William Pannal was among seven men who were charged with giving short weight with butter sales 'to the great loss of those who bought the butter'. They were fined one shilling each (A.127). Two years later, in 1614, the farmer of Pannal Rectory leased from the Duchy certain rights to extract marle, stone, slate and lyme (all used in building operations) from the royal forest (A.128). These examples of activity are not untypical, or sole cases, but are rather a sample of actions which were going on throughout the area of modern urban Harrogate in the years following 1571. Compared with other parts of the royal forest, Harrogate's food production industry seemed buoyant, and this can *only* have been because visitor numbers were creating a demand over and above that of the stable residential population. Further evidence for this growth occurs in the mid-seventeenth-century probate inventories, where the possessions of Widdow Jane Kanlor including fourteen shillings worth of 'routes growinge as cabige and the like'. The interest here lies in the fact that root crops were not listed in Harrogate or Nidderdale inventories before the beginning of the eighteenth century, so their singular listing in Widdow Kanlor's inventory is attributed to demand from widely travelled visitors coming to the spa (A.119). As for farmer Thomas Hill's interest in building materials, this occurred precisely at the time when illicit encroachments on the forest were increasing, and when the court was growing ever more concerned with their regulation.

An order had already been made in 1592 that all illicit dwellings within the forest should be seized by the Queen (as holder of the Duchy), but that the poor inhabitants should be permitted to live on rent free, subject to the proviso that at death, the cottage would be demolished and the site returned to the forest from which it had been taken. In practice this proved unworkable; as the poor inhabitants reproduced, their children still required shelter (A.III).

The court rolls also provide insight to the workings of local government. One of the oldest such posts was that of constable, the post being one of some antiquity, with pre-Conquest origins. The earliest known occupant of the post of constable in Bilton-with-Harrogate was Robert Matthew in 1496, but his accounts have not survived, as have those of none of his successors throughout the sixteenth century. The first accounts date from the appointment of Marmaduke Mathew (D.1) (no known relative) in 1637, which refer to the sum of £2 5s. 4d. being paid to 'the head constable', who can only have been head constable for the wapentake of Claro, rather than the royal forest, as the post was not in the gift of the Duchy of Lancaster, who, however, *were* responsible for the courts within the honour and forest of Knaresborough (D.23). The first recorded appointment of a constable for Pannal – as distinct from Beckwith-with-Rossett – occurred in 1715 when William Waite held the office, and it is likely that in the seventeenth and pre-seventeenth centuries, Pannal was contained within the constabulary of Beckwith-with-Rossett. It is also likely that the creation of a separate constable for Pannal, was occasioned by the early eighteenth-century development of Low Harrogate, especially the area around the sulphur wells, which was part of Pannal. Even a cursory glance at the constables' accounts for Pannal show how Harrogate affairs dominated his life: the earliest surviving accounts date from 1660, and include a charge of seven pence for carrying a cripple to Harrogate, and two shillings for taking ten people to Harrogate. In later years, references to the sulphur wells occur regularly, including one in 1675, when the Pannal constable Henry Bentley went 'twice to sulphur wells to cease quarrells' (D.10.13).

Functions of the office of constable included arresting lawbreakers, searching out men wanted for bastardy orders, escorting paupers to their legal parish of settlement, finding billets for soldiers, conducting ballots for calling up the militia, and ensuring that alehouses were closed at times of divine service. As the office was unpaid, it was highly unpopular, and lasted for a term of one or two years. The majority of the population at this time was illiterate, and it was not unusual for the constable to be the same – as may be seen by some of the surviving accounts! (D.10).

Bilton-with-Harrogate had been classed as part of Killinghall township at some time after 972, when the soke of Bilton was detached from Otley and when the geographical 'Harrogate' may not have been populated. When the royal forest was established, the internal communities were divided into three constabularies: Thruscross, with seven hamlets, Clint, with five hamlets, and Killinghall, with the three hamlets of Beckwith, Rossett and Bilton-with-Harrogate. Subsequent development changed this, and eventually, eleven separate constabularies were created. Beckwith-with-Rossett became a township, as did Bilton-with-Harrogate, and further change occurred when Pannal broke away from Beckwith-with-Rossett, becoming a distinct township in its own right, part of Pannal becoming Low Harrogate. The designation of Bilton-with-Harrogate as part of Killinghall township appears to have been significant only for purposes of taxation, as there is no evidence whatsoever to indicate that the relationship between Killinghall and Bilton-with-Harrogate covered anything beyond the established activities of pauper settlement, flow of labour, and co-operation under the wapentake of bridge, road and highway maintenance. For example, the 'tenthe' of 1475 for Claro itemised Knaresborough (manor), Killinghall (with Stubham), Bilton-with-Harrogate, and Pannal and Beckwith (A.75). This arrangement developed because the royal forest was divided into townships, which in turn sometimes included hamlets. This is why, and quite regardless of size of population, Bilton-with-Harrogate was classed as a hamlet within the township of Killinghall.

Local administration during the earlier part of the sixteenth century was affected by a number of statutes introduced by the government of Elizabeth I. Under the Acts of 1597 and 1601, the responsibility of finding work for the unemployed and relief for the needy devolved to the townships, with a corresponding rise in the role of the constable. In Harrogate, local authority was divided between the county and wapentake (with their officials) and the Royal Forest and Court (with its officials, such as the clerk, the bedell or provost). At local level, there was the vestry meeting. The vestry meeting was usually held in church, and between the sixteenth and seventeenth centuries, when the system developed, and its dissolution in 1894, when the civil functions of parishes were transferred to parish councils and parish meetings, many communities in England were controlled by the vestry meeting system. This system of government worked well, and when it did not there was always the discrete but powerful presence of the Duchy of Lancaster, representing the 'owner', whose impartial authority prevented the rise or undue influence of local grandees, aristocrats, or others whose whims could suddenly make or break a community. Harrogate would make its way without squire or lordling, prince of church or landed gentry.

The records of Pannal parish church (D.12) show that Low Harrogate's vestry meetings were held at St Robert's, until the building of St Mary's in

1825 (N.13), whereafter they were transferred to Low Harrogate (N.51). High Harrogate, however, had no church until the building of the Chapel of St John in 1749 (M.2). No early meeting records have survived, the first reference being that of 1780, when the town's meeting gathered in the Globe Inn (D.18). Further references indicate that meeting in public houses was customary (D.18, pp. 102, 117, etc.); the habit was established probably before 1749.

During the early sixteenth century, there were several families of significance living within the area of Bilton-with-Harrogate and Pannal, such as the Slingsbys of Bilton and Scriven, the Birnands of Harrogate Hall, the Trappes, the Dearloves, the Stockdales of Bilton Hall, and the Bensons – to say nothing of the Ingilbys of Ripley or the Tankreds, Herberts and Bentleys of Pannal. The rivalries of these families sometimes produced power shifts, such as that which occurred with the downfall of Sir Henry Slingsby, whose vacuum at Harrogate was filled by the Bensons (A.121).

Harrogate Hall was the principal residence on an estate in Bilton which by 1558 was held by the Burnand family, who also owned land in Knaresborough and Nidd.[9] Despite its impressive name, Harrogate Hall was simply a glorified farmhouse, to which were attached 143 acres of land, which in 1625 was leased by Francis Trappes Birnand to Thomas Wentworth (S.20) who was then within two years of receiving a barony from Charles I, and presidency of the Council of the North. His royalist sympathies were

PLATE 8
Architecturally undistinguished but historically significant, Harrogate Hall on Hall Lane, Bilton, was demolished in the 1970s.

therefore clear, but he was eventually abandoned by Charles I, who assented to his attainder and execution in 1641.

Two other significant properties at this time were Bilton Hall, and Crookisnab House, the former being in Bilton Park and the latter in Crookisnab, overlooking the open fields between the modern King's Road and York Place. Bilton Hall, although rebuilt substantially in 1853 (plate 9), appears to have been erected during the reign of Elizabeth I (most probably by the same Henry Slingsby who in 1588 was granted a lease of Knaresborough Castle) on the site of a much earlier structure which may well have been the lodge which John of Gaunt ordered be built in 1380 (E.50). By 1634 Bilton Hall, along with Bilton Park, was leased by Francis Slingsby, of Scriven, who had held it since 1602 (E.71). The Stockdales acquired the Bilton Park estate after Sir Henry Slingsby died without heir in 1634.

As for Crookisnab House, this was held by the Birnands, or Burnands, until the death of Richard Birnand in 1456 caused the estate to revert to the Duke of Lancaster (Henry VI) as an escheat, when it was leased subsequently to William Plumpton (A.37.158). Part of Crookisnab House still stands adjacent to central Harrogate's Oxford Street.

Although the history of Pannal township proper is beyond the scope of this narrative, it is appropriate to refer to Pannal Hall and families who possessed it, since some of these families held significant possessions in Bilton-with-Harrogate. Old Pannal Hall appears to have been built for the Tankred family, and the court rolls for 31 July 1594 show that at the death of Francis Tankred, the hall and its lands passed to his son William. The next family of owners were the Dougills, who held Pannal Hall for two generations, before it came into the hands of the Herbert family, who held it from 2 August 1638 until 12 June 1694, when the whole estate was mortgaged to Robert Bell, from whose family's hands it passed in 1724 to George Bentley.[10]

We have made reference to some of the principal local families at this point in our history because they were about to participate in the disastrous Civil War which had such serious ramifications for Harrogate, as for the entirety of the royal forest. Something of the state of Harrogate immediately prior to the Civil War can be gleaned from a letter sent by C. Fairfax to Lord Fairfax in London, who reported that shortly before Christmas 1639 the troops of one Captain Langley had been billeted about Harrogate, and that no good report came of them. Their Captain, 'a man of ill-government', had remained at Harrogate, but his men had marched on to 'the parish of Tewston [Fewston]' on Christmas Eve. The writer also noted that it was expected that when the landlords' provisions failed, the men would 'cater for themselves', and this may indicate that they had previously done so at Harrogate, where their dissolute Captain had remained, no

doubt to enjoy the more comfortable life at the spa. The writer also noted that at Fewston the constables were threatening the inhabitants with the courts if they refused to billet the soldiers and their wives, 'though some confess with a loathsome disease' (C.3.a).

The following year Thomas Stockdale wrote to Lord Fairfax that the regiment of Lord Marquis Hamilton had been disbanded after having committed continual spoils and thefts all over the local country, and that they 'did so overawe the civil subject, as they durst not complain of their suffering'. Stockdale also noted that the Earl of Holland had been at Harrogate but that, 'it seems he likes not the waters, for I do not hear any certainty that he comes to lie here, as once it was expected.' Mr Fairfax also added that, 'much other company, both of the gentry of the Country and of the commanders reformadoes, are now at the Spa' – in other words, Harrogate was busy, and its visitors were representative of both the King and Parliament (C.3.b).

The English Civil War, which had been brewing through the reign of Charles I, and the collapse of government authority during the double defeat by the Scots in the so-called Bishops' Wars, started in earnest on 23 October 1642, over control of the army raised to defeat the Irish rebellion. Evidence illustrating Harrogate's Civil War experience are sparse, and need to be considered in the light of the following facts:[11] Harrogate, and the forest and honour of Knaresborough, belonged to Charles I in right of the Duchy of Lancaster;[12] Harrogate was close to the royalist stronghold of Knaresborough Castle, as well as to York and Marston Moor, both of which played key roles as the Civil War developed.

On 16 February 1642 Thomas Stockdale, writing from Bilton Hall to Lord

Fairfax, advised that he had summoned all the ministers, churchwardens, constables and overseers of the poor in (the wapentake of) Claro to sign the protestation against popery (A.137). Among those summoned were the officials from Bilton-with-Harrogate and Pannal. Historians such as William Haythornthwaite claimed that Harrogate was a parliamentarian resort[13] and largely roundhead in sympathy,[14] but this is surely too much of a simplification, since the political alliances of the gentry must not be taken as typical of the lower orders, regardless of whether or not they were en-franchised. The reality was that so long as authority maintained order with the tenancy of land and supply of food, regulated the coinage, refrained from an excess of religious persecution, and protected the population from civil disobedience and foreign invasion, the mass of the population was more or less indifferent to the political nature of that authority.

The royalist Prince Rupert received a letter from King Charles dated 14 June 1644 which included the line 'If York be lost, I shall esteem my crown little less'. The situation in York was that following the defeat and capture of John Bellasis, Governor of York, on 11 April 1644, by parliamentarian Lord Fairfax, the king's ally, Lord Newcastle, entered York on 16 April, thus opening the way for Lord Fairfax's great siege of the city by Fairfax and Leven, during April, May and June of that year. Prince Rupert marched to relieve York from Skipton and had reached Knaresborough Castle by 30 June. It is likely that Prince Rupert's route from Skipton to Knaresborough Castle was via Harrogate, as he is known to have spent the night of 29 June 1644 at Denton Hall, the Wharfedale home of his enemy Sir Thomas Fairfax, and the most direct marching route from Denton to Nidd bridge at Knaresborough is the one via Askwith, Great Timble and Blubberhouses, and thence along the Skipton Road and into Harrogate at New Park, and so along the modern A59 through High Harrogate, Starbeck and between Bilton Park and Belmont Field. A second, and more likely possibility, given the condition of the roads, is that Prince Rupert left Denton, and via what later became the route of the modern A65, A660 and A659, marched through Otley and Poole, where the river Wharfe was crossed, and so on through Huby until Harrogate's southern boundary was crossed at the river Crimple, the army then reaching the Nidd via the modern A61 and A59; or, via Hookstone, Forest Moor and Calcutt. Whichever route Prince Rupert adopted, the impression made by his army on the residents of Harrogate must have been profound. From Knaresborough, Prince Rupert marched on York, which he reached on 1 July 1644, but the following day, he moved west of York to Marston Moor, where he met the forces of Cromwell and Fairfax, to which he eventually succumbed.

Thomas Stockdale, of Bilton Hall, witnessing the battle, wrote from Harrogate to the House of Commons that the parliamentarian victory 'was one of the greatest and most bloody since the war began' (A.138). Fairfax's siege of York lasted from 4 to 16 July, when Yorkshire's capital fell to the parliamentarians, and although the Civil War's first stage dragged on until 14 June 1645, when Charles I was defeated totally at the battle of Naseby, so far as Harrogate was concerned, it was as good as over.[15]

One incident during the siege of York had direct bearing on our knowledge – or lack of it – of Harrogate's early history. On 16 June 1644, during the siege of Royalist York by Fairfax's ally, the Earl of Manchester, the strategically important St Mary's Tower, part of York's fortifications, was blown up by an exploding mine. St Mary's Tower had been repository for records of the great monastic religious houses of northern England, deposited there the previous century at the dissolution of the monasteries. This incalculably valuable archive was being transcribed by Yorkshire antiquary and gossip, Roger Dodsworth, thanks to an annuity provided by Sir Thomas Fairfax. The explosion wrecked St Mary's Tower, and destroyed the documents, many of which were burned and scattered over the surrounding area, and although some public minded citizens attempted to retrieve those that were left, much was lost. It is possible that information about Harrogate's chantry chapel may have been among material destroyed, especially because the curious Dodsworth noted in one of his transcriptions a reference to Harrogate Chapel.[16] Sixteen folio and quarto volumes of Dodsworth's transcriptions came into the hands of Sir Thomas Fairfax, who presented them to the Bodleian Library at Oxford, where they remain to this day.

It seems that Harrogate's spa continued to function throughout the Civil War period. On 14 November 1644 Lord Morley and Mounteagle, staying at Knaresborough, found himself surrounded by the parliamentarian forces of Lord Fairfax, which hindered his travelling on to Harrogate for treatment for 'the inveterate malady of the spleen [which] enforced me to come to the Spa for my old remedy' (A.139). He 'betook myself with others to the castle not knowing what treaty [treatment] the common sort of soldiers might afford me . . .' After the battle of Naseby in June 1645, the area's parliamentary representative, Sir Henry Slingsby (whose estates were sequestered by Parliament), was replaced by Thomas Stockdale, a move of fortune which symbolized most eloquently the changes wrought by the Civil War (A.140). These same changes must also have created difficulties for visitors to the spa, especially for the king's supporters. In about 1645, one Lord Savile applied to the Earl of Holland begging him to 'procure him leave' to go to the spa waters for the benefit of his health. The Harrogate Spa at this time was invariably referred to as 'the Spa', or 'the English Spa', and it was usual for distant writers to clarify its location by adding 'near Knaresborough', or 'in the West Riding of Yorkshire' (A.141.a), but in the immediate post-Civil War years it became common to refer to it simply as Harrogate.

After the battle of Marston Moor, Harrogate, the Royal Forest, and the Honour of Knaresborough, along with all of the north of England including the great cities of Newcastle and York, were lost to the royalists. Knaresborough Castle surrendered to Lord Fairfax on 20 December 1644, and four years later was destroyed, or 'slighted', by Act of Parliament. After the battle of Naseby (14 June 1645), King Charles' cause in England was ruined, so he placed his hopes in the Scots, who eventually handed him over to the parliamentarians following the Newcastle compact of 30 January 1647. The king was marched south, with a strong escort of parliamentary troops, and on 6 and 7 February they were at Ripon, from where they departed for Wakefield on the morning of the 8th. Shortly before noon, they reached the approach to modern Harrogate, filing down the slope of Killinghall Moor to the narrow bridge over Oak Beck. Tradition later recorded that about five hundred yards from Burn Bridge the King's high hat was struck from his head by the boughs of an overhanging tree, and that the owner, a true monarchist, 'immediately caused its branching honours to be levelled with the ground' (A.143). Had Charles accepted his situation, he would probably have survived, but his intrigues led to the Second Civil War of 1648, and his eventual execution at Whitehall on 30 January 1649. One reference to Harrogate at this difficult period occurs in a letter of 28 March 1648, when it was claimed that 'the northern party are ready to join with the Scots in the King's Quarell ...', and that the speaker of Parliament was going to the Spa (Harrogate). By implication, speaker Clarendon was gathering information, in much the same way as Lord Walsingham's agents had looked to continental Spa and its 'spa rings' back in the 1560s (A.146).

In 1649, the year of the king's execution, when royalist sensibilities were particularly raw, a York chemist named John Taylor brought out a new edition of Dr Deane's *Spadacrene Anglica*. In reality, this was a pure piece of impudent opportunism, for despite the fact that Deane had died in 1640, the title page intimated that this was a new edition of his work. Not content with mangling Deane's writings, the York apothecary added considerable chunks from the writings of Michael Stanhope, who, as we have already demonstrated, was not above contradicting Deane. In his introduction, Taylor explains his purpose in re-issuing Deane was because the original had been 'almost lost and obliterated through the vacillation of these distracted and ruinous times'. Although the 'distracted and ruinous times' do not seem to have prevented Taylor from somehow knowing that Dr Deane's *Spadacrene Anglica* was scarce, they seem to have prevented him visiting Harrogate from York, as his editing of the work of Deane and Stanhope is so crude as to make the careful reader suspect that he had never been to Harrogate. The title page used by Taylor to replace Deane's original, referred to 'the English Spaw, or the glory of Knaresborough', which served to confuse generations that the spa was within Knaresborough town. Either Taylor chose these words because he wished to salute Knaresborough Manor (which like York had been royalist, and had suffered at the hands of Fairfax's parliamentarian forces) and snub Harrogate (which, thanks to such men as Thomas Stockdale, was perceived to be roundhead), or more probably because his 'Knaresborough' was simply shorthand for 'Royal Forest of Knaresborough', which he assumed had become redundant with the death of the king. Later editions of Taylor's forgery changed the most glaring errors, including the title page, which read '*Spadacrene Anglica, or, the English Spa. Being an account of the situation, nature, physical use, and admirable cures, performed by the waters of Harrogate ...*' We do not intend to labour this point unduly, but it has been necessary to provide an elaboration because careless interpretation has sometimes confused readers, and no matter how many inept references are quoted in support of the so-called Knaresborough Spa, the famous mineral wells were either in Bilton-with-Harrogate or Pannal.

The year before the Taylor forgery appeared, the tax assessments paid by constables Hogg and Marston (both of whom were members of old Harrogate families) to the county show some singular entries. Normally Bilton-with-Harrogate had but a single constable, but the exceptional disruptions caused by Civil War conditions seem to have forced the no-doubt unwilling community to provide extra help. In what seems to be an entry for 5 October 1648, Constable Hogg records that £0 14s. 4d. had been paid 'for the Mylitia here, A. 7,000'. This cryptic entry may refer to the constables' costs in dealing with the newly arrived militia, or the monies he had collected from certain of the inhabitants to enable him to deal with them. The entry 'A. 7,000' may refer to the number present, or, to some other military statistic, but whatever its meaning, it proves that the militia were in Harrogate at the time of the Second Civil War (D.35). An almost identical entry occurs at 16 October, but for 9 November, the figure increases to 'for the Mylitia 10,500' and the sum of £1 4s. 6d. Constable Marston's record of paid assessments has an even more tantalizing reference for 29th November 1648: 'Lt. General Cromwell, 3,500; Disbanding Mylitia 3,500, 50 prisoners Knaresborough Castle (assessment paid) £0 17s. 6d.' A further entry from constable Marston for 20 December 'Forces at Pontefract, Coll. Lambert (assessment paid) 10s. 6d. referred to Major General John Lambert, who, the previous summer, had been the parliamentarian commander in the north, and who had been obliged to despatch a force to besiege Pontefract Castle, which had been captured by Sir Marmaduke Langdale's royalist force. Pontefract Castle, like Knaresborough Castle, was a property of the Duchy of Lancaster, and both were the seats of courts under the Duchy's control.

The English Civil War created much lawlessness and disorder, and doubtless many of the forest's inhabitants, had they lived in the following century, might well have agreed with Goethe's observation, that it is easier to live under tyranny than under chaos. In February 1646, when the area was suffering at the hands of unpaid and discontented soldiers, Harrogate's population joined with those of other royal forest communities, as well as those of Knaresborough and other communities within the wapentake of Claro, in petitioning Parliament to maintain the fortifications and garrison of Knaresborough Castle. They wrote that the castle was, 'far from any other garrison, in a vast moorish part, and is a protection to the neighbouring inhabitants from outrages at the hands of straggling soldiers, is an assistance to the collectors of assessments [i.e., such as Constables Hogg and Marston] in the performance of their duties, and is the court house ...' (A.141.b). Apropos the court-house and its records, it is an interesting commentary on the disruption of the times that the usually punctilious entries in the court rolls become sporadic and inaccurate. The entries in the volume dated 31 October 1630 suddenly jump to 30 April 1645, and the entries for 1647 are incorrectly dated 1646, all of which indicates that the volume was compiled after the events recorded, probably from original loose drafts, some of which were subsequently lost (S. Class introduction).

When news reached Harrogate of the abolition of the monarchy, and the execution of the king, there may have been some who pondered over the related matter of the survival of the Duchy of Lancaster, and indeed of the no longer royal forest. Parliament passed an Act on 17 March 1649 which abolished the office of king, and prevented the former king's issue from holding the crown or its possessions, including, specifically, the Duchy of Lancaster. This Act was followed by the creation of the Commonwealth on 19 May, and by July, a further Act had been passed for the method and regulation of disposing of both Crown and Duchy lands. The Rump Parliament wanted no part in administering the Duchy's fee farms, or in collecting their rents, so in March 1648 it was decided to sell these, although the necessary Act was not obtained until 1650. Nothing, however, could be sold until accurate surveys had been prepared, and this huge task was given to surveyor general, Colonel William Webb, of whose monumental efforts over two thousand surveys survive into the present age.[17] The royal forest was surveyed by John Birchensha, Gabriel Taylor, and John Thorne, probably in the spring and summer of 1651, the return to Colonel Webb being made on 5 August 1651, and bearing the phrase 'survey of ... part of the possessions of Charles Stuart'. The return found that the annual worth of the 1,500 acres of the forest (termed 'wastes') which were rented legitimately was £750, and that some rents were not being paid, probably because of the recent disruption. For example, the surveyors found that the special rents paid for access to the enclosures of Fulwith, Harlow and Oakdale had not been collected. Whereas the rentals for Killinghall were calculated to be £11 18s. 2d., those for Rossett and Beckwith (including Low Harrogate and Pannal) were worth £16 12s. 7d. and those for Bilton-with-Harrogate were worth £17 10s. 0d. (A.150). When the sales took place shortly after completion and publication of the surveys, the Honour of Knaresborough produced £4,669, compared to the Honours of Bolingbroke's £888, Tickhill's £1,906, or Pickering's £5,966.[18]

There had always been far more to the Duchy of Lancaster than its ownership of land, as the Duchy's judicial responsibilities were widespread and effective, so even after the disposal of its estates, the Duchy's adminis-tration continued, because – quite simply – the Duchy Office was useful to the new Commonwealth, particularly in the County Palatine of Lancashire. There appear to have been some in Parliament who resented the Duchy's existence, as its continuation was usually approved for only six months at a time, but its light was never fully extinguished, even when Oliver Cromwell removed the remnant of Parliament in April 1653, and became 'Lord Ptrotector'.

The establishment of the Commonwealth and the apparent collapse of the royalist cause saw Harrogate involved with a system of blackmail, theft and compensation which under the victors' system of justice was known as 'compounding'. In effect, this enabled those on the winning side to steal the property of the vanquished. The homes of those of doubtful or proven hostility to the new regime were sequestered, a release being obtained only after swearing oaths not to assist the king in his struggle against parliament, and not to support the principles of 'solemn league and covenant', which among other things condemned church government by bishops. Sir Henry Slingsby, the area's member of parliament, was replaced by Thomas Stockdale of Bilton Hall, and William Hogg of Harrogate was forced to compound for his Harrogate holdings (A.148). Francis Trappes, a minor, had to have his guardians compound on his behalf on 18 March 1652, so that Harrogate Hall (see plate 8) could remain in his possession (A.149.b).

In 1651, the former royal forest, including Harrogate, was leased to Thomas Stockdale and three business associates (William Hardisty, Robert Atkinson, and John Burton), who promptly assumed the title of 'joint lords' and re-established the forest court. This enabled them to make some quick profits as they turned many illicit encroachments into copyholdings and gained from the entry 'fines' (S.55–S.96); they may also have sold Fulwith chase with its remaining timber.[19] The gap in the court roll entries from 1655 to 1668 may indicate that entries were deliberately destroyed after the re-establishment of the monarchy, although there is no direct evidence to prove this. Following the death of Cromwell in 1658, the resignation of Richard Cromwell in 1659, and the new 'Convention Parliament' of 1660, arrangements were made for the return of Charles II in May 1660, and at the following elections for May 1661, the canny William Stockdale – who was nothing if not a survivor! – was re-elected as representative for Harrogate and the rest of the Honour of Knaresborough.[20] The period of the Civil War and Commonwealth saw the Duchy of Lancaster very close to total extinction, especially in 1659, but thanks to the value of several of its offices, and the integrity of its officers, the Duchy survived to be returned to its rightful owner, Charles II. The greatest problem facing the Duchy was the recovery of lands and fee-farm rents which had been sold during the Commonwealth, and, perhaps wisely, Charles II left the matter to Parliament. Harrogate, the royal forest, and the Liberty of Knaresborough, were returned to full Duchy control with what appears to have been a minimum of effort, and although some lands were never recovered, the greater part of the pre-Civil War territory of the Duchy was salvaged. This did not include the former royal parks and chases which Charles I had sold in 1628 (E.78).

Before we conclude our chapter on Harrogate from 1571 to 1660, we must allude to matters spiritual, as such things dominated the minds and actions of men through this and succeeding periods. Following the religious struggles of the house of Tudor, England was an officially Protestant nation, and those members of the populace who practised Roman Catholicism were classed as recusants, or 'refusers'. Legislation from 1549 laid down a range of penalties, including fines, forfeiture of property, imprisonment, banishment and death, thus proving that the affair had nothing to do with the world of the spirit, but everything to do with the world of property and power. The Catholic Hogg family held property in Harrogate (S.17, S.37, S.46) and were persecuted during the 1630s (K.5). When the same family converted to Quakerism, they were persecuted for their non-conformity. In 1657, John Hogg was 'set in the stocks by the constable of Harrogate' for having attended a meeting on a Monday (K.8). These references to the Society of Friends are the earliest known references to non-conformity in Harrogate. John Hogg's term in the stocks does not seem to have been his first breach with the establishment, as he was one of three men brought before the Skipton sessions on 10 July 1655. Described as a linen webster of Harrowgate, Hogg was accused of interrupting a service at Knaresborough parish church by shouting at Minister Mathew Booth, '… runn not, keepe thy place, thou preachest false doctrine, thou arte antychriste … etc.' (A.135.h). Doctrinal difference had also fuelled the disputes between Charles I and Parliament, especially after the Bishops' Wars of 1639 and 1640, which is probably why his son and successor Charles II was considerably less intrusive in matters religious. During the reign of Charles I, the Common-wealth and the succeeding terms of Charles II, James II, William and Mary, Anne, and George I, Harrogate was without its own place of Anglican worship, but this changed during the reign of George II, thanks to the growing power of the visitors, and the goodwill of the restored Duchy of Lancaster.

Restoration to enclosure | *5*

T HE RESTORATION of the monarchy in 1660, although accompanied by widespread rejoicing, did not see an end to religious strife or civil unrest. One sign of this was the series of Acts from 1661 to 1665 which took their name from the Earl of Clarendon, and which were framed to appease the Anglican establishment and to circumscribe Roman Catholics and non-conformists. These Acts, which are considered in detail in the standard textbooks,[1] produced a simmering discontent among former puritans and parliamentarians, and led to all kinds of agitation and plotting, including the so-called Presbyterian plot of 1663 which produced the Farnley Wood rising, planned at Harrogate (A.153).

Meetings of discontents occurred at Harrogate throughout the spring of 1663 (A.154), at which one Dr Richardson appears to have been ringleader. Some of the conspirators were arrested in spring at County Durham, and about two hundred others went on to stage an armed rising at Farnley Wood, near Leeds, in October (A.155). It is clear from the subsequent depositions that men such as Richardson and Captain Atkinson assembled at Harrogate under the guise of visiting the spa (A.155.B). After the failure of the rising, twenty-one plotters were executed and the climate was ready to accept the oppressive Act of Conventicle, which imposed penalties for non-conformist worship. The Quakers were foremost among those targeted for religious non-conformity, and at Harrogate, the Hogg family suffered persecution. Back under the Commonwealth, John Hogg had been put in the stocks in 1656 for attending Quaker meetings and on 27 November he was sent to prison for his non-conformist practices. In 1664, Isabel Hogg of Harrogate was sent to prison, 'she being at the time of her confinement above eighty years of age' (K.7). The Hoggs held land near the Sulphur Wells, including an inn (S.299), for which an early reference is dated 1625 (S.17), and it is tempting to suggest that it was at just such an inn that the Farnley Wood plot was hatched, although there is no direct evidence supporting such a theory.

The first year of Charles II's reign coincided with the outbreak of a lengthy and tedious exchange of opinion over the merits of the Harrogate waters compared to those of Scarborough. The dispute may have been sparked by the appearance in 1652 of Dr French's important study *The Yorkshire Spaw ...* which described the waters of the Tewit Well, the Old Sulphur Well, the Petrifying Well, and St Magnus Well, the last of which was not in Harrogate, but at Copgrove. The Petrifying Well, located in the Little Park beneath Knaresborough Castle, on the Bilton-with-Harrogate side of the Nidd, was fast becoming a curiosity, but the Tewit Well and the Old Sulphur Well were thoroughly praised for their medicinal worth. The St Magnus Well was mentioned briefly by Dr Deane (F.3), who clearly regarded the Copgrove well as being of little worth, and it was not until Dr Short's promotion, in 1734, of a spring of plain and very cold water in what is now Cold Bath Road (F.24, p.296) led later writers to confuse it with the Cold Well at Copgrove. The Copgrove well was known as St Magnus (or Mungo, or Mungus), whose name was then mistakenly applied to Harrogate, causing writers such as Thomas Pennant, in 1777, to claim that it had been frequented by St Mungo in 'about 543' (C.52.d), a claim that was repeated by historian William Grainge.[2] The dispute, possibly sparked by Dr French's book, involved Drs Wittie, Simpson, and Tonstall, who between 1660 and 1679 issued a series of tedious publications (F.7–F.16) which were mostly point-scoring. Because these publications were intended for a national audience, most of whom would not have heard of Harrogate, the authors referred to the spa as being at Knaresborough Forest, or Knaresborough, and it was this fact, along with the Taylor forgery of 1649 (F.3) which sowed the seeds of later confusion. The Simpson, Tonstall, Wittie tracts all refer to bathing and drinking the Harrogate waters, and Simpson recommended hot sulphur baths in his discourse on sulphur water bathing (F.14). Venereal disease was one ailment for which Simpson recommended hot sulphur water (p. 25), and examination of various treatments recommended by the doctors at this time shows that specialization in the application of different waters for various ailments was increasing. In his *Hydrological Essays* of 1670, Simpson referred to the wells at Bogs Field, and also to a newly found sulphur well about twelve yards from the Old Sulphur Well (F.10), all of which indicates that the doctors were taking more and more interest in the range of Harrogate waters.

The most important and informative medical tract about late seventeenth-century Harrogate is that by Dr George Neale, who, with his son John Neale practised at the spa in the summer months between 1656 and 1723 (F.19 introduction). Tellingly, Neale entitled his fragment *Spadacrene Eboracensis* as if in emulation of Deane. Unlike Deane's 1626 *Spadacrene Anglica*. Neale's text was never published, and shows every sign of being an assembly of working notes compiled by a busy spa doctor with the intention of eventual incorporation within a larger text. After Dr Neale's death his widow lent the manuscript to

Dr Thomas Short, the greatest of all eighteenth-century British spa commentators, who summarised its contents (F.19) in his invaluable history of British mineral waters of 1734 (F.24).

Dr G. Neale began his account of the Harrogate spa with the 'Sweet Spa', which appears to have been the well discovered by Stanhope in 1631, rather than the Tewit Well. The 'Sweet Spa' was later dubbed 'St John's Well', or even 'John's Well', and almost from the time of its discovery eclipsed the Tewit Well in popularity. Neale noted with disapproval that the well had been surrounded with trenches and walkways done by some person to 'aggrandize himself with the benevolence of the benefactors', with the result that the waters of the well were being drawn away. According to Eli Hargrove, the sixty yards square terrace had been built in 1656, and was used by visitors to promenade, and the builder, one John Stevenson, had erected a stone with the inscribed words 'all this ground within these walkes belonges to the forist ...' to prevent anyone from claiming the inclosed land (G.3). This hardly supports Dr Neale's observation of a self-aggrandizer, although he continued by pointing out that in the immediate locality, 'many iron-stones were thrown up (all the ground thereabout being formerly digg'ed up, and all the wood destroyed in Queen Elizabeth's time, by iron forges),' which applied to the environs of both the Sweet Spa and the Tewit Well. Neale's forty years' experience with the Sweet Spa caused him to recommend the best time to drink as being from half, to two hours after sun-rise from May to August, which seems to be the first reference to what later became the spa season, the length of which was determined by the state of the highways and the weather (F.19, pp. 286–93).

Neale gave the sulphur waters careful consideration, noting that 'here are, and were, about twenty years ago, three springs, very low, and scarce of water, that all of them did not afford sufficient water for drinking and bathing.' Neale then described taking up the weakest spring, and creating a large basin, made from rammed clay and covered with a large stone, which provided what was possibly Harrogate Spa's first reservoir. The water thus collected proved stronger, and better suited for bathers and drinkers, who certainly included locals as well as visitors, for, as Neale added, 'It is surprising to see what quantities, and how much irregularity the Forresters, who flock thither in multitudes, on holidays, drink, contemning all advice, and vying with one another who can drink most ...' (F.19, p. 291) When Neale lifted the two stones which formed the basin of the 'upper (sulphur) spring' he encountered the flowers of sulphur which accrete to the mouth of the well, and which form such a remarkable phenomenon of nature as these words are set down. It was a sign of Neale's status as a trusted member of the community that he was able to lift the two stones, apparently without opposition, given the importance of the sulphur wells to

Harrogate's economy. On page 292 of his text, Neale refers to the habit of Harrogate's inhabitants of boiling the water for its salts, which were then sold in the country, some of it being sent to London. This shows that by the third quarter of the seventeenth century, the spa industry was expanding its services and, presumably, its profits. Such services also included warm water bathing, as Dr Neale refers to his having '... above thirty years ago [i.e. in *c.* 1663] ... I set up first warm water bathing in this water [sulphur], and procured one such vessel for a pattern, as are used beyond the sea for that purpose; and now there are above twenty bathing houses kept here, with all necessary conveniences, and all full employed in the season ...' (F.19). The bathing houses seem to have been established around the sulphur well at what became Well Hill, Swan Road, Royal Parade and its continuation, Cold Bath Road, the water being transported by means of barrels, or hogsheads. The will of John Canlove, dated 18 December 1692, made reference to 'a bathing tub ... in the west parlour and three hogsheads' (F.17), and the will of Francis Hardesty, who kept a Harrogate bathing house, listed a bathing room, and a bathing tub, with two hogsheads in the cellar (F.18).

Neale's fragmentary text ends with a recommendation that herbs be added to the water 'in some cases' (F.19, p. 292), probably to add to the efficacy of the water's action, rather than as a palliative against the smell of hot sulphur. Dr Neale's work, and that of his son, was recognised by several other doctors, who made reference to it in their own writings. One such was the anonymous author of a text written a century after the Neales, who praised them for being the first to set up 'regular' bathing (i.e. under medical supervision, and as a course of treatment) in warm water, followed by 'sweating', which became such a feature of the eighteenth-century spa (F.28).

The doctors' writings and publications were only made possible through the willingness of the public to visit Harrogate and submit themselves to the rigours of the water cure. Within a year of the restoration, John Ray was writing 'August 5th 1661 – we went to the spaw at Herrigate and drank of the water. It is not unpleasant to the taste ...' (C.6). Three years later, Marmaduke Rawdon wrote a more damning review of the waters: 'thir are two wells which they call the sulphurus spaw, of a most unpleasant smell and taste, and stinks like the smell of a sinke, or rotten eggs, but it is very medicinable for many diseases ...' (C.7). The year following, 1665, saw the penning of an even more graphic account by visitor Lady Elmes, who found the sulphur water as bad as could possibly be imagined, 'yet in my judgement, pleasant', by which she meant that although the smell was bad, the taste was not! Of her lodgings, however, she was unequivocal: 'The house and all that is in it being horridly nasty and crowded up with all sorte of company, which we eate with in a roome as the spiders are redy to drope into my mouthe (i.e. from the ceiling of her chamber), and sure hathe nethor been well cleaned nor ared this doseuen yerese ...' Lady Elmes' brother, Sir Ralph Verney, wrote to her on 5 June 1665, asking her to 'search out some hair to make me wiggs, and buy your coach full, if you can, for all sorts of commodities are cheaper in Yorkshire, and generally very good too ...' (C.8). Although the excruciatingly prim Ralph Thoresby found Harrogate in 1683 to be 'as formerly, a place very unfit for serious thought (C.13.w), others did not share his opinion, as Thoresby himself acknowledged in his diary for 1702 by noting, 'the place itself is so altered with new buildings ...' (C.13.bb), and that 'the Spa at Harrogate ... lately much improved in convenient buildings for the reception of strangers ...' (C.13.ff). Clearly, if Harrogate had been declining there would have been no demand for new buildings.

The reign of Charles II, from 1660 to 1685 is the most likely period at which Harrogate's first custom-built inns were constructed. When in 1782 Eli Hargrove published the third edition of his history and guide to Harrogate, he referred to the town's first inn as having been built in 1687 (G.2), and in the fourth edition of 1789 he identified this inn as the Queen's Head (G.3); he also noted that before this time, 'the water drinkers lodged in the cottages and farmhouses near the place. The company increasing every year, gave encouragement to the inhabitants to increase their accommodations, and before the year 1700 there were three good inns at High Harrogate.' For good measure, Hargrove added that when the Countess of Buckingham had visited Harrogate, the lack of accommodations had required her to have a tent pitched near the Old Spa (presumably the Tewit Well). This did not mean that the Countess spent more than a few hours each day in her tent, as she lodged herself and party in an acceptable inn at Knaresborough, Otley or Wetherby. The complaints of Lady Elmes shows that inns were available at Harrogate before 1687, and there is ample evidence for the existence of such establishments or 'houses'. The Skipton quarter sessions records include references in 1681 to Peter Hogg, John Stephenson, Mary Stayner, Urcilla Wharton, Jane Leedham, Edrus Plumpton, Robert Young, Sara Savage and John Chanter, all of Harrogate, 'alehousekeepers', who 'on 20 May at Harrogate did illegally, obstinately, willingly and without licence ... keep common Alehouses and Tipleing houses and there for the whole time did sell beer & ale' (A.135.q). The fines could be as much as twenty shillings. Marie Copley, a widow, was charged on 6 October 1691 with keeping a tavern in Harrogate and there selling ale and beere contrary to the statute, for which she was given the low fine of twenty pence, we hope because of her widow's status! Alehouses differed from inns and taverns in that they neither provided the meals and accommodation of the former or the 'respectable' drinking of wine and beer of the latter, and it has been estimated that by 1577, England had one alehouse for every 150 inhabitants.[3] Harrogate is unlikely to have conformed to this standard, certainly by about 1640, as the visitors who flocked to the spa were sufficiently wealthy to have their own means of transportation, and were therefore of the inn/tavern class. Yet it is equally unlikely that the ten Harrogate alehouse keepers indicted at Skipton in 1681 represented a population of 1,500, as this level seems to have been reached only by 1800, and such an estimate fails to take account of any other alehouse keepers who were not indicted. The most likely explanation for the high number of alehouse keepers in Harrogate may be that the trade flourished during and immediately after the Civil War, due to the presence of the military, and that once the Commonwealth was out of the way, the climate of the restoration encouraged a revival.

One obscure reference in the accounts of Marmaduke Mathew 'Constable of harrogate for this year 1637' points to the establishment of inns at Harrogate long before the time of Eli Hargrove: 'Item for charges for going to Isaac Peares, concerning the eating of partridges and such like, and carrying in the brewsters and innkeepers' (spelling modernised) (D.23). Isaac Pear may have been a landlord or tavern keeper who broke the laws of lent by serving fine game, but no doubt attaches to the last six words, which can only mean that the constable ensured that the tavern and innkeepers of Harrogate (i.e. not Pannal) attended the brewster sessions for their necessary licences. The key to this reference is the plural 'innkeepers'. A further reference to innkeepers occurs in the 1665 accounts of Pannal parish (which included Low Harrogate around the sulphur wells, and the precursor of Cold Bath Road), where an official (probably a constable) notes that he had to go before the justices of the Forest Court to present a list of all 'Inkeepers, alehouse keepers & butchers &c to enter bond ffor the due observation of lent' (D.12.4). As it would be stretching probability to grotesque extremes to argue that all of these 'Inkeepers, alehouse keepers and butchers &c.' were from the little-visited village of old Pannal, and none from thriving, busy and much frequented Low Harrogate, we suggest that this is further proof to support the opinion that there were inns at Harrogate long before the time mentioned by Eli Hargrove in his book of 1782 (G.2, pp. 76–85).

Hargrove's claim that visitors to Harrogate were accommodated in 'cottages and farmhouses' (G.2) is confirmed by the architectural evidence from the oldest hotels, which all contain, or contained, fragments of seventeenth- or early eighteenth-century origin: the Queen's Hotel core was revealed in 1988 when the dismantling of its central and south-westerly wing exposed seventeenth-century brickwork of a kind identical to that found under both the Granby and County Hotels.[4] Moreover, surviving

PLATE 18
Dragon Hotel,
c. 1870. The original
Dragon Farm is
visible, third from
left; the almost
organic nature of the
Dragon's growth
may be seen in this
photograph.

photographs of the Dragon Hotel show a typical late seventeenth-century West Yorkshire farmhouse at its core, surrounded by a host of later additions and accretions (see plate 18).

The Queen's Head was almost certainly the first of Harrogate's custom-built inns, although as we have shown it was unlikely to have been its first inn. Historian Grainge believed that the new inn, named the 'Queen's Head' (G.1), probably took its name from Charles II's queen, Catherine of Braganza (A.174), who died in 1705. This is a reasonable theory, as Catherine had been awarded the revenues of the Honour of Knaresborough in 1665,[5] and it would have made good sense to adopt a likeness of the royal forest's owner on the board of the new inn. However, if the Queen's Head replaced an earlier alehouse or tavern of the same name, Grainge's theory is still applicable, as Charles I's queen, Henrietta, had been awarded the revenues of the Honour of Knaresborough in 1629.[6] Hargrove's date of 1687 is contradicted flatly by Blind Jack Metcalfe, who wrote that in 1732 he had been invited to replace Morrison the fiddler at the Queen's Head, who had played there for *seventy* years, that is since 1662.

High Harrogate's three other principal inns appear to have been established within the same period as the Queen's Head, and were certainly active by 1700 (G.2); these were the Granby, the Dragon and the Salutation, with the smaller World's End (see plate 72) and Bay Horse (see plate 24) not far behind. The Granby Hotel (see plate 81) was especially well located, as it was not only adjacent to the town's most popular well, the Sweet Spa, but was also convenient for the junction of the highways to Skipton and York, and thus for passing custom. Although the Granby's later history, especially from about 1750, reveals that it was a somewhat exclusive address, and was patronised by the top level of society, its origins may have been those of an ordinary inn or even tavern, which sprang from farmhouse accommodation. The spread of 'house' or 'chain' public houses during the late twentieth century, with its plethora of pseudo ethnic or rustic inn names, devalued the historic significance of such labels, whereas in earlier times, they were an important guide to the establishment's history. On 12 July 1757, Christopher Benson's 'ancient and well-accustomed Inn, situated very conveniently for the Spaw at Harrowgate' (R.60) was put to auction, the name being revealed in a later advertisement for 26 February 1760, when 'the Royal Oak, many years kept by Christopher Benson' was advertised for letting (R.120). The Royal Oak was a name used to mark the incident in 1651 when the future Charles II, having invaded England and been injured during the battle at Worcester, had subsequently hidden in an oak tree at Boscobel while making his escape. The restoration of the monarchy in 1660 saw the spread of royalist names, which would have been impossible under

PLATE 72
World's End (later Skipton) Road, with Smithy Hill at far left, Grove House at right, ascribed to W. P. Frith, *c.* 1833.

the Commonwealth, the 'Royal Oak' being typical. However, the later Granby Hotel had an even older name, the 'Sinking Ship'[7] which recorded England's defeat of the Spanish Armadas of 1588, 1589 and 1597, a mere twenty years or so after Mr Slingsby's discovery of the Tewit Well. The Benson family appear to have had a long (but not necessarily unbroken) connection with the Granby, as they were mentioned a century later when Blind Jack wrote his memoirs (C.30.1). Neighbouring Granby Farm survived to the end of the twentieth century, its fields forming an important urban buffer between the thinly built frontage of High Harrogate and the former Bilton Park.

The third of the great High Harrogate inns was the Dragon, at the northernmost apex of the High Harrogate 'triangle', facing Devonshire Place. Sometimes known as the Green Dragon (B.31, R.130 etc.), the name probably derives from Charles II's racecourse of the same name, and we are fortunate in possessing a photograph of the building which shows a seventeenth-century farmhouse at its heart (see plate 18). Eli Hargrove, writing in the 1782 edition of his history, reported that there were three good inns at High Harrogate before 1700 (G.2), namely, the Dragon, the Granby and the Queen's Head. Hargrove's description has led some to think that there were only three inns at High Harrogate, whereas he was actually noting the existence of three *good* inns! It is likely that the former 'Salutation'

Inn (see plate 80) had a more significant role (C.31.b.13) than historians of the later nineteenth and twentieth centuries realised, in that its location between the Dragon and Granby, facing the common and directly opposite the carriage road to York Place, were all indicative of long establishment. By 1740, Richard Lund 'at the sign of the Salutation at Harrowgate Spa' advertised good grass, hay and corn and good stabling for their horses; and patrons 'may depend on the best entertainment, civil usage and a hearty welcome from their humble servant . . .' (R.20). The Salutation eventually changed its name to that of the Hope Tavern, and Gascoigne's hotel, but it is the earliest known name which betrays the inn's greatest historical interest. In 1959, historian Haythornthwaite drew the attention of the public to the link between the name of 'Salutation' and pre-Reformation chantry chapels, suggesting that the Harrogate Salutation may have been adjacent to the lost chapel that was dissolved in 1549. This was an extremely interesting observation, coming from a skilled historian, and one that offers the possibility of taverns, if not full inns, having been established over a century before the mid-seventeenth-century references in the quarter sessions records (A.135).

High Harrogate's Church Square (see plate 24) existed long before the Great Award of 1778 (B.31) and seems to have grown from an original building at the junction of the modern Skipton, Knaresborough and

PLATE 81
The Granby, with Granby lodgings on the left, and St Alban's Villa on the right.

PLATE 24
Church Square, or
Spa Hill, *c.* 1833,
ascribed to
W. P. Frith, with the
'Toy Shop', and Bay
Horse Inn

Wetherby roads, which at the time of writing is known as the Empress Hotel, but whose earliest known name was the Bay Horse. It would be stretching the bounds of credibility to an unacceptable point to posit that the Bay Horse Inn or its precursor was not in place by 1640, as of all Harrogate's inns, save perhaps the Crown, the Bay Horse had the best of all possible sites, being nearest of any to the popular Sweet Spa, and to the above named three highways. The original of the Bay Horse may have served visitors to the Sweet Spa, or the casual workers whose services were hired by users of the well. This possibility is given credence by the fact that in 1786 William Westmorland, who kept the Sweet Spa (by then known as the St John Well), also occupied the Bay Horse (S.d.2), part of the land being held by brewer Thomas Wilkes (S.345). The earliest surviving photograph (see plate 25) of the Bay Horse shows it to have been a structurally low building, constructed with coarse sandstone blocks and rendered with white-wash, although its interior was sufficiently spacious to accommodate a grand inquest of the Royal Forest Court in 1791.[8]

The final High Harrogate inn of which we have anything to note from the time of the mid and late seventeenth century, is the former World's End, more familiarly known in the nineteenth and twentieth century as the Grove, or Grove House. Although the first surviving reference to the World's End is as late as 1728 (R.1), when it was advertised as having 25 acres of good land (and thus betraying its agricultural connections), its location at the northernmost point of High Harrogate (see plate 72), and the inclusion of the highway verges of its western boundary in the Stray, along with a common watering place (B.31), show that it has been a structure of some antiquity and significance. The name 'World's End' has associations with the upheavals of the Civil War and execution of Charles I in 1649, so it is reasonable to suppose that the inn of that name was in existence at least from the time of Charles II, a hypothesis supported to this day by the structural evidence of the central section of Grove House, a building which later became famous as the home of Samson Fox.

The above-mentioned inns were located in High Harrogate, but the area of Low Harrogate around the Old Sulphur Well was also furnished with inns and taverns, although information is somewhat sparse, principally because of the attitude of Eli Hargrove, author of the first Harrogate guide books (G.1–G.3). The 1775 Hargrove (G.1) refers to the Dragon, Granby, Queen's Head, Salutation and World's End Inns, but makes no mention whatever of the Crown, which certainly existed, as it is mentioned on Joseph Thackwray's tombstone '... In 1740 I came to the Crown' (H.12). The second edition of 1782 refers to Harrogate having 'eight very good inns', but again it fails to name the Crown, which was not listed until the eighth edition of 1812, and then only in the most cursory manner. The reason for this neglect of the Crown, and indeed of all of Low Harrogate, must be

PLATE 25
The Bay Horse, precursor of the 'Empress', Church Square.

because Eli Hargrove was a bookseller and merchant whose businesses were all in High Harrogate, and whose interests most certainly would not have been served by diverting custom down to the rival resort of Low Harrogate (G.8). Whatever Hargrove's illusions as to his merits as an historian, we today should regard him, first and foremost, as a man of business.

The name 'Crown' is indicative of an establishment of some age, particularly the time following immediately upon the re-establishment of the monarchy in 1660. As a simple tavern, the Crown could have a longer history, possibly dating back to the Tudors but there are no clues as to when it evolved into an inn or hotel for the full accommodation of the public. Other establishments which may have developed with, or shortly after, the Crown, are the Bell, Promenade, and White Hart Inns, with the Globe, or Half Moon Inn (later known as the Crescent) following in the eighteenth century. The 1647 constable's accounts for 'the town of Bilton-cum-Harrogate' make frequent reference to the quartering of soldiers in Low Harrogate (D.34), as well as in Ripley and Ripon, which may have been influential in the development of alehouses and taverns into fully fledged inns. The Hogg family were among recipients of such custom, with Peter Hogg being paid as much as nineteen shillings for quartering men 'at several times'. In 1768 Joseph Hogg, landlord of the Bell Inn, was accused falsely of having murdered a customer (R.370), and it is likely that this Hogg and his inn were connected to the 1647 Hogg and his establishment.

The visitors whose patronage enabled the inns of High and Low Harrogate to flourish were provided with a powerful incentive in 1734 with the publication of Dr Thomas Short's two-volume account of British mineral waters, which paid particular attention to Harrogate. Dr Short wrote of the Tewit Well, noting correctly that it had been discovered in 1571 by Mr William Slingsby, as well as the 'Sweet Spa', although he later attributed its discovery to Slingsby rather than Stanhope. He also described the Sweet Spa as having a 'pyramidal roof, supported by four pillars each a foot and a half high', the whole structure being crowned with a stone knob or ball, 'the building have been done in 1656 ...' (F.24, pp. 251–2) (see plate 5).

Dr Short praised the sulphur wells of Low Harrogate, describing them as 'certainly ... the most incomparably strong sulphur water in Britain ...' (F.34, p. 285), and praised the pioneering work of Drs Neale, the senior of whose work he reprinted in his text. He also mentioned the Starbeck sulphur well ('in the middle way to Knaresborough, in a low ground, by a small brookside'), and that of Bilton Park ('half a mile north of this is Bitton [sic] Spaw'), and on page 297 he makes what may be the first reference to the wells at Harlow Carr, of which he is rather dismissive. More interestingly, he refers to the Cold Well (in what later became Cold Bath Road) and records that Dr

Neale had turned this into a very good cold bath with 'conveniences and accommodation for strangers'. But it was Dr Short's consideration of the mysterious bogs field that was of prime importance, as it directed the attention of the doctors to what became Harrogate's greatest supply of mineral waters. Dr Short described how one of these waters (most probably that of the later Alexandra Well) had been identified by a man named Robert Ward, 'about thirty years ago' (i.e. at about 1700) 'when the concourse of people was very great to this Spaw', had 'made a basin in the clay under the moss of a bog, where the strongest and briskest of these sulphur springs rise, and gathered half a hogs-head of these waters at a time, for the use of the poor.' Dr Short also noted that this had caused the three sulphur wells in Low Harrogate to dry up, by which he concluded that the sulphur springs within the immediate locality were somehow connected.

The three sulphur wells still exist beneath the Royal Pump Room of 1841–42, and continued to be popular long after the chalybeate, or iron springs of High Harrogate had fallen into disfavour. Dr Short mentions that each of the three sulphur wells had 'very pretty little stone basins laid for the water to rise up in to, and are each enclosed in a small neat building (i.e. well head) of stone and lime, about a yard square on the insides, and near two yards high covered over with two thick, smooth flag stones ...' (see plate 15). Evidently some work was done around the sulphur wells in the decade following Short's book, as the overseer for 1745, John Willans, noted in his accounts that one shilling and sixpence had been spent in surveying the ground at sulphur well (D.12.44), and two years later, constable Jeremy Wright noted payment of one shilling for further measurements at sulphur well (D.12.45). It is reasonable to assume from these payments that some sort of paved improvements to the sulphur well's environs were intended, and possibly executed.

Harrogate's visitors during the reigns of William and Mary, until that of George II, were still drawn from the two distinct classes of either the very rich or the very poor, the proto-middle class being represented by the town's resident population of people who serviced the inns and hotels, assisted by members of the medical profession, some of whom arrived and departed with the visitor season. In view of the economic importance of these visitors, it is instructive to consider their impressions of the Yorkshire Spa.

In about 1690 James Brome visited Harrogate as part of his three-year travels round Britain, and after writing about the various mineral waters, noted that he had arrived, 'when there was a great confluence of the gentry, who come hither to drink the waters from divers places' (C.16.f). Brome also mentioned St Robert at Knaresborough, and it is clear from his writing (C.16.c) that visitors regarded the story of St Robert, and the Harrogate

Spaw, along with other things encountered on national journeys, as curiosities worthy of note, quite regardless of any genuine medical properties that the waters may have possessed. A similar response may be seen in the writings of Celia Fiennes, who visited Harrogate during her journey of 1697–98, although the smell from the sulphur well so affronted her horse that she could not approach the well. Fiennes mentions two sulphur wells, and noted that they smelled like a 'carrion, or a jakes'. Others, however, visited Harrogate for business, either with spa visitors, or with those who found it a convenient place of resort. On 8 July 1699 Sir Walter Calverly 'went again to the spaws to Harrowgate' on legal business (C.19.b), and again on 15 July to meet Sir Walter Hawkesworth (C.19.c), a process he repeated on 11 August 1702 (C.19.d). Such patterns appear to have been typical of the use made of Harrogate by visitors, since the time of the Tudor 'spa rings' which so concerned the government of Elizabeth, right up to the time of writing this chronicle.

In June 1706 the Blundell family were in Yorkshire, Nicholas Blundell writing that they went to 'see the droping well at Knesbrough, thence we went to Harrogate, where I taisted both the sweet and stinking spa water. I saw there Morrison the riming musition, he played very well.' (C.21.b) This last was a reference to the Morrison who played his fiddle at the Queen's Head, and who was still active twenty-two years later when Sir Darcy Dawes stayed at the Queen's Head in 1728, noting in his travel journal that he tipped Morrison the fiddle player the very substantial sum of two shillings and six pence (C.24.b), a sum of repeated on 16 and 17 July. Sir Dawes Darcy's surviving accounts show that he visited Harrogate in June 1727, June and July 1728, and July 1730 (C.24), and that he not only tipped Morrison the fiddler, but also the servants (C.24.b), the maids and ostler (C.24.d), and that he paid for cards, bowls, raffles, bottles of 'sider', a barber, and the 'Spa women at Harriergate' (C.24.c), all of which reveals the extent to which the spa supported the local economy.

Perhaps the most celebrated and influential writer to visit Harrogate at this time, was Daniel Defoe, who visited Harrogate in 1717 during the tour he undertook in preparation for his book of 1724–27 *A Tour thro' the whole Island of Great Britain* . . .

Defoe's account is interesting not only because it comes from the author of *Robinson Crusoe*, but because it contrasts the remoteness of Harrogate with the numbers of visitors in attendance at the spa. 'We were surprised to find a great deal of good Company here drinking the Waters, and indeed, more than we found afterwards at Scarborough; this seems to be a most desolate out-of-the-world place, . . . that men would only retire to for religious mortifications, and to hate the world, but we found it quite otherwise.' (C.23.h) Defoe's remarks about the sulphur water indicate that

PLATE 40
The Sulphur Well,
c. 1770. The uneven
nature of the ground,
now covered by the
Royal Pump Room,
is apparent in this
drawing by a visitor.

he experienced it for himself, as well as seeing others drinking it, and he would certainly have called at one of the inns in the immediate vicinity of the Old Sulphur Well.

Harrogate's waters were still free to all comers, as they sprang from the ground owned in entirety by the Crown, through title of the Duchy of Lancaster, with the single exception of the wells on land which had been sold, such as Bilton Park. And it is also well to recall that the *effects* of the waters encouraged more than diuresis, bowel movement, suppression of worms, and healing of skin infestation. Dr Short, in his epochal 1734 treatise, complained that Harrogate was becoming 'the rendezvous of wantonness, and not seldom, mad frolics', and that 'luxury, intemperance, unseasonable hours, idleness, and gratification of taste and appetite, are become so fashionable', that prices were increasing to the degree that ordinary people were deterred from visiting the spa (F.24). We juxtapose these two points to illustrate again the supportive role of the Duchy with regard to Harrogate's development. As the Duchy owned Harrogate's freehold, including all the

mineral rights, the Duchy would have been entirely within its rights to have charged for the use of those mineral waters which sprang from its land. Yet in all the four hundred years between 1372, when the Duchy acquired the Royal Forest and Harrogate, and 1778, when the enclosure award was confirmed, there is not a single example of even an investigation into the possibility of levying such a charge on the inhabitants. It is doubtful whether such would have been the case with any other landlord.

When Dr Short touched on luxury and appetite, he identified a problem which continued to give concern to the medical profession, as witnessed fifty years later, when Dr Buchan deplored the monstrous meals devoured by invalids whose appetites had been unnaturally sharpened by the Harrogate waters: 'I have seen a delicate person, after drinking the Harrowgate waters of a morning, eat a breakfast sufficient to have served two ploughmen, devour a plentiful dinner of fish and flesh, and to crown all, eat such a supper as might have satisfied a hungry porter ...!' (F.33). Back in 1731, Thomas Amory had noted the expenses at Harrogate, by writing 'make haste then to Harrogate, if you are sick, *and have money*, and in all probability you will find the waters efficacious ...' (C.25.f). Amory proceeded to commend judicious exercise and regularity of diet, sleep and fresh air, which was becoming a recognised aspect of spa life nationally, a further attribute of which was wining and dining at the inns, along with dancing, gaiety and good humour (C.25). Thomas Amory concluded his description of Harrogate by noting 'of all the Wells I know, Harrogate, is in my opinion the most charming. The waters are incomparable, no air can be better, and with the greatest civility, cheerfulness, and good humour, there is a certain rural plainness and freedom mixed, which are vastly pleasing.' (C.25.g) Mention of this freedom recurs later with authors who were less enchanted with Harrogate's gay informality (C.76) than was Amory. But others confirmed and exceeded Amory's praises of Harrogate. Writing in about 1900, Yorkshire author Edmund Bogg quoted from a letter, now lost, of *c*.1731. 'Nothing can be more fine and agreeable than the intercourse here. Each strives to make another happy, and nearly as much is effected by good temper and cheerfulness ... as by the waters themselves. The mixture of families at the inns and boarding houses renders the entire company of a thousand individuals like one happy family ... the ladies, too, add the charm of their society to the entire time spent at Harrowgate, and both sexes vie with each other in the art of being mutually agreeable.' (C.26) The art of being mutually agreeable! – it is an entrancing picture.

By the middle of the eighteenth century Harrogate was at the peak of its rustic simplicity as a spa, although the interiors of the great inns must also have been, in contrast, home to a more sophisticated lifestyle. This was the time of the visit of Dr Pocock, who visited the town in 1750, and noted that at High Harrogate, one could lodge and board for one shilling and eight pence a day, breakfast excluded, whereas at Low Harrogate, charges were lower, at a shilling a day 'save tea'. Pocock also noted that High Harrogate had a 'long room' (C.29.1), which was a place of assembly for patrons and visitors other than those residing at the inn or hotel in which the room was located, although these latter would naturally have had unrestricted access. The 'Long Room' was a product of the pre-assembly room era, and in schedule 'C' of her authoritative study of English spas, Phyllis Hembry records that the earliest such room was Horn's Room at St Pancras, of *c.* 1700, with Hampstead and Epsom following in *c.* 1701 and *c.* 1707 respectively, and Bath receiving such an amenity in 1730, followed by Cheltenham in 1738. Harrogate is shown as having received its first long room in 1805, with the building of the Promenade Room,[9] but in fact, as Dr Pocock recorded, it had a long room by 1750, which may have been the one at the Queen's Head, referred to in 1732 by Blind Jack, the Yorkshire road-builder (C.30.c), which places Harrogate well at the forefront of English resorts with early long rooms. The same Dr Hembry also notes that there was evidence for a domestic trade in bottled natural mineral water in Harrogate in 1740,[10] although the Foley manuscript of 16 December 1700 points to Harrogate bottled water being available as 'physic', along with that of Bristol (C.20).

Visitors such as Sir Darcy Dawes (C.24) and Dr Pocock (C.29.1) cannot have failed to have noted a significant absence at Harrogate of a place of worship convenient, and suitable, for the increasing numbers of the aristocracy and gentry who attended the spa during the summer season. As the town's population was but a fraction of the annual total of visitors, and was without either a single pre-eminent wealthy resident, or a tax-raising local government capable of promoting and financing such an institution, it may have been obvious to all that Harrogate's first post-Reformation church would not be paid for by its own citizens. Accordingly, the visitors stepped into the breach.

As Harrogate was owned by the monarch, who was also the defender of the constitutional faith, and as the majority of the visitors were from that class of the aristocracy and gentry which was the defender of the monarchical establishment, it may be understood that the town's first post-Reformation church, when built, would be Anglican. When a survey was published of Roman Catholics having real estate in Yorkshire's West Riding between 1717 and 1734, Harrogate had only two entries: Sir Charles Ingilby, and Thomas Squire of Harrogate, tailor (K.20), and although the Society of Friends had had members and supporters the previous century (K.13, K.16), there were few signs of religious non-conformity in the town by 1740.

In the early 1740s there seems to have been a move by visitors to

Harrogate to provide funds for the building of a convenient place of worship, a key member being Lady Elizabeth Hastings, who left fifty pounds in her will towards the purpose. This benefaction was recorded in a 1743 list of subscribers 'agreeing to contribute towards cost of erecting a Chapel at Harrogate' (M.1). Inscribed 'to the glory of God and the good of Mankind more especially of the inhabitants of Harrowgate ...' the list included the names of visitors promising to contribute, including Edwin Lascelles of Harwood. As Bilton-with-Harrogate was, at this time, within the parish of Knaresborough, and diocese of Chester, the subscription list pledged payment to Thomas Collins, Vicar of Knaresborough. The site of the new chapel was to be at High Harrogate, in the centre of the common between the Queen's Head, Granby, Dragon and Salutation Inns, and despite later speculation, there is no evidence to suppose that the site was anything other than virgin. Building work may have been affected by the Jacobite rising of 1745, in which Blind Jack participated (C.30.n), but by 1749, the principal inhabitants were able to ask the Lord Bishop of Chester to dedicate and consecrate the new 'Chapel of St John', advising him that it contained seventeen yards in length and nine and one quarter yards in width, that it has been built with the leave and consent of the right honourable Earl of Burlington, and that it was constructed for the 'greater benefit of those who come to Harrogate to drink the Waters' and for the ease and convenience of the inhabitants (M.2). The reference to the Earl of Burlington was because the Earl had leased the Honour and Forest from the Duchy, as the Duke of Devonshire was later to do. This may explain why the Duchy's otherwise meticulous records contain nothing about the conveying of the site, or the process of designing and constructing the new Chapel of St John. And it is a moot point whether or not Lord Burlington really had authority to dispose of Duchy possessions in this way, although in later dealings with Harrogate Chapel the Duchy showed that it accepted without question the establishment and continuation of St John's Chapel (M.18). The Bishop of Chester consecrated St John's Chapel, together with its adjacent burial ground, on 18 June 1749, which from this time until 1755 was served by Thomas Collins, Vicar of Knaresborough. A curate, W. L. Williamson, was appointed in 1755 (M.5), and the Chapel of St John continued to thrive throughout the eighteenth century. Engravings (see plate 32) show the chapel to have been a simple stone structure built on an east–west axis, with a main entrance, surmounted by a bell turret, facing west. A plan of 1811 (M.64) depicts a rectangular structure with an eastern semi-circular apse for the sanctuary, and a projecting square vestry to the north.

St John's Chapel, with its vestry, provided the Bilton-with-Harrogate community with an obvious place for citizens to meet to discuss and promote the affairs of the township, and although the first surviving reference to such a vestry meeting is as late as the 1780 vestry book (M.30), it is clear that such meetings continued in their traditional venues of the Harrogate's inns long after the building of St John's. For example, the meeting of the High Harrogate churchwardens of 16 April 1784 took place at the Salutation inn, when it was agreed to levy a chapel rate of four pence in the pound (M.27). Similarly, in 1780, a town meeting was held at Thomas Linforth's inn, the Globe (see plate 83), which was at Low Harrogate, and therefore in Pannal, although it seems from the attendance list that with such names as Joseph Goodlad of the Dragon, Robert Gilbertson of the Queen's Head, and Thomas Benson of the Granby, the distinction between High and Low Harrogate, at least in township affairs, was blurring (D.18). Certainly, the unfortunate loss of the Pannal vestry books for the late eighteenth and early nineteenth centuries makes impossible any attempt to judge whether or not the Pannal vestry meetings continued to deal with Low Harrogate affairs, to the same extent they had done in the seventeenth century (D.12).

Local government during the late seventeenth and early eighteenth centuries was concerned primarily with ensuring that public responsibilities for law and order, taxation, and maintenance of highways and waterways, were observed, and of these, the working of the poor law was of special

PLATE 83
The Crescent Inn, with T. H. Walker's Leamington Well Pump Room of 1838 at right. The front gable of the Spa Rooms may be seen in the distance.

importance. One of the earliest surviving poor law documents for Harrogate is the assessment for sums to be collected each month during 1635 for use with the 'poor within the Hamblet of Bilton-cum-Harrogate', when sixty-four inhabitants were assessed as having to pay a total of five shillings and nine-pence halfpenny (D.21). In October of that year, an even more interesting document shows that one hundred and seventy five years before the big Starbeck Workhouse was opened (D.49.4), assessors John Matthew, Peter Benson, Robert Wayd, and William Hogg raised the sum of four pounds, thirteen shillings, and eight pence for 'the Towne of Harrogate ... for the buylding of a house and other messuages for the poor within Bilton & Harrogate ...' (D.23). The house in question was probably not a workhouse in the Georgian sense, but rather a single cottage for an individual or family fallen on hard times whom the community considered worthy of assisting.

Monies were raised to cover the basic provisions of local government alluded to in the above paragraph. The inhabitants of Bilton-with-Harrogate were also liable to national taxation, which during the reigns of Charles I, the Civil War, Commonwealth, and Charles II, grew at a dizzying rate. The first surviving reference to the name of Harrogate occurs during the reign of Edward I, in 1332 (A.35), in whose reign fourteen taxes were levied. Under Charles I, no fewer than one hundred and sixty 'collections, levys, taxes and loans' were raised,[11] and although some were purely regional, many were not, and the inhabitants of Harrogate were not spared the burden of seventeenth-century taxation (A.3).

A special forest tax appears to have been assessed in 1651, Bilton-with-Harrogate's share being £17 10s., and Rossett and Beckwith's (including Pannal with Low Harrogate) being £16 12s. 7d. When compared with Killinghall's £11 18s. 2d., or Felliscliffe's £10 14s. 5d., or Birstwith's £9 17s. 7d., Harrogate's fortunate economic status may be understood (A.150). More detailed records survive for the subsidies granted by the 'Cavalier' Parliament of 1663, which were payable by both clergy and laity. The tax threshold on moveable goods (*bonis*) was £3, on which a rate of 2s. 8d. was payable on each subsidy. For those taxed on land holdings (*terris*) a threshold of 20s. was set, with a rate of 4s. per pound per subsidy. Although cattle (*bovis*) were not specifically mentioned, their inclusion in the Honour subsidy rolls (A.157) indicates that they must have been classed as moveable goods. The high tax threshold meant that only a few citizens were liable to pay, including the Stockdales, Bensons, and Hoggs, who (as with their Pannal neighbours), were charged on land holdings, most of which reached the 20s. threshold.

The highly unpopular hearth tax, which lasted from 1662 until 1689, provides unique insight to the number and size of local properties. The 1664 returns show that Bilton-with-Harrogate had thirty-nine one-hearthed houses, compared with seventy-nine at Knaresborough, but as the number of hearths increased, the final count revealed that Bilton-with-Harrogate possessed four houses with more than six hearths, compared with Knaresborough's single example. The houses assessed consisted of fifty-seven at Bilton-with-Harrogate, and one hundred and fifty-six at Knaresborough (A.158). These tax returns reveal a state of affairs within the Honour of Knaresborough that is very different from the conventional view recorded by such writers as Hargrove or Grainge.

By the time of the mass taxation of Charles II, the hearth tax return for the wapentake of Claro for 1670 recorded empty houses across Yorkshire, save for Bilton-with-Harrogate, which had none, one explanation being that the assessment occurred during the visitor season, which was generally excellent as the reign progressed (C.161). The following year, for the poll tax subsidy, Harrogate's lands were assessed at £505 in value (where Bilton-with-Harrogate was £350 and the Low Harrogate part of Pannal may be assessed at one third of the total for Beckwith-with-Rossett), the same ratio producing an assessment of £25 5s. in tax. The figure of £505/£25 5s. when compared with Boroughbridge's £127/£6 7s. or Knaresborough's £720/£36 once again demonstrates Harrogate's economic significance, especially as this tax was payable by all, regardless of of wealth or degree (A.162). The same results may be had with further examinations of tax records, most notably with the window tax of 1697 (A.178), and the poll tax for 1698 (A.182).

Harrogate's low *resident* population, high visitor numbers, and sparse level of building in relation to total acreage (much of which was dedicated to the agriculture which fuelled the hotels and inns) makes difficult any attempt to calculate household density in the locality, although the standard study of hearth tax returns for greater Yorkshire suggests that for the period 1662–74, the number of households per 1,000 acres was 16.6 in Harrogate (presumably excluding Low Harrogate, as Pannal is estimated separately at 21.6 per thousand), compared with 13.3 at Scriven, 33.1 at Arkendale, 32.7 at Hampsthwaite, and 74.7 in dense Knaresborough.[12]

Bilton-with-Harrogate's tax assessments were clearly affected by the assessors' perception of community wealth, which in turn was determined by the rate of visitors to the spa. One of the greatest factors influencing visitor attendance was the state of the highways, and in the middle of the eighteenth century, these were subject to the widespread improvements introduced by the various Turnpike Trusts. These bodies were not created by central government, but rather by local initiative, the high-point being between 1751 and 1772, when 389 new Acts were passed by Parliament, the petitioners being local landowners and tradesmen, who saw 'economic advantage in improved communications'.[13] After the Enclosure Act of 1770,

Cruickshank Del.

Harrogate's highways and roads received further attention, but in earlier years, improvements were due entirely to the turnpike movement. Further, although the enclosure commissioners later would refer to laying out roads relative to the Great Award of 1778 (B.31), this did not mean that those same roads had not existed *in one form or another* before the Enclosure Act, either as forest tracks or paths. Complaints about the condition of Harrogate's roads were placed regularly. In 1710, the 'highway between Ripley and Harrowgate in a certain place called Killinghall ...' was found to be in poor condition, and the West Riding magistrates ordered it to be 'repayred before next sessions' (Q.3). The same year saw a complaint from Robert Byerley that 'fforest lane between the Town of Knaresborough and the Town of Harrogate [was] in a very ruinous state' (Q.4). Such complaints continued until 1751, when Parliament considered a bill for 'repairing the roads from the Town of Leeds, through Harwood, to the South West Corner of the Inclosures of Harrogate [the later Prince of Wales corner]; and from thence in two branches [one through Ripley ... the other through Knaresborough and Boroughbridge] to Ripon ...' (Q.5). The sponsors of the 1751 Bill included some of the greatest Yorkshire landowners, such as Sir Conyers Darcy, William Aislabie, Sir Henry Slingsby, Sir John Ingilby, Rev. Thomas Collins, and Edwin Lascalles. Note should be made of the verb 'repairing', as used in the Act's preamble.

The 1751 Bill referred to the fact that 'there are now two distinct roads from Harrogate to Knaresborough ... the one leading through Bilton Lane, to the High Bridge over the River Nidd, and the other over Belmen Lawn, to the Low Bridge, over the same river.' Although the latter is clear enough, having also been mentioned in 1648 (Q.2), the former has sometimes misled readers into believing that the Harrogate to Knaresborough Road ran down Harlow Hill as far as Starbeck, or Stockbrigge, where it terminated, before resuming at the junction with Bilton Lane and continuing to High Bridge at the river Nidd. The illogicality of this proposition is shown by the fact that for the Harlow to Stockbrigge 'great broade way' (see plan 6) to have developed in isolation, there would have to have been some very significant feature at Stockbrigge/Starbeck, and one, moreover, which was *not* of significance to the inhabitants of Bilton. Furthermore, if Bilton Lane had been the only route between the Nidd crossing and High Harrogate, it would have been Bilton Wells which developed between Charles I's sale in 1628 (E.78) and the Act of 1751, and not High Harrogate. An explanation for this apparent anomaly may be found in the term 'distinct road' which implies a foot path, cart track, way, or route, that was traversed regularly

PLATE 58
The Starbeck Toll House, near the junction of the Knaresborough Road and Forest Lane.

throughout the seasons, whereas the direct route between Bilton Lane, Forest Head, and Starbeck was used principally by seasonal visitors.

The 1751 Bill (Q.5) for the repair of the above-mentioned roads was followed in 1752 with an Act for the turnpiking of the road from Leeds to Harrogate and Ripon, with a branch from the later Prince of Wales corner to Knaresborough, Boroughbridge and Ripon (Q.6). One of the most visible results of the 1752 Act was the building, by the trustees, of toll houses at Forest Lane (for the road to the 'high' bridge at the Nidd), Belmont (to 'low' bridge), Buttersyke Bar (near Pannal on the Leeds Road), Killinghall, and later, bars in Harrogate itself on Ripon Road, just north of the George Hotel, and on Skipton Road at the junction of Bilton Lane. In 1753 the Bradford to Killinghall road was turnpiked, with a branch from Otley Road down to the Prince of Wales corner.

The first meeting of the turnpike trustees was held in Harrogate at the Queen's Head inn on 22 April 1752 (Q.5), and it must have been at this time that Jack Metcalfe, the famous blind roadmaker, entered the scene. Although 'Blind Jack' is a well-known figure in accounts of eighteenth-century Yorkshire, with claims for his having frequented a multitude of localities and buildings, hard documentary evidence to support these claims is noticeable by its absence, the principal source being the anonymously published *Life of John Metcalfe* (C.30). However, the 1795 *Life* was written by Metcalfe himself, and whatever his merits as a man of enterprise, and turner of diverting anecdotes, he was an execrable historian, as his memoir jumps from subject to subject and year to year with the undisciplined intensity of a jumping jack. Born in Knaresborough in 1717 (C.30.a), Metcalfe moved to Harrogate, following an invitation from the Queen's Head Inn to succeed Morrison, the fiddler, attracted no doubt by the opportunities offered by the thriving spa (C.30.c). Metcalfe distinguished himself at Harrogate not only by playing his violin in the hotels and inns (C.30.d), starting the town's first vehicle-hire business (C.30.l), and building the turnpike roads into Harrogate (C.30.p), but also by eloping with the daughter of the landlord of the Granby Hotel (C.30.k–l).

The newly improved roads enabled visitors to reach Harrogate in greater numbers (see plate 85), and also to extend their stay well into the season when inclement weather had rendered the old roads impassable. As the presence of these visitors played a decisive role in the move to protect the town from the excesses of the enclosure movement which swept England after 1770,[14] it is necessary to consider these visitors, before taking up the important matter of the enclosure of the royal forest.

One especially revealing official statistic enables comparison between Harrogate's pre and post turnpike / enclosure eras to be made: the War Office returns for 'spare' beds and 'standings' for horses, both of which were

PLATE 85
The arrival of the Harrogate stage-coach was a keenly anticipated event. One of the best places to view the arrivals was the crossroads opposite Hattersley's Hotel.

required for military billeting, and which have hitherto been totally ignored by historians of the royal forest and wapentake. By 1720, Harrogate with Sulphur Wells (Low Harrogate) was listed with 101 spare, or hireable beds, whereas busy Boroughbridge on the Great North Road had only 42, Knaresborough 67, and Northallerton (another important stop for travellers) a mere 38 (A.207). By the time of the 1756 return, these figures were 104 beds at Boroughbridge, 95 beds at Knaresborough, and an unknown figure of not more than 178 beds at Harrogate, which in the 1756 return was counted as an 'outride' of Knaresborough (Northallerton's separate figure was also obscured) (A.212.b). These official figures reveal yet again the growth of visitor accommodation in Harrogate during the seventeenth century.

The thriving condition of the spa as a rendezvous for 'fashionables' is demonstrated by the number of celebrities who frequented it, and of these, the most powerful was Lord Bute, who, on 26 May 1762, became Prime Minister. Bute visited Harrogate in the summer of 1763 (C.36.a–b), the same year as the philosopher David Hume (C.34), the diarist Dr Alexander Carlyle (C.38) and the novelist, Lawrence Sterne. Sterne revisited Harrogate in 1764, riding from Shandy Hall on horseback, and spending his week's visit at the

Dragon Hotel (C.40) where his friend Dr Kilvington was in attendance. Dr Carlyle's record provides the best insight to the resort at this time:

> Harrogate at this time was very pleasant, for there was a constant succession of good company, and the best entertainment of any watering-place in Britain, at the least expense. The house we were at was not only frequented by the Scotch at this time, but was the favourite house of the English nobility and gentry [i.e. the Granby]. Breakfast cost gentlemen only two-pence a piece for their muffins, as it was the fashion for ladies to furnish the tea and sugar ... The estates of the people at our table did not amount to less than £50,000 or £60,000 per annum, among whom were several members of parliament ... (C.38.b).

Carlyle also saw Lord Clive (of India) at the Granby, and witnessed his reception of the disastrous news that the government had confiscated his extensive Indian estates (C.38.d). 'Harrogate abounded with half-pay officers and clergymen. The first are much the same at all times, ill-educated but well-bred ... Of the clergy ... they are in general – I mean the lower order – divided into bucks and prigs ...' (C.38.g). Life at Harrogate was summed up by the author of *Humours of Harrogate*: 'Ah! Harrogate, that land of mirth, so famed of late for romp and riot, beaux and belles ...' (C.35), which may in part explain the spa's attraction to Tobias Smollett, the popular novelist, who visited the town in 1766 during preparatory work on *The Expedition of Humphrey Clinker*, his final novel. Smollett arrived in Harrogate in May 1766, midway on his journey between London and Scotland, where he hoped to convalesce after a serious illness. When *Humphrey Clinker* was published in 1771, the year of Smollett's death, it was clear that the author had made good use of his time in Harrogate. The novel relates the experiences of a group of gentlefolk who visit many spas, and it is proof of the importance of Harrogate at this point that it and Bath receive more attention that any other resort (C.44). Smollett's characters relate the stages of their 'expedition' in a series of colourful letters, and although *Humphrey Clinker* is primarily a work of fiction, the description of Harrogate is obviously based on the author's 1766 visit, and includes several important points.

The Melford character in *Humphrey Clinker* refers to five separate (i.e. principal) inns, which must be High Harrogate's Dragon, Granby, Queen and Salutation, and Low Harrogate's Crown, noting that the company at each inn visit the wells each morning in their own carriages. 'The lodgers of each inn form a distinct society that sat together; and there is a commodious public room, where they breakfast in dishabille, at separate tables, from eight o'clock till eleven, as they chance or choose to come in.' This reference to the extended breakfast period probably illustrates the early morning habit of water-drinking, followed by breakfast, followed by the effects of the purging nature of many of the waters. Equally, it may be proof of the habit of late nights!

Melford continued his letter: 'There is a public ball by subscription every night at one of the houses [i.e. hotels], to which all the company from the others are admitted by tickets [in the nineteenth century this habit led to the publication of lists of visitors]; and indeed, Harrogate treads on the heels of Bath, in the articles of gaiety and dissipation – with this difference, however, that here we are more sociable and familiar …' (C.44.b). This reference to Harrogate's easy informality was repeated by several later authors, not always with approval (C.56.c), and helps us appreciate why Harrogate was such a magnet to the higher aristocracy in search of a genuine health spa.

Smollett, as a medical man, did not pass the opportunity to describe in graphic and somewhat lurid detail the bathing practices at Harrogate, making his Mathew Bramble character spend an hour in a tub full of hot sulphur water, followed by an hour sweating in dirty blankets, which had been used by many previous occupants. As a consequence of this dire experience, Smollett give his character a 'violent haemorrhage' (C.44.h).

Smollett's dreadful description of spa treatments, admittedly in a vein of high humour, failed to frighten away visitors, and the Yorkshire newspapers continued to advertise improvements to Harrogate's inns (R.562) and transportation (R.490), which would only have been undertaken against a background of continued public patronage. Yet at this time, Harrogate did indeed face a threat, not from the pen of Dr Smollett, but from possible action from Parliament and the enclosure movement, which our next chapter will consider.

Harrogate and the enclosure of the Forest

6

IT IS NOT TOO FANCIFUL to claim that the threat which faced Harrogate in the mid-eighteenth century had implications as severe as those of the plague visitations of the fourteenth century, the difference being that whereas the latter had threatened the extermination of human life, the former threatened the destruction of human livelihood. The essence of the threat was this: Harrogate's lands were part of the royal forest, and apart from the copyhold enclosures on which people lived and farmed, all land was open and unenclosed, including that land on which the mineral springs arose. Consequently visitors to the wells enjoyed free and unhindered access, and the town's doctors, innkeepers, and much of its resident population derived their livings from the visitors and their requirements. However, if the open lands and their wells were to be sold, the new owners could enclose them, destroy the wells, charge high entrance fees, or generally discourage the visitors, ruining the residents' principal business. This an idle fear, as rich landowners such as the Lascelles of Harwood were well placed to purchase all the land they wanted, and then to manage it purely in the interests of agriculture, which was becoming ever more profitable, thanks to the twin problems of the wars with France and the growing population of England, whose food demands increased greatly with the industrial revolution and society's resulting urbanisation.

An important consideration of the enclosure movement was that British agriculture was hampered by adhering to the medieval practice of strip-cultivation, a system which favoured the poor, with their few strips of cultivatable land, often divided from one another by their neighbours' holdings, and supplemented only by access to the open common lands, and their grazing rights, which had been a boon to the poor 'from time immemorial'. The peak of the enclosure movement was between 1730 and 1794, and if this time is divided into five-year periods, the greatest number of enclosure acts occurred between 1770 and 1794, when 319 were passed by

Parliament.[1] Lands held by the Crown and by the Duchy of Lancaster were not immune to calls for enclosure, and indeed the Duchy had been considering the matter well before the eighteenth century, not so much to improve agricultural efficiency, but because of the increasing number of illicit enclosures which deprived the copyhold tenants of their grazing land and the Duchy of their rents. An enquiry of 1708 revealed that annual income to the value of two shillings and nine pence was lost within Bilton-with-Harrogate through the illicit incroachment of thirty land enclosures and four cottages (B.16.b), the scale of which may be understood by comparing it with the total yearly rent for the entire Honour of Knaresborough of £110 10s. 8¼d. Timble had an even higher loss at £1 13s. 4½d., so it was clear that controls were needed. A further report showed that Bilton-with-Harrogate and Beckwith-with-Rossett contained sixty-seven incroachments, by far the greatest number in the forest, save for Timble's seventy-five,. The report ending with the ominous note, 'besides many other Incroachments then making but not completed' (B.19.g).

Forty years later, the number of illicit cottages in Harrogate had reached approximately 28 (the highest in the forest) with land incroachments at 32 (surpassed by Thruscross, Felliscliff, Birstwith, Clifton, Menwith-with-Darley and Timble). A survey of 1766 revealed that some of these incroachments had been reduced, but as Harrogate's total figure was around 54, the loss of Duchy income was evident. (B.19.j). An earlier report of 5 December 1698 had shown that most of Harrogate's illicit cottage inclosures were around the Old Sulphur Well, and that although some of those responsible had been brought before the Court, few of the fines had been paid. (B.19.2).

On 15 July 1767 the Duchy issued a commission for a thorough survey of the forest, which began on 5 September (B.22), their return being made in January 1768. This return included reference to the important wells in Beckwith-with-Rossett (the Low Harrogate part of Pannal) and Bilton-with-Harrogate: 'the said wells or springs of water were of a medicinal nature the same being resorted to by persons of all ranks, several large inns have been built … the company resorting … being very numerous.' (B.23.b) The following month the Duchy announced its intention to apply to Parliament for an Act to enclose the forest, and that it would seek the opinions of the existing copyholders (B.24). Enclosure has generally been agreed as a controversial, even a retrograde development in British urban history, and the Act of 1770 for 'Dividing and Inclosing such of the open parts of the district called the Forest of Knaresborough, in the County of York, as lie within the eleven Constableries …' occurred at a time in British history which saw a surge of enclosure activity.[2]

Writers such as W. H. R. Curtler[3] and the Hammonds[4] agreed that the enclosure movement was best attributed to the greed of the landowners.

They also argued that in some places the labouring classes suffered a shocking deterioration of self-sufficiency, self-esteem, and standards of living, as the enclosure movement gathered momentum. In their important study of the government of England before the Reform Bill, the Hammonds certainly presented strong evidence in support of the claim that the enclosure movement was a disaster for the English peasant community: 'In England, the aristocracy destroyed the promise of . . . development when it broke the back of the peasant community . . . the peasant . . . standing in rags . . . makes way for the labourer with no corporate rights to defend . . . No class in the world has so beaten and crouching a history . . .' These were strong words, which – in many cases – appear to have been justified. Yet in their attempts to record the disadvantages of enclosure, they overstated their case with respect to Knaresborough Forest. For example: 'It would not have been very easy for a meanly inhabited man to make the journey to London from Wakefield or Knaresborough or Haute Huntre, even if he knew when a Bill was coming on . . .'[5] In fact, there was no need for the 'meanly inhabited man' to make the journey to London, as the Duchy surveyors held public meetings in the Royal Forest (B.29) and advertised the fact repeatedly (R.435).

The Hammonds also appear to have confused Knaresborough township, with the Royal Forest of Knaresborough, as in the above example. Knaresborough township was never in the Royal Forest of Knaresborough, and was therefore excluded from the enclosure process. Commenting on disappointed claimants, the Hammonds noted, 'At Armley and Knaresborough the final decision was left to arbitrators, but whereas at Armley the arbitrator was to be chosen by a neutral authority, the Record of Leeds, the arbitrators at Knaresborough were named in the Act, and were presumably as much the nominees of the promoters as the commissioners themselves.'[6] In fact, the arbitrators appear to have been selected by Samuel Powell, Under-Steward to the Forest, because they lived beyond its boundaries, and were therefore not affected by the Award. One of them, John Aspinal, was described as a 'Serjeant at Law' of Lincoln's Inn Field (B.29, entry 23/5/1773). Finally, the Hammonds claimed that commissioners 'can reject [the cottager's] claim on the ground of any technical irregularity . . . by several persons interested in the enclosure of Knaresborough Forest',[7] and that, 'at Knaresborough and Louth the poor got nothing at all'.[8] Yet the records of the commissioners are filled with correspondence from the foresters (B.29, entry 10/9/1773), which received due consideration by the Chief Duchy surveyor, Francis Russell (B.29, pp. 24–8). As for the poor, far from their getting 'nothing at all' they received, under the Great Award of 1778, allotments in all the Forest townships (e.g. 'Clint Poor', 'Killinghall Poor', 'Menwith-with-Darley Poor' etc.) including 'for the Poor of Bilton-with-Harrogate . . . incroachment 382 . . . incroachment 387' as well as money

payments for 'charitable uses', the right of access to 'common watering
place' and even to 'common stone quarries or places for collecting of stone'
(B.31, poor award clauses).

In Harrogate the orderly transference of unenclosed lands which were
subject to right of communal access and use, to enclosed lands which were
in the hands of individual owners, had advantages for both sides. First, the
Duchy, as owners of the freehold, often found themselves in the position of
having to maintain a complicated and expensive administration which
produced a low income (the 'fine' of tenancy agreements) effectively frozen
in tradition (the 'fine certain'). Conversely, the more ambitious tenants
were discouraged from undertaking much needed building or development
work, as they could not foresee a time when they might own outright the
subject of their labours or investment. Secondly, enclosure promised large
sums for those selling freeholds, the payment of which should thereby act
as an incentive to buyers to ensure the proper management of their
investment.

Moreover, the Duchy of Lancaster was not a common landlord. The
researches of Sir Robert Somerville have shown that in its actions as
landlord, the Duchy has always been more interested in long-term stability
than short-term gain. This was especially true during periods when the
monarchy was unpopular, or when republicanism was in the air – such as
the years of George III's illness, or Victoria's withdrawal from public life
after the death of the Prince Consort. Clearly it would have been dangerous
for the Duchy to have further alienated public opinion by forcing unpopular
enclosures on its holdings and tenants.[9]

This did not occur at Knaresborough Forest, despite the claims of the
Hammonds.[10] Apart from Knaresborough Forest, there are the examples of
Cowick and Snaith in 1752; Scalby in 1771; Enfield Chase in 1777; Pontefract
Park, in 1780; Pickering in 1785; and Needwood in 1801. In all of these areas,
enclosure was undertaken with due regard for the welfare of tenants, and in
all cases the outcome was generally regarded as an improvement.[11] For
example, at Pickering, the 1785 enclosure was described by Gilbert Slater in
the following words: 'I must here refer to the extraordinary act by which
Pickering Moor was enclosed in 1785 and divided equally among all owners
of common rights, the poorest cottager owning an ancient cottage getting
as much as the largest landowner.'[12]

The extent of the Duchy's public consultation was also unusual, as before
1774 it had not been necessary for a landowner to even notify his neighbours
that he was asking Parliament for permission to redistribute their land. In
1774, the House of Commons made a Standing Order providing that notice
of any such petition should be affixed to the church door in each of the
parishes affected.[13] The Duchy, as owner of the Forest of Knaresborough,

approached the subject of enclosure with great care. Such care was necessary, for along with the many advantages it might bring, enclosure would certainly threaten those landholders who had illegally encroached on the Forest (B.25). Moves taken in 1615 to enclose the Forest had met with failure, largely because of the resistance from the larger landowners, who feared that their illicit holdings would have to be paid for at full value. The Duchy Commissioners met the 'better sort of Bilton-with-Harrogate and Knaresborough to discuss the advantages of enclosure ... and do find them unwilling thereunto, as men respecting neither the king's profit nor their own' (B.13).

Survey

A thorough survey of the Forest was undertaken by the Duchy in 1767 (see plan 9), as a result of the king's commission of 15 July of that year, 'the commissioners thereto directed for perambulating and ascertaining the metes and boundaries of his Forest of Knaresborough ...' (B.23. b). When the return was completed in January 1768 the commissioners made special reference to the mineral wells at Harrogate:

> And we do further certify that upon a certain open part of the said Forest ... called the Sulphur Wells but now known by the name of Low Harrogate, it was some years since discovered that the Waters springing at the said Wells were of a medicinal nature and the same being resorted to by a great number of persons of all ranks, several large inns have been ... built near the same ... for their reception ... and the said Wells or springs of water being unenclosed and open have hitherto been and now are used in common, and the company resorting to the said two Hamlets (i.e. Bilton-with-Harrogate, and the Sulphur Wells part of Pannal) ... increasing and becoming very numerous ... (B.23.b)

Opinions

Having thus been advised of the significance of the mineral wells, the Duchy set about obtaining the opinions of the copyholders of the Forest, making it clear that, unlike earlier schemes for enclosure, there would be no requirement on purchasers to pay a continuing rent to the Duchy (B.24). Responses were mixed, but one return signed by 118 tenants included a specific request that any enclosure should safeguard the mineral springs. In view of the importance of this request, it is reproduced, as follows:

> We whose names are herewith subscribed being intitled as Freeholders or as customary tenants of the Forest of Knaresborough ... certain

springs of medicinal waters commonly called Harrogate Spaws to which during the Summer season great variety of genteel company constantly resort for the benefit of the water, to the great advantage not only of the Inn-Holders in the neighbourhood, but also of the farmers for many miles around on account of the extraordinary consumption of the produce of their respective farms occasioned thereby ... In order that such advantages may not be frustrated by the intended enclosure and division, may it be enacted that for the purpose aforesaid, 200 acres be left open and converted into a stinted pasture upon which such number of cattle shall be grazed by each of the freeholders and copyholders ... (B.24.b)

This plea was heard by the Duchy, and when the Act of enclosure of 10 George III, 1770, became law, it contained authority in section 44 for the commissioners to 'leave open 200 acres adjoining or near Harrowgate Spaws.' (J.1)

Opposition

Opposition to the proposed enclosure was described in colourful language:

these cormorants, dreading to be ... forced to disgorge such delicious morsels, began 'to form their own confederacies ... and draw in their unwary well meaning neighbours ... to oppose an enclosure, and to varnish over their own unwarrantable deeds with the specious pretences of public good (including) ... the care of the poor, whom they take care to keep poor enough. (B.25)

The opponents of enclosure got up a petition, which gave expression to a number of vague fears, of which the following extract is fairly typical:

... [we are] very sorry that we cannot concur with your Lordship ... [we] are of the opinion that the enclosing ... will be very prejudicial and detrimental ... High Roads will be a very great additional charge to most of the hamlets ... copyholders estates lessened ... expence of Commissioners ... so great ... no profit ... greatly affect the Woollen [sic] manufactory ... enclosure ... will make the poor more numerous and the rates lie very heavily upon the copyholders and their tenants ...

The petition was signed by 179 people, the majority of whom could only mark their signatures by means of a cross. In an accompanying note, the Chancellor of the Duchy was advised that

... there is ... [the] ... petition to the Chancellor, signed by a great

number of the lower classes of people praying that the Enclosure may
not be proceeded in. Upon enquiry, it is found that this petition had
been obtained and got signed at the instigation of eleven ... people ...
all of whom tho' in a low station of life are men of property, and are in
the possession of large incroachments of land of a few years standing,
stolen of the Forest ... they very well know that in the case of a general
enclosure ... their incroachments will be more than they will be intitled
to ... they have joined together and made it their business to go
amongst the lower class of people ... instigating and stirring them up to
an opposition of a Bill being passed for an enclosure ... (B.30,
pp. 56b–58b)

The opposition came to nothing, as it does not appear that the opponents
could persuade the Duchy to accept them as being representative of the
population at large.

Commissioners

Those charged with the implementation of the new Act soon found that
their problems had not ended with the Royal Assent. For once the Bill
became law, the matter of claims and counter-claims regarding plots of
land, water courses, stone quarries, etc. would inevitably be raised. The Act
of 1770 named and appointed commissioners 'for setting out, dividing,
assigning, and allotting all the open commonable grounds and waste lands
within the said eleven constabularies, and for putting this Act in execution'
(J.I). Those appointed were William Hill of Tadcaster, Gentleman, Joseph
Butler of Bowthorpe, Surveyor, William Chippendale of Ripley, Surveyor,
John Flintoff of Boroughbridge, Surveyor, and Thomas Furness of Otley,
Gentleman. None of these men was from within the Forest. The eighth
section of the Act required that the newly appointed surveyors should
survey the Forest, along with one Richard Richardson, surveyor of
'Darlington in the Bishoprick of Durham', who was appointed as an extra
commissioner by a separate Act of 1774. The Commissioners were to hold
their first meeting on 25 June 1770 at the Crown Inn, Harrogate, the meeting
to be publicised by means of notices affixed to the doors of churches and
chapels, as well as through advertisements in the *Leeds Mercury* and *York
Courant* (B.29). When the advertisement appeared in the *York Courant* for 5
June 1770 (R.435), it advised that the newly appointed commissioners
intended 'to set out and sell so much of the wastes as will raise a competent
sum of money to pay the expenses of obtaining the said Act and of carrying
the same into execution; of making the ring fences of all of the allotments,
and for making the new public roads and highways.' This proved

_____

PLAN II
1778 Enclosure,
Harlow Hill to West
Park. Note the
triangular 'Bogs
Field' at centre. The
King's lands to the
north later became
the 'Duchy' estate.

contentious, as some of the lands selected for sale were regarded as being more properly land for direct allotment. For example, when the commissioners identified a parcel of land between Harrogate and Knaresborough, called 'Belmont', as being suitable land to sell, Knaresborough objected on the grounds that since 'Belmont' had been traditionally farmed by Knaresborough, the application of sale proceeds would benefit communities within the Forest, which excluded Knaresborough. 'Belmont', they thought, should be directly allotted to Knaresborough township. An appeal to the arbitrators resulted in the judgement that the commissioners could not sell the land in question (B.26) – a further refutation of the Hammonds' contention that the Knaresborough Forest arbitrators would deal with pleadings in an unsympathetic manner.[14]

The Commissioners appointed by the Duchy went about their business in an open and fair manner, unlike the five Commissioners appointed by Parliament to oversee the enclosure of common lands at Leamington, under the 1767 enclosure act. Whereas the Leamington Commissioners were empowered to extinguish all rights of common, the Knaresborough Forest Commissioners were required, at Harrogate, to set aside two hundred acres of land to be 'forever open and uninclosed'. The Leamington

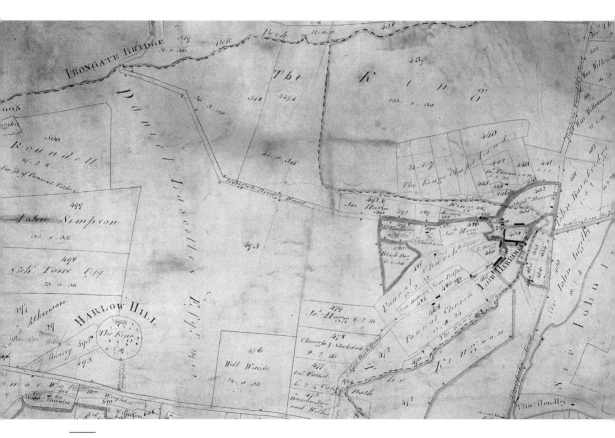

PLAN 12
1778 Enclosure,
showing the area
from Harlow to Park
Parade. Note the
boundary between
Bilton-with-
Harrogate and
Pannal townships.

Commissioners were excused the necessity for public meetings, and did not even have to maintain records of their proceedings, whereas the Knaresborough Forest Commissioners observed every opportunity to inform the public, and maintained meticulous records.[15]

The perambulation began at 9.00 a.m. on Monday 13 August 1770, meeting in Forest Lane, and thereafter the commissioners met frequently to complete the survey (B.29). In the course of their visits, the commissioners met with many disputes concerning properties, boundaries and rights of access, some of which they were able to resolve on the spot, others being recorded for future deliberation. In a few cases, deliberation meant obtaining counsel's opinion, for which a fee was payable. This in turn put pressure on the commissioners to resolve the question of which of the wastes could be sold to raise money for expenses. A major dispute arose on 10 September between the surveyors and several of the townships regarding the boundary of a piece of land on the river Crimple, near Fulwith Mill outside Harrogate. The commissioners judged this land to be part of the township of Spofforth, and therefore outside the Forest boundary. Local farmers, however, regarded the land as being within the Forest, and therefore ripe for enclosure and sale (B.29). Such disputes were commonplace.

It is clear from a reading of their recorded proceedings that the commissioners were uncertain as to their legal rights regarding the sale of waste lands to raise money for their various expenses, and that they sought advice from the Solicitor of the Duchy, Mr Russell, who replied on 9 December 1770 with a letter of clarification (B.29, separate letter attached).

The survey proceeded slowly, because of the unusually bad weather, and by 2 April 1771, the commissioners reported that their progress in the wilder rural parts of the Forest had been severely hindered. By way of compensation, they appear to have attended to much of that part of their work which could be dealt with on paper, such as the future layout of the road system, fixing the public roads in Harrogate 'to be sett out 60 feet wide ... and also the remainder of the eleven Constabularies' (B.29, entry of 27 December 1770).

A meeting on 23 December at the Crown in Harrogate minuted that 'the surveyors having not been able to complete their plans of the survey of the Forest ...' was followed on 27 December with a visit from Mr Russell himself, who advised that in view of the reported difficulties encountered by the commissioners in putting the Act of 1770 into effect, the Chancellor and Council of the Duchy had instructed him to draft a bill to put to parliament. Mr Russell then read the draft (B.29, minute of meeting of 27 December 1770) explaining that among other things, it would:

Repeal so much of the 1770 Act as directs any sale of land for raising expenses and for substituting a provision for charging upon every involved individual their respective shares.

To enact that the contentious portion of land called Belmont shall be subject to the same distribution &c. as the other waste lands.

To charge the lands inclosed for Harrogate Chapel with an annual stipend of £30 for the benefit of the Chaplain or Minister for ever.

The first item provided an alternative means of raising money for expenses other than that of selling part of the waste lands. The second item – which had been the real source of the contention about the sale of lands – was being suggested after consultation with the affected Townships (Knaresborough and Bilton-with-Harrogate), had revealed that this might be acceptable (B.29, minute of meeting of 27 December 1770) The third item safeguarded the stipend of the Minister of Harrogate Chapel, previously paid from the value of crops raised and sold on lands given by the Duchy for that special purpose, but which were now subject to enclosure and sale.

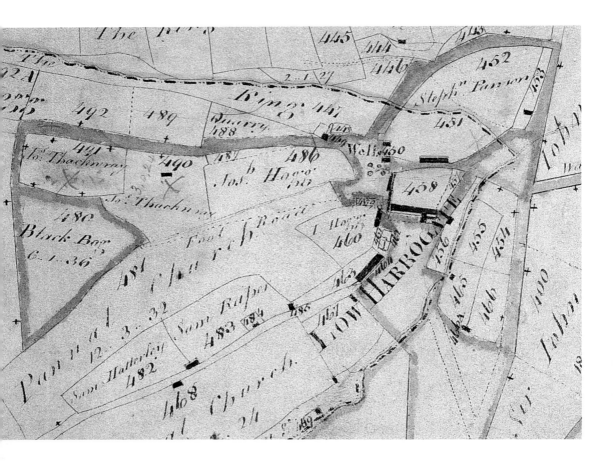

PLAN 13
1778 Enclosure, Bogs Field to Parliament Street. The thick line represented land that was part of the Stray. This included much of the modern Cornwall Road and all of Crescent Road.

The efficient Mr Russell then produced two engrossments of a petition proposed to be offered to Parliament in case the amended bill should be approved by the meeting. The outcome of all Mr Russell's work was that the first item was not adopted; the second – relating to Belmont – was left to the inhabitants of Knaresborough to consider (the inhabitants of Bilton-with-Harrogate already knowing that the commissioners regarded Belmont as being part of their Township); and the third item stood or was to be varied as the Vicar of Knaresborough thought fit. In other words, nothing was resolved and the whole exercise had been a waste of time. The commissioners went a stage further in their time-wasting at their meeting of 13 January 1772 at the White Horse Inn in Coppergate, York, when they recorded that Mr Russell's proposals had been entered in the proceedings book *without their formal permission*, and that they should accordingly be struck out! (B.29, entry for 13 January 1772).

One of the biggest landholders in the Forest of Knaresborough was the Duke of Devonshire, who had leased the whole of the Honour of Knaresborough from the Duchy in the eighteenth century, surrendering it only in

December 1897.[16] It is therefore not surprising to find that the duke's agents were among the most frequent complainants during the commissioners' proceedings. It is evidence for the objectivity of the commissioners that the complaints of the agents of the duke received the same degree of attention as was given to those of the poorest foresters.

The greatest part of the Harrogate area had been surveyed by the summer of 1773. The all important mineral wells, together with the lands on which they were situated, were visited by the commissioners on 7 April 1773, and the final bounds were determined of what later became known as the Stray (B.29, entry for 7 April 1772). This was to have a profound influence on the future growth of Harrogate, as it not only protected the wells, but provided a framework for both High and Low Harrogate around which controlled development could occur. Having attended to the Harrogate area of the Forest, the commissioners continued their work in the surrounding villages and Forest. At the same time, the commissioners dealt with claims and counter-claims from the Harrogate area about boundaries, rights of way, and a host of other matters relating to the enclosure.

PLAN 14
1778 Enclosure, Cold Bath Road. At the top may be seen the 'foot road' that became Valley Gardens.

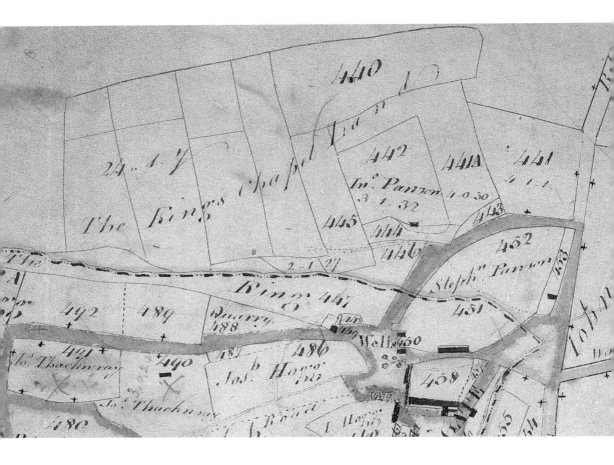

PLAN 15
1778 Enclosure,
King's lands, later
Duchy estate.

Allotments. The substantial task of setting out each allotment within the Forest appears to have been completed by July 1775, for in a letter dated 4 July 1775 John Bainbridge, a local surveyor who was also employed by the commissioners, wrote to Francis Russell at the Duchy:

> We have now set out every person's allotment on the plans throughout the whole Forest ... I have had a very tedious time of staking out the allotments under the new Act ... The Foresters are very riotous and have given me a great deal of trouble – the greatest thing we have to combat is their cutting up the soil for turves off the allotments, and the greatest part of the people who do this are not worth a shilling and of course cannot be prosecuted for a trespass ... (B.28.b)

Fortunately for Mr Bainbridge, he did not suffer the fate of a fencer of enclosures at Little Malvern, who was murdered, together with three of his family, for his innocent role in the enclosure of Malvern Chase.[17] It was shortly after Mr Bainbridge's complaint that the first sales of the 'waste' land within the Forest were held.

Sale

Surveyor Richardson advised the Duchy of the results of the sale of 19 July 1775, which was carried out in the form of an auction, with bids on slips of paper being handed in to the presiding officials. For example, a bid from one Cook:

> I agree to give seven pounds a year for ten acres, part of lot 15 on the west side as stacked [sic] out to run from the Turnpike Road to the utmost extent southwards, and on the terms mentioned, & to pay five pounds towards the lease. [signed] William Cook. (B.28.d.2)

At their meeting in the Horse and Groom Inn at Knaresborough on 1 June 1778, the commissioners minuted that they had '... proceeded further in examining the ingrossed part of the Award and contracted for a second reduction of the plan to be annexed to the Award, which is supposed to require six weeks to finish it ...' (B.29, entry for 1 June 1778)

Award

The final version of the Great Award was signed and sealed by the commissioners on 19 August 1778, with the copy having been made at the Duchy Office by 16 September. It was a formidable document, consisting of fifty-three closely written skins of parchment. The sections dealing with Harrogate were of such enormous significance for the future development of the town that they deserve to be considered in detail.

The Award opened with the naming of five stone quarries, which were to be public, identified by means of their extent in acres, roods and perches, as well as by a map reference. These quarries were in effect a gift from the King, and ringed the town in strategic positions. Almsford Bank lay to the south, Knox and Oak Beck to the north, Harlow Hill to the west, the eastern part of the area being served by the Hookstone quarry that was allotted to the existing tenant. Common watering places (nothing to do with the mineral wells) were then identified and described, the two most significant being at the 'Cold Bath', to the west, and at the 'World's End' to the north. The turnpike roads and other highways were then identified and measured, followed by an account of public bridle paths, public foot roads (i.e. footpaths), and waterways. These subjects formed only a short preamble to the main part of the Award, which consisted of descriptions of each allotment, with details of the person to whom the allotment was being made; a description of whether the land was an existing allotment or an encroachment; the number on the accompanying plan; the quantity in acres, roods, and perches; the type of tenure; where the land was situated; and the boundaries of the surrounding allotments. It must be appreciated that the commissioners were only too aware of their responsibilities to the

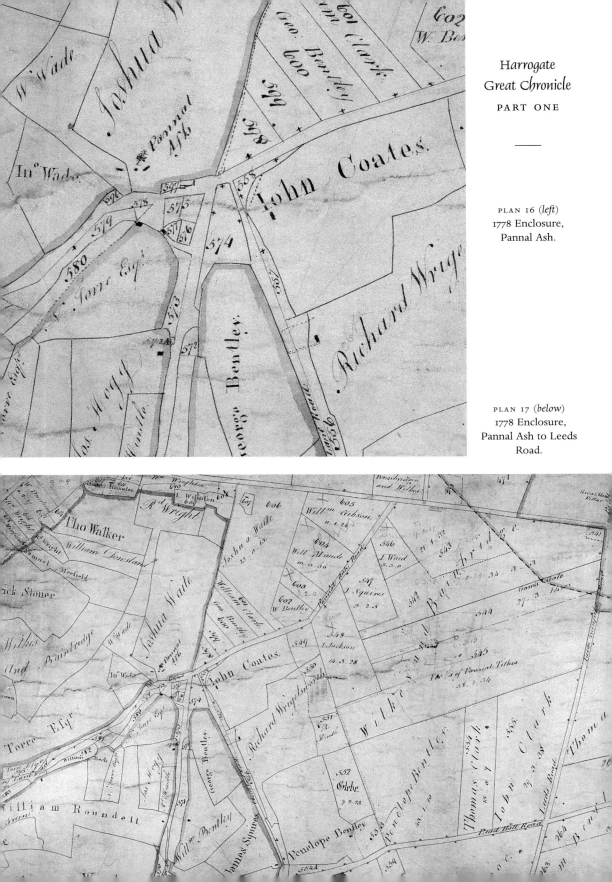

Harrogate
Great Chronicle

PART ONE

———

PLAN 16 (*left*)
1778 Enclosure,
Pannal Ash.

PLAN 17 (*below*)
1778 Enclosure,
Pannal Ash to Leeds
Road.

The handwritten labels on the map read: "Tho. Hendley", "Elizabeth. Hartl...", "398", "397", "396", "Tewit Well".

PLAN 18
1778 Enclosure, York Place to Tewit Well. The track at lower right later became Oatlands Drive.

king, as not all of the king's inheritance was to be given away or sold. What came to be known as the 'King's lands' were simply those parts of the Forest which were reserved for the king's use. Twenty such allotments were made to the king, the majority of them at Harrogate, with only two located beyond the boundary of the modern town, at Clint and Thruscross. The Harrogate lands allotted to the king remained under the direct control of the Duchy, including land near the wells (see plans 13 and 15), or overlooking the 200 acres (see plan 11), which was obviously of high value for development. The fact that such development would be under the direct control of the Duchy, with their high standards, meant there was every likelihood that key parts of Harrogate would receive buildings which were well designed and soundly built (B.31).

Allotments and encroachments formed two distinct categories. The former were lands leased to tenants, either for forty years, or in some cases for life, that were subject to a rent (or fine, as it was termed) which was recorded in the court rolls. It was possible under the Forest Customs to demise lands to sons, daughters, or wives. In such cases, the roll recorded '. . . and upon this cometh the said . . . and prays to be admitted to his fine' with a

note of the fine paid being entered in the margin. The majority of such allotments had their origins in illicit enclosures dating back to the earliest days of the Forest, the makers of which, when caught, were obliged to pay a fine. Over the centuries such fines were a useful source of income to whoever held the Forest, thus ensuring that the fines became translated into rents.[18]

Encroachments were allotments taken from the Forest without the legality of the customary fine having been paid. Such encroachments were disliked by the majority of copyhold tenants, because they were taken from the open 'common' upon which all Foresters had rights of access and grazing. In Knaresborough Forest, it was the sheer scale of illicit encroachment which brought about the enclosure, rather than the kind of incipient greed on the owner's part, as intimated by the Hammonds and others.

An investigation in 1766 revealed 37 illicit encroachments had been within the past forty years in Bilton-with-Harrogate, and about 20 in the Harrogate part of Beckwith-with-Rossett, or Pannal. Given that such encroachments had an average size of 3 acres, and included cottages and other buildings, it can be seen that they represented loss of both common grazing land for the regular copyholders, as well as rents to the lord of the Forest. The Award listed all the encroachments discovered by the commissioners and set out charges to be paid by the tenants if they wished to continue occupation. Naturally, the charges varied with the size of the encroachment and the perceived value of the land. A tiny encroachment up in High Harrogate made by 'Eli Hargrove at the Toy shop, number 286' was valued at a half penny, whereas an 'encroachment near the Sulphur Well in Low Harrogate, belonging to Jonathan Leatham, no. 484, we charge with the value of nine shillings and fourpence' (B.31).

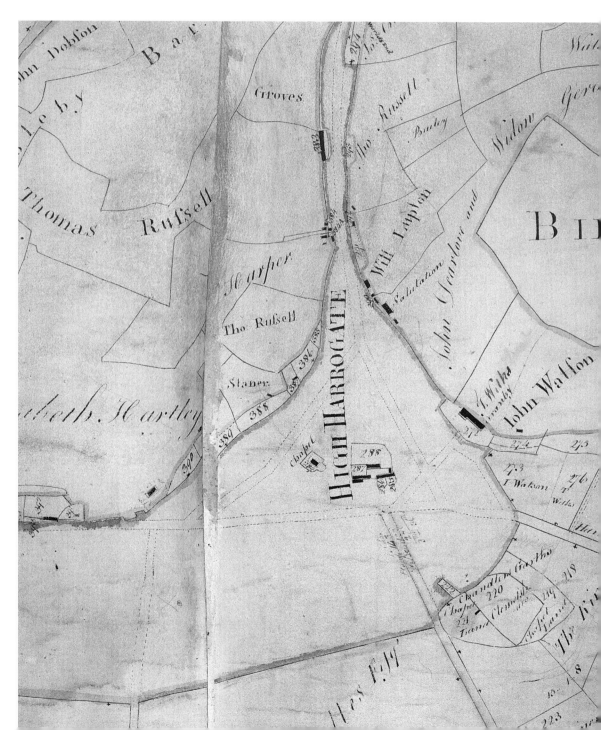

Any encroachments not taken by their occupant were sold at auction. The majority of parcels of land identified as either allotments or encroachments contained between one to two acres. Some, however, were much larger. Within Harrogate, Alexander Wedderburn, Lord Loughborough (later earl of Rosslyn and Lord Chancellor of England), held 271 acres, 2 roods, 38 perches, and Daniel Lascelles of Harewood House held 336 acres, 5 roods. The king's holdings in the wider Forest were 2,385 acres, those within Harrogate being little over 600 acres. In exchange for his hitherto valueless rights as lord of the Forest, George III secured a valuable inheritance for his Duchy of Lancaster.[19]

The main Award was followed with the identification of lands and buildings dedicated for charitable use, being awarded to the poor of Bilton-with-Harrogate, and other communities within the Forest, such as Killinghall, Clint, and Fewston. The penultimate section of the Award dealt with the important and special matter of the two hundred acres for the protection of the mineral wells. These two hundred acres were laid out in such a manner as to connect all of the *known* mineral wells on one great expanse of land, which had the dual effect of providing public access to each and every well,

PLAN 21
1778 Enclosure, Granby Corner to Forest Lane Head. Bilton Park at top right was excluded from the enclosure, as it had been sold in 1627 by Charles I.

PLAN 22
1778 Enclosure,
World's End Road.
The road leading
from the top later
became King's Road,
and the 'World's
End' later became
Grove House.

and also of setting out space on which exercise could be had by means of walking, running, riding or driving. The medical men had, since the time of Dr Deane's *Spadacrene Anglica* of 1626, recognised the importance of fresh air and bodily exercise as an adjunct to water drinking (F.3, pp. 127–31).

As may be seen on the plan of the Harrogate part of the Great Award (see plan 10), the two hundred acres lay between the two main thoroughfares of High Harrogate, surrounding the isolated buildings of the chapel and its neighbouring 'Spaw Hill', with a great expanse to the south of the Knaresborough and York road, and an area to the west which adjoined the old turnpike road to Ripon, leading down to the Sulphur Well and the so-called Bogs Field – this last in what is now the Valley Gardens The management of the two hundred acres was in the hands of the owners of a number of imaginary gates, fifty in all, each worth four acres. These 'gates' controlled the pasturing of animals on the two hundred acres, and strict rules for the kind and number of animals were laid down, as there were obviously limits to the amount of grazing which the land could support. Thus, cattle of more than two years old could each be depastured as one gate; three cattle of two years of age could depasture two gates; a calf represented half a gate; a horse of three years or more could have one and a half gates, but under that age such an animal needed only one gate; four sheep would have one gate and these included ewes with unweaned lambs. In the interests of pasture, however, only horses and cattle were to be pastured during the first seven years from 1778. Sheep and lambs could be brought on to the two hundred acres only after that time. As for asses, mules, goats, swine or geese, they were never to be pastured on the two hundred acres. (B.31) It

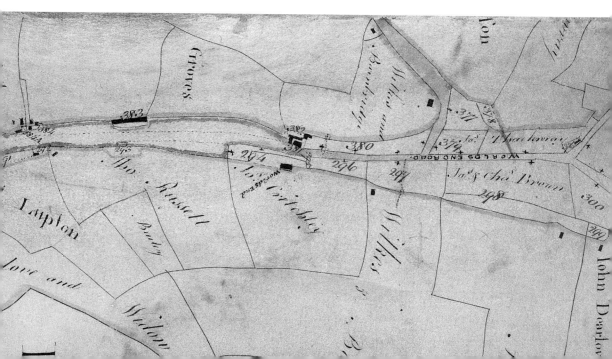

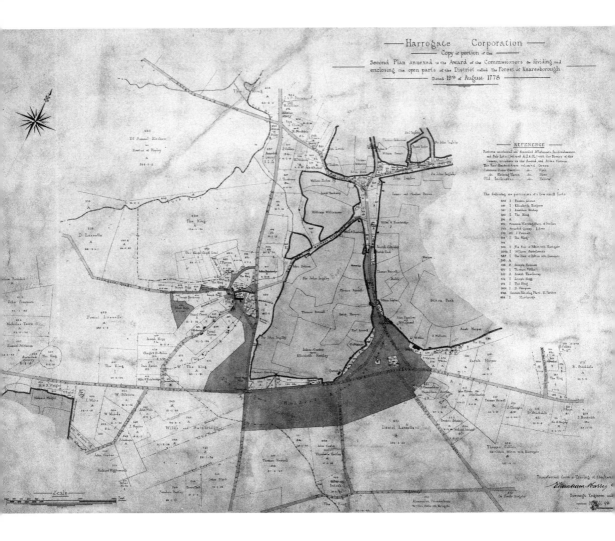

Harrogate Corporation
Copy of portion of the
Second Plan annexed to the Award of the Commissioners for dividing and
enclosing the open parts of the District called The Forest of Knaresborough
Dated 19th of August 1778

PLAN 10
Harrogate and the
1778 Award, copy of
1886.

was the opportunity for the animals depastured on the two hundred acres to roam freely, or to stray without tether, which gave rise to the popular name for the two hundred acres – the Stray.[20]

Although the Award gave the Stray's herbage rights to the gate holders (or Stray owners, as they unfortunately became known) the land, together with its mineral rights, remained the property of the Duchy of Lancaster, who to this day holds title to the freehold of the Harrogate Stray. Ownership of the imaginary 'gates' was determined by assessing the amount of lost grazing rights suffered by those landowners who had enjoyed rights of common over the unenclosed lands of the Forest (J.1, clause 53). Thus an owner such as Sir John Ingilby who had enjoyed extensive rights for grazing was compensated through the awarding of twelve gates. Although neither the 1770 Act, nor the 1778 Award had a word to say about responsibility for the upkeep or improvement of the Stray, the Award concluded with a memorable order which should be taught to every child in Harrogate:

> And we do Award that the said two hundred acres of land shall forever hereafter remain open and unenclosed and all persons whomsoever shall and may have free access at all times to the said springs and be at liberty to use and drink the waters there arising and take the benefit thereof without being subject to the payment of any acknowledgement whatsoever ... (J.31, clause 53)

The 1770 Act and the 1778 Award were not without their imperfections, as was discovered by the townspeople who wanted to effect later improvements. Nevertheless, when the Award became applicable in August 1778, Harrogate was guaranteed possession of two wonderful assets: the Stray, that unsurpassed area of rolling grassland; and a range of mineral waters which the nineteenth century would discover to be the richest supply on the known Earth.

Exclusions

The commissioners treated two areas of medieval Harrogate very differently. Bilton Park was excluded, simply because since its sale by Charles I in 1628 (E.78) it was no longer the king's to enclose. The other area was Belmont, and because of the gradual use of this land by residents and farmers of the Liberty of Knaresborough, following the actions of 1257 (E.8) and 1324 (A.27), as well a probable understanding of the symbolic importance to Knaresborough of the former 'Little Park' (with the Dropping Well and associations with the mythical 'Mother Shipton') much of Belmont land was awarded to residents of Knaresborough township. For example as many as eighty awards within the Belmont/Thistle Hill area were allotted to Knaresborough township (with about seventy-five on Belmont and twelve on Thistle Hill), whereas Scriven-with-Tentergate received only six on Belmont and two on Thistle Hill, Bilton-with-Harrogate a mere three, and Birstwith only a single allotment (B.31). Many of these non-Harrogate allotments were clustered around Belmont Road (later known as Forest Moor Road) which stimulated development at Calcut, although the area's links with Harrogate continued until 1841 and the establishment of the Improvement Commissioners, by which time an inn such as the Union was still within the Bilton-with-Harrogate tax area (W.14.18). The exclusion of the Starbeck wells from the two hundred acres of Stray can only be explained by the fact that by 1778, they were wholly neglected and forgotten (as were the wells at Harlow) by everyone save Eli Hargrove!

Conclusion

There is no evidence to support the opinion that the Duchy officials, in their framing of the Harrogate sections of the Award of 1778, had taken note of the acts which had affected the enclosure of Tunbridge Wells, in 1740,[21] or Buxton in 1771,[22] but in each case protection was given to the wells. At Tunbridge the 1740 Act ensured the integrity of the wells and land around them, which remained open and free for public use, but the rest of the affected land was divided between the new lord of the manor, Maurice Conyers, and the freeholders, led by Lord Abergavenny. At Buxton the Act of 1771 ensured the right of public access to the St Anne's Well and designated the public paths and roads leading to the well as being for ever open and unenclosed, for the use and benefit of nearby inhabitants. Finally the dual role of the Duchy and the Harrogate township authorities – be they Vestry, Improvement Commission, or Council – ensured that no single interest was followed to the harm of public interest. The Harrogate tenants did not suffer the fate of their counterparts in Bath, where seventy years before the Award, speculator Marchant had acquired a nineteen-acre common pasture meadow. Marchant promptly extinguished the tenants' common rights, and sub-let the land for housing, which then experienced a fifteen-fold rise in ground rents over thirty-five years.[23]

The enclosure of the Royal Forest of Knaresborough, which produced such beneficial results for the majority of those involved, was no isolated occurrence. The 1770s was a peak for the enclosure movement, with 321 such Acts being passed, ninety-two of which were in 1777.[24] In the early years of the twentieth century Gilbert Slater wrote – with respect to the enclosure movement – that it was not overstating the case to claim that, 'by nineteen enclosures out of twenty, the poor were injured, in some grossly injured …'[25] Despite their strictures, the enclosure of the Royal Forest of Knaresborough – at least as regards the Harrogate area – was advantageous for the majority of those affected. The Duchy received income for the sale of allotments; the tenants, dominated by no single individual, were able to become owner-occupiers, and embark on widespread improvements to their holdings, and the few Harrogate poor had recognition in the Great Award of 1778. More importantly the entire Harrogate community benefited from the enclosure, having received as a direct gift from the king the incomparable gifts of two hundred acres of open land at the heart of their community, and all the mineral wells which rose upon it (B.31). These benefits were the direct result of the town's association with the Duchy of Lancaster, which is why Harrogate's experience of the enclosure movement was both atypical and fortuitous.

7 | Harrogate spa after 1778

The visitors' view of Harrogate

The visitors who came to Harrogate in the wake of the Award of 1778 found that the spa possessed not only a splendid allotment of open land, over which they could walk or drive without charge, but also Eli Hargrove's new guide book, which had been published in 1775 (G.1). That this book was written for visitors, rather than residents, was a sign of the economic significance of the visitors to the town. An examination of Hargrove's guide book reveals something of what such visitors to Harrogate Spa might have discovered, in the years following the Act of 1770. Hargrove was a bookseller with a taste for antiquarian history, who owned businesses in Harrogate, Knaresborough and York. His Harrogate premises consisted of what today would be called a tourist gift shop, but what the 1778 Award described as 'the Toyshop' (B.31) (C.31.b.31). As a shrewd man of business, Hargrove recognised the sales potential that a guide to Harrogate would have among the many visitors who swarmed to the spa. Accordingly, his guide book passed into many editions. The fifth edition appeared as early as 1798 (G.5).

The wells described by Hargrove consisted of the St John's Well, which Hargrove called the 'Old Spaw', confusing it with the Tewit Well; the real Tewit Well, which Hargrove confuses with the St John's Well; the St Magnus Well; and the Sulphur Wells. This reference to the St Magnus Well was a further error on the author's part, albeit an understandable one. The confusion had really begun with another antiquarian, Thomas Pennant, who visited the Harrogate Cold Bath in 1777 and wrote, 'It appears that St Mungo, a Scottish Saint, who, about the year 543, driven by persecution from his See at Glasgow … visited this place, and left his name to a Well, which it still retains …' (C.52). Pennant had assumed that the Cold Bath at Harrogate was the same as the Cold Well near Knaresborough which had a strong traditional association with St Magnus (or Mungo, or Mongah). He was wrong, as the St Magnus Well was at neighbouring Copgrove, a few miles from Knaresborough. Dr French, writing in his 1652 treatise on the

Yorkshire Spa makes clear in the title: *The York-Shire Spaw; or, a Treatise of four Famous Medicinal Wells, viz, the Spaw, or vitrioline well; the stinking, or sulphur well; the dropping or petrifying well; and St Magnus-Well near Knaresborough ...*

Here French indicated that the first two wells are together at the Yorkshire Spa; the third well is at Knaresborough, and the St Magnus Well is *near* Knaresborough, i.e. at Copgrove (F.6). All of the early writers on Yorkshire wells place the Cold Well, dedicated to St Magnus, at Copgrove. The first definite reference to a Cold Well at Harrogate occurs in Dr Short's history of mineral waters, published in 1734. (F.24, p. 296). Short wrote, '... There is also a very cold well at Harrogate, famed for sore eyes. This, Dr Neale of Doncaster turned into a very good cold bath ...' This cold well at Harrogate must have enjoyed a high rate of use, as it was identified as a common public watering place in the Great Award of 1778 (B.31), the term 'at Cold Baths ... by Cold Bath Road ...' being used. At no place throughout the entire Award is there any mention of the name of St Magnus. It therefore seems likely that the enterprising Mr Hargrove took advantage of earlier confusion about the Cold Wells at both Copgrove and Harrogate, and took the centuries-old dedication of St Magnus from the decayed and forgotten former location, applying it to the popular location in Cold Bath Road.

Fortunately, there is no uncertainty over the sulphur wells mentioned by Hargrove, as these had been known for centuries, and were unique to Harrogate. The Survey of the Forest, which led to the Award of 1778, was completed in the summer of 1775. All of the then used sulphur wells were listed, being included within the two hundred acres 'to be for ever open and uninclosed' (B.31). Hargrove located the Sulphur Wells 'at Low Harrogate, each enclosed in a small neat building of stone. Hither the company resort from all the different Inns, early in the morning, to drink the water; the singular efficacy of which in curing a number of disorders, and particularly that universal one of scurvy, has been happily experienced by thousands of people.'

Hargrove then referred to two other wells, 'situated in the valley about one mile and a half from High Harrogate, near the road leading from thence to Knaresborough. These wells are only eighteen yards distant from each other, and yet as opposite in their natures as possible, the one being a chalybeate, the other a sulphur water. They were (many years ago) in great repute, but are now quite neglected.' (G.1, pp. 44–56). There may have been a mixture of commercial opportunism and antiquarian enthusiasm behind Hargrove's reference to the two neglected wells, which are clearly those at Starbeck, mentioned as having been discovered in late 1626 by a Dr Leake of York (F.4, p. 29). Hargrove's business could only have been improved by the revival of another well in Harrogate, and his historical research would have led him to the once popular Starbeck Wells. Yet his publicity for the Starbeck Wells had little effect, since they had to wait until the revival of 1822 before attracting custom (F.57, p. 12). Finally Hargrove mentioned the Bilton Park Spring, and commended a pamphlet on the Harrogate waters recently published by a Dr Alexander (F.37) – and published and sold by Eli Hargrove!

Having described the wells, Hargrove turned to the other amenities of Harrogate, beginning with the all important inns. 'The inns at Harrogate are large and spacious, and the accommodations, with respect to neatness and good entertainment, can hardly fail to recommend them'. (G.1, pp. 44–56) The inns named are the Granby, the Queen's Head, the Dragon, the Salutation and the World's End, all of which were in High Harrogate within reach of the chalybeate or iron wells. Of the inns of Low Harrogate, there is not a single mention, but then, Hargrove's 'Toyshop' was only located at High Harrogate. Hargrove went on to describe the lifestyle enjoyed by visitors at the High Harrogate inns. In view of the insight afforded the subject, it is instructive to reproduce the section in full:

> These Inns being at some distance from each other, their respective lodgers form distinct societies, and live in the most agreeable manner. Each House has a commodious public room, where the company breakfast on separate tables from eight o'clock till eleven, as they chance or choose to come in. Here also, in the afternoons, it has long been the custom for ladies to give tea in their turns. There are public balls every Monday and Friday (n.b. – there were also public balls at the Crown in Low Harrogate on Wednesday, but Hargrove does not refer to them!) at each House in its turn, to which all the company from the other Houses are invited. Each person pays one shilling on admittance, which is applied towards the expenses, the remaining part of which is paid by those Gentlemen who dance. (G.1)

Buxton, in comparison, possessed three inns, with a total capacity for three hundred guests.[1] And Cheltenham possessed one lodging house and two small inns, with a capacity of sixty-seven guests.[2] Lodging accommodation was even worse at Malvern, which in 1757 had 'only one old house in the town turned to that purpose' with a capacity for fifteen people.[3] At Royal Tunbridge Wells, it appears that in the late 1790s, the 'fashionable' visitors and residents in the season may have amounted to four hundred or so,[4] and Royal Leamington Spa had a single inn, built in 1793, where 'shortage of accommodation, combined with the hostility of local land owners [combined] to act as a brake upon progress'.[5]

Hargrove noted that 'at table each person takes their seat in the same order they arrived at the place, and ascend gradually as the others leave it ... As nothing contributes more to health than moderate exercise in the open air, when the weather will permit, it is usual to make excursions into the neighbourhood, which abounds in a variety of places well worth the attention of strangers [which Hargrove's guide then enumerates] ... Harrogate being only a small village, it cannot be expected to be so regularly supplied with shops as a market town, yet there are several good ones, during the Spaw season, and the deficiency in point of number is in great measure supplied by the numerous articles to be found in some of them ... Here is a circulating library (owned by one Eli Hargrove) where the company are accommodated with the perusal of books, pamphlets, and newspapers. The subscription book to this library is of great use, as a kind of intelligencer, to know where, and what company, are at the place.' (G.1, pp. 44–56)

The 1798 edition of Hargrove's book contained details of amusements which are not in the earlier editions: billiard rooms, archery competitions, a theatre – built in 1788 – and a race course, laid out in 1793 (G.5, pp. 98–9). Hargrove's description in many ways provided the essence of what late eighteenth-century Harrogate had to offer the visitors. First, the famous mineral wells, which were the source of visitor attraction, and the reason for their coming to Harrogate. Then the inns with their lifestyle, attractions and customs were described, followed finally by the other attractions and amusements – visits to neighbouring places, shops, libraries and the company. Tellingly, Hargrove's books give no account of entertainments provided by the inns, beyond a brief reference to the public ball nights; also, they give but scant attention to Low Harrogate (G.7, p. 127).

Hargrove was not the only source of information about amenities for eighteenth-century visitors. Carey and Smollett both left revealing descriptions of life in late eighteenth-century Harrogate. In his 1796 visit Carey referred to the lack of a strictly hierarchical method of ordering spa society, such as that which existed at Bath under the benign dictatorship of Beau Nash.[6] Carey noted:

> there is little etiquette at Harrowgate, nor are the company pestered with the officious & interested cringings of an obsequious Master of Ceremonies. They appropriate one from among themselves, such as may have good nature enough and ability to undertake the office during his visit ... (G.4, pp. 182–3).

Smollett also compared Harrogate to Bath:

Harrogate treads upon the heals of Bath, in the articles of gaiety and dissipation – with this difference, however, that here, we are more sociable and familiar ... (C.44.b).

The doctors' view of Harrogate

A number of significant additions to the spa literature of Harrogate appeared between the passing of the 1770 Enclosure Act and the end of the century. In 1773 Dr Ingram discovered a new well at Epsom, and undertook to publicise it by means of a scientific comparison with the sulphur water of Harrogate, which he described as 'celebrated'. (F.31) This was followed by a treatise by the Physician to the Leeds Infirmary, Joshua Walker, who published in 1784 a detailed scientific study of the Harrogate waters, including their effects in the treatment of various disorders, such as costiveness (p. 127), gout (p. 139), the itch (p. 150), the leprosy (p. 153), and of worms (p. 169). Tellingly Dr Walker warned that, 'the luxury of table, which of late years has become fashionable at Harrogate, should put the invalid on his guard, and serve him as a daily memento, that one error of intemperance may entirely defeat his designs ...' (F.32, p. 108). Over-indulgence at table, touched upon by Dr Walker, may have been encouraged by the action of certain of the Harrogate waters. Buchan writes,

> ... I have seen a delicate person, after drinking the Harrogate Waters of a morning, eat a breakfast sufficient to have served two ploughmen, devour a plentiful dinner of fish and flesh, and to crown all, eat such a supper as might have satisfied a hungry porter. All this indeed the stomach seemed to crave ... (F.33)

Small wonder that with such activity the Harrogate inns were noted for their splendid tables '... and the eating's so good, and the claret's so fine, 'tis worth riding post fifty miles just to dine' (C.91). Within a year of Walker's book, William Buchan published *A Treatise on Cold Bathing and Drinking the Mineral Waters* (F.33), and this was in turn followed by other writings on the Harrogate Spa in 1786 (F.34) and 1787 (F.37). The scale of such publication indicated a growing interest in the subject of the Harrogate waters both from the medical profession as well as visitors.

An important discovery was made by the landlord of the Crescent Inn in Low Harrogate in 1783. When digging in the garden at the back of the inn for a new source of fresh drinking water, he came across a sulphur well which was eventually investigated by a Dr Garnett (F.39). Named the Crescent Well, it soon became one of the most popular wells in Harrogate. It was also the first mineral well to be discovered after the Award of 1778, and consequently, was on private land, unlike all of the older mineral wells.

The existence of a well such as the Crescent within the curtilage of an inn was a valuable commercial asset, and other innkeepers began to search for similar wells. Whereas the wells given under the 1778 Award, being public, could never be subject to charges, wells not on the two hundred acres but on private property, could be the source of valuable additional income.

As to the sulphur water, Hargrove's guide book of 1775 (G.1) devoted more space to a consideration of the Iron, or Chalybeate Wells, of High Harrogate, than of the Sulphur Wells of Low Harrogate. By the time of Dr Alexander's 1787 treatise (F.37), however, consideration of the sulphur wells dominated the text. One reason for this may have been that all of the medical texts of the time refer to the efficacy of the Harrogate sulphur water as a means of arresting skin disorders and intestinal infestations (i.e. worms). It is possible that the strongly astringent nature of the sulphur waters may also have been used to treat infected flesh wounds, such as those caused by military action. This was the time of the French wars, and the lists of visitors arriving in Harrogate included a proportion of military titles not evident in earlier times (Class R). There is, however, no direct evidence to prove that the use of sulphur water increased as a direct result of the French Wars.

Dr Alexander offered insight into the use of the hot sulphur bath at Harrogate:

> Having got a bath prepared entirely of the Sulphur Water, and no part of which has been used by anybody before, ... go into the bath considerably cooler than it is intended to be made afterwards, and, while you are in it, keep pouring in more hot water from time to time, till it be almost as hot as you can bear it ... As soon as the patient comes out of the bath, and is rubbed dry, he is conducted into a small apartment adjoining to the bath-room. In this apartment there is a bed appropriated to sweating, and to the use of everyone who chuses to go into it Into this bed he is put between two blankets; three or four more blankets are laid over him, and he is ordered to sweat for an hour. After which he rises, shifts himself, and then goes into a low parlour, where he eats something light for supper, drinks a glass of negus. And then retires, through a long cold passage, to his bed.

Alexander did not condone some of these practices:

> I would advise all those who intend to go through this process, only to sit down five minutes and consider that they are not only going into the same bed, but into the same blankets, where hundreds have lain before them, and where hundreds have not only laid, but sweated; that these

blankets must be filled with sweat; and that it did not always arise from sound and healthful bodies, but from bodies diseased both internally and externally . . .

Much emphasis was given by all the doctors to the purge, and a corresponding discussion over stool evacuation – their frequency, size and condition – was given with enthusiasm (F.37).

Dr Alexander ended his treatise with a severe warning on the dire effects of buttered muffins, advice on drinking:

> it is the custom . . . at Harrogate . . . to drink sometimes several glasses of wine, or other strong liquors, during the time of dinner . . . such as have weak delicate stomachs, and are apt to throw up, should likewise be careful not to breakfast too soon after having finished their quantity of water, otherwise . . .

and

> the dinners at most of the Houses in Harrogate are furnished out in a manner much too luxurious for companies of invalids'. (F.37, p. 46)

At the period of Hargrove's greatest activity as publisher, between 1774 and 1818 (G.1–G.10), two professional classes held sway in the town: the innkeepers and the doctors. Of the two, the doctors were supreme. Indeed, Hargrove's 1775 guide mentions a total of thirteen people, of which one had been a benefactor of the Harrogate chapel fifty years before, two had been local landowners, and one the carver of an ancient stone fragment found near the St John's Well. All the other nine names are those of doctors (G.1). Despite Hargrove's neglect of their names, the innkeepers were a powerful force in the town, and they appear to have attempted to improve their establishments at every opportunity. The inns were – apart from the Harrogate chapel of 1744 – the only large structures of architectural pretension in the town. Writing in his diary for 1780, Sylas Neville noted that, 'The Houses here for the accommodation of the Company look more like gentlemen's seats than inns' (C.53).

The efforts of the innkeepers and doctors were directed towards securing the favours of the visitors, so it is appropriate to examine who these visitors were, and why they came to Harrogate.

The visitors, c.1760–1818

Shortly before the enclosure Lord Bute – an important politician – visited Harrogate. The earl of Bute visited Harrogate in the summer of 1763. He had become First Lord of the Treasury on 26 May 1762, and as a firm favourite of George III, was hated with a passion that was unusual even in eighteenth-century terms.[7] In a letter of 2 September 1763 to General Irwin, writer Lord George Sackville expressed the hope that if the unpopular earl, 'really does go abroad, he will equally please both parties. Had he never returned from Harrogate till all bustles were over it had been more prudent ...' (C.36.b) Lord Bute was typical of the class of visitors who had flocked into Harrogate since the time of the Civil War, a class of celebrities that also included the military and artistic sets, as well as a high proportion of gamblers and sportsmen. Of these groups, it was, naturally enough, the literary travellers who left the best accounts of their visits.

By 1763, 'Matinus Scriblerus' was describing Harrogate as 'that land of mirth, so famed of late for romp and riot, beaux and belles ...' (C.35), an opinion which did not prevent the great philosopher David Hume from staying in the town in the same year (C.34).

Laurence Sterne, writer and preacher, was seen regularly in Harrogate (C.40), and indeed the town appears to have been a favourite with 'literary lions', possibly because of its free and informal atmosphere. At this time Sterne was living at Coxwold's Shandy Hall, and he would ride over to Harrogate when so inclined, usually staying at the Dragon Hotel (C.41), where he entered into the spirit of the place with socialising, gossip, gambling and humour. On 19 July 1767, Sterne wrote to his mistress, Eliza, that he was at Harrogate, 'drinking the waters till the 26th. to no effect but a cold dislike of every one of your sex ...' (C.41.c).

A further famous author who visited Harrogate at this period (C.31.b.36) was shrewd professional author Tobias Smollett, whose jaunty, often coarse, travel novels were popular publications of the age. By 1766, Smollett was working on what some regard as his finest story, *The Expedition of Humphrey Clinker*, published in 1770, the year of the Enclosure Act (C.44). *Humphrey Clinker* provides what is perhaps Harrogate's best eighteenth-century example of spa satire, including social custom, water drinking and – above all – bathing, that it is worthy of closer examination, although we will leave Smollett's description of bathing until chapter eight. The accounts of Harrogate in *Humphrey Clinker* vary according to the nature and disposition of each character, so that whereas the dyspeptic Matthew Bramble refers to the accommodation and treatments of Harrogate in the most derogatory way, the more congenial Jack Melford finds the frivolous and racy society at Harrogate 'agreeable to his disposition', even being eulogistic about the waters!

Character Melford says that the company 'lodged ... in five separate inns ... from whence they go every morning to the well, in their own carriages', and that the lodgers at each inn form a 'distinct society, that eat together', breakfasting from eight until eleven o'clock, drinking tea in the afternoon, and dancing in the evening. 'There is a public ball by subscription every night at one of the Houses [i.e. hotels], to which all the company from the others [hotels] are admitted by tickets; and, indeed, Harrowgate treads on the heels of Bath, in the articles of gaiety and dissipation . . .' (C.44.b). The ill-tempered Bramble, however, describes Harrogate as 'a wild common, bare and bleak, without tree or shrub . . .' (C.44.d), and that 'one might expect indeed, that there would be no occasion for a fire at mid-summer, but here the climate is so backward that . . . I am fain to have my bed warmed every night.' (C.44.e) Bramble reported that he was lodged in the New Inn (C.44.c), which Smollett may have borrowed from the new inn at the corner of Skipton Road and Bilton Lane (S.760) (later known as the Dragon Inn, following the closure of the old Dragon Hotel) or more probably the Granby, which at this time was known as the New Inn (R.395). Inevitably, Bramble's account of the sulphur water was lurid: 'the only effects it produced were sickness, griping and insurmountable disgust. I can scarcely mention it without puking . . .' (C.44.g).

Humphrey Clinker is a work of fiction, despite Smollett's own experiences of Harrogate, so for a more accurate understanding of life at the Georgian spa it is necessary to consider the observations of visitors other than the 'literary lions', not all of which were flattering.

Judith Milbanke, who became Lord Byron's mother-in-law, was in Harrogate in 1784, accompanying her husband, Sir Ralph, who suffered from a leg ailment. Lady Milbanke's letters leave no doubt as to her opinions about the visitors she encountered 'we have . . . some characters that would be thought outre on the stage . . . Lady Liddell was splendid at the races – a coach and six very fine horses, six livery servants following & a chaise four in the evenings, dazzling all the room with her diamonds' (C.56.c). Harrogate, she wrote 'consists of six large public houses standing scattered on a bleak, desolate looking common . . . every House is now brim full of the most consumate vulgars I ever saw'. Reporting her guests' conversations:

> I think our table talk would match the purrings of catts, some squab-bling, some complimenting and some employing their teeth too much . . . I sit by Lady Danvers, who tells me all the time what a foine shape she once had – what beautiful auburn her hair was till spoilt by powder (not years). But poor women, I pity her for one thing, for that vile daughter of hers is come here, on purpose to plague her I believe, and she is leading the most infamous life possible . . . (C.56.c).

Some idea of the visitors' rank may be had from the Yorkshire newspapers, who followed the high life at Harrogate with avidity. The *York Herald* for 25 July 1801 listed: 'Arrivals at Harrogate: Lord Castlereagh; Lady Castlereagh;

Lord Adam Gordon; Colonel and Lady Tekel; Lord Selkirk; Lady Barbara Cooper; Sir William Milner; Lord Bishop of Down' (R.1075).

Castlereagh, who enjoyed visiting Harrogate in order to escape the worries of grand politics, wrote to a colleague on 29 July 1801:

> Amidst the sound of invasion on all sides, I have some difficulty in avoiding the fidgets so far as to remain here. The ... benefit I have derived from these Waters, and the calculation that I am within 3 days of Belfast makes me desirous of finishing the usual course (i.e. of the Waters) a month or five weeks. I have been very idle since I came, have forgot politicks, and am grown very fat ... (C.73)

Lord Castlereagh was probably then the single most powerful man in Britain. His visits to Harrogate occurred at the peak of his career, when he was rallying the government after the disastrous year of 1797. A few weeks after Nelson's victory at Copenhagen, Castlereagh collapsed through overwork, and spent the summer in Harrogate where he seems to have recovered his health. He returned during the crisis year 1805–6, by which time he was Secretary of State for War and the Colonies, at a time when Napoleon's defeat of Austria at Austerlitz had all of Europe in panic. In June 1805, Castlereagh summoned Nelson and Wellington to his office, and planned the downfall of Napoleon, and the following August – tense and depressed with overwork – he returned to Harrogate, where during his walks on the Stray, he contemplated attacking the French war fleets with Mr Congreve's new fangled rockets (C.74). By 1809 Castlereagh was out of office, due to a change of Prime Minister, and following riots in London he re-visited Harrogate in the autumn of 1810, where he again recovered his strength. For the ten years following 1812, when Castlereagh rejoined the government, as Foreign Secretary, he virtually carried the entire burden of that government in Parliament, when he also directed British foreign policy, dictating the post-Napoleonic peace terms to Europe in the manner of an emperor, the results of which lasted until the arrival of Bismarck (C.74).

During its immediate pre-revolutionary years, France may have witnessed an early example of the marketing of Harrogate water beyond the shores of England. On 16 October 1777, the medical newspaper *La Gazette de Santé* published an article[8] that told the story of the (later infamous) Jean-Paul Marat having returned to France from England, where he had stayed from 1770 to 1776, working in 1774 as a doctor in Newcastle, and becoming a graduate of St Andrews University in 1775. There is a mystery surrounding Marat's activities during the years of his British visit, but it is known that he travelled widely. The 1777 newspaper article relates that later, on his return to France, Marat saved the life of a young noble lady by means of a special water with properties identical to those of the Harrogate waters –

presumably the Old Sulphur Well. Later in the nineteenth century a story developed that shortly before the revolution's outbreak in 1789, Marat had sold bottles of 'Harrogate water' on the streets of Paris. It is not known whether this water was a genuine import or a locally manufactured synthetic version![9]

Many celebrities visited Harrogate at the time of the wars with France, including such disparate characters as Charles Dibdin (C.60), Lord Castlereagh (C.73), William Wilberforce (C.78), Lord Byron (C.79), Maria Edgeworth (C.93.b), and probably Sir Walter Scott (C.94). It is also probable that the distinguished antiquary and architect Sir John Soane also visited Harrogate at this period, as a guide book owned by Sir John, now part of the Soane Collection in London, indicates that during such a visit, Soane stayed at the Dragon Hotel.[10]

Lord Byron visited Harrogate in 1806, when he stayed at the Crown Hotel, wrote his 'Ode to a beautiful Quaker', attended the newly opened Promenade Room, enjoyed a visit to the theatre, dined with friends who were also visiting Harrogate, and danced the night away at the Granby Hotel's ball (C.79).

A newspaper description of Harrogate during the Regency gives a graphic account of the high life of the times:

> Harrogate – this celebrated Watering Place is assuming its wonted gaiety. Every day brings considerable additions to the number of fashionables; and it is expected that in a short time the Inns and Lodging Houses will be crowded with the first families of the United Kingdom. The company at the Granby gave a sumptuous entertainment on Wednesday evening in honour of the Prince Regent's splendid gala. Cards of invitation having been issued out to all the first families in the vicinity. The room was chalked out in the most tasteful manner, dancing commenced at ten o'clock, and about two, the company (amongst whom beauty, elegance, and fashion conspicuously shone) partook of an elegant repast; and the party broke up about four on Thursday morning, highly gratified with the entertainment. (R.1505)

Residents and visitors

The population of Harrogate in 1801 was about 1,400. By 1811 it had reached 1,700.[11] Given that the four big hotels (Crown, Dragon, Granby, Queen) would have had an accommodation for about 250 guests each, or one thousand combined, and that the other eight smaller inns could have accommodated nearly a thousand guests between them, so say nothing of the various lodging houses, it is probable that during the Regency there were more visitors than residents in Harrogate.[12] Among a considerable amount of description provided by the town's visitors, there is an almost total lack of any kind of reference to the Harrogate population, other than to the doctors and innkeepers. The former were mentioned occasionally in correspondence, such as in Mary Wordsworth's letter to Joanna Hutchinson, dated 20 July 1823, with its reference to Dr Jaques: 'Old Dame Jaques is a character that I delight in – I never saw such a good-natured, open hearted gossip' (C.101.a). The latter occur in more formal writings, such as diary or journal entries: '... when old Goodlad was host at the Dragon, during whose administration it was almost as impossible for a parvenue, or a party without four horses and liveried servants to match, to gain a footing at the hotel, as ...' (C.86.c). But apart from these references, the Harrogate residential population might have been invisible to the visitors, although there must have been contact at the spa, as well as the inns, shops, and entertainments. The residents left an equally blank record of their impressions of the visitors to whom their little community owed so much.

The Stray Act of 1789

The increased numbers of visitors after the Great Award of 1778 led to further building development around the newly laid-out Stray, especially in that part of High Harrogate between the Dragon, Queen and Granby Hotels. Alexandre de la Rochfoucauld, during his visit of March 1786, when he stayed at High Harrogate's Dragon Hotel, writes of Low Harrogate's 'dozen houses, all new, and arising from a recent land clearance' (C.56.H) – this last, presumably, a reference to the Award, so it is evident that both High and Low Harrogate were developing.

Chapter six has described the laying out, in 1778, of the Stray, or two hundred acres, and the control of the herbage by means of imaginary 'gates', the ownership of which enabled cattle to be depastured. The 'Stray Gates' became sought-after possessions, which could be handed down in wills (O.11) or mortgaged (S.1055), and it is possible that their value increased as the amount of grazing land in Harrogate decreased with continuing urbanisation. Consequently the fifty Stray gate owners resented any reduction in the extent of the two hundred acres, as this could result in remaining land being over-grazed. Alone, this resentment could not prevent reduction of the Stray, as its very existence invited use, and this use, in turn, led to the erosion of the herbage by pedestrians and carriages. Furthermore, the habit of builders constructing houses right up to the edge of their allotments, as on Regent Parade or Devonshire Place, meant that any connecting routes between house and public highway had to be at the expense of the Stray, and if a few more yards were enclosed to form a front garden, who would know or care!

Within a year of the Award of 1778, the discontented Stray gate owners prepared a deed (J.3) which betrays the hand of solicitor Samuel Powell, and which attempted to provide support for the gate owners' agents (Matthew Thackwray and John Dearlove) to proceed against those who infringed the stint, or who forcibly removed illicitly grazing cattle from the pound in which they had been placed by the Stray's pinder. The gate owners' difficulty was that the law recognised only two actionable offences in relation to the Stray: trespass and damage. The former was an offence if the stint defined by the Award of 1778 was infringed, and the latter was an offence if pits were dug, or rubbish dumped on the Stray, both of which acts were public nuisances. Action against trespass was possible only if someone was prepared to sue, and here it was not likely that all the gate holders would cooperate, as the owner of half a gate had far less at stake than the owner of five gates. This disparity tended to rule out the possibility that all the gate owners would conjoin in bringing a common action, and this explains why the deed of 21 October 1779 was signed only by fifteen gate owners. We do not know how long the deed's provisions were in force, but as gate owners died or sold their gates, opportunities for action diminished accordingly.

At some point in the later 1780s, public discontent at the reduction of the Stray, and the concern of the gate owners at the infringements of the stint, led to the realisation that the conflicts between private ownership of grazing rights, and public right of access to the two hundred acres, could be reconciled only by a new Act of Parliament. Accordingly a number of gate owners asked the Duchy of Lancaster (in their capacity as freehold owners) to support moves to insert 'certain clauses' into the 'said recited Act' (which, presumably, was the parliamentary bill for what eventually became the Act of 1789) which were thought would improve the situation (J.4). The request was signed by eight of the signatories to the deed of 1779 (J.3). This shows that moves were well under way for a new Act by the time the gate owners framed their communication to the Duchy.

The stray gate owners adhered to the basic principle that their own self-interest must be protected; however, they also implied that improvements were needed, and that the mineral wells should be protected more efficiently. The condition of the Stray was woeful, as the Duchy's earlier hope that moneys raised by gate owners would be ploughed back into the Stray through improvements, was never realised. The deed's framers suggested that the Stray should be levelled and drained via funds received as penalties for abuses or non-observance of the rules. Improvements to the Stray in the form of providing walks, and trees 'for the owners of cattle-gates and for the health, convenience and recreation of the company resorting to Harrogate' (note the sequence) were to be made possible by enclosing 'not more' than fifteen acres – presumably for cattle guards to protect saplings (J.4).

In a separate memorandum, one of the Duchy's agents in the area, Mr J. Bainbridge, suggested that the new Bill should enable 'such improvements and regulations about the wells as they shall think fit, so that the waters may be had in their original purity, freed from that indelicacy that now attends them' (J.4.b). This may be a veiled reference to the lack of lavatories, a situation alluded to by Michael Stanhope back in 1632: 'what unseemly shifts I have seen many strangers of note put to for want of a convenient place of retirement' (F.5), and one which a hundred and fifty years later had not been improved. Bainbridge's memorandum also touched on the controversial and significant matter of the status of the Award's allotments in terms of taxation, and of the imbalance experienced by the forest townships.

In the event, the Duchy of Lancaster steered a Bill through Parliament that was somewhat different to that suggested by the gate owners and Mr Bainbridge. The 1789 Act acknowledged that the 1770 Act had contained none of the necessary powers for improving the Stray, for planting trees, for securing the mineral wells from injury or to repair injury to the Stray as a result of footpath or road construction. The Stray was granted an additional fifteen acres of land along the verges of the forest roads (the property of the Crown) to compensate for the loss of herbage occasioned by such construction, and it is important to grasp the significance of this compensation. The fifteen acres were an *addition*, not an exchange, and the sub-soil beneath the roads and footpaths remained part of the Stray, although the surface herbage had been lost. Accordingly, the new fifteen acres were to compensate the stray gate owners for the loss of *herbage* (and the subsequent reduction in the value of each Stray gate by the diminution of grazing for cattle). The new fifteen acres, or 'Stray strips', as they soon became known, were in the form of long narrow stretches of land flanking the modern Otley Road, Wetherby Road, Knaresborough Road, and Hookstone Drive. The public's general interest was probably (though not specifically acknowledged) observed by the legitimisation of the footpaths and roads, while also acknowledging that the integrity of the two hundred acres would remain intact.

Instead of setting up a body of trustees who could manage and improve the land and the wells as the stray gate owners had suggested (J.4), the 1789 Act harked back to the same enclosure commissioners who had made the General Award of 1778 and required them, or any two of them, to make rules for (a) preventing and punishing abuses which arose from depasturing cattle without right (b) improvements (c) protecting the mineral wells from pollution or other injury. The commissioners were empowered to provide moderate penalties, not exceeding forty shillings for any one offence.

It is interesting to note that once the commissioners had made their rules, their authority would cease, and the power to amend, enlarge or vary the rules would devolve on the Duchy Court, 'as that Court from time to time should think expedient'. Two important restrictions applied to any deliberations of the commissioners: the regulations laid down by the 1778 Award for controlling the stint (i.e. the number of animals which could be grazed) could not be changed; and there must be no method whereby charges or assessments could be levied to provide for the improvement of the Stray or protection for the mineral wells. Any rules about expenditure had to be on the understanding that only monies raised by voluntary subscription could be used.

The remarkable thing about the 1789 Act was that its provisions for rules and regulations were never enacted. As the original commissioners vanished from the scene, one by one, no one remained to introduce rules and regulations that had the force of legislation; consequently, there was nothing for the Duchy Court to change, amend or enlarge. However, three years after the 1789 Act, three of the original commissioners from the 1778 Award (William Hill of Tadcaster, Richard Richardson of Darlington, and John Bainbridge of Pannal) did compile draft rules and orders for 'improving and ornamenting Harrogate Stray', and their work, although never ratified, provides insight as to the problems facing the community. The document's interest lies in telling us how, within the restrictions of the Act of 1789, the commissioners hoped to safeguard the public's interest. Under the draft rules, five gate owners were initially to form a committee for the dual purpose of improving the Stray and protecting the mineral wells. A special kind of vestry meeting of wealthier landowners or tenants was to be held each year to elect the committee, which, though its members could seek re-election, need not thereafter consist wholly of gateholders. Envisaged improvements included the draining and levelling of the Stray, the planting of trees, and the making of a dry ride on that part of the Stray known as the 'circle' (the race-course). As for meeting the costs of all these improvements, the principle of free access to the Stray and everything on it, previously enshrined in the Act of 1770, the Award of 1778, and the Act of 1798, was honoured. All must be by voluntary subscription. Consequently, and despite the Duchy's gift of the additional fifteen acres, the Stray remained little improved, and disputes continued to be raised. (J.7, J.8, J.9)

Spa developments from 1789 to 1818

On 16 June 1806 assembly rooms for visitors were opened in Swan Road (R.1300), at the instigation of several medical men (S.e.10), a full account of which is provided under chapter nine, 'Entertainments at the Spa'. That these assembly rooms were opened in Low, and not High Harrogate, was evidence of the increasing popularity of the sulphur waters, a popularity that appears to have increased during the French wars. It is therefore not surprising that the next improvements were at the Old Sulphur Well itself, a few yards from the new assembly room, and that whereas the assembly room (known as the Promenade Room) had been built through the exertions of the doctors, the sulphur well improvements were financed largely with help from the innkeepers (A.266).

On 29 June 1807, a number of 'Gentlemen, innholders and inhabitants', met at the Hope Inn (Salutation Buildings) in High Harrogate (A.266), 'for the purpose of taking into consideration the present state of the Sulphur Wells, to preserve them from external injury and destruction, and to promote such further improvements as may from time to time be thought expedient ...' Although both of High Harrogate's important wells (the Tewit Well and the St John's Well) were protected with stone basins, the latter also having a splendid pump room over it built at the expense of Lord Rosslyn, the increasingly popular Sulphur Wells at Low Harrogate were in a primitive state, having changed little since the time of Celia Fiennes' visit of 1697 (C.18). The meeting of 29 June determined to improve matters.

It is worth noting, however, that an earlier attempt to improve the Low Harrogate Wells was recorded in a subscription book, probably dating from 1807, which has the entry, 'Received of Mr Mitton, Treasurer, for a sum collected by the late Dr Adair in the year 1800, from the Bank of Harrison & sons, for improving the wells at Lower Harrogate' (A.266.b). The sum collected was £57 13s. 6d. Dr Adair is an interesting character, as he was a close friend of Robert Burns, and had studied medicine at Geneva and Edinburgh, before moving to Harrogate (A.249), where he occupied the former World's End Inn, then known as Grove House (S.702). It is likely that the 1801 death of Dr Adair slowed down the move for improvements at Low Harrogate.

Two designs for a new pump room were produced by Thomas Chippendale, one consisting of an enclosed structure with solid walls, doors and roof, the projecting eaves of which gave it a vaguely 'Chinese' look, the second being an open structure with a romaneque dome supported by Tuscan columns (plates 43 and 44). The committee appears to have favoured the 'Chinese' design, as Chippindale submitted his estimate of £230 7s. 9d. on 29 July 1807 (A.266.c). By 2 November 1807, however, the committee had changed its mind, noting that instead of the first plan drawn ('that is, according to the Chinese mode') the building would be covered 'by a dome after the Roman mode' (C.266.d). The change of heart can only have been the result of discussions with the Duchy, and as the Duchy archive includes drawings of the two plans, but no correspondence, it is likely that they came into the Duchy's hands after on-site discussions between the promoters of the scheme and an agent of the Duchy such as Samuel Powell senior, or the surveyor Villers (B.4). The problem with the 'Chinese' design was that it proposed to erect an enclosed building on Stray land, which was specifically prohibited by the Act of 1770 (J.1), and the exchange between the promoters of improvement and the Duchy must have produced an understanding that the current Act of Parliament would only enable an open pump room to be built, and that if an enclosed one was required, then a new (and expensive) Act of Parliament would have to be obtained.

The committee, chaired by Harrogate chapel's Rev. Mitton, decided on 2 November 1807 to proceed with Chippindale's 'Roman' building, and to allow an extra £30 above the £230 7s. 9d. of the estimate of 29 July 1807 (A.266.c). Collected moneys included generous gifts from the landlords of the Granby, Dragon and Crown Hotels, who each donated ten guineas (A.266.b), as well as a similar subscription from Sir John Ingilby of Ripley Castle. According to W. H. Breare, writing in the 1890s, one of the principal movers of the project to improve the Sulphur Well was the father of the Joseph Thackwray whose role in the great sulphur well case of 1835–37 had such an influence on Harrogate's development (R.3128).

PLATE 45
The Sulphur Well
Pump Room of 1808,
from Well Hill,
towards the back of
the Old Bell Tavern.
What later
developed into Valley
Drive may be seen
on the right.

Work on the new pump room began within days of the decision of 2 November, as Chippindale received his first payment on 5 November, other instalments following up to October 1808, when a total of £263 6s. 0d. had been disbursed (A.266.e). No doubt at the urgings of the landlords, Chippindale had originally been told to complete the work by 5 April 1808 (A.266.c), in order to be ready for the opening spa season, but the records show that structural work was still being undertaken on 19 April and that

PLATE 46
The 1808 Sulphur
Well Pump Room,
with Well Hill in the
background. Two
more stone-built
well-head enclosures
may be seen to the
right of the Old
Sulphur Well.

Chippindale had claimed a further £1 17s. which the committee refused to grant (A.266.e).

The lead dome of the new pump room stood upon twelve stone columns of the Tuscan order, six of which were ten feet six inches tall, and seven of which were seven feet three inches tall standing on a three foot high wall, the purpose of which was to act as a retaining wall for the earthen embankment which ran up steeply from one side of the well (see plate 45). This was where such celebrities of old Harrogate as Betty Lupton, the 'Queen of the Well', dispensed the waters to visitors (A.306).

The new Harrogate Pump Room shared certain features with that which had been opened a hundred years earlier at Bath. The first public Pump Room at Bath had opened in 1706, largely at the instigation of Dr Richard Bettenson. Designed by John Harvey, it had been built at a cost of £400 for labour alone.[13] John Fayram's copper engraving of the Bath Pump Room depicts a square, open building, about thirty feet by thirty feet, its main approach being via a flight of four steps. The flat roof was raised by means of screens, which incorporated four columns in the Corinthian order, each divided from the other with round arches which incorporated glazing bars. Plate 46 shows the Harrogate Pump Room as it appeared in c. 1820.

A more contemporary comparison between Bath and Harrogate may be made with the Hetling Pump Room of 1804, a square, enclosed building fronted by a four-columned Tuscan portico.[14]

Spa developments from 1818 to 1822

An important new source of mineral water was discovered in the autumn of 1818, when John Oddy, the owner of a lodging house in Low Harrogate undertook some borings in a field he rented opposite his property. The field was located at the corner of the busy turnpike road to Ripon, and the modern King's Road. Oddy's borings were prompted by a desire to repeat the success of the Crescent Inn and tap into sulphur water. Eventually, water was found, but it proved not to be sulphur, rather an iron, or chalybeate water, which analysis later showed to be the world's strongest Chloride of Iron well. A second well was discovered a few yards away from the first, and was given the name 'Cheltenham Spring' as its waters were found to be similar to those of Cheltenham. (F.48) These were important additions to Harrogate's range of waters in general, but more so to the waters of Low Harrogate, as their discovery now meant that Low Harrogate possessed valuable sulphur and iron waters, whereas High Harrogate had only the latter. Henceforth, the history of High Harrogate was to be one of steady decline in comparison with the rise of Low Harrogate. Between 1800 and 1900, Low Harrogate gained seven spa buildings, while High Harrogate received but one. Over the period between 1820 and 1860, when the newly opened central railway station transformed opportunities for speculative development, Low Harrogate was blessed with three new streets, High Harrogate none. All the new inns listed in the street directories were in Low Harrogate, none in High Harrogate.

Low Harrogate received a further boost to its reputation in 1822, when the owner of the Crown Hotel, Joseph Thackwray, discovered a sulphur well in the gardens to the east of his establishment. At the time of the Great Award of 1778, the existence of mineral wells in the Crown Hotel's garden was unsuspected; otherwise the Crown garden would have been designated part of the Stray, as occurred with the wells outside the George Hotel (B.31). An account of how the Crown's mineral wells came to light was related to W. H. Breare in 1892 by owner Joseph Thackwray's son. It seems that when the garden (which occupied what later became the Royal Bath's site) was but an empty field on which stood nothing save the Crown's billiard room, it was used to graze horses from the Crown Hotel's stud, and that children crossing the garden on their daily walk to Miss Parry's Strawberry Dale school noticed that hoof marks were filled with water of iridescent hue. On analysis, this water turned out to be sulphur water, the identification of

which caused the enterprising Joseph Thackwray to dig for the source (R.3129). The Crown Sulphur Well is first mentioned in the *Description and Analysis of a new Sulphur Spring at Harrogate* by Dr William West, published in 1823. Dr West noted that 'the proprietor of the New Crown Spa has made arrangements for affording to the public, at reasonable hours, the same facility of access which they enjoy at the Old Well [i.e. the public Sulphur Well], while he will be enabled wholly to prevent those unpleasant circum-stances to which the latter from its exposed position, must always be liable ...' (F.53)

The *New Harrogate Guide* of 1825 (G.13) also referred to the new Crown Sulphur Well: 'In 1822, Mr Thackwray of the Crown Hotel discovered a spring in the grounds east of his House, over which he erected a neat building after the manner of a Chinese Temple [see plate 54], and thrown the surrounding land into pleasure grounds, for the convenience of his visitors. The water is raised by a pump through glass tubes, and given to drinkers by a female who attends every morning for that purpose. The elegant baths of the Crown are also supplied from this spring ...' It is

PLATE 29
Strawberry Dale Academy, *c.* 1900. Under Miss Parry this became Low Harrogate's most important school.

PLATE 54
The Crown, or
Montpellier Pump
Room. The tall thin
building on the left is
the beginning of
Bath Terrace. The
gabled building on
the right marks the
corner of Montpellier
Parade and Gardens.
St Mary's Church
may also be seen on
the far right.

possible that the 'Chinese temple' built over the Crown Sulphur Well was the same that had been designed, and rejected, for the public sulphur well back in 1807–8 (see plate 43), as the Treasurer for the public scheme had been the Crown Hotel's owner, William Thackwray (A.266. d), who probably passed the unused design to his son at his death in 1814 (L.96).

Mr Thackwray not only provided his guests with an important new source of sulphur water, and 'pleasure grounds' in which to be amused; he discovered further wells in the gardens, and allowed non-guests into the estate on payment where they could drink the waters without any charge (F.55).

In touching on the exposed situation of the Old Sulphur Well, Dr West was dealing with a sensitive matter. His reference to 'unpleasant

PLATE 43
Designs for an
enclosed public
Sulphur Well pump
room.

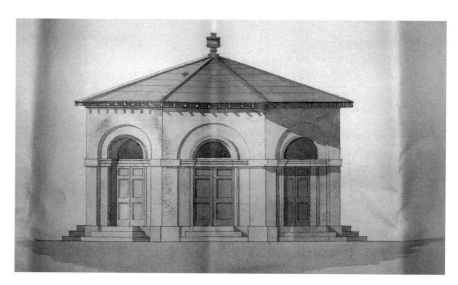

circumstances' may have had more to do with vandalism, than with the wind and rain which attended visitors at the well, and which the open cupola of 1807–8 did little to ameliorate. It seems that for some time before 1822, public concern had been growing at the deliberate pollution of the Old Sulphur Well. Things appear to have reached a crisis in 1821, when 'The Physicians, Medical Practitioners, Gentlemen, Innholders, Tradesmen, and other of Bilton-with-Harrogate and Beckwith-with-Rossett' organised a petition to the Duchy of Lancaster. After the preamble which relates the purpose of the legislation of 1770, 1778 and 1789, the petition states 'That of late years the interests of your petitioners ... have to a great degree been affected, and the persons resorting to the said Watering-Place, have been deprived of receiving the Waters in their pure state, inasmuch as on various occasions during the night time, some persons unknown to your petitioners have put into these Medicinal Springs quantities of dung, ashes, dead dogs, and other animals of a most offensive nature, by means of which the Waters thereof have been, and still continue to be, to a considerable extent polluted and unfit to be taken by any person ...' (H.2)

The petition went on to explain that it was impossible to guard the well through the night, and that the legislation designed to guarantee the public's right of access at all times prevented the well from being locked when not in use. The petition was compiled in 1821, with the assistance of the firm of Powell and Son, Solicitors, of Knaresborough, and printed for distribution in the following year. The petition was read before the Duchy Court on 2 February 1821 (B.192) instructed the Attorney General to provide

PLATE 44
Designs for an open public Sulphur Well pump room.

advice on whether or not the legislation would permit the Harrogate springs to be demised to trustees who could ensure their protection. The Attorney General gave his opinion on 13 September 1821, advising that only a new Act of Parliament could empower the provision of security measures to protect the wells against injury (H.3).

The townspeople took Mr Attorney's advice to their hearts, and with the assistance of Powell and Son of Knaresborough, a formal petition for a new Act of Parliament was prepared in the autumn of 1821 (H.4). It carried the signatures of twenty-one of the leading townsmen, including John Jacques, M.D., surgeons Robert Richardson and Croft Wormald, the incumbent of Harrogate Chapel, Henry Mitton, several leading landowners, and, most significantly, the owners of the leading Harrogate inns – Joseph Thackwray of the Crown, Thomas Ripley of the Dragon, Jonathan Shutt of the Swan, and Thomas Linforth of the Crescent. The name of John Greeves, owner of the Granby Hotel, was a notable omission from the list of signatories. The petition, dated 2 February 1822, was sent to the Chancellor of the Duchy of Lancaster (H.4). Five days later the Duchy received a second petition, signed by fifty-four townspeople, which stated: 'It being understood that a Petition is intended to be presented to his Majesty's Chancellor of the

Duchy of Lancaster to solicit his interest in obtaining an Act of Parliament for the Enclosure of the Wells at Harrogate ... We ... beg to state that no public notice whatsoever was given of such a Petition ... We ... request that you will postpone giving your consent to the alterations proposed until the same shall have had due consideration at a meeting to be convened for the purpose. We also think it right to observe that we are not desirous to oppose any improvements that may ... tend to the benefit of the place and convenience of the public ...' (H.5)

The counter-petition of 7 February produced a furious letter from Mr Thackwray on the following day. The powerful owner of the Crown Hotel, whose establishment faced the public sulphur well, wrote to the Duchy: 'Sir, I am sorry to inform you that a petition is handed about this neighbourhood in opposition to the one we sent up through the hands of Mr Powell, which has originated with Mr Greeves at the Granby and one or two more bad disposed persons in the place. They are getting many of the lower orders to sign it by misrepresenting the manner in which it is intended to protect the springs ...' (H.7) The 'bad disposed persons' and 'many of the lower orders' to which Mr Thackwray alluded in fact included many leading members of the community, including John Greeves of the Granby, Joseph Binns of Binn's Hotel, Michael Hattersley of the Cross-Roads Hotel, James Settle of the Queen's Head, J. T. Gascoigne of Gascoigne's Hotel, James Tengatt of the White Hart Hotel, several doctors, teachers, and tradespersons, and the rich landowner, James Franklin, whose signature headed the petition. The dispute most probably had its origin in the desire of people such as Joseph Thackwray of the Crown Hotel to press forward with necessary improvements as soon as possible, before the start of the next season for visitors. This high-handed approach inevitably annoyed some of his rivals, who felt that as persons with an equal interest in the welfare of the town, they should at least have been consulted. The Duchy Court agreed with them, and at its meeting of 11 February 1822, ordered that the petitioners be advised to hold a public meeting to discuss plans for protecting the wells at Harrogate, and that the result of such meeting be submitted to the court in writing. The same meeting of the court ordered that Mr Thackwray also be advised of their decision that a public meeting was necessary, adding that when the proposed improvements had been accepted by the public meeting, 'those persons who oppose it should be desired to send their objections in writing to me, fully stating the grounds upon which they oppose the proposed measures ...' (B.193).

The public meeting was not long in taking place, being held in the Promenade Room on 21 February 1822. A committee was formed, which at its meeting of 7 March resolved to apply for an Act of Parliament to protect the wells of Harrogate. On 18 March the same committee resolved to adopt the petition which had already been sent to the Duchy – presumably by Mr Thackwray and his associates – with the additional resolutions that the help of the Duchy be requested in carrying the Act into execution, and, 'that the expenses of obtaining the Act be defrayed by any sum not exceeding one shilling per week being raised on the public using the waters until the same is discharged.' (H.8) The levying of a charge for the use of the waters, to pay for the cost of a new Act, would only have been possible after the passing of any new legislation which permitted it. It is not known whether it was this concept of paying for a new Act, or some other factor, which was responsible for the whole subject of a new Act being dropped. The subject of the protection of the wells appears to have been left alone. When it was revived, it would be because Joseph Thackwray, and his new well of 1835, made it a matter or urgency for the entire community.

Harrogate was not alone in its attempt to counter vandalism and provide protection for the mineral wells. In Royal Tunbridge Wells, local gentry began meeting in 1816 to discuss local vandalism, which eventually resulted in the 1835 Tunbridge Wells Improvement Act, passed six years before that of Harrogate.[15] Similar moves were considered in Royal Leamington Spa, at the Old Well, but as this was on private land, the protection was provided by the owner, Lord Aylesford, who in 1804 defrayed the entire cost, presenting the restored well to the public in 1804.[16]

The visitors, 1818–1841

By 1818 Harrogate was clearly holding its own as a major national resort for the aristocracy, gentry, and aspiring members of both social groups. The *York Herald*'s edition of 12 September 1818 reported 'Harrogate – never was this celebrated Watering-place so crowded with visitors of the first distinction, as it has been for the last two months, and still continues. The spacious inns and boarding and lodging houses have been unable to accommodate all the families who have resorted here; and several have been under the necessity of remaining at Harewood, Knaresborough, etc., until vacancies occurred. It has been calculated that near 1,300 ladies and gentlemen have been assembled in a morning at the wells together ... The theatre, as well as the ballrooms and several other places of public resort, still continue to have their attractions ... from the Theatre Royal Covent Garden and Drury Lane ... should the fine weather continue, there is every prospect of Harrogate being very throng for some time to come.' (R.1790)

Travellers such as Sir Walter Scott, who along with Goethe was arguably the most famous living author, often referred to Harrogate in his correspondence (C.94), although it is difficult to know precisely when he was a visitor. In a letter of 1817–19, Scott refers to his dislike of being pursued by

PLATE 101
St John's Well, with
Christ Church at
right, and Park
Parade in the
background, drawn
by John Field in 1830.

'lion hunters' (what a later age would call autograph hunters, or groupies!)
'... so common at Harrowgate ...' (C.94.d) and more particularly provides
an exact description of parts of High Harrogate in his 1823 novel *St Ronan's
Well* when his character Lord Etherington leaves his apartments (probably
the Dragon) and 'took his way to the bookseller's shop, which also served
as a post office and circulating library [Library House]; and being in the very
centre of the parade [Regent Parade], for so is termed the broad terrace
walk which leads from the Inn to the Well [the St John's Well] formed a

convenient lounging place for newsmongers and idlers of every description.' (C.97)

Hitherto, the majority of the visitors' references to Harrogate had been about High Harrogate, apart from obligatory accounts of the Old Well and the sulphur water. However, as Low Harrogate developed after the 1806 opening of the Promenade Room (R.1300) and the 1807–8 building of the Old Sulphur Well Temple, Low Harrogate (A.266) featured in visitors' accounts with greater and greater regularity. When the Honorable W. H. Lyttleton wrote to Lady Sarah Lyttleton from the Queen's Head Inn on 15 September 1820, he mentioned that he was about to move down to Low Harrogate (hard by the spring in a sort of Rotton Row, just above where the eggs are perpetually steaming . . .).' (C.98.c.1) He wrote again, on 16 September, from Mr Shutt's, Low Harrogate (the Swan Inn) that 'I am established in my new quarters. It is, I assure you, a very tidy little room I am now writing in, fronting the south-east and looking out upon a neat little flower garden bounded by a low stone wall which divides us from the narrow road [Swan Road], along which pass at least a hundred foot-passengers for one horseman or carriage. Young untrimmed hedge-row trees beyond, between whose stems you look upon green fields [these would have been behind the George Inn] interspersed with houses, and a moving scene upon the cross-roads (the later King's Road/Ripon Road) which intersect them at a little distance.' (C.98.c.2). Before the extensions to the George Inn, and the Duchy's development of Swan Road in the later nineteenth century, most of Low Harrogate, south of Swan Road, presented a rural appearance.

In considering the development of High and Low Harrogate, and their attractiveness to visitors, the role of York Place and West Park must not be overlooked, and here, the location of the Cross Roads, or Hattersley's Hotel, was significant. In 1823 the Wordsworths emulated poets Byron (C.89) and Montgomery (C.100) in favouring Harrogate with their presence, staying at Hattersley's Hotel (C.101.a). Harrogate was so much to their liking that they enquired about the price of hiring lodgings, finding that they were so reasonable, that 'three could live as well as we should wish to do, at a less expense than Dorothy herself was at, at Hattersleys . . .' That William Wordsworth benefited from his visit is shown by Mary Wordsworth's writing, 'The Waters, and the mode of living, agreed well with William, his eyes were better and the heat in his face abated from the first, but a fortnight was too short a trial to expect any permanent benefit. He is still drinking the Water . . .' (C.101.a). As these lines were written from Rydal Mount, it is clear that the Wordsworths had obtained supplies of bottled Harrogate water.

References to Harrogate's relaxed and informal atmosphere continued to be noted well into the nineteenth century, as for example with the German Prince Pueckler-Muskau in 1827, who noted that 'this bathing-place is much after the fashion of ours, and more social than most of the English ones'. The Prince went on to make a most interesting observation about the treatment of rank, describing a conversation with an old General of eighty: 'He had met with Frederic the Great, Kaunitz, the Emperor Joseph, Mirabeau, and Napoleon ... he had likewise been Governor of Surinam and of the Isle of France ... and was now what we call a General of Infantry ... All this would give him a high station with us [i.e. in Germany]: here no such thing, and this he remarked himself: "here," said he, "the aristocracy is everything ... I am only a baronet, yet that empty and trifling title gives me more consideration than my long services or my high military rank ..."' (C.105.C)

The entertainment of visitors is the subject of our ninth chapter, and before we move to the particular matter of bathing at the spa (which forms the content of chapter eight), it may be well to return to the visitors' experiences of Harrogate as seen through the eyes and ears of an accomplished author. Catherine Sinclair published *Modern Flirtations, or a Week at Harrowgate* in 1841, and made much of Harrogate's associations with the marriage market: 'there is no place like it for young ladies ... it is a perfect emporium of beaux, you will live there at the rate of twenty new victims a day ... A downpour of marriages takes place at the end of every season. Several jewellers have made large fortunes at Harrowgate merely by providing wedding rings; and a confectioner is kept at each hotel with nothing else to do but to make marriage cakes.' (C.107.a) This enthuses the party to proceed with the visit, and when they arrive at the Granby Hotel, they find it appeared 'more like an entire street than a single house [see plate 11] ... and accommodation might be prepared in it for all the invalids in Great Britain ... the carriage was surrounded by a cluster of shabby waiters ... who were vociferous in their protestations that the house was already more than full, and that a hundred and fifty guests dined every day ...' (C.107.b). The visitors soon discover that 'the company [i.e. the other guests] is nearly of the same calibre as you might probably encounter in Margate, or in a second-class train on the Birmingham railway – or at a Bartholemew's fair, added Agnes, determined not to be outdone ... there should be door-keepers at Harrowgate to keep out the canaille.' (C.107.c) The visitors soon find more congenial company, and enjoy Harrogate's sociability, attend the wells, where they are amused by the faces of the drinkers, and finally take dinner at the Granby, where, 'the clock strikes five and the bell rings, and the instantaneous rush of company ... towards the dining room can only be compared to a congregation hurrying out of church ... elderly matrons advance, leaning on their gouty red-faced

husbands – troupes of marriageable daughters follow – the noise-meter then rises to a deafening pitch ...' (C.107.g). Although fiction, Catherine Sinclair's *Modern Flirtations* ... is quite obviously based on experiences of a Harrogate visit, especially as her descriptions are confirmed by many other authors, of whom Hofland (C.91), Curling (C.86) and Granville (F.58) are the most significant.

Conclusion

Thanks to the status and influence of the doctors and innkeepers of Harrogate, the irregular and modest nature of local government at the spa does not appear to have discouraged visitors. The informal and relaxed atmosphere at the inns, so different from the formality of Bath and Cheltenham, with their pompous Masters of Ceremony, seems indeed to have encouraged, rather than discouraged a good level of attendance at the spa. This was complemented by the natural rawness of the Harrogate waters, which were all available for consumption at source, a fact praised by the doyen of British spa doctors, Dr A. B. Granville, who in the late 1830s wrote, 'who can cavil at the nature, genuineness, and efficacy of the Harrogate waters! On the other hand, who has not cavilled, and cavils to this day, at the waters of both Leamington and Cheltenham? Those of Harrogate are unsophisticated because the place remains as it was. You dip your cup into the fountain-head and get your strong waters ... Elsewhere you have the complicated machinery of pumps, the ends of whose pipes may terminate heaven knows where … Harrogate is, in fact, a true and genuine Spa.' (F.58, p. 38). The spa was patronised by the visitors, and consequently, the visitors were the single most important factor in the town's economy. Everything was done to ensure that their interests were served, from the contents of the guide books, to life in the inns and hotels.

Residents and visitors have both left a scanty record of their impressions of each other. This reinforces the suspicion that the relationship between the two was very much what today would be called 'service industry' (with its providers and consumers), and that the Harrogate Spa was very much a visitor-led initiative. This in turn enabled the little Harrogate Spa to adapt to the profound changes that occurred after 1840, causing all other British spas to decline.[17] In other words, the Harrogate visitors had no need for the Harrogate population to adapt the spa's social life to the current fashion, because the visitors *themselves* undertook this task, aided by compliant innkeepers. And no doubt the doctors continued to provide their fee-paying patients with whatever was medically fashionable. In so shaping the social life of the spa, rather than merely consuming a ready-made product, the visitors made the Harrogate's history yet again atypical of British spas.

8 | Bathing at the spa

THROUGHOUT the period between 1770 and 1841, there was an increase in bathing facilities in Harrogate. This is demonstrated by the fact that in the year of the Enclosure Act there was only one public bathing house in High Harrogate, and none in Low Harrogate, whereas by 1841 Low Harrogate had four public baths and High Harrogate, including Starbeck, had two (G.26). The High Harrogate public bathing house had been established some time before the Award of 1778, which records that a 'Cold Bath' was sited next to the St John's Well (B.31, allotment 222.) It is not known who developed this bath, but it may have been one of the two Dr Neales, who practised in Harrogate between 1656 and 1723 (F.19). The 'New Cold Bath' is also mentioned in the third edition of Eli Hargrove's guide book: 'An elegant cold bath hath lately been constructed near the St John's Well in High Harrogate . . .' (G.2). Certainly Dr Neale of Doncaster also used the Cold Well in Cold Bath Road, as a bath, according to Dr Short in his treatise of 1734, who also recommended it to his patients (F.24).

The habit of bathing was well established before any public baths were erected at either High or Low Harrogate. Dr Neale, in his 1693 fragment *Spadacrene Eborencis* recorded that, 'It's now above thirty years ago, since I set up first warm bathing in this water, and procured one such vessel for a pattern, as are used beyond the sea for that purpose, and now there are above twenty bathing houses kept here, with all necessary conveniences . . .' Dr Neale was referring to bathing in the sulphur water, and the twenty bathing houses he notes were not public establishments, but private lodging houses which brought the waters to their premises in barrels for the convenience of guests.[1] The lodging houses on Well Hill, opposite the Sulphur Well, were particularly favoured in this respect, as were those of neighbouring Cold Bath Road. Tobias Smollett described the bathing process in his *Expedition of Humphrey Clinker*, published in 1771: 'By the time we reached Harrowgate, I began to be visited by certain rheumatic symptoms. The Scotch lawyer Mr Micklewhimmen, recommended a hot bath, which was a tub filled with Harrogate water, heated for the purpose.' (C.44.h)

Rather more impressive amenities than those offered by the lodging houses were available at some of the Harrogate hotels. In 1781, the landlord of the Queen's Head at High Harrogate advertised: '... as many objections have been made to the usual mode of bathing in tubs, in order to accommodate them in a more convenient manner, [the landlords] have been at considerable expense in erecting a Warm Bath, upon a similar construction to those used in the Medicated Baths in York, and have had the dressing room more commodious, which they hope will meet with approbation ...' (R.775)

When D. W. Smith visited Harrogate from Alnwick in 1816, he stayed at the Crown, and recorded in his notebook that, 'there are different baths in the House for Gentlemen and Ladies – the charge for the warm bath is 3 shillings, and the person who attends you expects not less than six pence.' (A.270.5) The bathing amenities at the Crown gained it a special nickname, noted by journalist Henry Curling: 'The Granby ... was called the House of Lords ... The Dragon ... was called the House of Commons ... The

PLATE 39
Moses Griffiths' 1772
drawing of Well Hill.

PLATE 49
The Crown Hotel, as
sketched in *c*. 1820.

Queen ... was called the Manchester Warehouse ... the Crown (see plate 49) was called the Hospital.' (C.86.e)

The Harrogate guidebook of 1825 referred to 'the elegant baths of the Crown, ... supplied from this spring' – i.e. the Crown Sulphur Well, discovered in 1822. The Crown Hotel baths received praise from Dr Hunter, in his *Treatise*, published in 1830: 'There are baths connected with all the principal hotels and some of the lodging houses; great credit is due to Mr Thackwray of the Crown Hotel, for the style in which he has furnished his baths.' (G.13) Indeed, the Crown certainly had provided hot baths since at least 1763, as one writer described: 'the infirmary – a room in Thackwray's House [see plate 50], so called as being always kept very warm, for the reception of ... those who were just come out of the hot bath (C.35). Having plenty of water upon the premises, his advantages are considerable: besides the usual hot and cold baths of Sulphur or common water, he has shower, vapour, fumigating, and medicated baths. Mr Thackwray also has it in contemplation *to erect a suite of public baths*, which would certainly be highly useful ...' (F.55). Here is one possible solution to the question of why the movement to protect the public wells came to nothing in 1822. Joseph Thackwray, prime mover of the petition to the Duchy, suddenly found himself owner of an important new sulphur well at the very period when his plan to safeguard the Old Sulphur Well was meeting opposition from his commercial rivals. Faced with this, what could have been more natural for him to have concentrated his activities on developing the sulphur wells on his own property, which he could furnish with every safeguard and

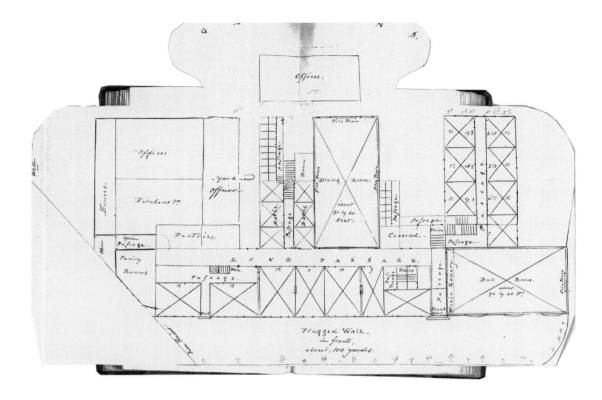

PLATE 50
Interior plan of the
old Crown Hotel,
c. 1820.

convenience? Mr Thackwray was not the only business man considering the erection of a suite of public baths in Harrogate. The 1834 *Yorkshire Directory* states that 'Harrogate is now considered the principal watering place in the north of England ... It is estimated that there have been of late years, upwards of 10,000 visitors annually, and many prolong their stay over winter.' (G.22) The appearance on the Harrogate scene of business man John Williams gave Joseph Thackwray an energetic rival.

The development of bathing in the Harrogate waters, as distinct from drinking them, was encouraged by Dr George Cayley, who wrote in 1809: 'Being in the constant habit of visiting Harrogate during the Seasons, I do not doubt but I can point out other improvements of equal value to the Company that resort thither with the assistance of my Medical Bretheren there, particularly the construction of Baths upon an improved plan; thus Harrogate may vie with the first Watering-place in the Universe ...' (F.45) The type and frequency of bathing was regulated by the Doctors, especially by those resident in Harrogate. In her *Season at Harrogate* published in 1811 for the amusement of visitors, Barbara Hofland named all the leading spa doctors:

> 'There's not one of them all that my fancy so takes',
> Cried a lady in black, 'as my good Doctor Jaques'

Says the next, 'Mr Richardson's wonderfully clever,
Tho' so busy, dear heart, there's no catching him ever'
Cries a third 'If you really want medical skill,
Mr Wormald will cure you if any man will',
'And I know', said a fourth, 'that whatever may ail ye,
You're sure of relief if you see Dr Cayley.' (C.91.b)

These men, Jaques, Richardson, Wormald, and Cayley, and their counterparts resident in the great inns during the spa season, recommended specific treatments for patients. Dr Jaques, in his revision of Garnett's treatise, lists various ailments and which kind of bath should be used in their treatment. For example, 'in 1803, I attended a young lady, who had been afflicted for four years with a dry, scaly eruption, covering almost every part of the body. Her appetite was bad, and very much debilitated. By drinking the sulphur water and using it as a bath, she soon got much better, and, in the course of seven weeks, obtained a cure.' (F.52) The people who drank and bathed in the Harrogate waters, appear to have done so under medical guidance. When Dr Granville published his monumental *Spas of England* in 1841, he warned against the random and uninformed use of the waters (F.58, pp. 51–2).

The majority of guidebooks to Harrogate which were published after 1834 give contradictory dates for the opening of the first suite of public baths in Low Harrogate. The 1834 directory (G.22) states that, 'Two suites of public baths are in the course of erection'; whereas the *New Harrogate Guide* of 1838 refers to, 'The Victoria Baths, erected by the late Mr

PLATE 65
John Williams used an elegant Ionic design for his 1834 Victoria Baths. On the right cano be seen the back of the Crescent Inn.

Williams, in 1833 ...' (G.24). Thereafter, all the guidebooks state that Mr William's Victoria Baths were built in 1832, and Mr Thackwray's Crown Baths were built in 1834 (G.25). The building of the Victoria Baths probably occurred between 1833 and 1834. Williams' solicitor, Samuel Powell, referred in his 1834 'day book' to securing Williams a further £1,000 to 'complete the baths'. (W.8.28)

The Victoria Baths were designed by John Clark, a native of Edinburgh who had settled in Leeds, and whose 1836 gothic design for the new Houses of Parliament was praised highly.[2] Clark, who went on to design the Spa Rooms for Williams, produced in his Victoria Baths a masterpiece of classical architecture, which combined aristocratic elegance with commercial practicality (see plate 65). Executed of the finest ashlar, with a single storey embellished with the Ionic order, battered architraves, and a central bay formed in a pleasing curve, the Victoria Baths were finally purchased by connoisseur Samson Fox, at the end of the century, and re-erected on his Grove House estate.

The Victoria Baths were built on land north of the old Crescent Inn and east of the Promenade Room of 1806. Williams had purchased the plot on 8 June 1833 for the sum of £615 (S.e.26). A clause in the surrender required that any new building on the site must not affect the natural lighting of the neighbouring Promenade Room. Accordingly Williams had to sink his new bathing establishment into the ground. Williams' Baths were described by the dyspeptic Dr Granville in his two-volume survey of England's spas:

> ... we find a very pleasing and creditable small building of the Ionic order, containing thirteen bathrooms, sunken below the level of the ground, as if erected at the bottom of a quarry, to which you have access by descending steps, and separate entrances for ladies and gentlemen. These are now called the Victoria Baths, the first establishment of the sort formed at Harrogate ... the arrangement of the baths themselves is very creditable. Although there is not a separate dressing room to each bath room, the latter is so large that it admits of a curtain being drawn across, to separate and conceal the bathing tanks, which are oblong and ample, and altogether sunken into the floor, and tiled. They are narrower than those at the Montpellier [Mr Thackwray's] and not so smart, yet very comfortable and clean. The terms are three shillings for each warm bath in both establishments. About 4,000 are used during the season at the Victoria, and 6,000 at the Montpellier. (F.58, pp. 57–8)

The Victoria Baths provided facilities for shower and vapour bathing, which cost 1s. 6d. and 4s. respectively, plus a recommended gratuity of 6d. to the attendant (G.26). All water used at the Victoria Baths came from

PLATE 66
Joseph Thackwray's
Crown, or
Montpellier Baths
favoured the Tuscan
order.

wells on the site, which were part of the same series to which belonged the Crescent Inn Well of 1783.

The Crown, or Montpellier Baths, seem to have been built between December 1833 and the summer of 1835 (H.14) and it is possible that their opening coincided with the closure of the baths which Mr Thackwray had built into the Crown Hotel. The new Montpellier Baths stood amidst the pleasure gardens of the hotel, and were in an austere Tuscan style of architecture, comprising a single-storey structure entered through a portico of four massive columns, which led into the central hall and ticket office (see

PLATE 67
The 1834 Crown
Baths, with the 1822
'Chinese' Crown
Pump Room.

Montpelier Baths & Pleasure Grounds Low Harrogate

W. Moore J.   H. Cove

plate 66). The architect of the new Crown Baths is alleged to have been one Andrews, although his name does not appear in surviving literature of the time. The Crown, or Montpellier Baths were built shortly before Joseph Thackwray obtained the services of Samuel Powell, solicitor (W.2.9), whose firm's records (Class W) would otherwise have contained the information.

There were six bathrooms each for men and women, and Dr Granville described them as being, '... exceedingly neat, being of stone of an elegant form, partly sunk into the floor ... The water for these baths is drawn from six different springs, by aspiring pumps. A small steam engine pumps the water through them into a reservoir, where it is heated by steam from the boiler of the engine. The supply of water, both of the sulphur and saline kind, is amply sufficient ...' (F.58). The digging of the foundation for the new Montpellier Baths brought to light six new mineral waters, including the Kissingen Well, which later became of one Harrogate's most popular waters, four sulphur wells, and a well of fresh water (H.14). In this way, Mr Thackwray was well able to capitalise on his fortune.

Starbeck, situated half way between High Harrogate and Knaresborough, had been identified as a source of mineral water by Dr Stanhope in 1626, who noted its discovery in that year by the appropriately named (in view of the water's diuretic power!) Doctor Leake of York. (F.4, pp. 29–30). Little appears to have been done to develop the Starbeck Wells (which consisted originally of a sulphur well and a chalybeate well) and the Award of 1778 transferred them from Bilton-with-Harrogate into Knaresborough township as a 'detached allotment' (B.31), after which they appear to have fallen into total obscurity, save for the efforts of Eli Hargrove (G.1). In the early years of the nineteenth century Knaresborough's economy declined, and consequently an 1822 plan by Knaresborough resident Michael Calvert to revive the Starbeck Spa, received much popular support in Knaresborough. A company was formed for the purpose of erecting a suite of baths, by means of issuing one hundred shares at 24s. each (F.57). Calvert claimed that the baths were built in 1828 (F.57), and they were certainly in use by 1829, as the Account Book for April to October of that year has an entry 'Credit – £137.01.10, including ninety-seven shares at 24s. each, & cash received for baths by 17 October: £10 15s. 6d.' (V.4)

The spa at Starbeck was promoted under the name of the 'Knaresborough Spaw' (F.57), although the official designation under the Great Award of 1778 was 'Starbeck Spa' (B.31). The earliest description of the Starbeck Spa comes in Dr Short's important *History* ..., which notes on page 257 that, 'there is another chalybeate spring in the mid-way between Harrogate and Knaresborough, on the south side of the brook, with a basin, and a little square place built over it.' Short also refers to the Starbeck sulphur well on pages 285–9, noting only that it is, 'in a low ground, by a small brookside' (F.24).

The 'little square place' was probably a typical seventeenth- or eighteenth-century well-head of vernacular appearance, in the form of a stone pyramid covering a basin and water spout water (V.67). Neither Short, nor any of the eighteenth-century writers, refer to any building at the Starbeck Spa, and the 1792 edition of Thomas Garnett's *Experiments* ... (F.39) intimates that the Starbeck wells were seldom used.

The history of the various buildings of the Starbeck Spa is complex, although it is likely that by 1700 there was some cottage accommodation in the immediate vicinity of the Starbeck sulphur well. The earliest hard evidence for building occurs on a post-1822 advertisement (see plate 12), issued by Langdale. A woodcut atop the advertisement shows, from left to right, a stone column, a single-storey cottage and a larger structure with a crenellated parapet, arched doorway, above which is a large window with intersecting tracery in the English decorated style of architecture. A singular cruciform device also appears on the façade to the right of the doorway, which may be connected with the 'Masonic Brethren', reported by the *York Herald* as having marched from Knaresborough to attend the spa's foundation stone laying in May 1822 (R.1985). The ceremony of 23 May 1822 can only have been for the rebuilding of the well-head, as the water was free to the public, and promoter Michael Calvert described the procession as being to the well, rather than to any pump room or larger building (F.57). The stone column was erected in 1823 to mark the location of the Starbeck Sulphur Well, the earlier one having been removed (S.994). The Langdale woodcut depicts a somewhat cruder structure than that which exists at the time of writing, and although this may be because of engravers' licence, an entry in the trustees' minute book for October 1843 records that the committee was to 're-affix the column in an ornamental manner', which implies a degree of change (V.64). The structures shown in the Langdale woodcut must have been erected after the 1822 formation of Michael Calvert's company; the smaller building at left is the cottage occupied by the keeper, mentioned in the 1825 accounts; whereas the larger structure at right contained the 1828 baths. The embellishment of the grounds, including the stone column, was undertaken between 1822 and 1825 (V.1).

The building that contained the baths is a curious 'gothic' structure and was developed at a period when the fashion for mock-gothic was strong, as the work of Wyatville, Pugin and Repton demonstrate, and it is likely that the Starbeck Spa's promoters favoured such a fashionable design, one element of which included an impressive traceried window, which was provided with stained glass in 1836 (V.41). As for the handsome structure in the Victorian-Tudor style (see plate 12) to the immediate north of the old baths, this was not built until 1852, to plans by Ralph Hodgson, who may also have been the architect.

It seems that by 1830 (by which time total income since 1822 had reached £282 12s. 5d.), demand had risen sufficiently to require the committee to install a new reservoir (V.28), and a stable, which were finished by the end of May 1831 (V.30). Three years later, in October 1833, the Annual General Meeting approved the construction of a major extension, with four extra bath rooms, a proper waiting room, and an enlargement of the reservoir to increase capacity to 1,500 gallons (V.37). The work was supervised by Mr Gott (V.39), who oversaw the Starbeck Spa's largest single annual outlay between 1822 and 1842, with no less than £191 13s. 2½d. being spent. The bounds of the Starbeck Spa estate were subject to a limited amount of alteration, the enrolment for which indicated the position of the various mineral wells. The estate was contained in allotment 208, which the Award of 1778 failed – unusually – to measure, describing it as 'Starbeck – Knaresborough detached'. Well number one, on allotment 209 (a twenty-three acre plot held by James Beckwith at the 1778 Award (B.31) but by 1832 held by Susannah Cockcroft (S.994), is marked as 'chalybeate spring destroyed'. Well number two, within the estate, is marked 'ancient chalybeate spring' and is shown to the north-west of the baths, next to the Star Beck (this survives to the time of writing, being protected by a traditional 'pyramid' type structure). Well number three is the sulphur well beneath the column.

It is evident from the committee minutes that attempts were made frequently to improve the baths (V.51), the estate (V.48), and the supply of mineral water (V.41), and that particular attention was paid to conserving water in adequate storage reservoirs (V.28, A.300, V.37). The most visible sign of the committee's desire to enhance the Starbeck Spa was the re-modelling of the entrance from the Harrogate–Knaresborough road. Following a meeting of 31 October 1837 (V.45), a special committee was instructed to obtain 'such plans and alterations as may be considered most conducive to the interests of the establishment', these plans being produced at the following year's annual general meeting (V.46). However, it took until the meeting of 8 December 1842 to confirm adoption of plan 'number three', for a new gateway in the form of a stone arch, the cost of which was not to exceed £75 (V.58). After further prevarication, agreement was reached as to the form and location of the arch, which was completed within the year (V.62–63). The superb masonry of the Starbeck Spa arch, with its delicate traceried panelling, buttresses and crenellated parapet, indicates workmanship of the very highest order, which may also be found on the neighbouring column, which was re-fashioned in 1843 (V.66). The well-head for the famous Starbeck sulphur well was replaced in February 1844 (O.22.28).

Rates at the Starbeck Baths were less than those in Low Harrogate. Warm baths cost 2s. 6d.; warm shower baths cost 1s.; cold baths or cold showers cost 6*d*. The minutes of the Starbeck Spa company show that money was put into effecting improvements over the next ten years, and that income for baths did not reach the hundred pound barrier until 1835–36, when £111 18*s*. 0*d*. was taken. By 1841 this had reached £162 2*s*. 10*d*. (V.18), and it is unfortunate that no comparable figures are available for either the Victoria Baths or the Montpellier Baths, although they would certainly have exceeded those of Starbeck. The local government changes of 1900 returned Starbeck to Harrogate.[3]

By the middle of the nineteenth century, a cluster of bathing activity had developed around the Cold Well in Cold Bath Road, then known as Cold Bath Lane (S.436). The prescribing of Cold Bathing is of ancient origin, as has been shown by Floyer in his texts of 1697 (F.20), 1702 (F.22), and 1715 (F.23), and although the Cold well in Cold Bath Road was alleged by Thomas Pennant to have been in use as far back as AD 543 (C.52.d) when it was visited by St Mungo (sometimes, Magnus), there is no supporting evidence for this claim, and Pennant was probably confusing Harrogate's Cold Well with that at Copgrove. The earliest reference to cold bathing in Harrogate occurs with the New Cold Bath built near St John's Well in Harrogate (G.2), whose existence is confirmed in the Great Award of 1778 (B.31, allotment 222). Dr Short's important text of 1734 refers to 'a very cold well at Harrogate, famed for sore eyes. This, Dr Neale of Doncaster turned into a very good cold bath ...' (F.24 p. 296). Dr French's 1760 text also praised the Cold Well's qualities in his *Pocket Companion for Harrogate Spaw*, writing on pages 52–56 that '... the well is built four-square, and has a house by it, to dress and undress in ...' (F.27).

The Great Award of 1778 identified the Cold Bath as a 16 perch allotment 474, directly beneath the public open space at 474A (see plan 14), and held by Samuel Hattersley, whose family interest in the estate may be traced from the time 'Samuel Hatterley' acquired it from Daniel Neal of Otley in 1736. (Sc.1)

By the time of the seventh edition of Garnett's *Treatise ...*, issued in 1822, the author was writing that 'St Mungo's or St, Magnus' Well, which is very pure water, and an excellent cold bath; though from what caprice I cannot tell, it has of late been very much neglected ...' (F.52). The 1833 *New Harrogate Guide* does not even mention the Cold Well (G.20), but the 1838 *Visitors' Vade Mecum* records that 'Mr Wordsworth, the proprietor, was induced in the spring of 1837, to have them completely rebuilt, and considerably enlarged and improved ... Further particulars may be known on application to L. Hobkinson, the occupier, who resides upon the premises (G.25). Although this account varies from that given by the Jennings WEA history, which claims 'In 1837, Joshua Holdsworth of Leeds bought the dilapidated buildings at Cold Bath and erected "a large lodging house, with suitable bathing rooms",' both agree that 1837 was the year of rebuilding. Just to make matters even more confusing, Dr Adam Hunter recorded in 1838 that 'St Magnus' Well or bath ... have lately become the property of Mr Joseph Dodsworth of Leeds who is actively engaged in improving the estate. He has already erected a large lodging house, with suitable bathing rooms and every other accommodation for bathers. The Bath and premises connected with it were previously in a very dilapidated condition ...' (F.63). So the reader may choose Wordsworth, Holdsworth or Dodsworth as being the identity of the Cold Bath owner,[4] although there is no doubt that it was Hobkinson who actually administered the establishment (Sc.16), or that the charge for 'plunging, shower and spouting baths' was one shilling. (G.26)

The Cold Bath, situated on the eastern side on Cold Bath Lane, had an interesting connection with a development on the western side, where the Great Award of 1778 had allotted a 6 acre 2 rood 4 perch plot to Isaac Forest (B.31, allotment 477) who purchased it from the commissioners in 1775 (Sc.2). This became the site of a large lodging and bathing house named 'Paris Pavilion', with associated cottages and stables, all of which catered to the Cold Bath's visitors. Paris Pavilion, which at the time of writing still stands adjacent to the site of the demolished Cold Bath, seems to have taken its unusual name from the 1814 Treaty of Paris and possibly the Brighton Pavilion built by Nash for the Prince Regent after 1815, and its association with the Cold Bath is shown in the enrolled entries for the Great Award of 1778 (B.31). The Cold Bath itself formed allotment 474, which together with the neighbouring allotment between the Cold Bath and Otley Road, numbered 473, was held by Samuel Hattersley, both allotments being described as 'at Cold Bath'. All other surrounding allotments – numbers 471, 472, 475, and 478, were described as 'near Cold Bath', and it is only allotment 477, the site of Paris Pavilion, that was described as being 'at Cold Bath'. Paris Pavilion consisted of a large single room at ground floor level, above which were a further two floors of lodging accommodation, reached via an external staircase. The ground-floor room appears to have been used originally as a separate bath house, possibly with internal wooden divisions and water storage devices. Adjoining were several detached structures which contained a wash house, stables, and cottages. It is possible that Paris Pavilion and its surrounding buildings, on the west side of Cold Bath Road, was the principal centre of activity at the Cold Bath, before the 1837 rebuilding by Dodsworth/Holdsworth/Wordsworth of whatever stood immediately adjacent to the Cold Well on the east side of the road. The likelihood of this is strengthened by the fact that the pre-1837 Cold Well (shown as allotment 474 on the Award map of 1778) had clearly been built on land designated as a 'common watering place' (allotment 474a). This meant that although the water of the Cold Well was used for medical

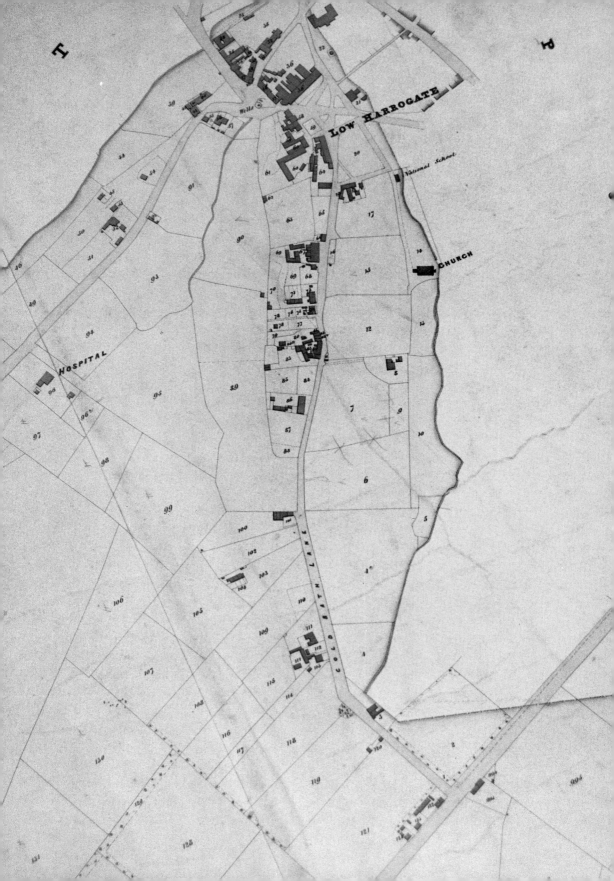

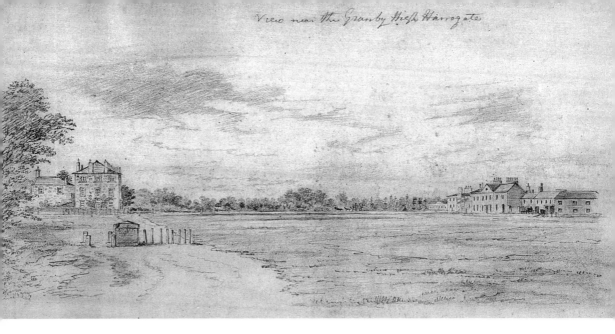

purposes, it was not a mineral water, so it was not deemed part of the Stray, but was, rather, recognised as a source of domestic water supply, open to all without charge. A similar public water source was identified at the World's End, with allotment number 295 (B.31).

The later Greeves' map (see plan 40) and survey (D.59) record that by 1839 Paris Pavilion had been re-named Harlow Cottage, but the older name lingered throughout the century, surfacing from time to time in the township records (D.43) and in newspapers.[5] Information about the decline of the Paris Pavilion and the Cold Bath is not available, but it is reasonable to assume from Grainge's comment, published in 1871,[6] 'now it is but rarely used', that the increasing popularity of both the Victoria and Montpellier Baths in convenient Low Harrogate, contributed to the Cold Bath's decline.

The *Visitors' Vade Mecum* of 1838 referred to a set of baths in Chapel Street, run by one Beck, and known as Clarke's Baths (G.25). This appears to have been nothing more than a lodging house which 'has been erected some years, and contains three or four warm baths … the terms … are very moderate.' (G.25) Clarke's Baths stood on the site which later became the junction of the modern Oxford Street and Station Parade, on which the Salvation Army built their Harrogate Citadel in 1897.

This is an area of Harrogate which has few, if any, natural springs or wells. Any baths given in the area were therefore dependent on having either a good supply of ordinary water, or the delivery of mineral water from the wells which the Award of 1778 had decreed must always be open and unenclosed. The drawing of water from the public mineral wells for use in private bathing houses – although entirely legal – put a strain on the supply for the drinkers. The proliferation of such establishments, as seen in

PLATE 102
The Granby at far left, and the Black Spring (High Harrogate's well of fresh water) with Church Square and Mansfield House at right, drawn in 1830 by John Field.
COURTESY OF MR R. BELDON

the pages of the early Harrogate directories, must have been a source of friction in the town.

Inevitably owners of bathing establishments sought to uncover fresh sources of mineral water by sinking wells on their land. In the case of Mr Thackwray, owner of the Crown Hotel, this activity produced initial success, with the number of wells increasing from one to eight within a period of about five years (H.14). However, the enterprising Mr Thackwray over-reached himself in 1835, when it was found that one of his new wells was affecting the supply from the public Old Sulphur Well. The resulting scandal and court case was directly responsible for the introduction of the Harrogate Improvement Act of 1841.[7]

Before we conclude our account of bathing at the Harrogate Spa in the years up to 1841, it is necessary to note that private houses, especially those in Cold Bath Road, Devonshire Place, Swan Road and Well Hill (S.595) (which last was known sometimes as Sulphur Well Mount), played an enormously important role in providing visitors with bathing facilities. Before the 1841 Improvement Act, which restricted the volume of mineral water which could be taken from the wells in containers (clause 88), it was standard practice to cart it in barrels pulled by donkey cart (see plate 17). Indeed, George Dawson, the epitome of Harrogate's Victorian builders, began life in Harrogate as a cooper for this self-same trade.[8] It was because nearly every house in Harrogate was used for purposes of lodging that there arose the habit of providing such houses with names. 'Britannia Lodge' was so much easier for a visitor to remember than number one Swan Lane.

The Harrogate Waters had been analysed and classified by medical men for centuries, with lists of various ailments and their treatment by means of bathing or drinking, included in their respective writings.

PLATE 17
Early photograph of
Harrogate water
carrier.

PLATE 55
Dr Thomas Garnett,
1765–1802, has been
credited with the first
scientific analysis of
Harrogate's waters.

Few doctors were more respected that Thomas Garnet (see plate 55). His 1792 treatise went into seven editions, the last of which was published in 1822. In this last edition, Dr Garnet recommended that the warm baths be at a temperature of between 94° and 96° Fahrenheit, adding that, 'I cannot forbear congratulating the company at Harrogate, on the abolition of the absurd and indelicate customs formerly in use, which afforded just grounds of complaint to Dr Alexander, and of ridicule to the facetious Dr Smollett ... The common sweating-bed, tainted with the effluvia of hundreds, is not now to be found even in the lowest bathing-houses at Harrogate.' (F.52) Given the widespread belief that the Harrogate sulphur water was so strong that *no* contagion could long survive its attention, it is not surprising that the common women who attended the sulphur wells were not celebrated for their observance of hygiene with either drinkers or bathers. Barbara Hofland, in her *Season at Harrogate*, first published in 1812, described drinking and bathing in the Harrogate Waters:

> From the sick to the well, the same cup travels round,
> From breath that would poison a Hottentot King,
> To breath that is sweeter than violets in spring,
> But as Sulphur prohibits all sorts of infection,
> The rational say there's no proper objection
> What a different thing was a Harrogate boiling,
> And astonished I saw when I came to my doffing,
> A tub of hot water made just like a coffin,
> In which the good woman who tended the bath,
> Declar'd I must lie down as straight as a lath,
> Just keeping my face above water so,
> I might better inhale the fine fume from below,
> But mistress, quoth I in a trembling condition,
> I hope you'll allow me one small requisition,
> since scrofula, leprosy, herpes, and scurvy,
> Have all in this coffin been rolled topsy-turvy,
> In a physical sense I presume it is meet,
> That each guest should be wrapt in a clean winding sheet
> 'Oh no! my good sir, for whatever's your case,
> You can never catch any thing bad in this place,
> And that being settled on solid foundation,
> We Harrogate bath-women spurn innovation.' (C.91.g)

Clearly, the period between Hofland, and the seventh edition of Garnet's *Treatise*, saw improvements in hygienic conditions for both water drinkers and bathers at Harrogate.

Conclusions

Comparison of the medical texts issued by the doctors on the subject of the use of Harrogate waters shows that between 1770 and 1841, bathing – as distinct from drinking – was recommended for a wide variety of skin conditions, arthritic complaints, muscular problems, and what today would be termed psychological states such as depression or hysteria. The bathing of internal organs (as, for example, the larynx by sprays of atomised sulphur water) appears to have been a later introduction of the last quarter of the nineteenth century. Doctors either visited patients at their hotels or lodgings, or received them for consultation in their surgeries. All the writings of the doctors stressed the folly of patients using the Harrogate waters without having first taken medical advice. All this required patients to possess means of remunerating the doctors, and – in view of the recommended length of most 'cures' – of remunerating also the hoteliers and lodging housekeepers. Those without means for such expenditure were still able to obtain access to the free waters of Harrogate, located on the two hundred acres, although bathing at the public wells would have been difficult. The growing fame of the Harrogate waters encouraged the provision – by the hoteliers or speculating businessmen – of specially built suites of baths for those who could pay for them, the most expensive being in Low Harrogate near the Old Sulphur Well, and the cheaper being at some distance, as for example at Starbeck. For the poor, who came from a wide area around Harrogate, the Bath – later the Royal Bath – Hospital was built in 1825, with separate bathing facilities of its own.

9 | Entertainments at the spa

T HE APPEAL of Harrogate's mineral waters was not sufficient to guarantee a continuing influx of new visitors or the regular return of the old. To be sure, the Award of 1778 had provided Harrogate with incomparable assets in the free and unimpeded right of access to the mineral wells, and also in the two hundred acres of land that surrounded those wells. Moreover, thanks to the doctors and their writings, visitors came to Harrogate in search of health, and, when they arrived, they found that the innkeepers had provided a range of accommodation suitable for most requirements. Yet something else was needed to attract new visitors, and to encourage the return of regular ones, as well as to entice all to prolong their stay; that 'something else' was entertainment. Throughout the years from 1770 to 1841, the provision of outdoor and indoor entertainments was in the hands of leading hoteliers or businessmen, and their response to visitor demand shaped an important aspect of contemporary spa life. Perhaps because of Harrogate's northerly location, its exposed situation, and the invalid nature of many of its visitors, much of the entertainment was of the indoor variety.

Indoor entertainments – Hotel life

The single greatest aspect of entertainment life at Harrogate for the visitors was undoubtedly that of the social world of the inns and hotels. One aspect of this social life, which distinguished it from other spas, was that Harrogate as a whole, uniquely, had no 'master of ceremony'. Instead, the guests at each of the great hotels appointed one of their own to regulate social life within each establishment (C.31.b.52) (G.17). The post of MC appears to have been first initiated at Bath, where the holder's function was to educate the sometimes uncouth provincial assemblies in standards of polite behaviour acceptable to fashionable London society. The Bath MC proved to be of such value that he was soon persuaded to share his services with Tunbridge Wells, and the precedent of having an MC was also copied at Bristol Hotwells, Cheltenham, Leamington, Scarborough and Southampton. The

MC received no salary, and his chief duties, as Richard 'Beau' Nash developed the post at Bath, were to preside over the functions in the rooms.[1]

At Harrogate, the absence of any MC produced an easier, less rigid society, which was remarked upon by visitors such as Thomas Amory in 1731, who noted that, 'of all the Wells I know, Harrogate is in my opinion the most charming. The waters are incomparable, no air can be better, and with the greatest civility, cheerfulness, and good-humour, there is a certain rural plainness and freedom mixed, which are vastly pleasing . . .' (C.25.g).

The freedom with which society mixed at Harrogate did not mean that formal divisions of rank were abandoned. Each of the biggest inns acquired followings from various groups of society. The Queen Hotel was nicknamed the 'Manchester Warehouse', as it was frequented by the manufacturing classes – 'the great Manchester millocrat, the Sheffield pin-maker, the iron-founder from Black Barnsley . . . folks who dared not . . . attempt admission either into the Dragon or the Granby, and who were hardly sufficiently assured in their position to venture even amongst the jewels of the Crown'. The Dragon was known as the House of Commons, because of its popularity with the gambling and fast-living set, including the military. The Granby had the enviable nickname of the 'House of Lords', because it was frequented by the nobility. As for the Crown in Low Harrogate, it was known as the 'Hospital', as it was frequented by those seeking the cure from the neighbouring Sulphur Well (C.86.f). This system of rigid class distinction between hotels did not survive very far into the nineteenth century. When Dr A. Granville visited Harrogate in the late 1830s, when researching for his monumental survey of all British spas, he noted:

> At one time your opulent Leeds, Sheffield or Manchester factors . . . no more dreamt of stopping at the gates of the Dragon, still less those of the Granby, than they would at the palace of my Lord Harewood . . . The Dragon and the Granby were sacred places. The Lords only graced the latter, while the wealthy commoner pleased himself in the former. Now [i.e. *c.* 1839] pretty little gauche misses and their snuff coloured papas boldly stalk into both houses without being 'called'; cutlers and cotton-spinners aspire to great assembly rooms and gigantic banqueting saloons, and nothing pleases the wealthy townsmen of Bradford and Huddersfield, Halifax and Rochdale, but the well-stuffed sofas of red damask, and the cuisine par excellence of those two crack hotels (F.58).

Thirty years before, one visitor to High Harrogate described the Dragon, and the efforts of its landlord to keep out the lesser orders:

The Dragon at Harrowgate (in those days) was unlike any other table
d'hote of the time; it was more like some nobleman's seat, where the
elite of the world of fashion had been invited to spend the summer
months ... there were personages whose names were familiar amongst
the aristocracy of the land ... when old Goodlad was host of the
Dragon, during whose administration it was impossible for a parvenue,
or a party without four horses and liveried attendants to match, to gain
a footing at the hotel ... (C.86.b–c).

The breakdown appears to have occurred because the class distinctions of
the three great High Harrogate hotels could obviously not be replicated at
Low Harrogate's single important establishment, the Crown Hotel, when
the fashion turned against High Harrogate in favour of Low Harrogate. The
former village possessed palatable iron water, but no sulphur water. Low
Harrogate possessed both iron and sulphur water, and its proximity – after
1848 – to the railway station ensured that it would be favoured with the
majority of attractive new developments.

PLAN 36
Charles Greeves' 1821
plan of the Granby
locality.

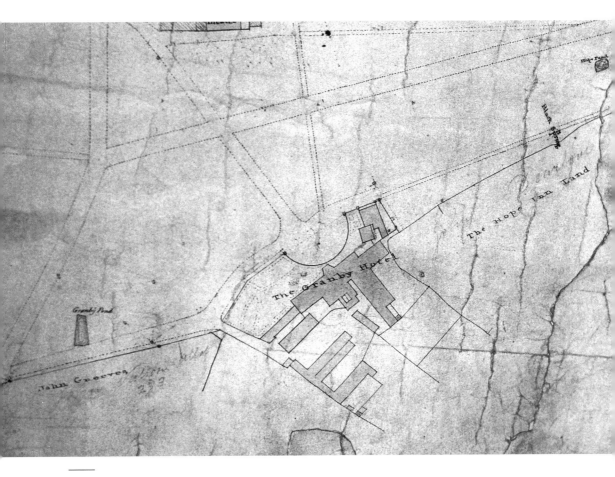

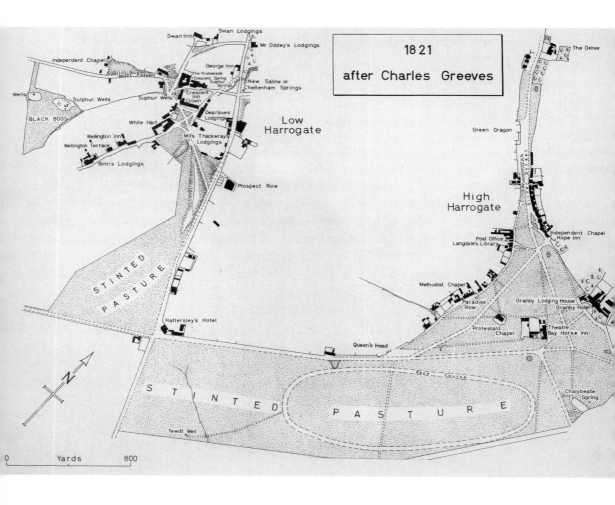

Indoor entertainments — Balls

During the visitor 'season', the series of nightly balls, held successively in each of the great hotels, required much planning. Special arrangements had to be decided on such matters as music making, candles, refreshments, and invitations to the guests of other establishments. Smollett noted that, 'there is a public ball, by subscription, every night at one of the houses to which all the company from the others are admitted by tickets; and, indeed, Harrogate treads upon the heals of Bath, in the articles of gaiety and dissipation, – with this difference however, that here we are more sociable and familiar.' (C.44.b) The balls were held, by tradition, at the Dragon on Mondays, the Crown on Wednesdays, the Queen on Thursdays, and the Granby on Fridays (see plate 88). (G.24). One of the visitors noted in 1813 that special charges were levied on ball nights, when the drawing rooms were lit with spermacete candles, and that two shillings and sixpence was the norm, which included a glass of negus. A singular charging system was employed, whereby the entrance money was collected by the head waiter, who had to pay the owner of the hotel for the extra candles, the food and drink, as well as settling the accounts of the musicians, who were paid seven shillings each for a single night's work. The waiters kept whatever was left from the entrance charges, after all costs had been deducted. By 1835, charges at the Crown Hotel had risen from two shillings and sixpence to three shillings (A.270).

Although the days of each ball were established through custom, it was still the habit for each hotel to post official invitations to the company at the other leading hotels. Each hotel supplied lists of company to its neighbours, in order to determine likely attendance figures at the balls (R.3100). It is likely that this habit led to the production of Harrogate's first newspaper, on Monday 18 September 1820, which was produced by William Langdale, who succeeded Hargrove at the High Harrogate 'Library'. The first issue of Langdale's paper was called *Weekly List of Company at Harrogate*, and it consisted of the names of all the visitors, followed by the names of the inns or hotels where they were staying (see plate 88). There were no advertisements, and no local news – this was a publication aimed at visitors, not for Harrogate residents (R.3100).

The pleasures of Harrogate at the time of the Napoleonic wars may be summed up by a contemporary description of *c.* 1810: 'What scenes of life have we not beheld at Harrowgate! what days of romance and nights of revelry and excitement, have we not passed at the far famed hotels, when on that bare, Scotchified looking common, were assembled in the huge stone built halls ... half the fashion and beauty of the kingdom; where the great sporting men of the day met; where mothers trotted out their daughters in all their charms, and country squires ... learnt the trick of

PLATE 88
All the great Harrogate hotels provided a weekly ball night for their guests and invited company.

wiving; where fortunes were won by the turn up of a card by old dowagers, whilst their radiant and exquisite daughters lost their hearts to some lord of sash and epaulette in the dance ...' (C.86.a).

Indoor entertainments — Gambling

Quite apart from the formal betting, which must have occurred on the Harrogate race course, and which is referred to frequently by Blind Jack Metcalf (C.30.f), organised gambling appears to have been a central pleasure for many visitors staying in the town's hotels.

> The Dragon was the house for those who came to seek for pleasure and amusement ... high play was constantly referred to, and the card-room was usually filled with players at this period ... Some dozen tables were filled with the oddest of all the oddities of the play men of the turf, the most celebrated sporting characters of that day, and perhaps the most determined gentleman gamblers in England ... So absorbed were some of the ... company in this vice, that we have known men pass a whole season in the card room ... seated at those tables morning, noon and night ... we remember a lady of rank, who after a life spent at the card table, died with the pack in her hand ... a rich Indian nabob who successively lost three fortunes at Harrowgate, Cheltenham and Buxton ... a devoted son of the Clergy, one of the finest preachers of his day, who was wont to treat his congregation with a sermon ... on the enormity of gambling, after which, he would ascend his curricle, drive to the Dragon, and pass the entire remainder of the sabbath behind the closed blinds of the card room ... (C.86.g)

Indoor entertainments — Assemblies

Harrogate did not possess a formal 'assembly room' until the close of the reign of George III. Unlike Bath and Cheltenham, which had Assembly Rooms by 1708[2] and 1738[3] respectively, Harrogate did not have a population of upper-class residents, with social ambition backed by wealth. In 1770, the number of innkeepers and doctors cannot have exceeded a dozen, the rest of the population of about six hundred being either servants or agricultural workers. However, 'assemblies' were provided on a nightly basis at the great inns (G.8). Moves to provide a public assembly room at Harrogate appear to have been made at the same time as the rigid demarcation between the inns was breaking down, with one inn inviting the guests of neighbouring inns to their ball nights (G.24).

The assembly room was the most common amenity for entertainment at a spa in the eighteenth and early nineteenth centuries. An assembly brought together the leading members of provincial communities, invariably being governed by a strict code of etiquette and demarcation. They provided a means for the public display of courtly manners and techniques – such as dancing – opportunity for courtship, and a means by which those attending could obtain a gratifying degree of public admiration. Although assemblies were open to subscribers or ticket holders, admission was nevertheless restricted to persons of quality and rank. By 1770 about sixty towns and spas provided regular assemblies for their visitors.[4] Bath's first assembly rooms had been opened in 1708, a century before those at Harrogate, having been developed by Thomas Harrison on the east side of Terrace Walk. Enlarged in 1749, the 'Harrison's Assembly Rooms' were part of the Royal Hotel, 75½ feet in length by 32 feet in width by 30 feet in height, and built in the style of Robert Adam. The Assembly Rooms at Cheltenham, first opened in 1738, were superseded in 1816 by the New Assembly Rooms, which measured 85 feet in length by 38 feet in width by 40 feet in height, and which were built in the classical style.[5]

There were two great differences between Bath, Buxton, Cheltenham and many other English spas on the one hand, and Harrogate on the other. First, Harrogate had a reputation for being remarkably informal (C.25.g), and therefore unsuited to the formality and regulation of assembly room life. Second, at Harrogate, all land was owned by the Duchy of Lancaster until the Award of 1778. After centuries of experience, the Duchy knew that its best interests lay in protecting the interests and traditions of established tenants, whether they were in Knaresborough Forest, Methwold, Needwood or Pickering – to name only four Duchy estates. This was certainly true during the difficult years of George III's insanity, or the disappearance of Queen Victoria from public view after the death of Prince Albert, when a whiff of republicanism was briefly in the air.[6] It would clearly not have been sensible for the Duchy to have made itself unpopular by appearing the grasping landlord; rather, the Duchy always adopted a long-term and moderate policy towards the tenantry of its estates.[7] In Harrogate, this policy ensured that before the Award of 1778, it was impossible for speculators to embark on any over-intensive developments.

The site of the first Harrogate assembly rooms had been allotted by the 1778 Award to the owner of the Crescent Inn (B.31). In 1804 part of the Crescent Estate was conveyed to two physicians, Dr Hunter and Dr Cayley, for the purpose of 'erecting and completing the said intended Promenade Room', which was to be 75 feet in length by 30 feet in width (S.e.10). Both Doctors Cayley (F.45) and Hunter (F.44) published treatises on the Harrogate Spa, and as a matter of course were in the habit of prescribing the waters to their patients. They must have recognised the need for assembly rooms in Low Harrogate, and identified the plot of land behind the Crescent Inn, which was only a few dozen yards from the Old Sulphur Well, as being a site ideally located for such a building.

Six years before Doctors Cayley and Hunter purchased the site in 1804, on Swan Road, for Harrogate's first assembly rooms, a plan for an assembly room at High Harrogate was completed, in the form of a watercolour drawing. Dated 1798, the drawing is neither signed nor costed, and if any ground plans or quantity surveys were completed, they have not survived. The drawing is entitled 'Design for Assemblin Rooms at Harrowgate', and shows a two-storey stone building in Palladian style, with a ground elevation in rusticated coursings, and an upper one decorated with pilasters and wide windows. Although the location is not identified, the drawing appears to show the Granby Hotel in the background, and may therefore be placed at High Harrogate (see plate 30). It is not known who – if anyone – actually commissioned the High Harrogate Assembly Rooms drawing; it may even have been done by a visitor as a diversion. But whoever the author was, Harrogate's first assembly rooms were fated to be erected in Low, rather than High Harrogate. Bookseller Hargrove opened a room at the back of his High Harrogate shop in about 1800, which was advertised as a place of assembly, and he even advertised for an MC from among the visitors, but the post carried no salary, and had authority only within the shop premises.

The *Leeds Mercury* announced the opening of the new assembly rooms: 'We understand that the Promenade, now being erected at Harrogate, is nearly finished, and will be opened on 16 June [1806] with some select pieces of music on the organ. This elegant and commanding building stands in the middle of a garden, and is intended as a morning Lounge for the Company who will assemble every morning at the Wells.' (R.1300) The financing of the new Promenade Room (see plate 53) was undertaken by a group of shareholders to a limited company founded by Doctors Cayley and Hunter. Sales appear to have been brisk, for by 21 June 1806 only ten shares of one pound each were remaining unsold (R.1310). The *York Herald* also reported the opening: 'To add to the harmony of the morning, the intervals between the pieces on the organ, were most tastefully filled up by the band belonging to Colonel Harvey's West Riding Cavalry.' Although Harrogate was without any formally appointed MC to order the niceties of social inter-course, rules were nevertheless composed for the proper use of the new assembly room. 'No servants be allowed to walk in the room, or gardens, at the hours they are frequented by the Company. Nurses attending young children excepted.' (R.1310) Annual subscriptions cost twelve shillings, with children of twelve or under paying six shillings. Special rates were available on request for occasional or short-term visits. The *York Herald* reported that

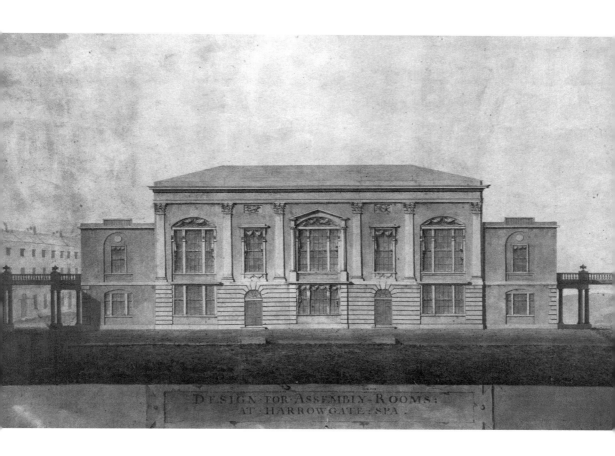

DESIGN FOR ASSEMBLY-ROOMS AT HARROWGATE SPA.

PLATE 30
1789 plan for an
Assembly Room at
Harrogate.

by 3 July, the subscribers' list totalled 55, reaching 221 by 23 August. Amenities at the Promenade included the use of the surrounding gardens, musical recitals, dances, lectures, card parties, and 'fashionable company'. Gossip, and ogling other subscribers, though not specified, must also have formed an important aspect of the Promenade's attractions! (C.91.k). A letter from the Rev. Robert Mitton, incumbent of High Harrogate Chapel, to the Duchy of Lancaster, provides insight as to the deportment of some of the fashionable ladies visiting Harrogate at this time '... My best respects to ... your sensible little daughter, and I hope she ... can walk, as the fashionable ladies do, with the back bent in, and stomach out.' (M.58)

Many of the entertainments available at the hotels were planned by senior visitors who acquired the status which was held at other spas by masters of ceremonies such as Simon Moreau at Cheltenham, or Richard Tyson at Tunbridge.[8] At Harrogate, alone of all the great British spas, each hotel had its own MC, and there is not a single recorded case of any person – guest or permanent resident – aspiring to, or obtaining, authority over the entire spa. Henry Curling, writing of Regency Harrogate, described the MCs of one hotel as being queen-bees, or lady-patronesses of high rank, whose glances of approval or rejection would be certain to either sanction the introduction of the newcomer into the *crème-de-la-crème* of society, or to keep them at so uncomfortable a distance, that they would be 'frozen into the necessity seeking the warmer climes of other houses.' (C.86.d) At table, precedence appears to have been determined by 'seniority of time', with 'the gentleman of longest standing [no matter how humble]' presiding at the head of the table, and the 'latest comer [no matter how grand] takes his seat at the bottom, and ascends gradually in turn.' (G.17) George Carey, describing the ceremonies at the spa in *c.*1796, wrote: 'There is little etiquette at Harrowgate, nor are the company pestered with the officious & interested cringings of an obsequious Master of Ceremonies. They appropriate one from among themselves, such as may have good nature enough and ability to undertake the office during his visit'. (C.31.b.45) (G.4)

PLATE 31
The unknown artist's
signature on the
unbuilt Assembly
Room plan of 1789.

Indoor entertainments — Music

The band and organ recitals provided in the new Promenade Room continued a tradition of music-making in Harrogate for the pleasure of the visitors. Sir Darcy Dawes noted that during his visit in June 1727, he paid Morison the fiddler two shillings and sixpence for his playing (C.24.a), Morison, who played in the long rooms of the Queen and Granby Hotels until he reached the age of one hundred, appears to have been superseded by Blind Jack Metcalf, who in his autobiography recorded that he had succeeded Morison, and continued to play the fiddle up to the end of the century (C.30.c). Concert recitals were provided for visitors in the High Harrogate Theatre. On 21 September 1802, a 'grand selection of sacred music from the works of Handel and Haydn' was provided by soloists, instrumentalists and chorus, with entry tickets priced at 5s. for boxes, 3s. 3d. for the pit, and 2s. for the gallery (R.1150). The press reported many such recitals, although they were less frequent than play performances.

Indoor entertainments – Libraries

The bookseller Eli Hargrove appears to have opened a subscription library
in High Harrogate shortly before 1775. Hargrove's guide to Harrogate
praises '… a circulating library, where the company are accommodated
with the perusal of books, pamphlets, and newspapers. The subscription
book to this library is of great use, as a kind of intelligencer, to know where,
and what company are at the place.' (G.1) At its location on Park Parade,
half way between the Queen and Dragon Hotels, and opposite the Granby,
the Chapel, and the St John's Well, Hargrove's library was conveniently
sited for the visitors. According to a surviving set of rules, subscribers paid
five shillings per annum, which entitled them to borrow up to two books at
any time for a maximum period of two months. The library opened with
the arrival of the earliest seasonal visitors on 1 June, and closed at the end of
September, when the last visitors were expected to depart. Like so much
else in Harrogate, the library was an amenity for visitors, rather than
residents.[9] George Carey visited a Harrogate library in 1796, noting that it
'… is not of the greatest magnitude, but is pleasantly situated on a rising
ground, between upper and lower Harrowgate; it is an agreeable lounge,
where you are accommodated with newspapers, hear the novelties of the
day, and sometimes form a good society.' (G.4) The first 'free' library seems
to have been Isabella Dunn's Westmorland Street Library, with 182 religious
works donated in 1828 by Mary Richmond of Hull.[10]

When Barbara Hofland published her racy and amusing *Season at
Harrogate*, in 1813, she noted:

> The place of all places for lounging away,
> In amusement and style the first half of the day,
> Is at each of the Libraries; where you may find,
> Books, Music, fine prints, in short all things combined
> … so to Wilson's I go every morning inquiring,
> 'What arrivals there are?' – and the papers desiring. (C.91.k)

No mention of Hargrove, let it be noted, who had asked Miss Hofland to
provide him with 'something connected with the place' that he could
publish. But then, Miss Hofland had quarrelled with the autocratic
Hargrove, who refused to give her the full third of profits she requested.
Instead, the enterprising Miss Hofland took her work to Wilson, owner of a
rival library, who produced it successfully (C.83.k). Angered by the loss of
the hugely successful *Season at Harrogate*, Hargrove commissioned a less
fastidious writer – David Lewis – to produce a rival work, which came out
shortly after Hofland's. Entitled *A Week at Harrogate*, Lewis's work was a
shameless plagiarism, even lifting the names of Miss Hofland's hero,

Benjamin Blunderhead. Hargrove's influence is obvious; whereas Miss Hofland provides a single allusion to libraries in Harrogate (as reproduced above), Lewis provides the reader with no fewer than six lengthy references to Hargrove's library! (C.92)

Indoor entertainments – Theatre

The provision of theatre was probably the most potent means of providing spa visitors with entertainment, along with balls and assemblies. Bath, in 1705, received a £1,300 playhouse from wealthy shopkeeper George Trim, followed in 1709 by a primitive playhouse run in a stable next to the Abbey gate, part of the estate of John Hall.[11] After the theatre retreated to Simpson's cellar in 1738, they began performing at inns such as the Globe, in 1747, and the George, in 1748. A new theatre opened in 1750 in Orchard Street, but rivalry with the Simpson's group led to difficulties, so when John Palmer, in 1768, obtained a royal patent for a theatre, under the first Act in England to secure theatrical property, it was claimed to be 'much wanted'.[12] The Bath Theatre Royal flourished in the 1790s. Cheltenham, in 1744, enjoyed visits from the Warwick company of comedians and their 'dramatic performances', and in July 1758 Mr Williams' company performed in an old malt-house in Coffee House Lane, which had been converted into a primitive theatre by Mr Pope, who also ran the Coffee House.[13] Buxton may have had a small, dirty theatre by 1776, which was demolished when the Duke of Devonshire built his famous stables on the site, replacing it in about 1792 with a new, modest structure, which opened on 1 July for three nights a week until the end of October.[14] A theatre was established at Tunbridge Wells in 1786,[15] and at Leamington Spa in about 1810, this last being replaced with Simms' Theatre in 1813.[16] Theatrical life was thus an integral part of life at an eighteenth-century English spa; indeed, as the researches of Phyllis Hembry have shown, a spa without a theatre was no spa at all.

Until our own research proved the contrary, the accepted history of Harrogate's theatrical life was that it began in the Granby Hotel's barn, and subsequently removed in 1788 to the specially built playhouse in Church Square that two centuries later became Mansfield House. It was historian William Grainge who first referred to Granby Barn, noting that, 'In 1788 ... a theatre was built at High Harrogate by Mr Samuel Butler. Previous to that time theatricals were enacted in a barn belonging to the Granby hotel.' On a further page, Grainge observed of the Granby Hotel: 'In the barn behind, the first plays acted in Harrogate were performed; traces of its fittings up at that time yet remain' (i.e. by *c.* 1870).[17]

There are several clear references to theatrical performances in Harrogate before 1788, and none of them refers to the Granby Hotel or its barn; instead, they use the term 'theatre'. Indeed, had it not been for Grainge, writing a century after the events he was recording, there would be no connection between Granby barn and the theatre in Harrogate. In 1774 Tate Wilkinson's company visited Harrogate 'under their own government' (i.e. at their own initiative rather than as guests of the Granby, or any other hotel). Wilkinson recorded that the company 'attended the Theatre on the opening. Not any regular company of players had then ever acted at Harrogate ... Mr Moody (an actor engaged from York) seated in the pit, as the only auditor in the whole theatre, either in box, pit or gallery.' Of time keeping, Wilkinson noted, '... at Harrogate ... the beginning of any stated hour was so little thought of, that the audience never went till the play ought to have been almost over ... However ... The performers were all prepared at half past six, the fiddlers played "Britons strike home", the bell was rung, and curtain drew up, and Mr Powell (one of the troupe) entered ...' (C.51.a)

The Wilkinson reference to boxes, gallery and pit surely indicate something more substantial than a converted barn!. Yet when the first edition of Hargrove's guidebook was issued the following year (1775), no mention was made of a theatre (G.1), though Hargrove also failed to refer to the Crown Hotel, which was definitely in existence by 1740 (R.3127).

The *Newcastle Courant* on 29 July 1775, reporting on Harrogate, noted that, 'We hear from Harrogate, that on Saturday last, was performed at the Theatre in that place, to a numerous and brilliant audience, a new farce, called "The Humours of Harrogate", written by Francis Meek Esq., which was received with repeated marks of the most uncommon applause.' (R.586) The following year saw the completion of a singular document which set down the circumstances under which money would be lent on certain copyhold premises at Harrogate. The premises were directly opposite High Harrogate's popular and busy Dragon Hotel, on allotment 291, which lay on the east side of Devonshire Place (B.31). This allotment was a small plot of one rood, thirty-eight perches, on which stood a building 'lately erected called the Playhouse', held by William Lupton (B.272.b), who was to surrender it to coachmaker George Burnand for one (or possibly four) hundred pounds, subject to conditions (S.273). The surrender was confirmed in the court rolls for 10 April 1776 (S.276), which repeated the term 'all that house or building lately erected called the Play House'. When, in 1793, George Burnand mortgaged the building to John Turnbull, the court roll recorded, 'all that house or building heretofore erected and used as a Playhouse, but which hath since been converted into a dwellinghouse ...' (S.403). After Burnand's death, the building passed to his family, the court roll recording that '... to Catherine and Jane Burnand ... all that building heretofore erected and used as a Playhouse …' (S.543) These references show that Harrogate possessed a custom-built theatre well before the Butler Theatre opened in 1788 at Church Square.

Although it cannot be proven, it is nevertheless probable that the earliest known Harrogate play bill, dated 15 August 1769 (P.1) refers to the Devonshire Place Theatre, and not, as was once supposed, William Grainge's Granby Barn theatre. A comparison of prices is instructive, in that the 1769 bill advertised boxes at three shillings, seats in the pit at two shillings, and one shilling in the gallery. Forty years later, the Theatre Royal in Church Square was charging identical rates (P.37), so it was hardly likely that in 1818 (P.37) prices in a custom-built theatre were identical to those charged forty years earlier in a mere barn!

The Devonshire Place theatre (see plate 21) was exceptionally well sited on the busy road between Harrogate to Ripon and Skipton (then known as World's End Road (S.342), and directly opposite the crowded Dragon Hotel and its colourful clientele (C.41). Such a favourable situation should have enabled the new theatre to survive, but as the covenant document shows, it had closed by 1776 (S.273). Identifying the theatre's builder and time of opening are more difficult. If the first known play bill (P.1) refers to Devonshire Place, then 1769 is the first known reference to a theatre in High Harrogate. The court rolls are unhelpful on the matter, as the earliest reference in the indices to the court rolls for the period 1764 to 1776 list William Lupton's allotment as being entered during the court of 27 December 1775 (S.272.b), but without mentioning the playhouse. The same indices have no earlier reference to William Lupton entering the Devonshire Place allotment of one rood, thirty-eight perches between 1746 and 1764,[18] so it is likely that the Lupton family had held the land for some time, and that it was William Lupton who was responsible for building the Devonshire Place Theatre, probably between 1765 and 1769. An engraving of 1829 by J. Stubbs (see plate 19) of the Dragon Hotel shows the former Devonshire Place Theatre at extreme left, facing Dragon Lodging House (also known as 'The Elms') and the rest of Regent Parade. Stubbs' drawing, and our knowledge of the theatre being on allotment 291 (B.31), show that the Devonshire Place theatre, quite remarkably, survived into the later nineteenth century, when it was held by Leeds architect George Corson, and then by the developer of the Regent estate, Amos Chippindale.[19] It was probably Chippindale who converted the traditional Georgian 'box' theatre, with its flat façade and high gable with central occulus window, into the Victorian-fronted building with swelling bay timber windows and solid stone lintels, which survives to the time of writing.

The design of the Devonshire Place theatre may have had much to do with its short life, although it had much in common with the successful

PLATE 21
The Devonshire Place, or 'Dragon' Theatre. The building was eventually acquired by developer Amos Chippindale, who converted it, adding the Victorian bay windows.

____

Butler theatre of 1788. The Butler theatre was built opposite the important Granby Hotel, the Lupton theatre being opposite the equally important Dragon Hotel. The Butler theatre fronted a yard with stables (S.d.23) as did the Lupton theatre (S.273), and both were designed with a central bay crowned by a high gable and central occulus, flanked by a pair of matching wings – although in the case of the Lupton theatre, it is uncertain if these wings were original, or added during conversion (S.403); the Butler theatre was adjacent to the Bay Horse Inn (S.d.2), the Lupton theatre was adjacent to the Salutation (B.31). There was, however, one great difference, and that was size: the Lupton theatre had three floors, the Butler had two. It may have been that the Lupton theatre was simply too ambitious for Harrogate in the 1760s, whereas the smaller Butler theatre was better able to cater to a public taste trying to come to terms with life during the era of the French Revolution and the wars which followed.[20]

As for Grainge's reference to Granby barn, it seems that he did not obtain this from original research, but from one of the Hollins illustrated hand-books, such as the 1858 edition, which notes on page 23 that before the erection of the Church Square Theatre, 'theatrical representations were performed in a barn behind the Granby Hotel; and there it was that the celebrated Miss Melon used to delight her audience, and where her genius shone forth in a blaze of triumph, which completely obscured the light of twelve penny candles flickering in bottles around her.'

The most likely explanation is that Granby barn did indeed serve as a makeshift theatre after closure of the Devonshire Place establishment in about 1776, and before the 1788 opening of the Church Square theatre for Samuel Butler. Weight is given to this theory by the fact that at the time of the Great Award of 1778, the Granby Hotel was owned by Thomas Wilks (as allotment 272,) who was also recorded as owning allotment 288 (B.31), having held it since October 1779 (S.d.1). Allotment 288 was, of course, the site of the theatre built ten years later for Samuel Butler (G.10).

The last known reference to theatrical performances at the Devonshire Place theatre occurs in 1775, with the *Newcastle Courant*'s review of 29 July (R.586). Lupton must have suffered financial reverses during the season of 1775, as he surrendered it to George Burnand in April 1776 (S.276), and here is one possible explanation for Hargrove's failure to mention the theatre in his 1775 guidebook (G.1). We therefore suggest that the Devonshire Place theatre served Harrogate from about 1765 until 1775, after which Thomas Wilks provided temporary accommodation in Granby barn, until the new theatre opened in Church Square in 1788.

PLATE 26
The Theatre Royal,
Church Square, built
in 1788.

Thomas Wilks, who died in April 1800 (S.486), obtained an annual rental of £188 2s. from his Granby tenant William Dinsley, which sum seems to have encouraged Wilks to improve his already lucrative business. By 1796, the tax on the Granby, known as Queen's rental, was only 10¾d. (A.242), so Wilks possessed sufficient means to proceed with plans for a new theatre. We do not know who designed the Church Square structure (see plate 26), but its erection on a site directly opposite the prestigious Granby Hotel is an elegant exercise in the same Georgian theatre design evident at the famous theatre at Richmond, which, indeed, served the same Samuel Butler and his troupe who visited Harrogate during the 'season' (P.c).

The theatrical performances were not intended for the resident population, few of whom could have afforded the price of the tickets, which cost one shilling for a gallery seat, two shillings for a pit seat, and three shillings for a box (P.2), all of which were very high rates for Harrogate's resident population, which in 1770 stood at about five hundred. Such a number was, of itself, insufficient to support a theatre without the spa visitors, and the theatre's performances mirrored the length of the visitor season between June, when the visitors arrived, and October, when the visitors departed (P).

The man brought in by Wilks to run the new theatre was Samuel Butler, and it is probable that the two had become acquainted during visits to Harrogate by the Butler company before 1788. Butler was born in 1750, joined a group of strolling players in *c.* 1770, marrying the wife of a former manager in 1773. With great energy, he built up a circuit for his players that included rights to perform at Beverley, in East Yorkshire, and to set up a base in Kendal. This was only three years before the change in the law which permitted players in the provinces to hire themselves as actors. Before this change, all such strolling actors were termed 'rogues and vagabonds', unless they had the protection of a royal warrant. Although there is no proof that Butler ever had such a warrant, he nevertheless adopted the title of 'His Majesty's Servants'.[21]

The High Harrogate Theatre closed in 1830, at a time when Low Harrogate was eclipsing High, and although the exterior remains unaltered to this day, the interior was gutted for conversion into dwelling houses. Some idea of the appearance of the interior of the High Harrogate Theatre may be had from the surviving one at Richmond, which opened the same year as Harrogate's, and for the same troupe of actors. The earliest surviving play bill for the Butler theatre in Harrogate dates from 12 August 1788, announcing a 'benefit' for Miss Wallis, a notable actress of the time. Possession of a ticket did not guarantee access to a specific seat, only admission to the building, and this resulted in the practice of sending servants to occupy the best seats until their masters and mistresses were ready to fill them. This in turn led to the management reminding patrons that 'servants cannot be admitted without payment' (P.7). The play bills show that for the first ten years, opening time was at 'half after six', changing to seven in 1799, which remained the case until the final few years of the theatre's life in the late 1820s, when it moved to 7.30 p.m.

Performances (see plate 27) were given on Tuesdays, Thursdays and Saturdays, probably in order to avoid clashing with the popular balls given at the Dragon on Mondays the Crown on Wednesdays, and the Granby on Fridays (G.11). Unlike twentieth-century practice, with management fixing programmes well in advance of performances, it was usual in the eighteenth century for programmes to be chosen by the customer. The great inns took turns to canvass their guests, with resulting requests then sent to the theatre. There was little that was democratic in this process, as the surviving play bills show that the preference of a single important guest held sway of that of an entire inn. Thus, for every time a play bill was published with a heading such as 'By the desire of the Ladies and Gentlemen of the Queen's Head' (P.16) or 'By desire of the Ladies and Gentlemen at the Granby' (P.76), it was three times more likely to be headed with a personal dedication such as 'By desire of the most Noble, the Marquis of Ely' (P.31). The players had little to fear from this arrangement, as the majority of requests were for popular ephemera or classics by Shakespeare or Sheridan.

The repertoire was seldom presented in the style intended by its creator, it being accepted practice that plays were to be cut and interrupted

according to whim. A performance of 'She Stoops to Conquer' on 16 July 1791 had acts one and two divided by a rendition of the 'French Revolution Song' (P.7). There is, however, no evidence that the Marseillaise was ever performed during Lord Castlereagh's visits to Harrogate!

If there were any English sympathies towards France, especially from the lower classes, they changed as the situation in France deteriorated. Samuel Butler, manager of Harrogate Theatre, reflected this change in the programmes he put on in accordance with visitors' tastes. In July 1793 he produced 'He would be a soldier', which although a comedy, introduced a military theme into the repertoire (P.13) In a performance of 'a new comedy, called, Management (never acted here)', the fourth act was interrupted by a song called 'The recruit', and such themes become more frequent as the Napoleonic era progressed (P.19). In July 1806, when England could boast only of naval victories, one of the plays was provided with a special 'naval duet, composed by Mr Shield expressly for the company, called "True Blue for ever"' (P.33), and this was followed a month later by a specially written narration entitled 'Trafalgar, or, Nelson's last triumph' (P.34).

Along with occasional pieces of contemporary interest, the Butler troupe performed more substantial pieces, and Shakespeare was seldom absent from the season's offerings. 'Hamlet' was given on 11 July 1811, with Mr Butler junior in the role of the ghost. The play was advertised as being the 'favourite tragedy', with acts one and two being separated by 'Master Phillips, who will sing 'The Bay of Biscay. Oh!' acts two and three by the melodrama 'The Forest of Hermanstadt', and acts three and four by Mr Butler junior singing the praises of mutton chops. Hamlet was performed by Mr Phillips, for whom the performance was a benefit – that is, he received all the box office takings (P.69).

The Butler connection with the Harrogate Theatre was a long and honourable one, extending to two generations. Samuel Butler senior died in 1812, after having bought the theatre from Mrs Wilks in 1805 shortly after the death of her husband (S.b.8). The theatre passed into the hands of Butler's widow, Frances Maria, and – on his maturity – their son, Samuel William Butler. Butler senior had already adopted the name of 'Theatre Royal', in 1805, and this name was thereafter used to advertise all productions.

The Butlers were not averse to recruiting outside talent on occasion, especially if it came from London. The celebrated Mrs Jordan acted the role of Lady Teazle in the performance of 'School for Scandal' of 15 August 1811 (P.70). Mrs Jordan was at this time nearing the end of her relationship with the Duke of Clarence, brother to the Prince Regent, who later became William IV, and the role of Lady Teazle was one of her favourites. Her stage husband, Sir Peter, was played by Samuel Butler himself. One of the Butler troupe was fortunate in obtaining powerful patronage in 1790, when, on 1 July, the play 'Tancred and Sigismunda' was performed with the sixteen-year-old Tryphosa Jane Wallis in the role of Sigismunda. According to a contemporary description, Miss Wallis was 'exquisitely fair, with expressive blue eyes, well controlled movements, a fine figure, and a voice of more sweetness than strength' (C.58). Her talent was recognised by the Lord Chancellor of England, Lord Rosslyn, and his wife, who had purchased land in Harrogate in order to build a residence half-way between London and Edinburgh. The relief obtained by Lady Rosslyn from the waters of the neighbouring St John's Well was a further attraction, in gratitude for which, Lord Rosslyn provided the well with an elegant pump room (C.71.b). Both the Rosslyns were regular visitors to the Harrogate theatre, and the support of such influential people proved extremely valuable to Miss Wallis. The diarist John Courtney recorded that at a performance on 5 June 1790, 'Miss Wallis played Sigismunda extremely well, indeed she had the richest dress on I think I ever saw on stage; it was given her by Lady Rosslyn and cost an hundred pounds; it was brilliant & most superb ...' (C.61). A later habitué of the Harrogate theatre, Harriet Mellon recorded that when Miss Wallis had established herself as a nationally celebrated actress, she interrupted her work at Covent Garden to visit Harrogate, to stay at Wedderburn House, the Harrogate mansion of Lord Rosslyn (C.58).

Harriet Mellon, born in 1777, has an interesting link with Harrogate, in that she not only attended theatrical performances at the spa, but she was also the mother of Angela Burdett Coutts, who donated the Potts clock to Harrogate market.[22] Harriet's mother remarried a Mr Entwistle in 1782, who was a musician who accompanied travelling players, and it was through the couple's travels that the young Harriet first attended the theatre in Harrogate. The child had already appeared on stage, when, in 1787, the Butler company had been in Ulverston, and shortly afterwards, when her parents were staying in Otley, they all walked over to Harrogate to see the 'London stars' who appeared occasionally at the spa. Many years later Harriet Mellon recalled a large sign in the Harrogate theatre, which was erected during performances by the famous actress Miss Wallis, the protégé of the powerful Lord Loughborough (Alexander Wedderburn). It seems that Miss Wallis did not believe in hiding her light under a bushel, and in consequence, the sign's text read ,'The Gentlemen of the theatre are requested not to wear their hats while Miss Wallis is in the house'. Harriet observed, however, that whenever the sign was erected, an unusual number of hats appeared, and on enquiring, was told by one gentleman that he had a cold – another that he had a headache – a third was liable to rheumatism – a fourth feared a sore throat that would prevent his singing – and a fifth having had his hair curled and powdered dreaded a wind that would disturb it. In fact every theatrical discomfort was made an excuse for wearing hats, even by those who did not do so habitually.

On one occasion, Harriet and her mother walked to Harrogate to witness a performance by the great Mrs Jordan, but were too poor to hire lodgings for the week, and all the inns and hotels were full. Being too tired to walk back to Otley after the performance, they asked the Butler company if any would accommodate the pair, and although young Harriet soon found a kind offer, her more ample mother (tactfully known as a full figured Rubens beauty) received none, requiring her to spend the night on the stage throne. The good lady's temper was so roused by this disagreeable experience, that when, the following day, she walked with her daughter back to Otley, she gave full vent to her asperity, telling her daughter, 'Miss Wallis is just that nice, clever young lady I should wish you to be, you stupid creature, but you don't mind the lessons in acting which I gave you. The day will come when she will have a carriage, you will be splashed by it, and I hope she will drive over you.' In fact, Harriet far exceeded Miss Wallis in fortune, as she became a celebrated actress in her own right, married Coutts, the richest banker in London, and after his death in 1822, went on to marry the Duke of St Albans. When Harriet died in August 1837, her entire vast fortune passed to her daughter, Angela, who then became the richest woman in England after Queen Victoria. (C.58)

Other prominent guest appearances were provided by the celebrated London actors Bannister, and his rival, Kemble. The former appeared on 1 August 1801 as Acres in 'The Rivals' (P.23). Kemble arrived on 15 July 1806, acting in a programme which included the usual mish-mash of light comedy (P.32), one of which was a dissertation on hobby-horses, in which the idiosyncrasies of various types were satirised – the minister, soldier, beau, lady, lawyer, Lord Duke, and theatrical manager. Harrogate audiences were probably well aware of the term 'hobby horse', as they would have been introduced to it by its inventor, Lawrence Sterne, who was in the habit of frequently riding over from Coxwold to meet friends at the Dragon or Granby Hotels. (C.40) The great actor Edmund Kean visited Harrogate on 2 September 1819, as star of the tragedy 'Alexander the Great'. On the play bill, the management advised that they had procured the services of Mr Kean for three nights, and that 'in consideration of the difficulty of obtaining the above unrivalled performer at this period, the great request that he is in, and the high terms which the display of his talent commands it is hoped that a trifling advance of the prices of admission will not be objectionable'. The trifling advance increased prices to five shillings for lower boxes, four shillings for upper boxes, three shillings for the pit, and one shilling, six pence for the gallery (P.79).

The attitude of the landlords of the great inns towards the actors – as distinct from their cooperative attitude towards the institution of the theatre – was nicely summed up by Thomas Dibdin: '1790 – from Beverley I went to Harrowgate, where we were joined for a few nights by Mrs Jordan, as also Miss Wallis of Covent Garden, who was patronised by, and domiciliated with Lord and Lady Loughborough [i.e. Lord and Lady Rosslyn]. What I principally remember of Harrowgate is the aristocratical dignity – of whom?, why, the landlords of the four principal inns towards actors I mean, – to their customers they were humble enough, but the members of the theatre were kept at such a distance by this quartet of the salver and the napkin, that it would appear they forgot how equally they were servants of the public with ourselves . . .' (C.60)

Outdoor entertainments – Sight-seeing

Such outdoor amusements as sight-seeing and touring were greatly stimulated by the doctors' encouragement of bodily exercise as an adjunct to the 'cure'. The doctors were uniformly of the opinion that drinking the mineral waters was an activity which had to be regulated, ideally by members of the medical profession, and preferably themselves, also that it formed but one element in the larger concept of the 'cure'. Exercise was recommended by such as Dr Alexander, who dedicated pages 57–62 of his 'directions' to the practice and advantage of bodily exercise (F.37). Visitors were recommended to take the air on the 'common' as 'there are few places in England, perhaps none, that can boast of a better air than Harrogate . . .', and to take their carriages to neighbouring beauty spots. The first edition of the first Harrogate guidebook advised the visitors that, 'As nothing contributes more to health than moderate exercise in the open air, it is usual to make excursions into the neighbourhood, which abounds with a variety of places well worth the attention of strangers.' (G.1) Writers usually recommended visits to neighbouring Boroughbridge, Harewood, Knaresborough, Ripley, Ripon, Studley and York, along with the pleasant countryside around Harrogate. (G.9)

Thomas Baskerville had written in 1675, 'As to Harricate, a village made good by reason of the resort of people to the Wells, it stands in a delicate place for pleasure in the summer time . . . where you have also a noble prospect over the large vale of Yorkshire . . .' (C.11). The pleasure of country visits appears to have been enjoyed by the majority of those guests who wrote about their experiences. Mary Hare, widow of Bishop Hare, wrote in a 1756 letter to her step-son, of an outing she had undertaken in the course of a visit to Harrogate: '[At] the beginning of the week some of our company, and from the Queen's Head, eighteen at least, hired a wagon with a tilt, put in benches, six horses in pairs, broad wheels and turnpike road, trotted away very expeditiously to see Studley, lay at a good inn at Ripon, danced 9 or 10 couple till two in the morning, and came home as gaily as they went, highly pleased with the frolic ...' (C.31). Such outings, organised by the 'company' of the various inns, do not appear to have been unusual. The autobiography of Dr Alexander Carlyle contains lengthy accounts of his visits to Harrogate in the 1760s, with much riding and walking through the town's surrounding countryside (C.38.e–f), and Henry Skrine wrote of 'the adjacent country, as at Buxton, produces a variety of objects; and the ornamented scenes of Harewood, Plumpton, Studley, Hackfall, and Newby, form perpetual sources of amusement to the strangers who visit Harrogate' (C.48). Provided with such a variety of beautiful countryside and historic sights, it is not surprising that outings were regarded as a most important means of entertainment in Harrogate.

The expense book of Sir Darcy Dawes, who visited Harrogate in 1727 and 1730, provides an insight to the range of amusements favoured by visitors. These included bowls, guided walks, card playing, and listening to Morison, the fiddler (C.24). All of these delights continued to be available up to the end of the century, save that Morison the fiddler was superseded by Blind Jack, the famous Yorkshire road maker (C.34.c).

Outdoor entertainments — Racing

The great expanse of the Stray was ideal for sporting entertainments. The tradition of racing on the Stray appears to have been established well before the construction of the race course. Blind Jack Metcalfe recorded in his memoirs that he had raced for bets on Harrogate common in the 1730s and 1740s. (C.30.f–g) However, in 1793, a race-course was laid out on the south Stray in High Harrogate, opposite the Queen and Granby Hotels (G.5). It had a circumference of one and a quarter miles, and a breadth of sixteen yards, and was constructed under the supervision of one of the visitors, Colonel Clement Wolsley. The *Leeds Mercury* and the *York Herald* published regular accounts of the Harrogate races,: 'Our race ground is at this moment crowded with horse, foot and upwards of three score carriages, to witness horse races, pony races, women running for shifts, and men trying to catch soap-tailed pigs. In short, the place seems to be all mirth and good fellowship' (R.1240). A few weeks after this report, the *York Herald* published a further account: 'Riding in the buff. Harrogate seems to outvie Brighton in the style of the amusements. Much interest was excited there by a race on Monday week, which was won by a boy who rode naked from the girdle upwards. All the fashionable of the place attended; and the ladies, *on this occasion*, were observed to be very numerous.' (R.1265)

Outdoor entertainments — Archery

Archery, according to the ubiquitous Hargrove, received a considerable encouragement at Harrogate on 2 August 1793, when the Yorkshire Archers held their first meeting in the town. They pitched their tent on the Stray, outside the fashionable Granby Hotel, and provided a contest that began at 11 a.m. and closed at 4 p.m. With their uniforms of green and white velvet, black gaiters, and ostrich-plume hats, the Yorkshire Archers must have provided visitors with a colourful spectacle (G.5).

Outdoor entertainments — Hunting

Hunting was one sporting activity which – if Barbara Hofland is a reliable witness – was practised by visitors of all ranks, although there can not have been many who emulated Colonel Thornton's habit of transporting large numbers of animals to Harrogate (C.86.l). Colonel Thornton, whose exploits at Harrogate were celebrated in Barbara Hofland's 'Season at Harrogate', was a famous sporting personality:

> The famed -r -n he is this moment arriving,
> To strangers well known by the style of his driving,
> For he sports his own mail, his own trumpet he blows,
> So he well may be known wheresoever he goes,
> He's the soul of good humour, of frolic, and whim,
> And High Harrogate owes half its pleasures to him. (C.91.n)

One writer described Colonel Thornton's sporting activities in Harrogate: 'The greatest sportsman of his day, Thornton, brought over his hawks upon one occasion and flew them of the common ... he made a progress through the land like some cavalier of olden times ... first came the huntsmen, whippers-in, and grooms with various packs of dogs ... next walked the falconers in their green attire, carrying the hawks, hooded upon their frames, after them marched the thoroughbreds, the trainers, racers, hunters, and hackneys, then followed the greyhounds, with terriers, water dogs and spaniels, followed up by innumerable serving-men and baggage wagons ... the gay Colonel with his green hat, and his partridge-coloured coat, was an actor at Harrogate ...' (C.86.l)

Probably the most regular out-of-doors activity favoured by the visitors was that of promenading round such frequented places as the Sulphur Well, or enjoying the great open expanse of the Stray, which until the tree-planting programmes of the Improvement Commissioners after 1860, had few trees around its perimeter. Memory of the former activity is preserved in the name of Royal Parade, where the Royal Pump Room was built in 1842. Barbara Hofland made her imaginary hero Benjamin Blunderhead, on his having to leave Harrogate, write 'no more must I saunter along the Parade' (C.91.z). Doubtless the flaunting of fashionable costume played a significant role in such pleasures! (C.91.x) And the Stray appears to have been used for more than just walking. In a letter of 27 November 1818 to a Mr Smith, Lord John Campbell wrote '... I have not made any progress in Ballooning, indeed I am quite lost for want of an assistant, & so constantly interrupted by other things that I have scarcely given it a thought since my return from Harrogate ...' (C.98.B)

Miscellaneous entertainments

Visitors to Harrogate, whether their interests were for entertainments of the outdoor, or indoor variety, were well served in the Yorkshire Spa. The guidebooks refer to diversions other than those described above, such as Billiard Rooms (G.2), or the colourful manoeuvres of the West Yorkshire Cavalry on the Stray. Billiards seem to have had quite a following, for apart from the provision of this amusement by hotels and inns, Harrogate had separate billiard rooms, such as that owned by David Simpson in 1796 (S.449) and managed by Jane Baines by 1809 (S.591), that was immediately to the east of the Crown Hotel, known consequently as the Crown billiard room (R.3129). By 1824 Jane Baines had become Mrs John Simpson Cartwright, whose husband was described as being a 'billiard room keeper' (S.850). It was this billiard room which was dismantled – probably when Joseph Thackwray was developing the Crown hotel gardens and moved across to the Old Bell Inn. (R.3129). Johnathan Shutt also kept a subscription billiard room (R.3120).

There were also, of course, the shops, the majority of which were located in High Harrogate between the Queen and the Dragon Hotels (see plate 78). Both Barbara Hofland and David Lewis made frequent allusions in their respective and rival epic poems about Harrogate, to the quality of the shops.

> At their shop, in New Bond Street, they'd most of them been,
> and had there some most elegant articles seen,
> Thus they all appeared certain, the best they'd bring down,
> To a place of such consequence, worth and renown.
> (C.92.l)

The shops opened at the start of the visitor season, in early June, and closed at its end, in late September. Local people were able to obtain the essentials of life from the few permanent shops in Old Bilton or Sulphur Wells (located in High and Low Harrogate respectively), but Harrogate had to wait until the 1820s for a permanent retailing life became established (G.11). By this time the population of Harrogate was about 1,800.

Conclusion

There appears to have been a general recognition by visitors to Harrogate that the place was a genuine health resort, and that the remote Yorkshire Spa was patronised either by people who believed that its regime would improve their health, or by people who accompanied them – be they family, friends or paid companions. The 'naturalness' and informality of Harrogate – which was mentioned by a variety of commentators – was one factor which encouraged visitors to consider the spa as a genuine health resort and place of relaxation. The other important factor was the lack of will by the Duchy of Lancaster (and after 1778, by the Duchy's tenants or successor freeholders) to encourage the kind of formal building development which could be used as a background against which 'society' could enact ritual formalities. In Bath, for example, the developments of John Wood or William Pulteney created 'environmental determinants' (or in plain language, a stage-set or architectural framework) for the pleasure of a select few.[23] This was one reason why, as social habits and fashions changed, Bath was unable to adapt, and why in the nineteenth century, the less architecturally developed spas of Buxton, Cheltenham and, above all, Harrogate, flourished. As Harrogate grew, so entertainments developed, and visitors became accustomed to higher rates of consumption, which – as Dr Granville observed – led to the contradictory activity of patients who had been ordered to Harrogate for the benefit of plain diet, exercise, and water drinking, leading lives of near-debauchery and gluttony (F.58, chapter two). This was an old complaint (F.24). Yet Harrogate, up to the close of the Regency, appears to have enjoyed a reputation as a resort both for health and pleasure, at which the visitor could share the imagined joys of a rural life, with all the comforts of the town. The lack of any strictly regimented system of etiquette, allied to freedom from the unwelcome attentions of hordes of local poor, gave Harrogate a reputation for rural charm which was vastly attractive to society of the time, and it is hardly surprising that visitor numbers continued to increase.

The local population, who worked as farmers, innkeepers, servants, builders, merchants, or labourers, seemed to understand that the visitors were a source of livelihood to the entire community. Throughout the entire period of Harrogate's history from 1770 until 1841, the records of the quarter sessions court at Wakefield, the Forest Court at Knaresborough Castle, and the reports of Harrogate affairs in the newspapers, do not contain a single reference to a visitor being duped, assaulted, or having being the victim of theft. Yet these same sources contain many references to local people being the victims of crime – of servants stealing from their employers, of the constables being sent to the wells to 'quiet disorders', of drunkenness, of apprentices having broken their indentures, of assaults on the mails. Put another way, at a time when conspicuous expenditure and consumption by visitors was the norm, no evidence has survived to show that the visitors were either resented, or considered 'fair game' by any of the Harrogate populace. Even at the height of the troubles associated with the Enclosure movement of the 1760s and 1770s, or the Luddite riots of the 1810s, or the 'Captain Swing' riots of the 1830s, life at Harrogate went its leisurely way. The only activity which affected the visitors adversely was that of vandalism at the wells, and even this appears to be occurred out of the regular visitor season (H.2). The visitors came to Harrogate for the proven healthfulness of the spa, the agreeable but informal society, and the diverting nature of

the entertainments. Some may also have attended Harrogate during the shooting season because of its convenient location. But it is clear that no matter which of the town's attractions predominated, the entertainments grew from the spa, rather than the other way round. Equally, all of the town's attractions were provided for the visitors, from the Theatre (the opening and closing of whose season was governed by the arrival and departure of the visitors) (P) to the 'Royal Cheltenham Spa and Concert Rooms' (see plate 68), which opened in 1835, next to Low Harrogate's Cheltenham Well (R.2705). This was a speculative venture by John Williams, which – like the Theatre – was provided for visitors, rather than residents, although by 1835, the town's resident population had also increased, to 4,000.[24]

Township administration and the Poor Law | 10

H ARROGATE, in 1770, possessed an unreformed Township administration, and a poor law that had been the result of centuries of piecemeal growth. By the time of the Harrogate Improvement Act of 1841, the
town had witnessed immense changes in the theory and practice of both
local government and poor law. Yet unlike so many other communities of
early nineteenth-century England, Harrogate absorbed these changes
without any appreciable social unrest. The following chapter will show why.

Community boundaries

The administration of the two villages of Bilton-with-Harrogate and Pannal,
which provided for the majority of the workforce at the spa, was concerned
with such mundane matters as the maintenance of law and order, the
suppression of nuisances, the condition of the highways, observance of the
requirements of the established church, complying with militia orders, and
the enforcement of the various measures for the protection of the parish
poor. In Harrogate, the greater part of these matters came under the
control of Bilton-with-Harrogate. The village of Pannal, consisting mostly
of farms, included a promontory of land bounded by Cold Bath Lane and
the modern Cornwall Road, with the Old Sulphur Well at its apex, which
was a very important part of the Harrogate Spa. Until the establishment of
the Harrogate Improvement area in 1841, a significant amount of Harrogate
matters were overseen by Pannal Township,[1] which itself was part of the
larger village of Beckwith-with-Rossett.

Parish boundaries

The two villages were also divided by parish boundaries. Bilton-with-
Harrogate was with the parish of Knaresborough, whereas Pannal was a

parish in its own right. A further complication arose from Bilton-with-Harrogate, and Knaresborough, being from 1541 until 1836 within the diocese of Chester, whereas Pannal was within the diocese of York. After 1836, when the new See of Ripon was formed, both Bilton-with-Harrogate and Pannal were placed under the jurisdiction of the new Bishop of Ripon.[2]

Local authority: the Pre-Reform system

The main centre of power in Harrogate was based neither in York or Chester – nor, after 1836, Ripon – but rather the Forest Court, which met at Knaresborough Castle. This was controlled by the Duchy of Lancaster. The Forest Court appointed the constables for all townships within the Royal Forest. It is possibly an indication of the relative importance of Bilton-with-Harrogate and Pannal that the first surviving record of the appointment of a constable for the former community occurs in 1496, whereas Pannal had to wait until 1715 (D.1). The rolls show that from 1770 until 1819 single constables were appointed both to Bilton-with-Harrogate and to Beckwith-with-Rossett; and that in 1819 Bilton-with-Harrogate gained a deputy constable, whereas Beckwith-with-Rossett had to wait until 1825 for the creation of the post of deputy.

The other important local official, along with the constable, was that of overseer of the poor. These officers were selected at the vestry meetings held within St Robert's Church – for Pannal – and St John's Chapel – for Bilton-with-Harrogate; their names being then submitted to the Justices of the Peace for approval. Office usually lasted for a year, and an important part of his work consisted of collecting taxes for the relief of the poor. The overseer had to submit his accounts at the end of his year of office, for approval by the vestry meeting, which always included the principal landowners of the district.[3]

Constables

The office of constable is of some antiquity, dating from pre-Conquest times, and the principal source of information about the office is the annual account, of which only a few have survived for Bilton-with-Harrogate and Pannal. The functions of the constable were many and varied, including the arrest of law-breakers, searching out men wanted for bastardy orders, escorting paupers to their legal parish of settlement, finding billets for soldiers, conducting ballots for calling up the militia, and ensuring that alehouses were closed at times of divine service. The constable was appointed by the local vestry meetings, but as the office was unpaid it was highly unpopular, lasting for a term of one or two years. The majority of the population were illiterate, so it was not unusual for the constable to be the same.[4]

The earliest surviving reference for Harrogate business within the accounts of the Pannal constable is dated 1800, and contains much 'passenger' business. 'Passengers' were those paupers or vagrants who had no right of settlement in the community and – to prevent them becoming a burden on the parish – were returned to their community of origin. It was an important part of the constable's work to identify such people, and to accompany them to their place of legal settlement. Such journeys often involved expenses for transportation, food, or other 'necessaries'.

> relievg. And conveyg 3 pasengers to Killinghall, 8d.
> To conveying 7 persons from workhouse, and exps. To Killinghall, 7s. 6d. (D.2)

The constable also attended coroners' courts, served militia papers, and attended the pinfolds to supervise the release of impounded cattle (D.2). He appears to have worked in co-operation with the surveyors of highways and bridges, who, since an Act of 1555, were usually appointed by townships or parishes. In view of the generally low ability of the average eighteenth-century constable, it was possibly fortunate for Harrogate that levels of civil crime or disorder appear to have been negligible. The only evidence for any public demand for improvements in the numbers or efficiency of the Harrogate constables occurs in the late 1840s, when the construction of the first Harrogate railways brought gangs of navvies whose presence was disruptive. This, however, lies beyond our period of study.[5]

Surveyors

The position of township surveyor was an old one, having been created under the provisions of the Statute of Highways Act of 1555.[6] The post, like that of constable, was unpaid until 1773, when the General Highways Act permitted the payment of a salary if two-thirds of the vestry meeting agreed. The principal duty of the surveyor was to supervise the work which all adult parishioners were bound to do in person or by proxy for six days a year on the parish roads. After 1773 parishioners could pay a 'composition' rate in lieu of statute duty. In Harrogate the condition of the roads was a matter of some importance, given that the highways were the only means by which visitors could arrive in town, and so fill the pockets of the doctors and innkeepers. Proof of this may be found in the records of the High Harrogate vestry meetings, which were dominated by the doctors and innkeepers, and which contain frequent reference to the highways and their maintenance (D.18). Although little evidence exists to show if the Harrogate surveyors were paid, it is reasonable to assume that the vestry considered their work to be of such importance as to merit payment. The fragmentary surviving highways accounts for Pannal contain an 1823 reference to the surveyor being paid two shillings and sixpence a day for his attendance (D.6.16).

Responsibility for all bridges and highways within the Royal Forest lay with the county authority, that for Harrogate being the West Riding of Yorkshire. However, the large size of the West Riding ensured that its highways and bridges were administered by smaller units, which in Yorkshire were based on the traditional 'wapentake' of Anglo-Saxon times. Harrogate came within the wapentake of Claro, in common with the rest of the Royal Forest. For example, in 1779, the county surveyor recorded 'received of the constable of Harrogate towards repairs of the wapentake bridges &c. 5s. 3d. ¾d. by me Peter Harrison.' (D.3) Within the parish each parishioner was required to give so many days' labour towards maintaining the highways, with the possibility to avoid or 'commute' this obligation by means of a payment. After the Act of 1835 abolished statutory labour, this obligation was transformed into a regular highways rate. For example, in 1816, the accounts of Bilton-with-Harrogate surveyors John Stott and David Stoner recorded that £54 9s. 6d. had been taken in 'composition payments', and £38 1s. 0d. 'in lieu of statute duty', whereas after 1835 a straightforward 'Highways Rate' was levied (D.45.14).

Harrogate's roads and highways had for the greater part been established before the Great Award of 1778. This may be seen by comparing a map such as that drawn up by Charles Greeves for the Bilton-with-Harrogate surveyors in 1821 (see plan 37) with the roads mentioned in the Award (B.31). The expansion of the town's internal road system occurred under the administration of the Improvement Commissioners, from 1841 to 1884, with great impetus being given by the Victoria Park Company's work in 1860, which linked up the two villages of High and Low Harrogate. Before this time, High and Low Harrogate were linked by the turnpike roads – which themselves had grown from much older routes – or by crude paths across the fields, such as that which grew into the present route between the Sulphur Well and High Harrogate chapel – the Ginnel, Oxford Street, Park View, Stray footpath. The turnpike roads were constructed after a series of Acts passed by Parliament in the 1750s. The road from Harrogate to Knaresborough was turnpiked as part of the 1751 'Act for repairing the roads from the Town of Leeds, through Harwood, to the south west corner of the inclosures of Harrogate; and from thence …' (Q.5) A further Act was passed in 1752 to provide powers for the turnpiking of the road from Harrogate to Ripon (Q.6). The next significant Act was that of 1777, which led to the turnpiking of the busy road from High Harrogate to Skipton (Q.12). It is clear that this Act of 1777 had been framed to coincide with the passing of the Great Award of 1778. The turnpike roads through Harrogate were built as a speculative venture, being financed by trustees comprising such important landowners as the Earl of Harewood (Q.5).

The surveyors for both Bilton-with-Harrogate and Pannal townships were concerned, in their duties towards roads and bridges, to ensure the maintenance of the turnpikes through the properly appointed turnpike trusts, and for the rest, that other public roads and ways were kept open and in repair. Much of the road work consisted of laying stones across the surface. For example, the surveyor's accounts for 1796 record 282 loads of stones, at 3*d*. a load, being laid on Skipton Road, Bilton Lane, Low Harrogate Road, and Chapel Road (D.45.6).

The parish constables and the county surveyors appear to have had a close working relationship. For example, the county rate for highways was collected by the parish constable. In 1779 the county surveyor recorded receipt of five shillings, three pence and three farthings, paid by the Harrogate constable as contribution towards the cost of repairing all the bridges within the wapentake of Claro (D.3).

Militia

The period of this study of Harrogate, before 1841, includes the whole of the French Wars from 1793 until the final defeat of Napoleon in 1815. The modern militia had come into being in 1757.[7] Local constables were required to draw up lists of all able-bodied men of a certain age in their parishes or townships. Ballots were then held to establish which of the men should be called upon to serve; or else pay for a replacement. Only a few of the militia lists for Harrogate, drawn up by the constable, have survived, in common with those for most of England. In the earliest surviving record, 1778, the constable William Shutt claimed 3*d*. for attending to the warrant for Pannal men (D.9.1). The next entry of significance occurs in 1781, when Samuel Hattersley supplied a bill for 'Bileting Sir G. Savill's Malitia [sic]' (D.9.2). Hattersley received land in the Award of 1778 (B.31) which later became the site of 'Hattersley's Hotel', and it is reasonable to assume that he was accommodating militia men in similar circumstances as early as 1781. One of the greatest problems resulting from the militia system was the burden it placed on families whose sole breadwinner was called away to serve. The overseers of the poor had responsibility for such families, although they tried to transfer responsibility on every possible occasion. For example, when one William Barker of Knaresborough, who worked in Harrogate (probably as a waiter) was called into the Bilton-with-Harrogate militia, the overseers charged Knaresborough township with his 'wife and two children at 4s. 6d. a week being nineteen weeks from the 27th day of November to the 9th day of April 1799: £4 5s. 6d.' as they lived in Harrogate but did not have settlement papers (D.9.7). The account was recognised and settled by Knaresborough township. Fortunately for the poor, the magistrates kept watch on the overseers, having power to amend or cancel some of their decisions. In the case of Mary Grimstone, wife of a serving Harrogate soldier, and her three children, the overseers' decision not to provide her with relief was countered by an order from magistrate John Watson of Bilton Park, who in an order dated 16 May 1801 required the overseers to 'shew cause why you refuse to relieve Mary Grimstone . . .' (D.9.15).

The practice of providing substitutes appears to have caused the authorities considerable problems. Substitution was a generally acceptable means for a man to avoid military duty while ensuring that militia numbers were maintained. However, in a small community such as Harrogate, where many of the most able men worked in such service industries as the inns, it seems that substitution may not have occurred because of the reluctance of an individual man to serve his country, but rather because his services to the community were regarded as being more valuable than military service. The case of the Leeds worker, Thomas Taylor, is an example. In 1794 the Harrogate township paid the Leeds township the sum of two shillings a week for the family of Thomas Taylor, a substitute for the militia for Harrogate, from 20 February 1793 until 20 August 1794. It is not known for whom Taylor was substituting, but somebody must have valued his services (D.9.9).

During the difficult year before the celebration of the battle of Trafalgar on 21 October 1805, the militia quotas for the wapentake of Claro recorded that Bilton-with-Harrogate (and also, for some unknown reason, Minskip) had been told to produce six men, who were accordingly identified, four of whom then deserted (A.252.b). So much for the defence of the realm. Patriotic effusion had its place, but not when it interfered with business. In April 1805 the landlords of the Granby, Queen, Crown, Bell, Crescent, Swan and Bay Horse Inns petitioned against the billeting of volunteers during the visitor season, remarking that the previous year they had been much injured by their presence, with one establishment having had no fewer than one hundred and twenty men to accommodate. The authors added that they would, 'cheerfully contribute their best endeavours after the Season or during the winter', presumably in the belief that Napoleon would arrange his military campaign to suit the requirements of the Harrogate season (A.252.c). The authorities' response to the petition is not known, but in 1805 the county authority fined Bilton-with-Harrogate forty pounds for 'deficiencies in vacancies in the militia and army of reserve.' (D.3)

Occasionally Harrogate had to billet militia from other towns, such as from 8 to 9 June 1812, when the Bilton-with-Harrogate constable recorded charges of seven shillings for 'billiting Halifax local Militia' (D.9.29). Possibly the arrival in Harrogate of large numbers of militia men may have had some effect on the inns and hotels, especially if they arrived out of the regular visitor season from June to September. From what is known of the Harrogate landlords, however, they would probably have regarded the militia men with suspicion.

Overseers of the poor

The accounts of the overseers of the poor are among the earliest Harrogate township records to survive. They include a 1635 'assessment for the Town of Harrogate ... for the buylding of a house ... for the poore within the said hamblet ...' (D.22). Yet the Award of 1778 does not contain any references to a Harrogate poor house, or workhouse. On the other hand, it does list a number of 'incroachments from the Forest', such as that near to the World's End Inn, which were for the 'Harrogate poor' (B.31). An earlier document of 1730 contains a reference to a 'Cottage and Intack belonging the township of Bilton-with-Harrogate', adding that the township had made a gift of £6 10s. to the daughter of the late tenant, William Marsden, as they both 'did very much improve it', and because the daughter assisted him and his wife in their sickness and 'took care to bury them without troubling the Township' (D.50.2). The overseers' papers contain several references to repairs or building work at various of the town's houses for the poor (D.10.5; D.50.35). The time must have come when the 'poore houses' were insufficient for the needs of the town, for in 1784 and 1785, the township of Bilton-with-Harrogate paid the township of Pannal two guineas per annum rent for the accommodation of paupers in Pannal workhouse (D.50.35). By 1790 Pannal workhouse was receiving as much as £31 6s. 0d. from such outside communities, with Boroughbridge, Harwood, and Bilton-with-Harrogate paying each two guineas (D.63). Clearly the building of a proper workhouse in Harrogate could not long be postponed.

The first significant reference to the building of a workhouse in Harrogate occurs in the vestry book for High Harrogate, when an entry of 24 April 1801 resolved that:

1 a well regulated workhouse will be extremely beneficial to the township;
2 it is expedient to build a workhouse;
3 that funds be raised by sale of property belonging to the Township;
4 that a committee be appointed to consider the proper situation for a workhouse. (D.18, p. 51)

A vestry meeting of 6 April 1802 appointed a committee to enquire into possible sites for a workhouse, which had twenty-one days to complete their enquiry. The committee was able to report by 24 April that the property of the township adjoining Peter Dalby's was 'superior to any situation offered to the committee'. Peter Dalby must have been co-operative, for the meeting of 28 May saw an agreement to exchange land between Dalby and the township, and on 18 November a minute recorded that the agreement had been confirmed and that the township's property could be sold (D.18, p. 59). The matter appears to have rested there, because work on the Harrogate workhouse did not begin until 1809 (D.18, p. 101). The delay may have been occasioned by the failure of the sale of township property to raise the necessary sum. On the other hand, it might have been because of opposition from local landowner, William Williamson, who – in a letter dated 4 March 1803 – wrote that '... it will be a very unpleasant thing to have a building of that sort so near my barn.' (D.50.18)

Despite local opposition, a vestry meeting of 4 July 1805 resolved that the erection of a workhouse in Harrogate was necessary. It fixed upon a plot of land opposite the World's End Inn as a suitable site, yet it was not until the meeting of 1 June 1809 that the specially appointed committee agreed to 'the expediency of opening or erecting a Workhouse in order to reduce the poor rates, and render the aged poor more comfortable.' (D.18, p. 96) The committee appointed to supervise the building of the workhouse included the tenants of the Crown, Dragon and Granby hotels (Joseph Thackwray, Joseph Goodlad and John Greeves), and a leading Harrogate physician, Dr Jaques, a membership which demonstrates the continuing role of the inn-keepers and doctors in the town. The site chosen was just about as remote from fashionable High and Low Harrogate as was possible to find, being at Starbeck, which at that time was still part of Bilton-with-Harrogate township. Having at last decided to proceed, the committee fixed upon 12 May 1810 as a deadline for the completion of the new building (D.18, p. 102) and – in a most business-like manner – required that their inspectors monitor building progress and pay for the various stages of construction when they were satisfied that the work was satisfactory. The Harrogate workhouse (see plate 57) appears to have been completed by 12 May 1810.[8]

Throughout the summer of 1810 the committee concerned itself with equipping and furnishing the new workhouse. The accounts show that such objects as a yeast can and grater, a candle box, an iron coal pan, and a pudding dish of tin were purchased from William Swales for the total of three shillings and six pence (D.49.5). Money for these purchases came from the poor rate via the township. Occasionally, however, the records show that the poor rates were paid by local people 'in kind'. Bilton-with-Harrogate carpenter Thomas Ripley paid four years' back rent to the township 'chiefly by five coffins'. The committee does not appear to have been able to meet all of its financial requirements by means of the poor rates, as their surviving records make frequent references to loans, interest charges, and repayment dates. In 1815 one of the overseers, Thomas Emmatt, paid £120 to Mr Terry of the Knaresborough Bank, apparently as repayment for a loan. In 1817, a further £7 11s. 6d. was paid to Mr Terry as interest, which suggests a loan still outstanding of about £150. In 1822 the township borrowed £100 from John Eteson, with a further loan of £200 from George Abbey appearing in the accounts for 1825–1831.[9] These may have been to pay off the debt to the bank, but whatever their purpose it seems that the workhouse was the only liability which could have caused the township to go into debt.

Having by the summer of 1810 a well-built and suitably remote workhouse at their disposal, the township next had to appoint a master. This was obviously a matter of some importance, as the performance of the master would determine whether the erection of the new building could be justified or whether it would turn into a drain on the local rates. At a vestry meeting at High Harrogate church on 11 October 1810 Edmund Whitehead was appointed master, his term of office being until the following March, carrying a salary of £10 per annum. Whitehead was to be allowed to continue to work at his business (unspecified), 'but by no means to neglect the superintendence of the House.' (D.18, p. 109) It is not known how long Mr and Mrs Whitehead remained in office, but the vestry meeting of 20 April 1812, held at 'Mrs Kindalls', the present master and mistress were ordered to resign immediately 'as persons unfit for the situation'. Thomas Shaw and his wife were appointed as replacements. (D.18, p. 117)

Rules for the workhouse have survived among the workhouse papers. Although they are dated 1830, it is unlikely that they are very different from those of the 1810 establishment. The workhouse provided the necessities of life – daily sustenance and shelter – subject to an austere regime that was designed to discourage the idle from taking advantage of the community. The orders of 1830 reflect this attitude to a nicety.

No occupant was permitted to leave the workhouse without permission from the master, on penalty of forgoing dinner. In the event of any inmate bringing spirituous liquors into the workhouse, 'he or she shall be confined in a dark room, and shall be allowed nothing but bread and water for the next day following.' The master and mistress were to ensure that the poor be kept at work from six in the morning until six in the evening, making reasonable allowance for age, abilities and infirmities. Attendance at church was required 'twice every Lord's day', with no loitering on the way back to the workhouse. And woe betide any person who should pretend to be sick, lame or blind in order to be excused labour; they were to be 'severely punished, as the law directs.' (D.50.25) Although the master and mistress were in charge of the workhouse, they were directly responsible to the workhouse committee, which consisted of a dozen prominent citizens elected at vestry meetings of the local church. It was they who examined the accounts, and were thus able to monitor the cost of the operation. An early grocer's bill from trader John Stott (himself an overseer from 1809 to 1810), a butcher's bill from John Dearlove, and a milk bill from John Pennington, were of sufficient size to indicate an occupation of about forty persons. (D.49.8)

The provision in 1813 of a smithy (D.49.9), and of a loom in 1824 (D.49.16), ensured that the occupants were able and obliged to do useful work. The accounts, however, show that not all purchases were for strictly utilitarian requirements, such as the purchase in October 1811 of a bottle of wine for two shillings and sixpence (D.49.6). The year 1825 saw the appointment of a new master, Mr Henry Peacock, who inaugurated his new administration with an order for rose shrubs and poplar saplings to be planted in the grounds, as well as the construction of an 'arbour' in the garden. Mr Peacock also ordered the numbering of all the workhouse rooms. (D.49.17)

Henry Peacock's period of office lasted until 1838 (D.20.26). He appears to have been a person with sufficient energy to better his position, while sailing very close to the wind in matters of finance. On several occasions he came close to ruin. His surviving correspondence shows him to have been a man capable of arousing affection and contempt from those with whom he had contact. It is also probably true that his possession of three excellent wives in succession was his salvation. The Peacocks enjoyed a joint salary of £50 per annum, and the record of their appointment shows that they had come from the Aldborough and Boroughbridge workhouse in order to better themselves. Elizabeth Peacock died after a brief illness in 1826. As the duties of the workhouse master clearly required that he be married, Henry Peacock remarried in August 1828. His new bride was Jane Dodd, a former maid to Harrogate visitor Sir Charles de Voeux of Woodhall, and it is instructive to note that at the time of her marriage she possessed a savings account with the York Savings Bank of nearly £150, which by March 1830 had dwindled to £20. At the same time Henry Peacock's debts were considerably reduced (D.20.10).

An important part of the overseer's work consisted of disclaiming responsibility for as many paupers as possible, in order to save his township expense. The zeal with which Henry Peacock applied himself to this aspect of his work may be seen in some of the correspondence he received. One letter from an 'F.H.' of Knaresborough included the line, 'For God's sake

don't waste our time – you know the man belongs [to] your township!'
Another correspondent wishes that, 'other Overseers gave me as little
trouble.' (D.20) A man less confident than Henry Peacock would have
destroyed much of his personal correspondence, as some of it hardly
reflects to his credit. His own mother had been on poor relief in Holbeck for
the three and a half years previous to her death in 1834 (D.20.18), and had in
consequence received a pauper's funeral. Her 'settlement' being in Pateley
Bridge, that community was obliged to reimburse Holbeck for the funeral
expenses. Not surprisingly, that township then attempted to recover the
costs from the late woman's apparently wealthy son at Harrogate, hinting
that if Peacock failed his duty, the Pateley Bridge overseers intended to put
their case before the Poor Law Commissioners in London (D.20.19). The
outcome is not known.

The average weekly cost per pauper in 1821 had been 3s. 1¾d. (D.49.13).
In 1822 and 1823 this was reduced to 2s. 8d. (D.49.14–15). By 1836, near the
close of Peacock's reign as master, the average weekly cost had been
reduced still more, to 2s. 2¾d. (D.49.24). This remarkable reduction, at a
time of national inflation, was achieved by the simple act of spending less,
a fact which no doubt endeared Peacock to the committee of the
Harrogate workhouse. It is possible that Jane Peacock, with her training
in frugality as a maid, may have assisted her husband in the practice of
economy – at least with regard to expenses at the workhouse, for in his
private affairs Peacock appears to have been anything but frugal, running
up bills for newspapers, among other things (D.20.5). Peacock's replies to
a questionnaire sent in 1832 by the Poor Law Commissioners in London,
provides information about conditions in the Harrogate workhouse. The
Peacocks reported that they had established a regular weekly diet: Sunday:
meat and potato pies; Mondays and Saturdays, rice milk; Tuesdays and
Thursdays, boiled beef; Wednesdays, pea soup; Fridays, suet dumplings
(D.50.33). This diet was probably enhanced with produce from the
extensive gardens of the workhouse, as for example in 1821, when the
accounts record the expenditure of three shillings for three hundred
cabbage plants (D.49.13).

If the orders of the workhouse prevented 'spirituous liquors' from being
brought into the building by the inmates, they did not imply abstinence by
the master or the committee. Even before the opening of the Harrogate
workhouse, the accounts for April to October 1809, entered by overseer
Barker, record under 1 June: 'Paid for liquor at the meeting choosing a
Committee for the Workhouse … 13s.' (D.10.7). The deliberations of the
worthy gentlemen must indeed have been thirsty work, as what appears to
be a set allowance of ten shillings per meeting increased with time. In 1815,
the vestry and workhouse committee refreshed itself liberally at the Black

Swan in High Harrogate, receiving a bill from landlord Joseph Waite for £5 6s. 10d. The gentlemen then crossed the Stray to the Bay Horse Inn (later, the Empress), where landlord Mrs Kendal eventually presented a bill for 'etceteras' (D.49.10).

In 1829 the refreshments were on so lavish a scale that they were itemised by grateful landlord Joseph Waite, whose Black Swan Inn must have prospered under the deliberations of the workhouse committee: 'wine and water – 1s. 4d.; liquer [sic – i.e. spirits] – 12s.; tobacco – 6d.; cheese and bread – 3s. 6d.; extra rum – 6d.' (D.49.20).

The scale of these refreshment charges came to light in 1832, when in the course of a national enquiry into the administration of the Poor Law, the commissioners' London representative asked the Harrogate commissioners and master to meet with them at the Crown Hotel in Low Harrogate; also that they should bring their account books with them. The interrogation dragged on for two years, largely because of the inaccurate replies emanating from Harrogate, including the information that the Workhouse had been built 'about eighteen years ago at a cost of near £2,000' (D.50.33).

Peacock's success in keeping down the cost of the workhouse enabled him to enjoy the favour of the overseers. This did not prevent their dismissing him on 20 May 1838 (D.20.26), following the death of his wife, Jane, in 1837. An entry in the *Harrogate Advertiser* for 1 September 1838, records the next stage in Peacock's career: 'Marriage to ... Mrs Waudby' (D.20.27). As the widow of the late owner of the busy Brunswick Hotel, the wealthy Mrs Waudby must have been quite a 'catch' for the ambitious master of the workhouse. Henry Peacock joined the ranks of one of the two most powerful groups of men in Harrogate, the innkeepers.

Some of the receipts surviving in the workhouse papers record payments made from townships, other than Bilton-with-Harrogate, which lay within a distance of about twenty miles. These seem to indicate that townships such as Hampsthwaite and Follifoot which were without workhouses, sent their paupers to Harrogate after the opening of the workhouse in 1810 (D.18). In 1830–31 the accounts of overseer William Lister include an income of £90 4s. 6¾d. for 'paupers belonging to out Townships'. In 1836 the receipts include payments from sixteen neighbouring townships, including Ripley, Clint and Spofforth (D.10.9). These receipts may provide an answer to why the Harrogate workhouse of 1810 was built on so large a scale. With its massive stone walls, three storeys, and dozens of rooms, the workhouse seems to have been far larger than was needed to accommodate the paupers of early nineteenth-century Harrogate. With its population of about one thousand people, most of who worked for the seasonal service industry associated with the spa – and who moved out of Harrogate when the 'season' ended – the township did not have a large indigent population. It may well have been the case that the promoters of the workhouse saw an opportunity not only to provide their own wealthy little community with provision for a limited number of local paupers, but also to charge surrounding communities for the reception of their own indigent population. The vestry and the overseers were, after all, dominated by the canny businessmen who ran the local hotels and inns. The Harrogate workhouse closed in 1854, with the establishment of the Union for the surrounding area in 1854 (D.50.37). This no doubt pleased the township authority, which since 1841 had been the newly elected Harrogate Improvement Commissioners. The danger that the town's wealthy and fashionable visitors might come into contact with inmates of the Harrogate workhouse was now removed.

The above examination of Harrogate township and the operation of its Poor Law, covers the period before the Harrogate Improvement Act of 1841 which led to the establishment of a board of Improvement Commissioners, elected by local inhabitants or property owners. To qualify as a candidate, an occupant had to be rated for the relief of the poor at £35 per annum. Owners of property without the Improvement District had to be 'seised or possessed or in the enjoyment of rents and profits of lands and hereditaments for an estate not less than a life in being, for his own use, or of leasehold lands or tenements held under demise of not less than 31 years, within the district, to an annual value of twenty pounds.'[10]

Only persons who occupied or owned property rated at £3 or more per annum, and who had paid their last Poor Rate assessment, could vote. This was within a few years of the 1832 Reform Act, which had so changed the patterns of British enfranchisement. The real beneficiaries of the Reform Act were the prosperous middle classes,[11] who in Harrogate both before and after 1841, were largely the innkeeping and medical classes. As another writer claimed, The Great Reform Act 'strengthened the institutions of the country by bringing [government] into the representation of the prosperous middle classes'.[12] In Harrogate these same middle classes formed the majority of the population. In other words, Harrogate before the Reform Act of 1832, the Poor Law Amendment Act of 1834 (which removed responsibility for the relief of the poor from the vestries to boards of elected guardians), and the Municipal Corporations Act of 1835, was not the scene of a discontented, unfranchised populace, frantic for reform. In the nation as a whole, the local government reform case rested on four planks:

- the growing problem of law and order[13] which even affected the electoral process.[14]

- the political and religious exclusiveness of the unreformed corporations, which had become an increasingly irritating thorn in the side of the new commercial and industrial elites in the towns.

- the mode of appointment to the corporations, being for the most part self-elected through co-option.

- the link between the 1832 Reform Act and the corporations, by means of the ancient office of freeman, who were often corrupt and anti-reform.[15]

None of these problems existed in Harrogate, thanks to the fact that the community lay within the ancient Royal Forest of Knaresborough. Harrogate was, therefore, never subject to the whims or greed of aristocratic landowners or grasping industrialists; it had never been at the centre of religious struggles or subject to the ambitions of any great prince of the Church (being divided until 1836 by the dioceses of Chester and York). It had a small number of poor, set against a larger number of the comfortable and rich, and when both were combined, the total population was still less than half of the total annual influx of wealthier visitors (G.5, p. 101). Most significantly of all, large parts of the town continued – after the Award of 1778 – to be owned by the powerful Duchy of Lancaster, which, as a Crown possession, exercised its authority in a benign and progressive manner. This was of course in the Duchy's interest. The very extent of the Duchy's national estates meant that they were administered by scrupulous officials, some based in far-away London, who knew of the need to run the monarch's estates in an efficient and fair manner, so as to produce a maximum profit to the Crown, without upsetting local people.

By 1810 the management of Bilton-with-Harrogate's poor laws were entrusted to a workhouse committee, which was so successful that by 1814, Pannal gave up its own workhouse, and sent its paupers to Starbeck. By 1815, eight townships joined the scheme, a number that by 1832 increased to eighteen.[16] Once again, the profit motive behind the innkeepers and doctors was a significant driving force.

The demand for change, when it arrived in 1835, came because one of the leading members of the Harrogate community, Mr Joseph Thackwray – owner of the Crown Hotel – threatened the sanctity of the Old Sulphur Well, which had been given to the public via the Crown through the Duchy of Lancaster. Those who responded to that threat were not the local poor, but Mr Thackwray's business rivals, the other innkeepers and hoteliers, as well as the doctors. The 1841 Harrogate Improvement Act was the outcome of awareness of the need for reform, by both the Duchy and the majority of the Harrogate population.

The Harrogate township had concerns other than for the workhouse, Poor Law, constable, and highways, the chief of which were religious life, education and the Bath Hospital. These three subjects will be examined separately in later chapters.

11 | Religious life and church building in Harrogate, 1770–1841

ETWEEN 1770 and 1841 the two villages of High and Low Harrogate experienced a growth in their combined populations from about 1,200 to 3,064.[1] This growth occurred at a time of unparalleled national unrest, as well as a formidable increase in the numbers of visitors to the spa, bringing with them various and alternative ideologies, beliefs and customs which influenced the community. The first – social unrest – was manifest at home by the demands for Catholic emancipation, parliamentary reform, and the repeal of the Test and Corporations Act, as well as the French Revolution and Napoleonic Wars abroad.[2] The second – spa development and the increase of visitors – was manifest in the work of the innkeepers and doctors in improving and enlarging the spa,[3] and in the continuing newspaper reports of growing visitor numbers (Class R). Yet, as this chapter will show, at a time when non-conformity made considerable progress, especially in Yorkshire, Harrogate remained firmly Anglican. The national unrest occurred at a time that also saw the declining influence of Anglicanism,[4] and the increase of religious dissent throughout the social structure.[5] Faced with all this unrest, change and influence, religious life in Harrogate from 1770 to 1841 might have been expected to reflect national trends. But the town's religious life did not conform to either national or even regional patterns. Rather, it was the result of a unique mixture of three factors: visitor status; royal patronage through the Duchy of Lancaster; and working-class seasonal migration.

On the eve of the Enclosure Act of 1770, Harrogate ocontained only one place of worship. This was the Anglican chapel of St John (see plate 32), built in 1749 (M.3) in High Harrogate, on land donated by the Duchy of Lancaster (M.2), and paid for largely by subscriptions from the visitors, including the opening one of £50 from Lady Elizabeth Hastings (M.1). There is no evidence to show that this chapel was built for any other purpose than to provide a place of worship convenient to the visitors who were resorting in ever increasing numbers to the wells of Harrogate. The original list of voluntary subscriptions collected to pay for the erection of a place of worship for 'such as thither resort for the use of the Minerall Waters' contains ninety-eight names, of which only twelve were local, and those twelve included the Earl of Harewood and Sir Henry Slingsby (M.1). Moreover, the Duchy of Lancaster order of 1771 to authorise payment of a £30 stipend to the Minister of High Harrogate chapel states that the chapel was 'by voluntary contributions erected ... principally for the use of the Nobility and Gentry resorting to Harrogate ...' (M.18). Local people, after 1749, were of course able to use the High Harrogate chapel, but had it not been for the visitors, they would have continued to attend either the two-mile distant church of St Robert's, at Pannal, or the equally distant Knaresborough parish church. At one time Harrogate had a pre-reformation chantry chapel, but this closed in 1549 and its remains have vanished.[6]

The curate of High Harrogate chapel – in the parish of Knaresborough – appears to have been given some of the enclosed lands in the Royal Forest of Knaresborough, for his 'use and benefit', in about 1749. It is not known who authorised this 'gift', as it is not recorded in any of the Duchy land registrations. The Enclosure Act of 1770 confirmed their status as 'illicit encroachments' (J.1). A subsequent report on these lands, issued in 1775, noted that the tenants had previously paid the vicar of Knaresborough about £16 per annum (B.30). This unsatisfactory means of producing a stipendiary contribution had already been corrected by the 1770 Act, which allowed for the reversion of the lands to the Duchy in exchange for a regular stipend of £30 per annum, payable from the Duchy's revenue office (M.18). The former 'chapel lands', comprising 63 acres, 2 roods, 25 perches, were purchased on 24 February 1781 by Lord Loughborough (Alexander Wedderburn, or 3rd earl Rosslyn), for £230, who added them to his already extensive Harrogate estates (B.33). Along with the annual stipend of £30, the 'clerk', Robert Mitton, who had been nominated to the curacy of Harrogate chapel on 24 February 1769 by the Reverend Thomas Collins, vicar of Knaresborough, also received 'contributions given by the company who attend Harrogate during the summer season.' (M.48)

By 1770 the influence of both the Crown and the visitors on the religious life of Harrogate was strongly apparent. The resident population included a handful of local landowning families, identified in the Award of 1778, as well as the innkeepers. Both groups employed workers with varying degrees of remuneration – farmers, smiths, stewards, farm-hands, full-time inn staff, for example, who either lived in accommodation provided by the farmer or innkeeper, or as copyholders of the Royal Forest. There were also the self-employed traders, listed in the early directories, as, for example, butchers, saddle makers, milliners, boot and shoe makers, laundresses, and cabinet makers listed in Baines' *Yorkshire Directory* (G.11). However, there were also the workers who flooded into Harrogate during the spa season,[7] which, before the coming of the railways, began in early June and ended in late September (G.1). Hargrove noted that in 1781 the annual number of visitors totalled 1,556, whereas in 1795 it had grown to 2,458, these figures being exclusive of servants. In each case, the annual visitor total exceeded the town's total resident population (G.5). By the time of Dr Granville's visit in 1839, visitor levels between June and October had increased to 20,586, or five times the population of Harrogate at the time of the 1841 census (F.58). The dramatically fluctuating employment requirements of the spa season were, therefore, met by the in-migration of workers from the communities surrounding Harrogate, such as Beckwithshaw, Knaresborough or Spofforth, who either commuted between their homes and places of work, or took up accommodation in the servants' wings of the great inns and hotels. Some workers appear to have had their homes in places as far away as Leeds and York, at distances, respectively, of 17 and 21 miles. A study of the patterns of employment in Harrogate and Knaresborough in 1851 shows that whereas more than 80 per cent of domestic servants employed within Knaresborough had been born in that village, only about 10 per cent of domestic servants employed within Harrogate had been born there, with the majority of servants being born outside the spa.

Similarly, with the hotel servants; more than 80 per cent appear to have been born north of the river Nidd, which separated the two communities of Harrogate and Knaresborough. The same pattern is evident with stone masons.[8] At the end of the spa season, the hotel workers were paid off, receiving a share of the tips left by visitors throughout the season. The 'Inn Master' entered all such tips in a book, the shares being paid out in a proportional system approved by the innkeeper. One writer in the *Harrogate Advertiser* for 1893 wrote: '... the tips often amounted to fabulous sums in the course of a season ... the Knaresborough waiters worked hard in the summer, earned lots of money, and drank and took things easy in the winter ... one was a tapster at the Crown Hotel ...' (R.3138) From this it is clear that a very considerable proportion of Harrogate's workers were not permanently domiciled in the town. The very groups of workers who in other communities supported non-conformity from within those communities, appear to have left their non-conformity at home. For example, Hampsthwaite, some two miles from Harrogate, is known to have had a Methodist meeting house in 1764, some sixty years before Harrogate. Consequently, there was no reason for Hampsthwaite's Methodist workers, migrating to Harrogate for the season, to have campaigned in Harrogate for what they already had at home – home being only some two miles away. The same applied to other sources of migratory labour – Knaresborough, Killinghall, and Beckwithshaw.[9]

The spirit of evangelical revivalism is completely absent from any of the surviving accounts of religious life in Harrogate before 1841. Such revivalism usually flourished either in very cohesive communities, such as mining settlements, or among rural migrants to industrial towns. Neither description is appropriate to Harrogate. It has also been noted that certain forms of non-conformity, such as Primitive Methodism, emerged as religious protest against the harsher aspects of labouring life, and the oligarchical troika of parson, squire and farmer.[10] Harrogate never had a squire; its parsons were appointed by two different princes of the Church: Chester and York, and most of the farmers had become innkeepers. And even if such a troika had existed, there were always the doctors, to say nothing of the Duchy, as counter-balance.

The religious affiliations of the High Harrogate population were assessed in 1789 with a questionnaire issued by the Diocese of Chester: 'Are there in your parish any presbyterians, independents, anabaptists, quakers or other sectarians?' The minister replied in the negative in each case, save for a single family of presbyterians, adding by way of explanation that they were 'farmers'. Of Methodism or Baptism, not a single reference was made, and Quakerism, which was recorded in Harrogate in the seventeenth century, appeared to have been extinguished (M.32). Yet these questions were made in respect of the resident population, and had they been directed to the migrant population, a different answer might well have been given. The accuracy of Mitton's replies need not be doubted, since Robert Mitton served his Harrogate cure from 1769 to 1818, leaving detailed and accurate accounts of proceedings in the Vestry Book (D.18).

The pioneer of Methodism in Nidderdale, Thomas Lee, visited many of the Nidderdale communities in the 1740s and 1750s, including such villages as Hartwith, Pateley Bridge, Hardcastle, Greenhow, Lofthouse, Birtswith and Menwith, but he left no record of even a single visit to Harrogate. John Wesley, a regular traveller in Nidderdale, preaching at Pateley Bridge in 1788 in his 85th year, visited Knaresborough on at least three occasions, 1743, 1744 and 1761,[11] but the nearest he got to Harrogate was in 1788, when he preached at Pannal.[12] Non-conformity did not take early root in Harrogate. One of Harrogate's rivals, Malvern, built four non-conformist meeting-houses between 1806 and 1820, at a time when its resident population rose from about nine hundred to fifteen hundred. In Harrogate over the same period, no nonconformist chapels were built, although the town's resident population had increased from 1,500 to 2,800.[13]

Then there were the great industrial towns. Only twenty miles to the south-west, Bradford in 1841 has been described as being one the most intensely non-conformist towns in mid-Victorian England. At the time of the 1851 census, only 23 per cent of Bradford's morning worshippers chose to attend Anglican churches, compared with 60 per cent attending different non-conformist chapels.[14] Similarly at Leeds, 17 miles south of Harrogate, the strength of non-conformity was such as to ensure that by 1829 the Anglicans had lost control of the Improvement Commission, and by 1835 they had lost control of the town council. Indeed, after the Kilhamite schism of 1797, Leeds became one of the principal centres of the new sect, the Methodist New Connection.[15]

The often uneasy alliance of Church, Crown and State was the target for all those who wished to reform Parliament, repeal the Test and Corporations Acts, and abolish the legislation against Roman Catholics. The agitators for these changes were, by and large, middle-class dissenters, Roman Catholics, and the articulate poor. The alliance between the establishment and Anglicanism was countered by that between the agitators for reform and non-conformity. According to John Wesley, the earliest Methodist converts were 'poor almost to the man', and 'a low, insignificant people'.[16] The best places in which to preach, explained Wesley, were those which 'have the greatest number of quiet and willing hearers'. For these reasons, Methodism found more converts in the lower, rather than the upper levels of society.[17] Or, as the Duchess of Buckingham remarked to the Countess of Huntington, Methodism, even in its somewhat less plebeian Calvinistic form, was 'much at variance with high rank and good breeding'; both ladies – incidentally – were visitors at High Harrogate.[18] The overwhelming mass of evidence indicates that until the railways came to Harrogate in 1849, visitors were either from the wealthy middle or upper classes, and that apart from the charity patients at the Royal Bath Hospital (who were sent on the recommendation of wealthy and titled donors, or by Anglican clergymen), the majority of poorer workers were from settlements outside the twin boundaries of Bilton-with-Harrogate or Pannal.

The innkeepers, as a class, being used to receiving such arch-conservative members of the establishment as Lord Bute, who first visited Harrogate in 1763 (C.36.b), or Lord Castlereagh, in 1801 (C.73), would naturally have taken some trouble to ensure the town – at least outwardly – remained free from anti-establishment feeling. The same may be said of the doctors. Had Harrogate been home to a large number of poorer workers, it is likely that Primitive Methodism would have been established well before 1855, when the first chapel was built in a poor area of High Harrogate,[19] regardless of the feelings of the innkeepers or doctors – but by then, High Harrogate was in decline. Earlier in the century non-conformists had worshipped in their home villages.

Anglicanism in Harrogate enjoyed the direct support of the Duchy of Lancaster, which since 1399 has been linked to the Crown of England. The Duchy retained large and important estates in Harrogate after the Great Award of 1778 (B.31), and continued to take an interest in their development, as well as in the development of the town as a whole (B.238). This was important, politically, for the continued prosperity of the church in Harrogate. Newspaper descriptions of Harrogate's spa season between 1800 and 1820 contain many references to the increasing numbers of visitors. For example, in September 1808, 'Never was this place remembered to be so full ...' (R.1425). During the season of 1811, the *York Herald* reported, 'this celebrated watering-place is assuming its wonted gaiety. Every day brings considerable additions to the number of fashionables, and, it is expected that in a short time the Inns and Lodging Houses will be crowded with the first families of the United Kingdom.' (R.1505) In 1817 the *York Herald* reported that 'notwithstanding the long continuance of the wet, this celebrated watering place has to boast of a greater number of visitors than for some years past.' (R.1745) The effect of these increases on High Harrogate chapel had been observed in 1791, when the Duchy of Lancaster issued a fiat and commission to Lord Loughborough to improve the building: '... whereas it has been represented unto ... our Duchy ... that some of the main walls and other parts ... are much decayed ... and that by means of the great increase of the ... great concourse of persons who annually resort to Harrogate for the benefit of the Medicinal Waters ... the said chapel hath been found to be insufficient for the reception of the congregation assembled ...' (M.35).

A number of improvements were completed the following year, including a new vestry (D.18), but by 1810 a larger programme of rebuilding was under consideration. This seems to have been in part stimulated by a visit to Harrogate made by the Duchy Clerk, Robert Harper, who, in the company of his little daughter, visited Harrogate in September 1810, staying at the Crown Hotel. He met the curate, Robert Mitton, and as a result of the curate's remarks, requested that details of the condition of High Harrogate chapel be forwarded to London as soon as possible. (M.58). The reply included details of the previous twelve months' use of the building, with records of thirty-four christenings and fourteen funerals, and that the Bilton-with-Harrogate part of the parish contained 1,443 people. Of the visitors, he wrote, 'so full a season I never knew during my residence of forty-two years'. The average voluntary contribution over the previous ten years had been the not inconsiderable sum of £150 per annum, but he did not specify the sources of these donations. Mitton sent a second letter to the

Duchy on 26 November, enclosing estimates for the proposed work of enlargement, which came to £150 for the new roof, ceiling, and pews, and £130 for the stonemason's work. Commenting on the ground-floor accommodation, he wrote, 'I could wish may be preserved for the lower order of those who attend divine service'; and, of the seats in the new gallery, that they should be preserved '... for the accommodation of the people resorting to Harrogate for the use of the Waters.' (M.59)

The proposed enlargement of High Harrogate chapel was considered by the Duchy Council between 1810 and 1812, who eventually approved plans produced by the Duchy's own Surveyor General (B.188). The curate, Robert Mitton, had asked for an increase to his stipend (M.60), and on 8 December 1810 the Duchy Council agreed to hold over consideration of his request until the cost of the proposed alterations had been ascertained (B.179). Mitton sought increases to his Duchy stipend regularly (B.248), which was eventually raised from £30 (B.244) to £50 (B.267) per annum (8). Robert Mitton had held his cure since 1769, and, having achieved the moderate success of improvements to his chapel, as well as an increase to his stipend, he retired in January 1818, with his son, the Reverend Henry Mitton being licensed to the stipendiary curacy of Harrogate (M.92). The pews of High Harrogate church were largely rented by local residents, dominated by the doctors and innkeepers. A plan submitted to the Duchy at the time of the enlargement of 1810–12, showed that the proposed gallery included twenty-three pews, and that ten of these were appropriated by innkeepers (M.60). It is not certain whether these pews were intended for the sole use of the innkeepers and their families, or whether they were rented to ensure that important guests of the innkeepers could be provided with sittings. The former is more likely, since the Duchy Court wrote to Robert Mitton in June 1813, pointing out that as only two persons had agreed to rent pews, it might be sensible to write to the innkeepers suggesting that they should consider taking unlet pews for the visitors at their hotels, proportional to the contributions each hotel collected for the benefit of the minister. Their reply is not known. (M.85). The vicar of Knaresborough also wrote to the Duchy, grumbling at the attitude of the Harrogate innkeepers: '... the plan for recent allotment of pews in Harrogate Chapel has lain a long time at this Vicarage ... for inspection ... but only a few have called ... only Mr Thackwray of the Crown and Mr Wormald (the surgeon) have assented to the conditions ... Mr Greaves of the Granby, and one or two more, have formally declined their pews ...' (M.80). High Harrogate chapel had probably contained seating for about 200 people, at its opening in 1749, which increased by 50 with the enlargements of 1792 and 1806. The enlargements of 1812 provided a further 107 sittings, which brought the total up to about 350.[20]

The 1812 improvements to High Harrogate Chapel gave the 1749 building

PLATE 100
The Queen Hotel at
left, with Christ
Church and Church
Square at right,
drawn by John Field
in 1830.
COURTESY OF MR R. BELDON

a further ten years of life, but when the Bishop of Chester visited it on 28 August 1822, he found that the east end was 'in a very ruinous and dangerous state & will require taking down and be rebuilt.' (M.99) This was the opening shot in a campaign to replace St John's chapel with a completely new building, and it occurred at the very time when church building was a big issue nationally. The unrest which followed the Peterloo massacre of 1819 saw the Whig opposition increasingly identify the Church of England as a pillar of the discredited social order, which in turn increasingly bracketed Whiggery[21] with dissent. Membership of the Church of England had, over the previous 90 years, gone into decline, and the church building rate had been insignificant. Between 1801 and 1821 the Church of England increased the number of its churches and chapels from 11,379 to 11,883, or by 4.24 per cent at a period when the population of England and Wales had increased from 8,893,000 to 12,000,000, or by 29.89 per cent.[22] Anglican revival, negligible before 1830, generally post-dates the establishment of the Ecclesiastical Commission in 1835.[23] In Harrogate, however, the assistance of the Duchy of Lancaster ensured that the improvements began considerably earlier, in the 1820s.

Discussions about a new church for High Harrogate occurred regularly at vestry meetings, and on 1 September 1825 Rev. Henry Mitton was appointed 'to take the opinion of an architect upon the state of the chapel.' (D.18) The following year the Duchy agreed to contribute £300 'towards the repairs of the chapel at High Harrogate, as soon as it shall appear that there shall be so much money raised by subscription in the neighbourhood, or from other sources, as with that sum may be sufficient to put the chapel into substantial repair' (M.148). The Duchy chose its words with care, as it was at this time receiving other requests from High Harrogate for contributions towards a hospital (B.293) and a school (M.295), as well as from Low Harrogate for a new church (B.298). Contributions from residents included the landlords of all three of High Harrogate's great hotels – the Granby, the Dragon and the Queen – as well as leading doctors and landowners, but not (so far as can be ascertained) from any of the artisan class. Other contributions came from visitors, as well as from the 'Incorporated Society for promoting the enlargement, building and repair of churches and chapels'. In 1827 the new curate, the Reverend Thomas Kennion, was able to advise the Duchy that the township had collected £500, which, when added to the £200 promised by the church building society, and the £300 promised by the Duchy, came to £1,000 for the building fund (M.151).

The decision to proceed with the building of a new church, rather than to enlarge the old one, was taken by the parishioners at a vestry meeting of 17 December 1829 (M.168), attended by the Rev. Thomas Kennion, chapel warden Thomas Frith, who held the Dragon Hotel, William Sheepshanks, a wealthy landowner, and nine others, including the vestry clerk Henry Peacock (M.169), who at this time was still master of the workhouse and still spending his wife's money with alacrity (D.20.10.). Building work seems to have been under way by the spring of 1830, using stone from Hookstone Quarry (W.7.24). Eventually, the new church was consecrated on 1 October 1831 by the Bishop of Chester. The old church had been fitted with an organ in 1806,[24] without any of the argument which had occurred at Hollingwood Church, Oldham, or at many non-conformist places of worship in Lancashire and Yorkshire at this period.[25] Similarly, the new church had an organ, and the services appear to have been appropriately 'high' rather than 'low' church.[26] This was possibly reflected in the very full description – not of the church, but of the congregations' apparel – which the Yorkshire newspapers published, after the consecration service of 1 October 1831 (M.189). Of Primitive Methodist austerity, there was not a trace. The new church provided free sittings for the poor, as requested by the Clerical Commissioners in 1831, although they do not appear to have been used regularly (M.191). All the evidence points towards High Harrogate church being a church for the upper and middle classes.

In the early years of the nineteenth century Low Harrogate began to eclipse High Harrogate, primarily because it possessed both sulphur and chalybeate water, whereas High Harrogate had no sulphur water. The growing use of sulphur water as a medical treatment ensured that the doctors sent more of their patients to Low Harrogate, and, accordingly, the numbers of visitors began to increase (F.58, pp. 36–8). The example of the innkeeper Joseph Thackwray, is typical; the sulphur well he discovered in

1822 in the grounds of his Crown Hotel was advertised as an important new amenity which was proving popular with his guests (G.13). In the same year as Joseph Thackwray discovered the 'Crown Well', and the Bishop of Chester inspected the decayed chapel in High Harrogate, Low Harrogate progressed towards a church of its own. The previous year, 1821, a petition had been sent from the 'Vicar, Churchwardens and principal inhabitants of Pannal for scite of ground to build a church at Low Harrogate'. The petition was addressed to the Chancellor of the Duchy of Lancaster, Henry Bathurst and its precise wording explains its nature with admirable clarity:

> ... the great want of a place of public worship in connection with the established church at Low Harrogate in the Parish of Pannal, which is nearly three miles from the Parish Church, hath been proven to the satis-faction of the Archbishop of York, in consequence of which his grace has given his consent to the erection of a Chapel of Ease to Pannal Church at Low Harrogate, and has promised a liberal donation towards the expense of building the same ... the Parish ... have agreed to raise the sum of £500 towards effecting the above object. By voluntary subscrip-tions and otherwise your petitioners have no doubt the same will be effected, provided a proper scite can be procured for such chapel. Your petitioners therefore humbly pray your Honour will be pleased to advise a grant from His Majesty of a piece of ground suitable for the erecting of such chapel ... which would be very great convenience to the inhabi-tants of Low Harrogate ... and who are much more numerous than those residing in the village of Pannal ... Your petitioners beg leave to suggest that a small field ... given to his late Majesty in right of his Duchy of Lancaster, would be a most suitable scite ...

The petition was signed by the Vicar of Pannal, Ralph Bates Hunter, and nineteen prominent citizens of Low Harrogate, of which at least ten were landlords of inns, including Joseph Thackwray of the Crown, the only inn at Low Harrogate (N.2).

The new churches in both High and Low Harrogate were a sign not only of increasing numbers of visitors, but also of an increasing confidence and sense of community by residents. No longer were the people of Low Harrogate content to walk to distant Pannal for Anglican services; High Harrogate had its own place of worship, so why should Low Harrogate be lacking a church? The support shown by Joseph Thackwray for the idea of a Low Harrogate Church may have had something to do with the habit of visitors parading themselves on the way to and from church:

> This leads me to mention (by association)
> No people go better to church in the nation

_____

Than we Harrogate folks, for many go here
Never seen in such places before I much fear,
We go jostling and crowding for seats and quite free,
Turn out the poor possessors sans ceremonie,
And should the poor wretches presume but to grumble,
Look down with contempt and so bid them be humble ...
(C.91.x)

Barbara Hofland's poem about the pleasure of the Harrogate season in the Regency made much of the behaviour of the fashionable visitors. As the Crown was the only one of Harrogate's four great hotels not to be within easy reach of a church, it may be that Joseph Thackwray supported the idea of building one in the field opposite the Crown Inn, to supply this need. Whatever the reason, Joseph Thackwray and two other local businessmen, and the vicar of Pannal, took out a bond with wealthy landowner Henry Wells of Scriven-with-Tentergate, on 25 February 1824, for the loan of £1,600 for the express purpose of building the Low Harrogate church (N.8). This was after the foundation stone had been laid on 4 September 1822 (N.7), and before either the Duchy had consented to transfer the site (which had been surveyed after 11 February 1822 (B.81) to the vicar of Pannal, or before satisfaction of the Archbishop of York's demand that the new living should include provision of a stipend of £50 per annum (N.3).

The 1821 petition to the Duchy did not meet with initial success, and two further petitions had to be submitted – in 1822 (N.6) and 1824 (N.12) – before success was achieved in the conveying of the site. Unlike the first and unsuccessful petition, the two subsequent ones include the phrase:

... The Inns and Lodging Houses which are yearly increasing at present accommodate upwards of 1,500 visitors to the Mineral Springs ... The want of an Episcopal place of worship according to the doctrine and discipline of the Church of England has for many years been the cause of serious public regret. Under the strong impression of the importance of advancing the religious interest of so many individuals from the highest to the lowest rank of society, who reside at Low Harrogate and who come from all parts of the United Kingdom. The Rev. R. B. Hunter, Vicar of Pannal, Captain Bainbridge, Mr Crosby and Mr Thackwray, decided friends to the established church, seeing dissenting Meeting Houses of different denominations rise up on every side, and attended by such number of members of the Establishment (who having no Episcopal place of worship to attend, will of necessity resort to the meeting house) formed themselves into a committee for the purpose of endeavouring to accomplish so desirable an object ...

PLATE 99
Low Harrogate
church, a drawing by
John Field.
COURTESY OF MR R. BELDON

The reference to dissenting meeting houses appears to have been an exaggeration, but it was made at the very time when Whig politicians were involved in an increasingly acrimonious dispute with Anglican churchmen, and when the establishment was increasingly sensitive to its weakening support.[27] The 'strong impression of the importance of advancing the religious interest of so many individuals ...' mentioned in the above petition most probably refers to comments addressed by individual visitors to individual promoters of the Low Harrogate church scheme.

The new St Mary's church (see plates 64 and 99) was intended to serve a Low Harrogate population of five hundred, together with visitors, who were estimated to number three thousand per year. A plot of two acres was identified, the church's external dimensions being 78′ 2″ by 51′ (N.11), with a capacity for between seven to eight hundred seatings, of which four hundred were to be free. Work appears to have begun on the church in 1822 (N.7), and concluded in 1825 (N.39), and on 11 October 1825 the Duchy of Lancaster issued a warrant for payment of an annual £50 stipend for the curate (B.296). This warrant was issued only a few weeks before the Duchy made a similar payment to High Harrogate church (B.294) and a payment of £50 to High Harrogate School (B.295). These expenses were noted by the Duchy Chancellor, Lord Bexley, who wrote to Harrogate

PLATE 64
Low Harrogate's
parish church,
St Mary's, was built
in 1825.

PLAN 38
Surrender of site for
St Mary's Church, 1
August 1825.

agent Mr R. Harper, regarding the work done by Duchy surveyor Smirke that, 'I am sorry to see that we are all in so much debt to Mr Smirke, but expenses which have been incurred must be paid. It however makes it less convenient to do what would be desirable at the Savoy Chapel ...' At a time when Duchy resources were needed for George IV's Chapel of Savoy, they were diverted to Harrogate, in a further example of Duchy munificence.

The new church was within the parish of Pannal (see plan 38) and therefore under the control of the vicar, Ralph Bates Hunter (who of course

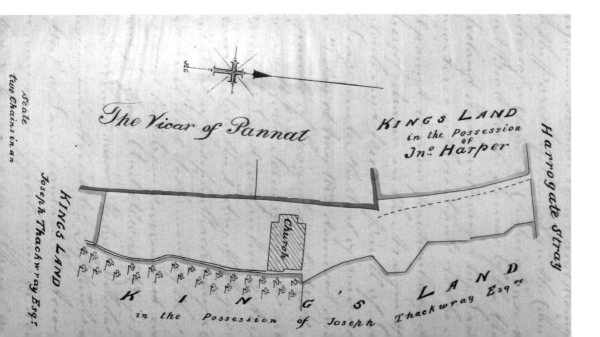

was subject to his superior, the Archbishop of York) who wrote to the Duchy on 18 July 1826 asking that St Mary's be transferred to the Duchy, subject to the Duchy reimbursing all expenses (B.195). The matter was laid before the Privy Council, who at their August meeting intimated their agreement to Hunter's request, and their readiness to reimburse the sum of £1,852 8s. 5d. subject to approval from the Archbishop of York, but the move was suspended after the Duchy learned that the commissioners for building churches would not sanction such a move without the Duchy agreeing to increase the stipend, which in view of their previous generosity they declined to do (B.95). This decision seems to have been based on a realisation that the pew rents would not be as great as originally estimated. Hence Hunter's wish to transfer St Mary's to the Duchy; hence the Duchy's refusal to accept it; hence the commissioners' refusal to sanction its conversion into a separate district church (B.205). The new St Mary's, for the time being, would have to remain a chapel of ease to Pannal church and its vicar, Ralph Bates Hunter.

The architect of St Mary's church was Samuel Chapman (N.48), who produced a well-mannered exercise in the early English style of architecture, complete with a massive square tower, and crisp lancet windows (see plates 64 and 99), which was an ornament to the town until its dismantling in 1923. The surviving accounts for the building of St Mary's church provide insight to the source of materials. Thomas Mears, a bellfounder, was paid £84 9s. 10d. for his work on the church bells, and A. T. Smith received £29 for 'stained glass'. The occupant of Wedderburn House, Dr Jacques (D.41), received £13 0s. 10d. for 'Scotch fir poles', no doubt for use as scaffolding, and the largest payment, £1,282, went for masonry and plaster work (N.48). The final cost of the new church, excluding the value of the land conveyed by the Duchy, came to £3,137 11s. 8¾d. (N.50). Building costs were met from subscriptions, including a £500 grant from the Church Building Society, £652 from general subscriptions, £115 from collections after sermons and £202 from what was termed a 'brief', all of which came to £1,469 approximately, leaving a shortfall of £1,669 approximately (N.50). This shortfall seems to have been met eventually by further donations and pew rents, although not before Rev. Holme had applied to the Duchy yet again for further land and another stipendiary increase (B.108).

The post of curate at the new Harrogate church proved to be one that was highly sought after, as demonstrated by the fifty-nine letters from hopeful applicants which flooded into the Duchy office between June 1828 and September 1829, written mostly in cringingly servile or self-righteously effusive style (N.44). Matters were not eased by the new Duchy chancellor, the Earl of Aberdeen, who succeeded Lord Bexley in January 1828,[28] and who promised the living of the new Low Harrogate church to one

Reverend James Arnold (N.43). The Archbishop of York's preferred choice was Rev. T. H. Madge (N.29) whose ministry, according to William Grainge, was succeeded by those of James Holme, James Heyworth, and, in 1839, by George Digby (N.51), although these dates are almost certainly inaccurate (e.g. compare N.51 with B.116). Grainge also recorded that the first three ministers resigned suddenly, and it is possible that the difficult character of their vicar, Hunter (who was a lush[29]) had something to do with this.

An interesting insight into the somewhat Trollopian state of church affairs in early nineteenth-century Harrogate, is revealed in a letter sent to the Duchy by the minister at High Harrogate, Reverend Mitton, on 23 April 1825, who asked if he could be the appointee, if the new church became vested in the Duchy (N.17). Three months later the Archbishop of York wrote to the Duchy Chancellor, Lord Bexley, noting that the Rev. Hunter, vicar of Pannal, had opposed the patronage of the new Low Harrogate church passing to the Duchy, because he feared that it would be awarded to the Rev. Mitton, who 'he says, had made himself extremely unpopular at Low Harrogate from his having done everything in his power to prevent the building of the chapel ...' (N.29).

The new St Mary's church was ready for consecration by the Archbishop of York in August 1825. The archbishop wrote to the Duchy on 7 August that '... I consecrated the chapel at Low Harrogate on Thursday last, in the presence of a most numerous congregation, containing I should think nearly a thousand ... Mr Hunter preached a very good sermon, somewhat flowery, but calculated to make a considerable impression on an extremely attentive auditory ...' (N.39) Of the total of seven hundred and fifty 'sittings' at St Mary's, no fewer than five hundred were free, for the greater convenience of the visitors (G.17).

When a field, tenanted by one Harper (N.2), had been identified in 1821 as being a suitable site for Low Harrogate's church, it was conceived as a site for a chapel of ease to Pannal church, and that it would, therefore, be without its own surrounding or adjoining burial ground. However, when the promoters forwarded their petition to Lord Bexley, the Duchy chancellor, in July 1824, they referred specifically to 'His Majesty having been graciously pleased to give land sufficient for a Burial Ground and site for a new Church ...' (N.12).

The Duchy warrant which authorised the issuing of a deed for the granting of the site, made reference to 'building a church or chapel thereon with a burial ground annexed thereto ...' (N.24), terms which were repeated in the particular of 2 August 1825 (B.298) and the actual grant (N.38) which refers to a burial ground or cemetery. Having already made a gift of the land, and contributed towards the curate's stipend, the Duchy may have been surprised to receive a rather disingenuous letter in May 1837, from

Rev. Holme, at the Low Harrogate parsonage, in which the curate asked the Duchy to provide his churchyard with a 'good substantial wall' as the fences were in a dilapidated state, and that Mr Thackwray's cattle were in constant occupation of the churchyard (B.114). This sparked off a series of letters concerning boundaries, rights of access and general grudges and grievances (B.115–120), all of which the senders appear to have expected the Duchy to settle. Eventually the Duchy agreed to pay for the building of the requested wall, the Duchy clerk commenting somewhat acidly that, 'as it appears however that it is the practice on occasions similar to the present for the district or parish or committee to fence the church yard round, I have to observe that the present liberality on the part of the Duchy must not lead to the expectation that the repairs in the wall in future time will be undertaken by this office.' (B.121) A local mason, Winterburn, was contracted for the job (B.122), and when his wall was finished, the churchyard required only to be consecrated, before interments could occur.

St Mary's eventually became a parish church after an order dated 19 July 1830, which assigned to it a large portion of Pannal parish, the Rev. Holme (B.108) being the first vicar, whose early resignation was followed by the installation of Rev. George Digby in 1839 (N.51). In 1836, the new diocese of Ripon was created, which drew High Harrogate (which had been an independent parish since 1828) out of the diocese of Chester, and Low Harrogate out of that of York (K.30), placing both within the responsibility of the new see. Accordingly when Rev. Digby decided to undertake the consecration of the cemetery at St Mary's, he wrote to the Duchy clerk, Mr Dawes Danvers, asking if it would be possible to use part of the proposed site for a garden to the parsonage, by reason of the fact that the two-acre plot was far bigger than was currently required for the Low Harrogate population (B.136). When Danvers replied on 14 April 1840, he advised that although he could not alter the terms of the original grant of land, he passed on the Chancellor's observation that the Duchy would not object to such usage (B.137). Although the parsonage garden seems to have been made, there are no references to a single interment ever having taken place, or indeed to an official consecration by the Bishop of Ripon. The reason for this omission may well have been touched on by Rev. Digby in his letter of 9 April 1840 (B.136), when he claimed that the land needed to be levelled and drained 'more than we could possibly afford'. Eventually Low Harrogate interments occurred at both Grove Road and Harlow Hill cemeteries, the land at St Mary's walk being filled with housing and the St Mary's school room. We have related the history of St Mary's church at such length and detail in order to demonstrate once more the extraordinary role of the Duchy of Lancaster in the town's affairs.[30]

Non-conformity, which had become so powerful in neighbouring

Bradford, Leeds and indeed the entire West Riding of Yorkshire, made few inroads at Harrogate. For example, High Harrogate increased its population between 1821 and 1831 from 1,934 to 2,812 (an increase of 31.22 per cent) in the same period enlarging its old Anglican church; Low Harrogate increased its population from approximately 800 to 900[31] and received an entirely new church – St Mary's. However, Bradford, with its population increasing from the 1821 level of 13,064 to 23,223 in 1831 (an increase of 43.74 per cent),[32] built no Anglican churches. Over the same period Harrogate built one non-conformist chapel, whereas Bradford built eleven.[33] The view that, by 1830, the Church of England was on the point of becoming a minority religious establishment, was certainly not applicable to Harrogate.[34] Harrogate's single non-conformist chapel, built in the 1820s, was located neither in High nor Low Harrogate, but in the newly emerging community known as central Harrogate, which had developed after 1800 along the footpath between the two villages. At this rural spot, sheltered from the gaze of visitors, using land owned by the speculative developer James Franklin or the innkeeper Joseph Thackwray, Methodist builder James Simpson erected terraces of cheap housing, which were subsequently occupied by the labouring classes.[35]

With names such as Beulah Place, Elim Court, and Gilead Place, the non-conformist character of central Harrogate was marked (see plan 45). Here, in 1824, Harrogate's first custom-built Methodist chapel opened. The Wesleyan Methodists had rented a room in a private house in High Harrogate in 1796 (see plate 92), but this does not appear to have been very successful. Although historian Grainge referred to it as being built, the architectural style suggests that it was probably converted from another use (K.23). The 1824 chapel, however, appears to have attracted a growing congregation, probably because of its appeal to the lower orders of society, who lived in its immediate neighbourhood.[36] An article in the *Harrogate Advertiser* of 13 September 1899 claimed that Primitive Methodism had arrived in the town in 1819, with the Rev. John Abbey, followed the same year by Rev. William Plowes, who re-visited in 1820. Services were first held in 'barns and cottages' in Bilton and Bachelor Gardens.

The growth of Methodism in Harrogate occurred at the precise time and place that cheap housing appeared, built to accommodate the increasing number of permanent resident workers at the spa (D.42). Earlier attempts to promote the Methodist cause do not appear to have met with success. When the fiery Methodist irregular Mary Barritt wrote of her 1799 Nidderdale experiences as a preacher, she noted that she had made some impact in Knaresborough with her sermons, but that she was not confident of having achieved anything in Harrogate.[37]

Congregationalism seems to have appeared in Harrogate through the

Sunday school movement, of which more will be said in the next chapter. The first church – the so-called 'Cross Chapel' was built in 1821 in the poorest part of the town, at Smithy Hill (see plate 72), a location which seems to be contrary to the established opinion that, like Baptists, Congregationalism enjoyed greatest support from the middle classes of society.[38] One explanation for this may be that the land on which the Cross Chapel was built was the nearest plot to High Harrogate's fashionable Regent's Parade not owned by the great innkeepers, who do not seem to have been non-conformists. Smithy Hill may have been chosen simply because no other location was available (B.31).

Congregationalism and Baptism flourished in Harrogate only after the arrival of the railways in 1848, when a number of middle-class Bradford, Leeds and York commuters established themselves in the town. Congregationalism, however, seems to have been introduced to Harrogate in about 1775, when Henry Thornton, of Clapham, Surrey, visited the town. At Mr Thornton's direction, one Richard Johnson, a member of the independent church at Knaresborough, moved to Harrogate to instruct children, his efforts finding support from similarly inclined people. It was from the early meetings of these groups that Congregationalism in Harrogate had its true beginning, assisted by the Rev. Howell, minister at Knaresborough. In 1813, a large room was rented, next to the Hope Tavern (later known as Gascoigne's or the County Hotel) which soon became known as the 'Hope Chapel', and when this became too small, a building was erected in 1821 at Smithy Hill (see plate 72, left side), on what was often called World's End Road. Opening on 17 October 1821, the new 'Cross Chapel' survived for ten years, before being purchased by the Anglicans, for conversion to a National School (K.33). At about the same time as High Harrogate's Cross Chapel had opened, a similar institution had been provided in Low Harrogate by Major Thackwray, known as the Rock Chapel, which was sited behind Well Hill overlooking Iron Gate Bridge Road (G.11). The Congregationalists of High Harrogate, having sold their Cross Chapel to the Anglicans, then moved to central Harrogate's James Street, where, on 26 April 1832, they acquired a prime site from Franklin's trustees (S.989), on which they then re-erected the materials of the old St John's Chapel, having purchased them from the Anglicans for £100 (K.36). The Congregationalist's James Street Chapel, known as the 'Providence Chapel' served until the opening of the Victoria Avenue Church in 1862.

As for the Baptists, their very first recorded meeting took place as late as October 1880, the first Baptist church being built three years later.[39]

The Society of Friends, commonly known as Quakers, appears to have been active in Harrogate since 1656, when John Hogg of Harragate was condemned to be set in the stocks for attending Society meetings (K.7), an experience which seems not to have deterred him, as he suffered another term in the stocks for a similar offence the following March (K.8). Writing in his diary for 1666, Oliver Heywood recorded that he had 'preacht at Widdow Hogs', and that on a following day he had preached to a number of Christians at 'one Francis Ingles, near the Wells ...' (K.10). These references to the Hogg family may refer to the same branch as that of John and William Hogg, who are recorded as tenanting land in Bilton-with-Harrogate in May 1625 (S.17), and who later are known to have been running the Bell Tavern (R.370). References to the Quakers in Harrogate during the eighteenth century are all but non-existent, but in 1820 the noted Liverpool minister, Elizabeth Robson, visited Harrogate during a tour and noted that 'some of the gay people then at that place attended and it was a favoured time.' (K.26) By 1835 the Quakers were meeting at 'Skaife's school room' (K.37), but the first specially built meeting house, in Chapel (now Oxford) Street, seems not to have been opened until 1854.[40]

In 1789, the curate of High Harrogate chapel informed the Bishop of Chester that there were within his parish '8 papists – farmers and day labourers; and one family of presbyterians – farmers' (M.32). By the time of the visitation of 1814, the record refers to '6 or 7 papists in High Harrogate'

PLATE 76
Park House, Park Parade.

(M.87). The identity of these 'papists' is not known, although it is possible that they may have belonged to the Roman Catholic communities associated with the Ingilbys of Ripley Castle. What is certain, however, is that they did not belong to any of the innkeeper class, nor to that of the Harrogate landowners, who were all Anglican. The growth of post-reformation Roman Catholicism in Harrogate appears to have been an essentially post-1841 phenomenon.

Conclusion

Religious life in Harrogate between 1770 and 1841 was influenced by the role of the Crown, through the Duchy of Lancaster, the religious character of the visitors, most of whom were of the establishment Anglican class, and the absence of significant numbers of lower-middle-class or poor resident population. The migratory lifestyle of the spa's seasonal workers – otherwise promising soil for the development of non-conformity – also failed to threaten the supremacy of Anglicanism in Harrogate. It was only with the building of a working-class community in central Harrogate in the 1820s, and the introduction of mass transportation after 1848, when the first railway ran into Harrogate, that there was an increase in non-conformist worship, both among the residential population, as well as the visitors. For the period of the *Harrogate Great Chronicle*, however, the town suffered none of the religious convulsions which affected so many of its neighbours – Bradford, Leeds, or the other manufacturing towns of West Yorkshire. Nor did Harrogate share with these neighbours their high mortality rates, grinding poverty, groups of oppressed workers, nor any great social cause – problems with which non-conformity identified itself, and which were such good recruiting grounds for their respective causes. Harrogate did not even have a cholera scare.

One sign of the strength of the established order in Harrogate, was that when the 1841 Improvement Act was passed, the newly elected Board of twenty-one commissioners had but a single minister, the Reverend Thomas Kennion, and he was minister of the Anglican High Harrogate church, in receipt of a stipend paid by the Duchy of Lancaster (B.267). The visitors to Harrogate, from the time of Lords Bute and Castlereagh, to the time of Wordworth, Southey and Van Mildart, were Anglican and establishment. Indeed, this final troika have been described as being the last distinguished defenders of the Catholic question, argued as a case of political theology – and all three were regular visitors. Van Mildart (the last Lord Bishop of the County Palatine of Durham) even settled in Harrogate, buying a mansion (see plate 76) facing High Harrogate's Christ Church (G.22).

12 | Education in Harrogate, 1770–1841

T HIS CHAPTER will describe the state of education in Harrogate between 1770 and 1841: who it served, how it changed, and why it changed. It will also show that the principal agents for change were different from those of much of the West Riding of Yorkshire. At the time of the Enclosure Act of 1770, the twin villages of High Harrogate and Low Harrogate possessed a number of inns and other businesses which clearly employed people capable of reading, writing and arithmetic. The baptism registers of the time reveal that local resident families – innkeepers, saddlers, surveyors, coachbuilders, ministers, joiners, etc. – produced children, some of whom would certainly have been expected to work, eventually, in the family businesses, all of which required basic educational attainments (D.55).

Details of the simple 'Dame schools' were not recorded in the Harrogate's guide books, as such information would have been useless to the kind of visitor for whom such books were written. Eli Hargrove's publication of 1775 – the first such production – contains a full description of Harrogate's inns and wells, but not a single reference to any kind of school (G.1). Yet by the time of the 1838 *Visitors' Vade Mecum*, ten schools are described (G.25). Dame schools were little more than places for working parents to leave their children, usually in the charge of an elderly female, who might, for a few pence, teach children letters, numbers, and simple catechism. They needed no licence, and have left sporadic evidence for their existence. These Dame schools received children below working age, which, at the time, was usually seven years, the maximum age for school leaving being ten for boys (in rural areas), and fifteen for girls.[1] The practice in Nidderdale seems to have been for Dame schools to accommodate about twenty pupils, who, for a fee of 2*d*. or 3*d*. a week, received basic instruction in reading.[2]

In Harrogate, Education was required for two quite different classes of children. First, there were the local children; second, there were the visitors' children. A third class may also have existed: the children of workers who migrated to Harrogate during the summer season. Nothing is known about the education of such children, but it is likely that if they stayed with their parents in Harrogate during the season – between May and October – they would have received the same type of education as that of the other local children of similar status. On their parents going back to their home villages, the children would have moved with them. The period between 1770 and 1841 was one that saw a phenomenal increase in the provision of both charitable associations and schools, particularly Sunday schools. In London, a total of 243 medical, religious, educational and moral charities were founded, and the number of specially endowed educational establishments alone increased from 255 to 334 between 1760 and 1800. The English Sunday school movement, in 1788, claimed that it had enrolled 59,980 children, but by 1841 this had increased to 1,679,000.[3] The rivalries between the Anglican Church, and non-conformist religious practice, also played a significant role in the development of education between 1770 and 1841, especially as they provided parents of lower- and lower-middle-class background with an element of choice.[4]

The Sunday school movement in Harrogate, 1770–1841

The earliest known reference to the teaching of children in Harrogate occurs as late as 1775, in the writing of John Peel Clapham, who described a member of the Knaresborough Congregationalist movement, Henry Thornton, visiting Harrogate and being '... greatly troubled to observe on his daily walks, many ignorant and neglected children.' Seeking someone to instruct them, he was directed to Richard Johnson, a member of the Knaresborough Independent Church. Johnson accepted Thornton's offer of a teaching appointment, and was supported by him for several years afterwards.[5] This account has been regarded with scepticism by some, who have considered Thornton's accounts to be exaggerated, and the writings of Clapham as simple panygeric.[6] There is no evidence to support the claim that the streets of Harrogate were filled with 'many ignorant and neglected children'. Nor is it likely that the town was without at a teacher, no matter how humble. Thornton's school was a Sunday school, established at the time when the Church of England was undergoing an era of disaster, unlike the non-conformist churches, which were enjoying a period of sustained growth.[7] The Sunday schools established by the non-conformists were connected root and branch with the expansion of non-conformist chapels. Nationally, between 1750 and 1800, the number of Congregationalists almost doubled, and increased almost fourfold by 1838. But not in Harrogate. The Baptists almost tripled their membership in the second half of the eighteenth century, and more than trebled it again during the next thirty-eight years. But not in Harrogate. The Methodists, numerically the most important, expanded from 22,642 in 1767 to over half a million by the middle of the nineteenth century.[8] In Harrogate, the Wesleyan Methodists built a single chapel well away from either High or Low Harrogate, which never succeeded in eclipsing the Anglican Church in its levels of attendance.

Attendance at Sunday school was motivated by a variety of reasons. Because instruction was primarily religious, both the Anglicans and non-conformists saw the schools as a basic means of spreading Christianity, of rescuing poor children from corrupt parents – and possibly of influencing parents via their children. However, whereas the Anglicans believed that their schools should buttress society, teaching respect for the Church, the monarchy and the establishment, the non-conformist schools stressed a slightly different mixture of evangelism, self-improvement and the importance of the bible. Some Sunday schools were run on purely inter-denominational lines, but what was common to all the Sunday schools was that they were part of the evangelical revival of the 1780s and 1790s which was supported by all ranks of society, and not just by the lower and middle classes.[9] Indeed it seems that there existed in Yorkshire in about 1812 a prejudice amongst the better-off members of the working classes against sending their children to Sunday school, as such schools were considered suitable only for the lowest and most needy poor.[10] It is likely that the majority of children attending Sunday school in Harrogate from 1770 to 1841, came from the middle or lower middle classes, and – unlike many other parts of Yorkshire – the children of the poor were not much in evidence. This was simply because Harrogate did not possess a significant number of poor residents. The absence of poor, or pauper children, probably ensured that the first Harrogate Sunday schools were the resort of children from the better-off labouring and middle classes.

In a community such as Harrogate, where trade and spa growth were so important, the Sunday schools must have included elements of utilitarian and secular education in their teaching, so that along with reading, elementary writing and arithmetic (perhaps even the calculation and presentation of bills to customers!) may have been taught. Although such secular teaching was opposed by Anglicans, it was also opposed by many dissenters. The rector of Almondbury, near Huddersfield, 'regretted that a great number of children are tempted to go to Sunday schools of the dissenters owing to the inducement being held out by teaching writing on Sundays'.[11] Before the 1870 Education Act, it was the demand for cheap secular education, rather than for religious instruction, which ensured the popularity of Sunday schools among the working classes. Those schools which taught literacy and numeracy appear to have attracted more pupils than those which did not.[12] In so competitive a world as early nineteenth-century Harrogate, it is likely that the demand for secular education could not have been resisted by the Sunday schools. By 1831, when returns were sent to a House of Commons enquiry into education, High Harrogate was recorded as having three Sunday schools. One for the Anglicans taught 90 boys and 100 girls; one for the Wesleyans taught 55 boys and 33 girls; and one for the Independents taught 30 boys and 41 girls. Low Harrogate, by contrast, had one Sunday and day school teaching 119 children, and a separate Sunday school teaching 62 children of both sexes. All the schools were free, run by contributions, and catered to the educational needs of the poorer elements of Harrogate society (X.7).

Charity schools in Harrogate, 1770–1841

The first charity school appears to have been established in Harrogate in 1785 (see plate 28). It was provided by Richard Taylor, a local resident land-owner. The purpose of the school was the 'teaching and instructing such number of poor boys and girls of the township of Bilton-with-Harrogate, in reading, writing and arithmetic and in the church catechism.' (K.27) The school was endowed with 15 acres, 3 roods, 20 perches of land, as well as two beastgates upon Harrogate Stray, the rents being used to support the schoolmaster. Taylor bequeathed the school and land to a local teacher, John Inman, in his will of 8 June 1785 (K.27), and Inman appears to have run

PLATE 28
Bilton Endowed School, subsequently converted into residential use.

BATCHELOR GARDENS SCHOOL HARROGATE

the school until 1824, taking gratuities from those parents who could afford to pay them. The Charity Commissioners' report of 1820 referred to Inman instructing 'thirty children, boys and girls, in the manner directed by the deed of 1785, and makes no charge to their parents, except a shilling a year for each child, which is received with the sanction of the trustees.' Any resident of Bilton-with-Harrogate (High Harrogate) could apply for admission of their child, although the trustees vetted all such applications by means of interviewing the children, those selected being admitted at six or seven years of age. 'The number of applications generally exceeds that of the vacancies in the school by six or seven, and occasionally by a larger number.' The schoolmaster was permitted to take other children – generally numbering from fifteen to twenty – whose education was paid for by their parents. The principles under which charity children were admitted are not known, beyond having to satisfy the trustees that they would benefit from admission to the school (K.27). By 1828 John Inman had been replaced by his son, Robert (G.18).

Low Harrogate, until the first decade of the nineteenth century, was peopled with servants and tradesmen associated with the spa and hotel business; unlike High Harrogate, it had no grand houses, and hardly any properties that rivalled the villas and terraces of the upper village (D.37). It was, however, undergoing expansion, and it is therefore likely that it had a greater proportion of lower–middle income families than had High Harrogate. In 1817 moves were made to provide Low Harrogate with a charity school of its own. On Monday 8 December 1817 the Duchy of Lancaster Court read a petition presented to them by the vicar and principal inhabitants of the parish of Pannal (of which Low Harrogate formed part) praying that '... his Majesty contribute towards the erection of a tenement to be appropriated as a Sunday and day school, for the education of the poor children of the ... parish ... and further, that this court would also contribute towards a sufficient salary for a competent teacher ...' (B.191). The Duchy Court approved payment of £25 towards the cost of building the school (B.252), which should be 'of such benefit to the children of Low Harrogate'. The order for the warrant was signed in 1818, but it did not refer to any contributions towards a stipend, as the court felt that this should be raised locally (B.252). The petition sent to the Duchy referred to the proposed school costing £100, and that a site had been given by the Duke of Devonshire (who was a Duchy tenant) in the vicinity of Pannal church. Late in 1818 the national committee appointed to enquire into the education of the poor, were advised by the vicar of Pannal that a school now existed, serving a population of 914 (as compared with Bilton-with-Harrogate's population of 1,583) and that it had about fourteen scholars, and a Sunday school with about 150 scholars. 'The master's salary is about twenty shillings per annum, but he derives some employment from extra tuition' (X.3). A document of 1815 refers to a 'school house close' in Pannal, situated at Lund House Green (S.680).

The Richard Taylor charity school was, at its old Bilton location, about a mile from the centre of High Harrogate, and when High Harrogate's population began to increase in the second decade of the nineteenth century (it grew from 1,583 in 1811 to 2,812 by 1831),[13] calls were made for provision of a more convenient charity school. In 1825 a petition was sent to the Duchy of Lancaster requesting their assistance with the cost of building a school at High Harrogate. It had been sent by the newly appointed minister, Thomas Kennion, who – in a letter of 5 September – explained, 'having recently been appointed to the care of this chapelry, I find that in a population of about 2,000 persons … there is no provision made for the education of the lower classes beyond what is afforded by a Sunday school … I cannot but think that the establishment of a National School in this place would be of the utmost advantage … I propose that the school should contain 200 children. A fund of £160 is already collected towards the object, £60 of which was subscribed two of three years ago, the remainder since my residence in the parish. It is expected that £300–£400 will cover the whole expense.' (M.135)

Although the Duchy agreed to donate £50 towards the projected High Harrogate school, they withheld payment until 1831 (B.212), probably because the Duchy was more concerned with the rebuilding of High Harrogate church, the campaign for which had begun on 1 September 1825 (M.134), just four days before the Reverend Thomas Kennion's letter requesting Duchy assistance with his school project. Some may consider this as evidence to support the opinion that the Crown considered the building of the new church to be of greater importance than the provision of a school at High Harrogate, but in the event, the Duchy contributed towards both amenities.

The school was opened at a time when Anglicanism was becoming increasingly disturbed at the success of non-conformity in attracting pupils to their Sunday schools. In West Yorkshire the percentage of the population enrolled at Sunday schools rose from 6.5 per cent in 1818, to 16.8 per cent in 1851, and within this rise, the role of non-conformity was particularly significant. For example, by 1851, Anglicanism could boast an enrolment of only 42 per cent, with the Wesleyan Methodists alone claiming 19.16 per cent, and the Independents 13.33 per cent of the total. Accordingly, it is not surprising to learn that many Anglican clergyman saw non-conformist Sunday schools as a direct threat.[14] The so-called National Society, formed in 1811 by members of the Society for the Promotion of Christian Knowledge, existed to assist the education of the poor in the principles of the established church throughout England and Wales. As such, it was a natural ally of clergymen such as High Harrogate's Thomas Kennion, who applied for assistance on 19 January 1831. Kennion advised the National Society that he and his supporters had agreed to purchase a site in High Harrogate for the sum of £360, and that to date, they had collected £195. Kennion's sincerity may be judged by the fact of his having already established a school in his own home 'on a temporary footing, giving for the purpose the use of a large room on my own premises'. The same letter refers to a further £50 having been given towards the project by 'Dr Bell, on a visit of that respected individual to the place a few years ago'. Dr Andrew Bell, a former Anglican chaplain to the Indian army, had developed a method of dealing with large numbers of pupils by the monitorial system, and he – along with his London colleague Joseph Lancaster – was an important figure in the history of early nineteenth-century British education. His £50 donation must therefore have carried some weight in Harrogate (X.4).

When Rev. Kennion came to complete the application of the High Harrogate school for pecuniary aid from the National Society, he explained that the population of High Harrogate had increased from 1,235 in 1821, to about 2,500 in 1831, and that it was his intention that the school should receive 100 boys and 100 girls, that it should be a day school, and that it should be supported by annual subscription and collections in the High Harrogate church. Tellingly Kennion recorded that, 'it has been found that the small payment is an exclusion from the school of a very considerable number of children.' It is not known to which school he was alluding, but it was probably the temporary one he had opened in his own premises. The sum for books and school mistress was estimated to be about £50 per annum. The efforts of the school's promoters must have been successful, as the new High Harrogate school opened in 1835 in the former 'Cross Chapel' – built in 1821 by the Congregationalists – at Smithy Hill. (X.23). The site had been conveyed to the trustees of the new school on 17 September 1834 for payment of £360. (X.23)

The new school taught its pupils reading, writing, arithmetic and the 'accepted tenets of the Church of England'. The children were from seven to thirteen years of age (X.6), and excluded infants. This exclusion was made good in 1837 by the provision of a special infants' school at High Harrogate, paid for and endowed by the same local landowner who had assisted with the construction and embellishment of Christ Church – William Sheepshanks. This Infants School, built at the centre of High Harrogate, in Church Square, under the shadow of Christ Church, was an important advance in the provision of education in High Harrogate (X.31). Low Harrogate, meanwhile, had not been tardy in promoting its own interests, and in the same year as the new High Harrogate Infants school opened – 1837 – a new school opened in Low Harrogate which provided local children with a school that was far more convenient than the one in Pannal village (X.31). In 1834 the minister of Low Harrogate church (St Mary's) sent a memorial to the Treasury Commissioners in London, in which he requested an 'education grant' towards the erection of a school in connection with his church (X.10). Something of the rivalry between the Anglicans and the non-conformists is evident in the correspondence regarding the new Low Harrogate school. The minister, Rev. Holme, in writing to the grant body, advised that, 'It is remarkable that immediately after we had collections in the church for the building of a daily school room, the Methodists not only began to collect for a school of their own but actually commenced building one which is now completed and suitable to the accommodation of several hundred children. Nothing, however, but the absolute want of a school in union with the church would induce the greater part of poorer parents to send their children to the Methodist school, so that I am convinced of the imperative necessity of having a room built immediately.' (X.17) Rev. Holme's efforts succeeded, and the new Low Harrogate school opened in 1837 (X.31). It was built next to St Mary's Church on land which had been conveyed to the church by the Duchy of Lancaster (N.38).

The Methodist school referred to by Reverend Holme had been built in 1835, in the newly emerging area of central Harrogate. It was near to the small Wesleyan chapel (S.1256), erected in 1824, and served a community of lower income labourers and traders, who raised the impressive sum of £400 for the construction of the school, control of which was vested in seventeen trustees. These trustees elected a committee to run the school, and in the first instance decided to admit only the children of the recently established Wesleyan Sunday school. However, they subsequently decided to open it to the children of parents of all denominations, 'irrespective of sect or party'. By 1840, 120 children were entered on the register, of whom 90 were in daily attendance. The master, Henry Hardwick, was brought from Borough Road, London, and the school was conducted on the same Lancastrian system used in Borough Road by Joseph Lancaster (X.31). Like Bell's system, the Lancastrian favoured mass instruction by means of monitors. The Harrogate Wesleyan school appears to have been genuinely non-sectarian, and in this, they followed the lead of much of Yorkshire (save, perhaps for Leeds, where the clergy took the lead in the schools). At York, for example, an important step in the spread of education was taken in 1786 with the opening of several Anglican schools, but in 1791, the Wesleyans increased the number, insisting that they were 'free to servants, apprentices and children of every denomination'.[15]

The British School – as the Harrogate Wesleyan school became known –
was a member of the British and Foreign School Society, an organisation
which differed from the National Society of the Anglicans, in that it was
originally founded by two Quakers, and supported by Methodists.[16] The
Society's report of 1841 advised that the Harrogate school now had the
services of 'a committee of ten ladies … two of whom … attend every
afternoon to instruct the girls in plain needlework knitting, &c.' (X.28) The
following year, the Society's report noted, '… the children are improving in
useful knowledge, such as will enable them to pass through life respectably;
and it is hoped the instruction they receive will prove a blessing to their
souls.' (X.30) Such a mixture of utility and idealism was typical of the
Victorian educational system.

Private, fee-paying schools

The 1838 *Visitors' Vade Mecum* referred to 'four schools established for the
gratuitous education of the poor of both sexes', describing Richard Taylor
endowed school at Bilton, the High and Low Harrogate schools, and the
'British School opened by the Wesleyans'. Note was also made of the Infants
school in High Harrogate.[17] However, the guide also mentioned several
private schools and academies which grew throughout the nineteenth
century to become an important part of the town's economy.[18] In 1838 four
private schools were listed, two being boarding schools 'for young ladies',
and two being boarding schools 'for young gentlemen'. All of these
boarding schools were in High Harrogate, or its immediate environs, and
all appear to have been located within convenient reach of the great High
Harrogate hotels. The oldest of these private schools, Grove House (see
plan 72), was an eighteenth-century establishment, which occupied a
seventeenth-century inn, the World's End, about 200 yards to the north of
the Dragon Hotel.[19] Indeed, the Grove House school appears to have drawn
most of its pupils from the visitors who stayed at High Harrogate's hotels.
In May 1809 the new head teacher, Barbara Hofland, writing to a friend in a
Sheffield school, admitted that she intended to charge the visitors the same
rates as her Harrogate predecessor – Mrs Addison – had charged, thirty-five
guineas a year per child (C.83.c). Some of the visitors were not above
haggling with Mrs Hofland, as the latter recalled in a letter of 21 October
1809. 'Lady Meredith, the notorious gambling lady, came to me yesterday,
to tell me her children should come in the spring and stay some months, if
I would bargain to take them for a guinea a week and pay all the masters
out of it. She said, 'Mrs Addison did it last year, and she, Mrs Addison, was
a sweet creature.' Said I, '… she had a right to please herself, but I shall not
alter my terms a single shilling, for I know that I can not do it.' I never felt

so disgusted with any woman in my life as this beautiful young Lady, who could be twisting at a bargain with me, when every night she stakes fifty or one hundred guineas on an odd trick, till she is poorer or richer by a thousand pounds – she won 700 guineas with a coach with four fine boys, of a young baronet this week on a wager of his driving a figure of 'eight' before the Dragon ...' (C.83.f). The minister of Low Harrogate Church, Rev. Holme, issued a printed bill which his services as a private teacher:

> The Rev. J. Holme ... receives into his house a limited number of pupils. Terms for board, and instruction in English, Writing, Classics and Mathematics – fifty guineas per annum. Ditto for pupils above the age of fourteen: eighty guineas per annum. (X.9)

His pupils may have included not only the children of long-term visitors, but also those of wealthy residents such as the doctors and innkeepers. The increase in the provision of schools of all kinds in Harrogate, from charity to private, over the period 1770 to 1841 was the result not only of an increasing population, but also of a growth in the numbers of whole families who visited Harrogate during the spa season from June to October. This may be seen in the rapid increase of lodging houses which were built after the Award of 1778, for the accommodation of such families (Class S). Although many wealthy families would certainly have sent their children to public school, many also brought their children to Harrogate, where they hired the large lodging houses, built round the Stray in High Harrogate especially for their accommodation. For a family of perhaps eight people (excluding servants, cooks, coach drivers etc.) it was a more sensible action to hire a lodging house for the season, rather than to pay the innkeeper's often high bills. The rapid growth of such lodging houses after the Award of 1778 (B.31) is proof that there was a real demand for such accommodation, which continued until the arrival of the railways in 1849, which then produced a change in the length of visits. Up to this time, the children of such families would have represented a golden opportunity for private education in Harrogate.

Conclusions

The growth of education in Harrogate from 1770 to 1841 appears to have been affected less by the ideological battle between Anglicanism and non-conformity, and more by the requirements of local market forces for an educated workforce, as well as the requirements of visitors for suitable private schools for their own children. The struggle to put down Sabbath teaching of writing and arithmetic, which had been such a *cause célèbre* in, for example, Macclesfield,[20] found no counterpart in Harrogate. Equally, the absence in Harrogate of any appreciable numbers of pauper children ensured that the forces which led to the success of ranterism in other areas of Yorkshire failed to gain even the slightest of footholds in the spa. Increasing numbers of poor children appeared later, when the railway altered for ever the seasonal nature of the spa, and thus did away with the concept of a migratory, or seasonal workforce. But when pauper children did appear, in the 1850s and 1860s, Harrogate had a system of education, developed between 1770 and 1841, which was able to deal with the problem.[21] Thanks to the role of the Duchy as holder of Crown property, and defender of the Established Church, the town had a powerful source of assistance. It was thanks to the Duchy that in Harrogate Anglican education was able to keep abreast of non-conformist education.

A *hospital for the poor* | 13

B ETWEEN 1770 and 1841, the provision of medical services in Harrogate
changed from that of being two wholly separate concerns: first, medical
relief under the Poor Law administration; and, second, that of fee-paying
patients consulting private medical practitioners, to a system which
included an important charitable hospital – the Bath Hospital. The creation
of this hospital, in a community which did not appear to have required such
facilities for its own residents (who were indeed specifically excluded from
being admitted) was sign of a change in public attitudes towards the medical
needs of the poor. As such, the Bath Hospital, both in the story of its
creation, and subsequent operation, has a special significance in the history
of Harrogate's spa.

Commenting in relation to the old Poor law and medical relief in the West
Riding of Yorkshire and Lancashire in 1839 a writer noted, that 'with scarcely
any exception, through the whole district, the medical relief of which any
district account could be found in the township books, bore an extremely
small proportion to the population, and to the general expenditure on the

PLATE 61
The old Bath
Hospital, photo-
graphed from Bogs
Field, *c*. 1860. On the
left can be seen the
old Magnesia Well
Pump Room.

poor.'[1] By 1831 Poor Law relief in the West Riding of Yorkshire cost only 5s. 7d. per head of the county's population, compared with 18s. 3d. in Suffolk, or 15s. 4d. in Norfolk. The explanation for this imbalance was 'a close spirit of economy in relieving the poor on the part of the assistant overseers and vestries, a degree of hardihood and independence in the mass of the people, the existence of numerous clubs and societies, providing against the contingency of sickness, and embracing large numbers of the operative classes ...' A further explanation was that despite the dislocations caused by trade depressions in the north, it was wealthier than many southern and midlands regions. Overall there was less poverty and fewer permanent paupers. By 1843 the cost of Poor Law relief in the West Riding was calculated at 1d. per head of the population – the lowest in the country – the highest being in Essex at 6d. per head.[2]

By the time of the 1834 Poor Law Amendment Act, which abolished the old system of administering local poor law through the vestries, and introduced a new system based on unions of parishes, run by boards of elected guardians,[3] Harrogate had – for ten years – been home to a remarkable charitable institution: the Royal Bath Hospital. The remarkable fact about the establishment of the hospital was that for many years no person resident within three miles from the hospital was allowed admittance. This prohibited the residents of High and Low Harrogate from using the facilities that many of them had paid for.[4] The history of hospital provision in Harrogate during the early nineteenth century was to a large extent governed by a spirit of genuine philanthropy, which was quite different from the concept of self-interest that led other communities to attempt to curtail the local threat of epidemic disease and to provide only for the poor of their own neighbourhoods.[5]

Thanks to the spa, the residents of High and Low Harrogate were able to call on the services of several local doctors, some of whose names were so familiar that they were included in both Barbara Hofland's *Season at Harrogate*.

> There's not one of them all that my fancy so takes,
> cried a lady in black, as my good Doctor Jacques,
> says the next, Mr Richardson's wonderfully clever,
> tho' so busy, dear heart, there's no catching him ever.
> Cries a third, if you really want medical skill,
> Mr Wormald will cure you if any man will,
> And I know, cries a fourth, that whatever may ail ye,
> You're sure of relief if you see Doctor Cayley' (C.91.b).

and David Lewis's *Week at Harrogate*, which refers to Dr Jaques, Dr Merry, Dr Campbell, Dr Cayley, Mr Richardson, and Mr Wormald (C.92.e). Harrogate's population at this time was little over 2,000, but these doctors were there not primarily to serve the local population, but rather the visitors to the spa.

The evidence from the records of Harrogate workhouse (see plate 57), which opened in 1810, shows that doctors were called in as and when the master considered their services necessary. For example, in 1811, there is an entry, 'Dr Habbershaw, for delivering a woman in the workhouse, September 1811: 7s.' (D.49.6). Such references are, however, few and far between, and there are only the sparsest indications to show that inmates were ever sent to hospitals such as those at Wakefield, Leeds or York. Indeed, the same applies to the residential population of High and Low Harrogate, where individual residents would certainly have required occasional access to hospitals, although at this time such institutions were regarded as being a place of last – desperate – resort. In short, for the time from 1770 to 1825 when the Bath Hospital was being planned and eventually built, there is little surviving evidence to show that the population of Harrogate had any need of a hospital for its own immediate use.

The association between a spa and charitable hospital had been established in Bath by 1738, when Richard 'Beau' Nash encouraged the creation

of the hospital which later became the 'Royal Mineral Water Hospital', opened in 1742 to make the mineral wells available to sick and poor strangers,[6] 'provided they had proper credentials'.[7] Even so small a place as Leamington Spa (population about 400) had opened a charity in 1806 to enable the sick poor from any part of the United Kingdom to have free use of the waters.[8] In 1816 Leamington built a small hospital and dispensary in Regent Street, which was in turn replaced with a proper hospital in 1831.[9] All of these charities were supported by visitors' subscriptions, and in the course of ten years provided 2,000 free baths to poor invalids.[10]

Nationally, the background against which plans for the Harrogate Bath Hospital developed, was – especially in the West Riding – one of increasing charitable involvement with the health of the poor. One writer has observed that such charity was motivated by four considerations: first a fear of social revolution; second, a humanitarian concern for suffering; third, satisfaction of some psychological or social need; fourth, a desire to improve the moral tone of the recipients.[11] The first of these considerations was hardly applicable to Harrogate; the last three, more so. General infirmaries had been established in Leeds in 1767, Sheffield in 1797; and Dispensaries in Wakefield in 1787, Doncaster in 1792 and Halifax in 1807. All of these West Riding communities had experienced an enormous increase in accident cases, as a result of the development of manufacturing machinery in the region.[12] Harrogate had no manufacturing industry, and a population level (3,064 in 1841) that was only a fraction that of the great cities of Doncaster, Leeds, Sheffield or Wakefield, yet by 1841 it had a special hospital to which all of these cities were sending patients (U.53).

The first of the minute books of what later became the Royal Bath Hospital records that about fifty years before the opening in 1825, subscriptions were raised 'for the benefit of the poor resorting to the place for the benefits of the Waters.' (U.2) It is probable that the majority of these subscriptions were raised by means of 'subscription books' which were placed in the town's various inns by supporters of the scheme (U.2).

The problem faced by the sick poor was not one of access to the wells, since the 1778 Award had ensured that all the known mineral wells were designated part of the Stray. Rather, it was the cost of accommodation and – to a lesser extent – transportation. In the absence of any evidence to indicate that the innkeepers reduced their charges for the sick poor, it is reasonable to assume that some of the subscription monies were used to reimburse local people who admitted the sick poor into their homes. Such sick poor were probably sent to Harrogate on the recommendation of a patron, who may even have contributed directly towards their journey, for philanthropic reasons that were the result of considerations both religious and social. The accessibility of the wells changed after the 1778 Award, in that the majority of the new wells were discovered on private land. For example, the Crescent Well was found in the grounds of the Crescent Inn in 1783 (G.10); the Cheltenham Well was found in a private field in 1818 (F.48); and the most significant of the Crown Wells were sunk in the gardens of Thackwray's Crown Hotel in 1822 (G.13). Yet the medical texts of the time show that the doctors still regarded the public wells as being the most important, especially the wells of the so-called Bogs Field, the ancient iron wells of High Harrogate, and the Old Sulphur Well, or stinking spa (F.58).

It is possible that the landlords supported the provision of a special hospital in Harrogate for the sick poor, not only because their important customers favoured the idea, but also because some of them may have wanted to tidy up the public wells, to ensure that their guests were not offended or inconvenienced by the crowds of sick and poor visitors taking the waters. As early as 1632, Dr Michael Stanhope had written

> Is it not a shame that the Sulphur Spring (whereof many of the best sort have occasion to drinke) should lie open for the promiscuous use of all sorts, without any due order observed in the keeping of it, so that poore Lazer, impotent people, doe dayly environ it, whose putrid rags lie scattered up and downe, and it is to be doubted whether they doe wash their soares, & cleanse their besmeared clouts (though unseene) where many diverse after dippe their cupps to drink. Not that I would have the poore debard the use of the spring … (F.5).

A further reason for the landlords' support may have been simply one of genuine philanthropy for the sick poor, as well as an element of pride in the little Harrogate community, which caused them to co-operate with the other promoters of the Bath Hospital project. The publicity accorded to such charitable institutions as Bath's Royal Mineral Water Hospital, and Leamington's Regent Street Hospital and Dispensary, may have encouraged some in Harrogate to consider it was time for a dispensary of their own.

By 1818 some sort of committee appears to have been in existence which distributed monies to the sick poor resorting to Harrogate to benefit from the waters. Such payments were primarily for accommodation costs and medical fees. Then, in August of that year, a number of regular subscribers met in the Promenade Room (see plate 53) to discuss means of 'improving the collection and application' of subscriptions. They resolved to open a special new subscription for the building of baths for the exclusive use of the sick poor, and, over the following year, to encourage as wide as possible an interest in the scheme. Their efforts succeeded on the 3rd and 10th of August 1819, when, with the Earl of Harewood in the chair, the meetings resolved, 'with the view of enabling the poor to receive the full benefit of the proposed charity, to erect a hospital as well as baths, and a subscription for this purpose was immediately commenced.' (U.2) The Earl of Harewood not only chaired the early meetings of the subscribers' committee, but, when it became clear in 1823 that the target figure of £1,000 was going to be raised, he donated – on 2 October – one and a half acres of land on which to build the hospital. This land did not consist of low-value agricultural land, set in a remote part of the Lascelles' extensive holdings, but rather of a plot within a few yards of the 'Bogs Field' on Low Harrogate Stray. The Bogs Field (see plan 13) was described in 1652 by Dr French as possessing many important wells: 'if any Gentleman would be pleased to expend some costs in digging up this bog, and erecting some new wells there, he would prove an acceptable benefactor to his Countrey, and it may be some new kind of water might be discovered hereby, having yet more vertues than of any former.' (F.6) Further wells were discovered, and by the time of Harrogate's incorporation as a borough in 1884, thirty-six unique mineral wells had been identified on the Bogs Field, the greatest single concentration of unique and varied mineral wells in the world. Many of these wells had been known in 1823, and affected the value of the surrounding land, as the terms of leases granted by the Forest Court show so clearly.[13] The choice of this site, in close proximity to the wells of Bogs Field, demonstrates the extent of commitment shown by promoters of the scheme. Lord Harewood remarked, at the time of his gift, that he had given the land, 'in contiguity to the medical springs. And in so doing, I have done my best ... to make it a permanent possession to the poor, and I hope I may answer for the benevolence of my descendants.'[14] Subscriptions and gifts were not the only means of raising funds for the hospital scheme, as is shown in the treasurers' reports: 'profits of a concert in 1819 ... £32 8s. 0d.' (U.3)

Harrogate was a popular resort for visitors from Scotland, a fact noticed by Dr Carlyle of Inveresk in his journal of 1763 (C.38), as well as being recorded in the weekly lists of visitors published in the Yorkshire newspapers between 1770 and 1841. This was understandable, as it was the most northerly of all the English health resorts, and Scottish resorts with spa facilities, such as Strathpeffer or Moffat, were, in the late eighteenth century, no rivals to Harrogate.[15] Scotland's approach to charitable work was different from that of England's. Before the industrial revolution, funds for the relief of the poor in Scotland were composed of either church door collections or charitable monies in the form of gifts and bequests. If these two sources failed, then local landowners – the heritors – were required to assess themselves, and if they failed to do this, the Statutes provided that a legal assessment could be imposed upon them. The essence of the old Scottish poor relief system was its voluntary nature, which automatically gave charity a more elevated status than was the case south of the border.[16] It may therefore be that Harrogate's popularity with wealthy visitors from Scotland was an important factor in the successful raising of funds for the promotion of the Bath Hospital charity.

At progress meetings in January and February 1824, at the Crown Hotel, the trustees reported that the list of principal subscribers was headed by the king, with a donation of £52 10s. 0d., and further donations of £50 each by the Earls of Harewood, Fitzwilliam, and Scarborough as well as the Archbishop of York and the Bishop of Llandaff. Plans submitted by Yorkshire architect Samuel Chapman were considered, whose estimated cost for the building was £958 10s. Chapman was then working on the new

St Mary's church in Low Harrogate (N.48), so it is likely that his presence in the town marked him as a suitable candidate for the task. Work began on the new hospital in the spring of 1824, being completed by the spring of 1825, when the committee learned that they had exhausted their funds. Faced with the need to furnish and equip the hospital, the Committee decided to stop any subscription disbursements to the poor for a year so that all income could be devoted to completing the building. By the spring of 1826 the Committee were satisfied that the hospital was completely finished, and that costs incurred had been £1,147 19s. 8d. for the building; £155 7s. 3½d. for the furnishing, and nearly £50 for miscellaneous items. With paid-up subscriptions at £1,547 3s. 5d. this left £194 6s. 4½d. in the treasurer's hands (U.2).

The first annual report of the new 'Harrogate Bath Hospital' (as it was originally known) reprinted twenty-two rules of management which the committee established for the administration of the charity, and several of these provide insight as to the founders' intentions:

(1) That this hospital having been built solely with a view to afford to the poor, free of expense, the benefits of the Harrogate Waters, be denominated the 'Harrogate Bath Hospital' and that no patients be admitted therein but such as, in the opinion of the Medical Officers of the establishment are suitable cases.

This rule shows that despite the power given to external patrons and subscribers to recommend patients, admission remained firmly in the hands of the local committee. 'Suitable cases' did not include those suffering from medical ailments that were untreatable by the Harrogate waters, such as the entire range of infectious diseases.

(3) Every donor or benefactor of £15 or upwards shall be a member for life; and every subscriber of not less than £1; every Medical officer of the Institution, and any person who has collected £10 or upwards, and paid the same in one sum to the Treasury of the Institution, shall be a member for that year, with the privileges hereinafter mentioned.

This rule demonstrates the Victorian belief that the pleasures of philanthropic patronage were determined by the monetary level of such patronage. It was an open way of encouraging greater philanthropy.

(4) Every Benefactor shall be allowed during his life to recommend one patient annually for every £15 contributed: and every Member shall be allowed to recommend one patient annually for every pound per annum subscribed.

(5) Every Incumbent of a church or Minister of any denomination Congregational, who shall transmit a congregational collection to the

Treasurer, shall be allowed to recommend one patient for every £5 so contributed during that year.

(6) Every hotel, or innkeeper, boarding-house keeper or lodging house keeper in Harrogate, shall be allowed to recommend one patient for every £5 collected at his or her house during the season.

These two last rules encouraged specific classes of patronage, one at national, the other at local level.

(17) The parties to be admitted to the benefits of the Hospital shall be poor persons of good character who shall have a recommendation from a member. Each patient shall in all respects conform to the Rules of the Institution, and it shall be in the power of the Committee to dismiss any patient not conducting himself or herself properly.

(18) No person resident within the distance of three miles from the Baths except at the discretion of the Committee; no woman far advanced in pregnancy; no person of insane mind, labouring under any infectious disorder, or subject to fits, shall be admitted into the hospital.

This rule is perhaps the most interesting, in that it demonstrates the desire of the writers to keep Harrogate free of those of the sick poor who might offend the sensibilities of the wealthier visitors, become a burden to the poor laws, cause an increase to the bastardy rate, or be the means of introducing an epidemic (U.1). For sound medical reasons, it also excluded those whose ailments could not be treated successfully by the Harrogate waters.

A separate set of rules was compiled for the use of patients. As well as having to obey such sensible injunctions as keeping themselves, whenever possible, clean and tidy, and obeying the matron, patients had also to remember 'not to loiter about the Wells, nor in the public walks frequented by the visitors'; and, 'not to beg on any account; nor under any pretence whatever to frequent a public house.' (U.1) It is possible to see the hand of the innkeepers in some of these regulations, given their long established custom of discouraging anything that might discourage the upper classes from visiting the town (F.58).

The innkeepers continued to support the institution after its opening, and throughout the period under study the subscription books placed in the inns and hotels played a major role in financing the Harrogate Bath Hospital. The largest sums were not always collected in the greatest hotels. In the accounts for the 1821–22 deposits from the Crown Hotel (in Low Harrogate, and directly overlooking the public Old Sulphur Well) were £40 2s. 6d. whereas the lordly Granby (nicknamed the 'House of Lords') in High Harrogate raised a mere £4 16s., and the Dragon Hotel, also in High Harrogate, raised £12 0s. 6d. (U.5). These proportions remained representative throughout the first half of the nineteenth century, and indeed the fifteenth report, for 1840, included a note: 'It is no wonder that the Granby subscriptions make such a poor figure on the general audit of the charity, as the book does not appear to be presented much to the notice of visitors at the hotel.' (U.51) The greater part of donations towards Harrogate's Bath Hospital charity appear to have come from the visitors, among whom such munificence was an expected responsibility and social obligation. It would, therefore, have been difficult for any unsympathetic landlord to refuse to provide a subscriptions book in his establishment.

The new Harrogate Bath Hospital, with a capacity of twenty-five beds, appears to have been opened for patients on Thursday 6 April 1826, a date fixed by the meeting of trustees and subscribers on the previous 21 March.

The March meeting confirmed the appointment of the institution's medical officers – Mr Richardson and Mr Wormald – a matron – Mrs Winterburn – and a secretary – Mr Pickersgill Palliser (U.2). This last was a particularly happy choice, as Mr Palliser (see plate 56), who had settled in Harrogate in March 1821, became a fervent supporter of the charity.[17] The importance of Palliser's support lay not only in the length and quality of his service, but also from his position as founder of the *Harrogate Advertiser* in 1836, which subsequently promoted the cause of the Bath Hospital at every opportunity.

Annual income for the hospital fluctuated between 1826 and 1841

PLATE 56
Pickersgill Palliser, founder of the *Harrogate Advertiser* and Secretary of the Royal Bath Hospital.

from a minimum of £362 1s. 6½d. in 1831 (U.29), to a maximum of £844 3s. 7d. in 1841 (U.53), and the occasional reference in the reports, of donations from special sources, indicates that a high level of fund-raising was practised. There was, for example, a collection in Pudsey church in 1830 (U.27); and in 1838 similar collections were made at Halifax and Huddersfield (U.45). The practice of publishing names of donors may well have encouraged some benefactors, although the source of 'penalty for disturbing a place of worship' (five shillings) would hardly have come under that category. The frequency with which communities outside Harrogate contributed towards the Harrogate Bath Hospital is in part accounted for by a singular clause in the charity's regulations: 'No person resident within the distance of three miles from the baths, except at the discretion of the Committee … shall be admitted to the hospital.' Those of the sick poor who resided at Harrogate, who were not occupants of the workhouse, but who required access to a hospital, must have been recipients of local charity, some of it provided by the township. A hint of this may be found in the vestry book of High Harrogate church on 19 March 1840 – when the 'Town's surgeons' were appointed – which refers to 'The medical gentlemen will be expected to attend the paupers belonging the Township both in the Workhouse and out in sickness and labour at a fixt salary of £25 per year, including attendance on casual paupers not belonging this Township, the journeys not to exceed three miles from Harrogate Church.' (D.18) In 1828 the township had also to agree to paying £77 9s. 8d. for the discharge of debts incurred by the incarceration of townsman Fred Stoner, a lunatic, in York Asylum. From these examples, it is reasonable to suppose that the few of Harrogate's sick poor – themselves a minority group – who required admittance to hospital, would have been sent to the institutions at Leeds, York or Wakefield, with the township picking up the bill.

The Harrogate Bath Hospital was a charitable institution for the north of England, and the annual reports contain evidence for the levels of admittance and rates of treatment success. Admittance occurred not only under the terms by which subscription monies were collected, but also by petition. In 1820, for example, the minister of Haworth Church, Patrick Brontë, petitioned the 'Committee of the Charity at Harrogate for the purpose of enabling the afflicted and distressed poor to receive the benefit of the waters at the place', on behalf of one of his parishioners, James Parker, a woolcomber, who was 'afflicted with a severe scorbutic complaint' (A.273). During its first season, in 1826, the Bath Hospital admitted 147 patients, with a further 37 being admitted as 'out-patients' (U.17). This balance was not typical of the rest of the West Riding, in that the comparatively high costs of accommodating, feeding and caring for an in-patient produced a bias in favour of out-patients, whose lower costs were less of a burden on the responsible community. In Huddersfield, for example, an 1833 calculation showed that whereas an in-patient was costing £3 7s. per head to maintain, an out-patient cost only 3s. A similar balance appears to have pertained in Wakefield.[18] The explanation for the Bath Hospital's unusually high proportion of in-patients must lie in the fact that the majority of patients were indeed the sick poor, who had been sent from communities outside Harrogate, and who were lacking either family or friends to provide them with accommodation, or sufficient funds to hire suitable lodgings.

The 1826 annual report noted that, 'of the in-patients, thirty-nine have been cured, fifty-two much relieved, forty-nine have derived a little benefit, and seven have received no benefit. All the out-patients have benefited.'

(U.17). The treatments provided at the Bath Hospital were intended to cope with five principal conditions: (a) skin disorders; (b) internal parasites; (c) defective kidney action; (d) anaemia; and (e) costiveness. The original intention had been to provide the poor with free baths, the hospital wards being an afterthought, according to the public meeting of 1819. (U.1). The mineral water for the baths was supplied from neighbouring 'Bogs Field', which the Award of 1778 had incorporated in the Harrogate Stray, thus ensuring ease of public access (B.31). The water was probably obtained in the time-honoured way of carting via a barrel on a donkey cart (see plate 17). The growing demand for water by the hospital eventually produced a crisis, and by the 1870s the Harrogate Improvement Commissioners took upon themselves the task of controlling the use of the public well of Bogs Field, even going so far as to charge the hospital an annual rent of £5 for the exclusive use of three of the Bogs Field Wells. This sensible, but undoubtedly illegal action, regularised what had, since the opening of the hospital in 1826, been a cumbersome method of supplying mineral water.[19]

Some insight into the diet of patients is provided in the 1826 annual report, when details of expenditure were published. General 'groceries' topped the bill at £47 1s. 5d., followed by 'butcher's meat' at £36 4s. 5½d. Malt liquor is entered at £11 8s. (U.17) and the following year, 1827, the entry 'malt & hops' £8 6s. 7d. indicates that the hospital had begun to do its own brewing (U.20). By 1841 the costs for butcher's meat had risen to £180 14s. 0d. and other costs included flour and meal, malt and hops, tea and coffee, sugar and treacle, rice and sago, potatoes, cheese and fish. Apart from an apparent lack of green vegetables (which may have been supplied from the grounds surrounding the hospital) this appears to have been a healthy diet, although precise dietary proportions for each patient are not known (U.53). In 1826 Dr Richardson prepared what he regarded as a standard diet: eight a.m. breakfast consisted of tea or coffee with bread, toast and a little butter. One p.m. dinner provided boiled beef or mutton, with potatoes or another vegetable, on Sundays, Tuesdays and Thursdays; broth and bread, with rice or bread pudding, or dumplings, on Mondays, Wednesdays, and Fridays; and meat & potato pies on Saturdays. 'Afternoon' fare, at six p.m, included tea or coffee, with bread or toast, or gruel with bread, or bread and cheese. Beer was to be allowed only 'to such as are employed in the work of the house; or to those for whom it may be ordered by the Medical Attendants.' (U.19)

Expenditure on food and drink was not for a full twelve months, as the hospital closed for the winter, usually in November, and re-admitted patients the following March or April. Details were published in the Harrogate and other Yorkshire newspapers. For example, the 1830 *York Herald*: 'Harrogate Hospital. The enlargement of the hospital having been completed, and twelve beds added to the establishment, it will be opened for the admission of patients, on Thursday, the 18th instant. The Committee attend at the hospital every Thursday during the season, at two o'clock, to examine and admit patients [signed] Pickersgill Palliser, Secretary.' (R.2315) In November 1834: 'Harrogate Bath Hospital ... will be closed on Thursday the 13th instant ... the annual meeting of trustees ... will be held ... on Thursday the 20th instant ...' (R.2630). The above reference to enlargement refers to the works carried out in the autumn of 1832. As early as 1827, the annual report refers to 'many distressing and proper cases were rejected for want of accommodation,' (U.20) and the report for 1828 (U.22) repeated this observation. Consequently the 1829 report minuted that '6th July 1829. At a meeting of the Trustees & Subscribers ... held at the hospital this day to determine on the expediency of its enlargement, Sir Thomas Slingsby, Bart. In the chair, it appearing that there was a balance in the Treasurer's hands of not less than £300, it is resolved to proceed with the enlargement of the hospital according to a plan & specifications given in.' A separate enlargement fund appears to have been started in 1829, which received a generous opening from the Lord Bishop of Durham, with £25. The builder of the original hospital, Benjamin Horner, put in a bid of £267 18s. 8¾d. for the work of enlargement, which was accepted as the lowest offer (U.24). The York newspapers carried an advertisement on 3 October 1829 that 'the benevolent public will no doubt be highly gratified to learn that this truly valuable institution, after having undergone considerable improvement, by the enlargement of the building, was re-opened for the admittance of patients on Thursday last.' (R.2305) The advertisement failed to report that the new enlargement had no furniture or equipment, and the annual report of 3 December 1829 noted, 'resolved – that the gentlemen who formed the committee for superintending the erection of the new building, be requested to extend their services to superintend the furnishing of the same.' (U.26)

The philanthropy of the Harrogate Bath Hospital did not extend to the admittance of patients who qualified for admittance under the regulations, but who might also be carriers of infectious diseases. In 1832 much of Yorkshire fell victim to a dreadful outbreak of cholera. The Industrial Revolution, fuelled by those of the poorest classes who had been impoverished by the eighteenth-century Enclosure movement, produced concentrations of squalor in many northern communities.[20] The unsanitary living conditions, which lacked such basic services as rubbish removal, clean water supplies, and – perhaps most significantly – an understanding of the causes of infectious disease, were the breeding ground for the contagion that often frightened the upper classes into defensive action. Such defensive action, which occurred elsewhere in England – at Cheltenham in 1786 and

PLATE 86
Doubtless the
Harrogate doctors
also dealt with
patients whose
ailments were more
of mind than flesh!

1806,[21] Bath in 1788,[22] Malvern in 1830,[23] and Tunbridge Wells in 1832[24] – was also practised in the West Riding of Yorkshire at Huddersfield, which opened an infirmary in 1831,[25] and Wakefield in 1841 and 1853, when the city introduced compulsory vaccination, and 1848, when its Board of Guardians constituted themselves as a sanitary authority.[26]

With the widespread knowledge and fear of the dangers of infectious diseases, it is therefore reasonable to suppose that the Harrogate innkeepers were particularly keen to ensure that the town's reputation as an oasis from infection remained intact. On 17 September 1832 the Committee of the Bath Hospital decided, 'not to open the hospital for the remainder of this Season, in consequence of the prevalence of the cholera in those places whence the patients are chiefly supplied & Harrogate still enjoying the privilege of remaining quite free from that frightful malady.' (U.31) Harrogate appears to have experienced an especially busy summer during the cholera year of 1832. The *York Herald* commented, 'we are not surprised at this, for the health of the place was never better and it has long been considered a most safe refuge from the dangers of infection and the ravages of the pestilence.' (R.2435) The 1837 report notes that, 'during this season, 304 patients have been admitted, many of them very bad cases of cutaneous disease. Two-thirds have been cured and the remainder greatly benefited. About fifty out-patients have been admitted, and derived great benefit from the baths.' (U.42) When these figures are compared with those for 1827, with admissions at 147 in-patients and thirty-seven out-patients, the rate of growth over the ten-year period may be appreciated. Even with the enlargement of 1829, the facilities appear to have been under pressure, so much so that in 1838 it was found necessary to abandon the practice of allowing clergymen or ministers to recommend patients, restricting this privilege to trustees only (U.45).

Conclusion

The Poor Law Amendment Act of 1834, described by some historians as being a distinct watershed in the provision of medical services for the poor,[27] does not appear to have had much impact in Harrogate. The Bath Hospital report for 1834 does not even refer to the Act (U.36), nor do any of the local newspapers. The 1834 Act made local medical services much more formalised and strictly regulated. Local medical officers lost any powers they had previously held to authorise medical treatment. Medical authorisation became the preserve of newly appointed relieving officers, who based their decisions on the financial position of the applicant, rather than on medical data, and if a charitable doctor treated a patient without formal authorisation he might have had to carry all the costs himself. In Huddersfield and Wakefield, for example, the poor lost many of the old forms of medical provision – fringe practitioners such as midwives or bone setters were no longer employed, and the payment by the parish of subscriptions to friendly societies also ceased. To quote Hilary Marland, 'there does seem to have been a decline in the quality and range of Poor Law medical relief offered after 1834'.[28] By contrast, early nineteenth-century Harrogate, with its relative lack of poverty, and a developing hospital supported by the charity of wealthy supporters, appears to have been an oasis of good health care provision, certainly when compared to such contrasting communities as either Haworth[29] or Leeds.[30]

14 | The building of Harrogate, 1778–1841

Part one – 1778 to 1810

The Great Award of 1778 regularised the occupation of Harrogate's land, either by means of direct allotment to individuals whose bids were successful, or, to those who became copyhold tenants of the lands remaining in Duchy hands – the so-called 'King's Lands' (B.31). Historians have tended to concentrate on Harrogate's urban development during the Victorian age, especially the post-1860 boom, but it is essential to grasp the fact that the infrastructure on which this urbanisation was able to occur was in place because of developments which had taken place during the period from 1778 to 1841. In this chapter we will examine the patterns and processes of this urbanisation, beyond that which has already been described in connection with the spa, education, health and religion.

High Harrogate

In 1778, High Harrogate consisted of the triangle formed by what are now known as Park Parade, Regent Parade, Devonshire Place (previously, Silver Street R.2825) and Church Square, including the St John's and Tewit Wells. Each apex of this triangle was formed by a great hotel – the Queen's Head, the Dragon and the Granby, with the important Salutation Inn half way between the Granby and the Dragon, and two other significant inns, the Bay Horse at Spaw Hill in Church Square, and the World's End, a little north of the Dragon.

The Queen's Head (see plate 22), whose origins have been considered in chapter five, had, by the time of the 1788 Award, grown to an estate of some size, with plot number 268, held by John Coates, containing twenty-seven acres (B.31) but by the time the estate was sold in 1828, it had increased to seventy-one acres (R.2109, S.932). The advertisement of 7 July 1827 referred

to the Queen's Head containing a breakfast room, dining room, ball room, billiard room, forty lodging rooms, 'suitable bathrooms', butler's pantries, and stabling for forty-six horses. Much was made of the fact that the hotel was surrounded by excellent building land, including 'poor folks close', which was still subject to the payment of one pound per annum to the poor of Harrogate (S.1035). A reference to part of poor folks close already being staked out for building, points to an established demand for housing in this part of High Harrogate. Lots 2, 3, 4, 5, 6, 7, 8, and 9, measuring ten yards in width and forty yards in depth were all laid out on the north-west side of

PLATE 33
High Harrogate after the 1831 building of Christ Church.

PLATE 34
High Harrogate's Park Parade (*left*) and Devonshire Place (*right*).

PLATE 22 (*above*) Queen Hotel, *c.* 1833, attributed to W. P. Frith.

PLATE 23 (*below*) Queen Buildings, AD 2000.

the hotel (i.e. at what later became Queen Parade and York Place), rather than towards High Harrogate proper, which by 1827 was well developed. Development around Harrogate's inns was not restricted to housing, and there is much evidence for retail and commercial development occurring, although in the case of the Queen, it had vanished by the mid-nineteenth century. An earlier advertisement in the *York Courant* of 1767 had described, 'next to the Queen's Head, two dwelling houses, ... fit for a milliner, jeweller or other shopkeeper ...' (R.335). High Harrogate's retail activity was concentrated at Regent Parade, Devonshire Place (C.91, C.92) and to a lesser extent at Spaw Hill, in Church Square, where Hargrove's 'Toy Shop' (see plate 24) was located (B.31, incroachment 286). The status of an inn as a coaching stop also encouraged urbanisation, as passengers, goods, postal services, horses and innkeepers all required facilities or premises from which to operate. As such activities could not occur on the Stray which faced all the great High Harrogate inns; they tended to develop along flanking frontages, of which Park Parade, Regent Parade and Devonshire Place were prime examples. The majority of visitors to Harrogate were also visitors to the spa, so the development of the Queen's Head mirrored the development of Low Harrogate's Crown. Even before the Enclosure Act of 1770, landlord Gilbertson announced that he had instituted many improvements at the Queen's Head, including new stables, coach houses, and other conveniences, and that the long room had been 'finished and fitted up in a genteel manner' (R.400). By 1775 John Gilbertson had retired, and was succeeded by his son Robert, who subsequently offered his guests the

PLATE 78
Regent Parade. The second building from left was known as 'Library House', run by Langdale. The board to the left of the window probably announced newly purchased stock.

PLATE 79
Park Parade was developed mainly for residential use, as distinct from neighbouring Regent Parade, which was largely commercial.

luxury of specially warmed baths. By 1781,Gilbertson announced that, 'he had ... been at considerable expense in erecting a warm bath ... and have made the dressing room more commodious ...' (R.775), an improvement which reinforces the image of the Harrogate hotels as wholly self-sufficient communities.

It was because Regent Parade (see plate 78) was favoured over Park Parade (see plate 79) for the location of retail premises, that the face of this thoroughfare was developed as a continual urbanised strip, whereas the more residential nature of Park Parade determined its growth as a setting for detached villas.

Although it is known that the Queen's Head possessed a separate lodging house (S.932), its precise location is unclear. No such doubt exists as to the site of Dragon Lodging House, to the north, as the building still stands at the time of writing (see plate 20). In May 1790 a reference was recorded for the 'lodging house belonging to the Green Dragon' (S.375), and it is likely that this building, which was directly opposite Harrogate's first custom-built theatre (S.273), was erected at the busiest spot in Harrogate. Following the closure of the 'Green Dragon Theatre', it is possible that, by 1782, the

PLATE 20
Dragon Lodgings, occupied by the tenant of the Dragon Hotel, was used to accommodate the hotel's most important clients.

building became the King's Arms Inn (R.800), which was further converted, in 1784, into Harrison's Hotel, Coffee House, Inn and Tavern (R.840) by J. Harrison of the New Hummums, Covent Garden, London. At High Harrogate's northerly extremity, the Congregationalists had built their 'Cross Chapel' in 1821 (K.33) which was located on World's End Road, almost opposite the former World's End Inn, which shortly before 1816 changed its name to 'The Grove' (S.702), and which was occupied by a school (C.83), and it is likely that this period saw the establishment of the community which later developed into Smithy Hill (see plate 72).

By 1778, Devonshire Place[1] was developing as a major link between the Skipton and Ripon turnpike roads and the route to Knaresborough and York; as such, it was central to the coaching runs, and establishments such as the Granby (G.18), Gascoigne's (Q.27.43), and Black Swan (Q.28) featured in the timetables as important coaching stops, with the resulting growth in service industry. Along with the movement of goods and passengers, the transportation of mail was long associated with the age of the coach, and it was a sign of High Harrogate's eighteenth-century development that in 1797 the Post Master General agreed to create the town as an 'independent post town', the postmaster's salary being eight pounds per annum (A.309.3). Before 1797 the Harrogate mails were handled at Wetherby, where the volume of Harrogate–London mail caused some to suggest that Harrogate should have a separate London bag (A.309.2). A member of the numerous Thackwray family was appointed to the office of postmaster (A.309.5), but by 1803 it passed to Thomas Ripley (A.309.8) after one Goodlad failed in his bid for the position (A.309.7). Then, in 1817, Sarah Goodlad was appointed postmistress of Harrogate (A.309.10). These names have one thing in common – the Dragon Hotel. In 1778 the Dragon estate was held by Thomas Russell (B.31, allotments 292–3), who mortgaged it in 1786 (S.346), being then occupied by Matthew Thackwray, who became postmaster in 1797. In 1807, Russell surrendered the Dragon estate to Joseph Goodlad (S.564), the failed postmaster applicant of 1802 (A.309.7), whose wife, Sarah, had become postmistress by 1817 (A.309.10). Four years later the same Russell sold part of his High Harrogate estate to one Thomas Ripley (S.616), who in 1803 succeeded Thackwray as postmaster (A.309.8). These facts all point to the location of Harrogate's first post office being the Dragon Hotel (see plate 18).

The frequency with which the World's End/Devonshire Place/Knaresborough Road route was used may be gauged from the number of inns and hotels that had developed by 1841. These included, from north to south, the Star Inn (S.1226), the New Inn (S.760), the World's End Inn (S.342), the short-lived King's Arms Inn (R.800), the Devonshire Inn (more of a

PLATE 32
High Harrogate,
1829, Granby Hotel
(*left*), Church Square
(*centre*), St John's
Chapel (*right*).

lodging-cum-beer-house), the Black Swan Inn (S.902), the ancient Salutation Inn (R.20) and the lordly Granby (R.60), well placed opposite the St John's Well and the junction between the turnpike roads to Leeds, Otley, Skipton, Wetherby and York. All of these inns, with the possible exception of the Star, appear to have developed before the year 1810.

The southern part of the High Harrogate triangle was formed by Church Square and the Chapel of St John (see plate 32), to which the St John's Well and Wedderburn estate were an integral part. The building of the Chapel of St John has already been considered in chapter eleven, and it is likely that the existence of this amenity stimulated the further growth of adjacent Church Square, which at the time of the forest's enclosure was known as Spaw Hill, or Spawhouses (B.31, allotment 287). Scrutiny of the enclosure map (see plan 20) shows that it was the southern and eastern boundaries of Church Square which were the first to be developed, the likelihood being that the first building on the site stood where the Bay Horse Inn (later known as the Empress) was located. In 1786 the Bay Horse was tenanted by William Westmoreland (S.d.2), the site of which was owned by Granby Hotel proprietor Thomas Wilkes (S.345). Westmoreland's name appeared in the Brewster Sessions lists for 1777, so he appears to have been a settled tenant, a fact made more likely as he also ran the neighbouring St John's, or Sweet Well. William Westmoreland was something of a local celebrity, dying in 1842 at the age of ninety-nine. He was reported as greeting ladies to the St John's Well (see plate 37) with the following verses:

> Dear ladies, believe me, this water is blest
> When conscious charity gives it a zest,
> When charity tempers its steel, you will find,
> It strengthens the body and braces the mind.
> Then open your purses as you open your jaw;
> Fine feeling imbibe as you swallow the Spa;
> If to charity then you've a little to spare,
> I, poor William Westmoreland, sue for a share. (A.301)

Ely Hargrove's Toyshop stood next to the Bay Horse Inn, on the Knaresborough Road side of 'Spawhouses' (B.31, incroachment 286), which was probably a much-frequented place of attraction for Harrogate's visitors. The 'toys' in question were not exclusively objects for the diversion of children, but amusements and novelties for adults. It is known that in about 1811 Hargrove attempted to persuade authoress Barbara Hofland, then running her school at The Grove on Skipton Road, to write her *Season at Harrogate* for sale at his shop (C.83.k), and that when she refused his terms, he hired another author, David Lewis, to write a similar work, *A Week at Harrogate*, which turned out to be a shameless plagiarization of Hofland's work (C.92).

Hargrove did not establish the Spa Hill Toyshop, as the memoirs of Blind Jack Metcalfe, the Yorkshire roadmaker, refer to his having run up against a sign post, 'near the Toy Shop', at the same location (see plate 24), back in about 1738 (C.30.g).

We have already recorded the 1788 building of a theatre (see plate 26) in Church Square, which probably stimulated more neighbourhood development. According to unpublished evidence[2] gathered in 2001, a structure to the immediate north of the rear courtyard was used, during the 'season' to accommodate actors visiting Harrogate, and it is likely that this, in turn, stimulated further development.

In his 1789 *History*, Hargrove reported that the St John's Well had been given an elegant domed pump room in 1786 by Lord Loughborough (Alexander Wedderburn), who was then embellishing his neighbouring estate (G.3). Built to an octagonal ground plan, with a high dome, the St John's Well pump room was the first such enclosed pump room to be built in Harrogate (see plate 7). The post-1778 date of building may seem to indicate that Duchy consent was obtained, as the St John's Well was located on the two hundred acres, or Stray, but there is no evidence to suggest that his Lordship ever approached the Duchy for permission. Strictly speaking, the building of the St John's Well pump room was an illicit enclosure! The delightful print of *c.* 1790 depicts visitors to the St John's Well, probably including Lady Loughborough (who is known to have benefited from the

PLATE 37
Lady Wedderburn and her circle at the St John's Well, *c.* 1790. Note the lady on the right right, who appears to be drinking from an outside, and presumably free, supply.

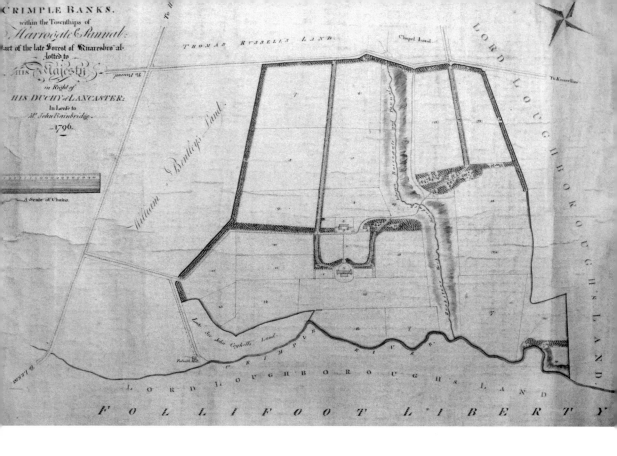

PLAN 28
The King's
allotments,
Hookstone to
Crimple (see B.31 and
B.32). Wedderburn's
closes 243 and 245
granted 1781.

chalybeate water) and well attendant William Westmoreland (see plate 37). Alexander Wedderburn, MP (1733–1805) was an ambitious politician, who in 1771 became Solicitor General, later advancing to the positions of Attorney General, Chief Justice of Common Pleas, and, in 1793, Lord Chancellor, a post he held until 1801. Wedderburn earned a place in history when he grilled Benjamin Franklin on his role during the unrest in the American colonies. His meteoric career earned him many enemies, and his friendship with David Garrick and Richard Brindsley Sheridan was evidence for his great interest and support for the theatre. Wedderburn's titles included those of Baron Loughborough and first Earl of Rosslyn.

In 1775 Wedderburn acquired allotment 242, under the Great Award process, as compensation for the loss of tithes occasioned by the enclosure of the forest (B.31). The 271 acres of allotment 242 were located *south* of Hookstone Road.[3] The 154 acres of allotment number 270, to the immediate *north* of Wedderburn's allotment, lying between Hookstone Road and the Stray, were allotted to Daniel Lascelles of Harewood, and it is likely that Wedderburn also rented allotment 270 from Lascelles, as he is known to have occupied Woodlands House, which stood near to the junction of Hookstone Road and Wetherby Lane (see plan 28).

The building that later became Wedderburn's principal residence, and known as 'Wedderburn House' has a complex and uncertain history (see plate 36). Credited as being designed by the eminent architect Carr of York, the building was clearly an enlargement of an earlier structure, which internal evidence[4] suggests had been erected earlier in the eighteenth century as a farmhouse, possibly for the Lascelles family. Although the existence of a carriage road across the Stray from Church Square to Wedderburn House may point to pre-1778 construction, in that neither the 1778 Great Award (B.31) or subsequent Duchy documentation relating to the Stray contain any reference to the building of such a road, the example of the St John's Well can also point to post-1778 construction by the autocratic Wedderburn as a further illicit inclosure! The western wing of Wedderburn House was probably converted by Carr from the original farmhouse, the vanished front door of which would have closed the view along the Stray carriage road.

The estate acquired by Wedderburn from Lascelles (allotment 270) was subsequently landscaped and planted, the resulting parkland being opened occasionally to public use. The 1789 edition of Hargrove's *History* refers to 'Lord Loughborough, whose rising plantations on his estate, consisting of oaks, ashes and sycamores, affording a very agreeable shade to a walk eight feet wide and two miles long, is one of the greatest and most useful improvements ever yet made at this place.' (G.3) Public admittance to the homes of grandees such as Alexander Wedderburn was not unusual in the eighteenth and early nineteenth centuries. Even after Wedderburn had died in 1805, when the estate was purchased by a local doctor (Dr John Jacques), the grounds remained open to the public during the spa season, a fact

PLAN 29
King's allotments,
Low Harrogate
c. 1810. Russell's
Survey, p. 132.

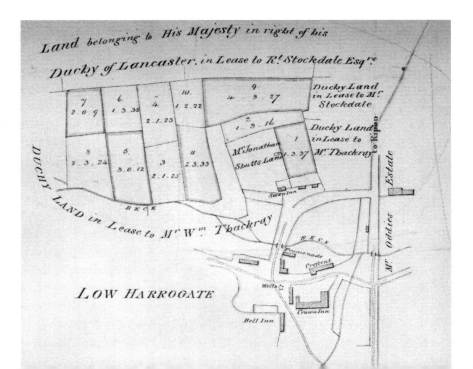

alluded to in David Lewis's *A Week at Harrogate*: 'The day being hot, we were tempted to rove, beneath the cool shade of great Wedderburn's Grove, to the Woodlands we wandered, which all must admire, who wish from the bustle of life to retire.' (C.92.0) The retention, in very few private hands, of the majority of lands south of the Stray, ensured that this area would not be developed for housing until the arrival a more democratic (but not necessarily better) age.

Wedderburn acquired more land in Harrogate in January 1787 (S.352), and in 1790 paid one thousand pounds to his neighbour John Bainbridge of Crimple House, who mortgaged nearly twenty acres of land on Jenny Plain to his lordship by way of security (S.370). These transactions, along with his support for Harrogate's Theatre Royal (see chapter 9) and the developments on the Wedderburn estates, show the extent of his long-term commitment to the town. The land due south of the Stray, bounded by Wetherby Lane and Leeds Road, was entirely in agricultural use, save for the Hookstone Quarry, which was not identified as a common stone quarry in the Great Award of 1778, but which seems to have been worked largely in the earlier nineteenth century (B.31 – preamble). Consequently the first buildings to appear, other than Wedderburn House and Woodlands Cottage, were cottages for the estate workers, which were erected on what later became Oatland's Drive, but which in the eighteenth century was called 'Intack' or 'Intake' Road. This road connected York Place with Hookstone Road, joining the latter at the 'Intake' (a common term), which was a ten-acre plot (number 269) bounded by what in the twentieth century would become Hookstone Road, Oatland's Drive, Wheatland's Road East, and Hornbeam Crescent. The 'Intake' can be traced back long before the Great Award, an early reference being in 1653, when this area of Harrogate was credited by the singular map of 1587 (see plan 5) as being part of the

PLATE 35
Woodlands House at the junction of Hookstone and Wetherby Roads was probably home to Alexander Wedderburn during the construction of Wedderburn House. It was, most regrettably, demolished in 1966.

PLATE 36
Wedderburn House
was said to have
been remodelled for
Alexander
Wedderburn by the
architect Carr of
York, who
incorporated the
older farmhouse (the
right wing) into the
new building.

Manor of Plompton (A.110), and leased by 'Henerey Plumpton' (S.83). It is reasonable to assume that the 'Intake' was an incroachment which was used as a plantation for produce used in connection with the surrounding agricultural lands, or even as a pen or pound for cattle. (See also W.14.11.)

West of Leeds Road, as far as the later Pannal Ash Road, the boundaries of the intervening fields, as recorded on the 1778 enclosure map (see plan 17), are indicative of ancient usage, which seem to have remained intact and dedicated to agricultural use until the development of the area after the opening in 1848 of the Brunswick Railway line.

Before we leave High Harrogate, it is necessary to consider two small pieces of land that were of special significance to the development of the locality. Allotments 282 and 283 ran due east of the Granby as a long thin parcel of land containing a little over nine acres of land, a shape which points to a medieval origin. As both allotments were awarded to the King as a unique example of King's lands on the east side of Harrogate, the surveyors must have had some special purpose for their designation (B.31). These King's lands are all the more puzzling when it is realised that their basically medieval outline was allowed to split in two the post-medieval field boundaries of the larger fields which were allotted to John Watson (allotments 273 and 274) and Sarah Harper (allotments 278, 280 and 281). Access to the cigarette-shaped King's lands in the east was via Bilton Park Lane Road and in the west by what later became Roseville Road, and Silverfields (see plan 30). The Great Award of 1778 (B.31) records that these King's lands, 282 and 283, had been enclosed under fifty years, for the benefit of Harrogate Chapel, so it is likely that such enclosure from the Royal Forest occurred shortly after 1749 (M.3). One possible hint to their original purpose may be found in the names which accompanied the 1749 petition to consecrate the new church at High Harrogate, which includes the Bensons (M.2), who occupied the neighbouring Granby (R.60) which was then known as the Royal Oak (R.120). It would have been quite acceptable for the tenant of the popular Royal Oak inn to have piously dedicated a portion of the extensive open lands behind his establishment for the benefit of the minister of the new church which he was keen to have consecrated.

We must also direct the reader's attention to the status of allotments 218–222, all of which lay to the immediate south-east of the St John's Well, and which in the nineteenth century became the location for several aristocratic villa residences, and in the twentieth century provided a site for the District Hospital. Allotment 222 was a small, one rood plot on which stood the Cold Bath, a structure which pre-dated the Stray Award of 1778, and which, according to Hargrove, had been built to enable visitors to bathe in the cold 'Steel Waters' of the St John's Well, when such visitors had had

PLAN 30
Chapel lands, *c.* 1810.
Russell's surveys,
p. 132.

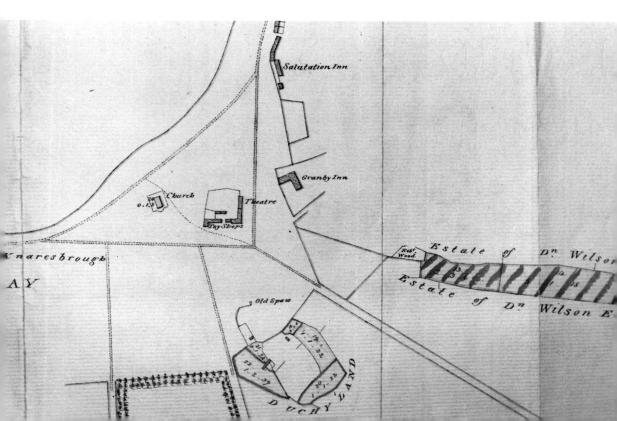

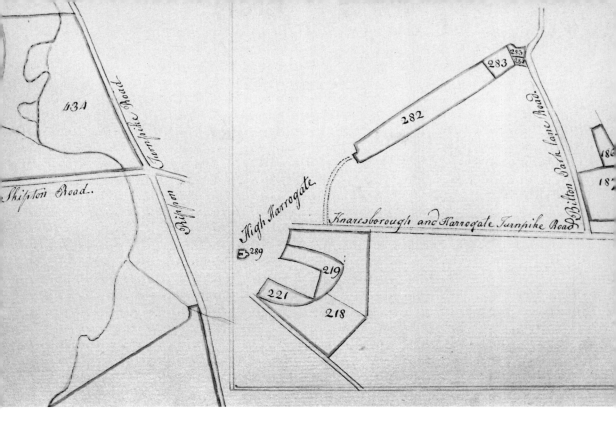

PLAN 26
King's High
Harrogate
allotments, 1778.
Russell's survey,
p. 122 (see also B.31
and B.32).

their health undermined by too much warm bathing (G.2). Allotments 218, 219, 220 and 221 were described in the Award as being at, or near, Chandler's Garths, and of these allotments, numbers 218, 219, 221 and 222 were allotted to the King, with allotment number 220 being awarded to Elizabeth Clemenshaw. The recording of these special allotments varies from map to map, as the King's lands tended to be recorded without regard to their relation to other lands (see plan 26). The significance of these allotments lies in their irregular and unusual shapes, which may have been the result of specific occupational usage. Allotments 219 (the King), 220 (Elizabeth Clemenshaw), and 221 (the King) were all classed as 'incroachments', which points to someone once having thought that it was worth their while to have encroached land from the Royal Forest in close proximity to the St John's Well, which itself was classed as the sole allotment within this group of 'Kings Chapel lands'.

What all this demonstrates is that at the time of the 1778 Award, the land nearest to the St John's Well was used for several purposes, and it is impossible to escape the conclusion that at least some of these purposes may have been connected with visitors to the St John's Well. The Duchy's retention of the ownership of the freehold of the King's Chapel lands at this location meant that they would only be developed when the Duchy believed the time was ripe, and then only to the highest standard. In fact the time became

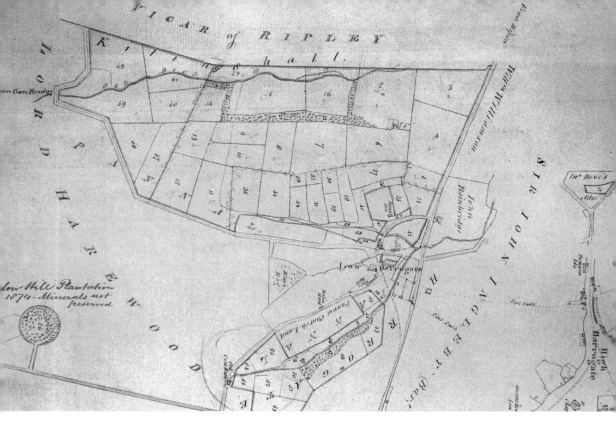

PLAN 27
The King's Low
Harrogate
allotments, *c.* 1782,
Russell's survey,
p. 122. Note the
Harlow Hill
plantation at lower
left.

ripe only in the middle of the nineteenth century, because even by the time
of the 1778 Award, it must have been clear that the future of the town lay in
proximity to Low Harrogate's Old Sulphur Well. This was why the great
majority of the Duchy's 'King's lands' lay between Otley Road and Ripon
Road, rather than between Wetherby Road and Skipton Road.

The south-western quadrant of modern Harrogate, flanked by Leeds and
Otley Roads (see plan 17), between 'Harrogate Corner' (Prince of Wales'
roundabout) and Pannal contained at this time only a scattering of farm
houses, most of which (east of Pannal Ash Road) were held by the Bentleys,
Clarks, Wescoes, Wilkes and Bainbridges. The modern Stone Rings Avenue
was known in 1778 as Quarry Road, as it led to the quarry in allotment 563,
which the Great Award had designated as a common stone quarry (B.31).
Inevitably the working of this quarry led to some associated building in the
vicinity, but it was never anything other than small scale. Further north,
Lead Hall Road (today, Lane) led to Lead Hall, which must have received
its name from the material forming the roof. Described as a farmhouse in
the 1762 will of George Bentley (S.238), Leadhall seems by 1778 to have been
the only substantial building between the modern Lead Hall Lane and Otley
Road.

At the crown of Otley Road, Richard Wright's allotment 610 may have
been of considerable antiquity, as it was situated at the junction of the old

Harlo-gatte (see plan 11) as well as the road which led to the common quarry (allotment 495) and the circular 'King's Plantation' in allotment 494 (B.31), which latter features may well have led to the establishment during the final quarter of the eighteenth century of a beer house at this spot.

Although it is tempting to speculate whether Irongate Bridge Road and Cold Bath Road may together have formed the northern and eastern boundaries of the old Harlow woodland, no firm evidence exists to support this theory. The junction of Cold Bath Road and Otley Road (see plan 14) has been filled with a public house, the New Inn, since at least the late eighteenth century, judging from surviving architectural evidence. The Great Award describes allotment 465, held by Wilkes and Bainbridge as being 'in Pannal, near Cold Bath' rather than 'at New Inn' (B.31), and the only intimation that the New Inn existed at this time is a reference to Pannal innkeeper Leonard Buck (this part of Harrogate being then within Pannal), being granted £10 surety for good behaviour by Thomas Wilkes in the Brewster sessions of 1777 (A.223).

The land between the east side of Cold Bath Road and the two hundred acres was filled with the small Cold Bath allotment 474 and the public watering place 474a, Pannal Church lands allotment 468, and the two allotments to the King, numbers 467 (the later 'Esplanade') and the very much larger 471, where the Red Hill, or Beech Grove, Lancaster Road, Victoria Road, Queens Road development would later occur – see plan 11). Apart from the developments at the Cold Bath (see chapter 8), the land between east Cold Bath Road and the later Beech Grove was firmly in agricultural use up to the 1841 Act. The western side of Cold Bath Road, however, experienced a very different type of development.

It is likely that Cold Bath Road was originally a simple lane which connected the Old Sulphur Well with Harlow in the south west, and Bilton (via the modern King's Road) in the north-east, and that its urbanisation occurred after 1752 and the construction of the Otley Road turnpike (Q.6), with the development of a number of inns and lodging houses on the higher and sunnier south eastern side of the road. The Cold Bath Road inns grew in importance and size the nearer they were to the Old Sulphur Well. The establishments beyond the New Inn were known as Binns' (later the Lancaster), the Robin Hood (later the Wellington), and the White Hart. Neither the Adelphi nor the Beechwood hotels existed before 1841.

Binns' Hotel had an interesting history as it was one of Harrogate's most important coaching inns. One Joseph Binns resided in Cold Bath Lane in 1795 (S.436), living on allotment 482, held by Samuel Hatterley (B.31), and although the first reference to Binns' Hotel occurs in 1835 (S.1060), Binns' establishment features in *A Week at Harrogate*, written in about 1812, where allusion is made to the overcrowded Granby, Dragon and Crown sending

PLATE 47
Woodcut of old
Wellington Inn, Cold
Bath Road, c. 1850.
Originally known as
the Robin Hood, the
inn was an important
destination for
coaches.

people down to 'dwell with Mrs Binns' (C.92.0). It is therefore reasonable to assume that Binns' lodgings were established well before 1810, and indeed an advertisement of 1825 intimates that the business had been established for nearly forty years (R.2130), which rather confirms the implications of document (S.436) above.

The Wellington Inn was probably older than Binns' Hotel. An entry in the court roll for 14 May 1828 (S.928) refers to land behind the Wellington with the name of Robin Hood field, Robin Hood being the earlier name by which the Wellington Hotel (see plate 47) was known. David Lewis' *A Week at Harrogate*, written in about 1812, refers to the 'famed Robin Hood' which 'commands a fine prospect around' (C.92.b), and, again, it is likely that the Robin Hood (which gave its name to the earliest known name of Cold Bath Road (R.3123)) was well established by 1810. Early coaches which would have passed Low Harrogate on their regular runs were the Leeds to Newcastle 'Diligence', which began in 1791 (Q.27.22), the Alexander from Leeds to Harrogate and Knaresborough, which began in 1807 and ran from the Wellington in Low Harrogate, and continued to the Hope Tavern (Gascoigne's) in High Harrogate (Q.27.31). By 1815, the 'True Briton' coach was running between Halifax, Leeds and Bradford, arriving at the 'Lord [sic] Wellington Inn, Low Harrogate at 12.00 noon. (Q.27.58). Cold Bath Road's last inn, the White Hart, was its most important, and although a case can be made for including the Bell Inn within Cold Bath Road before the building of Royal Parade in the 1840s, there is no evidence to indicate that it was ever regarded in this light.

The White Hart (see plate 42), located at the foot of ancient Robin Hood Lane, and convenient for the much frequented Old Sulphur Well, was functioning in 1765, when an advertisement in the *York Courant* offered a reward of fifteen shillings for the return of a dappled grey mare 'stray'd or conveyed on the 14 August from Thomas Wray's, at the White Hart in Low Harrogate ...' (R.290). Although several twentieth-century writers stated that the White Hart was visited by John Wesley during his visit to Nidderdale of July 1766,[5] we know of no contemporary evidence to support this claim. It does seem, however, that the White Hart was frequented by members of the Methodist faction, as Mary Bosanquet's 1773 journal refers to her travelling to Harrogate to stay at the White Hart Hotel (K.21). Four years later the White Hart was the setting for an auction of land in Low Harrogate, which seemed, 'peculiarly adapted to the building of a pleasant and commodious inn ...' (R.650). That this was no single occurrence is shown by the fact that in 1781, the Half Moon (later, Crescent) inn was auctioned at the White Hart (R.780). By 1801, the White Hart was the destination for the York to Harrogate 'Diligence' coach, for which passengers were charged 9s. 6d. inside, 6s. outside.

The inns and lodging houses were not the only structures lining Cold Bath Road, as the court rolls record a great increase in the number of houses erected on the south-eastern side between Binns' lodgings and the Wellington in the years around the 1770 Enclosure Act. In 1795 John Harper of Leeds purchased a mortgage from Samuel Hattersley for land in 'Cold Bath Lane ... with all houses, erections, and buildings ... save and except one dwelling house ... lately converted into two dwelling houses ...' (S.436). It is clear from examinations of the nineteenth-century street directories, and aerial photographs, that the south-western frontage of Cold Bath Road was densely urbanised between 1770 and the middle of the nineteenth century, and that what little space was left between the frontages of various buildings was occupied by a few courts (Wellington Square, Kensington Square, Cold Bath Place, Diamond Court, St Peter's Square), which ran back towards Bogs Field (this was before Valley Drive was constructed in the 1890s). Further surrenders emphasise this trend (S.469, S.473, S.522 S.569).

The presence of the Crown Hotel had a particularly important role in determining Low Harrogate's pattern of urbanisation, and it is instructive to compare the building density which surrounds High Harrogate's Tewit and St John's Wells, with that around Low Harrogate's Old Sulphur Well.

At High Harrogate both wells and their pump rooms stand amidst the two hundred acres, the neighbouring Granby and Queen Hotels being at some distance. At Low Harrogate, the Old Sulphur Well is also on the two hundred acres, but so overshadowed by building as to be almost hemmed in by stone. The source of this disparity may be that the older chalybeate wells of High Harrogate fell into neglect in the early seventeenth century, but that when the revival occurred, it was Low Harrogate's sulphur water that enjoyed the public's esteem, which encouraged the local small-holders to make their enclosures around the Old Sulphur, rather than the Tewit Well. Although we have already noted above that some of the enclosures near to the St John's Well may have had spa associations, they never surrounded it on four sides, which, later, was indeed the case at the Old Sulphur Well.

Although some writers on the Crown (see plate 49) allude to its having been established in 1740, their sole basis for this claim appears to be the singular inscription on Joseph Thackwray's gravestone in Pannal church-yard: 'In 1740 I came to the Crown ...' As there must have been a Crown in 1740 to which Joseph Thackwray 'came to', it had clearly existed for some time before 1740. By 1770, the Crown was sufficiently important to be the scene of the first public meeting held by the commissioners charged with the enclosure of the Royal Forest (R.475). Ideally located at or adjacent to the junctions of roads to Bilton, Harlow, Haverah, Ripon and Leeds, as well as the Old Sulphur Well, and with a southerly view across the two hundred acres, the very name of the Crown Inn, or Hotel, intimates a long history.

We suggest that the Crown developed from a building erected in the early seventeenth century by forest tenants, who viewed the visitors to the Old Sulphur Well as a source of profit. Such a building may have been a farmhouse, or some structure associated with a farmhouse. What is certain is that by 1770 the Crown was the most significant building in Low Harrogate. The inscription on Joseph Thackwray's gravestone does not rule out the possibility that the Thackwray's had held the Crown *before* 1740, but with the lack of any positive evidence to prove their association, the year 1740 is as good a date as any to fix for the start of their family's association with the Crown. One reason for the Crown's supremacy in Low Harrogate (as distinct from High Harrogate, where at least three, and possibly four hotels, struggled for supremacy) may have been that the owners engaged in programmes of enlargement and improvement on a regular basis. The Crown's record of mortgaging (W.14.9) and land conveyancing (S.303 to S.1230) between 1770 and 1841 demonstrates this trend amply. The drawing reproduced as plate 50 shows how the Crown was laid out when Lord Byron was a visitor in 1806 (C.89.b–c). The Crown was mentioned by other visitors with a literary or theatrical bent, such as James Tate (C.80).

Some six years before Byron's visit, Richard Colt Hoare wrote of the Crown, 'The Crown Inn, at Lower Harrogate, since its late improvements is perhaps superior to any of the houses [i.e. Harrogate's hotels] in point of rooms ...' (C.72) Writing of the Crown in the Regency era, Henry Curling noted that it was known as '... the Hospital, ... erected close to a well of the most foetid and foul smelling water ...' Curling, remarking on the Queen Hotel, said it was a place resorted to by people who would not dare enter the Granby or the Dragon, and 'who were hardly sufficiently assured in their position to venture amongst the jewels of the Crown.' (C.86.f) The habit of promenading round the Crown Hotel's west side seems to have begun at this time (C.68.f), which may have stimulated the later development of Royal Parade. The Great Award of 1778 had allocated to Joseph Thackwray incroachments 452, 453, allotment 454, incroachment 455, allotments 456, 457, incroachment 458, and allotment 459, all of which were copyhold. Plots 452 and 453 were – roughly – between Ripon Road, Swan Road, and the site of the George Hotel, and were probably used by Thackwray in connection with the Crown Hotel (see plan 13). Plots 454 and 455 were the fields bounded later by Parliament Street, Crescent Road, and the Ginnel; 456 was a thin oblong strip flanking Montpellier Road, separating it from the aforementioned two fields 454 and 455; and 458 was the site of the Crown Hotel proper. Allotment 459 was a small plot next to the Bell Inn across the later Royal Parade, opposite the Old Sulphur Well. From these allocations may be seen the Crown Hotel's role in determining the future development of Low Harrogate.

As with the great High Harrogate inns, the Dragon (S.375), the Granby (S.1207) and the Queen (S.932), the Crown Hotel had its own lodging house, known as Ashfield House, and although the first known reference to 'Crown Lodgings' occurs as late as 1839 (S.1211), it is likely that a building within the immediate vicinity of the Crown Hotel existed well before this time. An advertisement in the *York Chronicle* of 15 October 1790 for the sale of the Crown Inn estate, does not refer, specifically, to a separate

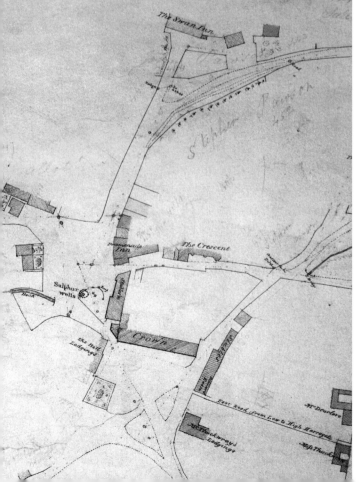

PLATE 48
Promenade Inn,
photographed *c.* 1890,
long after its closure.

lodging house (R.990), but the map accompanying Charles Greeves' 1821 survey (see plan 32) shows 'Thackwray's lodgings' on the Ashfield House site, and it is reasonable to suspect that Crown Lodgings were built on what later became Lower Montpellier Parade at some time during the boom years of the Regency.

Crown Lodgings and the Crown Hotel formed half of a square, the third side of which was formed by the Bell Inn (the fourth side being the open Stray), the site of which was later incorporated within Royal Parade. The Bell (see plan 32) seems to have been smaller than its White Hart neighbour. An article in the *York Courant* for 1768 advised readers that the Bell's landlord, Joseph Hogg, had been accused of murdering one of his customers, but that, 'there does not appear to have been the least foundation for such a rumour, and the report has been solely owing to the distempered brain of a woman, who many years ago when big with bastard child, imposed greatly upon the public under the pretext of sympathy.' (R.365) Sometimes known as the 'Blue Bell', from its display board, the Bell was a stage for the York to Harrogate coach. On 27 May 1777 an advertisement informed the public that 'the York and Harrogate machine will begin from Mr Featherstone's, the White Swan, York, and go to Mr Hogg's, the Blue Bell, in Low Harrogate, in time for dinner.' Too much should not be made of the fact that the Bell was excluded from the early editions of

Hargrove's guidebooks, since Hargrove was prone to neglect Low Harrogate in favour of High, where he had a shop. The Hogg family continued to be associated with the Bell after the death of Joseph Hogg (R.700), and it is very likely that these were from the same family who lived at 'Sulphur Wells' in 1758 (S.236) and who had been brought before the magistrates in 1681 for keeping an alehouse without licence (A.135.q). By 1805, the Bell was run by Mrs Clayton, and was still on the coaching run between York and Harrogate (R.1235).

The Promenade Inn (see plate 48), like the Bell, was convenient to the Old Sulphur Well, which it faced on the well's northern side, at the junction of Swan Lane (later Road) and Crescent Road. The Promenade's origins are not known, but its central location points to very early establishment, possibly in the seventeenth century, when it may have been one of the alehouses which in 1676 caused the constable to go 'twice to Sulphur Well to cease quarrells' (D.12.13). The map which accompanied the Great Award of 1778 showed a building on the site of the Promenade Inn, part of tiny allotment 460 (see plan 13). This was held by Joseph Hogg, the publican who also held allotments 461 and 462 (the Bell Inn) to the immediate south of the Old Sulphur Well. As for tiny allotment 460, this was an incroachment from the very much larger 2 acre, 3 rood, 33 perch allotment 451 held by Stephen Pawson (B.31) whose family held the Blacksmith's Arms, precursor of the Swan (R.795). It is therefore reasonable to assume that the precursor of the Promenade Inn was run by the same publican who ran the adjacent Bell Inn. The Brewster sessions for 1773 (A.215) record a Joseph Hogg and a Robert Cocker as being licensees in Low Harrogate (part of Pannal); it is possible that this Cocker is the same man as the Robert Corker who in 1829 was referred to as having once held the Promenade Inn (S.943). Joseph Hogg's joint control of the Bell and – via a sub-tenant – the Promenade, would appear to have made him a wealthy man, and a victim for the kind of malicious fabrication alluded to above. As there are no references to the name 'Promenade Inn' before 1822 (G.11) it is likely that around the year 1810 the inn took the name of the adjacent Promenade Room of 1806 (R.1310) rather than the reverse. The Promenade later became Hales' Bar.

As the Promenade Inn was the nearest of all Harrogate's inns to the Sulphur Well (nearer even than the Bell Inn or the old Crown), it may have been a well frequented establishment, the absolute centrality of which led to its being adopted as a coaching stop. The coaches do not appear to have actually called at the Promenade Inn itself, probably because of the extremely cramped nature of the site (tiny allotment 460), but rather at the Promenade coaching office, which stood behind the Bell Inn on allotment 459 held by Crown Hotel owner Joseph Thackwray (B.31) and which continued to be held by the Thackwrays well into the 1830s (S.1089). The

Promenade Inn had its principal façade towards Swan Lane, and with its northerly neighbour the Promenade Room of 1806 (R.1310), the Old Sulphur Well to the south, the Bell Inn, and the great bulk of the Crown Hotel, formed the heart of Low Harrogate.

A little to the east, along what later became Crescent Road, a fourth inn added to Low Harrogate's growing list of attractions. The Crescent Inn (see plate 83) underwent a series of name changes throughout its history. An advertisement of 1775 advised readers that a coach departed from York for 'Mr Pawson's the Half Moon in Low Harrogate to dinner ...' (R.625). Under the Great Award of 1778, Stephen Pawson received allotment 451, an incroachment, on which the Half Moon stood. Shortly after, he seems to have leased from the King's lands two further allotments, number 440 (a little over three acres), and number 452 (a little over two acres), which no doubt were used to supply the inn with consumables (see plan 13).

Stephen Pawson did not long survive his new status at the Crescent, as he died shortly before December 1778 (S.e.1), to be succeeded by his son Matthew, who seems to have enjoyed his inheritance for only a very short period. It was at this time (i.e. 1779 or 1780) that the inn's name changed to that of the 'Globe', as an interesting reference in the diary of Sylas Neville to the imposing appearance of the Harrogate inns refers specifically to 'the Globe' (C.53). A further reference in the township records alludes to a town's meeting being held at 'Thomas Linforth's, the Globe Inn, Harrogate, the 28 October 1780 (D.18). An explanation for Thomas Linforth's sudden appearance is answered by a stark reference in a document of 1781 to 'Matthew Pawson, late of Low Harrogate ... But now of the castle of York'! By 1781 the full Globe was demoted back to the status of 'Half Moon' (S.309), and it was as the Half Moon that the inn was auctioned at the White Hart Hotel on 1 August 1781. The sale description referred to 'a commodious Barber's shop also contiguous, now occupied by Mr Yates ... for the recovering whereof ... the assignee will serve an ejectment ...' (R.780). History does not record whether or not the unfortunate Barber was indeed ejected from his premises!

Thomas Linforth announced his retirement in 1801 (R.1275), but evidently he retained financial interest in the inn, as by 1804, when Dr Cayley and others acquired part of the inn's garden for their Promenade Room venture, he was described as 'owner of the equity of redemption of the mortgage' (Se.9). A new landlord, James Stettle, held the Crescent's tenancy by 1806 (R.1285), and the same year saw the continuation of the York Harrogate coaching run advertised as 'the new Diligence coach from York to James Settle's Crescent Inn' (R.1320); it was still running in 1810 (R.1460). In 1810 Linforth re-mortgaged the Crescent for a further £900 from his associate John Lofthouse (Se.11). The frequent borrowings by Linforth appear to have

RIPON RD HARROGATE

been typical of the financial dealings of Harrogate innkeepers at this period, and the apparent willingness of the moneyed classes to lend is evidence for the dynamic state of the local economy, even during the economically difficult years of the French wars. This state is demonstrated by the glowing descriptions of the Harrogate season by such newspapers as the *Leeds Mercury* (R.1425) and the *York Herald* (R.1495).

The George Hotel (see plate 52), which became such an important address by the middle of the nineteenth century, was credited by Grainge as having been a simple tavern with the name of 'The Chequers'.[6] No precise date can be set for the establishment of the George Hotel's precursor, although it is likely that given its location adjacent to the Ripon Road turnpike bar, it was opened in about 1752 (Q.6). In an entry for February 1816, Samuel Powell, the solicitor, recorded that John Oddy purchased a piece of land 'near the Chequers' (W.3.7), and it is reasonable to suppose that the change to the 'George' occurred either with the accession of George IV in 1820, or with William Barber's purchase in 1828 (S.926), or even to commemorate George III's 1778 gift of the Stray.

To the north-west of the Old Sulphur Well, at the crown of Well Hill, a small cluster of buildings had developed, known sometimes as Sulphur Well Mount (S.595), which was ideally placed both to serve the visitors and to house workers at the neighbouring quarry (B.31) or local hotels. Eventually this favoured locality became a popular location for lodging houses (see plate 16), but it is reasonable to assume that its point of vantage over the old sulphur well, and its situation on Iron Gate Bridge Road meant that its origins were connected with travellers, in much the same way as the neighbouring Promenade Inn. Swan Lane, from the old sulphur well round to its junction with Ripon Road, had been designated part of the Stray by the Great Award of 1778 (B.31), and the Swan Inn's origins may have had something to do with the forges and smithies connected with the ancient Iron Gate Bridge Road (see Chapter 2). By 1777 the plot of land occupied by the Smith's Arms (Allotment 442) was held by John Pawson (S.281) who was probably related to the Stephen Pawson who held the Crescent (B.31). Plan 13 shows a building on the site. In May 1782 the *York Courant* advertised that the 'Blacksmith's Arms' had been taken by Jonathan Shutt and 'fitted up in the neatest manner for the Spaw Season ...' (R.795) Like High Harrogate's Dragon, the name and colour of the Smiths/Blacksmiths Arms seemed to change with different writers, and the new owner adopted a new name – the White Swan – as if to signify a complete break with the plebeian past (R.795).

The Swan Inn overlooked the rear of the George Inn, whose frontage faced Ripon Road at a point immediately adjacent to the turnpike bar erected as a result of the 1751 Act (Q.5). The precise date for the establishment of the George is not known, but historian Grange recorded that it had once been known as 'The Chequers'.[7] Probably no more than a simple public house, the George only became of importance to Low Harrogate after the 1828 surrender (see below).

PLATE 16
Thomas Rowlandson's drawing 'Dr Syntax at Harrowgate'.
COURTESY HARROGATE MUSEUMS AND ART GALLERIES

To the north of the Swan Inn, and reaching up to Oak Beck and beyond, the King's lands (see plan 15) covered much of what later became the Duchy estate, including Jenny Plain, which is referred to in a document of 1790 (S.370), but which is certainly far older. Beyond, on the western side of the Ripon turnpike road, lay Rattle Cragg and the great rabbit warren (T.3162) (B.28.d, entries 13 and 14) while the eastern side, north of World's End Road, lay Knox, which at this time was a community isolated from Harrogate. The Knox gritstone beds had been designated as a public quarry by the Great Award of 1778 (B.31), and when, in 1613, Solomon Swale had surveyed the Harrogate area for the Duchy as part of an early and abortive scheme to enclose the Royal Forest (B.11), he calculated that 'Harrigat Knocks' contained 201 acres. In 1789 stone cutter William Voackes mortgaged his land in the locality to John Oliver of Knox Mill for £40 with interest (S.369). It is possible that Voackes wanted the money to improve his stone cutting work, which was in demand during the post-Award period. The miller at Knox must have been a man of means, for in 1790 he acquired land at 'the Toyshop' (Church Square) (S.377), which he sold quickly to innkeeper William Dinsley (S.381). Voackes provided further mortgage loans (S.387, S.418) in the years up to 1810.

Bilton, to the south and west of Knox, does not appear to have been greatly affected by the events of 1778, save for the all-important matter of regularising the ownership and tenancies of land. The greater part of Bilton between the World's End (later Skipton) Road to the west, Bilton Lane Road to the north, and Bilton Park to the south, was awarded to James and Charles Brown, Sir John Ingilby, and the families of Dearlove, Dobson,

Wilkes and Bainbridge (jointly), Taylor and Gerard. Although the greater part of Bilton was in agricultural use, there is evidence to show that coalmining was practised before 1744, for as was shown by historian Haythornthwaite, one James Smith 'collier at Bilton Park was buried this year at Knaresborough', so it is likely that he was working as a miner for some years before this date.[8] A letter of 1730 refers to there being 'little good husbandry' about the Bilton estate, which had 'ordinary coal in it, fit for burning lime' (E.94.b), which in 1783 was being undertaken by Clough and Stockdale at New Park (D.5). Two years later Bilton Park was acquired by John Watson (E.95), and by 1766 one John Dobson was leasing the mine for £88 10s. per annum (E.106). A report of 1777 stated that the Bilton coal seam was within 200 yards of the park's boundary, and that it had been won by means of cuttings from the banks of the river Nidd. The spoil heaps from the Bilton mines were still evident two hundred years later in Bilton Fields.

Evidence for the prosperity of old Bilton may be seen from the high architectural quality of many of the locality's surviving houses, such as Red Cat Cottage, Prospect House Farm, or the handsome structures on Bilton Lane (see plate 11). Red Cat Cottage (see plate 10), from both internal evidence, and its location at the junction of Knox Lane, Crab Lane and Bachelor Gardens, shows signs of having been an inn or beer house, an activity that its central location between Killinghall, Knox and Old Bilton was well suited to promote. A deed of 1777 refers to it as '... the Red Cat' (S.285), and the Great Award of the following year mentions 'the Red cat' as a sixteen-perch incroachment (number 326), held by a John Metcalf (B.31), who may possibly have been the famous roadmaker Blind Jack (see also C.30). Old Bilton's principal public house, the Gardeners Arms in Bilton Lane, contains architectural evidence which indicates a seventeenth-century construction date, which would make it a contemporary of the three neighbouring stone cottages, on which the date 1700 is inscribed. The site directly opposite the Gardeners Arms also being of interest in that it was once used to bleach flax for the local flax mill, as shown by eighteenth-century maps.

One of the locality's most interesting buildings was the impressively named Harrogate Hall, located on Hall Lane, almost equidistant between Knox Mill and the Gardeners Arms, and a little to the south east of the Bilton Endowed School (see chapter 12). The location of Harrogate Hall – a former Slingsby property, acquired by the Birnands *c.* 1450 (A.69) – clearly affected the type and rate of post fifteenth-century agricultural development as well as the pattern of nineteenth-century urbanisation. These factors were reflected in the locality's field dimensions and the occupations of cottagers (Classes D and E). Over-hastily torn down in the 1970s, Harrogate Hall probably acquired its undistinguished architectural face at the hands of the Inglebys. At the time of the 1664 Hearth Tax, Sir William Ingleby was assessed for nine hearths, which points to a considerably larger structure than a conventional farmhouse of the time. William Grainge reported that Harrogate Hall had been rebuilt in about 1820, after the Greenwood family of Swarcliffe Hall had purchased it from the Inglebys in 1809.[9]

It may be that Harrogate Hall, located at the heart of the busy Knox–Old Bilton locality, pre-dated Bilton Hall, but the reverse is the more likely to have been true, in that Bilton Hall has a close connection with Bilton Park, which is of irrefutable antiquity (Class E). In other words, had Bilton Hall not existed when Harrogate Hall was built and named, it would have been the latter structure that would have probably carried the name 'Bilton Hall'.

By 1810 Bilton Hall was in the hands of the Watson family, who had held it since 1734, after acquiring it from the Stockdales (E.99). When the house was rebuilt in 1854, historian Haythornthwaite claimed that it was rebuilt in Victorian Tudor style to match the earlier structure, and there is an element of truth in this assertion (see plate 9). The real point of interest about Bilton Hall is not one of architectural style, but that the existence of such an important structure, sited in Bilton Park at the eastern extremity of Bilton Lane, together with the adjacent Bilton Sulphur Spa, did *not* result in the

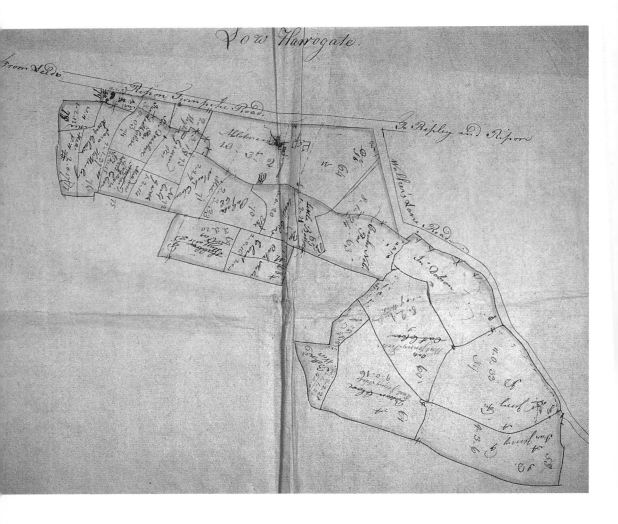

Low Harrogate.

development of a third spa village to match those of High and Low Harrogate. The reason for this non-development, as we have previously noted, originated with the sale of Bilton Park in 1628 by Charles I (E.78). With the wells in private hands by 1770, it was not possible for the enclosure commissioners to dedicate the land about Bilton Wells to the public – as occurred in High and Low Harrogate – as it was no longer their land to dedicate.

Before we consider the building development of Harrogate between 1810 and 1841, it is necessary to consider one final area of the town, which after 1810 was the area subject to the greatest degree of urbanisation: the so-called 'central Harrogate' area.

The undated map of Ingilby holdings in central Harrogate (see plan 23) pre-dates 1810 clearly, and reveals the layout of the field system that had been part of the ancient Crokisnab. A footpath, more or less contiguous

PLAN 23
Ingilby estates, central Harrogate, pre-1810. The present Parliament Street, Ripon Road, and King's Road can be seen at the top of the plan.

PLAN 34
Charles Greeves' 1821 plan of the Leeds to Ripon turnpike road.

314

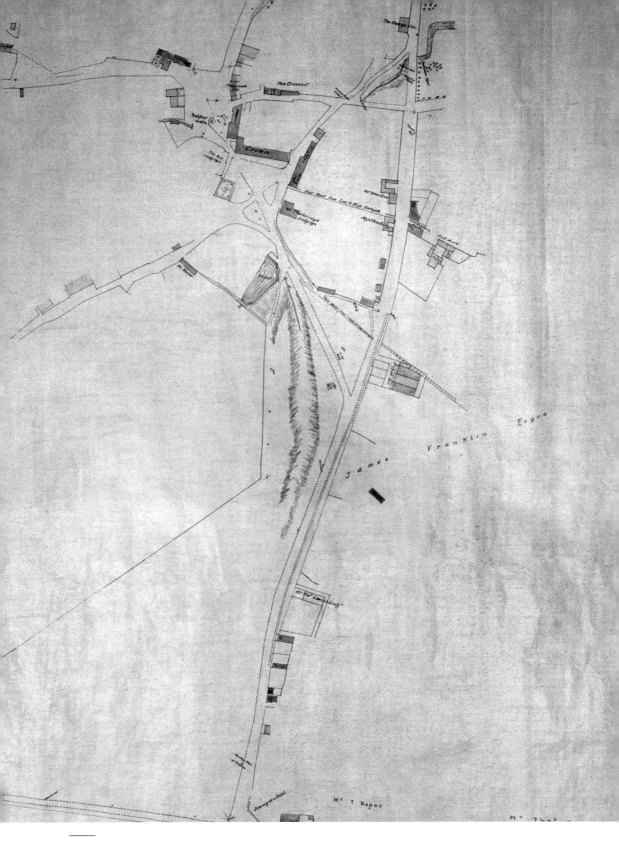

with the later Cheltenham Crescent, may have led to a number of agricultural buildings, but the only one for which firm evidence can be
produced is Prospect Cottage, on a 13 acre, 3 rood, 2 perch site. Prospect
Cottage stood slightly east of Parliament Street (which before the Great
Reform Act of 1832 was known as the Leeds and Ripon turnpike road), and
with its back to a narrow route between the old Sulphur Well and High
Harrogate's Chapel of St John. This route later became that of the several
thoroughfares known respectively as the Ginnel, Chapel or Oxford Street,
Park View, and Walker's Passage. Prospect Cottage appears to have been
the principal farmhouse of Crokisnab, which was included with the Ingilby
allotments under the Great Award of 1778 (B.31). From its principal south-
facing elevation could be commanded a view towards York Place uninter-
rupted by any buildings, save for the occasional barn. For some reason, the
route between the Old Sulphur Well and St John's Chapel, as it passed
behind Prospect Cottage, was known as Cranbourne Alley (see plan 34).

Part two: 1810–1841

On 10 January 1810 Sir John Ingilby sold central Harrogate to James Franklin
for the sum of nine thousand pounds, and thereby ensured that the town's
rate of urbanisation would occur along lines determined by a new
phenomenon – the speculative developer. (T.263) James Franklin was
described as 'of Beer Ferris in Devon . . .', and nothing is known of him prior
to his extraordinary purchase in 1810. One explanation may be that Franklin
first arrived in Harrogate as a visitor, possibly for reasons of health, and that
he soon assessed the town's potential for speculative development. After
1810 he was well placed to realise his assessment. In 1814, Franklin moved
into Prospect Cottage, which he occupied with his daughter until his death
in 1826,[10] after which his daughter, Elizabeth Bailey, appears to have
emulated the local habit of letting the place during her summer absences.
An advertisement of February 1820 announced the furnished letting of 'a
very desirable summer residence called Prospect Cottage . . . 200 yards from
the Wells, at the above fashionable watering place . . .' (R.1865).

We do not know whether James Franklin was influenced by the Duchy of
Lancaster in their own careful policy for building development, but examination of the surviving land and building leases reveal that Franklin was not
only a man of vision, but also one of patience and caution. That by 1860 and
the arrival of the Victoria Park Company, central Harrogate did not consist
of a large number of architecturally impressive but land-greedy detached
properties, was largely due to the efficient Franklin's clear determination to
maximize rentals from each site. This policy may be seen in a conveyance
of 4 October 1825 (S.884) which envisaged the construction of dwelling

houses' in what later became Beulah Street; a clause to the effect that the new building must provide a four inch 'resting place' for further building material. In reality, this was the construction of terraced property by instalment. The requirement for 'resting places' was introduced on many subsequent occasions by Franklin and his executors (S.898, S.912, S.922 etc.)

The development of Chapel Street (the name can be traced back in the Court Rolls to only 1833 (S.1002)) was given considerable impetus with the building of the detached mansion Belle Vue, on part of the old Sandy Close, by Captain Thomas Thrush, RN. Captain Thrush (see plate 60) belonged to the profession which after Lord Nelson's great victory in 1805 over Napoleon at Trafalgar was regarded widely as the national salvation.

Consequently, when, in 1822, Captain Thrush published an essay on the incompatibility of Christianity and war, addressing it to the king on the occasion of his Coronation Oath, the national shock can be imagined. For three years Captain Thrush struggled with his conscience over the matter of his essay, whose findings he re-enforced by reading the scriptures in the Greek of their earliest surviving form. On 14 January 1825 Captain Thrush resigned his prized commission, to the scandal of his friends and the ridicule and hostility of society.

Captain Thrush appears to have suffered from rheumatism, and it is possible that at the onset of that disagreeable complaint, he had visited Harrogate in search of a cure. When the affliction returned in the 1820s, he and his wife moved to Harrogate, and in 1824, at the very time he was struggling with the incompatibility of Christianity and war, purchased the Chapel Street plot (S.867), which enjoyed fine views across Low Harrogate. The mansion built by Captain Thrush was capacious so that it could accommodate fee-paying guests during the spa season, the income from which supplemented the Captain's meagre pension, which indeed ceased altogether after 1825. (A.304). It was from Belle Vue that Captain Thrush published a number of polemical tracts, now in the British Library, although their subject matter and titles were hardly designed to attract mass readership, e.g.: 'Letters addressed to the Rev. J. Richardson . . . on his vindication of the Athanasian creed and the primary visitation charge of Archdeacon Wrangham, with a supplementary letter addressed to the Rev. G. S. Fabian M.A., on his sermon preached before the London Society for promoting Christianity among the Jews.'

Information about Harrogate's famous Captain may also be found in such local sources as jury lists (D.8), directories (G.18), or the poor rates lists (D.43). Captain Thrush's connection with Harrogate came to a close on 10 July 1843, when an entry in Charles Greeves' diary records, 'Captain Thrush died this morning – Monday' (O.22.19).

Land to the east of Captain Thrush's Chapel Street residence was developed by the Simpsons, and although their family is usually credited with work in the Cheltenham estate (by James Simpson), as well as by the most famous Simpson, David (who built the Duchy estate), their contribution in the development of early central Harrogate has never been acknowledged. An earlier David Simpson had, in December 1779, surrendered a parcel of land in central Harrogate half-way down Montpellier Hill on which stood 'houses and buildings' (S.301). By 1793 David Simpson, described as a 'mason' was credited owning tenements (i.e. lodging houses) in the vicinity of Parliament Street (S.417), and by 1806 he was described as 'David Simpson the elder' in a surrender by his son, 'David Simpson the younger' of a house next to that of his father, in the vicinity of the Crown

PLATE 91
By 1831 much of
Lower Parliament
Street had been
developed. The
three-storeyed
building on the left
was also known as
'Oddy's Lodgings'.
The residential
nature of Parliament
Street is clear from
this photograph.

Hotel (S.540–1). When David Simpson the elder died in 1808, his eldest son, Benjamin, inherited the property (S.605). Simpson interests in central Harrogate may be seen in surrenders of 1813 (S.644), 1817 (S.714), 1820 (S.769), 1822 (S.813), and 1834 (S.1024), all of which were on or adjacent to Parliament Street. It was, however, with an 1832 surrender further east along Chapel Street that can be recognised the role of the Simpsons in the development of central Harrogate. In this surrender, innkeeper John Harrison mortgaged his Chapel Street property to Samuel Powell, solicitor, for £450, including three newly erected cottages and a public house known as the Belle Isle Tavern, with adjoining brew-house and stables. This sale reserved rights of

access to a road to the immediate west of the tavern which connected with Chapel Street, the road being the later School Court and, in 1914, Cambridge Place (S.1045). The land at the south-eastern corner of this road, on the junction with Cambridge Street, was long held by the Simpson family, who much later in the nineteenth century built a further public house, the Ebor.[11] John Harrison's Belle Isle Tavern may be seen on an 1835 plan of Cambridge Terrace (S.1063), which also shows the Methodist School, on a site used in the 1920s for Woolworth's department store.[12] The Belle Isle, which seems to have been built by Harrison in c. 1832 (S.1078), had become the Ship Inn by November 1839 (W.11.1), by which time it was well established as the principal public house of central Harrogate. The road over which David Simpson retained right of access to Chapel Street indicates that in 1834 the road that later became Cambridge Street was little more than an unmade track.

We have alluded to the building of the Chapel Street Methodist Chapel at the junction with Beulah Street, in chapter eleven of our history, but it is necessary at this stage to examine the process of its construction in further detail, so that its place in the urbanisation (rather than the purely sacred life) of central Harrogate may be understood.

As has already been stated, Harrogate's first Methodist chapel was opened in 1796 at 20 Park Parade (see plate 92), but when the circuit came to enlarge their premises, a site (at the corner of what later became Beulah and Chapel Streets) was chosen in the newly developing locality of central Harrogate. The new chapel was built in 1824 by James Simpson, and served the Wesleyan Methodists until their largest chapel was erected in 1861–62 at the corner of Chapel Street and Cheltenham Crescent (K.32). The site of 'Beulah Chapel' had been part of James Franklin's 'Sandy Close', and had been surrendered in November 1823. A document of August 1827 contains a simple plan that shows Beulah chapel to have been a square structure, flanked to the east by a 'foot-road to High Harrogate', which later grew into Beulah Street proper. (S.915). The 725 square yard site was sold to the trustees for £95 10s. in 1827 (S.919), and the court rolls record much subsequent building activity in Chapel Street (S.953, S.958 etc.). A deed of November 1825 referred to Chapel Street as 'the road leading from the Leeds and Ripon turnpike road (Parliament Street) to the new Methodist Meeting House' (S.886), which indicates the landmark status of Simpson's newly built 'Beulah Chapel'.

Perhaps the most striking evidence for the rise of central Harrogate was the construction of a bathing house more or less at the junction of Beulah and Chapel Streets, adjacent to the new 1824 Methodist Chapel. Known as 'Clarke's Baths, the 1838 guide refers to their being kept by one J Beck: 'it has been erected some years, and contains three or four warm baths.' (G.25)

PLATE 92
Park Parade's
Methodist Chapel of
1796. The arched
carriage entrance
which led to the rear
was filled in around
1977. By the turn of
the nineteenth and
twentieth centuries,
the building had
become the studio of
the great
watercolourist
Bernard Evans.

––––

The Chapel Street Baths were minor, and only became known at the end of the nineteenth century as 'Volta House', but their true significance was as an indicator for the area's increasing urbanisation. The Chapel Street Baths were proof that visitors were frequenting central Harrogate for reasons other than the enjoyment of rural walks across the agricultural fields between High and Low Harrogate.

Within ten years of the erection of Beulah Chapel, a school followed, and the building of a schoolhouse at the junction of what later became Cambridge Street and School Court was proof that by the 1820s central Harrogate was frequented by locals for purposes other than agriculture. The plan accompanying a document of January 1835 (S.1063) shows that the new school was to be erected on land held by John Emmerson, and a contemporary agreement (X.24) reveals that the Methodists were behind the project, including Richard Ellis senior.

Central Harrogate's other important thoroughfare was James Street, although its most significant development did not occur until the later 1850s and the arrival on the scene of the Victoria Park Company. James Street seems to have grown from a foot route which ran from Low Harrogate up Montpellier Hill, across the turnpike road and along what later became James Street, Station Bridge, North Park Road, and a footpath behind the Queen's Hotel to York Place; a plan of 1813 shows this foot route crossing what later became Prospect Square and entering what later became James Street. (S.651). It so happens that 1813 was a key date in the evolution of

PLAN 33
Charles Greeves' 1821 plan of Prospect Place. The beginning of Prospect Place may be seen above the name Franklin. At centre right is the junction of Montpellier Parade and Parliament Street.

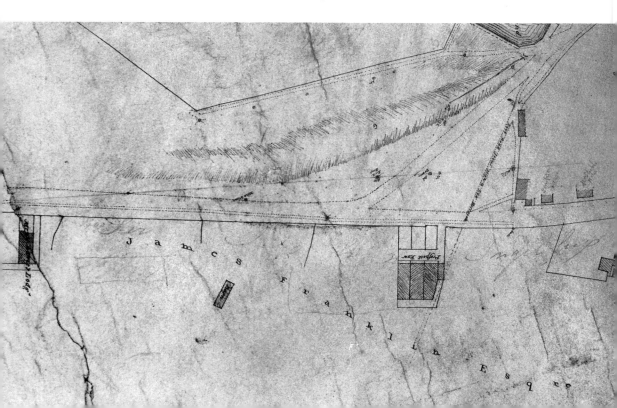

James Street, for in that year it received its first determining structure, with the building of Nicolas Carter's Prospect lodging house, which later became the Prospect Hotel, first mentioned as such in 1828 (G.18). Nicholas Carter purchased land from James Franklin for £137 which had hitherto been part of the enormous 'allotment meadow' (S.650), and by March 1815 he was mortgaging it for the sum of £300, presumably to pay the costs of building (S.679). From that moment, the infilling of the whole length between the Prospect and York Place became inevitable. The Prospect seems to have been known as 'Carter's' for a brief time, for in 1837, a meeting was held at Carter's to raise funds for the discharging of debts incurred during the great Thackwray Well case trial of that year (H.11). Similarly, the 1840 guidebook also refers to 'Carter's' in its list of inns and hotels (G.26). The 1821 Greeves map (see plan 33) shows only two properties had been constructed south of Prospect Place from Carter's (see plate 70), so urbanisation did not immediately follow Nicholas Carter's initial development.

It is, however, almost certain that the further development of Prospect Place was personally stimulated by James Franklin, who did not die until 1826 (L.100), and this is demonstrated in an advertisement of February 1820, which advised the public that 'to remedy the great inconvenience arising from the scarcity of good lodging-houses at Harrogate ... a plan is now in agitation for building five spacious lodging houses at Low Harrogate in

PLATE 62
The Brunswick
Hotel, left, with York
Place, right, ascribed
to W. P. Frith, *c.* 1833.

Prospect Row ... by way of tontine ...' (R.1865). We do not know if the handsome terrace of houses between the Prospect and Albert Street were indeed built to conform to Franklin's tontine, but they certainly conformed to his wishes. By 1849 the junction of Prospect Place with Albert Street was occupied by a further hotel, the Albion, held by one Thomas Barf (G.28), which in 1863 became the Alexandra, in honour of the new Princess of Wales. As the Albion is not listed in the 1840 visitors' handbook (G.26), it must be presumed that it was established shortly after this time, and that it was built by the Simpsons (W.11.9–11).

From the point of architecture, the most significant development on the Prospect Place/West Park strip was that between the later Albert and Raglan Streets, where James Franklin's foresight in demanding continuous terrace construction eventually produced a handsome example of urbanisation in the fashionable neo-grecian style of building. The land, again, was part of the former 'Barn Close', which in turn had been part of the medieval 'Crokesnab' (see plan 23). Work was under way by 1841 (S.1252), but subsequent sections of the terrace were not completed until about 1855, by which time the elegant neo-grecian style of the first properties had deteriorated into crude copies.

Brunswick Terrace, to the immediate south of the later Victoria Avenue development, is arguably Harrogate's finest terrace in the Georgian style of architecture, and seems to have been started in the early 1830s (S.1077) on land formerly held by James Franklin (the former Far Laith Close) and his trustees. 'Brunswick' derived from the Hanoverian succession, which ensured that after 1815, all British monarchs were also kings of Hanover,

BRUNSWICK TERRACE HARROGATE.
Published by P. Palliser, Post Office, Harrogate.
1841

15. Lord Street Liverpool

PLATE 95
West Park, 1841, with
Brunswick Terrace
on the left. The
buildings on the far
right are probably
meant to depict the
Clarendon Hotel.

until the accession of Queen Victoria in 1837. In Harrogate, the 'Brunswick' name seems to have first been used at the neighbouring Brunswick Hotel, which adopted the title in 1830 (R.2325), rather than from the Brunswick railway station, which did not open until 1848.[13] The distinction between residential and commercial properties on West Park may be seen clearly even as these words are set down at the start of the twenty-first century: by and large, those properties built up to the public highway were intended for commercial use, whereas those set back behind gardens were built for residential occupancy (see plate 95).

The 1839 Powell survey map reveals the state of infilling between Brunswick Terrace and the crossroads by Brunswick Hotel (see plan 44). South of Brunswick Terrace stood the detached property of Lion Cottage (S.1023), which seems to have been built at about the same time as Brunswick Terrace (see plate 95), and was occupied for a period by Mary Thackwray, a lodging house keeper (G.11). Immediately south of Lion Cottage began the commercial properties proper, the first of which was established in 1836,[14] and shown on the 1839 Powell map (see plan 44) as being held by Mary Thackwray. The construction of 'Thackwray's Vaults' directly on the West Park frontage may well have determined the position

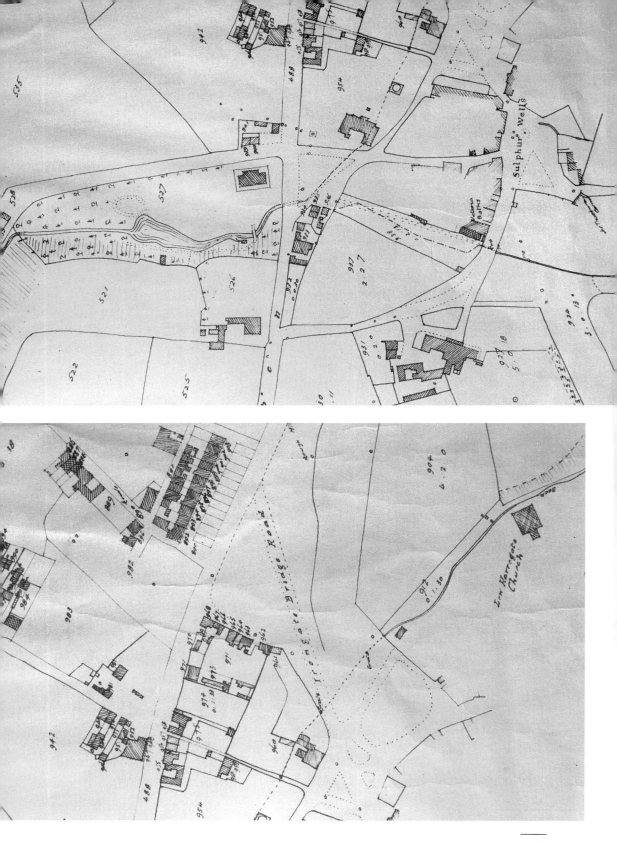

PLAN 42 (*left, top*)
Powell survey,
c. 1839. Low
Harrogate. The large
building at the centre
is the Crown, or
Montpellier Baths; a
little to the left are
the Spa Rooms at the
junction of the
modern King's and
Ripon Roads; and to
the lower right are
the buildings of the
Swan Inn.

PLAN 43 (*left, bottom*)
Powell survey,
c. 1839, Montpellier
Quarter to Prospect
Place.

PLAN 44
Powell survey,
c. 1839, West Park
and York Place.

of later West Park frontages to the south, many of which were also inns and beer houses (see plate 95).

Tower Street, so called from its clear view of the Harlow Hill Observation Tower of 1829 (A.283), seems to have been developed during the 1830s as a working-class housing street. It is not shown on the Greeves' 1821 map (see plan 33), but by the time of the 1839 Powell survey map, some seventeen or eighteen properties were marked (see plan 44). The first appearance of the name of Tower Street that we have been able to discover in the court rolls appears in records for the Court of 21 November 1838 (S.1206). The builder Riley Fortune may have been responsible for much of the Tower Street development (W.10.69), which began at West Park and edged eastward towards the site of the then un-built Albert Terrace. A mortgage of October 1840 reveals that Riley Fortune borrowed £200 from the Reverend William Barker of Cold Bath Road on security of property in Tower Street (S.1241). The Tower Street development may have been a result of the accommodation needs of the growing number of workers employed between Prospect Place and West Park, a situation that also explains the high number of inns and taverns in the locality.

The southern corner of the Tower Street junction with West Park was occupied by The Coach and Horses, which may have started life as a tavern, but which soon advertised itself as a fully fledged inn.[15] The site of the Coach and Horses is shown to be occupied in the 1839 Powell Map (see plan 44), so it is reasonable to suppose that along with its southern neighbour, the Golden Lion Inn, the construction date was around 1830. Indeed, the 1827 Brewster Sessions refer to one Thomas Wood at the Coach and Horses (A.282). The *Harrogate Advertiser* for 17 June 1847 contains a sale

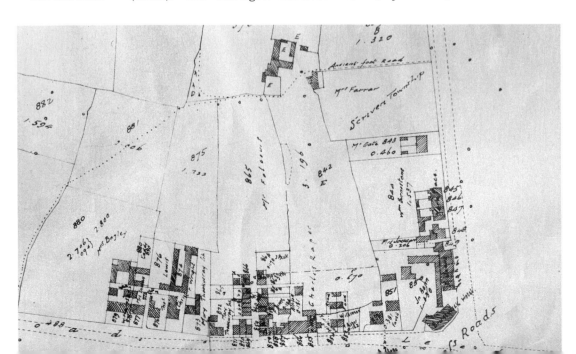

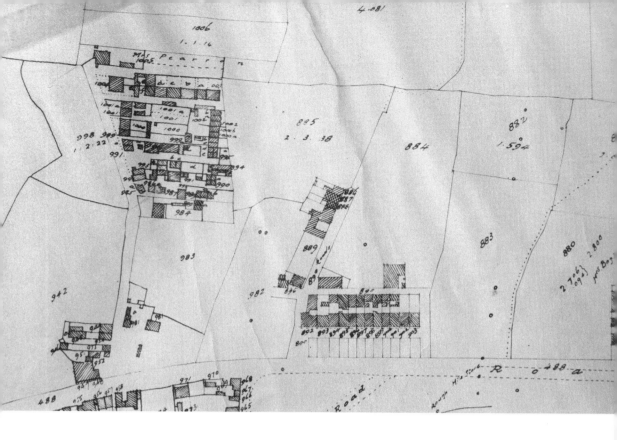

advertisement for Blenheim House 'occupied as offices by Mr Isaac Thomas Shutt', which was to be sold by auction at Thomas Sissons house, 'The Golden Lion Inn'.[16] Although the Golden Lion does not feature in the list of 'Inns & hotels, taverns & public houses' printed in the 1828 *Yorkshire Directory* (G.18), it does appear in the 1849 Torrance *Directory* (G.28), and the property is shown on the 1839 Powell survey map (see plan 44). The Golden Lion stood to the immediate north of the Commercial Hotel, which was West Park's most important inn between Tower Street and the crossroads. An enrolment of December 1839 refers to 'all that newly erected dwellinghouse ... called ... the Commercial Inn ... and ... adjoining ... Ale House ...' (S.1227), the alehouse being the Golden Lion. Something may be gleaned of the value of land at this part of the busy Leeds–Ripon turnpike by the fact that both the Commercial and its smaller neighbour were built right up to the frontage, requiring coach traffic to the Commercial to drive through an archway which separated the inn from the alehouse. The Golden Lion's landlord, Abraham Wilson, seems to have been something of an eccentric, as recounted in an amusing story by W. H. Breare (R.3138), which also names the builder of the neighbouring Commercial as being one Holdsworth.

Historian William Grainge refers to the Commercial having been 're-built' in 1838 from an earlier inn known as the Obelisk.[17] A further note in Cary's coaching itinerary of 1821 mentions that the mail coach stopped

PLAN 45
Powell survey, *c*. 1839, Central Harrogate and West Park. The line of the modern West Park and Parliament Street may be seen at the bottom, with Prospect Place at lower centre, and the beginnings of James Street at dead centre. At upper left, the growing area known as Central Harrogate formed below the junction of the modern Oxford and Beulah Streets.

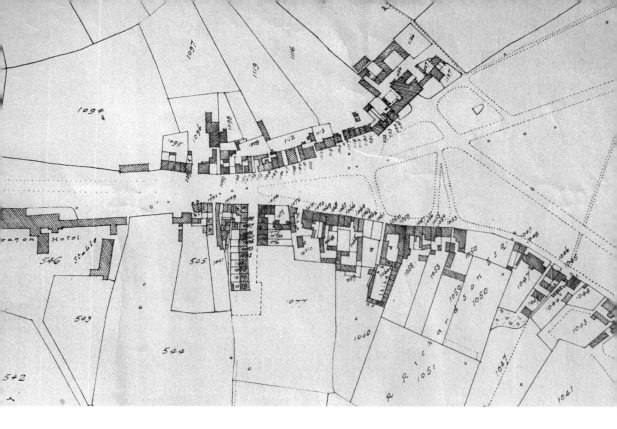

there regularly (Q.28). Indeed, the Commercial (which became the West Park Hotel in September 1899) soon established itself as an important stop on the coaching run (Q.27.30, Q.27.37). The Commercial Inn was to be the scene of a macabre event in 1848, when the abominable Stubbs sisters, Abigail and Sarah, of neighbouring Tower Street, were present at the inquest on their father, at which they were committed to trial for his murder.[18] The Bishop of Chester's transcripts for 1817 record their baptismal entries (D.55).

The ante-penultimate gap on West Park before the corner plot occupied by the hotel at the crossroads, was filled by the Clarendon Hotel, which William Grainge described as having been 'enlarged and adapted to its present use in 1847'.[19] This implies that something had stood on the site before that year, and indeed the architecture of the upper storeys was contemporary with the regency style of several properties in Cold Bath Road, Parliament Street, and above all Brunswick Terrace. The adaptation of this structure in 1847 may have been a piece of clever speculation by those who knew the proposed location of the new Brunswick railway station of 1848, but no documentary evidence survives to confirm this theory.

Between the bulkier structures of the Clarendon and Brunswick hotels, a smaller lodging-house was built in about 1829 (S.952) which was set back from the turnpike road, fronted by a large garden, and which was known as

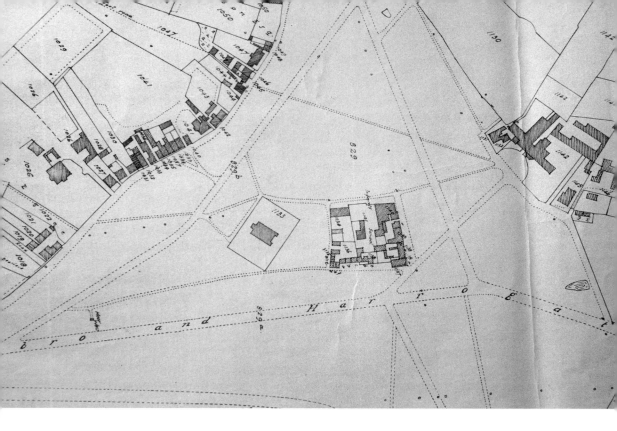

'Lancaster House'. According to an advertisement of 1830, Lancaster House had been 'fitted up in a most elegant manner', almost certainly by the Hattersleys, but following Michael Hattersley's bankruptcy and Dorothy and Joseph's term in office, Lancaster House was sold to Charles Favill or Faviel (S.1033), who retained it until the Improvement Commissioner period (S.1265).

The termination of West Park at its junction with York Place became a significant location after the Great Award of 1778 made it the first site beyond the new Stray that would be reached by visitors arriving via coaches from Leeds and the south. Although the Powell firm's documents (relating to what later became the Brunswick Hotel) trace back the title deeds to November 1797, when Samuel Morell surrendered it to Dorothy Hattersley (W.14.6), the earliest evidence for an inn or hotel at 'Harrogate Corner' does not occur until April 1815, when 'Michael Hatterley [sic] many years waiter at the Granby, begs to inform the nobility and gentry that he has opened an Hotel at the Cross Roads ... which he has fitted up in a handsome and commodious manner ...' As the Powell listing records Hattersley ownership of the site since 1797, it is likely that the inn or hotel grew from a private house, in much the same manner as the Prospect had done.

By 1817 Michael Hattersley was advertising 'two genteely furnished Lodging Houses, adjoining the hotel ... where families may provide

PLAN 47
Powell survey,
c. 1839, Church
Square and Granby.
The future North
Park Road would be
built on land to the
right of plot 1022. The
large square building
on plot 1026 was the
Park House that was
sadly demolished in
1961.

themselves, or be supplied from the hotel [with sulphur water brought from the well every morning].' Michael Hattersley's initiative did him no favours, despite his attempts to raise money through mortgages in 1816 and 1818 (W.14.6), as he was declared a bankrupt in February 1819, probably because he over-extended himself in building and improving the Brunswick (R.1800). The hotel was taken over by Dorothy and Joseph Hattersley, who employed Mr Gascoigne as landlord, who, however, crossed the Stray in 1821 to run the old Hope Tavern on Devonshire Place, which he renamed 'Gascoigne's' (R.1910).

Hattersley's Hotel was the Harrogate address of the lake poets during their 1823 visit to the spa, when Mary Wordsworth wrote of the low price of accommodation at Hattersley's Hotel (C.101), but by 1825 the party were staying at the Crown (C.101.b). The location of Hattersley's made it an ideal stopping place for stage coaches, and the timetables in class 'Q' reveal that coaches such as the 'Age' (Q.27.30), the 'Defiance' (Q.27.37), and the 'Union' (Q.28) ran from the hotel at the 'cross-roads', the arrival and departure of which provided scenes of the utmost animation. A memoir of the old coaching days in Harrogate was published in an 1874 edition of the *Barnsley Times*, possibly by a member of the Carter family,

> ... the visitors in town gathered at the [hotel's] corner, at about four o'clock, to gaze up at the Leeds Road for the distant cloud of white dust which heralded the approach of 'the Mail' [coach]. What excitement there was, and anxiety to catch the first glimpse of the leading bays, what anticipations for expected friends, and what a perennial joy was the toot of the pleasant horn ...

For the visitors, too, crammed up in the great coach, with perhaps eight more passengers atop on the roof, the rambling buildings and courtyards of Hattersley's Hotel was their first glimpse of Harrogate. Barbara Hofland described the reaction of many of the visitors

> from a Cumberland Castle I find they have slept
> where from ages to ages their ancestor's slept,
> and tis vastly amusing to see how they look,
> on the Harrogate world as a new opened book,
> where many new faces appear to delight 'em,
> but many new manners to wound and affright them.
> (C.91.0)

By 1830, Dorothy Hatttersley had retired, her hotel being taken by Abraham Huddleston, who moved up from Low Harrogate's Crescent Inn, refitting the place 'with a view to the comfort of those who may please to honour him with their favours' (R.2325). Huddleston paid £3,500 for the hotel, and also purchased the neighbouring Lancaster House on West Park, which may well have been the hotel's lodging house (W.7.3.). To mark the changes, the hotel was re-named as the Brunswick, a name which later came to be applied to the railway station opposite, and to the handsome Brunswick Terrace further north along West Park. It is not known how long Huddleston stayed at the Brunswick Hotel (see plate 93), but in 1833, William Waudby announced to the public that he had taken possession, and that 'no expense had been spared in fitting it up with good beds . . .' (R.2465) Waudby's name does not feature from this point in the hotel's deeds (W.14.6), so he must have occupied the Brunswick as landlord rather than owner, and it seems that the proprietor was the powerful Mr Benn (W.14.6), who in 1835 also bought the Granby Hotel (W.9.30). After Waudby died, his widow stayed on at the Brunswick, and was eventually married by the opportunistic workhouse master Henry Peacock (D.20.27), who in so doing became a member of one of the town's 'aristocracy' – the landlords.

York Place, between the Brunswick and the Queen Hotel properties, seems to have been largely un-built until the later 1840s, when Thomas Salt built the Royal Hotel and its neighbouring houses. The two handsome developments of Albert and Alexandra Terraces, and slightly north along what, after 1860, became Station Parade, were also constructed at this post-1842 period, and therefore do not come within the chronological scope of our book.

York Place did, however, have one development in the pre-1842 period,

PLATE 93
The Brunswick Hotel
at Harrogate corner.

which was based on land between what later became Holmstead Road and Queen Parade, and this was Shutt Hill. Although later nineteenth-century urbanisation diminished the viewer's sense of the natural geography of Shutt Hill, it is still possible to sense the locality's elevated altitude by walking along Knaresborough Road in a westerly direction from Granby corner. The attentive observer will note the sudden incline of the ground at a point before the Queen Hotel; this incline marks the beginning of Shutt Hill. The name of Shutt Hill implies a strong association with the Shutt family, and this is proved by a newspaper recollection of 1893 (R.3134), which also states that Shutt Hill covered quite an extensive area. The development of Shutt Hill as an isolated working-class community can have had little to do with the Swan Inn, as it developed well before Jonathan Shutt acquired the old Blacksmith's Arms in 1782 (R.795), and in any case it is unlikely that homes for the Swan's labour force would have been provided at a spot so distant as the land behind the Queen Hotel. It is surely more reasonable to suggest that the homesteads at Shutt Hill grew around the existence of a bequest of land for the relief of the poor. In their report of 1820 the Charity Commissioners recorded that a Mr Baxter had given the rent charge, worth twenty shillings per annum, of a two and one half acre field, for the relief of the poor of Harrogate, and that this field, once known as Small Acres but by 1820 known as 'Poor folks' close', was owned by Mary Glenton (K.27). Fifty years later, when William Grainge noted the existence of this close, it had reverted to its old name (M.208). It may be that the poor themselves had access to this field, for the production of basic foodstuffs, following the enclosure of the Forest in 1778, and that the homestead grew in turn to provide basic accommodation. There is however no direct evidence to support this theory, although the existence of a seven yard wide public right of way from York Place, down to the start of 'Poor Folks Close' (which started more or less at the later North Park Road) shows that the public were in the habit of passing this way frequently. The route, which became Homestead Road, is shown on the plan accompanying S.1035. Shutt Hill even possessed its own school (R.3140) although it is a mystery who established it, the munificent Mr Sheepshanks of Park House being a likely candidate. Shutt Hill was completely overwhelmed by the growth of Queen Parade in the 1850s and was all but obliterated by the Victorian infilling of York Place in the 1860s and 1870s, although fragments remained along Homestead Road until the 1980s.

Although the above mentioned developments in central Harrogate and along the fringes of West Park and York Place were of very real significance for the nineteenth-century urbanisation of the town, they were not as important as those on the 'King's Lands' in Low Harrogate which also occurred during the post 1810 period. As the Duchy development of the so-

called 'King's lands (allotments 170, 449, 452, 453, 464, 466, 467, 485 and 491 –
see B.31) will be considered in chapter 15, it is necessary only to observe that
until the implications of John Tolle's 1829 report had been fully absorbed by
the Duchy, the importance of the King's lands lay in ensuring that many of
the most obviously valuable sites in the town were kept free of the ill-
planned speculative building frenzy which harmed other British resorts. In
other words, the Duchy was biding its time.

Post-1810 developments in Low Harrogate were far more considerable
than in High Harrogate, and the years up to 1842 saw much growth in areas
such as Cold Bath Road, Well Hill, the Crescent and Cheltenham estates,
and Parliament Street, especially with individual inns and hotels. In Cold
Bath Road, Binns' Boarding and Lodging House was being run by Mrs
Binns, following the death of her husband, and by 1825 she was expressing
her gratitude to the public for their support (R.2130). Although her son took
over the running of the establishment in 1828 (R.2220), Mary Binns' troubles
came to a head in 1834, when she was declared a bankrupt (R.2620), and an
advertisement of 1835 shows that another son had taken over from his late
mother (R.2645). Clearly the running of an inn or hotel in nineteenth-
century Harrogate was no sinecure, as the earlier case of the Crescent Inn
has already shown. Binns' survived, and in the years following the 1841
Improvement Act, it developed further, becoming the Lancaster Hotel, and
favoured resort of Charles Dickens, who may have been attracted by the
establishment's rich coaching atmosphere (or more likely by its low prices!).
Indeed, Binns' establishment featured heavily in the coaching timetables of
the day, being Low Harrogate's equivalent of High Harrogate's Gascoigne's
Hotel on Devonshire Place. In 1839, the Binns' Hotel coaches were the Earl
of Zetland to Redcar via Ripon and Thirsk; the Celerity, which went direct
to Manchester; the Mazeppa and also the Earl of Zetland, both of which
went to Leeds (R.2945). Further down Cold Bath Road, 'at the House of Mr
Joseph Cullingworth', the Wellington Arms (see plate 47) was, in 1815, the
location for an auction of some cottages near Hattersley's Hotel (R.1640).
According to the recollections of W. H. Breare, Joseph Cullingworth had
entered the Wellington as a tenant, the oldest portion of the building having
been built for him, and the Cullingworth connection with the Wellington
was typical of that had by many Harrogate families with the town's inns and
hotels (R.3123).

The importance of the White Hart lay in it popularity with the
fashionable and wealthier members of society, and a sign of this was evident
with the post-Waterloo ball of September 1815, when the *Leeds Mercury*
reported that

we are happy to learn that Harrogate still continues to be the centre of

PLAN 48
Duchy of Lancaster's
proposed
developments, Low
Harrogate, John
Howgate's 1839 plan.
The two plots at
lower right, 'Red
Bank Crown Lands',
later became Beech
Grove.

____

Plan
OF THE GROUND
Proposed to be built upon
AT
LOW HARROGATE,
Belonging to the
Duchy Court of
LANCASTER

TO RIPON

CROWN LANDS

Exrs of the Late
Jonathan Shutt.

SWAN HOTEL

PROPOSED
BUILDING GROUND

GARDENS

7 6 5 4 3 2 1

Road 60 Ft Wide

8
9 BUILDING GROUND
10 7 6 5 4 3 2 1
11

CROWN LANDS

12 12
13 13
14 14
15 15
16 16
BUILDING 17 17
GROUND 18 18
19 19

Bath Gardens

BATHS

Old Promenade Room

New
Promenade
Room
To High

Drain

CROWN LANDS

20 25 24 23
BUILDING
26 25 24 23 22
20 21

Major Quarry

COMMON

THE LEEDS AND RIPON TURNPIKE ROAD

BATHS

Iron Gate Bridge Road

Wall

CROWN
HOTEL

Well

Water Course

WHITE HART INN

GARDEN

A

PART OF THE STRAY OR 200 ACRES

B

27
28
29
30 26
31 32
33 34 35

BUILDING GROUND

From Otley

Cold Bath Lane

The Vicar of Pannal

RED BANK

Drain

Church

CROWN LANDS

FROM LEEDS

C D

A

Scale of Chains.

fashionable attraction. Amongst the varied amusements which have of late enlivened that celebrated Watering Place, none have afforded more real satisfaction than the Ball given by the company at the White Hart last Monday night. An unusual assemblage of beauty and fashion graced the rooms on that occasion, after partaking of an elegant supper provided by the unwearied attention of Mr. Tengatt, separated at 2.00 o'clock in the morning, highly delighted with the evening's entertainments (R.1660).

One year later, Tengatt was mortgaging his White Hart for £600 (S.698), which he seems to have used in improving his property, as by the time of his retirement in 1832, the estate was clearly valuable (S.983).

The junction of Cold Bath Road with what was later known as Providence Green (eventually, the Esplanade) was formed by part of the King's lands (see plan 48), which were tenanted by one Harper, who in 1809 took a thirty-one-year lease from the Duchy, at a rent of £10 per annum. Harper not only leased a plot of 1 acre, 2 roods, 23 perches, but also a house and stables, which was almost certainly the same 'Providence Green' boarding house in which one 1893 writer claimed to have been born in 1815 (R.3140). In 1808 the Harper interest in Cold Bath Road was considerable (S.582), but the properties he occupied were scarcely commensurate with the building standards of the Duchy, and by May 1834 the Duchy Clerk wrote that the land 'is eligible for building purposes' (B.109), which eventually resulted in the construction of a

PLATE 42
Low Harrogate
c. 1815. From left to
right, the White
Hart, Old Bell, Well
Hill and Sulphur
Well.

TO BE SOLD
By Auction,
AT THE
House of Mrs. Clayton, the Bell Inn,
AT LOW-HARROGATE,
On TUESDAY, the Twenty-eighth Day of NOVEMBER 1815,

At Three o'Clock in the Afternoon, subject to such Conditions as will then be produced,

ALL THAT
Valuable Old-established
INN,

Situate at *LOW-HARROGATE*, called the *BELL INN*,

With the Coach-House, Stables, Outbuildings, two Gardens, and Croft therewith occupied, now in the Possession of MRS. CLAYTON, (except a small Part of the Building adjoining the Dwelling-House occupied by MRS. THACKWRAY, with a Piece of Ground behind the same, as now staked out.)

Also all that CLOSE of MEADOW GROUND at Low-Harrogate aforesaid, called the Beck Garth, containing three Acres or thereabouts, now in the Possession of MRS. CLAYTON, with the Blacksmith's Shop thereto adjoining and belonging, which Close is staked out and divided into convenient Lots of Building Ground, being the best adapted Situation for Building upon at Low Harrogate, great Part whereof fronting and situate very near to the Sulphur-Wells.

Also all those three CLOSES of rich MEADOW LAND, called the Intacks situated at Low-Harrogate aforesaid, adjoining southward upon Iron Gate Bridge Road, and containing together 9 Acres or thereabouts, now in the Possession of MRS. CLAYTON.

And also all those three other CLOSES of LAND, situate near Low-Harrogate aforesaid, in Cold Bath, containing together 9 Acres or thereabouts, now also in the Possession of MRS. CLAYTON.

*** *The Premises will be shewn on Application at the BELL INN, and further Particulars may be had at the Office of*

Mr. Powell, Solicitor, Knaresbrough.

WILSON, PRINTER, HIGH-STREET, KNARESBROUGH.

PLATE 59
Notice of sale, the
Old Bell Inn.

boarding house known as Briggs' Boarding House, and later as the Victoria Hotel. The point about both Harper and Mary Thackwray (widow of Joseph) was that when the Duchy came to consider the development of their Low Harrogate holdings in the later 1830s, they had to contend with the fact that some of their choicest sites already contained a few isolated buildings occupied by properly constituted tenants, which then raised the tricky matter of compensation (B.54).

The Stray fronting Providence Green was filled with a large pond, known locally as the 'fishpond', into which children were, apparently, in the habit of falling (R.3140). Also overlooked by the Crown Hotel, the Providence Green pond was used by post-boys to wash the legs of their horses, as well as being home to local families of ducks and geese, who no doubt scattered in panic as one of the huge stagecoaches rolled down Cold Bath Road, all straining leather, groaning timber, and jingling brass, to disgorge their passengers into the arms of the apron-clad, beaming landlords, who received their guests with obsequious attention. A 'Pantheon Bazaar' was also established at Providence Green by William Williams, which seems to have been a 'cabinet of curiosities and novelty shop (R.3136). Williams paid Duchy tenant Harper the sum of £20 per annum for his sub-lease (B.148).

Next to the White Hart stood the Bell Tavern (see plate 42), whose landlords from May 1786 (R.880) until *c.* 1793 were Francis and Mary Haw. In a move typical of the Harrogate landlord class, the Haws then moved to the Queen's Head (R.1570), at which the Claytons arrived as the Bell's last landlords (R.1210). In August 1810 the Bell was the destination of a letter sent by authoress Barbara Hofland to her friend James Montgomery (C.83.h). Hofland's literary rival, Lewis, mentioned the Bell, along with the Crescent, Crown, Swan and White Hart, in a verse of his *A Week at Harrogate* (C.92.d).

After William Clayton's death in 1810 (L.100), his widow Margaret (S.419) moved to a house on Well Hill (see plan with S.937) which may have been shortly after the inn's closure in 1815 (W.3.6) (see plate 59). As a coaching inn (R.1235), the Bell would have been well equipped, so there may be some truth in William Wheater's claim about the post-closure auction of its content (C.112.i), part of which included a separate billiard hall that had been dismantled from its original site (S.641) in the gardens of the Crown Hotel (at the entrance to the later Montpellier Gardens) and moved across the Stray to a new site behind the Bell (R.3129), the property of which was purchased by a Mr Bolland, who appears to have used it for commercial purposes until its demolition in c. 1846, when Royal Parade was built (W.14.2).

Important as were the Wellington, White Hart, Bell and Binns', they were all dwarfed by the Crown Hotel, which with its unrivalled position overlooking the famous Old Sulphur Well, and its glittering social position, was Low Harrogate's most prestigious place of accommodation. The Powell record of Crown mortgages shows that the Thackwray family (Joseph, William and Joseph) were assiduous in their attempts to finance improvements to their properties (W.14.9). The Thackwray improvements such as the building of the 1822 Pump Room (G.13) and Crown, or Montpellier Baths of 1833–35 (H.14), have already been considered in our seventh and eighth chapters. A fascinating recollection of the old Crown Hotel was provided by W. H. Breare in 1892, who wrote that,

> the Crown ... was an Inn of remarkable resources, and it enjoyed a brilliant connection. The best people in the land travelled in state in those days, attended by gorgeously apparelled servants, and made the Crown their temporary abode. The establishment was equipped with far greater completeness than are many important estates now [i.e. 1892]. It had its own joiners, butcher, stone mason, bakers, blacksmith, and needed little service from without ... (R.3127).

After the death of William Thackwray in 1814 (L.100), his son Joseph succeeded in the property, and it was this Thackwray who created such a stir with his 1835 attempt to create a new sulphur well within yards of the public one beneath the 1807–8 temple (see Chapter 15). Joseph Thackwray should also be remembered as the man who generously supported the building of St Mary's church (N.8), and who was acknowledged by his rivals (such as the Greeves of the Granby Hotel) to be a sound man of business. In 1835, shortly before the affair of the well, Joseph Thackwray's income from his hotel, lodging houses, posting business, and wine trade was a huge £3,000 per annum (O.21.14). Plate 49 shows the old Crown Hotel, as it was before its rebuildings of 1847 and 1870, in a view which would have been familiar to Lord Byron during his visit of 1806 (C.86.b). Another visitor to the Crown, D. W. Smith, arrived with his family in 1816 and returned in 1835, keeping detailed records of his expenses on each occasion (A.270). In 1816 Smith noted that Wednesday was the Crown's ball night, as distinct from the Dragon on Mondays, the Queen on Thursdays, and the Granby on Fridays (A.270.4).

Smith's journal contains the most detailed insight into the services and costs which were experienced by visitors to the Crown during the earlier nineteenth century, and are eminently worthy of study. Tellingly, Smith noted that whereas accommodation prices at High Harrogate used to be higher than at Low, by 1835 their prices had fallen into line with the Crown. This again demonstrates the eclipsing of High Harrogate by Low Harrogate.

Reverend James Tate frequented the Crown during his Harrogate visits between 1807 and 1836, which indicates a certain loyalty to the establishment, and also the Crown's unwavering high standard (C.80). The Crown may have been where the famed Maria Edgeworth stayed during her Harrogate visit of 1826, when she enjoyed the company of Sir Humphrey Davy (C.103). Were it not for the existence of Jane Austen, Maria Edgeworth would today be regarded as England's greatest woman novelist of the time before Mrs Gaskell and George Eliot. Maria Edgeworth's finest novel, *Belinda*, contains many references to Harrogate, its high living, and gambling, not all of which (we fear) are entirely flattering![20]

We cannot leave the Crown without re-telling William Grainge's story about Lord Byron, the poet, which appears on page 200 of his history. In the autumn of 1806, Lord Byron with his friend Miss Pigot, and his dogs, Nelson and Boatswain, took up their abode at the Crown. The shy poet and his companion always dined in the public room, but returned very soon to their private one. They lived retired, and made few acquaintances. While here his lordship met with Professor Hailstone, of Cambridge, who called on him one evening, and took him to the theatre; and sent his carriage for him another time to the Granby. The dogs of the poet had a mortal antipathy to each other, and whenever they met, a battle was the consequence, and they were only parted by thrusting poker and tongs into the mouths of each. One day. Nelson escaped out of the room without his muzzle, and going into the stable yard, fastened on the throat of a horse, from which he could not be disengaged. The stable boys ran in alarm to find Frank, the valet, who, taking one of his lordship's pistols, shot Nelson through the head, to the great regret of the poet. Byron wrote here his poem, entitled 'Ode to a beautiful Quaker'.

The Crown Hotel's farmlands seem to have been spread around the Low Harrogate basin. Allusion has already been made in our eleventh chapter to Joseph Thackwray's surrender of his lease of land in St Mary's Walk, to enable a new church to be constructed in 1825 (N.26). This field was part of

LIBRARY, HIGH-HARROGATE, Monday, September 18, 1820.

WEEKLY LIST of the COMPANY at HARROGATE.

KNARESBROUGH: PRINTED by W. LANGDALE, HIGH-STREET; and sold at LANGDALE'S LIBRARY, HIGH-HARROGATE, and at Mr. BATCHELOR'S, LOW-HARROGATE.

Names of the Company Alphabetically arranged. P. L. signifies private Lodgings.

Askew Capt. P L
Anderson Mrs. Crown
Askew Mrs & Miss, P L
Ancotts Lady, Granby
Ayton Mr, Crown
Atkinson Mr, White Hart
Andrews Mr, Mrs and 8 Misses, Queen's
Bischoff Mr T & E. Crown
Bolding Mr, Crown
Bates Mr & Mrs. Queen's
Bates Mr G. Queen's
Blackburn Mr, Queen's
Broadman Mr, Queen's
Boyd Mrs, Granby
Blacket Mrs & family, P L
Broadley Mr, Crescent
Bousfield Mr. Mrs & Miss, P. L.
Bolland Mr, Crown
Bellamy Miss, P L
Barlow Miss, P L
Bealby Mr & Mrs.
Boswell Mr. Mrs & family, P. L.
Bayley Mrs, Queen's
Belgrave Rev C, Wt Hart
Brown Miss, Queen's
Brounhill Mrs, Queen's
Browne Mr, Crown
Brooks Mr, Crescent
Barnard Mr, Granby
Booth Mr, Crescent
Barrett Mr, White Hart
Belling Mr, White Hart
Berwick Mr, Queen's
Battell Mr, Crescent
Best Mr. T. R. P L
Bower Dr. and Mrs, P L
Bancroft Miss, P L
Burgess Mr & Mrs, P L
Birmingham Mr, Dragon
Bancroft Mrs, Queen's
Bagwell Dean and Mrs, Granby
Blacket Mr, Crown
Bennet two Misses, P L
Briggs Mrs & Miss, Crown
Buckanam Mr & Mrs, Crown
Buckanam Miss, Crown
Billingham Mr, Granby
Briggs Mr, White Hart
Bray Mr & Mrs, Binns's
Blake Mrs, P L
Bayldon Mr, White Hart
Bradley Mr, White Hart
Candles Mr S & G. Crown
Campbell Rev Dr. P L
Crampton Mr, Dragon
Collett Mr, White Hart
Croker Major, Granby
Clark Mr, Granby
Craster Miss, Granby
Coates Mr, White Hart
Currie Mr, Dragon
Cheap, Mrs & family, P L
Colthurst two Misses, Crown
Carr Mr & Mrs, Wt. Hart
Cook Miss, Crown
Chapman Mr, Crown
Carr Mr G. White Hart
Cane Miss Du, Granby
Cassedy Major, Wt Hart
Crack Mr, Hotel
Crosley Mr. Hotel
Colven Mr, Crown
Collier Mr, White Hart
Coleman Mr & family, P L
Clay Mr, White Hart
Cleghorn Mrs, Granby
Courtney Mr. Mrs & family, P. L.
Cleghorn Mr. Granby

Campbell Mrs and family, P L
Clayton Miss, Queen's
Cooper Mrs & Miss, Crown
Clarke Mr, Crown
Charnock Mr, Crown
Dudgeon Miss, P L
Dowker Mr, Crown
Doncaster Miss, Wt. Hart
Dudding Miss, Crown
Dickson Col. and Miss, Dragon
Denshire Major & Mrs, Dragon
Deacon Capt. Granby
Dibbs Mr, Binns's
Delaval Lady, P L
Dalbiac Mrs & Miss, P L
Drabble Mr, Wellington
Dallas Mr, Binns's
Davenport Rev. W. Mrs and family, Dragon
Douglas Miss, Granby
Dibb Mr, Binns's
Dobson Mr, P L
Daniel Miss, Granby
Deeres Mr. Rt. Hon. Lord Crown
Dunn Capt. & Mr, Dragon
Eden Mr, Granby
Erskine Rev. Mr, Crown
Elwood Mr, Binns's
Ellice Mr & Miss, Binns's
Ellice Mrs & Miss, Binns's
Egelstone Mr, P L
Ellison Mr. Mrs & family, Granby
Evans Mr & Miss, Dragon
Foster Mr, P L
Forster Mr, Crown
Ford two Misses, P. L.
Fletchers 2 Misses, Crown
Fowler Sir J. and Lady, Crown
Flintoff Mr, P L
Fiott Miss and Miss L. Dragon
Flintoff Mr & Mrs, P L
Geidart Mr C. Crown
Gill Mr, Crown
Greenwood Mr, Wt. Hart
Goodwin Mr, White Hart
Green Mr and Mrs, Crown
Green Mr G. Crown
Gaskill Mr, Crown
Groves Mr, Crown
Gibson Mr & Mrs, Crown
Gibson Mr J T. Crown
Gibson two Misses, Crown
Green Rev. T. Wt. Hart
Greame Mr, Granby
Graham Mr & Mrs, Crescent
Graham Mr & Mrs, P L
Greaves Miss, Crown
Greener Mr, Binns's
Gibson Mrs, Binns's
Groves Mr & Mrs, P. L.
Gray Mr, Crown
Greenwood Miss, Binns's
Grape Mrs, P L
Goodwin Mr, Crescent
Goulding Mr, P L
Garforth Mr, Wellington
Hodgson Mr E. Hope
Horabon Mrs & Miss, P L
Hapburse Miss, P L
Hodgson Mr. Mrs & family, P. L.
Hamilton Mr and Mrs, White Hart
Hargrave Mr, Queen's
Haigh Mr. Mrs. & family, Granby
Hastings Mr, White Hart

Harvey Mrs, Crescent
Holroyd Mr, Crescent
Hall Mr & Miss, Wt Hart
Hewgill Rev F. Queen's
Hemingway Mr, Wellington
Holmes Mr, Binns's
Hall Mr, White Hart
Harrison Mr G E. Crown
Hall Miss, White Hart
Henson Mr & Mrs, Queen's
Hilton Miss, Queen's
Hustler Mrs, P L
Hinkley Miss, Crown
Holmes Mrs, Binns's
Henderson Mr, P. L.
Harrison Mrs and Miss, Crown
Hodgkinson Mr, Crescent
Haynes Mr, Crown
Hunter Mr, Crown
Harreman Miss, Crown
Harrison Mr & Mrs, P L
Hutchinson Lady, Granby
Hale Miss, Granby
Horaban Mrs & Miss, P L
Hand Mrs & Miss, Crescent
Hollings Mr, Crescent
Honer Mr, White Hart
Hobson Mr, P L
Hobson Miss and Miss C. Crown
Hulton Mrs, Crown
Hartley Mr. Mrs & family, Crown
Hebain Mr, Queen's
Heath Mr, Queen's
Hetheringtou Mr, Crescent
Hewson Mr, Crown
Hardy Mrs & family, Crown
Hobson Mr, Crown
Hartley Mr & Mrs, P L
Hartley two Misses, Crown
Hartleys two Mr, Crown
Hall Mr & Mrs, Wt. Hart
Jameson Mr, Crescent
Johnson Mr, Wt. Hart
Jepson Mr, White Hart
Johnson Mrs F, P L
Johnston Mr and Mrs, Queen's
Johnson Miss, P L
Johnson Mr, Wellington
Green Mr and Mrs, Crown
Jarfat Mr, Dragon
Jackson Mr, Hotel
Jameson Mr, P L
Jackson Mr H. Crescent
Kirk Mrs, P L
Kay Mr, White Hart
Kay Mr J. White Hart
King Capt. Royal Artillery Dragon
Kelly Mr E. Hotel
Kay Mr and Mrs, P L
Kenwick Mr and Mrs, P L
Kemme Miss, P L
Lodge Mr & Miss, Crown
Lodge Mr, Crown
Lambert Mr & family, P L
Lambe Mrs, Queen's
Lee Mr and Miss, Binns's
Leigh Mr & three Misses, Granby
Littledale Mr, Crown
Lally Capt. Mrs. & family, P. L.
Lucas Rev T. B. Crown
Lutwedge Mr, Crown
Lunn Miss, Crescent
Lee Mrs, Swan
Lorimer Miss, Dragon
Law Mr. Mr. & Miss, Granby

Lynam Rev. H. P. L.
Lang Mr, Binns's
Lister Mr, Crown
Lonsdale Miss. P L
Littleton Hon Mr, P. L.
Lister Mr, Crown
Lonsdale Miss. P L

Making Mr, Hotel
Marsh Mrs, P. L.
Mayor Mr and Miss,
Matthews Capt. Granby
Matthews Mr, Granby
Morwate Mr, Swan
Makins Mr, Hotel
Marsh Mrs, P L
Mayor Mr & Miss, Crescent
Murray Mr A, P L
Murray Mr Mrs & 2 Misses, Crown
Monkhouse Miss, Crown
Montgomery, Miss Dragon
Mackland Mr, Crown
Maude Mr & family, P. L.
Murray Mr, P L
Moore Mrs & three Misses, Granby
Mold Mr, Crescent
Moore Mr and Master, Queen's
Matthewman Mr and Mrs. P L
Moore four Misses, P.L.
Mussenden Mr, Granby
Mussenden Mr W. Granby
Matthews Capt. Granby
Nixon Mr, Crown
Netherwood Mr, Crescent
Norton Mr, P L
Nichols Mr, Wellington
Naylor Mr, White Hart
Norris Mr & Mrs, P. L.
Ormston Miss, P L
Oldis Mr J & T, Wt Hart
Ogden Mr & four Misses, P. L.
Ostler Mr Mrs. & F. Hotel
Oakey Mr & Mrs, Queen's
Payn Mrs, White Hart
Pollt Miss, Crown
Pea 2 Mr, Granby
Poyer Mr, Granby
Pinkney Miss, P L
Phillips Mr, P L
Pollck Mrs. & Miss J. P L
Pigney Miss, P. L.
Philips Mrs, P. L.
Prichard Mr, White Hart
Pocock Mrs & Miss. Granby
Pea Mr & Mrs, Crown
Pirson Mr A. Wt. Hart
Pearson Mr, White Hart
Puris Mrs, P. L.
Pargr Mr, Promenade
Parkinson Mr, Binns's
Paulin Mr, Swan
Parkin Mr, Dragon
Priestly Mrs, Crown
Priestly Mr, White Hart
Pearson Mr and Miss, White Hart
Pierson Mr, Queen's
Powell Mr, Mrs. & Mr G. P L
Pearson Mr, Wt. Hart
Phillipt Mr, Crown
Pulleine Mr and Mrs,
Pulleine Mr & Miss,
Peters Mr and Miss, Crown
Panther Mr, White Hart
Reeve Miss, P L
Robertson Mr, Dragon
Rothwell Mr, White Hart

Richardson Mr, Crown
Remington Mr, P L
Roberts Mr, Swan
Reynolds Mr & two Misses, Crown
Robson Mr, White Hart
Reed Miss, Queen's
Rayner Rev Mr, Wt Hart
Robinson Mr and Miss, Binns's
Ross Mrs, P. L.
Robinson Miss, P. L.
Roberts Mr. Mrs & family, P L
Ridsdale Mr, Crown
Ramsay Mr, Crescent
Remington Mr, Crown
Remington Mr T. Crown
Ramsay Mr, Granby
Ridsdale Mr, Crown
Royle Mr, Crown
Richardson Mrs & Miss, P L
Ross Mr, Crown
Ranson Mr, Crescent
Remington Miss, P L
Richardson Mr & Miss, P L
Remington Miss, P L
Ross Mr, Crown
Salmond Mr, Crown
Stewart Mr. Mrs & Miss, Crown
Smith Miss, Crown
Scholefield Mr, Wt. Hart
Stamper Mr, Queen's
Sladen Mr, Queen's
Sutton Miss, Granby
Scarff Mr. Mrs & Miss, P L
Sanday Mr, Crown
Smithson Rev T. Hope
Simpson Miss, Crescent
Shildon Mr, P L
Slates Mr, Crescent
Scarf Mr. Mrs & Miss, P L
Sanday Mr, Swan
Smithson Rev. L. Hope
Scott Mr, Crescent
Swinton Mr, P L
Speight Mr and Mrs, White Hart
Smith Mr, Dragon
Scott Miss, Hotel
Smith Mrs, Binns's
Smith Mr, P. L.
Smith Mr & Mrs, Binns's
Simpson Mrs, Crescent
Stoney Mr, Crown
Smith Mr A. White Hart
Stewart Miss E. Queen's
Scott Mr, Queen's
Sowby Mr and Mrs, Wellington
Smith Mr, Hotel
Stevenson Mrs and Miss, P. L.
Smith Miss, Crescent
Smith Miss, Queen's
Smith Mr, White Hart
Sadler Mr. Mrs & Miss, P L
Smith Mr, White Hart
Stoven Dr. Mrs. & family, P L
Stewart Mr and Mrs, Crown
Sheradan Mr & Mrs, P L
Smithson Mr, Crown
Sinclair Mr, P L
Smith Mr,
Sykes Mr. Mrs N. & family, Dragon
Scott Mr, Queen's
Sinclair Mr, P L
Schofield Miss, P L
Settle Miss, P L
Taylor Mr, White Hart
Thorpe Mr, White Hart

Turnor Rev. Mr. Mrs. and Miss, P L
Thompson Mr and Mrs, Queen's
Thompson Mr and Miss, Queen's
Torry Mr, P L
Townsend Mr, Granby
Todd Mrs & family, P. L.
Thompson Mrs and Miss, Crown
Tyne Mr, Wellington
Todd Mr R. Queen's
Taylor Mr, Binns's
Thorpe Mr, White Hart
Tenker Mr & Mrs, P L
Taylor Mr, Crown
Thornhill Leut. Col. Crown
Trebeck Rev. Mr and Mrs, Crown
Toosey Mr, Crown
Thompson Mr & Mrs, P L
Theakston Rev. Mr, P L
Tatham Mrs & Miss, P L
Tweedy Mr, Crown
Toosey Mr, Crown
Thompson Mr & Mrs, P L
Tiff Mr, Queen's
Tyas Mr, Queen's
Thorothon Miss, Granby
Townshend Mr, Granby
Urns Miss, Crown
Vacars Mr & Mrs, P L
Vicais Mr & Mrs, P L
Varley Mr, Crown
Whitfield Mr. Mrs and family, P L
Wainman Capt. Granby
Watson Mr, Granby
Wilson Mrs, Hotel
Worth Miss, Hotel
Walker Mr & Mrs, Queen's
Wainwright Mr, Queen's
Wright Mr, Crescent
Wood Mrs & family, P L
Warner Mrs & family, P L
Wood Mr, Crescent
Williamson Mr J. Wt Hart
Walwyn Major, Granby
Walton Mr, Crown
Walker Mr I. Crown
Waller Mr, Crown
Wilson Mr, Wellington
Wiggins Mr, Queen's
Wright Miss, P L
Waring Mr, Binns's
Wall Hon. Mrs, Dragon
Walker Mr, Binns's
Watson Mr, White Hart
Walker Mr, Queen's
Wood Mr, Queen's
Wainhouse Mr and Mrs, P. L.
Watson Mr & Mrs, Wt Hart
Williamson Mr J. Wt Hart
Wescombe Mr and Mrs, Granby
Ware Mr, Wellington
Williams Mr, Wellington
Wilkinson Miss E. Wt Hart
Wood Mr W. and family, P L
Woodward Miss, P L
Whitfield Mrs, Granby
Wainman Col. Granby
Weir Mrs and Miss, P L
Ward Mrs and Miss, Crown
Wamsley Mr W. Queen's
Welton Mr, Queen's
Walker Mr, Crown
Weir Mrs & Miss, P L
Young Miss, P. L.
Young Mr, Queen's

340

a larger plot leased by Thackwray from the Duchy's 'King's lands', and a document of 1837 referred to the continuing problem of Joseph Thackwray's cattle straying into the churchyard to graze (B.114). In 1829 Thackwray was also leasing a 120-acre farm from the Duchy on Irongate Bridge Road (B.308) which was clearly used to supply the Crown Hotel. His widow Mary was also recorded in 1840 holding extensive lands in the Harlow Hill/Oakdale area (B.305). The Crown's agricultural pursuits may have been practised within the immediate curtilage of the hotel, as Joseph Thackwray senior was reported as having erected a barn, in what later became Crown Place, in about 1770, a fact which was revealed at his grandson's trial in March 1837 (H.12). The Bishop Landaff recorded that a new sulphur spring had been uncovered in the digging of the barn's foundations (F.34).

The Crown was the setting for a splendid fancy dress ball in October 1828, reported by the *York Herald*, when

> ... the spacious ballroom, at the Crown Hotel, was thrown open to upwards of two hundred fashionables, amongst whom were not a few whose rank, beauty, taste, and correctness of costume had attracted notice at the brilliant festival of the preceding week ... the scene was not wanting in the usual splendid military and naval uniforms, court dresses and varieties of national costumes. Greeks and Turks, Spaniards and Egyptians mingled in most amicable alliance ... the strains of Weber animated the dancers, that here had found the enchanted ball ... the elegant quadrille and sprightly waltz succeeded each other with unabated spirit, to far beyond the witching midnight hour, when the dining room received the party to a supper equally distinguished by excellence of fare and tasteful decoration. The company separated after an evening passed in the highest gratification ... (R.2255).

The public appetite for news of Harrogate's high-life was such that the *York Herald* was obliged to print a more detailed account of the following year's fancy dress ball (R.2295).

At this point, it is worth recalling that each hotel in Harrogate provided its guests with a ball, to which friends from other inns could be invited, and it was this custom which led to the printing of 'lists of visitors', which eventually became newspapers. William Langdale (see plate 38) published a list of visitors in 1820 (R.3100), as did Pickersgill Palliser in 1834 (R.2735). In September 1836, Palliser announced that in future he would publish his list as the *Harrogate Advertiser* (R.2755), which soon developed into a fully fledged newspaper, to be joined in 1847 by Robert Ackrill's rival *Herald*. Palliser arrived in Harrogate in 1828 with only half a crown in his pocket, plus 'a good education, steady habits, and good intentions'. He set up a private school at Smithy Hill, subsequently moving to Northumberland

PLATE 38
Langdale's *Weekly List of Company*, precursor of the Harrogate newspapers.

_____

341

Place (off Chapel Street) and then to Cornwall Road. After prospering as a schoolmaster, he obtained the post of postmaster shortly before 1836, combining it with the business of bookseller and printer, and set up his printing works on Devonshire Place, in a building later to be the Spread Eagle Inn. Eventually he moved into larger premises at 31 Devonshire Place.[21] Hotels such as the Crown, Dragon and Granby played an important part in creating a market for the Georgian broadsheets which in Victoria's reign transformed themselves into newspapers, which in turn played such a role in shaping public opinion.

The back of the Crown Hotel, and its adjacent public sulphur well, were overlooked by Well Hill, which formed the high part of Promenade Square. The open public sulphur well was, of course, the square's heart, with one side formed by the rear of the Crown, the Promenade Inn (which was purchased by Thomas Humble Walker in May 1840, W.11.25)), and the Promenade Room, and the other side formed by Well Hill and the building of the old Bell Inn on the site of Royal Parade. The character of the square was changed irrevocably in the 1840s with the building of the Royal Pump Room, and Royal Parade.[22] Well Hill possessed a blacksmith's forge, located next to the start of the footpath to Bogs Field (R.3122), which was well placed for custom from the area's many visitors. Some of the other houses and their occupants of about 1820 were described in W. H. Breare's recollections (R.3122), and an enrolment of 1829 confirms that they were in use as lodging houses (S.949; see also S.937).

A little to the west of Well Hill, on the north side of Cornwall Road, stood an independent chapel known as the Rock Chapel, probably because of its location next to the common stone quarry awarded to the public in 1778 (B.31). The Rock Chapel was built in about 1821 by Mr Major Thackwray, a mason who lived on Well Hill (S.756), and who was credited with having erected the chapel especially for the Rev. T. B. Wildsmith, who was principal of the Grove House school (K.33).

The importance of Swan Road increased dramatically between 1782, when Jonathan Shutt took over the Blacksmith's Arms, turning it into the Swan Inn, and 1806, when the new Promenade Room was opened (R.1300). This process continued, and on the eve of the 1841 Harrogate Improvement Act, Swan Road was central to the development of the Duchy of Lancaster's Harrogate holdings.

In the summer of 1839 the Duchy approached their Attorney General, Mr Ellis, to ask his opinion as to a suitable person to produce a plan for the development of Duchy lands at Low Harrogate (B.47), with the result that John Howgate, who had previously been involved with the great well case of 1835–37 (W.10.39), was selected. The Duchy advised that it was not their intention themselves to build, but rather to grant building leases to suitable applicants (B.47). Howgate's proposals were based essentially on land on each side of Swan Road (see plan 48). On 26 November 1839, the Duchy's clerk, Mr Dawes Danvers, was able to reply to Howgate, advising him that his proposals had been received at the Duchy office, and that several questions had to be answered (B.49), especially with reference to existing tenants, whose isolated enclosures (e.g. such as those of Mr Thackwray or Mrs Harper) would have to be incorporated with the overall master plan.

The plan John Howgate forwarded to the Duchy on 29 October 1839 proposed the building of eleven houses on the field tenanted by Mary Thackwray (roughly bounded by the modern Swan Road, Crescent Gardens and Ripon Road, but excluding the strip on which the George Hotel was located). The first seven, and best of the houses, were to face south, with their backs to Swan Lane, thereby ensuring a capital view over the Low Harrogate basin. Four more were to face Swan Lane, from a position between Back Victoria Baths Road and Crescent Gardens, and on the west side of Swan Lane, between what later became York Road, and the existing houses on Well Hill, eight houses were planned, which however were not to end at the junction with Well Hill, but somewhat short of it, the space being filled with a further three houses which were an eastward extension of the older Well Hill properties. Finally, four more houses were planned west of Well Hill, on Cornwall Road (B.285 and plan 48). South of the above developments, Howgate divided up the square of land behind Providence Green with nine smaller plots, facing the Stray and Cold Bath Road, for 'respectable lodging houses, and shops for that immediate neighbourhood which I believe will readily be sought after and taken upon leases

for the term of ninety-nine years.' Interestingly, Howgate did not recommend the development of the Duchy's large possessions on 'Red Bank', between what later became St Mary's Walk and Otley Road, as he wished to 'avoid overstocking the market with too many lots now to be let ...' (B.285). Howgate's plan was adopted by the Duchy Court on 11 December 1839 (B.229), and one year later he recommended that the Duchy employ the young Isaac Thomas Shutt as superintendent of building (B.232). The Duchy Council offered young Shutt the fee of two per cent of the cost of each building he was required to inspect (B.63), informing him of their offer on 26 March 1841 (B.65). Shutt's task was to ensure that buildings erected on Duchy land met the high standards prescribed by the Duchy specification (B.68). All was now ready to begin the planned urbanisation of Low Harrogate.

On 27 October 1841 the Duchy Court was informed of an offer from Thomas Humble Walker that he was willing to lease lots 19, 20, 21 and 22 (at the corner of Well Hill and Swan Lane), subject to certain minor changes to Howgate's plan, and this offer was accepted (B.238), the Duchy clerk notifying the Harrogate agent of this fact on 2 November 1841 (B.158). Walker's development work evidently disturbed the older neighbouring property on Well Hill, as the following year he received a letter from the Duchy clerk, Mr F. Dawes Danvers, explaining that the Duchy could not compensate a Mrs Jackman for damage to her house resulting from Mr Walker's building works. The Duchy also reminded Mr Walker that 'great caution should be exercised in digging your foundations ...' in order to prevent damage to the mineral wells, and it was probably for this reason that Mr Walker's Swan Lane terrace was placed on an elevated plinth (B.163).

Swan Lane's central feature was the Swan Inn (see plate 51) developed successfully from the old Blacksmith's Arms after it was acquired by Jonathan Shutt in 1782 (R.795). Indeed, it is difficult to see how the Swan could have failed, save for the incompetence of its landlord, as it was not only well placed near the Old Sulphur Well – being close enough for the convenience of visitors, yet sufficiently removed from the well's malodorous fumes – but was surrounded by the King's Harrogate estates which, thanks to the Duchy, would be built only as high-class developments.

When, in September 1820, Lady Lyttleton visited Harrogate, she began her visit with accommodation at the Queen's Head, but soon moved down to Low Harrogate, where she lodged herself in a 'very tidy little room at Mr Shutt's ...'. From her south-easterly facing room, she looked out at 'a neat little flower garden, bounded by a low stone wall which divides us from a narrow road, along which pass at least a hundred foot passengers for one horseman or carriage. Young untrimmed hedge-row trees beyond, between whose stems you look upon green fields interspersed with houses, and a moving scene upon the cross roads which intersect them a little distance ...' (C.98.C). This description of the land south of Swan Lane as far as Crescent Road was to be transformed not by Thomas Humble Walker, but by George Dawson, whose later nineteenth-century developments adopted many of Howgate's 1839 proposals (B.285; see also plan 48).

One of the buildings visible in Lady Littleton's south-eastern view from the Swan Inn, was that which housed the George Inn, which seems to have been no more than a public house which a land surrender of 1815 does not even mention by name (S.686). Built on incroachment 453 (B.31), the George's landlord Henry Hopps may have been supplied by brewer Thomas Tuton (S.674), but by 1816, when Hopps sold out to innkeeper Hall Sanderson, the brewer was William Thackwray, who lent Sanderson the £400 he needed to complete the purchase (S.701). A sale of 1823 referred to the inn having a coach house and stables, in the possession of Abraham Huddleston (S.827), who later worked at the Brunswick Hotel (S.1001). The most significant date for the George Hotel was the arrival of William Barber – described as a 'waiter' – who in 1828 bought the inn for £1,290 from Hall Sanderson (S.926), and then immediately re-mortgaged it back to Sanderson for £500 (S.927), presumably to cover refurbishment costs. Barber then installed landlord W. J. Dickinson (S.941). Property adjoining the George (probably lodging houses and shops) was referred to in a surrender of February 1834 (S.1027), which also seems to have been the first recorded use of the name 'Cheltenham Place', following the discovery of the neighbouring Cheltenham spring in 1818 (F.48, F.50).

South of the George, almost overlooking the Old Sulphur Well, was the Crescent Inn (see plate 83), whose fortunes appear to have waned as those of the George waxed. Indeed, it would be tempting to equate the fall of the one with the rise of the other, were it not for the fact that this was at the time when the neighbouring Bell Inn closed, and when there was no obvious decline in visitor numbers. In 1814 Thomas Linforth junior advertised that he had entered the Crescent (R.1580), and by 1822, it was reported that the inn's daily rate of 6s. was the same as that of the Swan. The following year the Crescent was advertised as being available for leasing, which indicates that Thomas Linforth junior had, or was about to decline business (R.2010), and in 1825 there were references to the Crescent estate possessing barns, stables and coach-houses, as well as an inn (S.882), which indicates a property of some size. It is probable that the Crescent Inn had remained open after 1823, but under new management, for in 1831 and 1832, advertisements were appearing for the important coaches the 'Tally Ho' (R.2360) and the 'Prince Bluecher' (R.2430) departing from the Crescent for York. The days of the Crescent Inn were, however, numbered, for in January 1833 the entire Crescent estate was put up for sale, including garden ground, houses, the inn, cottages, and what was termed 'building land'. The newspaper advertisement referred to the Crescent being 'well adapted ... for carrying on an extensive and respectable business ...' (R.2460), but when the same advertisement was re-run in a later issue, the wording had been amended to include '... or if preferred the same might be converted into shops, lodging houses and public rooms.' (R.2470) This same advertisement mentions a valuable mineral spring in the cellar of the inn 'to which a pump has lately been added', and two more springs in the garden of a house behind the inn, one of which was a sulphur well and the other a chalybeate well called 'the Crescent', enclosed by stone pillars and a cupola. Yet another spring of 'Cheltenham Water' (i.e. chalybeate) was to be found on the piece of building ground adjacent to the inn (R.2470). This reference to the Crescent cupola was repeated in 1834 (S.1053), so it does not appear to be a mistake, although no likeness of the Crescent cupola is known to us. Moreover, the Crescent cupola was not the same as the pump-room erected over the old Leamington Well by the new proprietor, Thomas Humble Walker, who was credited in 1838 with having 'erected a neat pump room in front of his house adjoining the road leading to the Old Sulphur Well' (G.24) (see plate 83 on page 115). A further guidebook of 1838 announced that the Crescent had ceased to be occupied as a hotel about two years ago: 'it is now called Northumberland House, and is occupied by Mr T. H. Walker, wine and spirit merchant, adjoining whose warehouse is the pump room, containing the above named [i.e. Crescent] spring.' (G.24) There is an element of confusion in these statements. The original 1783 Crescent Inn Well of sulphur plus a small quantity of iron water, was discovered by the 'master of the Half Moon ... in the field behind his house' (F.32), whereas the second well of strong saline water was found in the inn's cellar (in 1790, according to Grainge[23]). It was this second spring which was nick-named the 'Leamington spring', because of its similarity to the famous saline well at Royal Leamington Spa, which had been known since 1480.[24] The official Edwardian plans[25] of central Harrogate's mineral water piping network show that only two of the mineral wells from the former Crescent estate were incorporated in the system. One of them, the furthest away from the site of the former inn, is located directly behind the former Promenade Room, on a site which in 1783 was a field behind what was then called the Half Moon Inn. The second well is shown to be on a site which formerly had been within the curtilage of the inn, i.e. within the cellar, and although the Edwardian plan names this well, confusingly, the old Crescent Well, it was in fact the Leamington Well. These facts show that the well beneath the 'cupola' was the original 'Old' Crescent Well, and the well found within the

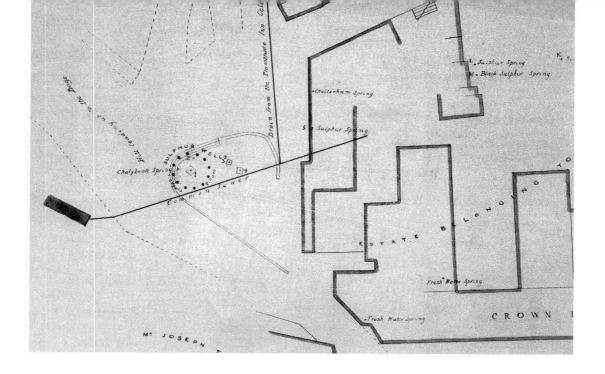

The Thackwray well
case plan, *c.* 1837. The
buildings at the
centre were
demolished by
George Dawson to
make way for Crown
Place. The corner of
the Promenade Inn
may be seen at top
centre.

former inn was the original Leamington Well. No less an authority than Dr
Granville, in his monumental 1841 study of British spas, noted that on the
occasion of his Harrogate visit, probably during the late 1830s the Crescent
Old Well was in a state of 'utter dilapidation and neglect', whereas the
Leamington Well 'now called Walker's strong saline spring' could be
obtained by pump in a small room adjoining Mr Walker's premises in
Northumberland House (F.58). Plate 83 shows the Crescent Inn, with Mr
Walker's pump room of *c.* 1838 adjoining to the right. The map used in the
1837 well case confirms this identification (see plan 39). Although the
Crescent must have closed as an inn by about 1833, it seems to have re-
opened by 1848, as it is listed in a guidebook as being run by James Slater
(G.28). We have dealt at length with the Crescent, as its history demonstrates that the success or failure of an inn was not determined solely by its
location, or possession of an important mineral well. Nevertheless, it was a
mineral well which was responsible for the development of what came to
be Harrogate's most important town centre site: the Spa Rooms estate.

   To the east of Ripon Road, slightly south-east of the George Hotel, lay the
open fields which had been allotments 401 and 402 in the Great Award of
1778, and which encompassed virtually all of the land which in the twentieth
century came to be filled with the Harrogate International Centre (B.31).
One of these fields, near the junction of Ripon Road and Walker Lane,
possessed a couple of chalybeate wells, discovered in 1818 (F.60). These
lands were held by John Oddy, who leased them for farming use (S.544), but
within months of the discovery of the new wells Oddy bought back

possession (S.747), and also extended his land holdings in the locality of the George Inn (S.806). He then bided his time, allowing the public to drink at his wells for half-a-crown a week (R.3120). Oddy seems to have a man of foresight and substance, and like James Franklin before and George Dawson after, he had faith in the town, and knew when was the best time to exploit his holdings. In 1829 Oddy agreed to sell allotments 401 and 402, then termed part of the Portugal House Estate (Sf.8), to Thomas Williams (W.7.13), a wine and spirit merchant, formerly of London (S.957), who lived at Beckwith Lodge Farm, due west of Harlow Hill (S.963). Soon afterwards, Williams died (S.977, W.7.9), leaving his estates to the son of his sister, Ann Wood, along with an unusual bequest, which was that the young John would inherit his uncle's estates subject to his agreeing to pay certain annual sums to his mother, and that he would adopt the surname of Williams. The petition, drafted by Samuel Powell (W.8.28) was forwarded to King William IV, whose consent was received on 26 February 1833 (S.1007). Young John Wood, now Williams, was now able to exploit his inheritance (W.7.28), but not before taking action against Mr Benn of the Granby Hotel, for 'defamatory language he had used regarding your house-keeper and requiring an apology.' (W.8.28)

John Williams' first activity in Harrogate seems to have been the building of the Victoria Baths, on a site next to the Promenade Room, and only four months after receiving authority to change his surname (and presumably coming into his inheritance), he bought the land through Samuel Powell for six hundred and fifteen pounds (S.e.26), after it had been advertised for sale by auction along with the rest of the Crescent estate (R.2460). John Williams then proceeded to borrow money in a manner which showed either great faith in his business ability, or great recklessness. Powell's day books noted the borrowings: '27 February 1833, £1,500 to complete purchase of Crescent Garden and erect Baths ...' '[date incomplete] 1834 ... a further sum of £1,000 to complete the Baths'; 'September 1835, ... £1,500 ...'; '24 December 1835, ... £1,000 ...'; 'August 1836 ... £500 ...' (W.8.28). Other entries relating to Williams' Spa Rooms development were also recorded by Powells (e.g. W.2.6). The pattern of spa development in Harrogate at this time has already been considered in our eighth chapter, but from the point of the town's urban growth in the 1830s, it is useful to note that the order of building was Williams' Victoria Baths, Thackwray's Crown or Montpellier Baths, and Williams' Spa Rooms.

In a memoir of 1895, a writer recorded that, 'it was in a spirit of rivalry that the new Spa Rooms were built, and, I understand, they about ruined the promoter, who, I am told, carted all his stone from Leeds ...' (R.3123) Although this was clearly hearsay, it seems nevertheless to have been true, as was indicated by the record of John Williams' borrowings. The rivalry

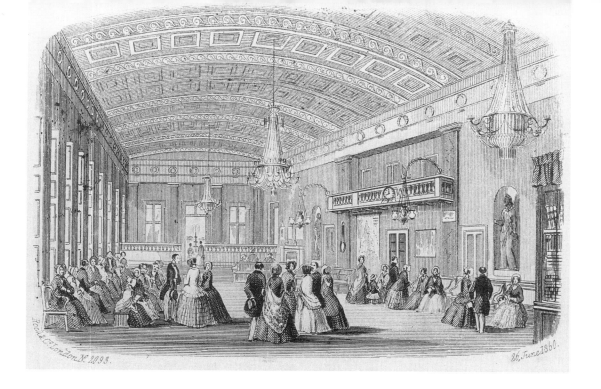

PLATE 69
The interior of the
Spa Rooms, looking
towards the east.
The windows on the
left admitted
northern light, and
the windowless wall
at right included a
musicians' gallery.

can only have been between John Williams and Joseph Thackwray, and may account for the splendid architectural character of the buildings they erected respectively, which were put up at the height of the provincial fashion for the neo-classic. If this rivalry was indeed a battle, then John Williams was the victor, as his Spa Rooms may be credited with being the most magnificent public building erected in Harrogate (see plate 68). The original title of the 'Royal Promenade and Cheltenham Pump Room' (R.2695), provides insight as to the building's purpose and function. 'Royal' denoted the desire of promoter Williams to establish his building at the summit of the town's facilities. So far as is known Williams had no authority for the use of the Royal prefix; 'Promenade' indicated that the building enabled its users to practise the social activity of promenading, and all the term denoted; 'Cheltenham' reminded the visitor that the waters of the estate were similar to the famous saline chalybeate wells of that town (although if Dr Granville is to be believed, the Cheltenham spa was then in decline[26]); 'pump room' told the public that they could drink the estate's mineral waters within the building in a properly equipped pump room. It was only later in the nineteenth century, after the estate was acquired by the Corporation in 1897 that the short title of 'Spa Rooms' was adopted.

John Williams' 'Spa Rooms' was designed by the same Clark who had built the Victoria Baths, across the Ripon Road and behind the Crescent Inn. Architect John Clark 'son of modern Athens', who died in May 1857, was a Scotsman, who practised in Bradford, Doncaster, Harrogate, and –

principally – in Leeds.[27] An exponent of the neo-classical revival, Clark lavished great care on client Williams' new Spa Rooms. Built by Iredale & Co. (who later built the Royal Pump Room) (W.8.41) of beautiful massy stone, the Spa Rooms' main space was a long saloon, illumined on the north side by a range of windows, battered in the Grecian style. This great space had a vaulted coffered roof, from which hung a range of magnificent chandeliers, and an elevated platform rose at the eastern wall, from which glazed doors admitted guests on to the rear terrace and gardens (see plate 69). A musicians' gallery formed a centrepiece for the south internal façade. The western front of the Spa Rooms contained a pump room, from which could be dispensed the estate's well waters. But Clark reserved the most spectacular architectural effect for the building's main, western façade, in the form of a mighty hexastyle Doric portico, between whose exquisitely fluted columns passed generations of Harrogate visitors, from Charles Dickens to Edward Elgar.

Readers of the *York Herald* for 1 August 1835 were advised that

> the period is now fast approaching when the numerous visitors to this deservedly celebrated and fashionable Watering Place, will have an opportunity of witnessing the grandest scene ever witnessed in Harrogate, or its vicinity – the opening of the Royal Promenade. The style of this superb edifice, whether we regard its external or its internal structure, is pre-eminently superior to any similar erection in the neighbourhood, having been built at an expense of several thousand pounds, and being capable of accommodating upwards of five hundred persons … (R.2695).

The opening of the 'Royal Promenade' took place on Friday 21 and Saturday 22 August 1835, the former day being the birthday of King William IV, when the new building was packed with society 'fashionables'. During the king's birthday, displays of archery were mounted in the gardens, and a glittering ball was held that evening, at which the band of the Scots' Greys performed alongside a celebrated quadrille band; both groups 'displayed some of their finest specimens of musical talent'. On the following evening, the gardens and pleasure grounds were 'elegantly illuminated with variegated lamps, after the style of Vauxhall Gardens in London', and Professor Southby from Vauxhall arranged an elaborate exhibition of fireworks (R.2705). So successful were the opening festivities that in time-honoured fashion, the proprietor was obliged to repeat them with 'another splendid public ball to be held on the evening of Thursday 3rd September' (R.2715).

The Spa Rooms gave Harrogate a social amenity that was the equal of any in the kingdom, and a good many abroad. It also determined the future development of the whole site at the junction of the later King's and Ripon

Roads. Within its noble walls, the elite of the age amused themselves and performed their gilded rituals, probably without any thought or knowledge of its progenitor, John Williams, who did not long survive his creation. We have found no notice or obituary for the man to whom Harrogate owed so much. The Harrogate press had closed at the time of his death, and neither the York nor Leeds newspapers carried any tribute. It is our opinion that John Williams' death may in part have been induced by stress resulting from financial worries caused by the building and equipping of the Spa Rooms (W.8.36). Certainly Samuel Powell's day books noted on 2 June 1837 that Williams was ill, and, more ominously, on 21 September, that he had attended John Williams 'upon the matter of his Will ...' (W.8.42). On 9 November, Mr Gordon, the Spa Rooms' tenant, summoned Samuel Powell, in order to confer with him about the course of action to be taken following Mr Williams' death (W.8.44), which had occurred five days earlier (L.100), although his will was not entered in the court rolls until March 1839 (S.1210). The Powells' account for dealing with the late John Williams' affairs was not closed until before Christmas 1839, by which time the estate owed Powells some £357 (W.8.52).

In one respect, the Spa Rooms provided Parliament Street with a real focal point and purpose, as before 1835 it had been nothing more than an urbanised section of the Leeds to Ripon turnpike road. Parliament Street's name seems to have originated with the great parliamentary reform act of 1832, which extended the electoral franchise, and abolished some pocket and rotten boroughs. The map which accompanied the great enclosure award of 1778 depicted no structures on the eastern side, comprising lands awarded to the Ingilby family (see plan 13). However, by the time of the big Greeves

PLATE 41
John Field's drawing of Low Harrogate, c. 1820, showing the White Hart on the left and Hopewell House on the right. Hopewell House later became the site of Betty's café.

PLATE 71
Prospect Place, right,
Parliament Street,
centre, Montpellier
Parade, left,
attributed to
W. P. Frith, *c*. 1833.

survey of 1821 (see plan 34), the eastern junction with Cranbourne Alley (later incorporated with Chapel, subsequently Oxford Street) had been flanked with buildings on both the north and south sides. The western side of Parliament Street had also received buildings at the junction of the Ginnell, those to the north being held by Mrs Dearlove as lodgings, and those to the south by Miss Thackray (sic?) also as lodgings. The old Somerset Hotel and lodging house may also be discerned, and the junction with the latter named Montpellier Parade was also filled by Hopewell House, which featured in a Powell schedule of 1828, but which may only have been built as late as 1831 (W.14.10). Certainly it was an address in August 1832, as Samuel Powell recorded that he had met resident Mary Simpson there, to receive on her behalf some property from James Simpson (W.7.33); indeed, it is possible that James Simpson was the builder of Hopewell House, which may be seen in the remarkable drawing alleged to be by the young Frith (see plate 71). Hopewell House was of particular importance in the development of Harrogate as it determined clearly the junction of two very important public thoroughfares, and was also the first building on the left since Spacey Houses to be seen by visitors arriving in Harrogate.

The origin of the Somerset Hotel is unclear, although a newspaper reference suggests it may have been connected with the Pullan family.[28] It is probable that the neighbouring property at number seven (modern numbering) was the original Somerset lodging house, which at the time of writing was the oldest surviving property in Parliament Street, the architecture of which typified the period from 1770 to 1810, other examples of which existed in Cold Bath Road, West Park and Parliament Street itself.

The development of the eastern side of Parliament Street seems to have taken off in the 1820s and 1830s. Parliament Street's northern section, from Cranbourne Alley to Walker Road, received a significant boost in 1828, when Richard Kay and William Matterson (sometimes Masterson) purchased a 631 square yard plot (S.922) from James Franklin's trustees. The surrender included the standard Franklin clause about any building erected to the south (i.e. up Parliament Street) having a 'resting place' for future southern developments. This surrender also made reference to an intended new road already staked out to the east of the turnpike road, which is the first known allusion to what later became Back-Parliament, or Union Street. A building surrender of the following month referred to the site's having 'buildings ... thereupon ... lately erected ...' (S.923). The residential nature of Parliament Street at this time may be seen in a mortgage surrender of 1816 (S.697), which referred to 'dwelling-houses', a term which was again used when the property was re-mortgaged in 1827 (S.908). However, as Low Harrogate developed, Parliament Street's commercial life began to grow, as was seen with the 1834 opening of a business by ironmonger England, whose Parliament Street shop soon became a landmark.[29]

Development in Harrogate from 1810 to 1841 was not restricted to the low and central parts to the town, and although High Harrogate experienced a lesser rate of urbanisation, that rate was still significant, and we shall now consider this matter before bringing our chapter to its conclusion. Before

the central Harrogate railway link crossed Skipton Road shortly after 1860, the term High Harrogate was applied to the whole of 'World's End Road' up to the inn at the corner of Bilton Lane, which hostelry was then known as the New Inn, certainly by 1819. At this time, the New Inn included a stable, a barn, 'other outbuildings', and 'all that cottage house adjoining' (S.760), being a development that was probably typical of the area between High Harrogate and old Bilton. Across World's End Road, the estate of Peter Dalby occupied the large corner site at the junction of what later became Skipton and King's Roads, containing several buildings, including a dwelling house, a blacksmithy, and orchard and a joiner's shop (S.1066). It was the southern section of this estate that eventually became Smithy Hill, and which in October 1821 saw the opening of the Congregationalists' 'Cross Chapel', which ten years later was acquired by the Anglicans and converted into a National School (K.33). Smithy Hill faced east towards the old 'World's End', directly opposite across Skipton Road (see plate 72).

The World's End seems to have been converted into a residence before the 1780s (S.342), and indeed by 1758, the *York Courant* was advertising 'the late well-accustomed Inn ... now rebuilt in the modern taste ...' (R.70). By 1807 the World's End had been renamed 'Grove House', and converted for use as a school under the direction of Mrs Addison (R.1375). It was this establishment that was taken in 1809 by Barbara Hofland, the future celebrated authoress of *A Season at Harrogate*. (C.83.c). Grove House had been rented by Barbara Hofland's predecessor, Mrs Addison, from Dr James Adair, who was a close friend of poet Robert Burns, and after Adair's death in 1801 (A.249) it passed to his two sons, James and Charles, who cleared a debt of £250 in the process (S.702). Grove House was sold in 1819 for £2,200 (S.772), and shortly afterwards (in 1824) it passed into the hands of wealthy landowner John Greenwood of Swarcliffe Hall (S.863). Ten years later Grove House (see plate 72) was being rented as a lodging house (R.2560), and by 1837, as a school (R.2780), and this mixed usage continued until the 1880s, when Grove House was acquired by its most famous owner, Samson Fox.[30]

Probably the most important building in the northern part of High Harrogate was the Dragon Hotel (see plate 18). Indeed there were times when the Dragon could fairly claim to be the most important building in the whole town! When we last considered the Dragon in the Napoleonic era, it had been the seat of Harrogate's post office, but this role was really incidental to that of being one of the great spa hotels of England. Let Henry Curling's famous description be related:

> What scenes of life have we not beheld at Harrowgate! What days of romance, and nights of revelry and excitement have we not passed at the far-famed Dragon, even a quarter of a century back, where ... were

assembled half the fashion and beauty of the Kingdom; where the great sporting men of the day met; where mothers trotted out their daughters in all their charms, ... where fortunes were won by the turn-up of a card by old dowagers, whilst their radiant and exquisite daughters lost their hearts to some lord of sash and epaulette in the dance. The Dragon ... was ... more like some nobleman's seat, where the elite of the world of fashion had been invited to spend the summer months. A constant succession of guests were continually arriving and departing, and there were personages whose names were familiar amongst the aristocracy of the land ... old Goodlad was host of the Green Dragon, during whose administration it was ... impossible for a parvenue, or a party without four horses and liveried attendants to match, to gain a footing at the hotel ... the Dragon was the house for those who came to seek for pleasure and amusement ... high play was constantly resorted to ... there they sat, hour after hour ... some dozen tables ... filled with ... the most celebrated sporting characters of that day, and perhaps the most determined amongst the gentlemen gamblers in England ... the road before the terrace of the Dragon presented a most animated scene, being filled after breakfast with gay equipages – fours-in-hand, curricles, and tandems, whilst whole bevies of ladies and attendant cavaliers were seen mounting their palfreys to excursionise to the various places of interest in the neighbourhood ... (C.86).

The Dragon was known to Lord Byron (C.88.b) and Lawrence Sterne (C.41.a), and countless other celebrities, and was, as we have already observed, nicknamed 'the House of Commons' (C.75). 'Old Goodlad' seems to have 'entered' the Dragon in about 1803 (R.1160), but it is possible that he had worked there for some years previous to this (A.225). Joseph Goodlad may well have been responsible for maintaining the establishment's eminence, and following his death in 1809 (L.100) his widow tried to carry on the business (R.1515). A reference in May 1816 to the Dragon's sale by auction indicates that she had continued for at least five years (R.1675). The sale announcement referred to the neighbouring Dragon Lodging House (see plate 20), and fifty acres of land, all of which indicates that the Dragon was an establishment of some size. Sadly Widow Goodlad's attempts to maintain the business did not succeed, as not only did the auction fail to produce a buyer, but an advertisement of 8 June 1816 shows that the widow then attempted to carry on herself (R.1685), the outcome being that by December she was declared a bankrupt (R.1710). Such was the Dragon's fame, with so good a potential for return, that it was soon taken by Thomas Ripley, a former head waiter to the Thackwrays (R.1725).

Ripley's management of the Dragon Hotel succeeded so well that by 1819 the *York Herald* reported that, 'the Dragon has lately been obliged to reject several families *with carriages* ...' A description from this time says it was

> a large rambling structure, the extensive basement [i.e. ground floor] consisting of an entrance hall; a bar; an immense kitchen; reception rooms of all sorts and sizes; 'parlours', rejoicing in names such as 'the Green', 'the George', 'the Angel', 'the Bear', etc., together with a ball-room of enormous length, where the visitors of the three great hotels of the day – the Granby ... the Queen's Head and the Crown, gathered frequently to trip the light-fantastic toe ... here, I fancy I see Dr Smollett, the novelist, with his bright eyes twinkling all agog, Thomas Pennant, the great English naturalist ... Sarah, the famous Duchess of Marl-borough playing cards in a cost corner, stern, dour-faced Lord Clive, the conqueror of India, who visited Harrogate then ... at one time, lovely gardens were attached to the hotel, and charming fields stretched away beyond to Low Harrogate, so that with the wild common in front, and a beautiful prospect behind, visitors were never at a loss for a pleasant promenade and lovely scenery ... but these were the palmy days of High Harrogate, and the Dragon flourished in those palmy days ... (A.303).

The great artist, William Powell Frith, spent his boyhood at the Dragon, when his parents moved to Harrogate from Aldfield in about 1826, and took over the hotel (C.99.b). It was at the Dragon, in about 1831, that Frith's artistic skills were discovered (C.99.d) and before he left Harrogate for London in March 1835 (C.99.f). In his autobiography, Frith mentioned that some of his early drawings had been displayed around the town, and that a selection had been hung on the walls of the Granby Hotel (C.99.g). For many years these early Frith works were thought to be lost, but in 1937 a collection of twelve drawings, alleged to be by Frith was presented to Harrogate Corporation. The unsigned drawings, although undated, depict Harrogate street scenes in about 1833, and are entirely consistent with the Harrogate of Frith's youth.[31] Their reproduction in this book provides valuable information as to the appearance of Harrogate in the early years of William IV.

In 1833 the Dragon staged a great coup by obtaining the services of the famous violinist Paganini, the most celebrated instrumentalist of his day. Paganini was no stranger to Yorkshire, having performed at Leeds in January 1832,[32] but his special appearance in Harrogate in September 1833 was indeed a unique occasion. A newspaper report described the event: 'On Saturday evening last, Mr Watson [the promoter?] gave a concert in the Ball-room of the Dragon Hotel, Harrogate, at which Paganini was the principal attrac-tion ... praise would be superfluous ... we have never witnessed him in greater force ... the room was crowded to excess, so much so that the signor seemed to suffer greatly from the heat during his performance ...' (R.2520).

It is highly unlikely that such a celebrity as Paganini was accommodated anywhere other than in Dragon lodging house, where he could be cosseted by Thomas Frith, the landlord, away from the curiosity of the Dragon's other guests. Dragon lodgings was a handsome detached mansion south of the Dragon facing Skipton Road, which was in existence by 1790 (S.375) and which had probably been built around 1750. In earlier times, Dragon lodgings may also have been the home of the Liddle family, who kept the Dragon in 1764, and who were reputed to have been recipients of the Dunmow fitch. This was a prize consisting of a whole side of bacon, awarded to a married couple who swore an oath to the effect that they had passed an entire year without brawling, quarrels or ill-words. The Liddles affirmed that they had spent not one, but seventeen years of wedded bliss, in consequence of which they not only won the side of bacon, but also the admiration of the 'gentlemen of the neighbourhood', who contributed extra dishes for a banquet in honour of such 'conjugal felicity' (A.234).

Before the mid-1870s, when Richard Ellis built East Parade as an extension of Westmoreland Street, High Harrogate's only road links with Low Harrogate were those via Skipton Road and King's Road, or York Place and West Park (or after 1860, Victoria Avenue). Westmoreland Street is referred to in a surrender of 1833 as 'a new street called Westmoreland Street ...' (S.1012), which may have developed from 'Westmoreland Garth' (S.962), and it is tempting to suggest that the Westmoreland association derived from either William Westmoreland, who was keeper of the St John's Well (A.301) and who had property in High Harrogate (S.345), or the earls of Westmorland. The building of Westmoreland Street was clearly well under way by 1833 (S.1022, R.2590), much of it connected with the landholdings of the Thackwray family, and indeed the sheer volume of Thackwray developments entered in the court rolls during the later 1830s led to our reluctant decision to exclude them from Class S.

Regent Parade was all but fully built up by the time of the 1839 Powell survey (see plan 46), the name being adopted some time soon after 1811, as was Devonshire Place opposite, which contained many commercial properties. Some of the businesses that established themselves on Regent Parade are named in Hofland's *Season at Harrogate* (C.91.z) and in Lewis's *A Week at Harrogate* (C.92.k–m), most of which were to be found on Regent Parade and at Low Harrogate's Royal Parade. Fattorini, the celebrated jeweller set up shop at both locations, starting in 1831 at 14 Regent Parade, with his 'oriental lounge',[33] which appears to have soon established itself with discerning visitors, in much the same manner as Hargrove's lending library had done.

Devonshire Place's largest building was the former Salutation Inn (see plate 80), which by 1803 was known as the Hope Tavern, when it was held by George Life and his son John (R.1180). Tragically, John Life was killed in 1804, when he was struck by the pole of a chaise (R.1220), and by 1806 George was bankrupt (R.1355). The Hope was then taken by George Burnand (R.1380) who was charging his guests half a guinea a week, which although expensive by national standards, was advertised as being 'lower than any other house in Harrogate' (R.1455). An interesting advertisement of 1813 refers to the inn having 'bath-rooms', which almost certainly implies rooms for batheing in mineral water imported from the town's wells (R.1520). One of the Hope's greatest innovations occurred in 1815, when a separate wine vault – also known locally as a wine 'safe' – was built behind the main building. This was a massively constructed stone box, with typical 'bonded warehouse' windows on the side facing the Hope, and more open windows on the side facing the lane, security being maintained by an internal dividing wall. An advertisement in the *York Herald* on 15 July 1815 announced that the Hope's proprietor had 'opened a wine vault, where the choicest wines may be had on liberal terms' (R.1645), presumably from the half of the building that had been fitted up as a shop.[34] Another advertisement of 11 May 1816 notified visitors to Harrogate that their 'wine vault and porter warehouse' was able to supply 'the choicest of wines . . . and best London porter.' (R.1680)

The association of the Gascoinge family and the Hope began in about 1820, when John Turner Gascoigne purchased the establishment from bankrupt Michael Hattersley (S.792), at whose crossroads hotel he had previously worked as landlord (R.910). It was at this time that the Hope was re-named 'Gascoigne's', being at the peak of its fame as a coaching inn. At this time, Gascoigne's probably looked much as depicted in the Frith drawing of about 1833 (see plate 80) with a central gable flanked by two wings, but the building's antiquity is betrayed by the irregularity of the fenestration and proportions of the wings, with another clue provided in the carriage road which crosses the Stray from the former Salutation building until the junction with York Place.

Important as was the above establishment, it never reached the status of the Dragon, the Queen's Head, Low Harrogate's Crown, or above all its neighbour to the south-east, the lordly Granby. So renowned was the Granby that when in the later nineteenth century Improvement Commissioner Richard Ellis was making the case for Harrogate's incorporation as a borough, and drawing a comparison between the changed times of Harrogate then and Harrogate now (i.e. 1883) he referred to the fact that times had changed from those when visitors came to the Granby with grand equipages and four horses.[35] Equally, the opponents of incorporation urged their case by reporting that the Granby was experiencing hard times, and that the seeking of incorporation was therefore inappropriate![36] The hotel's nickname said it all; whereas the Queen was the 'Manchester Warehouse' (popular with those in 'trade'), the Crown was 'the hospital' (popular with genuine invalids taking the sulphur water cure), the Dragon was the 'House of Commons' (popular with the fast-talking, high-living sporty set, the military and celebrities), the Granby was 'the House of Lords', frequented by the higher echelons of society (C.75.a).

In September 1801 the landlord of the Granby was reported as paying the owner three hundred and sixty-five guineas for the privilege of renting the hotel, including its forty acres of adjoining farmland, and that during the season the daily receipts could be as much as sixty pounds per day (C.75.d). Granby staff were reputed to earn fabulous sums, and indeed one of them, Michael Hattersley, did so well that in 1815 he was able to open his own hotel at the crossroads (which later became Brunswick, then Prince of Wales' corner) (R.1625). It was ironic that in 1820 and 1821 Hattersley's bankruptcy was discussed at a meeting of his creditors in the Granby (S.787). At this time the Granby (see plate 81) was still held by John Greeves, but in 1824 he decided to retire, and an advertisement was placed in public places throughout the country. Since 1823 the Granby had been leased to Jonathan Benn, who was described in the advert as being 'a most eligible and respectable tenant ... [who paid a] ... low rent of £400 per annum ...' (A.277). Benn eventually was to buy the Granby outright, but in 1824 he was content to remain as a tenant.

The Granby's notice of sale described it as 'one of the first inns in the

United Kingdom' with full printed particulars being available at the principal inns of Bath, Cheltenham, Doncaster, Leeds, York etc. and also at Robbins' auction mart, Covent Garden piazza, London. Two or three lodging houses were included, one of them being the detached, square mansion to the north-west of the principal structure, which before the rebuilding of 1900 was not connected to the Granby (A.278). An account has survived from this time, presented by Benn to guest Sir Henry Fitzherbert, which charged a bill of £33 5s. 5d. for a family of nine with unspecified servants, on a seven-day visit to Harrogate (A.279). These charges, while high, were probably no more than would have been charged at the Crown or Dragon. Clearly the Granby was seen as a good investment.

The auctioning of the Granby occurred at a time when William Charles Macready, a famous actor, was 'looking out for investments for my little savings', and was advised to put in a bid of £6,000 for the Granby estate. Macready had £3,000 available, but decided to raise the remainder on mortgage, which he secured with a loan of £2,900 from Knaresborough solicitor Samuel Powel (S.859). The extent of the Granby estate can be appreciated by examining the plan accompanying the surrender of 16 August 1824, which shows that the detached Granby Cottage (or lodging house) was retained by John Greeves for his own use (S.859). As it turned out, Macready did not consider his ownership of the Granby a success, and in his memoirs, he made the revealing claim that 'it would have been a very profitable investment, if I had had a solicitor faithful to my interests ...' (A.106.a) Thanks to a successful acting tour in southern England in 1825, Macready was able to 'pay off one mortgage on the Granby property of £720 ...' (A.106.a), but by 1833 it was evident that he wished to be rid of the property. In September of that year Macready walked across to the Granby 'thinking of Lear', to meet his tenant Jonathan Benn, who 'gave me no assistance in furthering my wish to dispose of the property' (A.106.b). The following year, Macready was walking across the Stray to the Granby, recalling, 'how exultingly I had first entered it, and how blindly and unresistingly I had been led to the purchase of it' (A.106.b).

Macready's regrets over his Harrogate investment were probably the result of temperament rather than economics. The Granby continued to attract the cream of society throughout the increasingly popular spa seasons. In 1824, when the previous owner, John Greeves announced his retirement, the Granby's tenant, Jonathan Benn, thanked the public for 'the most liberal patronage he has received since he entered upon the above Inn – a patronage which far exceeded his most sanguine expectations – [and he] respectfully informs the nobility and gentry visiting Harrogate that no expense or attention shall be spared on his part, to make the Granby Hotel,

PLATE 75
Park Parade, c. 1833,
with Christ Church
at the right. In the
distance in the centre
can be seen the gable
of Salutation
Buildings, also
known as
Gascoigne's Hotel.

in every respect, one of the most genteel and fashionable residences in the north of England . . .' (R.2040).

Moreover, when, in 1833, Macready decided to sell the Granby (W.9.15), it was tenant Benn who bought it, and if anyone really knew the truth about the Granby's economic performance, it was Benn, who had already purchased the Brunswick Hotel in 1833 (W.8.30.) The reality was probably that Macready, who was still working as a successful actor, and away from Harrogate for long periods, was unsuited to the role of owner of a great hotel, and that he expected too much from his investment. He does, however, seem to have learned from his initial poor choice of solicitor, as he employed the highly respected firm of Samuel Powell to oversee the sale of the Granby (W.9.15). On 18 October 1834 Benn agreed to pay Macready £4,900 for the Granby, which points to a net loss of £1,100 (W.9.30). Benn, who was one of the major players in nineteenth-century Harrogate, and who earned the town's everlasting gratitude for his role in supporting the prosecution of his rival Joseph Thackwray over the case of the sulphur well (H.10), commissioned Richardson and Clunn to compile a detailed inventory of the Granby (W.9.30), the result being reproduced – down to the last pair of sugar tongs – in document A.289, which provides an incomparably accurate insight into the furnishing of a great spa hotel during the reign of William IV. Macready's connection with the Granby did not end with his sale to Benn, as he went on to lend Benn £2,900 (S.1069), which Benn repaid by November 1838 (S.1204).

Jonathan Benn did so well out of the Granby that when he retired he was able to build a splendid mansion, St Alban's Villa, on land to the hotel's

south-east, which he reserved for himself when he sold the Granby estate to Thomas Hall in 1841 (S.1254). St Alban's, which appears to have been built shortly before 1830, may be seen on the Frith drawing reproduced as plate 81. It was named after one of the Granby's most illustrious guests, the Duchess of St Albans, or Baroness Burdett Coutts, who fled to the Granby from the Queen Hotel after being opportuned by the fortune-hunting Irish barrister Dunn (A.292), and whose subsequent patronage was greatly to Jonathan Benn's advantage.

Church Square, across the Stray opposite the Granby, experienced much change during the early part of the nineteenth century (see plate 24). The Theatre Royal closed in 1830, the last surviving play bill for which is dated 30 July 1829 (P.84). Victim to the declining public taste for theatrical entertainment and the growing popularity with visitors for Low Harrogate's sulphur waters, the theatre building was soon the subject of an application for conversion into a public house, which was opposed by Samuel Powell on behalf of Jonathan Benn.

As has been observed above, Church Square developed along its southern and then its eastern edges, but it was not until 1810, when Thomas Emmet bought a plot of land from William Thackwray at the

———

PLATE 77
Bilton House, Park Parade. The fake 'Georgian' windows with their panes of multiple mullions and transoms were replaced in *c*. 1975. The original whole panes of plate glass, with a single transom, were such an admired part of quality Georgian buildings.

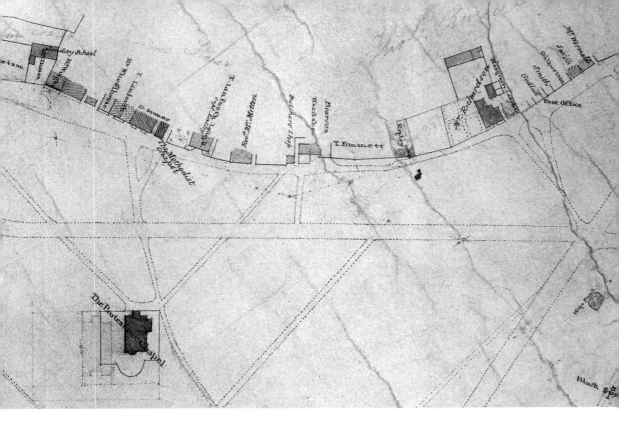

Charles Greeves' 1821
plan of Park Parade.
The Chapel of
St John (later Christ
Church) is at lower
left, and the Black
Spring at lower right.

north-western corner of the square, that the infilling of the north side began seriously (S.608). Emmet, usually described as 'stone mason' (S.744), subsequently built the handsome terrace of Georgian properties which so embellish the northern side of Church Square (Sd.20), and also built property in central Harrogate (S.781). He may also have been the builder of Silverfields Cottages south-east of the Granby, into which the Greeves family moved in 1836 (O.21.90).

The building of Christ Church in 1831 as a replacement for the chapel of St John has been considered in our eleventh chapter. The church's new tower provided High Harrogate with an important architectural focal point, just as the new parsonage on Park Parade (which was known for a time somewhat facetiously as Paradise Row (K.23) provided that locality with an architectural counter-balance to the impressive Park House. Park Parade's development had been stimulated with the building in the very early nineteenth century of a number of imposing residences, such as Park Place (which was a mini-Rudding Park) and just beyond the footpath to Low Harrogate known as 'Walker's Passage,' the austerely neo-classical Bilton House (see plate 77). Walker's passage was named after Walker, the tea dealer and coffee roaster, who had premises on the northern side of the junction of Park Parade with the footpath. In 1830 Park Parade received an important addition in the form of an Italianate palace, which would not have been out of place on Venice's Grand Canal. Such buildings as these reinforced High Harrogate's image as a resort of refinement and substance.

Park Parade and Regent Parade both grew from the footpath which connected the Dragon Hotel with the Queen's Head Hotel, each thoroughfare dating back probably to *c.* 1700. In 1837 the footpath outside the Queen's Head became the first in Harrogate to be paved (D.18), probably as a result of pressure on the vestry meetings by the Dearloves, who had taken the Queen's Head in 1829 (R.2270). For some time previous to this, and certainly by 1810, the Queen's Head had been held by Francis Haw (R.1575), and known as one of the four best hotels in Harrogate, as well as being the oldest custom-built establishment in the town (G.2). It was under the Dearloves, however, that the Queen's Head played a more significant role in local politics, especially with regard to the matter of the Thackwray Well Case (H.10) and the move towards obtaining the 1841 Improvement Act (H.15) (I.5). The proposal to pave the footpath invited (inevitably) opposition, as the footpath was on Stray land, given that the boundary of the Stray was seen by many as reaching up to the façades of the houses built on former allotments or incroachments. This was despite the Act of 1789 (J.5) which had compensated for the loss of land to the two hundred acres occasioned by the making of roads and footpaths, by awarding the Stray extra land in the form of the Stray slips. A letter of 23 January 1837 from Charles Greeves of Granby House set forth the opposition view (J.21).

The Dearloves were an old Harrogate family, their names featuring frequently in the court rolls (A.37.61; S.237 etc.), and it was under their control that the Queen's Head hotel probably enjoyed its greatest success. When the great public meeting at the Queen Hotel took place on 24 November 1840 (I.5), the building had not yet been subjected to the major refrontings of 1855–56 and 1861,[37] and it appeared much as it had when young W. P. Frith had allegedly drawn it (see plate 22). There is a delightful character sketch of old Dearlove, set down in February 1893, to which we direct the curious (R.3138). Of more historic interest is the account of Angela Burdett Coutts's experiences at the Queen Hotel, which we now relate to illustrate by how little human nature changes!

We have previously encountered Angela Burdett Coutts in our ninth chapter amidst pages on the theatre, where, it may be recalled, Angela, on her mother's death in August 1837 inherited the immense fortunes her mother had received following that lady's marriage to the banker Coutts and then to the Duke of St Albans (C.58). The unmarried Angela was now the richest woman in England (apart from Queen Victoria) and a target for every fortune-hunter in the land.

Before her death in 1837, Angela's mother Harriet had brought her daughter to the Yorkshire Spa on several occasions, mostly connected with the Theatre Royal, and consequently, Angela Burdett Coutts developed a strong affection for the place. Harrogate was therefore a natural refuge for the grieving daughter, who also seems to have been on friendly terms with the wealthy Mr Paley, who had acquired Captain Thackwray's Oatlands estate in the autumn of 1837 (W.10.33).

The worst fortune-hunter to trouble Angela at this time was an improvident Irish barrister, appropriately named Dunn, who throughout her visit in 1838 to the Queen Hotel, persisted with his unwanted attentions. Angela Burdett Coutts' annoyance was the talk of Harrogate during the 1838 spa season, and it was only after she asked Mr Paley to consult solicitor Samuel Powell, that any real action was taken against the tiresome Dunn (W.10.79), who continued to pester Angela so much that she was obliged to summon help from her London friend Mr Marjoribanks, who came to Harrogate with a policeman. Meanwhile, Angela had been obliged to quit the Queen for the more exclusive surroundings of Granby House, where she was attended to by Mr Benn (A.292). The long and unfortunate story of Dunn's pestering of Angela Burdett Coutts has been told by her biographer,[38] who related that when Dunn had been released from prison, he claimed compensation on the grounds of being encouraged in his pursuit of Angela by some absurd poems she had allegedly written to him:

PLATE 87
The presence of the militia and rich elderly female visitors inevitably produced unlikely pairings.

when to Harrogate sweet papa beats a retreat,
to take Spa waters sulphurious,
I could hear your heart thump as we stood by the pump,
While you bolted that stuff so injurious.

The reading of these verses caused great amusement in court.[39]

At this time Harrogate was celebrated as a paradise for fortune-hunters, and one has only to recall Catherine Sinclair's lines about it being a 'perfect emporium of beaux' (C.107.a) to take the point. Additionally the presence in Harrogate of large numbers of impoverished but personable military officers (A.252.c), and the attraction of the spa for wealthy female hypochondriacs, must have encouraged many otherwise unlikely pairings! (see plate 87).

The Dunn case was probably regarded as a scandal in Harrogate not because of Dunn's pursuit of an heiress, but because his pursuit was unwanted, and that, consequently, a visitor had been incommoded. Given

Thompson's Observatory

the importance of the visitors to the local economy, any behaviour which might discourage guests (especially wealthy ones) must have been regarded as treasonable.

We shall conclude our consideration of the building of Harrogate between 1778 and 1841 at a high point: the Harlow Hill Observation Tower, as its history connects the perceived needs of the visitors with the speculations of the builders and the concerns of the Duchy of Lancaster.

On 11 March 1829 the Duchy of Lancaster's clerk, Mr F. Dawes Danvers wrote to the Duchy's Harrogate agent Mr Tolle, notifying him of an application by a Mr John Thompson for eight to ten yards of land at the top of Harlow Hill for the purpose of building an observation tower. The Duchy Council would be obliged to Mr Tolle for his opinion as to the propriety of such a request (B.94), which was received in time for their meeting of 4 May 1829, at which Mr Tolle's recommendations were accepted (B.206). Writing in c. 1870, historian William Grainge claimed that John Thompson then constructed a tall square tower (see plate 82), probably using stone from the Harlow Hill quarry, and equipped it with seven large telescopes made by the Leeds optician Davies, who claimed that they had a magnifying power of seventy-five, and that a clear view could be had for forty miles. Thompson paid over £700 to build and equip his tower, and obviously reckoned on recovering his costs from entry charges, which in 1843 were six pence each (A.283). This same statement by Grainge needs to be used with care, as it contains several errors, especially with reference to the Earl of Harewood. Guidebooks such as Pigot & Co.'s 1834 directory indicate that soon after it opened, the Harlow Hill observation tower became an important amenity for visitors.

A puzzling reference in the Duchy correspondence for 1843 shows that having built an observation tower atop Harlow Hill, John Thompson subsequently attempted to construct a second one. Writing on 20 January 1843, Thompson stated that '... I wish to take a ninety-nine years lease ... to erect an observatory ...'. In his reply of 31 August 1843 (the delay presumably having been occasioned by an exchange of further correspondence between the Duchy Clerk and the Harrogate agent), Mr Dawes Danvers explained that before they could make an answer the Duchy Council would require more detailed plans, and that they would not in any case permit a portion of the premises to be used as a public house. Mr Dawes Danvers also asked Thompson, '... perhaps you would have the goodness to state whether you have reason for thinking that the inhabitants of Harrogate generally wish for another observatory on a larger and better scale in addition to the existing one ...' (B.169). It is tempting to conclude that Mr Thompson's proposed second observatory was an excuse to install a public house, and that the Duchy's disfavour ensured the scheme's abandonment.

15 | Obtaining the 1841 Improvement Act

T HE 1841 Harrogate Improvement Act was the culmination of a process of spa development which had begun with the 1778 Award. The Award not only stimulated the growth of the spa by means of providing free access to all the known mineral wells, but it also created an asset of considerable proportions in the form of the 200-acre Harrogate Stray. The Stray protected the mineral wells, guaranteed unrestricted public access, provided sufficient space for the exercise recommended by the doctors as an essential adjunct to mineral water drinking, and created a link between the two Harrogate villages in the form of an urban spine, around which building development could subsequently occur.

The Duchy of Lancaster had promoted the Enclosure Act of 1770, and in the Award of 1778 it received several parcels of land: the so-called 'King's lands' (B.31, allotments 170, 449, 452, 453, 464, 466, 467, 485, 491). Because of the proximity of these lands to the Low Harrogate Spa, any development undertaken by the Duchy's tenants was significant. The majority of these tenants were innkeepers and doctors, the two professions of most significance to the growth of the spa. By about 1835 the successful development produced under this partnership eventually placed strains on what was, to all intents and purposes, still an eighteenth-century system of local government. Accordingly, there were calls for a new Act of Parliament. Such demands were not unique to Harrogate, and had – over the same period of 1770 to 1841 – been heard in other spas. However Harrogate's urban development during this period was atypical, thanks to the unique influence of the Duchy, the role of the professional class of innkeepers and doctors, and, thirdly, the visitors. This final chapter describes the process of obtaining of the 1841 Improvement Act under the influence of this powerful trio, and its transformation from a conception of simple protective legislation as envisaged in 1835, into a comprehensive piece of local government reform six years later.

The legislative system

Private Bill legislation had acquired an unenviable reputation for expense by the time the Harrogate community decided to pursue the objective of a new Act. It was usual for a country solicitor to charge five guineas a day for attendance in London, and the average cost of an unopposed town improvement bill was £1,627; opposed bills cost very much more, as for example at Manchester, where a failed water bill cost the city £6,000.[1] Recognition of the needs of smaller communities to pursue reforming legislation for specific concerns came with the passing of a number of model Bills, such as the 1828 Act for lighting, cleansing and watching of towns in Ireland, or Scotland's 1833 'general system of police'.[2] In England, the Whig government reworked the permissive 'Lighting and Watching Act' enacted by the Wellington administration, and John Tidd Pratt, the Whig lawyer who drafted the new England Act, declared that it was to 'enable parishes … with the consent of ratepayers, to make a rate for the purposes of lighting and watching, without the necessity of incurring great expense necessarily attendant in obtaining a local act'.[3] The development within Harrogate of a movement in favour of reforming local legislation arose at a time when special local acts for such things as water and gas supply, street cleansing and sewering, policing and other significant matters, were commonplace. Consequently it is not surprising that the local promoters of a new Harrogate Bill were contemplating legislation for the better protection of the wells and Stray, and very little else (I.4), in much the same way as the promoters of legislation in Cheltenham in 1786 for footpaths,[4] Leamington in 1828 for paving,[5] or Tunbridge in 1835 for water supplying and market provision:[6] all supported Bills which were narrow and specific, rather than comprehensive in the urban sense. Harrogate, however, unlike Bath, Buxton, Cheltenham, Leamington, Malvern or Tunbridge, had to submit its draft legislation to the Court of the Duchy of Lancaster, with its Attorney General, Surveyor, and Chief Clerk, and it was this requirement which led to the comprehensive nature of the Harrogate Bill, which eventually became the Harrogate Improvement Act of 1841.[7]

Duchy policy and Harrogate

Before considering the approaches made by Harrogate to the Duchy of Lancaster about an Improvement Act, it is necessary to examine the Duchy's interests in the town, as these interests naturally affected their response to the townspeople's application. As will be shown, the Duchy influenced the content and scope of the 1841 Harrogate Improvement Act by expanding the original draft clauses which dealt specifically with the protection of the mineral wells, into a comprehensive piece of local government legislation. The final version of the 1841 Improvement Act – with Duchy help – enabled Harrogate to adapt into a successful Victorian spa, in contrast to the townspeople's earliest draft, which in its narrow and special content would only have addressed the problem of protection for the mineral wells.

The official history of the Duchy of Lancaster records that revenues throughout the eighteenth and nineteenth centuries did not reflect the value of the Duchy's holdings, which included 38,301 acres of land in sixteen counties, the greatest area and extent of which, at 17,172 acres, lay in Yorkshire.[8]

Attempts to improve this situation and to reform the administration of the Duchy occurred at a time in the 1830s when, to quote Sir Robert Somerville, 'the parliamentary rumblings over the Duchy's administration and finances which had been heard, however faintly, in 1820, and again more loudly in 1830 and 1831, broke into something of a roar in 1837, after the death of William IV'.[9] This was at a time when feeling in Harrogate was developing in favour of new legislation, especially after the shock of the Thackwray well case of 1835–1837. Consequently the Duchy was already in a frame of mind both to improve its revenues and to consider legislation conducive to such improvements.

The Duchy holdings in Harrogate consisted of several parcels of land in close proximity to the Low Harrogate Spa. In 1829 the deputy receiver of Duchy farm rents, John Tolle, sent a report to the Duchy Council in which he reported several applications to lease some of this land for building purposes, and recommended that the Duchy should act (B.269.b). No action was taken, however, other than noting the contents of Mr Tolle's report; but ten years later, in June 1839, in an atmosphere of improving revenues, the report was re-examined. The Duchy Council considered two options: first, to sell individual plots; and second, to adopt a local plan. Consultant John Howgate, land surveyor of Knaresborough, who became involved with the Thackwray well case, was called in. He advised that the best option would be to divide the 'King's lands' at Low Harrogate, containing six and one half acres, into thirty-five building lots with building leases being granted for ninety-nine years. At one point Howgate advised that he had

> divided [this lot] it for respectable lodging houses and shops for that immediate neighbourhood, which I believe will readily be sought after ... there are other lands belonging to the Duchy very desirable for building ground, namely the Red Bank marked upon the plan ... my reason for not yet allotting these at present is to avoid overstocking the market with too many lots now to be let, being of opinion that it would be more advantageous not to do so until there is further demand (B.285).

The contrast with Leamington Spa, which in 1839 was suffering from a glut of property – the result of the uncontrolled building boom of the years between 1806 and 1815 – could not have been greater.[10] The Duchy Court accepted Howe's report at their meeting of December 1839 (B.229).

The lots identified by Howgate were all in Low Harrogate, and lay chiefly along Swan Road, which today leads from the Royal Pump Room to the former Ripon turnpike road, via the Swan Hotel (see plan 48). The terms and conditions under which building leases were to be granted were published in 1840 and distributed throughout the town. They laid down strict standards for construction, design, materials, proportions, walling and fencing, road and sewer making, and the prevention of nuisances – this last by means of restricting such activities as rendering, tanning or fat boiling. Granting of leases depended on the obtaining of certificates of approval from 'the superintendent to be appointed by the Duchy' (B.68).

Thomas Humble Walker seems to have been the first of many builders to take up the Duchy's proposals. Walker was a lodging house keeper and wine and spirit merchant, who asked to take four lots in Swan Road, opposite the Sulphur Well and Promenade Assembly Room, at a total annual rental of £5 1s. 1d. This rental was called a building rent, but in reality was for the land, as it was the Duchy's practice to require a second or revised rent on completion of the building. The length of the lease was then reduced by the length of the time of construction. For example, the rental for an initial lease of ninety-nine years was increased on completion of the building, to reflect the increased value of the land, but the term would be reduced to 97 or 98 years, depending on how long it had taken to complete the building. This was a sensible arrangement, as the builder would not profit from the building until it was ready to be occupied (B.238).

The Duchy, through its terms and conditions of building leases (B.68), demonstrated its desire to encourage the construction of high-quality villa-type dwellings, which could not be expected to stand in isolation, but which would be occupied by residents who would expect provision of proper footpaths and highways, running water, street lighting, adequate maintenance of law and order, regulation of public conveyances; and an authority capable not only of protecting and regulating the historic mineral wells and Stray, but also one which could administer the town in a manner appropriate for the development of the Duchy's extensive Harrogate assets. The Duchy itself did not build roads, lay down sewers, provide public gas illumination or maintain a police force. However, it did not oppose or discourage such amenities when it was clear not only that local people wanted them and were prepared to pay through a local rate, but also when the provision of such amenities would increase the value of the Duchy's own holdings. Accordingly, when the Duchy received a letter from Samuel

Powell, solicitor, advising them that a public meeting in Harrogate on 24 November 1840 had resolved to seek a new Act of Parliament for the better protection and management of the Stray and wells, it was in a receptive frame of mind (B.143).

Harrogate in comparative perspective

The atypical nature of Harrogate's growth up to the time of the public meeting in November 1840 is well demonstrated by comparing it with trends in Bath, Buxton, Cheltenham, Malvern, Royal Leamington Spa and Royal Tunbridge Wells, when both similarities and differences are apparent. However, the progress made after 1840 by all of these communities, in terms of the success of their spas, took two clear directions: whereas only Harrogate's spa prospered and continued to develop, those of all the others declined. 'Leamington, Cheltenham and Malvern had, by 1840, become the retreat of those seeking retirement ... at Leamington and Cheltenham, purveyors of commercialised entertainment failed, invalids took over and their interests became the first concern.'[11] As for Bath – again, to quote Dr Granville, it was 'now a town with a Spa, rather than a Spa with a town'.[12]

Before explaining this phenomenon, it is instructive to compare a few random similarities and differences between Harrogate and its rivals, which show that although some aspects of spa growth were typical of other British resorts, Harrogate's early nineteenth-century development was unusual. At the same time, it must be emphasised that growth of resident population did not constitute either a guarantee of success, nor a promise of failure. For example, in 1801, Buxton's population was 760, compared with 1,600 at Harrogate, 819 at Malvern, 315 at Leamington, and 33,196 at Bath. By 1841, these figures increased to 1,569 at Buxton, 4,200 at Harrogate, 2,768 at Malvern, 12,864 at Leamington, and 53,206 at Bath.[13] After 1841, Harrogate, armed with its Improvement Act, developed its spa successfully; unlike the other resorts, whose populations were both smaller (Buxton and Malvern) and larger (Leamington and Bath) than Harrogate, and whose spas all declined, despite having Improvement Acts of their own.

Cheltenham

At the 1801 census Cheltenham had a population of 3,076, compared with Harrogate's 1,600, but by 1841 its population had increased nearly eleven-fold, reaching 31,411. Harrogate's population, however, did not even treble, reaching a mere 4,200 by 1841.[14] The development of public amenities in Cheltenham appeared to match and exceed those of Harrogate. Cheltenham provided a general hospital and dispensary in 1848, based on a fund opened in 1813.[15] Harrogate provided a restricted hospital in 1825, based on a fund opened in *c.* 1775 (U.2). At Cheltenham, the Church of England opened five new churches between 1770 and 1840, and by 1840 Cheltenham had eleven places of worship for dissenters.[16] Harrogate over the same period saw the opening of two new churches for the Anglicans, and three chapels for non-conformists.[17] Harrogate, from the passing of the 1770 Enclosure Act to the 1841 Improvement Act, was subject to only the General Award of 1778, and the amending Act of 1789, both of which dealt with Knaresborough Forest in its entirety, rather than just Harrogate town. Cheltenham, by comparison, was subject to the 1786 Improvement Act, the 1811 Enclosure Act, the 1821 Improvement Act, the 1833 Sewage, Draining and Cleansing act, the 1824 Waterworks Act, and the two Gas Acts of 1786 and 1819.[18] Thanks to the Duchy of Lancaster, Harrogate's Improvement Act would be comprehensive, rather than piecemeal, thus obviating the need for a string of special legislation. Cheltenham's Improvement Act of 1786 had been called for by the town's leading traders, who wished to provide new and improved footpaths and highways, and to enable their cleaning and lighting. The act was framed to satisfy the immediate demands of local traders and the wealthier residents, who attended the public meetings held in the town. In the event, this act was found to be too narrow, and in 1806 it was necessary to adopt a further Act for 'amending and enlarging the powers of the previous act'.[19]

Royal Leamington Spa like Harrogate, but unlike both Bath and Cheltenham, was still administered by the vestry meeting process; and, like Harrogate, this system in Leamington was inadequate for either protecting the mineral wells or for providing improvements. A public meeting held in 1818, at Copps Hotel, focused on the desire of residents to provide Leamington with an Act of Parliament for the 'paving, watching, cleaning and improving the town'. Various resolutions were passed, but no legal opinion was sought, nor was any timetable laid down for attaining the proposed Act. A parish meeting in 1820 resolved that 'a paving and lighting act ... would be highly beneficial to Leamington, followed by a public meeting called by the proprietors of houses and land in Leamington ... for paving, lighting and improving the town'. Unfortunately, timidity and irresolution appear to have delayed fulfilment of this move, which once again demonstrated the inability of the vestry meeting system to introduce necessary improvements. Eventually, after further delays, the leading townsmen agreed to apply to Parliament, and on 10 June 1825 the new statute came into force, which enabled the election of twenty-one Improvement Commissioners. They were known as the 'Paving Commissioners', to emphasise the real nature of the Act. The 'Paving Act' was too narrow in scope, and the commissioners could not prevent the further decline of Leamington as a spa,[20] nor could they solve the problem of the housing glut and the failure of the Leamington Bank.[21]

Harrogate's first post office opened in 1797 (A.309.1), Cheltenham's in 1800.[22] But when a comparison is made of the improvement to the spas and entertainments in both Harrogate and Cheltenham, the following results are apparent. Whereas two important mineral wells were discovered in Cheltenham in 1803 and 1809[23] at least twenty were discovered in Harrogate between 1770 and 1841 (G.25). Harrogate opened its race course in 1793 (G.5, pp. 89–92) whereas racing in Cheltenham began in 1819.[24] At Cheltenham between 1770 and 1841 pump rooms were erected over the Montpellier, Pittville and Cambray springs,[25] whereas in Harrogate, over the same period, the Old Sulphur Well, St John's Well and Crown Well were given pump rooms.[26] Visitors were able to arrive in Cheltenham by railway by 1842,[27] whereas in Harrogate they had to wait until 1848 for the opening of the first railway station.[28] Cheltenham was developing more as a town, whereas Harrogate was developing as a spa. From the above it may be seen that development in Harrogate and Cheltenham had both similarities and differences. Yet for Cheltenham, to quote Dr Hembry, 'in the 1850s the momentum behind its expansion was spent, and a period of near stagnation set in'. Dr Granville, however, writing of Harrogate, said 'it has the elements ... of becoming a spa of the first magnitude, even to the extent of attracting foreign travellers ... at present the condition of Harrogate is quite primitive, ... a spirited capitalist would find an unexplored mine of wealth [there] which is not one of your ephemeral spas, dependent on fashion.' (F.58)

Cheltenham was not the only British spa to experience decline and stagnation after 1841. At Malvern the promise of eighteenth-century Malvern wells was not fulfilled in the nineteenth century, as the residential character of Great Malvern swamped its smaller neighbour. Following the Act of 1664 which permitted the enclosure of Malvern Chase, the biggest and best estates passed into the hands of the Horneyolds, the Foleys and the Russells,[29] whereas in Harrogate, the Duchy, playing a key role as an improving landlord, ensuring that all tenants – including themselves – had the opportunity to acquire land (B.31). The result of these different methods of apportionment was that in Malvern realisation of the spa's potential depended on the business acumen of wealthy families, whose principal concern appears to have been maintaining the status quo. In Harrogate, however, the innkeepers acquired extensive parcels of land under the 1778 Award (B.31), being thereby enabled to institute improvements to their newly acquired holdings (B.31, entries 272, 276, 288, 292, 293, 296, 383, 384, 385, 386, 389. Note, these examples refer only to awards made to the innkeepers at High Harrogate, overlooking the Stray.) In Malvern, the two hotels established before 1770, the Crown and the Well House, were insufficient for the needs of the visitors, and by 1841, their number had been increased by only one – the Belle Vue. Surrounded by land held by a few wealthy families, the hotels had few opportunities to develop.[30] In Harrogate, the Duchy of Lancaster retained control of large areas of land in proximity to the wells of Harrogate, the development of which was under-taken wisely in accordance with the Duchy's long experience as one of the nation's oldest landlords (B.31).[31] In Malvern the great landowners committed unprecedented encroachments against the remaining common lands; in 1806, for example, no fewer than twenty actions were instituted in one day.[32] In Harrogate, between the Award of 1778 and the Improvement Act of 1841, only one threat of action for encroachment had to be issued – against the tenant of the White Hart Hotel – thanks to the Duchy's vigilance (B.186).

Royal Leamington Spa

The 1801 census at Royal Leamington Spa revealed a total adult population of 315, which was one-fifth the size of Harrogate. By 1841 Leamington's population had increased to 12,864, an astonishing forty-fold rise, whereas Harrogate's had reached just 4,200.[33] Yet despite this very considerable difference in population growth, the history of both communities has much in common. Leamington's Enclosure Act dated from 1767, with the award being rushed through the following year.[34] Harrogate's Act was passed in 1770, the award taking a full seven years to complete – admittedly forming part of the much bigger Forest of Knaresborough enclosure. The enclosure commissioners responsible for Harrogate, appointed by the Duchy, published their programme of surveys, advertised their meetings – most of which were public – and made full provision for petitions and complaints to be heard. In addition, they maintained a full record of their business (B.29).

Leamington received a General Hospital and Dispensary in 1826, one year after Harrogate's Royal Bath Hospital opened. New mineral wells were discovered, and new spa facilities introduced, more or less at the same rate as at Harrogate.[35] The great difference between the two communities, however, was that in Harrogate the best sites for residential development were held by the Duchy, who encouraged the building of small numbers of top-quality villas, the successful sale of which determined the course of subsequent developments, in that the leases had to be taken before further building could begin (B.68). At Leamington no such restrictions appeared to control the building boom which occurred after 1810, at the very time when the rest of the nation's building industry was suffering a depression.[36] The activities of building speculators produced a glut of property, so that in 1821 the Leamington census recorded no fewer than 60 out of 400 houses unoccupied.[37] This was development by speculators. At Harrogate, speculation similar in purpose if not in scale, was driven by the innkeepers. The great difference was that at Leamington the speculators built their houses *after* the opening of new bathing establishments,[38] whereas in Harrogate the innkeepers first provided new spa amenities before extending their establishments to accommodate extra visitors. Harrogate's speculative development was thereby undertaken by innkeepers and others, working with a regular influx of visitors, whereas Leamington's speculators relied on an increasing population of wealthy house buyers. In the event, Leamington's failure to transform its speculations to market requirements led to the collapse of the Leamington Bank, the degeneration of much of the speculative housing into appalling slums, and 'the decay of the Leamington Spa as a fashionable institution in the 1840s'.[39] Harrogate, by contrast, did not have sub-standard housing until ten years after the railway cut into the new centre in 1860, and slums have never existed within the town's boundary.

Royal Tunbridge Wells

The villages which grew into Royal Tunbridge Wells also shared points of similarity with Harrogate, and by the 1801 census Tunbridge Wells' population of about 1,000 was only 600 fewer than Harrogate's.[40] Included within the Tunbridge population were a considerable number of poor and improvident people, whose presence had been recorded in the reign of Charles II and for whom the Presbyterians had, in 1698, formed a chapel.[41] This stimulated other non-conformist groups to activity, so that the Independents, Baptists and Methodists were all well established by 1800.[42] At Tutty's village, a 'God-forsaken cluster of shacks', two women attempted in 1836 to open a Sunday school, an action for which there was no counterpart in Harrogate.[43] But then Harrogate was a different type of community, which lacked any appreciable population of resident poor, and where non-conformity seems to have had little support. In consequence, the township authorities were not required to divert resources from basic improvements to such things as roads and footpaths (which were used by the visitors), towards poor relief (which was of no use to the visitors). The failure of non-conformity to establish itself in Harrogate was not only a sign of the scarcity of the social groups which were usually its strongest supporters,[44] but it also ensured that the broad class of visitors, drawn as they were from the establishment, did not have their peace or consciences disturbed by the often intrusive rantings which were one of the hallmarks of non-conformity.[45] Harrogate's lack of any appreciable population of resident poor also meant that the mass marches reported in Royal Tunbridge Wells in 1760,[46] the disturbances of the Leamington slums,[47] the Chartist meetings of 1839 which so scandalised much of Cheltenham and which resulted in the firing of shops in the town's centre,[48] the disturbances at Malvern following the enclosure of the former Chase, when four innocent people were murdered,[49] or the riots in Bath following the Gordon disturbances of 1780, or 1839 when the authorities faced a demonstration by 3,000 Chartists[50] had not an echo in Harrogate. The town was also free from the epidemics and infections which took 151 smallpox victims at Bath in 1837,[51] or which in 1829 scared Tunbridge Wells into establishing an inoculation scheme against smallpox.[52] Freedom from the breeding grounds of disease – slums and industrialisation – allied to a remarkably pure supply of drinking water[53] and the refusal of the Bath Hospital to admit patients with infectious diseases (U.1) were the principal reasons for Harrogate's happy freedom from the scourges of early nineteenth-century urbanisation.

Buxton

According to Dr Phyllis Hembry, 'despite its increase in population, early nineteenth-century Buxton, like Matlock, declined relatively in fashion, though the actual number of visitors may have only slightly decreased. Harrogate's dominance as a northern spa, and its development in the 1820s and 1830s, overshadowed Buxton and Matlock'.[54] In Buxton the role that the Duchy of Lancaster played in Harrogate was filled by the Cavendish family, particularly the sixth Duke of Devonshire. In 1818, the sixth Duke provided a remedy for Buxton's serious lack of a hot bathing establishment by building the Hot Baths. Apart from this, and endowing a National School with one hundred pounds, the role of the Cavendish family in promoting and developing the Buxton Spa, was minimal. Even by 1840 Buxton lacked a pump room, and the very first edition of the *Buxton Advertiser*, in 1842, emphasised Buxton's failures, asking why it was so behind other watering places. Again, to quote Dr Hembry, 'Buxton had possibly by the 1820s been overbuilt for its requirements'.[55] The ubiquitous Dr Granville wrote that although Buxton had 'the fragrance of aristocracy, it was a very dull place, lacking amusement and even more, society, in its present apparent desertion'.[56] Complaints were made about the dirty condition of the wells and the state of the attendants, who were either 'decrepit old women' or a 'young male attendant looking like a grubby labourer called from plough'.[57] Although the Cavendishes' role in Buxton affairs grew after 1842, the fluctuating interest of this powerful family's interest was very different from the stable interest of the Duchy of Lancaster in Harrogate, which as we have seen was a crucial factor in Harrogate's growth.

Bath

The Bath Improvement Act of 1789 seems to have grown from a desire by the leading traders and doctors to escape the depression caused by the

Gordon riots of 1780. Surgeon Symons, writing in 1783, noted that the Bath waters were under threat from the digging of drains by private house-holders, but the Bath Corporation was in no financial position to seek a new Act to prohibit such work, because of its debt from the Guild Hall project of 1765–1783, when the corporate debt had risen from £3,100 to £26,000. Nevertheless the improvers persisted in their demands, until in 1784 a committee was appointed to enquire into thirteen clauses for the better governance of the city. These clauses provided an ingenious and optimistic plan to refurbish the city centre, improve the Baths and Pump Room, and create access between the corporation owned facilities and the rapidly expanding upper town. However, as the financing depended upon an increase in the turnpike charges, it provoked massive public opposition, which delayed the proposed legislation until June 1789, when the Bath Improvement Act was passed.[58]

The elaborate improvements to the city of Bath – as distinct from improvements to the smaller Bath Spa – did not produce the expected upturn in Bath's fortunes. '[the] ... earnings ... show ... the failure of Bath to fulfil the expectations of its developers ...'[59] In 1841 Dr Granville put forward an explanation of this stagnation in the demand for Bath and of its decline as a place of resort, which is probably reliable. First there was the rising cost of treatment by Bath's doctors. Second, the growing preference for private, as distinct from public, entertainment, which had been Bath's speciality. But above all, after the boom of 1788–98, Bath was just too big and bustling to attract the exclusive company who had made it popular seventy years earlier. Its size was particularly damaging because of competition from newer and more fashionable resorts, especially at a time when the 'naturalness' of a resort was being prized as an asset.[60] In some respects, the Bath Improvement Act may actually have hastened Bath's decline as a spa, although it undoubtedly produced some handsome buildings.

The role of visitors

Before 1840 Harrogate differed from other British spas in a unique way. Visitors to other spas, including large ones such as Bath, or tiny ones such as Malvern, all found themselves in a planned, ordered world with pre-ordained patterns of behaviour, routine and fashion. Upon being discovered, a well would be encircled with a pump room, piped to a dispensing counter, and sometimes bottled and exported. Entrepreneurs provided entertainments in premises erected to attract a clientele. Masters of ceremony dictated fashion and behaviour. Building speculators threw up architectural frameworks which provided a backdrop before which ritualistic promenading and socialising could be enacted. The success of all this depended on the continuing support of the visitors. When tastes changed, visitors looked elsewhere, and those British spas which could not adapt began their long decline. Harrogate, however, developed in a different manner. The waters were administered informally. Emphasis was placed on naturalness, on drinking at the source or well-head. Before 1778 all of Harrogate's wells were on Duchy land, so pump rooms could not be built, nor could the waters be piped or bottled on anything other than the smallest of scales. After 1778 all of the known wells were on the Stray, or 200 acres, which the Award ensured could not be built upon or enclosed, so the open and undeveloped nature of the wells remained undisturbed. Consequently, when doctors began to emphasis the value of waters from natural sources, Harrogate was in a strong position to exploit this fashion. Here is Dr Granville's striking observation of *c.* 1840:

> it remains a village ... this is precisely the circumstance that has saved the reputation of Harrogate. Who has not cavilled at the waters of Leamington and Cheltenham? Those of Harrogate are unsophisticated, because the place itself remains as it was. You dip your cup into the fountain-head and get your strong waters. Elsewhere you have the complicated machinery of pumps ... Harrogate is, in fact, a true and genuine Spa. (F.58, p. 38)

Entertainments at Harrogate were equally informal. Newly arrived visitors were not faced with a formal 'ritualised leisure industry', bearing the approval of a pompous MC, as at other spas.[61] Certainly there was the theatre, built by a local innkeeper (G.3) and, after 1798, a race course, to which no admission fee could be charged owing to its Stray location.[62] But for the rest, visitors provided and controlled their own entertainments (C.38). Consequently, when entertainment taste changed, the entertainments at the inns changed accordingly. Harrogate, unlike all other British spas, had no institutionalised master of ceremonies.[63] Instead, each inn appointed a master of ceremonies, who naturally ensured that the tastes and wishes of his co-guests were paramount. Since the appointment of each MC was determined by the length of their visit at the inn, rather than of aristocratic rank, entertainments tended to reflect the broad taste of the majority of each inn's guests (G.4). This extraordinarily democratic system meant that a butcher could – within the inn – have precedence over a duke, a state of affairs that was deeply offensive to some visitors such as Lord Byron's mother-in-law (C.56).

The 'naturalness' of the Harrogate spa was emphasised by the lack of any impressive architectural backdrop against which formal ritual could occur. Thanks to the role of the Duchy, both before and after the Award of 1778,

Harrogate had no equivalent of Buxton's Crescent of 1781,[64] Cheltenham's colonnade of 1791,[65] Tunbridge Wells' Upper Walk of 1793,[66] Leamington's Royal Baths and Pump Room of 1812,[67] still less of Bath's Circus of 1754[68] or Royal Crescent.[69] Indeed, until the advent of the Victoria Park Company in 1860, Harrogate consisted of two geographically separate communities: High Harrogate and Low Harrogate.[70] Consequently, when the fashion for ritualistic promenading died out and was replaced by one for 'natural' waters in a rural setting, Harrogate was well placed to benefit, as will be examined in the next section.

Early nineteenth-century visitors were affected by two further matters which influenced spa development within the United Kingdom: first, the changing scientific climate; second, the threat of the new seaside resorts. The former had been growing since the public disputes of the 1780s between the Swedish Chemist, Torbern Bergman, and the Cheltenham Doctor, John Barker.

The former, writing in the late 1770s, claimed that a water's 'naturalness' was of little consequence, and that equal results would be obtained by analysing chemical contents, and adding the elements to a plain water. Dr Barker, however, claimed that this was too hasty and simplistic, and that chemistry was a 'good servant though a very bad master'. Further, the composition of mineral waters was so complex that a true analysis was beyond the means of science.[71] The dispute between the rival adherents of Bergman and Barker continued well into the nineteenth century, and was deepened, rather than resolved, by the discovery – by analytical chemists – that the mineral waters contained many more salt-forming elements than had been known in Bergman's day: manganese, zinc, strontium, potassium, lithium, phosphoric and flouric acids and, most importantly, bromine and iodine.[72] Whereas other spas, with a few mineral wells, might attempt analysis and then publication of their waters' contents, Harrogate, with the world's greatest known supply of natural mineral waters – some of which were notoriously irregular in their compositional nature – could not, before 1841, embark on such exercises. The Harrogate spa survived the increasingly sceptical opinions of the nation's medical analysts, because water drinking was only one facet of the spa experience, and one, moreover, which had all the advantages of a natural, undeveloped setting, and none of the disadvantages of the sceptical scrutiny directed to the handful of mineral wells in other resorts ... In any case, the purgative power of the Old Sulphur Well was secure to the doubts of the analytical chemists.[73]

Moreover, the other great threat to British spas – the growing popularity of seaside resorts – did not harm Harrogate to the extent it harmed its rivals. As Dr Hembry put it:

During the 1840s the effects of over-building and over-investment in Spa towns were being felt more markedly ... Competition of the growing seaside resorts and the coming of the railways killed the small inland watering places. By the mid-nineteenth century the fervour for spas increasingly declined ...[74]

Compared with the social rigidities of Bath, Buxton or Cheltenham, the freedom and informality of Scarborough, Bournemouth or Eastbourne were infinitely preferable to the newly mobile middle classes. This freedom and informality was precisely what all classes of visitor found so refreshing at Harrogate. From the time of Edmund Bogg's 1731 description:

> nothing can be more fine and agreeable than the intercourse here. Each strives to make the other happy, and nearly as much is effected by good temper and cheerfulness ... as by the waters themselves ... the mixture of families at the inns and boarding houses renders the entire company of a thousand individuals like one happy family. (C.26)

Until the complaint of Charles Dibdin in 1802 that at Harrogate, 'everything is too full of freedom and too much in common. A man may, according to the routine, sit down at dinner between a Countess and a Milliner, a species of levelling which cannot happen even in a stage coach.' (C.76) Harrogate presented an appearance of informality and freedom in which the entertainments were shaped by the visitors themselves, rather than by any external authority. As Catherine Sinclair wrote, shortly before the passing of the 1841 Harrogate Improvement Act, 'this is the only spot in all the earth where English people attempt the ease and sociability of foreign manners.' (C.107.c)

The innkeepers at Harrogate benefited from the company resorting to the spa, and it was clearly in their best interests to maintain the status quo, which was that although all the inns shared the visitors, no single inn had a monopoly of the town's most celebrated mineral waters, the most popular of which was the Old Sulphur Well. The significance of the Old Sulphur Well as a means of attracting the visitors to Harrogate, cannot be under-estimated. This was the well chosen by Dr J. Hannath as the subject of his lecture to the Royal Society of Physicians in 1831 (F.56), and it was also called 'the glory and pride of Harrogate' by Dr Granville (G.58, p. 42). From the time of its first recorded use in the seventeenth century, the Old Sulphur Well had always been open to all the visitors, regardless of whether the land on which it was located, belonged to the king or those who benefited from the Enclosure of the Forest in 1778.

Its importance had already been confirmed in 1806, when the landlords of all the significant inns of High and Low Harrogate contributed towards the

fund for building a pump room, in the form of an open Doric temple, over the well (A.266). However, when one of the innkeepers threatened the sanctity of the publicly owned Old Sulphur Well, he set in motion developments which culminated in the passing of the 1841 Harrogate Improvement Act.

The Thackwray Case and its aftermath

On 1 December 1835 the owner of the Swan Hotel, Jonathan Shutt, was walking past the Old Sulphur Well, when his attention was caught by a pile of earth outside one of the shops which formed the rear premises of the Crown Hotel (see plate 89). This lay only a few yards from the public Old Sulphur Well. On investigating, Mr Shutt found that two men were digging a pit which had reached a depth of about seven feet six inches, which was filling with sulphur water. Mr Shutt then crossed to the Old Sulphur Well, where he found the water level to be falling. Thoroughly alarmed by his discovery, Shutt called upon his innkeeper colleagues, Dearlove of the Queen, Frith of the Dragon, Benn of the Granby, as well as John Williams, owner of Low Harrogate's Victoria Baths and newly opened Royal Cheltenham Pump Room (H.10).

Together the men decided to take some sort of action against the owner of the Crown Hotel, Joseph Thackwray, believing that he was either trying to divert the water of the publicly owned Old Sulphur Well into his own property, or that his actions would injure the old well. The presence of Samuel Powell, a solicitor, was sought. This was a wise move, given that Samuel Powell was the Steward for the Royal Forest, appointed by the Duchy of Lancaster, and consequently regarded as the most influential legal mind in the area. When Powell arrived, a notice was drawn up, calling on Joseph Thackwray to desist in the making of his new well; otherwise, legal proceedings would be taken against him. One fact which may have motivated the group was that none of them owned mineral wells on their hotel properties, unlike their formidable business rival, Thackwray, who possessed many wells on his Crown estate. For Thackwray to gain control additionally of the water of the famous Old Sulphur Well, would be for him to gain a dangerous commercial monopoly. Mr Powell subsequently called on Mr Thackwray, who gave the assurance that his intention had not been to damage the public sulphur wells, and that he would not be deepening his own new well any further as the current depth of 9 feet was quite adequate (H.10).

The following day, after receiving Samuel Powell's report, the hoteliers called on Joseph Thackwray in person, their number having been increased by the presence of Nicholas Carter of the Prospect Hotel (who, like his colleagues, was not the happy owner of a mineral well!). The landlord of the Dragon asked Mr Thackwray if he knew the clause in the 1770 Enclosure Act which banned the digging of pits likely to result in damage or pollution to the public wells, to which Mr Thackwray replied in the affirmative. The landlord of the Granby then asked Mr Thackwray if he would refill his well, as that would 'satisfy the town and prevent legal proceedings', to which Mr Thackwray replied that he 'didn't like law, but would protect his private property, and all Yorkshire should not make him desist.' (H.11) The sides were now drawn for a legal battle, and the hoteliers decided to ask Samuel Powell to represent them in a prosecution of Joseph Thackwray. Unfortunately for them, Mr Powell advised that he had, the previous day, been appointed to act as Joseph Thackwray's solicitor. The astute Mr Thackwray had moved quickly (W.10.6).

The leading Thackwray opponents assembled on 7 December 1835 at 'the committee room, High Harrogate' to formalise their opposition. Throughout the Thackwray affair, the role of the High Harrogate innkeepers and doctors demonstrated that the subject of the Old Sulphur Well was not just a matter of concern to Low Harrogate, but to all sections of the Harrogate community (H.8.b).

A formal committee was established, consisting of Benn of the Granby, Frith of the Dragon, Dearlove of the Queen, Shutt of the Swan, Williams,

PLATE 94
Betty Lupton – could
this be the Betty of
'Betty's Café' fame?

owner of the Victoria Baths and Royal Spa Rooms, and two wealthy land-owners, Charlesworth and Sheep-shanks (H.8.b). Throughout 1836, as evidence was gathered, water from the new well was piped into the newly built Crown Baths, whose opening in 1834 (G.25) may have prompted Mr Thackwray the following year to search for more mineral water (H.14). One question seemed to be paramount: were the Harrogate wells inter-connected at depth, or were they wholly independent of each other? The evidence of Thomas Coates (a pro-fessional 'well sinker') was sought, who claimed that the Harrogate wells were always vertical, and whenever one was pumped dry, its neighbours continued their yields unabated (H.14). Land surveyor John Howgate produced for the prosecutors a thorough set of plans and measurements of the yields of respective wells in the area, which appear to have involved much sampling, e.g. 'self and clerk filling the old spring and tasting like draughts of ale the fresh water spring in the neighbourhood.' (H.9) Meanwhile, Joseph Thackwray's solicitor, Samuel Powell, was also active, and between 15 and 30 February 1836, he collected no fewer than twenty-three affidavits, including reports from Professor Phillips, 'the eminent London geologist', and from old Betty Lupton (see plate 94), the 'Queen of the Wells' (W.10.14).

In early 1836 an injunction had been made to the Court of Chancery to restrain Joseph Thackwray from deepening or widening his well, but it was granted only after the well had been finished and provided with a pump. Armed with the injunction, the plaintiffs obtained a true bill for nuisance against Joseph Thackwray at the October 1836 session of the Royal Forest Court (H.12).

Eventually, on Tuesday 14 March 1837, the trial of Joseph Thackwray, on grounds of nuisance, was held at York assizes (H.12). The presiding judge, Baron Alderson, sought immediate clarification of one point: would Joseph Thackwray give up the new well if that was all the prosecutors sought? The defendant's counsel replied that their main purpose was to defend Joseph Thackwray against the charge of injuring the public, and that he would offer to put a pump into the new well, to which all the public could have access, but that as he had expended thousands of pounds over the past few years for the benefit of the public, and had already dug about a dozen other wells, he could not give up all his other wells. Thackwray also undertook not to deepen his new well, but to leave it as it was. After some further cross-examination, which resulted in Joseph Thackwray confirming that he would not deepen any of his other wells, Baron Alderson directed the jury to return a verdict of not guilty. The effect of the verdict was to secure Joseph Thackwray's right to the rest of the wells on his premises, at his engaging not to make them any deeper (H.12). One point which had been made repeatedly by Thackwray's counsel, Mr Cresswell, was with regard to 'the groundless jealousy the Queen had for the King', the Queen being co-plaintiff John Dearlove's hotel, and the King being, of course, Joseph Thackwray's Crown Hotel! (H.12). There may indeed have been a element of truth in this assertion, but the reality was that *all* the innkeepers had been alarmed by Thackwray's actions, as is so clearly shown by the later subscription lists to reimburse his prosecutors (H.11).

The rule of court was distributed throughout the town, the following extract in the form of a printed handbill:

> It is ordered by and with the consent of the parties, their counsel and attorneys, that there be entered a verdict of not guilty; and that the defendant shall appropriate the well in Mr Husband's shop to the public, by putting a pump into it, and that the room be converted into a public pump room, but that it shall not be maintained at the expense of the defendant, unless he thinks fit; and the room be opened to the public from six o'clock in the morning until six o'clock in the evening of each day, and that the defendant shall only use the pump and water in common with the rest of the public ... (H.12).

Joseph Thackwray enjoyed his victory – if indeed he regarded it as such – for a short time, for, within a few weeks of the death of William IV, the *Harrogate Advertiser* carried news of his death (R.2795). The same newspaper also reported the deaths of one of Thackwray's prosecutors, Thomas Frith, of the Dragon hotel. Finally, the death in November 1838 of John Williams, owner of the Victoria Baths and Royal Spa Rooms, had considerable implications for the remaining prosecutors, on whom fell the burden of the trial costs (W.8.44).

Although they had lost their prosecution, Benn, Charlesworth, Dearlove, Frith, Sheepshanks, Shutt and Williams had reason to be pleased. First, they had ensured that the new well would not be used; despite the court's ruling, it would have been obvious that no businessman such as Joseph Thackwray would choose to give the public free access to a shop with a well in it, instead of obtaining a rent from a tenant shopkeeper. Second, the prosecutors had won the sympathy and support of the town. On 21 March 1837, one week after the trial closed at York, a meeting was held at Carter's Hotel to 'take into consideration the propriety of raising a fund for the discharge of the expenses incurred in the recent law proceedings at York ...' This meeting, after thanking the prosecutors for 'their very great exertions' on behalf of the common interest, agreed to open a subscription to assist in the payment of the costs of £1,339 1s. 3d. (H.11). By 19 April the names on the subscription lists included all the leading hoteliers, doctors, traders and gentry in Harrogate. It even included the widow of Joseph Thackwray (H.11).

Township mood

In 1834, a year before the digging of the Thackwray well, the holders of the majority of 'Stray gates' – those imaginary gates which entitled their owners to depasture specified cattle upon the Stray – instructed their solicitor, Samuel Powell, to write to the Duchy of Lancaster. Mr Powell's letter reported that, 'the neglected state of the Common at Harrogate has long attracted the attention of visitors, and several attempts have been made to get the same into better order without success, owing to the gates being vested in twenty or thirty individuals who could never agree upon any plan'. Mr Powell also observed that the value of the land surrounding the Stray, which was still in Duchy ownership, would be increased if the Stray could be improved – a point not lost on the Duchy Council (J.14). This letter was attached to a more detailed memorial, which outlined the history of the Stray and the relevant legislation from the 1770 Enclosure Act. The memorial closed with a proposal that the entire Stray be drained, levelled, and that bylaws for the regulation and protection of the wells – which had been permitted under the legislation of 1789, but never implemented – should be introduced as soon as possible (J.15).

There seem to have been two sources of this attempt to put the Stray into better order. The 'gate holders' who communicated with Samuel Powell included the landlords of the larger Harrogate inns. If the Stray could be levelled, drained and otherwise improved, the value of each 'gate' would be increased, because of the improved yield of the land. Also, an improved Stray would be a further attraction, and a positive response to those visitors whose adverse remarks were mentioned in Samuel Powell's letter to the Duchy. In the event, this attempt at improvement failed, due to opposition to the proposed means of paying for the necessary legislation. The supporters of the proposed legislation suggested that fifty new gates should be created, which could then be sold for £80 each. Charles Greeves, owner of High Harrogate's Granby Hotel, and an important gate holder, complained to the Duchy Court that this would drastically reduce the value of existing gates because it would mean that more livestock could be pastured on the same two hundred acres. The Duchy Court agreed with Charles Greeves, and in any case had a dislike of legislation that was narrow and special rather than general and comprehensive (B.219).

After the 1837 Thackwray trial, Harrogate appears to have experienced something of a mood of hyper-sensitivity so far as threats – real or imagined – to the Stray and wells were concerned. For example, in the spring of 1839 a row blew up regarding the placing of some seats on the Stray. These had been paid for by public subscription, to provide visitors – many of whom were invalids – with convenient seats. The sum of £130 was raised by popular subscription, and the seats were in place by the opening of the Harrogate season of 1839. The fact that the seats prevented access to every single square inch of the Stray, and therefore could be held to be an illegal enclosure of grass, caused some people (their names are not known) to indict the benefactors at York assizes for committing a nuisance. Historian William Grainge, writing in 1870, noted, 'we cannot find that this piece of ill-feeling and malevolence produced any effect, or for that matter came to a public trial.' (J.22)

A dispute of a more serious nature occurred in 1839, when a woodsman named Richardson entered a field in Low Harrogate, bordering the Stray, and marked for felling a row of fine trees which overhung a public footpath. The trees provided a sheltered walk for visitors, and were regarded as a valuable amenity to the community. The field and trees were owned by the Duchy of Lancaster, and Richardson was their employee, so the butt of local fury fell on the Duchy. A memorial of protest was prepared and dispatched to the Duchy's Chancellor, Lord Holland, signed by 160 of the town's leading citizens, and fifty-two visitors. It claimed that the trees were 'forming an agreeable shade to a public walk, the only one protected from the declining sun which the visitors can gratuitously enjoy.' (B.42) After making several enquiries, the Duchy Surveyor of Woods, Mr Gillett, found that 'some person has unwarrantably marked a number of oaks', probably to cause mischief (B.42, letter of 2/6/1839). The Duchy Court ordered that the line of mature trees be left standing, and that the woodsman be compensated with timber from 'other parts' (B.227). The strength of local feeling against the proposed tree felling was shown not only in the many letters of protest, but also in a report from the woodsman, who wrote to the Duchy surveyor Mr Gillett, that '... the inhabitants of Low Harrogate comes to my house and said it was at my peril that I set another foot in the above ground' (B.42, letter 20/5/1839). For the townspeople, here was further proof that the town's amenities were under threat. Throughout 1839 and 1840 feeling seems to have grown that something needed to be done about this perceived problem, which culminated in the approach to solicitor Samuel Powell on how best to approach the Duchy of Lancaster to obtain the necessary legislation (B.234).

Support for a new Act

Perhaps the most valuable outcome of the Thackwray case was that it helped to focus the attention of the community on the matter of protecting and improving the mineral wells. At a public meeting of 21 March 1837, held by Thackwray's prosecutors for the purpose of considering ways to defray the cost of the trial, a resolution was passed that, 'this meeting regret the very inadequate protection to the Antient Wells, which the original statute afford, and take this opportunity of expressing their full determination, at the earliest opportunity, of applying to the Legislature for an Act, whereby the above Wells, so valuable to the community, may in future be guarded against similar attempts, either of encroachment or injury.' The individuals behind this resolution included the landlords of all the principal inns of High and Low Harrogate, the secretary and surgeon of the Royal Bath Hospital, the principal and medium landowners (excluding the Duchy of Lancaster), builders such as Riley Fortune and T. H. Walker, shopkeepers and traders such as George Wright the coachmaker, and Miss Blackburn of the High Harrogate Library, influential local residents such as Captain Thomas Thrush, RN, and Mr Salt, and the proprietor of the *Harrogate Advertiser*, Pickersgill Palliser. The only substantial omissions from the list were the incumbents of High and Low Harrogate churches, Reverends Kennion and Digby, who probably excluded themselves on grounds of propriety, rather than opposition, and because they wished to consult the Duchy (who paid them both a stipend) before making any public comment on so significant a thing as a movement for a new Act (H.11).

The individuals who supported the proposal to obtain a new Act of Parliament were certainly representative of the commercial and social life of Harrogate. But there is little evidence to show that, initially, this support was for anything other than safeguarding and improving the mineral wells. If the high level of public interest in the Thackwray case is anything to go by (H.11, H.12), the affair of the Crown Hotel well seems to have shaken the town's commercial classes, and at the meeting of 21 March 1837 they demonstrated this concern by calling for fresh legislation. It is not hard to understand their concern. All of Harrogate depended on the annual success of the season, and even a remote threat to the attractions of the unique mineral wells was a direct threat to the livelihoods of every tradesman. innkeeper, and workman in the town. Although the minutes of subsequent meetings of the committee have not survived, sufficient progress had been made by 1840 for Samuel Powell to make his approach to the Duchy of Lancaster for assistance in securing new legislation (W.11.32).

Obtaining the 1841 Improvement Act

During the autumn of 1840, Mr Powell met with 'many of the principal inhabitants' relative to the protection of the wells, and drainage and improvement of the Stray. Mr Powell advised the Duchy of the level of local support for a new Act, and succeeded in persuading the Duchy's Secretary, Mr Danvers, and the Surveyor General, Colonel Fox, to visit Harrogate so that they might support the application if it came before the Duchy Council. Some of the 'principal inhabitants', including the leading innkeepers and doctors, met on 9 November 1840, to discuss various proposals for resolutions which were to be put to a public meeting (W.11.33), and the following day Mr Powell met with the chairman and leading gentlemen to go over the proposals and brief them on how the meeting should be conducted, so that it should be taken seriously by the Duchy. Mr Powell also posted copies of the agenda to the London *Gazette* and two Leeds newspapers (W.11.34).

Events now moved as quickly 'as possible, there not being a day to be lost', and on 15 November, Mr Powell fixed public notices of the meeting of 24 November on the doors of High and Low Harrogate churches (I.4). The meeting, held at High Harrogate's Queen Hotel, advised those in attendance that the committee had, the previous day, met with the owners of the Stray gates, who had engaged to improve and drain the Stray at their own expense, on not being called upon for any part of the expense of the intended Act. This showed the attitude of part of the Harrogate community towards new legislation. Considering that the Stray gate owners had, since 1778, had sixty years to improve the Stray, and had failed so to do, their statement must have been heard with scepticism by others at the meeting. The Stray gate owners were not even unanimous at their meeting of 23 November. In all, they represented ownership of thirty-six and a half of the total of fifty gates. At one point five members, representing thirteen gates, retired, objecting to some point of procedure, but not before having supported the first two resolutions for improving the Stray and the expediency of applying for an Act of Parliament. The remaining fifteen owners were, in terms of a show of hands, still a majority, but they represented only a minority of gates. Samuel Powell undoubtedly acted in a high-handed manner at the two meetings of 23 and 24 November 1840. With the Stray gate owners on the 23rd, he insisted that the voting be on the basis of one man per vote, regardless of the number of gates each vote represented. However, by the time he distributed the printed resolutions of the meeting to proceed with the application to Parliament, a number of Stray gates had been sold by those opposed to change, and bought by those in favour of it. Mr Powell was then at pains to stress that the application was supported not only by the majority of votes, but by the majority of gate owners as well.[75] He was clearly the right man for the job.

The public meeting of 24 November 1840 decided in its sixth resolution that costs incurred in the obtaining of a new Act should be met by laying a new rate upon the Stray, and on all lands, houses, buildings, gardens and yards within the geographical limits of the new Act. Costs for actually carrying the Act into execution were to be paid for by a further rate on the Stray, and on all lands and houses within the Act. These proposals were at variance with those of the previous day, agreed to by the gate owners, who wanted to have a rate of about £5 per annum on each gate, after five years each owner to have extra gates in proportion to the number they possessed (J.25).

On 5 December 1840 Mr Powell wrote to the Duchy, forwarding the resolutions agreed by the public meeting of 24 November, adding that it 'was exceedingly favourable to the proposed improvements, and was attended by a large proportion of the higher classes in the two villages'. He estimated that the cost of the proposed Act was £600, and expressed 'the hope that the Council of the Duchy will be induced to make a liberal grant, particularly as Duchy land will be so much improved by the proposed drainage.' (B.143) The Duchy considered the matter on 19 December 1840, which it supported, subject to various questions being satisfied about other contributions, and the extent of the area to be affected by the new Act. Between 19 December 1840 and 30 March 1841, many letters passed between Mr Powell, in Harrogate, and the Duchy's secretary, Mr Danvers, which – little by little – extended the scope of the draft Bill so that it eventually included machinery for the election of twenty-one 'Improvement Commissioners' (clauses 2–18); with powers to borrow up to a ceiling of £3,000 (clause 56); to protect and control the mineral wells (clauses 87–94); to construct and maintain roads and footpaths (clauses 95–97); to construct sewers and drains (clauses 98–101); to license carriages (clauses 140–148); to appoint constables (clauses 157–165); to purchase or rent buildings (clause 77); definitions of responsibilities of Stray gate owners, and confirmation of their power to make and enforce bylaws for the Stray (clauses 194–212); and, powers to light the streets (clause 135). Although many of these powers were permissive, rather than obligatory, the Duchy had widened the scope of the Bill from a simple means of protecting the mineral wells and controlling the Stray, to a blueprint for a modern system of local government such as was suitable for a rapidly developing community like Harrogate.[76]

It is worth emphasising that the influence of the Duchy at this key stage in the progress of the draft Bill was absolutely critical. Given the original objective of the innkeepers of obtaining improved protection for the wells – especially in the light of the recent Thackwray well case – and the prevalent wish to improve the Stray, piecemeal legislation would have been quite in keeping with their requirements and vision. Nor would it have been unusual. In 1770 Worcester had obtained an act to empower the city to supply water, cleanse sewers and drains.[77] This act had to be amended, and its powers extended, by subsequent Acts dated 1780 and 1823. Gloucester, in 1819, promoted a special Bill to empower the authority to light the streets with gas, a move vigorously opposed by the vestry of the specific parish involved. At Banbury in 1824 a group of professional men promoted a bill to enable the authority to pave the streets of the central area, but with no powers for lighting the same streets.[78] For the Duchy, however, such piece-meal legislation does not appear to have been favoured, most probably for the sensible reason that in the long run a comprehensive piece of local legis-lation was less demanding of valuable resources than a whole series of individual Acts.[79] This attitude enabled Harrogate to develop beyond the self-interest of the innkeepers and doctors, as it provided a comprehensive piece of legislation which would benefit the entire community. It was of course of great benefit to the Duchy, because – as the owner of the best tracts of land in the vicinity of the mineral wells – the value of their holdings would increase as the town developed.

On 30 March 1841 the Duchy Court ordered that the sum of £150 be contributed towards the cost of obtaining a new Act for Harrogate (B.235). The sum was not paid over to Mr Powell until October (B.237), because of a difference of opinion between the Harrogate committee and the Duchy over the right of the latter to appoint the minister of High Harrogate Chapel as an ex-officio member of the new board of Improvement Commissioners. After receiving objections from Harrogate, the Duchy agreed to withdraw their requirement (B.236).

Throughout his dealings with the Duchy, Mr Powell quoted extensively from the original resolutions passed by the public meeting at the Queen Hotel on 24 November 1840. The signatories of this document represented the leading members of the community, including the incumbents of High Harrogate Church – Reverend Thomas Kennion – and Low Harrogate Church – Reverend George Digby, as well as leading landowners Charles Charlesworth, John Bainbridge, Samuel Carrington, Matthew Thackwray, and John Green Paley (all 'esquires'). Tradesmen such as Joseph Waite, dispensing chemist, and Thomas Humble Walker, wine and spirit merchant, signed their support, as did the builder John Thompson. But one class dominated the signatories – that of innkeeper, or hotelier, as the trade was increasingly known. Headed by Staning of the Crown, the list included the new tenant of the Granby, Hall, as well as its old owner Mr Benn, Carter of Carter's Hotel, Peacock, the former workhouse master but now landlord of the Brunswick, Forrest of the White Hart, and Harper of the Wellington. The resolutions had been put together in the Queen Hotel, owned by Dearlove, who was also contributed financially (I.5). The absence of both the Dragon and Swan was no doubt because Frith had died in 1837, and Jonathan Shutt had died in 1840.

The Harrogate Improvement Act was passed on 10 May 1841,[80] and the first meeting of the newly elected twenty-one Improvement Commissioners took place on 7 June 1841, at John Dearlove's Queen Hotel.[81] Harrogate's population in 1841 was about 3,064,[82] which represented an increase of 600 per cent since the 1770 population figure of about 500.[83] The town, with its new Act, its reformed system of local government, protection for the mineral wells, and powers for the Stray gate owners to make and enforce bylaws, was well set to advance into the nineteenth century.

At the time when the ubiquitous Dr Granville was writing his great study of British spas, in which he praised Harrogate for its naturalness, while condemning its lack of progressive government (F.58, p. 83), the townspeople, led by the innkeepers and doctors, were taking steps to introduce the very form of government whose absence Dr Granville so criticised. Thanks to the self-interest of these men, and the wider influence of the Duchy of Lancaster, Harrogate obtained an Improvement Act which enabled it to develop as a town and as a spa, and – moreover – to do so successfully at the very time other British spas were declining.[84] So much so that by 1884, Harrogate sought and obtained the status of a Municipal Borough, with Mayor and Corporation.[85]

The continuing success of Harrogate was in no small part due to the Improvement Act of 1841, which was itself the culmination of a period which had opened with the Enclosure Act of 1770. That Act had provided Harrogate with limited means for providing access to the unique mineral wells, and the townspeople had, in co-operation with the Duchy of Lancaster, ensured that the potential of the 1770 Act had been exploited to the stage when only a fresh act could take them any further. As such, Harrogate's history from 1770 to 1841 is significant, and no more so than in the role of the innkeepers, doctors, and the Duchy of Lancaster. No other community in England was subject to the influence of such a group of interests, which is the explanation for the particular and largely atypical nature of Harrogate's urban development.

The precise boundaries of the new authority that came into being in 1841 excluded much of medieval Harrogate, and as the official 1841 census returns classed such traditional Harrogate localities as Sulphur Wells, Cold Bath Road, Harlow and Crimple as part of Pannal township, and Starbeck as a detached portion of Knaresborough, it is necessary to re-examine the commonly accepted figures. If the 80 resident patients at the Bath Hospital, and the 71 inmates of the workhouse are added to the totals for Bilton-with-Harrogate and the Cold Bath Road and Sulphur Wells parts of Pannal; and Harlow Hill (29) and Birk Cragg (12), Crimple, Fulwith, Hornbeam and Lead Hall (48) and Starbeck (62) (but excluding Pannal Ash) a population of 3,064 persons is the result.[86]

The period between the Enclosure Act of 1770 and the Improvement Act of 1841 was critical in determining the quality and direction of Harrogate's growth. If, at the opening of the Victorian age, the days of the town's glorious exclusivity seemed to have ended with the fading of the Regency era, the new age nevertheless presented its own challenges and forged its own answers. Although historians may consider that the new age opened with the passing of the 1841 Harrogate Improvement Bill, it is probable that for the citizens, a new age had dawned with the coronation of the youthful Queen Victoria, on 28 June 1838. According to historian William Grainge, it was

> kept as a general holiday in Harrogate, all the shops were closed, and the whole day was observed as a time of general festivity and rejoicing. The public wells and buildings were decorated. The children attending the National and Sunday schools, with many of the inhabitants, were sumptuously feasted to the number of upwards of five hundred, at tables set out on the Stray in front of Prospect Place, while those who had provided the treat for the children and their poorer neighbours, afterwards dined together at tables similarly set out in the open air in front of the White Hart ... The joyous company afterwards paraded the town in all directions, singing and playing by turns. Towards evening they were all regaled with tea – one portion in front of Prospect Place, another in the Cheltenham (Spa) Room, which along with the grounds, was freely thrown open for the recreation of the children and the public. Dinner parties were held at the Queen and Black Swan in High Harrogate, and a grand ball was held at the Crown ... All went merry as a marriage bell (A.293).

One thing was certain, Harrogate's future could never be as great as its past – it could only be greater.

16 | Conclusion

T HE KEY to understanding the urban development of Harrogate from
1770 until 1841 lies in the nature of the relationship between both
residents and visitors, as well as the influences exerted upon both groups by
one external, and two internal interests. This troika of interest embraced
two professions (doctor and innkeeper), and the Duchy of Lancaster. In
combination, the troika was unique, which is why Harrogate's urban
history is unique. No other British spa or resort was subjected to such a
combination of interest.

In early nineteenth-century Britain spas were in decline. Although they
made much of such aristocratic patronage as the Cavendish family at
Buxton,[1] or Queen Adelaide at Leamington,[2] their principal source of
income seems to have come from the enriched middle classes, who aped
the aristocracy's habit of attending fashionable watering places.[3] Their rise
had been brought about, as Corfield wrote, 'by a new and more broadly
based consumer society [which] created urban markets for specialist
entertainments previously confined to courts, the capital and great country
houses'.[4] When applied to British spas, this consumerism comprised
elements of (a) the identification of ailments, real or imaginary and their
appropriate treatment – which involved the doctors; (b) lifestyle, by means
of accommodation at an inn, plus a wide range of associated entertainments
– which involved the innkeepers and those in their employ; (c) the local
conditions under which both elements of consumerism operated, and
which in Harrogate were determined by the principal landowner, the
Duchy of Lancaster. At Bath, Buxton, Cheltenham, Leamington, Malvern
and Tunbridge, the spas thrived in urban environments, some of which
were the result of uncontrolled speculation and over-development,
including an element of architectural 'frameworking' for ritualistic
promenading. Entertainments, equally, were prescribed and formal, being
determined by tradition and supervised by Masters of Ceremony. Alone of
major British spas, Harrogate had neither a formal urban environment, nor
a system of prescribed entertainment. It simply had the mineral wells in
their natural state, plus the visitors, who themselves determined the spa

lifestyle. Consequently, when fashions changed, the developed urban spas were put out of sympathy with the times, whereas 'naturalistic' Harrogate continued to function with all elements of its spa being determined by the visitors themselves. As Dr Granville put it, the seven or eight thousand visitors who were in Harrogate in 1839 at the peak of the season, were 'a larger number than at any other English spa'.[5] The visitors were 'the lords of the place ... what does not suit them, that must not be'.[6]

Resort towns in nineteenth-century Britain underwent phenomenal transformation. Increasing urbanisation concentrated ever larger populations within towns and cities. Yet between 1801 and 1851 the aggregate rate of growth of English manufacturing towns was slower than that of English spas and resorts.[7] It was a case of English spas and resorts rising to meet the challenge of the new centres of urban population, possessed of desire to emulate the lifestyle of the aristocracy, as well as the means of paying for it. Throughout England, spas and resorts were increasingly urbanised, a process which affected (a) building development, (b) local government, (c) education, (d) religious life, (e) health and medical welfare. Harrogate's experience, in all five areas, was unique.

Building development was the most obvious process of urbanisation. By 1841 Harrogate's population was 3,064,[8] whereas Bath's was 53,206.[9] Yet size of population did not determine the success or failure of a spa. In 1841 Bath was declining as a spa, whereas the Harrogate spa was enjoying increased popularity, thanks to the fashion for 'natural' waters at natural settings, and the swing of taste away from the eighteenth-century formality, in favour of the freedom of nineteenth-century consumerism.[10] Equally, Malvern, with its 1841 population of 2,768, below Harrogate's 3,064, was also in decline, thanks to the results of the faulty Enclosure Act of 1664 which placed the best plots of land under the control of three local families.[11] Harrogate, by contrast, benefited from the favourable terms of the 1770 Enclosure Act, which saw the uniform distribution of plots of land to local people balanced by Duchy retention of key central plots, which were developed slowly and carefully (B.31). Urban development at Harrogate was therefore planned and careful, and the catastrophe of over-development, which harmed Leamington in the 1820s, was avoided at Harrogate.[12]

Local government, so necessary for the regularisation of the living conditions of an urban population, was primitive in early nineteenth-century Harrogate, because the town had a small residential population (*c.* 1,600 in 1801),[13] which was swollen by migratory workers during the spa 'season' and who were consequently not a drain on the township. The vestry meetings, dominated by local innkeepers and doctors, ensured that those aspects of local government which had the most direct bearing on the visitors – such as maintaining highways and footpaths likely to be used by visitors – were enforced (D.18). Equally, the lack of any appreciable numbers of impoverished local residents meant that the workhouse was treated almost as an adjunct to the inns and hotels, in that the innkeeper-dominated vestry was able – for a fee – to take in paupers from surrounding villages which were without workhouses of their own (D.50.26). Also, the existence of the Harrogate workhouse ensured that any genuine local paupers could be kept away from the gaze of the visitors to the spa (D.18). The town's small-scale local government was in contrast to that of other spas such as Bath or Cheltenham. At Cheltenham, local government negotiated no fewer than seven Acts, each piecemeal and particular,[14] none of which halted the town's decline as a spa.[15]

At Harrogate, by contrast, calls for similar local legislation were transformed by the Duchy of Lancaster into an Act much broader than envisaged by the local innkeepers.[16] In other words, at Harrogate, lack of a properly developed system of local government did not result in failure to obtain the comprehensive legislation necessary for the town's future development. Once again, the peculiar balance between the innkeepers, who started the move for local government reform with the 1835–1837 Thackwray well case, and the Duchy of Lancaster, who ended the process by steering the 1841 Harrogate Improvement Act through Parliament, was to Harrogate's advantage.[17]

The division of education at Harrogate between 1770 and 1841 was a division between charity education provided for the poorer classes, and private education provided for the affluent classes. The former category included children of agricultural workers and manual workers, who lived away from the spa, in the rural areas of Bilton-with-Harrogate and Pannal. This was why the first charity school was established in rural Bilton.[18] By contrast, the first known private school in Harrogate was at 'the Grove' (C.83.c), adjacent to the prestigious Dragon Hotel at High Harrogate, which taught the children of visitors, as well as the children of affluent local residents, such as doctors and innkeepers (C.83.f). The Award of 1778, made at the time of the Enclosure of the Royal Forest, was done by the Duchy commissioners in such a manner as to ensure that the innkeepers were able to acquire parcels of land in the immediate vicinity of their establishments (B.31). Consequently the innkeepers were able to control the uses which prospective tenants could make of their holdings. Even if there had been a need for much charity education in Harrogate, it was unlikely to have been located within sight of the great inns.

Education appears to have been stimulated at Harrogate more by the need to provide a workforce capable of meeting the basic requirements of the spa – especially the innkeepers and traders – than by the ideological battles between Anglicanism and non-conformity, which were such a feature of life in other urban areas.[19] As the urbanisation of High and Low Harrogate increased between 1821 and 1841, the population increasing from c.2,000 to 3,064,[20] and commercial activity developed correspondingly (G.18), so too did educational provision. In Low Harrogate, which – since c. 1800 – was becoming increasingly fashionable (R.1310), a call was made for a charity school of its own. This call, made in 1818, was directed to the Duchy of Lancaster, who provided a grant to enable such a school to be built (B.191). In 1825 High Harrogate also received help from the Duchy, when a petition sent to elicit assistance with the building of a new school, produced a grant (B.212). Once again, the intervention of the Duchy proved critical in an important area of Harrogate's urban development.

Religious life in Harrogate between 1770 and 1841 was atypical of that of other English communities, in that it experienced neither a decline in Anglicanism, nor a rise of non-conformity.[21] Thanks to the Crown, via the Duchy of Lancaster, the structural and pastoral requirements for active Anglicanism were maintained: the Duchy funded the building of Low Harrogate Church (N.24) and High Harrogate Church (M.179), as well as contributing towards the stipends of the curates of St Mary's church (B.296) and Christ Church (B.267). Thanks to the town's principal businessmen, the seasonal spa employed labour on a seasonal basis (R.3138), so Harrogate lacked a permanent population of those classes of society who were the mainstay of non-conformity (D.59). The principal class was, of course, the visitor class, and it was for this class that both of Harrogate's Anglican churches were primarily built. High Harrogate's Christ Church, built on land given by the Duchy (B.31), was erected for the convenience of the visitors (M.185). Equally, Low Harrogate's St Mary's was built on land owned by the Duchy (N.24), and voluntarily surrendered by the owner of the Crown Hotel, Joseph Thackwray (N.38). Between 1770 and 1841 non-conformity failed to make any impression on the religious life of Harrogate until the creation of a separate community of central Harrogate in the 1820s led to the building of the first purpose-built Methodist chapel.[22] This experience was very different from that of other communities, where non-conformity expanded as Anglicanism declined.[23]

One of the most important matters faced by post-industrial urban development was that of health and medical welfare, since no class, economic or social system, or religious faith, could withstand the onslaught of infection or plague. Harrogate, which had no industrialisation beyond the spa industry, and no impoverished resident population which might be a source of infection, nevertheless had, by 1825, a hospital that was famous as a refuge for the sick poor of other towns (U.1). In this Harrogate followed the example of Leamington, which in 1806 had opened a charity to enable the sick poor from any part of the kingdom to make free use of the waters.[24]

Thanks to the Duchy of Lancaster, Harrogate's waters were free for all to drink, so the Harrogate charity concentrated on providing facilities for patients (U.12). However, the innkeepers, who sat on the Hospital's Board, were a further influence. First, they ensured that when the visitors left (taking their source of funding with them), the hospital closed, re-opening only at the start of the following season (U.20). Second, they ensured that no patients with any infectious disease, nor any lunatics, could be admitted at any time. Third, they ensured that each inn contained a subscription book for guests to record hospital donations (U.20). The influence of the visitors was also apparent by the regulation which prevented any of the Harrogate sick poor from being admitted (U.1, rule 17). Power to admit was determined by size of subscription, and as the visitors provided most of the subscriptions, and admittance was limited by the size of the hospital, the visitors were very influential (U.1, rules 3, 4, 5 and 6.)

The defensive action against infection, which urbanisation had produced (or, if not produced, at least exacerbated) at Cheltenham in 1786 and 1806,[25] Bath in 1788,[26] Malvern in 1830,[27] and Tunbridge in 1832,[28] as well as in the larger industrial centres such as Huddersfield in 1831,[29] or Wakefield in 1841,[30] was never necessary at Harrogate. As the *York Herald* noted, 'the health of the place [i.e. Harrogate] was never better, and it has long been considered a most safe refuge from the dangers of infection, and the ravages of the pestilence.' (R.2435) In health matters, as in so many other areas, Harrogate's urban development was atypical.

The broader picture

The phenomenon of urbanisation in Britain between *c.* 1750 and 1914 was so great that by 1914 the United Kingdom was the world's most urbanised nation. Describing this process, R. J. Morris wrote, 'British towns of the industrial revolution period were substantially the creation of their middle class, and in turn provided the theatre within which that middle class sought, extended, expressed and defended its power'.[31] This was true for Harrogate, save that at Harrogate, the spa created by the professional middle classes – the doctors and innkeepers – continued to attract the aristocracy and nobility.

Spas were only one kind of resort, and as the nineteenth century progressed, their rivals enjoyed increased patronage. In 1806 a guidebook to English watering places listed thirty-four sea bathing resorts, of which only four – Bridlington, Brighton, Scarborough and Southampton – were also known as spas. Sea bathing, known to be pleasurable and believed to be healthy, was a serious challenge to traditional inland water places.[32]

The industrial revolution, which was such a stimulus to urbanisation, also provided its antidote in the form of mass transportation, which enabled people to escape the greater urban areas, and travel widely. Whereas other British spas lost much of their custom, as the middle classes took up the seaside resorts, and the aristocracy patronised the continental spas with their casinos and imperial society,[33] Harrogate continued to attract the wealthy middle classes, the landed families of the north, country squires from the old stone granges of the Yorkshire Dales,[34] as well as the aristocracy and royalty.

The source of Harrogate's success as a flourishing, urbanised spa, lay in the key period between the 1770 Enclosure Act and the 1841 Improvement Act, in which the principal movers were the doctors, the innkeepers, and the Duchy of Lancaster.

Notes *and* references

Notes to Chapter 1: Genesis of a community

1. Bernard Jennings, *A History of Harrogate and Knaresborough* (Advertiser Press, 1970), p.24.
2. J. L. Coles, H. Coutts and M. L. Ryder, 'A late Bronze Age find from Pyotdykes, Angus', *Proceedings of the Prehistoric Society*, xxx (1964), pp. 186–92.
3. William Wheater, *Harrogate the Antique* (Parliament Street, 1900?), p. 1.
4. Richard Muir, *Landscape Detective: Discovering a Countryside* (Windgather Press, 2001).
5. *Harrogate Advertiser*, 5 July 1952.
6. Bernard Jennings, *History of Harrogate and Knaresborough*, p. 26.
7. William Grainge, *History and Topography of Harrogate and the Forest of Knaresborough* (Smith & Co., 1871), p. 248.
8. Peter Salway, *Roman Britain* (Oxford, 1981), p. 434.
9. Bernard Jennings, *History of Harrogate and Knaresborough*, p. 27.
10. Ibid., p. 28.
11. Ibid., p. 30.
12. Ibid., p.30.
13. Pipe Roll, 31 Henry I, p. 31.
14. English Place-name Society, vol.

15. 34, p. 117. See also West Riding Place Names, vol. 4, 32.
15. For example, Ordnance Survey, Explorer 27 (Lower Wharfedale), 1:25000.
16. M. Chibnall, *Ecclesiastical History of Orderic Vitalis*, II (Oxford, 1969), pp. 231–3.
17. W. E. Wightman, 'The Significance of Waste in Yorkshire Domesday', *Northern History*, x (1975), pp. 55–71.
18. The Domesday Book.
19. Ibid., ref. SW, Bu. 31; 46.
20. A bovate is one-eighth of a ploughland or carucate, varying in size from 10 to 18 acres, according to the condition of the land.
21. The Domesday Book.
22. Bernard Jennings, *History of Harrogate and Knaresborough*, p. 36.
23. The Domesday Book.
24. William Grainge, *History and Topography of Harrogate ...* (Russell Smith, 1871), frontispiece map.
25. Early Yorkshire Charters, no. 513.
26. David Hey, *Yorkshire from AD 1000* (Longman, 1986), p. 4.
27. Bernard Jennings, *History of Harrogate and Knaresborough*, p. 78.
28. Richard Muir, *Landscape Detective:*

29. *Discovering a Countryside* (Windgather, 2001), pp. 22–5.
29. Charles Young, *Royal Forests of Medieval England* (Leicester University Press, 1979), pp. 18–19.
30. Pipe Roll, 15 Henry I, p. 37.
31. Pipe Roll, 31 Henry I, p. 31.
32. *Early Yorkshire Charters*, volume one, pp. 390–2.
33. Pipe Rolls, 7 John, p. 59.
34. Bernard Jennings, *History of Harrogate and Knaresborough*, pp. 96–7.
35. Calendar of Patent Rolls, 1216–1225, pp. 64, 315, 425.
36. Calendar of Close Rolls, 1227–1231, pp. 315; 1231–1234, pp. 238, 438.
37. *Yorks Inquisitions*, volume III, p. 126.
38. Bernard Jennings, *History of Harrogate and Knaresborough*, p. 108.
39. Calendar of Patent Rolls, 1317–1321, p. 310.
40. Court Rolls, National Archives, D.L. 42/129.
41. Bernard Jennings, *History of Harrogate and Knaresborough*, p. 65.
42. Ibid., pp. 66–7.

Notes to Chapter 2: Harrogate and the Royal Forest

1. Charles Young, *Royal Forests of England* (Leicester University Press, 1979), p. 19
2. Pipe Rolls 15 Henry II, p. 37.
3. William Grainge, *History and Topography of Harrogate and the Forest of Knaresborough* (Russell Smith, 1871), p. 97
4. Bernard Jennings, *History of Harrogate and Knaresborough* (Advertiser Press, 1970), p. 78.
5. Pipe Roll of 15 Henry II, p. 37.

6. H. R. Schubert, *History of the British Iron and Steel Industry from 450 BC to AD 1775* (Routledge & Kegan Paul, 1958), p. 104
7. Bernard Jennings, *History of Nidderdale* (Advertiser Press, 1967), p. 62
8. Yorkshire Archaeological Society Record Series, volume 1, p. 66.
9. H. R. Schubert, *History of the British Iron and Steel Industry*, p. 112.
10. Ibid., p. 122.

11. Bernard Jennings, *History of Nidderdale* (Advertiser Press, 1967), p. 62.
12. Bernard Jennings, *History of Harrogate and Knaresborough*, p. 92.
13. Oyer and Terminer – a commission to justices of the royal court to hear and determine specific cases of treason, murder and other serious crimes.
14. William Grainge, *History and Topography of Harrogate and the*

Forest of Knaresborough, p. 345.

15. In J. J. Bagley and P. B. Rowley, *Documentary History of England*, volume one (Pelican, 1966), pp. 70–3.

16. Sir Robert Somerville, *History of the Duchy of Lancaster, volume one, 1265–1603* (Duchy of Lancaster, 1953), p. 137.

17. J. C. Holt, *Robin Hood* (Thames & Hudson, 1989), chapters 2–5.

18. G. Phillips and M. Keatman, *Robin Hood: The Man Behind the Myth* (O'Mara Books, 1995), pp. 72–8.

19. Leland's Itinerary, 1769 edition, vol. V, p. 101.

20. British Library Department of Manuscripts, Sloane manuscript 715.

21. *Lytell Geste of Robyn Hood*, 1495.

22. Public Record Office. D.L. 42/15 f. 101.

23. Ibid., f. 12.

24. Sir Robert Somerville, *History of the Duchy of Lancaster, volume one, 1265–1603* (Duchy of Lancaster, 1953), p. 395.

25. Ibid., p. 460.

26. Ibid., p. 396.

27. Sir Robert Somerville, *History of the Duchy of Lancaster, volume two, 1603–1965*, privately printed for the Duchy, 1970), pp. 16–29.

Notes to Chapter 3: Early Harrogate, 1332–1371

1. Bernard Jennings, *History of Harrogate and Knaresborough* (Advertiser Press, 1970), p. 54.

2. Ibid., p. 67.

3. Bernard Jennings (ed.), *History of Nidderdale* (Advertiser Press, 1967), p. 57.

4. J. F. D. Shrewsbury, *History of Bubonic Plague in the British Isles* (Cambridge, 1970), pp. 2–3.

5. Bernard Jennings, *History of Nidderdale* (Advertiser Press, 1967), p. 90.

6. Sir Robert Somerville, *History of the Duchy of Lancaster, volume one, 1265–1603* (Duchy of Lancaster, 1953), p. 52.

7. G. H. Cook, *Medieval Chantries and Chantry Chapels* (Phoenix House, 1932), p. 21.

8. *Valor Ecclesiasticus.*

9. J. R. Lunn, *Eccl. Rur. Deanery of Boroughbridge*, p. 32.

10. G. H. Cook, *Medieval Chantries and Chantry Chapels* (Phoenix House, 1963), p. 21

11. *Early Yorkshire Charters* volume one, pp. 390–2. Calendar of Charter Rolls, volume one. p. 191.

12. Rollo Clowes, *Notebook*, Duchy of Cornwall archive, p. 117.

13. Yorkshire Chantries, volume 92.

14. A tax levied on a person's belongings, collected between 1181 and 1623, based on one tenth of total value.

15. A selion was a cultivated strip in an open field consisting of a ridge with a furrow on either side.

16. Court Roll D.L. 30/487/1.

17. Bernard Jennings (ed.), *History of Nidderdale* (Advertiser Press, 1967), p. 63.

18. H. R. Schubert, *History of the British Iron and Steel Industry from 450 BC to AD 1775* (Routledge, 1957), p. 181.

19. Ibid., p. 227.

Surtees Society. 1893. p. 259.

Notes to Chapter 4: Rise of the spa, 1371–1660

1. P. Lafagne, *Spa et les Anglais ou l'influence anglais dans l'historie de Spa.*

2. There was a Sir William Slingsby, but he was only nine years of age in 1571, and lived at Kippax, rather than the Bilton Park mentioned by Dr Deane.

3. Calendar of State Papers Domestic, additions 1547–1565, p. 571.

4. See entry for Bright in Dictionary of National Biography.

5. W. J. Carlton, *Timothe Bright, Doctor of Phisicke* (Elliot Stock, 1911), p. 153.

6. Phillis Hembry, *The English Spa, 1560–1815: A Social History* (Athlone Press, 1990).

7. Ibid., p. 366.

8. Dr G. West Piggott, *Records of Cures Effected by the Harrogate Waters in the Reign of Charles the First* (Palliser, c. 1855).

9. William Grainge, *History and Topography of Harrogate ...* (John Russell Smith, 1871), p. 204.

10. Ibid., pp. 217–22.

11. *Harrogate Advertiser*, 15 February 1958.

12. Ibid., 16 January 1960.

13. Note 13.

14. Note 14.

15. Peter Wenham, *The Siege of York, 1644* (Sessions, 1994).

16. Dodsworth Transcriptions, volume 129 (H), c. 1619–1630, ff. 62 verso, Bodleian Library.

17. Sir Robert Somerville, *History of the Duchy of Lancaster, volume two, 1603–1965*, Chapter 4, Commonwealth and Restoration.

18. Sidney J. Madge, *Domesday of Crown Lands: A Study of the Legislation, Surveys and Sales of Royal Estates under the Commonwealth* (Routledge, 1938). (This work provides the most detailed analysis of the whole process of disposal, and is invaluable for purposes of comparison.)

19. See entries in National Archives: D.L. 30/500/4–6.

20. P. H. Atkinson, *Political History of Knaresborough*, box 3, Harrogate Reference Library.

Notes to Chapter 5: Restoration to enclosure

1. Sir George Clarke, *Later Stuarts, 1660–1714* (Oxford, 1956) Chapter one.

2. William Grainge, *History and Topography of Harrogate ...* (Russell Smith, 1871), p. 149.

3. J. Gardiner and N. Wenborn, *Companion to British History* (Collins and Brown, 1995), p. 17.

4. Author's collection.

5. Calendar of State Papers Domestic, 1664–65, p. 423.

6. The lease was signed with the Duchy seal on 13 November 1629 – D.L.41/83.

7. William Grainge, *History and Topography of Harrogate* (Russell Smith, 1871), p. 187.

(The recording of this fact by historian Grainge almost as a casual aside is a typical and infuriating example of the man's approach to historiography; yet he could happily devote time and space to recording endless lists of useless church inscriptions!)

8. *Harrogate Advertiser*, 8 August 1959.
9. Phillis Hembry, *English Spa, 1560–1815* (Athlone, 1990), p. 365.
10. Ibid., p. 366.

11. Lay taxes in England and Wales, 1188–1688. Public Record Office.
12. John Purdy, *Hearth Tax Returns for Yorkshire, 1662–1674*. Volumes 1–2, Theses A, Leeds University M.Phil.

pp. 346, 661, 728.

13. *Oxford Companion to Local History* (Oxford, 1996), p. 454.
14. Michael Turner, *Enclosures in Britain, 1750–1832*, pp. 68–70.

Notes to Chapter 6: Harrogate and the enclosure of the Forest

1. Michael Turner, *Enclosures in Britain, 1750–1830* (Folkstone, 1980), p. 68.
2. Ibid., p. 70.
3. W. H. R. Curtler, *Enclosure and redistribution of our land* (Oxford, 1920), pp. 238–50.
4. J. L. and B. Hammond, *Village Labourer, 1760–1832* (London, 1927) p. 28.
5. Ibid., p. 73., 81, 30–31.
6. Ibid., p. 35.
7. Ibid., p. 40.
8. Ibid., p. 62.
9. Sir Robert Somerville, *History of the Duchy of Lancaster, volume 2, 1603–1965* (1970), pp. 155–65.
10. J. L. and B. Hammond, *Village Labourer* (1927), pp. 31, 35, 40, 62.
11. Sir Robert Somerville, *History of the Duchy of Lancaster, volume 2*

(London, 1970), p. 283.

12. Gilbert Slater, *English Peasantry and Enclosure* (London, 1907), p. 128.
13. J. L. and B. Hammond, *Village Labourer* (1978), p. 15.
14. Ibid., p. 40.
15. T. B. Dudley, *Complete History of Royal Leamington Spa . . .* (London, 1901), pp. 50–2.
16. Sir Robert Somerville, *Office Holders in the Duchy and County Palatine of Lancaster, from 1603* (London, 1972), biographical table.
17. Brian Smith, *History of Malvern* (Leicester, 1964), p. 167.
18. The National Archives, Duchy of Lancaster, Forest of Knaresborough Court Rolls, Class D.L.30.
19. Sir Robert Somerville, *History of the Duchy of Lancaster, vol. 2, 1603–1965*

(London, 1970), p. 158.

20. Such a term is not, of course, unique to Harrogate. It is a north country term, examples of which occur at other nearby locations, such as York.
21. Rustall Manor Act, 29 April 1740. See Hembry, *English Spa, 1560–1815 . . .*, p. 233.
22. Fairfield Act, 1770 – See Hembry, *English Spa, 1560–1815 . . .*, p. 219.
23. R. S. Neale, *Bath 1680–1850: A Social History* (London, 1981), p. 61.
24. David Hay (ed.), *Oxford Companion to Local and Family History* (Oxford, 1996), p. 151.
25. Gilbert Slater, *English Peasantry and the Enclosure of Common Fields* (London, 1907), p. 128.

Notes to Chapter 7: The spa after 1778

1. Phillis Hembry, *The English Spa, 1560–1815* (London, 1990), p. 94.
2. Ibid., p. 183.
3. Brian Smith, *History of Malvern* (Leicester, 1964), p. 175.
4. Alan Savidge, *Royal Tunbridge Wells* (1975), p. 97.
5. M. A. Simpson, and T. H. Lloyd (eds), *Middle-class Housing* (1977), p. 119.
6. Phillis Hembry, *English Spa*, pp. 234–5.
7. J. A. Lovat-Fraser, *John Stuart, earl of Bute* (Cambridge University Press, 1912).
8. Mess. Filassier, 'Marat and the Marchioness of L'Aubespine' in *La Gazette de Sante*, no. 46, 16 October 1777, p. 189.
9. *Proceedings of the Royal Society of*

Medicine, vol. 34, no. 1. November 1945.

10. Despite frequent pressing enquiries made at the Soane Museum between 1997 and 1999, as to the possible identification of this book, no acknowledgement was ever received by the author, making it the only such unhelpful response in the making of the entire *Harrogate Great Chronicle*.
11. 1841 Census and Victoria County History of the County of York. (1913) (the figures are approximations, as there was no distinction between the inhabitants of Pannal Village, which lay outside Harrogate, and the Sulphur Wells part of Pannal, which lay within Harrogate).

12. These figures are based on an inventory of the Granby Hotel taken in 1835 which recorded 130 bedrooms. Given an average of two per room (servants often slept in dormitories), the figure of 250 per hotel is a conservative one. The Crown, Dragon, Granby and Queen were all of similar size).
13. Phillis Hembry, *English Spa, 1560–1815*, p. 280.
14. Ibid., p. 280.
15. Alan Savidge, *Royal Tunbridge Wells* (London, 1975), pp. 121–2.
16. T. B. Dudley, *Complete History of Royal Leamington Spa* (London, 1901), p. 93.
17. Phillis Hembry, *British Spas 1815 to the Present*, pp. 146–206.

Notes to Chapter 8: Bathing at the spa

1. Armstrong's *Harrogate Almanack*, 1891 – 'Memories of old Harrogate'.
2. *Building Chronicle*, May 1857, obituary on p. 197.
3. The most likely candidate, in view

of Class Sc., but there again, D.59 shows Joshua Wordsworth!

4. Ibid.
5. *Harrogate Advertiser*, 17 July 1912.
6. William Grainge, *History of Harrogate and the Forest . . .* (John

Russell Smith, 1871), p. 150.

7. H. H. Walker, *History of Harrogate under the Improvement Commissioners, 1841–1884*, pp. 20–2.
8. Ibid., p. 286.

Notes to Chapter 9: Entertainment at the spa

1. Phillis Hembry, *English Spa, 1560–1815*, p. 309.
2. Ibid., p. 117.
3. Ibid., p. 180.
4. John Brewer, *Pleasures of the Imagination* (London, 1997), p. 547.
5. Phillis Hembry, *English Spa, 1560–1815*, p. 365, schedule C.
6. Richard Williams, *Contentious crown ...* (Aldershot, 1997), p. 35.
7. Sir Robert Somerville, *History of the Duchy ... vol. 2*, chapters 12 and 17.
8. Phillis Hembry, *English Spa, 1560–1815*, p. 139.
9. Catalogue of Hargrove's Library, no. 9, *c.* 1816, including earlier set of rules. Location: Harrogate Reference Library.
10. Public Library and Art Gallery, Diamond Jubilee, 1887–1947, leaflet.
11. Phillis Hembry, *English Spa, 1560–1815* (Athlone, 1990), p. 116.
12. Ibid., p. 148.
13. Ibid., p. 184.
14. Ibid., p. 224.
15. Ibid., p. 239.
16. Ibid., p. 295.
17. William Grainge, *History of Harrogate and the Forest of Knaresborough* (Russell Smith, 1870), pp. 119, 187.
18. Index to surrender book five, 1746–1764, National Archives.
19. Owner's deeds, examined May 2001.
20. Sybil Rosenfeld, *The Georgian Theatre of Richmond, Yorkshire, and its circuit ...* (1984), Introduction.
21. Ibid.
22. See H. H. Walker, *History of Harrogate under the Improvement Commissioners, 1841–1884*, p. 294.
23. Phillis Hembry, *English Spa, 1560–1815*, pp. 281–3.
24. Author's estimate based on census returns, mostly 1841.

Notes to Chapter 10: Township administration and the Poor Law

1. Harrogate Improvement Act, 1841, HMSO.
2. *Historic Ripon* (Ripon, 1890), p. 79.
3. David Hey, *Oxford Companion to Local History* (Oxford, 1996), p. 361.
4. Clive Emsley, *English Police: A Political and Social History* (Hemel Hempstead, 1991), pp. 8–15.
5. H. H. Walker, *History of Harrogate under the Improvement Commissioners, 1841–1884*, p. 88.
6. Act of 2 & 3 Philip and Mary, clause 8
7. Act for establishing ... Militia ... 1757. 31 George 2nd
8. William Haythornthwaite, *Harrogate Story*, p. 53.
9. Ibid., p. 49.
10. Harrogate Improvement Act, 1841, Clause V.
11. Michael Brock, *Great Reform Act* (1973), p. 335.
12. John Cannon, *Parliamentary Reform, 1640–1832* (Cambridge, 1973), p. 250.
13. Derek Fraser, *Power and Authority in the Victorian City* (Oxford, 1979), p. 3.
14. Norman Gash, *Politics in the Age of Peel* (London, 1953), pp. 137–53.
15. Michael Brock, *Great Reform Act*, pp. 22–3.
16. Bernard Jennings (ed.), *History of Harrogate and Knaresborough* (Advertiser Press, 1970), p. 335.

Notes to Chapter 11: Religious life, 1770–1841

1. Census 1841, including Low Harrogate, Starbeck, etc. and population statistics in *Victoria County History of the County of York*.
2. J. C. D. Clark, *English Society, 1688–1832* (Cambridge, 1985), p. 350.
3. Chapters 7 and 8 of this book.
4. Alan Gilbert, *Religion & Society in Industrial England* (London, 1976), p. 27.
5. Ibid., p. 30–48, and graphs on pp. 38–9.
6. DLOA Jura Regalia of the Duchy of Lancaster: Edward VI Commission to enquire concerning chantries in Lancashire & Yorkshire, ff. 210, 354–357.
7. J. A. Patmore, 'Harrogate & Knaresborough, a study in urban development', unpublished MA Thesis (Oxford, 1959), Appendix tables.
8. Ibid.
9. Bernard Jennings, *Nidderdale*, p. 409.
10. David Hempton, *Religion and Political Culture in Britain and Ireland* (Cambridge University Press, 1996), pp. 30, 36.
11. Bernard Jennings, *Harrogate and Knaresborough*, p. 370.
12. Ibid., p. 371.
13. Brian Smith, *History of Malvern* (Leicester, 1964), p. 190.
14. Theodore Koditschek, *Class Formation and Urban-industrial Society: Bradford, 1750–1850* (Cambridge, 1990), p. 252.
15. Nigel Yates, 'The religious life of Victorian Leeds', in Derek Fraser (ed.), *History of Modern Leeds* (Manchester University Press, 1980), p. 264.
16. John Wesley, 'Advice to people called Methodists', in *Works*, volume 6, 1745, p. 410.
17. Alan Gilbert, *Religion and Society in Industrial England ... 1740–1914* (London, 1976), pp. 59–60.
18. A. C. H. Seymour, *Life and Times of Selina, Countess of Huntington* (London, 1839).
19. H. H. Walker, *Harrogate 1841–1884 ...*, p. 352.
20. K. J. Brock, *History of Christ Church, High Harrogate* (Harrogate, 1981), p. 1.
21. J. C. D. Clark, *English Society, 1688–1832* (Cambridge University Press, 1985), p. 359.
22. Census returns for 1801 and 1821.
23. Alan Gilbert, *Religion and Society in Industrial England ... 1740–1914* (Cambridge University Press, 1976), p. 29.
24. Walter Kaye, *Records of Harrogate*. Handwritten note in Kaye's annotated copy, 1922. HRL.
25. Mark Smith, *Religion in Industrial Society. Oldham and Saddleworth, 1740–1865* (Oxford University Press, 1994), p. 55.
26. K. J. Brock, *Christ Church*, pp. 24–5.
27. J. C. D. Clark, *English Society, 1688–1832*, p. 359.
28. William Grainge, *Annals of Harrogate*, unpublished manuscript,

Harrogate Reference Library.
29. Ibid.
30. Sir Robert Somerville, *History of the Duchy of Lancaster, volume 2*, p. 248.
31. H. H. Walker, *Harrogate, 1841–1884*, Appendix Three, p. 463.
32. Bradford Reference Library, The population of Bradford (statistics).
33. Theodore Koditschek, *Class Formation and Urban-industrial Society: Bradford, 1750–1850*

(Cambridge, 1990), p. 253.
34. Alan Gilbert, *Religion and Society, 1740–1914*, p. 27.
35. Leases and enrolments from Royal Forest of Knaresborough Court Rolls, National Archives class D.L.30, vols 1796–1838.
36. H. Hitchen and T. E. Dawson, *Non-Conformist Churches – Wesleyan* (Harrogate, 1962), pp. 8–10.
37. *Memoirs of the life of Mrs Mary Taft,*

formerly Miss Barritt (privately published, 1827) p. 91.
38. Alan Gilbert, *Religion and Society*, pp. 62–3.
39. Anon., '70 years of baptism in Harrogate', *Harrogate Advertiser*, 20 September 1950.
40. William Grainge, *History of Harrogate ...* p. 176.

Notes to Chapter 12: Education in Harrogate

1. T. W. Laqueur, *Religion and Respectability ... 1780–1850* (Yale, 1976), p. 97.
2. Bernard Jennings, *Nidderdale*, p. 453.
3. T. W. Laqueur, *Religion and Respectability*, p. 2.
4. S. J. D. Green, *Religion in the Age of Decline* (Cambridge, 1996), pp. 214–15.
5. J. P. Clapham, *Registrar of the West Riding Congregational Union* (Leeds, 1861).
6. William Haythornthwaite, *History of the Harrogate Congregational Church* (Harrogate, 1962).
7. Alan Gilbert, *Religion and Society in Industrial England ... 1740–1914* (London, 1976) pp. 27–30.
8. T. W. Laqueur, *Religion and Respectability ...*, p. 3.
9. Ibid., p. 21.
10. Society for bettering the condition of the Poor. *Reports*, volume 6 (SBCP, 1812), pp. 139–46.
11. T. W. Laqueur, *Religion and Respectability ...*, p. 149.
12. S. J. D. Green, *Religion in the Age of Decline ...*, p. 214.
13. *Victoria County History of the County of York*. Census tables. 1913.
14. T. W. Laqueur, *Religion and Respectability ...*, p. 48.
15. Ward, *Religion and Society in England, 1790–1850*, p. 15.
16. *Oxford Companion to Local and Family History*, p. 146.
17. Bernard Jennings, *Harrogate and Knaresborough*, p. 393.
18. Ibid., p. 399.
19. William Grainge, *History*, p. 185.
20. Ward, *Religion and Society in England, 1790–1850*, p. 94.
21. H. H. Walker, *Harrogate, 1841–1884*, pp. 372–5.

Notes to Chapter 13: A hospital for the poor

1. Report of the Poor Law Commissioners on the further amendment of the Poor Laws, appendix B, Mr Power's report, 1840.
2. Hilary Marland, *Medicine and Society in Wakefield and Huddersfield, 1780–1870* (Cambridge, 1987), p. 56.
3. *Oxford Companion to Local and Family History*, p. 362.
4. RBHA, Royal Bath Hospital, rules and regulations, section 17.
5. Hilary Marland, *Medicine and Society*, p. 172.
6. Phillis Hembry, *English Spa*, p. 271.
7. *Bath Journal*, 1755.
8. *Leamington Spa Courier*, 5 May 1832.
9. Phillis Hembry, *British Spa*, p. 29.
10. T. B. Dudley, *Royal Leamington Spa*, p. 95.
11. Derek Fraser, *The Evolution of the British Welfare State* (Manchester, 1973), pp. 115–23.
12. Hilary Marland, *Medicine and Society*, p. 130.
13. National Archives, Duchy of Lancaster, Forest of Knaresborough Court Rolls, volumes 22–23, 1824–1828. D.L. 30.
14. E. P. L. Dixon, *Harrogate Royal Bath Hospital Historical Review* (Harrogate, 1956).
15. Phillis Hembry, *British Spas*, pp. 207–15.
16. Olive Checkland, *Philanthropy in Victorian Scotland* (London, 1980), pp. 12–13.
17. Obituary notice of 1883, reprinted *Harrogate Advertiser*, 9 August 1933.
18. Hilary Marland, *Medicine and Society*, p. 102.
19. E. P. L. Dixon, *Historical Review*.
20. Sir Llewellyn Woodward, *Age of Reform, 1815–1870* (Oxford, 1962) pp. 462–3.
21. John Godding, *Norman's History of Cheltenham* (London, 1863), p. 511.
22. R. S. Neale, *Bath 1680–1850: A Social History* (London, 1981), p. 251.
23. Brian Smith, *History of Malvern* (Leicester, 1964), p. 250.
24. Alan Savidge, *Royal Tunbridge Wells* (London, 1975), p. 121.
25. Hilary Marland, *Medicine and Society* (Cambridge, 1987), p. 101.
26. Ibid., p. 81.
27. Ibid., p. 70.
28. Ibid., p. 93.
29. Juliet Barker, *The Brontës* (London, 1994), pp. 95–7.
30. David Hey, *Yorkshire from AD 1000* (London, 1986), pp. 260–1.

Notes to Chapter 14: The building of Harrogate, 1778–1841

1. Named after the Duke of Devonshire's purchase of the tenancy of the Royal Forest from the Duchy of Lancaster.
2. Given to the author by the owners of Mansfield House, December 2001.
3. The leadwork around one of the chimneys has been inscribed with the names of Eleanor Tickell and ? Wardell – presumably servants – and the date of 1776.
4. William Grainge, *History of Harrogate ...* (Russell Smith, 1871) p. 197.
5. Ibid., p. 204.
6. Ibid., p. 197.
7. *Harrogate Advertiser*, 26 May 1897.

8. Malcolm Neesam, *Bygone Harrogate* (Breedon Books, 1999), p. 17.

9. Malcolm Neesam, *Harrogate History and Guide* (Tempus, 2001), p. 42.

10. Thackwray's Vaults changed to George Muckle's Vaults only after 1873, but continued to advertise as est. 1836.

11. *Harrogate Advertiser*, 6 May 1847.

12. Advertisement from nineteenth-century commercial directory, photcopy in Neesam Archive.

13. William Grainge, *History and Topography of Harrogate* . . . (Russell Smith, 1871), p. xx.

14. *Harrogate Advertiser*, 19 July 1848.

15. William Grainge, *History and Topography of Harrogate* . . . (Russell Smith, 1871) p. 191.

16. Maria Edgeworth, 'Belinda', in *Tales and Novels in ten volumes* (Bohn, 1870).

17. In 1858, Palliser sold his newspaper business to T. Hollins, who in turn re-sold to Robert Ackrill, who had founded the rival *Herald* in 1847. H. H. Walker, *History of Harrogate under the Improvement Commissioners, 1841–1884* (Manor Place Press, 1986).

18. Further changes occurred in 1930 when buildings next to the Valley Gardens entrance were demolished.

19. William Grainge, *History of Harrogate* . . . (Russell Smith, 1871), pp. 136–7.

20. Lyndon Cave, *Royal Leamington Spa* (Phillimore, 1988), p. 4.

21. Harrogate Reference Library, copies in Walker-Neesam archive.

22. A. B. Granville, *Spas of England*, volume two (1841, Adams & Dart, reprint 1971), p. 284.

23. John Clark – architect. Obituary notice in 'the Builders Chronicle', May 1857.

24. *Harrogate Advertiser*, 'Freelance', 28 June 1952.

25. *Harrogate Herald*, 21 November 1923.

26. M. Neesam, *Samson Fox Chronolgy*, Walker-Neesam archive.

27. The twelve drawings were presented to Harrogate Corporation by Mr J. Carter of Kirbymoorside, receipt of which was acknowledged by Librarian George Byers in a letter of 28 April 1937.

28. *Leeds Intelligencer*, 19 January 1832.

29. Fattorini moved to no. 2 Royal Parade in c. 1875. Fattorini Archive.

30. This unique early nineteenth-century wine vault and shop have survived to the time of writing, and were listed in November 2000.

31. H. H. Walker, *History of Harrogate Under the Improvement Commssioners, 1841–1884* (Manor Place Press, 1986), p. 425.

32. Ibid., p. 437.

33. Ibid.

34. Edna Healey, *Coutts & Co., 1692–1992* (Hodder & Stoughton).

35. *The Times*, Law report of trial, 27 February 1847.

Notes to Chapter 15: Obtaining the 1841 Improvement Act

1. John Prest, *Liberty and Locality* (Oxford, 1990), p. 5.

2. Ibid., p. 8.

3. Ibid., p. 12.

4. M. A. Simpson and T. H. Lloyd (eds), *Middle-class Housing in Britain* (London, 1977), p. 511.

5. T. B. Dudley, *Leamington Spa* . . . , pp. 174–8.

6. Alan Savidge, *Royal Tunbridge Wells*, p. 122.

7. H. H. Walker, *Harrogate 1841–1884*, pp. 30–43.

8. Sir Robert Somerville, *History of the Duchy*, vol. 2, p. 326.

9. Ibid., p. 283.

10. M. A. Simpson and T. H. Lloyd (eds), *Middle-class Housing in Britain*, p. 120.

11. Phillis Hembry, *British Spas*, pp. 146–7.

12. Phillis Hembry, *British Spas*, p. 147.

13. Census tables.

14. Census tables and author's estimates.

15. John Godding, *History of Cheltenham*, p. 442.

16. Ibid., p. 456–70.

17. William Grainge, *History*, pp. 151–76.

18. John Godding, *History of Cheltenham*, chronology appendix.

19. M. A. Simpson and T. H. Lloyd (eds), *Middle-class Housing*, p. 511.

20. T. B. Dudley, *Royal Leamington Spa* . . . , pp. 174–8.

21. M. A. Simpson and T. H. Lloyd (eds), *Middle-class Housing*, pp. 120–31.

22. John Godding, *History of Cheltenham*, chronology appendix.

23. Ibid.

24. Ibid., chronology appendix.

25. Ibid.

26. William Grainge, *History*, pp. 127–43.

27. John Godding, *History of Cheltenham*, chronology appendix.

28. Bernard Jennings, *Harrogate and Knaresborough*, p. 306.

29. Brian Smith, *History of Malvern*, pp. 185–6.

30. Ibid., p. 179.

31. Forty-four awards were made to the Duchy, from award number 170 up to award number 2080a.

32. Brian Smith, *History of Malvern*, p. 247.

33. Census tables, HMSO, and author's calculations.

34. T. B. Dudley, *Royal Leamington Spa* . . . , p. 50.

35. Ibid., pp. 79, 226.

36. M. A. Simpson and T. H. Lloyd (eds), *Middle-class Housing in Britain*, p. 119.

37. Census tables.

38. T. B. Dudley, *Royal Leamington Spa* . . . , p. 99.

39. M. A. Simpson and T. H. Lloyd (eds), *Middle-class Housing in Britain*, p. 120.

40. Census tables, HMSO.

41. Alan Savidge, *Royal Tunbridge Wells*, pp. 48–9.

42. Ibid., pp. 92–5.

43. Ibid., p. 148.

44. Alan Gilbert, *Religion and Society*, pp. 59–60.

45. A. C. H. Seymour, *Life and times of Selina, Countess of Huntington* (privately published, 1839), p. 59.

46. Alan Savidge, *Royal Tunbridge Wells*, p. 92.

47. M. A. Simpson, & T. H. Lloyd (eds), *Middle-class Housing in Britain* . . . , p. 124.

48. John Godding, *History of Cheltenham*, chronology appendix.

49. Brian Smith, *History of Malvern*, p. 167.

50. R. S. Neale, *Bath 1680–1850*, pp. 91, 372.

51. Ibid., p. 291.

52. Alan Savidge, *Royal Tunbridge Wells*, p. 121.

53. William Grainge, *History* . . . , p. 124.

54. Phillis Hembry, *British Spas*, pp. 115–16.

55. Ibid., p. 119.
56. Ibid., p. 120.
57. Ibid., p. 120.
58. R. S. Neale, *Bath 1680–1850 ...*, p. 251.
59. Ibid., p. 263.
60. A. B. Granville, *Spas of England*, p. xxxix.
61. Phillis Hembry, *English Spa*, p. 136.
62. William Grainge, *History*, p. 120.
63. Murial Searle, *Spas and Watering places* (London, 1977), pp. 96–7.
64. Phillis Hembry, *English Spa*, p. 220.
65. Ibid., p. 195.
66. Ibid., p. 240.
67. Ibid., pp. 300–1.
68. Ibid., p. 122.
69. Ibid., p. 125.
70. H. H. Walker, *Harrogate 1841–1884*, p. 353.
71. Christopher Hamlin, *Chemistry, medicine and the legitimization of English Spas, 1740–1840* (London, 1990), pp. 72–4.
72. Ibid., p. 78.
73. William Bain & Wilfrid Edgecombe, *Physiology & therapeutics of the Harrogate waters, baths and climate* (London, 1905) p. 20–25.
74. Phillis Hembry, *British Spas*, p. 241.
75. H. H. Walker, *Harrogate 1841 to 1884*, pp. 23–4.
76. Harrogate Improvement Act, 10 May 1841 (London, 1841).
77. Worcester Improvement Act, 10 Geo. 3, c. 22.
78. Derek Fraser, *Power & authority in the Victorian City* (Oxford, 1979), chapter one.
79. Sir Robert Somerville, *History of the Duchy vol. 2*, chapters 14, 15, & 18.
80. Harrogate Improvement Act, 1841 (London, 1841).
81. Harrogate Improvement Commissioners, Minutes of the meetings of 1841–2, transcribed by H. H. Walker. Harrogate Reference Library.
82. *Victoria County History of the County of York*, 1913, plus H. H. Walker's calculations in his mss, plus 1841 Census.
83. Estimate by author.
84. Phillis Hembry, *British Spas*, chapter nine 'Victorian Finale'.
85. Harrogate Borough Council, Charter of Incorporation, 1884.
86. 1841 Census returns, extracts from Harrogate, Knaresborough and Pannal returns.

Notes to Chapter 16: Conclusion

1. Phillis Hembry, *British Spas*, p. 119.
2. T. B. Dudley, *History of Royal Leamington Spa*, p. 139.
3. A. B. Granville, *Spas of England*, pp. 73–4.
4. Corfield, *Impact of English Towns*, p. 51.
5. A. B. Granville, *Spas of England*, p. 61.
6. Ibid., p. 72.
7. Corfield, *Impact of English Towns*, p. 64.
8. Census figures, plus author's calculations, including Starbeck, Low Harrogate and Cold Bath Road, Birk Cragg, Harlow etc.
9. Census figures, plus author's calculations.
10. R. S. Neale, *Bath, 1680–1850*, p. 263.
11. Brian Smith, *History of Malvern*, pp. 185–6.
12. Lloyd, 'Royal Leamington Spa', in T. H. Lloyd, *Middle-class Housing in Britain*, p. 120.
13. Census tables, and author's calculations.
14. John Godding, *History of Cheltenham*, chronology appendix (section between 1786 and 1833).
15. Phillis Hembry, *British Spas, 1815 to the present*, p. 43.
16. DLOA, Letter Books, 1838–1840 and 1840–1843.
17. Act for improving ... High and Low Harrogate, 1841.
18. Charity Commissioners, Third Report, 15 January 1820.
19. Alan Gilbert, *Religion and Society*, pp. 30–48.
20. Census tables, plus author's calculations.
21. Alan Gilbert, *Religion and Society*, p. 27.
22. H. Hitchen and T. E. Dawson, *Non-conformist Churches* (Harrogate, 1962), pp. 8–10.
23. Theodore Koditschek, *Class Formation and Urban Industrial Society*, p. 252.
24. *Leamington Spa Courier*, 5 May 1832.
25. John Godding, *History of Cheltenham*, p. 511.
26. R. S. Neale, *Bath 1680–1850*, p. 251.
27. Brian Smith, *History of Malvern*, p. 250.
28. Alan Savidge, *Royal Tunbridge Wells*, p. 121.
29. Hilary Marland, *Medicine and Society in Huddersfield and Wakefield*, p. 101.
30. Ibid., p. 81.
31. R. J. Morris, 'The Middle Class and British Towns, 1780–1870', in Derek Fraser and Anthony Sutcliffe, *Pursuit of Urban History* (London, 1983), p. 286.
32. John Myerscough, *The Pursuit of Happiness Abroad* (lecture to the Anglo-American conference of historians, 1979).
33. Phillis Hembry, *British Spas*, pp. 6–7.
34. Kenneth Young, *Music's Great Days in Spas and Watering Places* (London, 1968), p. 34.

Index to part one

Acts, Parliamentary, 1649 (Duchy) 92
Acts, Parliamentary, 1752 (Turnpike) 120, 227
Acts, Parliamentary, 1770 (Enclosure) 117, 125, 129, 144, 147, 239, 240, 259, 393
Acts, Parliamentary, 1778 (Award) 14, 132, 144, 137–146, 148, 165, 177, 195, 211, 227, 274, 285, 296, 298, 311
Acts, Parliamentary, 1789 (Stray 'slips') 158, 159, 160, 161, 374
Acts, Parliamentary, 1828 (Test and Corporations) 239
Acts, Parliamentary, 1832 (Reform) 236, 237
Acts, Parliamentary, 1834 (Poor Law Amendment) 236
Acts, Parliamentary, 1835 (Municipal Corporations) 236
Acts, Parliamentary, 1841 (Improvement) 258, 369–394
Adair, Dr James 162, 354
Addison, Mrs 267
Adelphi 301
Agistment 36, 42
Albert Street 324
Albert Terrace 327, 332
Albion Hotel 324
Alderson, Baron 385, 386
Alexander, Dr 149, 152, 153, 192, 217
Alexander's Hill 9
Alexandra Terrace 332
Allotment meadow 323
Almsford Bank 132
Alrome 149
Amory, Thomas 112, 196
Andrews (architect) 184
Archery 150, 218
Archill 13, 14
Assarting 53, 55
Ashfield House 305, 306
Assembly rooms 113, 162, 200, 201, 203; see also Promenade Room
Atkinson, Captain 96
Augustini, Augustine 69

Bacon, Sir Francis 50

Bailey, Elizabeth 316
Bainbridge, John 136, 160, 249, 296, 392
Bains, Jane 220
Balls and assemblies 198, 201
Banbury, Act of 1824 392
Barf, Thomas 324
Barber, William 228, 309
Barn Close 324
Barrels 191, 281
Barton, John de 42
Baskerville, Thomas 217
Bath 146, 150, 164, 175, 195, 200, 201, 221, 272, 283, 373, 378–9, 381
Bath hospital 243, 247, 270–84, 373, 389, 394
Bath hospital, diet 281
Bath hospital, rules 277, 278
Bath hospital subscription books 273, 274, 276
Bath Improvement Act of 1789 379
Bath Theatre 206
Bathhurst, Henry 248
Bay Horse 102, 106, 210, 229, 235, 292
Beaker Cottages 9
Beckwith Lodge Farm 348
Beckwith-with-Rossett 10, 13, 14, 15, 19, 58, 84, 107, 125, 140, 225
Bell Inn 108, 220, 229, 257, 302, 306, 307, 337, 338, 345
Belle Isle Tavern 319, 321
Belle Vue 317, 318
Belmont 28, 30, 31, 32, 120, 131, 145
Benn, Jonathan 332, 348, 359, 360, 361, 365, 383
Benson, Christopher 103
Benson, Henry 50
Benson, John 59
Benson family 85, 116, 298
Benson, Thomas 67, 115
Bentley family 86
Bergmann, Torben 381
Beulah Chapel 321
Beulah Place 255
Beulah Street 317
Bexley, Lord 250–1, 252
Billiards 150, 220, 378

Bilton 3, 4, 7, 10, 11, 13, 14, 15, 18, 20, 49, 54, 63, 67, 119, 237, 311, 312, 313
Bilton Banks 52, 55, 312
Bilton coal 67, 312
Bilton Endowed School 262, 267
Bilton Hall 86, 87, 93, 313
Bilton House 362
Bilton Lane 61, 120
Bilton Mill 36, 82
Bilton Park 18, 28, 33, 36, 37, 41, 46, 48, 49, 20, 51, 52, 54, 63, 71, 76, 78, 86, 108
Bilton Park sulphur well 18, 73, 76, 108, 111, 119, 149, 313
Binns, Joseph 170
Binns Hotel 170, 301, 302, 334
Binns, Mary 334
Birnand, Ralph 46
Black death see plague
Blacksmiths Arms 310, 333, 342
Black Spring 190
Black Swan 235, 292, 394
Blower, Richard 48, 49
Blue Bell Inn see Bell Inn
Blundell, Nicholas 110
Bogs Field 97, 143, 271, 275, 276, 281, 303, 342
Bollingbroke, Henry (see also Henry IV) 43, 59
Bosanquet, Mary 303
bottling, see Spa water, bottling
Bradford 243, 255
Brig, John 59
Brigantes 4
Briggs Boarding House 337
Bright, Timothy 70, 71
Britannia Lodge 191
Broad Way, Great xxvii, 9, 62, 119
Brome, James 109
Brontë, Patrick 280
Bronze Age 14
Brunswick Hotel 235, 324, 325, 329, 332, 345
Brunswick Terrace 324, 325, 329
Brunswick Railway station 325, 329
Brunswick Terrace 332
Buchan, Dr 151

Buckingham, Countess of 80, 100, 243
Burdett Coutts, Angela *see* Coutts,
   Angela Burdett
Burns, Robert 162, 354
Bogg, Edmund 112, 382
Burun, Erneis de 14
Burgh, Serlo de 18
Burgshire 16
Burlington, Earl of 114
Burnand, George 207
Burns, Robert 354
Bute, Lord 121, 153, 243
Butler, Samuel junior 214
Butler, Samuel senior 211, 212, 214
Buxton 149, 201, 206, 221, 373, 378, 381
Buxton, Act of 1771 145
Byron, Lord 157, 338, 339, 354

Calcut 145
Calverly, Sir Walter 110
Calvert, Michael 184, 185
Cam, William 20
Cambridge Place 321
Cambridge Street 321
Carey, George 150, 204
Carlyle, Dr Alexander 121, 122
Carr of York (architect) 295
Carrington, Samuel 392
Carter, Nicholas 323, 384
Carter's Hotel *see* Prospect Hotel
Castlereagh, Lord 155, 156, 157, 214, 243
Catherine, Queen 102
Cave, Ambrose 48, 49
Cayley, George 180, 181, 201
Chalybeate waters 72, 106, 247
Chandler's Garth 298
chantry chapel 52, 59, 60, 61, 62, 63, 65,
   66
Chapel Street 317, 319, 321
Chapel Street Baths 190, 322
Chapman, Samuel 252, 276
Charles I 49, 50, 51, 73, 87, 88, 89, 90,
   92, 95, 107, 116, 119, 314
Charles II 94, 95, 96, 100, 102, 103, 104,
   117
Charlesworth, Charles 385, 392
Cheltenham 149, 175, 200, 201, 203, 221,
   282, 320, 373–6, 381
Cheltenham estate 165, 316, 347
Cheltenham Spa Rooms *see* Spa Rooms
Cheltenham Square 345
Cheltenham Waters (Harrogate) 165,
   223, 274, 345
Chequers Inn *see* George Hotel
Chester, Bishop of 114, 247
Chester diocese 2, 114, 225, 237, 247,
   254
Chippindale, Amos 208
Chippindale, Thomas 162
Chloride of Iron Well 165
Christ Church *see* Church, High
   Harrogate

Church, High Harrogate 62, 85, 114,
   115, 134, 153, 225, 239, 244, 246, 247,
   257, 264, 292, 363, 384
Church, High Harrogate, Minister 240,
   245, 257
Church, High Harrogate, stipends 134,
   240, 245
Church, Low Harrogate 84, 248, 249,
   250, 253, 254, 276, 389
Church, Low Harrogate, burial ground
   253, 254
Church, Low Harrogate, curate's
   stipend 249, 250, 253
Church Square 105, 106, 211, 212, 291,
   292, 362
Civil War, English 87–95, 101
Clarendon Hotel 329
Clark, John 182, 349, 350
Clarke's Baths 190, 321
Claro Wapentake 83, 84, 88, 117, 227,
   228
Clayton, Margaret 307, 338
Clayton, William 338
Clemenshaw, Elizabeth 299
Clive, Robert (of India) 122
Coach and Horses Inn 327
coaches 302, 303, 306, 307, 308, 331, 334,
   345
Coates, Thomas 385
Cold Bath 62, 109, 137, 147, 148, 151,
   177, 187, 188, 298, 300
Cold Bath Lane/Road 45, 61, 101, 109,
   148, 177, 187, 191, 224, 300, 302, 303,
   334, 337
Cold Bath Place 303
Collins, Rev. Thomas 114, 119, 240
Colt Hoare, Richard 304
Colvile, Balam 48, 49
Commercial Inn 328, 329
constables 83, 91, 92, 101, 108, 109,
   225–6, 227, 228
Cornwall, earldom of 20, 31, 33, 34, 37,
   60
Cornwall Road 34, 224, 342
Cotton, John 65
Court Rolls 53, 55, 66, 83, 93, 139, 208
Coutts, Angela Burdett 216, 362, 364,
   365
Cranbourne Alley 316, 352
Crab Lane 52
Crescent Cupola 346
Crescent Gardens 4
Crescent Estate 345, 346, 348
Crescent Inn 85, 108, 115, 151, 169, 182,
   201, 229, 274, 308, 310, 331, 334, 345,
   346
Crescent Inn Well 274, 346, 347
Crescent Road 308
Crimple beck 18, 28, 48, 62, 67, 132
Crimple House 296
Crokesnab 53, 57, 58, 63, 54, 86, 314,
   316, 324

Cromwell, Oliver 91, 94
Cross Chapel 256, 265, 290
Crossroads Hotel 170, 330, 359
Crown, or Montpellier Baths 179, 182,
   183, 184, 187, 338, 348
Crown Hotel 106, 108, 133, 149, 157,
   163, 165, 169, 170, 178, 179, 180, 196,
   198, 220, 229, 235, 237, 241, 244, 248,
   274, 276, 278, 303, 304, 305, 307, 338,
   339, 341, 383, 385, 394
Crown Hotel, baths (within) 179, 183
Crown Hotel billiard room 165, 220
Crown Hotel Sulphur Well 166, 167,
   179, 248
Crown Sulphur Well Pump Room 166,
   183, 338
Crown Hotel wells 165, 183, 184, 383
Crown Lodgings 305, 306
Crown Place 341, 383
Cullingworth, Joseph 334
Cumberland, Earl of 48, 67
Cures without care 79
Curling, Henry 199, 200, 203, 305, 354

Dalby, Peter 354
dancing 199
Danvers, Dawes 254, 343, 368, 390
Davy, Sir Humphrey 339
Dawes, Sir Darcy 110, 113, 201, 218
Dawson, George 345
Deane, Edmund 69, 70, 71, 72, 76, 90,
   97, 142
Dearlove family 311, 314, 383
Dearlove, Mrs, lodgings 352
Dearlove, John 159
Dearlove, Robert 58
Defoe, Daniel 110–11
Devonshire, Duke of 114, 134, 263
Devonshire Inn 291
Devonshire Place 191, 207, 208, 211, 290,
   291, 342, 358
Diamond Court 303
Dibdin, Charles 157
Dibdin, Thomas 217
Dickens, Charles 334, 350, 382
Digby Rev. George 254, 392
Diocesan boundaries 1, 2, 254
Disturbance of 1507 47
Dodd, Jane 233; *see also* Jane Peacock
Dodelow 44
Dodsworth manuscripts 88
Domesday book 3, 7, 12, 13
Doufbiggyng, Robert 44
Dragon Hotel 102, 104, 105, 107, 114,
   115, 122, 149, 154, 155, 157, 158, 163,
   169, 172, 178, 196, 197, 207, 208, 216,
   220, 247, 268, 285, 289, 291, 305, 353,
   354, 355, 356, 383, 386
Dragon Lodging House 208, 289, 290,
   357
Dunmow Fitch 357
Dunn, the fortune hunter 365

East Parade 357
Ebor Hotel 321
Edgeworth, Maria 339
Edmund, Earl of Cornwall 20, 33, 34
Edward I 20, 25, 33, 34, 60
Edward II 9, 37, 38, 39, 45, 60
Edward III 26, 40, 42, 43, 45, 58, 61
Edward IV 63
Edward VI 65
Elim Court 255
Elizabeth I 25, 48, 68, 86
Ellis, Richard senior 322
Elmes, Lady 99, 100
Emmatt/Emmet, Thomas 362, 363
Empress see Bay Horse
Enclosure movement (see also Acts;
    Royal Forest, Enclosure 124, 125
England and Son, ironmonger 353
English Spa 71, 72
Esplanade 301, 336

Fairfax, Lord 86, 88, 89
Farnley Wood plot 96
Fattorini 358
Faviel, Charles 330
Fiennes, Celia 110, 162
Follifoot 9
Follifoot ridge 9
Forest Head 120
Forest Lane 31, 118
Forest Moor Road 31, 88, 145
forges 20, 34, 55, 58, 67, 98
Forrest, Isaac 393
Fortune, Riley 327, 389
Fox, Colonel 390
Fox, Samson 107, 182, 354
Franklin, Benjamin 294
Franklin, James 170, 256, 316, 317, 323,
    353
French, Dr 97, 147–8, 187, 275
French Wars 214
Frith, Thomas 247, 357, 383, 386, 393
Frith, William Powell 352, 353, 356
Fulwith 28, 41, 42, 46, 47, 48, 63, 67, 132

Gam prefix 14, 15
Gambling 200
Gamelbar 13, 14, 15, 36
Gamels wath 15
Gammell gate 14, 28
Gardners Arms 53, 313
Garnet, Dr Thomas 187, 192, 193
Gascoigne, John Turner 170, 331, 358
Gascoigne's Hotel 170, 331; see also
    Salutation, Hope Tavern
Gaveston, Peter de 36, 37, 60
Gaye, William 57
George II 95, 109
George III 142, 154, 200, 201, 309
George IV 251
George Hotel 173, 309, 310, 345, 347
Gilead Place 255

Gilbertson, Robert 115, 288
Gillett, Mr 388
Ginnel 227
Glenton, Mary 333
Globe Inn see Crescent Inn
Golden Lion Inn 327, 328
Goodlad, Joseph 115, 197, 231, 291, 355
Goodlad, Sarah 291, 355
Gordon, Mr 351
Grainge, William 97, 102, 206, 253, 255,
    394, 397
Granby Farm 104
Granby Hotel 101, 102, 103, 104, 107,
    114, 115, 120, 122, 149, 157, 158, 163,
    169, 170, 174, 178, 196, 197, 204, 205,
    206, 207, 210, 211, 212, 213, 216, 218,
    221, 229, 245, 278, 285, 292, 298, 305,
    332, 356, 359, 360, 361, 362, 383
Granby Hotel inventory 361
Granby Lodging House 364
Granville, Dr A. 175, 182, 184, 196, 347
Greenhow Hill 4
Greeves, Charles 227, 306, 318, 322, 364,
    388
Greeves, John 169, 170, 190, 231, 245,
    359, 360
Greistenwra 27
Grove, The see World's End
Grove House school 292, 342, 354; see
    also World's End
Grove Road 254

Half Moon Inn see Crescent Inn
Halifax 279, 302
Hall, Mr 362
Hare, Mary 217
Haregate Head 71, 72
Hargrove, E 55, 100, 101, 104, 107, 141,
    145, 147, 148, 149, 153, 205, 206, 207,
    288, 292, 293, 295
Harlow Carr Wells 108, 145
Harlow Hill 7, 8, 9, 14, 18, 27, 28, 34, 44,
    61, 62, 71, 119, 137, 271, 368, 394
Harlow Hill Tower 327, 366, 367
Harlow Woodland 28, 41, 42, 46, 47, 301
Harper family 251, 253, 336
Harper, John 244
Harper, Sarah 298
Harpur, Constantine le 37
Harrison's hotel 290
Harrison, John 319, 321
Harrogate, agriculture 52, 58, 65, 82, 143
Harrogate, alehouses 100, 101
Harrogate, Anglicanism in 113, 239–258,
    260, 264, 374
Harrogate, Baptists 256
Harrogate, architecture 380, 381
Harrogate, assarting 23, 53, 55
Harrogate, Baptists 256
Harrogate, boundaries 244
Harrogate, building development 100,
    158

Harrogate, bridges 227
Harrogate, Catholicism 257, 258
Harrogate, central 314, 319, 321, 322,
    333
Harrogate, central, school 322
Harrogate, Civil War 88–94
Harrogate, Congregationalism 256, 260,
    265
Harrogate, Constables 83, 101, 225, 226
Harrogate, definition 1, 3
Harrogate, development in 135
Harrogate, diet at 112, 153
Harrogate, doctors 112, 237
Harrogate, diocesan boundaries 1, 225
Harrogate, education in 259–269
Harrogate, entertainments 195–223
Harrogate, etymology 3, 7, 8, 9, 21, 53
Harrogate, farms, conversion 80, 100,
    101
Harrogate, gambling 200, 355
Harrogate, High 1, 51, 69, 102, 104, 107,
    119, 158, 165, 196, 197, 220, 227, 243,
    285, 304
Harrogate, High, School 264, 265
Harrogate, hospitals see Bath hospital
Harrogate, hotels, nick-names 178, 196,
    359
Harrogate, Improvement
    Commissioners 236
Harrogate, informality at 112, 123, 150,
    174, 196, 221, 380, 382
Harrogate, Innkeepers 80, 100, 101, 217,
    245, 256, 332, 375, 382
Harrogate, law and order 15, 82, 92, 115,
    225, 236
Harrogate, Libraries 150
Harrogate, Low 1, 51, 85, 107, 115, 121,
    149, 158, 165, 173, 197, 227, 247, 255,
    263, 304, 305, 336, 342, 351, 379, 394
Harrogate, Low, School 263, 266
Harrogate, Methodism 242, 243, 255,
    261, 262, 264, 321
Harrogate, non-conformity 254, 255,
    258, 260, 264, 265, 374
Harrogate, Overseers of the poor 225
Harrogate, peopling of 21, 37
Harrogate, population 53, 56, 57, 92,
    117, 157, 221, 223, 239, 241, 255, 263,
    265, 272, 373
Harrogate, postal services 290, 291, 354,
    375
Harrogate, Presbyterians 257
Harrogate, Quakerism see Harrogate,
    Society of friends
Harrogate, religion 59, 239, 240
Harrogate, roads and footpaths 5, 118,
    119, 120, 121, 137, 227, 357
Harrogate, sanitary accommodation 79
Harrogate, Schools 259–269
Harrogate, servants 200, 217, 221, 222,
    241
Harrogate, shops 220, 221, 222, 241

Harrogate, Society of Friends 94, 242, 256, 257
Harrogate, Stocks 94
Harrogate, Sunday Schools 256, 260
Harrogate, surgeons, town's 272
Harrogate, surveys of 48
Harrogate, trades and professions 241
Harrogate, visitors 79, 80, 87, 99, 100, 109, 110, 112, 121, 122, 123, 153, 154, 156, 157, 171, 174, 176, 180, 196, 198, 199, 222, 240, 241, 244, 276, 379
Harrogate Advertiser 279, 341
Harrogate corner 332
Harrogate Hall 52, 85, 313
Harrogate Head 73
Harrogate Hoard 4
Harrogate Improvement Commissioners 393
Harrogate Workhouse 230, 231, 232, 233, 234, 235, 236, 272, 273, 394
Harrying of the north 12
Hastings, Lady Elizabeth 114, 240
Hattersley, Dorothy 330, 331
Hattersley, Joseph 331
Hattersley, Michael 170, 330, 331, 359
Hattersley, Samuel 228
Hattersley's hotel 173, 228, 334; *see also* Brunswick Hotel
Haverah 20, 27, 32, 33, 34, 36, 37, 41, 43, 45, 47, 48, 49, 50, 51, 63
Haverah forge 20, 34
Haverah castle *see* John O'Gaunt's castle
Haw, Francis 337, 364
Haw, Mary 337
Haworth 280
Haya Park 24, 28
Haythornthwaite, William 88, 105
Hearth Tax 116, 117
Henrietta Maria, Queen 50
Henry II 17, 18, 24, 33
Henry III 20, 25, 27, 33, 42
Henry IV 43, 59, 61
Henry V 64
Henry VI 63, 64, 86
Henry VIII 60, 65
Hetling Pump Room, Bath 165
Heyworth, Rev. James 253
highways and roads, maintenance of 226, 227
Hilda, Saint 19
Hile's Nook, St 19
Hodgson, Ralph 185
Hobkinson, Leonard 187
Hofland, Barbara 193, 205, 206, 267, 292, 331, 337
Hogg, Isabel 96
Hogg, John 94, 96, 256, 257
Hogg, Joseph 108, 306, 307
Hogg, Peter 66
Hogg, William 93, 116, 257
Hogg family 91, 96, 116, 257, 307
Holland, Earl of 89

Hollins, Thomas 230
Holme, Rev. 254, 268
Holmstead Road 333
Holy Wells 70
Hookstone 88
Hookstone Quarry 296
Hookstone Road 296
Hope Chapel 256
Hope Tavern 162, 256, 302, 358; *see also* Salutation, Gascoigne's
Hopewell House 352
Hopps, Henry 345
Hornbeam 296
Horner, Benjamin 282
Hospital, the 179, 196
House of Commons 178, 196, 355
House of Lords 178, 196, 359
Howgate, John 342, 343, 344, 371, 372, 385
Huddersfield 196, 279, 280, 283, 284, 399
Huddleston, Abraham 331, 345
Hume, David 121, 154
Humours of Harrogate 207
Hundredskelde 11
Hunter Dr 201, 253
Hunter, Ralph Bates 248, 249, 251
Hunton, Anthony 71
Hunts 40, 219
Husband's shop 386
Hyrpe tribe 6

Ingilby, Sir John 58, 119, 144, 163, 311
Ingilby, Sir William 313
Ingram, Dr 151
Inman, John 262, 263
Inns and Hotels 195–197
Intack (Intake) Road 296, 297
Iredale & Co. 350
Iron Gate Bridge Road 256, 341
iron ore 48, 56
Iron water *see* Chalybeate waters
Iron works 56, 67

Jacobite rising 114
James I 48, 49
James Street 256, 322, 323
Jaques, Dr 158, 169, 181, 252
Jenny Plain 296
John of Gaunt 42, 58, 59, 61, 86
John of Gaunt's castle 33, 38, 39, 44
John of Harrogate 1, 7, 19, 21, 52, 53
John, King 17, 25, 27, 33
John, Saint, of Knaresborough 62
Johnson, Richard 256, 260
Jones, John 71

Keane, Edmund 216
Kemble 216
Kennion, Thomas 247, 258, 264, 265, 392
Kensington Square 303
Killinghall 7, 13, 14, 55, 57, 83, 226, 242

Killinghall Moor 90
Kilvington, Dr 122
Kings' Arms Inn 290, 291
King's lands 139, 141, 285, 295, 297, 298, 311, 333, 334, 341, 371
King's plantation 301, 366
Kirkby, Robert 66
Kirby Overblow 65
Kissingen Well 184
Knaresborough Castle 2, 9, 10, 16, 18, 36, 49, 86, 87, 88, 91, 92
Knaresborough, etymology 10
Knaresborough Forest *see* Royal Forest
Knaresborough Honour 2, 18, 19, 20, 33, 50, 87, 102
Knaresborough Liberty 2, 25
Knaresborough manor and township 13, 24, 32, 72, 109, 126, 131, 133, 134, 145
Knaresborough Road 120
Knaresborough, Vicar of 240
Knox 52, 311, 313
Knox House Farm 52
Knox Mill 311

Lancaster, Duchy of 18, 26, 31, 42, 43, 45, 46, 48, 49, 50, 51, 58, 59, 60, 63, 67, 84, 87, 91, 92, 93, 94, 95, 111, 125, 127, 133, 139, 143, 146, 159, 160, 161, 163, 169, 170, 201, 221, 225, 237, 239, 240, 244, 245, 246, 247, 251, 252, 253, 254, 258, 264, 316, 335, 336, 337, 342, 344, 368, 369, 370, 371, 372, 375, 376, 384, 388, 391, 393
Lancaster, Earldom of 42
Lancaster House 330
Landaff, Bishop of 341
Lanercost, chronicle of 22, 37
Langdale, William 199, 341
Lascelles, Daniel 142, 294
Lascelles family 275
Lead Hall 300
Leake, Dr 78, 148–9, 184
Leamington Spa 149, 175, 346, 373, 374, 381
Leamington Spa, bank crash 374, 377
Leamington Spa, Enclosure Act 1767 131
Leamington Spa, hospital 273, 274, 374
Leamington Spa, Improvement Act 370, 374
Leamington Spa Theatre 206
Leamington Well at Harrogate 346, 347
Leeds 243
Lewis, David 205, 206, 220, 292, 296
Liber Regis 60
Libraries 172, 199, 205
Linforth, Thomas 115, 169, 308, 345
Lion Cottage 325
Lisleburn, John de 28
Little Park 28, 30, 31, 97, 145
Littleton, Lady 344, 345

Lodging Houses 157, 177, 268, 309, 323, 342
London, city of 50
Long rooms (see also Assembly Rooms) 113
Lund House Green 52, 264
Lupton, Betty 164
Lupton, William 207, 208, 385
Lyndley, Thomas 59

Macready, William Charles 360, 361
Madge, Rev. T. H. 253
Malvern 136, 149, 242, 283, 373, 375
Manchester, water bill 370
Manchester Warehouse 179, 196
Marat, Jean-Paul 156
Marl 54, 55
Marston Moor, battle of 90
Masters of ceremonies 150, 175, 195, 196, 203, 204, 380
Matlock 378
Mellon, Angela see Burdett-Coutts, Angela
Mellon, Harriet 215, 216, 364
Metcalf, John ('Blind Jack') 5, 102, 104, 113, 114, 120, 204, 218, 293, 313
Milbanke, Judith 155
militia 83, 91, 228, 229
Milner's Lane 52
mineral water see spa water
Mitton, Henry 162, 169
Mitton, Robert 203, 240, 242, 244, 245, 253
Monarchy, restoration of 96
Montpellier Baths see Crown Baths
Montpellier Hill 322
Montpellier Parade 352
Moore, John 62
Morley and Mounteagle, Lord 89
Morrison the fiddler 102, 110, 120, 204, 218
Mowbray, Richard 63
music 204
musters, military 65

Naseby, battle of 89, 90
Nash, Beau 272
National School 264
National Society 265
Neale, Dr G 48, 68, 97, 98, 108, 148, 177, 187
Neale, Dr J 97, 108, 109
Neusom, John de 40
Neusom, William de 40, 59
Neville, Sylas 153, 308
New Cold Bath 62, 177, 187
New Inn 291, 301
News out of Yorkshire 76, 79
Newspapers 199, 244, 341
Nidd 10, 24, 30, 52, 76, 79, 97, 120
Normans 11, 12, 30
Normanville, Roger de 39, 40

Norse 7
North Park Road 333
Northumberland House 346, 347

Oak Beck 90, 311
Oakdale (Ockden) 28, 33, 34, 41, 42, 43, 46, 55, 58, 63
Oatlands Drive 296
Oatlands Estate 365
Obelisk Inn 328
Oddy, John 165, 309, 347–8, 348
Old Bell Inn see Bell Inn
Old Victoria Baths see Victoria Baths
Olrome see Alrome
Oswald, Archbishop of York 10, 20, 28
Otley 10, 11, 20
Overseers 230, 233

Paganini, Nicolo 356, 357
Paley, John Green 365, 393
Palliser, Pickersgill 279, 341, 389
Pannal 3, 18, 41, 51, 82, 86, 101, 115, 140, 224–5, 237, 242, 243, 248, 249, 394
Pannal Ash 52, 300
Pannal Church 37, 47, 55, 61
Pannal constables 226
Pannal forge 20, 34
Pannal vicar 248, 249, 253
Pannal Workhouse 230
Pantheon Bazzar 337
Paradise Row 363
Paris Pavilion 188, 190
Park House 333, 363
Park Parade 205, 286, 289, 320, 321, 361, 363
Park Place 363
Parliament Street 319, 329, 351, 352
Parry, Miss 165
Parsonage 363
Pateley Bridge 234
Pawson, Matthew 308
Pawson, Stephen 307, 308, 310
Peacock, Elizabeth 233
Peacock, Henry 233, 234, 235, 247, 332
Peacock, Jane 233
Pendragon, Uther 6, 7
Pennant, Thomas 97, 147, 187
Pensax, Robert de 59
Pensax, Thomas 63
Pensax, W. de 57
Petitions 129, 168, 170, 248, 253
Petrifying well 72, 97
Philippa, Queen 39, 61
Philips, Professor 385
Pigeon Spring 76
Pippin castle 8, 33
Pierriers, Aegidius 69
plague 54, 55, 56, 57
Plumpton 21, 45.61, 297
Plumpton, Nigel de 18, 19, 32
Plumpton, Robert 45, 46

Plumpton, Sir William 45, 64
Plumpton Park 45
Pocock, Dr 112, 113
Poll tax 117
Poor Folks close 286, 333
Poor Houses 116, 230
Poor Law Commissioners 234
Portugal House estate 348
Powell, James 327
Powell, Samuel 159, 163, 170, 182, 184, 309, 319, 351, 384, 387, 390–1
Presbyterian plot 96
Proctor, Thomas 67
Promenade Inn 108, 307
Promenade Room 162, 170, 173, 182, 201, 275, 307, 342, 348
Prospect Cottage 316
Prospect House 175, 312
Prospect Hotel 323, 384, 387
Prospect Place 324, 327, 394
Prospect Row 324
Prospect Square 322
Providence Chapel 256
Providence Green 336, 343
Puddingstone Cross 18, 61, 62
Pueckler-Muskau, Prince 174
Pullan family 352

Quakers 96, 242, 256, 257
Quarries 137, 300
Queen Hotel 100, 101, 102, 107, 110, 113, 114, 115, 120, 157, 158, 170, 173, 178, 196, 205, 213, 218, 220, 229, 247, 285, 286, 287, 288, 289, 337, 364, 365, 383, 392, 394
Queen Parade 333
Queen's Head see Queen Hotel

rabbit warrens 311
race course 150, 218, 375
railway 354, 375
Rattle Cragg 311
Rawdon, Marmaduke 99
Ray, John 99
records of cures 81
Red Bank 301, 344, 371
Red Cat Cottage 312
Regent Parade 172, 288, 289, 358, 364
Richard I 18, 33
Richard II 18, 43, 58, 59
Richard III 42, 46
Richard, Earl of Cornwall 20, 31, 33, 39
Richardson, Dr 96, 169, 181, 279, 281
Richardson, Mr 137
Richardson, a woodman 388
Ridings 15
Ripley 62
Ripon diocese 2, 225, 254
Robert, Saint 19, 109
Robert, Saint, church at Pannal 55, 64, 84, 225, 252
Robin Hood 45, 301, 302

Rock Chapel 256, 342
Rokley, Robert de 44
Roman artefacts 6
Roman roads 5
Romans 4
Roseville Road 207
Rosslyn, Lord see Wedderburn. Alexander
Rossett Acre school 62
Royal Oak see Granby Hotel
Royal Bath Hospital see Bath Hospital
Royal Cheltenham Spa and Concert
    Rooms see Spa Rooms
Royal Forest 1, 2, 16, 18, 24–51, 58, 61,
    72, 81, 84, 87, 101, 125, 126, 127, 237
Royal Forest – agriculture 125
Royal Forest – Court 1, 101, 106, 276
Royal Forest – Court, inquests 31
Royal Forest – customs, law &
    regulations 16, 25, 26, 27, 40, 50, 55,
    66, 139
Royal Forest – deer 25, 32, 39, 46, 47, 48
Royal Forest – disturbing ground in 46,
    48, 68, 98
Royal Forest – enclosure 124–146
Royal Forest – enclosure, allotments
    131, 136, 137, 139, 140, 304
Royal Forest – enclosure, allotments to
    poor 126, 140, 146
Royal Forest – enclosure, Award; see
    Acts, Parliamentary, 1778 (Award)
Royal Forest – enclosure, commissioners
    128, 130, 131, 132, 135, 137, 304
Royal Forest – enclosure, opposition 47,
    129, 130
Royal Forest – encroachments 18, 125
Royal Forest – foresters & forestry 42,
    47, 65, 68
Royal Forest – parks and woodland
    chases (see also under individual
    named parks) 16, 32, 36, 38, 47, 51,
    58
Royal Forest – rentals 81, 82
Royal Forest – stud see Stud
Royal Forest – surveys 48, 62, 92, 125,
    128, 132, 133, 135, 148, 311
Royal Forest – tenants 32, 53, 125
Royal Forest – township workhouses 235
Royal Hotel 332
Royal Leamington Spa see Leamington
    Spa
Royal Oak see Granby
Royal Ontario Museum 4
Royal Parade 220, 306, 338, 342
Royal Pump Room 73, 109, 220
Royal Tunbridge Wells see Tunbridge
    Wells
Rupert, Prince 88
Russell, Francis 133, 134, 136
Russell, Thomas 291

St Alban's Villa 105, 361
St Hilda 19

St John's Chapel see Church, High
    Harrogate
St John's Well (or Sweet Spa) 4, 18, 48,
    76, 79, 98, 103, 106, 147, 153, 162,
    172, 205, 215, 292, 293, 298, 299
St Magnus Well 73, 97, 147, 187
St Mary's Church see Church, Low
    Harrogate
St Mungo's Well see St Magnus Well
Salt, Thomas 389
Saltergate Hill 34
Salutation 102, 104, 105, 107, 114, 115,
    149, 210, 292, 358, 359; see also Hope
    Tavern, Gascoigne's
Salvation Army 190
Sanderson, Hall 345
Sandy buts 63
Sandy close 321
Sanitary accommodation 79
Sarah, Duchess of Marlborough 356
Savoy Chapel 251
Scargill reservoir 8
School Court 321
Scott, Sir Walter 171, 172
Scottish invasion 11, 22, 37, 38, 55
Scriblerus, Matinus 154
Scriven, Henry de 36
Scriven-with-Tentergate 145, 249
Settle James 170, 308
Settlement 225–6
Sheepshanks, William 247, 265, 333, 385
Ship Inn 321
Short, Dr Thomas 98, 108, 109, 111, 112,
    148, 184
Shutt family 59, 228
Shutt, Isaac Thomas 328, 344
Shutt, Jonathan 169, 173, 220, 310, 342,
    383, 393
Shutt Hill 333
Silver Street 285
Silverfields Cottages 363
Simeon of Durham 11, 12
Simpson, Dr 97
Simpson, Benjamin 319
Simpson, David 319
Simpson, James 318, 352
Simpson, Mary 352
Sinclair, Catherine 174, 175, 366
Sinking Ship see Granby
Skaife's room 257
Skipton Road 52
Slingsby, Sir Henry 49, 85, 86, 89, 119
Slingsby, Richard 63
Slingsby, Sir Thomas 282
Slingsby, William 69, 70, 71, 72
Small Acres see Poor Folks close.
Smirke, Robert 251
Smith of Alnwick 178, 339
Smithy Hill 256, 265, 290, 354
Smollett, Tobias 122, 123, 150, 154, 177,
    198
Snawe, William 38

Soane, Sir John 157
Somerset Hotel 352
Spa (in the Low Countries) 69, 70
Spa, first English 71
Spa, bathing 97, 99, 177–194
Spa, bathing houses 99
Spa Hill 106, 142, 288, 292, 293
Spa Lane 62
Spa promenading 220, 221
Spa rings 70, 110
Spa ritual 221
Spa Rooms 222, 223, 348, 349, 350, 383,
    394
Spa Rooms estate 347
Spa season 241
Spa treatments 123, 154, 193
Spa water, analysis 192, 381
Spa water, bottling 80, 81, 113, 156, 173,
    379
Spa water, reservoirs 98, 99
Spa water, salts 99
Spa wells (see also under individual
    named wells) 17, 165, 169, 170, 197,
    276, 382
Spadacrene Anglica 70, 71, 72, 74, 90, 91,
    97, 143
Spadacrene Eboracensis 177
Spofforth 132
Stanhope, Dr Michael 13, 76, 78, 90, 160,
    184, 274
Stanhope, Richard 67
Stanhope, William 74
Stapleton, Miles de 36
Star beck 49, 52, 62, 119, 187, 231, 237,
    394
Star Inn 291
Starbeck Spa 73, 84, 75, 78, 145, 148,
    184, 185, 186
Starbeck Spa Chalybeate Well 78, 148,
    184
Starbeck Spa Sulphur Well 73, 78, 108,
    148, 184, 185, 186
Steele Well 298
Sterne, Lawrence 121, 154, 216, 354
Stevenson, John 98
Stewarde, Ralph 65–6
Stockdale, Thomas 50, 87, 88, 89, 93
Stockdale family 85, 116, 313
Stokbrigge 9, 18, 61, 62, 119
Stone Age 4
Stone Rings beck 6, 18, 61, 62
Stone Rings road 300
Strawberry Dale 166
Stray 144, 145, 158, 159, 160, 161, 218,
    262, 275, 337, 369, 387, 389, 391
Stray footpaths 160, 391
Stray Gates 142, 158, 159, 262, 387, 388,
    389
Stray Gates, cattle 142, 143
Stray seats 388
Stray 'slips' 160, 161
Stray trees 388

Stubbs sisters 329
Stuart, Esme 149
Stubbing Field 53
Stud, in Royal Forest 16, 39, 40, 42
Stuteville, William de 18, 19, 27, 32, 33, 34, 60
Sulphur bathing 97, 99, 152
Sulphur waters, general 74, 98, 152, 162, 362
Sulphur Well, Low Harrogate 1, 5, 73, 76, 77, 78, 79, 80, 83, 97, 101, 107, 109, 110, 111, 121, 125, 147, 148, 152, 157, 162, 166, 167, 168, 169, 170, 173, 177, 179, 227, 274, 278, 307, 310, 343
Sulphur Well Mount 191
Sulphur Well Pump room 164, 166, 168, 173
Sunday Schools 260–2, 264
Surveyors 31, 128, 226, 228
Swale, Solomon 311
Swan Inn 169, 173, 229, 310, 311, 333, 342, 343, 345
Swan Lane/Road 173, 191, 342, 343
Sweating 123, 192
Sweet Spa see St John's Well

Tanckarde, William 86
Tate, James 339
taxation 116
Taylor, John 90, 91
Taylor, Richard 292, 267
Tengatt, James 170, 336
Tenth tax 63
Tewit Well 18, 69, 70, 71, 72, 73, 76, 78, 79, 80, 97, 98, 147, 162, 191
Thackwray family 291, 338, 358
Thackwray, Captain 365
Thackwray, Joseph 163, 165, 169, 171, 179, 180, 182, 184, 220, 231, 237, 248, 255, 304, 307, 338, 341, 384, 385, 386
Thackwray, Major 256, 342
Thackwray, Mary 325, 343
Thackwray, Matthew 159, 291, 392
Thackwray, William 167, 362
Thackwray Well Case 371, 353–387, 389
Thackwray's Vaults 325
Theatre, Church Square (Theatre Royal) 150, 204, 206, 208, 210, 211, 212, 213, 214, 365
Theatre, Devonshire Place 207, 208, 209, 210, 211
Theatre, Granby Barn 206
Thedmarsh Edmund de 40
Thistle Hill 145
Thoresby, Ralph 9, 100
Thompson, John 368, 393
Thornton, Colonel 219

Thrush, Captain Thomas 317, 318, 389
Tison, Gilbert 13, 14, 15
Tithes 294
Toll Bars 120
Tolle, John 368
Tonstall, Dr 97
Tower Street 327, 329
Towton, battle of 64
Toy Shop 106, 141, 147, 149, 288, 292, 293
Trappes, Francis 93
Trinitarian Friars 30, 31, 32, 33
Tunbridge Wells 149, 171, 203, 283, 370, 377, 378, 381
Tunbridge Wells, Act of 1740 145
Tunbridge Wells Theatre 206
Turner, William 71
turnpike roads 118, 310
Turnpike Trusts 117
Tuton, Thomas 345

Union Inn 145
Union Street 353

Venereal disease 97
Verney, Ralph 100
Vestry meetings 84, 115, 226, 231, 233
Victoria, Queen 201, 325
Victoria Baths (old) 181, 182, 187, 348, 383
Victoria Park Company 227, 316, 322, 324
visitors 99, 100, 110, 121, 122, 123, 147, 150, 151, 153, 154, 155, 157, 158, 171, 174, 176, 180, 196, 198, 199, 222, 240, 241, 276, 309, 340, 379
Vitalis, Oderic 12
Voackes, William 311
Volta House 322

Waide, Robert 66
Waite, Joseph 393
Wakefield 222, 272, 273, 280
Walker, Dr 151
Walker, Thomas Humble 342, 345, 346, 347, 372, 389, 393
Walker Road 353
Walker's Passage 363
Wallis, Tryphosa Jane 212, 215, 216
Walton Head 65
Wapentakes 15, 83, 84, 88
War Office returns 120
Warm Baths 178, 179, 192, 288, 299, 321
Waste 12, 13, 133
Watson family 313
Watson, John 297
Waudby, Widow 235

Weaving 66
Webb, William 92
Wedderburn, Alexander 142, 162, 215, 240, 293, 294, 295
Wedderburn House 252, 295, 297
Well Hill 99, 177, 178, 191, 256, 309, 310, 342, 343
Wellington Inn 45, 301, 302, 334
Wellington Square 303
Wesley, John 242, 243, 303
West, William 166
West Park 325, 327, 329
West Yorkshire Cavalry 220
Westmoreland, William 62, 106, 292, 294, 358
Westmoreland Street 205
Wheater, William 4
Wheatlands Road East 296
White Hart Inn 108, 170, 302, 303, 334, 336, 337, 376, 394
Wilberforce, William 157
Wildsmith, Rev. T. B. 342
Wilkes, Thomas 106, 211, 212, 301, 383
Wilkinson, Tate 207, 381
William III 109
William IV 356, 371
Williams, John 180, 182, 223, 348, 349, 350, 351, 383, 386
Williams, Thomas 348
Williams, William 337
Wills 66
Wilson, Abraham 328
Window tax 117
Wittie, Dr 97
Windsor Castle 42
Wolsley, Colonel Clement 218
Wood, John 348
Wood, Richard del 53
Wood, William del 57, 58, 59
Woodlands Cottage 296
Woodlands House 296
Wordsworth, Mary 158, 173, 331
Wordsworth, William 173, 253
World's End 102, 103, 106–7, 137, 149, 162, 182, 230, 231, 256, 267, 290, 291, 311, 354
World's End Road 103, 354
Wormald, Croft 169, 181, 279
Wright, George 389
Wysham, John 22

York 81, 90
York, Archbishop of 22, 33, 252, 253
York diocese 2, 237, 254
York Place 9, 105, 324, 332, 333

Zouche, Archbishop 55, 56